Shopping Environments
Evolution, Planning and Design

Shopping Environments
Evolution, Planning
and Design

Peter Coleman

AMSTERDAM • BOSTON • HEIDELBERG • LONDON • OXFORD • NEW YORK
PARIS • SAN DIEGO • SAN FRANCISCO • SINGAPORE • SYDNEY • TOKYO
Architectural Press is an imprint of Elsevier

Architectural
Press

Architectural Press is an imprint of Elsevier Ltd
Linacre House, Jordan Hill, Oxford OX2 8DP, UK
30 Corporate Drive, Suite 400, Burlington MA 01803, USA

First edition 2006

Notice

No responsibility is assumed by the publisher for any injury and/or damage to persons or property as a matter of products liability, negligence or otherwise, or from any use or operation of any methods, products, instructions or ideas contained in the material herein. Because of rapid advances in the medical sciences, in particular, independent verification of diagnoses and drug dosages should be made

British Library Cataloging in Publication Data
A catalogue record for this book is available from the British Library

Library of Congress Cataloging in Publication Data
A catalog record for this book is available from the Library of Congress

ISBN 13-978 0 7506 6001 3
ISBN 10-0 7506 6001 5

06 07 08 09 10   10 9 8 7 6 5 4 3 2 1

For information on all Architectural Press publications visit our website at www.books.elsevier.com

Typeset by Cepha Imaging Pvt. Ltd., Bangalore, India

Printed and bound in Italy

Contents

Foreword

It is likely to be provocative and self-defeating to suggest that no one individual person actually fully understands all the issues and considerations in the formulation and design, from start to finish, of a typical shopping centre. Having undertaken the research and completed the writing, I feel well positioned to make this observation. Shopping centres are big, complex developments involving the skills of a large team of designers and specialist consultants who contribute at particular stages throughout the project. Typically, the process of forming a shopping centre can last, from inception to completion, for a period of 10 years or more, involving the contribution of many specialist consultants. Invariably, those best placed to understand all the issues in the process of making a shopping centre are likely to be a combined team consisting of the client, architect and retail team. The process can be compared to a cross between a marathon and a relay race – where the project is the baton and a gradually changing team of runners carries it through the race. Although the architect will be involved in most stages of the race, it is likely that supporting runners will come alongside at different stages and may even carry the baton at some points. While a stakeholder or consultant is carrying the baton, the architect may be required to run alongside as part of the team for this stage. The challenge to the architect will be twofold: first, to understand at which stages to run with the baton or to run alongside; and second, to maintain sufficient tenacity to be the custodian of the vision through the different stages until completion.

This book will hopefully help all those involved in the design of shopping centres to recognise the format of the event, when to run or just to jog, and with whom they should be running.

Preface

This book was instigated from a need to update the original book *Shopping Centres: Retail Development, Design and Management* written by Nadine Beddington in 1981 (with a second and revised edition published in 1991, published by Architectural Press). However, much has happened in the development of shopping centres since the update of the original book, responding to social, planning, economic and technological changes. Key influences upon the development of the building type have been, for example:

- working patterns – requiring more convenience and customer specific shops
- more discerning customers – expecting greater value and more memorable experiences
- government policies – restricting out-of-town development and requiring more sustainable and inclusive town centre shopping development
- technological advancement:
  - aiding retailers with bar code sales and corresponding automated 'just in time' deliveries
  - increasing the availability of information, facilitating the monitoring of turnover rents
  - generating greater competition from alternative modes of shopping (Internet shopping).

General progress, since the original book, has seen a new type of shopping centre emerge and the opening of many exciting new centres. Such is the rate of progress and change in the retail industry that it has been necessary for the book to be totally re-researched and rewritten.

The overall aim and objective of this book is to identify the principal issues and considerations an architect is likely to encounter in the design of a shopping centre. With the average shopping centre taking some 10 years to complete from inception, a key characteristic of this building type will be found in understanding the influence of the lengthy process upon its design and planning. Shopping centres are complex public buildings, meeting the needs of several different stakeholders and users, and involving clients, retailers, customers and the general public.

The book aims to build up an understanding of the building type through the examination of the following:

- an outline of the background and development of facilities for shopping
- an identification of the different types of shopping centre and the ongoing evolution of new formats
- an outline of different client requirements and the influence of various stakeholders
- the influence of the process and how the brief will evolve over the length of the project
- the (key) issues to consider in initiating the project and preparing the brief
- the types of accommodation to be included in the building
- the organising qualities of the public spaces
- the elements of the building to be designed by the architect
- the provisions to be made in the building for completion by others
- the importance of the back of house areas which support the operation of the shopping centre
- the economic principles involved with the viability of a project.

Through the examination of the above issues the book aims to assist and equip those involved with the creation of shopping facilities to develop the following skills: the ability to balance the requirements of different stakeholders; to anticipate the requirements of elements to be designed by others; to provide the vision and act as the custodian of the design throughout the length of the process.

This book is principally aimed at all those involved in the creation, extension and alteration of shopping centres: architects, designers, technical consultants and developers. It is organised into three principal parts.

Part 1 The Development and Nature of Shopping Environments. Chapters 1 and 2 identify the big issues facing the shopping centre industry which are likely to influence the design of all new shopping facilities.

Part 1 also examines the historical evolution of shopping activity leading up to the first purpose planned shopping centre.

Part 2 The Contemporary Types of Shopping Centre. These chapters (3–6) outline the development of contemporary shopping facilities, explaining (with illustrations of example projects) the different types of shopping centre and the ongoing evolution of new shopping formats.

Part 3 The Design Guides. In this part the focus changes from the analytical to the more practical guidelines to be used in the design of shopping facilities, starting with an explanation of the different stakeholders, identifying the types of commissioning client and the issues to be considered.

■ An examination is made of the key issues at the initiation of the project and in the preparation of the brief, including the involvement of the appropriate specialist consultants.

■ The different types of retail, catering and leisure accommodation to be incorporated into the layout are identified.

■ The significance of public spaces in providing the organisational framework to the layout is examined, along with the characteristics of different types of public space.

■ The elements that make up public spaces are individually examined to assist the architect in designing these spaces.

■ The back of house (non-public) areas are examined with an outline explanation given the role these areas play in the operation of a shopping centre.

■ An explanation of the economic principles and commercial considerations involved with the viability of a project are also examined.

Part 3 concludes with the consideration of future places for shopping.

Exclusions: this book focuses on the different types of planned shopping centre and the various considerations and elements that the shopping centre architect is usually required to design and accommodate. It does not include the design of individual shops and their interiors nor the design of individual catering or leisure facilities. The design of food stores and supermarkets is also excluded.

Peter Coleman

Acknowledgements

As a practising architect in a busy, London-based, company of designers, Building Design Partnership, this book has largely been prepared and written in my spare time. The venture has taken some three years to research, write, prepare the illustrations, and eventually to produce. Such an undertaking has involved the assistance, advice and contribution of many experienced and talented individuals. Without their generous help and support during the preparation of the book it would not have been possible.

My gratitude, thanks and acknowledgement are therefore extended to all those who gave the following help and assistance.

Architectural Press have been understanding in recognising my professional responsibilities, extending deadlines and in their continual support and encouragement throughout the process.

All the many architects, designers, development companies, centre managers and commercial agents, who are too numerous to mention individually, who readily provided information, drawings and photographs referred to and illustrated in the book. Particular thanks to those who have provided information relating to several projects. Specifically the development companies – Amstel Multi, Capital Shopping Centres, The Grosvenor Estate, Hammerson, ING, Lend Lease, The Mills Corporation – and architects – Building Design Partnership, Chapman Taylor, Jerde and RTKL.

I would like to give extended thanks to the following key individuals in the industry who generously provided advice, guidance and suggestions for projects: Ken Christian for suggesting examples and information on projects in the USA; Neil Mitchenall for the cosmopolitan examples in Europe and the Americas; John Bullough and Mike Prentice for collaborating and assisting with the writing of the chapter on commercial and economic considerations; and Nigel Woolner for his personal advice, help and encouragement throughout the preparation of this book.

The use of archive images, professional photographs and the complete colour reproduction of illustrations has been assisted and made possible by the generous sponsorship of The Grosvenor Estate and Henderson Global Investors.

I am indebted to the following individuals for their assistance with the preparation and format of the book: Charlotte Kelley for researching information on the example projects; Helen Wilkins for researching the sources of illustrations and in obtaining permissions; Mark Moore for editorial advice with the written style; Caroline Field for allowing use of her photographs; and Catherine Anderson for her dedication with the proof-reading of the manuscript.

General thanks to my colleagues at Building Design Partnership for their support with my involvement with this project.

In particular, my thanks are extended to those colleagues at work who went beyond the call of their daily responsibilities: Andy Borzyskowski for advising and setting up the framework for the digital images; Sean Dooley, Architect, for technical advice with the front and back of house areas and fire-safety; Martin Lupton, Lighting Designer, for advice regarding luminaire types; Jane Messinger for researching, collating and obtaining the BDP illustration permissions; Bob Spittle, Building Services Engineer, for technical advice relating to space heating and cooling; Vivien van Namen for assistance with tables and manuscript format; Carole Amelinck, Richard Austin, James Cheung, Sean Dooley (technical diagrams), Shyuan Kuee, Joyce Lam, Robert Palmer and Walter Wang for helping with the preparation of the drawn illustrations and diagrams.

Special thanks to Anne Wyatt for her continual patience and organisation with the typing of the manuscript and illustration notes.

Last, but not least, James Cheung for helping to collate, prepare and organise all the illustrations and for volunteering support and encouragement in bringing it all together.

Most of all I recognise the sacrifices made by my family who have provided support and encouragement to enable me to complete this challenging project. Thank you all.

Figure Credits

Source/Credit	Figure number
AA	2.5, 2.34, 2.41, 2.53, 2.54, 2.56
Adam Wilson	5.103
Adrian Price	5.36
Adrian Price/BDP	5.3
Adrian Wilson	14.2
AJN Architect	5.18, 5.19, 5.20
AKG	2.2, 2.3
Alexei Naroditsky	10.5, 11.26, 11.30
Allies & Morrison/ Miller Hare	4.49
Allies and Morrison/BDP	8.10
AM Developments	11.19
AM Development/Avec Fotografie	5.80
AM Development/Tom de Rooij Fotografie	5.76
Amalgam	10.61, 10.62, 10.63, 10.64
Amstel Multi	3.9
Andy Borzyskowski	1.4, 1.5
Andy Borzyskowski/BDP	11.2, 11.10, 11.15
Anthony Baker Artwork	6.24
Anthony Belluschi	4.61, 4.62, 4.63, 4.64
Anthony Belleuschi Architects/Hedrick Blessing	3.4
Anthony Belluschi/BDP	4.60
AP/Wide World Photos	6.45
Arcaid/Richard Bryant	1.15, 2.20
Architech, Gallery of Architectural Art	2.35
Archivio Fotografico Tourismo, Torino	2.18
Arquitectonia	4.96
Art Directors	2.28
Art Directors/Martin Barlow	2.13
Art Directors/Michael Good	2.12
Art Directors/Tibor Bognar	2.9
Austin-Smith Lord	8.11
Avery Associates/Richard Holttum	9.43
BAA	6.43
Bayer Properties Inc	4.58
BDP	2.29, 2.39, 2.55, 3.11, 4.5, 4.8, 4.11, 4.13, 4.51, 4.52, 4.81, 4.93, 5.4, 5.15, 5.16, 5.81, 5.95, 5.99, 5.105, 5.106, 5.110, 5.111, 5.112, 5.113, 5.114, 5.115, 5.116, 5.118, 5.119, 6.29, 6.30, 7.1, 7.2, 7.3, 8.2, 8.3, 8.7, 8.9, 8.12, 8.14, 8.15, 8.17, 8.18, 8.25, 8.27, 8.29, 8.31, 8.35, 8.36, 8.37, 9.3, 9.32, 9.41, 9.60, 9.62, 10.6, 10.16, 10.17, 10.67, 11.16, 11.32, 11.36, 11.50, 12.4, 12.5., 12.6, 12.10, 12.34, 13.2, Opening figure to Chapter 14
BDP/Cesar Pelli	5.117
BDP/David Balbour	6.33, Opening figure to Chapter 13
BDP/David Barbour	Opening figure to Chapter 3, 9.33, 10.75, 11.28

(Continued)

Source/Credit	Figure number
BDP/Miller Hare	Opening figure to Chapter 11
BDP/Paul Chapman	9.54
BDP/Peter Hutton	5.107, 5.108, 5.109
BDP/Sean Dooley	11.33, 11.34, 11.35, 11.37, 11.38, 12.1, 12.13, 12.15, 12.21, 12.23, 12.24, 12.27, 12.29, 12.31
Benoy/BDP	4.25, 5.26
Benoy/GMJ	Opening figure to Chapter 8
Benthan Cronwell	1.13, 6.18, 6.19, 6.20, 6.21, 6.22
Benthem Cornwel	10.71, 11.12, 11.31, 11.39
Bettman/Corbis	2.49
Bibliotheque Nationale de France	2.21, 2.23, 2.24
Bildarchiv Foto Marburg	2.6, 2.7, 2.8, 2.36, 2.37
Birmingham Picture Library	11.53
bpl photo/Jonathan Berg	4.110
British Architectural Library, RIBA	2.30, 2.31, 2.32, 2.33
Buddy Mays/Corbis	10.1
Callison	4.65, 4.74
Callison/Chris Eden	4.66, 4.67, 4.68, 4.75, 4.76, 4.77, 11.7
Capital Shopping Centres	4.14, 5.10, 10.69
Capital Shopping Centres/Haskor	5.11
Capital Shopping Centres/Newcastle City Council	5.13
Caroline Field	3.1, 9.13, 10.55, 11.47
Catalyst	9.49
Chapman Taylor	1.18, 4.15, 4.16, 5.12, 5.14, 5.29, 5.91, 5.92, 6.26, 6.44, 8.1, 8.26, 9.19, 9.38
Chapman Taylor/Hopkins Architects	5.104
Charlotte Wood	4.9, 10.48, 11.3, 11.5
Charlotte Wood/BDP	5.5
Chetwood Associates	4.91, 4.92
Company Archive, Harrods Ltd, London	2.38
Corbis Picture Library	2.44
Corbis/Robert Holmes	4.12
Corbis/Robert Landau	3.2, 4.59, 6.4
CTP	6.46, 6.47, 6.48, 6.49
Daniel Hopkinson	5.96
Daniel Hopkinson/BDP	4.87, 4.88
Davi Deepres/Hammerson	5.34
David Barbour	1.6, 1.14, 1.16, 4.41, 5.54, 5.98, 5.100, 5.101, 5.102, 9.44, 10.85, 10.86, 10.87, 10.88, 11.29, 11.48, 12.3, 12.7, 12.8, 12.9, 12.11, 12.16, 12.17, 12.18, 12.19, 12.22, 12.25, 12.30, 12.32, 12.33
David Barbour/BDP	3.5, 6.28, 8.32, 9.9, 10.18, 10.54, 10.59, 10.74, 11.13, 11.22, 11.46
Dover Publications	1.1
Dover, Kohl & Partners	4.56, 4.79, 4.80
EDAW/Chapman Taylor	5.90
ELS Architects	6.14
Entertainment Development Group	9.36
Entertainment Development Group/Stan Obert	6.3, 6.15, 6.16, 6.17
Faulkner Brown	4.112, 4.113, 4.114, 9.34, 9.55
Finnish Tourist Board	1.10
Fitzroy Robinson	5.57, 5.60
Fitzroy Robinson/Peter Cook	5.58, 5.59, 5.61
Framingham Historical Society	2.48
Getty Images	Opening figure to Chapter 12
Glasgow City Council	2.43
GMW	4.47
Guildhall Library	2.14, 2.16, 2.19, 2.22
Hammerson	5.21, 5.22, 5.23, 5.24, 5.30, 8.13, 8.34

Source/Credit	Figure number
Hassell	4.104
Highwoods Properties	2.46
HOK	4.83, 4.84, 4.85, 5.8, 5.9, 9.59
Ian Latham	5.70, 5.71
Index Stock Imagery/Ralph Krubner	5.38
Irvine Company	4.89
J Salmon Ltd	2.52
James Cheung	10.42, 10.43, 10.60, 10.68, 10.82, 12.2, 12.12, 12.13, 12.14, 12.20
Jean Nouvelle/BDP	5.17
Jerde Partnership/Stephen Simpson	1.9
Jerde	4.17, 5.62, 5.63, 5.74, 5.75
Jerde/Stephen Simpson	6.2
Jeremy Sweet/ BDP	4.42
Joe Low	10.49
Joe Pie Picture Library	2.4, 2.25
John Lewis Partnership Archive Collection	2.42
Justin Parsons	Opening figure to Chapter 7
KaDeWe	9.21, 9.22
King Kullen	2.45
Kone	10.53
Lend Lease	4.26, 4.27, 4.28, 4.29, 4.30, 4.31, 4.32, 8.5, 9.63, 10.46, 11.4, 11.20, 11.27, 11.44, 11.45
Lyons, Sleaman, Hoare	4.94
Martin Charles	3.8
Martin Donlin/Hammerson	11.43
Martine Hamilton Knight	5.97
Martine Hamilton	4.7
Mary Evans Picture Library	2.1
McArthur Glen/Michael Hart	4.95
Michael Betts/Hammerson	5.28, 5.31, 10.12, 11.8
Mills Corporation	4.43, 4.44, 6.5, 6.6, 6.7, 6.8, 6.9, 6.10, 6.11, 6.12, 6.13
Mills Corporation/Parque de Nieve	9.58
Minnesota Historical Society	2.50
Mithun	6.51, 6.52, 6.53
MKDC/BDP	4.45
Montagu Evans	8.19
Museum of History and Industry, Seattle	2.47
Nicholas Grimshaw/Hayes Davidson	1.17
Patricia Fisher/Mills International	4.97
Patrick Lim	8.20, 8.24
Paul Harmer	4.82
Peter Coleman	1.2, 1.3, 1.8, 1.12, 2.26, 2.27, 2.57, 3.3, 3.7, 4.2, 4.4, 4.6, 4.18, 4.22, 4.23, 4.24, 4.35, 4.39, 4.86, 4.90, 4.100, 4.101, 4.102, 5.2, 5.6, 5.32, 5.33, 5.35, 5.37, 5.52, 5.53, 5.56, 5.64, 5.66, 5.67, 5.68, 5.69, 5.72, 5.77, 5.78, 5.79, 5.86, 5.94, 6.23, 6.25, 6.27, 6.31, 6.32, 6.50, 8.4, 8.8, 8.16, 8.21, 8.22, 8.23, 8.30, 8.33, 8.38, 8.39, 9.1, 9.2, 9.4, 9.5, 9.6, 9.7, 9.8, 9.10, 9.11, 9.12, 9.14, 9.15, 9.16, 9.17, 9.18, 9.20, 9.23, 9.24, 9.25, 9.26, 9.27, 9.30, 9.35, 9.37, 9.39, 9.42, 9.56, 9.57, 9.61, 10.2, 10.3, 10.11, 10.13, 10.14, 10.19, 10.20, 10.21, 10.22, 10.23, 10.24, 10.25, 10.26, 10.27, 10.28, 10.29, 10.30, 10.31, 10.32, 10.33, 10.34, 10.35, 10.36, 10.37, 10.38, 10.39, 10.40, 10.41, 10.44, 10.50, 10.51, 10.52, 10.56, 10.57, 10.58, 10.65, 10.66, 10.72, 10.73, 10.76, 10.77, 10.78, 10.79, 10.80, 10.81, 10.83, 10.84, 11.1, 11.6, 11.9, 11.11, 11.14, 11.17, 11.18, 12.26, 14.1
Peter Cook	4.48
Peter Durant/ArcBlue	9.28, 10.7, 11.52
Peter Pearson/eStock Photo	5.39
Peter Renerts	4.19, 4.20

Source/Credit	Figure number
Photogenics	9.40
PJC	10.9
Platform Group/Carl O'Connel	9.50, 9.51, 9.52, 9.53
Port of Portland	6.42
Raf Makda/BDP	11.49
Ravi Deepres	13.1
Ravi Deepres/Hammerson	5.27
Reid Architecture	4.98, 4.99, 4.111, 8.6, 9.31
Reid Architecture/BDP	4.109
Richard Allen	12.28
Richard Bryant/ David Lock Associates	4.46
Richard Rees/BDP	4.103
Richard Rogers Partnership	6.41
RKW	5.44, 5.45, 5.46
RKW/H Esch	5.47
RKW/H G Esch	5.43, 5.48, 5.49, 5.50, 5.51
Robert Frerck, Odyssey Productions	2.10, 2.11
Rochester Public Library	5.7
Roger Ball/Image Photo Ltd	4.10, 10.47, 10.70, 11.51
Roger Vaughan Picture Gallery	2.17
RTKL	3.6, 4.33, 4.36, 4.37, 4.38, 4.40, 4.69, 4.70, 4.71, 4.72, 4.73, 4.105, 4.106, 4.107, 4.108, 5.73, 5.93, 6.34, 6.35, 6.36, 6.37, 6.38, 6.39, 6.40, 9.29, 10.15, 11.24
RTKL/BDP	4.21, 4.34
Rui Morais de Sousa	4.50, 4.53
Rui Morais de Sousa/BDP	4.54, 4.55
Selfridges Collection	2.40
Sheffield City Council	11.40
Shops of Saddleback	4.57
Simon Williams	9.45, 10.45
Sjaak Henselmans	1.11, 5.83, 5.85, 5.87, 5.88, 5.89, 8.28, 11.23
Soeters/BDP	5.82
Spacedecks	9.48
St Martins Property Corporation Ltd	1.7, 10.8, 11.21
Stephen Anderson/BDP	14.3
Stephen Simpson	10.4
Stephen Simpson/Jerde	5.65
Taubman Company	4.3
The Birmingham Alliance	5.25
Thomas Heatherwick Studio	11.25
Toyo Ito/Nacasa and Partners Ltd	Opening figure to Chapter 9
Tsogo Sun Gaming	9.46, 9.47
TUI Interactive	11.41, 11.42
Van den Broek and Bakema	2.51
Vera Yanovshtchinsky	5.84
Vito Palmisano	6.54
Von Gerkan, Marg	10.10
Westfield	4.78
Westminster Archive	2.15
Wilkinson Eyre Architects/James Brittain	10.89
Zeidler Partnership	5.55
Zeidler/Grinnel Partnership	5.41, 5.42
Zeidler/Grinnel	5.40

Biography

Peter Coleman was born in 1954, and studied architecture at Brighton University School of Architecture, UK.

Peter is a practising architect and urban designer who worked for a range of London practices involving public and civic buildings before he turned to specialising in the design of shopping environments. His work has been awarded for prospective new projects and successfully completed work in the UK and Europe. His work and career have involved travelling and studying shopping development in America, Europe, the Far East, Australia and South Africa. He is currently involved in the design of major, leading-edge shopping developments in the UK, Europe, the Far East and Australia.

Peter is a member of the International Council of Shopping Centres (ICSC), British Council of Shopping Centres (BCSC) and is actively one of the BCSC Annual Award judges. Peter is director and leader of retail design for Building Design Partnership (BDP), the internationally recognised architects and designers of shopping centres. BDP was awarded Retail Architect of the Year in the Architect of the Year Awards by Building Design in 2004.

This inaugural book brings direct and observed experience to an often under-estimated building type.

PART 1

The Development and Nature of Shopping Environments

THE MAIN AVENUE—EAST,

Figure 1.1 The Grand Exposition/Crystal Palace – a showcase for manufacturers to sell their wares. *(Source: Dover Publications)*

The Big Issues

1

Issues Facing Shopping Centres Today

As we enter the 21st century there are new challenges facing designers with the continual emergence of new types of shopping facility. New urban types of shopping facilities prevail today which are designed as integral parts of our town centres, combining traditional high street qualities with the commercial efficiency, convenience and operational benefits of a planned shopping facility. These new types challenge the conventions and preconceptions of existing shopping centres to the point where new criteria and new types of centre emerge.

Each new type of shopping centre that emerges does not replace the existing formats of shopping, but adds to the diverse range of shopping facilities that already exist. This reinvention and diversification are further reflections of the dynamic nature of this building type.

Many different types of shopping facility already exist. These can be defined by product (e.g. white goods shops and fashion) and by places (e.g. by type of environment, whether its in town, out-of-town or a retail park). Despite this vast range of facility there is a public wish for more interesting and more unique types of shopping environment.

Before going on to examine how shopping centres are created and designed, it is necessary to achieve a general understanding of their nature, together with an awareness of the big issues facing those involved with forming a shopping centre development.

This chapter gives an overview of the dynamic nature and complexity of shopping centres and examines the issues facing the industry. These issues are examined in three strands: social; planning; and retail economics. The chapter concludes

with the recognition that reinvention and diversification will continue as these key challenges are addressed.

Shopping facilities are an expression of a market. Fundamentally, they provide a showcase for manufacturers to sell their wares. They are part of a large, sophisticated and dynamic industry tied into the economy of a country, its regions and districts. They also reflect basic human activities, such as consuming and trading. They have been integral to our settlements from earliest times and have grown at the heart of our towns and cities. Basic trading stalls in markets have grown into the various shopping formats we have today. The development of the different types of contemporary shopping environment is examined in detail in Part 2 of the book (Fig. 1.1).

Those employed in the retail industry make up a large proportion of a country's workforce. In the UK, for example, 20 per cent of the workforce is employed in the retail industry (British Council of Shopping Centres Report, 2001). This makes the retail industry the second largest employer in the country, only marginally exceeded by a declining manufacturing industry. This figure does not include the many consultants and development teams involved in creating and bringing together the shopping centre, nor those who build them.

Retail property is one of the most important investment categories in the UK. Plans in the pipeline to meet a demand for 11 million m^2 (119 million ft^2) of new floor space by 2012 ensure this is likely to continue for the foreseeable future (British Council of Shopping Centres Report, 2001).

Shops generally form the heart of a town or city centre. They affect our environment and become the places we identify with, serving as backgrounds to our social and leisure lives. They often form the memories we grow up with and look back on as pleasant parts of our lives (Fig. 1.2).

Figure 1.2 Town centres form the heart and backdrop to a community's social life, illustrated by Eastgate Street, Chester, UK. *(Source: Peter Coleman)*

Figure 1.3 A new urban community featuring a library, church, housing and shops, Marienburg, Nijmegen, The Netherlands (2000). *(Source: Peter Coleman)*

In the planning and design of shopping environments, consideration needs to be given to the great number of visitors passing through the centre each day. In the largest centres at weekends this volume can be over 100 000 visitors a day and can reach several hundred thousands per week. Only major football stadiums and some of the largest railway stations and airports achieve a similar footfall. In addition to the shopping public that must be catered for, shopping centres employ large numbers of staff who run the shops, numbering from 3000 to 5000 people, depending on the size of centre, and they require facilities as well.

Retail centres generate large traffic volumes derived from public access to the shops, and from servicing, including private and commercial service vehicles. Public transport serving shopping centres needs to be integrated and made applicable and relevant, available and accessible to those who are likely to use it. All these people – and goods-moving factors – must be considered and accommodated into the surrounding highway and transport network.

Although shops can be the sole use, they are more usually grafted into a mix with other complementary uses such as food consumption and, increasingly, with leisure facilities, creating a broad spectrum of consumer use. Shopping facilities are changing in nature, with more activities and uses incorporated into them. Over a third of all new developments considered in 2002 included a significant leisure element. Now, with more town centre schemes in the pipeline involving the new urban type of shopping environment, this format is often a mixed-use development requiring an understanding of other building types such as housing, offices, transport hubs and civic buildings. These mixed-use developments require design skills, which include the different building types, town planning and public realm design capabilities.

The key issues governing design and development of shopping centres fall into three main areas:
1 social and human
2 planning
3 retail economics.

Social and Human Issues

Public sentiment is potentially the single most important factor that designers need to consider. Although there is a need for comfort – including protection from bad weather – and security, there is also a need for convenience, especially ease of access both by car and public transport. Although shopping centres in the past met many of these criteria, recent focus group research indicates that the public has a dislike for enclosed, internalised shopping environments and would prefer to go shopping in more natural environments where there is daylight, a feeling of contact with the outside and something unique or particular about that town or city.

Public opinion has expressed a preference and a wish for arcades, market halls and even simple glazing covering existing streets. There seems, therefore, to be a difference between what the public prefers and what development world has traditionally been providing in the form of interior based shopping environments.

This shift in public feeling, together with planning requirements, which are also moving in the same direction, presents one of the greatest challenges to designers of shopping environments. It seems, therefore, we have reached a key moment in time, in that any scheme that is now presented has to take on board these new criteria and most shopping facilities will have to address the urban agenda.

Society today finds itself with a shortage of time. And time, together with attention and trust, have been categorised as the 'new scarcities' (Dr David Lewis at the British Council of Shopping Centres Conference, 2002). The scarcity of time is one of the results of modern day pressure-cooker living and fast lifestyles. When people use some of their scarce time to go shopping they expect the right retail offer and the right level of amenity and comfort.

The British Council of Shopping Centres Report, *Shopping Centre Futures*, identifies that people also have shorter attention spans. (British Council of Shopping Centres Report, 2002, p. 9). In a world of channel-hopping and net-surfing, there is a constant bombardment of images. Society's attention span has been reduced and shopping has to compete in a visually oriented world. It has to be exciting to respond to that competition (Fig. 1.4).

Trust in institutional authority has diminished and has also become a scarce commodity. The public's trust in institutions, politicians and the monarchy has declined. Perhaps the converse of the decline in trust is also a decline in gullibility, and a public less deferential and less prepared to be patronised. They

Figure 1.5 Generation X are less deferential and prepared to be patronised. *(Source: Andy Borzyskowski)*

are more challenging and discerning and shopping centre facilities have to recognise and reflect this.

Buying an Experience

The activity of shopping for this kind of public has moved on, for example, from 1945 when it was mainly buying a product or a commodity, to the 1960s and 1970s when the focus was on services, to the latter part of the 1990s when shopping was about going out and obtaining an experience. Now, shopping is about transformation, or collecting a thought – about collecting aspects of a lifestyle or things that contribute to a person's mental well-being. Shopping expeditions are continuing to progress from providing experiences to transformations, for instance, by incorporating opportunities for the visitor to participate in a civic or cultural activity. Some of these activities would traditionally be found in historic town or city centres, which favourably suit the trend towards new integrated urban shopping environments in town centre locations (Fig. 1.6).

The activity of shopping now contains aspects of knowledge-giving, teaching and mind-changing

Figure 1.4 Dual screen imaging and digital technology have raised visual expectations. *(Source: Andy Borzyskowski)*

Figure 1.6 Shops providing knowledge and displaying goods in a gallery-like context, Apple Store, Regents Street, London (2004). *(Source: David Barbour)*

that were previously remote or unconnected to it. The challenge for designers is how to make a shopping environment a memorable experience. This applies both to the shopping environment and to the individual units. Examples of shops providing knowledge have already been developed in New York and Tokyo, where goods are displayed as artefacts in contemporary environments, and where there is plenty of space for shoppers to walk around and look at the goods from different angles. There might also be informative explanations of the manufacturing process or the technologies involved, as in Nike Town and Sony stores. In these sort of shops the purchasing is carried out in a separate dedicated area.

The challenge is how to bring this knowledge-making experience to a shopping environment. Shopping places will need to exploit this and make the visit memorable, even to the extent that the shopping trip becomes more important than the purchase. It will need to be a fulfilling experience and it should provide something that is unique and different to visiting another place. It should have a sense of place and this will also require the architecture to be of sufficiently high standard to be memorable and fulfilling.

Increasing Expectations

Familiarity and travel have raised public expectations about the retail offer and the ranges available. Now the public expects more of the right kind of shops to be grouped together to facilitate comparison shopping, together with larger units displaying full product ranges. Shopping environments should be examples of good urban design. It is very important for designers to be responsive to a place, its history and culture, and make their designs respond to it. The designer's skill will manifest itself in taking these requirements on board without making the end design patronising.

The quality of the environment of shopping amenities from arrival to departure has been improved, and will continue to be so, because people will vote with their feet and shop elsewhere if it is not right.

Making a Destination

As part of a shopping trip, attractive shopping places can double up to provide a civic destination space which forms the hub to a centre or town. These spaces can have both local and regional uses. They are particularly important as local social meeting points and as tourist destinations. Forming

such spaces is a key element of shopping centre design. The opportunity for creating a civic destination can be one of the most rewarding aspects of being involved in the design of retail environments.

Customers Become Guests

With competition between centres increasing, providing the right level of facility can make the difference to success. Developers have recognised this and new benchmark levels of customer care continue to raise the standards from customer arrival through to departure. The level of amenities in some

Figure 1.7 Shopping places double up to provide a civic destination space, Hays Wharf Galleria, London, UK (1988). *(Source: St Martins Property Corporation Ltd)*

shopping environments now parallel that in hotels. This level of consideration given to customer quality is part of the package from entrance to exit. Provision of drinks and refreshments, cashpoints, seating, design of toilets, disabled facilities and crèches are all important customer requirements that can no longer be positioned in remote and inaccessible parts of a centre, or added to a design as a necessary but non-integral afterthought. They are fundamental to the planning and organisation of a centre and must be considered at the outset.

Demographic Change

With more of the population aged over 60 than under 16, and this older percentage being healthier and wealthier, society is more youthful for longer. This trend towards an increasingly older and more active population means the right retail and catering offers in the places they shop must be tailored to fit their requirements and characteristics. Although this group might be grey, it is not necessarily dull and its retail demands are diverse and discerning. It is careful of its use of time and when these consumers go to a shopping centre they want it to have the right facilities, in the right environment, with the right levels of safety and security. It is this particular generation, which is generally well-travelled, experienced and knowledgeable, that wants shopping to be a positive, memorable experience. It also has high expectations allied to close attention to detail.

Catering Facilities

The amount of catering as a percentage of the total retail area in shopping centres has been steadily increasing over the past 20 years. The main reason for this has been to increase 'dwell-time' – the length of time shoppers stay in a centre. If they enjoy the experience more, they will stay longer and will spend more per visit.

Centres must provide broad ranges of catering facility from cafés to fast-food, plus a range of restaurants and bars. Catering in shopping centres has progressed from simple fast food in food courts to a sophisticated broad-spectrum of food offers being provided.

The range of different types of food outlet can be categorised:
- simple refreshment, such as small outlets, kiosks, stalls and vending machines
- fast-food and snack areas

Figure 1.8 The archetypal fast food court, Canal Walk, Century City, Cape Town, South Africa. *(Source: Peter Coleman)*

- light meal, which might be fresh food, salads, or sushi
- medium-stay meal
- comfortable or memorable meal.

The nature and size of the catering depends on the size and location of the centre. Each centre will determine a catering offer to suit the size and nature of the centre and will not necessarily need to provide this full range.

Safety and Security

With increasing exposure to crime and terrorist threats, providing a safe and secure environment has become a major factor in shopping centre design. But shopping centres are not fortresses and designers must achieve a balance. Security, therefore, must be incorporated as a necessary but discreet element as far as possible. Entrances have to remain inviting and encourage access. In an urban setting, entrances and thresholds often need to be made invisible to maintain integration and permeability within their context of the town centre.

Leisure and Entertainment

With shopping being increasingly combined with leisure activities – especially in the large regional retail destinations to encourage a long stay or a full-day visit – a range of good quality leisure facilities increasingly need to be provided.

Shopping combined with leisure is not restricted to large regional centres. For example, 38 per cent of all planned new shopping centres include a large leisure component. Society is participating in more out-of-home leisure time, including dining out.

Leisure facilities build on the correlation between enjoyment and the feel-good factor which, in turn, encourages people to spend. Such facilities would include:

- cinemas; ranging from multi-screen complexes down to single-screen arts film theatres
- theatres or music venues
- events spaces
- gyms and health clubs
- climbing walls
- bowling alleys
- slot and electronic games machines
- casinos
- surfing, swimming and other sports.

Leisure facilities relate well to catering and dining and to leisure-based retail such as book or music shops, but such facilities have to be carefully thought out and provided. They tend to be space hungry and bring in lower rents than shops and therefore are often better suited to locations in lower-value areas, perhaps on floors above the shops or in the more remote locations of a centre. When including leisure with shopping it is important to ensure compatibility. For example, leisure activity may focus at a different time during the opening period to avoid a conflict with the use of car parking facilities.

Figure 1.9 Retail entertainment centres where retail catering and leisure facilities are equally arranged, illustrated by Universal City Walk, Los Angeles, USA (1993). *(Source: Jerde Partnership/Stephen Simpson)*

Women Shop Most in the UK

According to The Future Foundation, two-thirds of shopping is currently undertaken by women, which reinforces the need for a safe and secure environment. (Grosvenor/British Council of Shopping Centres Report, 2002, p. 11). Leisure elements in a centre can therefore be tailored to attract and cater for different sex and age-group preferences. It also means that when families go shopping, other facilities for men and children must also be provided. To minimise in-family stress, facilities will range from in-store amenities, such as seating areas adjacent to fitting rooms, to in-centre facilities, such as specific male or youth-oriented shops, crèche facilities and leisure activities.

As the social trend for men taking a more active role in parenting and cooking is borne out in the future, they are likely to become more active shoppers. Future shopping centres will need to cater for this change without alienating women. Another major demographic change is that there are now more single-person households and providing facilities for these 'singletons' is also something designers and developers need to take into consideration.

Figure 1.10 In Northern Europe most shopping takes place in the four months with least daylight – emphasising the importance of artificial lighting. *(Source: Finnish Tourist Board)*

Shopping Habits

It is commonly recognised in northern Europe that most shopping takes place in the four months with least natural daylight. The months of October, November, December and January generally account for 80 per cent of all retail sales. This emphasises the importance of providing high standards of artificial lighting in public spaces.

The shopping seasons also influence the completion and opening dates of developments. Building programmes will be tailored to target such key trading periods. Developers and owners will aim to complete their centres in time to maximise their impact, and allow rental income returns to start as soon as possible. If aiming for the Christmas shopping period, for example, centres will need to open at the end of September or early October at the latest.

Planning Issues

Planning legislation has had a significant influence over shopping centre design. This has been particularly so in the UK and Europe since the mid-1990s. Planning is obviously necessary to protect the countryside and to prevent urban sprawl. In this way out-of-town shopping development has been stemmed and strictly controlled. This has refocused attention back to the city heartlands and caused the development of a new generation of retail centres in urban environments.

At the same time, to protect the character of town and city centres in the UK, new legislation and

design guidance has come in which has influenced the nature of shopping design in towns. For example, the scene for urban-led regeneration and the formation of urban communities was set by the seminal report, *Towards an Urban Renaissance*, chaired by Lord Rogers, which illustrated design-led ways of improving the quality of our towns (and countryside) through design excellence, social well-being and environmental responsibility within a viable economic and legislative framework (Department of Environment, Transport and the Regions, 1999). The Urban Task Force report led to more specific design guidance from both the national consultative body, the Commission for Architecture and the Built Environment (CABE) and the retail industry, the British Council of Shopping Centres (BCSC).[1]

The design guidelines challenge the conventions of traditional shopping centres. They encourage open streets, with potential for covered streets and smaller building blocks; they promote individual buildings, designed by a mix of architects; and there is a desire to create a variety of architectural styles. In general they discourage large inward-looking, impermeable, internalised shopping environments and, instead, seek integration with other parts of a town centre, incorporating a mix of uses in addition to retail.

The result is a new type of urban centre designed as an integral part of a town centre, which combines the outward appearance of open or covered streets with the convenience and operational benefits of a planned and centrally managed shopping environment. In other words, something which has the benefits of both worlds; combining the best of town centres, with their cultural and civic qualities, with the comfort and convenience of a shopping centre. As yet there are only a few completed examples, but these will undoubtedly increase over time.

The new type of centre is complex in its nature:
- it has invisible boundaries
- the public spaces do not have recognisable thresholds separating them from other parts of the town

---

[1] CABE has produced several guidance publications referred to by planning authorities, for example *By Design – Urban Design in the Planning System; Towards Better Practice*, Department of the Environment, Transport and the Regions, CABE, 2000; *Creating Successful Masterplans: A Guide for Clients*, CABE, 2004. The BCSC, in recognition of CABE's guidelines being for the purpose of general urban design guidance, produced a specific guideline for town centre retail development – *Urban Design for Retail Environments*, BCSC/BDP, 2002. The principle to these guidelines recommends more sustainable and integrated development in town and city centres.

Figure 1.11 A masterplanner architect and two other architects designed the successful mixed use development, Marienburg, Njimegen, The Netherlands (2000). *(Source: Sjaak Henselmans)*

- it provides modern convenient retail spaces of the right size and variation
- it is safe and secure
- it has integrated service vehicle access even though it is part of the city streets
- it has user-friendly and convenient car parking
- it has a good close relationship with an integrated transport network.

This new type of centre is encouraging significant proportions of town centre retail environments to be centrally managed. This can be a combination of the developer's management team and the local authority team. Architects and designers are becoming accustomed to the idea of shopping centres being designed to be integral parts of town centres.

Such an approach, combining urban design with the technical knowledge of modern retail facilities, which is often referred to as the 'urban agenda', requires a broader range of skills than was common with traditional large out-of-town centres. Skills required include urban design and town planning, as well as architecture.

To create a town-centre-based shopping centre having a similar organic quality to that of a town that has grown over several hundred years, demands an architectural approach with a variety of treatments. And, although it is possible for a single architect to bring a variety of architectural approaches to different buildings, the new urban shopping centre tends to encourage the involvement of different architects working on individual buildings or blocks within a masterplan. On such projects a lead architect, or masterplanner, will work with other architects, with the lead architect acting in a coordinating role. The lead architect may also undertake a proportion of the detailed design work.

Environmental Awareness

A greater awareness of the environmental impact of a large shopping project causes designers positively to incorporate such criteria as:
- ways of consuming less energy
- using more passive means of controlling the use of energy, e.g. using greater insulation, using natural ventilation and daylight, the careful positioning of glazing, and avoiding solar gain
- using locally sourced materials
- re-using waste materials
- ensuring less dependency on cars and promoting an integrated transport system.

Integrated Transport Policies

All sorts of means of access and modes of transport must be considered when planning a shopping centre. Such modes include:
- cars
- public transport – bus, tram and train
- bicycle
- pedestrian.

All these modes must be brought together to operate in a single integrated network.

Economic Issues

Maturity of the Market

In northern European countries the population is generally well provided with retail facilities. Shopping centres began to appear in the UK some 50 years ago and now, in Britain, there are around 1500 centres, which is the largest number in any country outside North America (BCSC Report, 2001). Therefore, opportunities for building new centres in the UK are few and any new facility has to be better than those preceding it.

Competition

The density of urban development in some regions of the UK creates competition between adjacent centres, which inevitably attract the same potential visitors from within a 40 to 60 minute drive-time. A centre often finds it necessary to keep up with a neighbouring new competitor in order to maintain the centre's asset value, which can generate the need for refurbishment. The shopping public only has so much disposable income and time available to shop, therefore competing centres must capture that urge to spend by providing the right retail offer in comfortable and secure surroundings.

Need to Modernise Town Centre Facilities

Despite the boom in building out-of-town shopping centres in the 1990s, over 80 per cent of shop floor space in the UK is still located in town centre high streets. However, only 35 per cent of town centre space has been built since 1985 (Bridget Roswell at BCSC Conference, 2002). Therefore, more than

Figure 1.12 Typical European high streets with premises which do not meet modern retailer requirements, illustrated by an early shopping precinct, Market Way, Coventry, UK (1955). *(Source: Peter Coleman)*

half of all UK retail space is either old or out of date and does not meet the needs of current retailers. It is clear that there is a great need to rebuild and modernise town centre retail facilities. Much of architects' work in the future will involve modernising existing space and great care will be needed to integrate these modernised facilities into town centres in a sustainable and sensitive way.

Expectations

Public expectations of what makes a good shopping centre have been raised by advertising, ease of travel and greater mobility. Failure to meet these heightened expectations will result in shoppers going elsewhere and a centre losing its market share. The public is well aware that there is usually another centre within a radius of 40–60 minutes drive-time.

Value

Consumers expect best value and will search until they find it. Retailers need to operate from efficient premises to provide this. Unit sizes need to be larger to achieve economies of scale and the larger unit also allows fuller ranges to be displayed, thus improving the offer.

Importance of the Customer

General market demand, based simply on measures of affluence, has developed into more sophisticated means of categorising customers. Among these measures, shoppers are now characterised into lifestyle types by habits, activities and age. This more realistic and accurate model of customer or predictability is taken into account when deciding on the retail mix to be provided in shopping facilities.

A new micro-social science has emerged through the work of several consumer researchers such as David Lewis, joint author of *The Soul of the New Consumer*, which has given new insights into consumer behaviour (Lewis and Bridges, 2001). Using such studies has enabled centres to be specifically customised to suit local catchment area characteristics, both in terms of retail mix and in the core values of the design. It has allowed themed retailing, where bespoke groups of shops are created within a centre, for example, by providing shops focused on youth fashion, ladies fashion, leisure activity or homewares, and which are specifically tuned to the aspirations of the particular catchment area.

Taking 'tuning the mix' further means that entire centres can be themed, where the buying characteristics of the likely catchment area justify it. Examples include Fashion Island in Newport Beach, California, which focuses on high profile fashion labels, or Villa Arena in Amsterdam where the whole centre provides solely homewares.

Figure 1.13 Focusing the mix of a single centre to one type of retailing. A whole centre for homewares, Villa Arena, Amsterdam, The Netherlands (2001). *(Source: Benthan Cronwell)*

Tenant Mix

Shoppers are looking for more product variation and a broader tenant mix. This requires centres to be of sufficient size to be able to provide this mix and the careful selection of tenants to get the right retail offer. Size and mix are key to getting the centre right.

Constant Change

Retail provision is a dynamic industry where the drivers of change extend beyond the seasons and operate, to some extent, outside standard changes in fashion criteria. New types of retail constantly emerge requiring new types of facility and new standards.

Trading patterns too are evolving all the time and these also influence design requirements. For example, stock changes are now more frequent which, in turn, involve corresponding changes in display and fit-out and more frequent delivery and handling of goods.

Retail supply patterns have altered. Computerised tills linked directly to stock control and warehouses have allowed just-in-time delivery methods, resulting in less on-site storage and a greater reliance on regular delivery from centralised hub warehouses.

Global Retailers

Many retailers now expect to operate across more than one country. They have set new standards in shopfront and fit-out, and have often been at the forefront of raising benchmarks and taking new ideas from one country to another. Not least among these new standards is their willingness to trade on several levels. Familiar examples include Mango and Zara of Spain and Benetton of Italy.

Figure 1.14 An example of Global retailers, The Apple Computer Store, Regent Street, London, UK (2004). *(Source: David Barbour)*

Economies of Scale

As shop units become larger, shopping centres have correspondingly become larger in order to accommodate them, and they remain viable by maintaining a balance and range of retail offers. Large stores are often encouraged to take space in centres by low rents or other financial incentives. For the centres to afford making these beneficial deals with key tenants and to build up a viable critical mass, they require a necessary amount of other units to pay the full rent.

Emerging Competition

Shop units have to compete with other methods of shopping, such as catalogue purchasing and 'e-tailing', which is available in a variety of electronic formats. Though alternative forms of shopping may increasingly impinge on the market share of non-comparison shopping, such as books, music and general foodstuffs (as long as delivery and security issues can be adequately addressed), there will always be a strong demand by people to go shopping when seeking comparison goods where sight, size and feel are all important.

Yet, while Internet sales currently have little impact on traditional sales proportions, we should not overlook the impact of the IT-savvy generation (sometimes called 'Generation X'). This generation will come of age with real spending power, probably after 2010, and these techno-consumers will have a great influence on future modes of shopping.

Technology, that is now at the leading edge will, in time, become commonplace. By 2020, for example, 80 per cent of the British population is likely to have adopted interactive services in the home (Grosvenor/BCSC, 2002). The three technological developments of interactive TV, mobile Internet and Broadband are the most likely to impact on shopping and the future of shopping centres.

Advances in technology will not replace traditional shopping activity, just as the cinema has withstood television and video formats, however, it will influence how we shop. IT will combine with traditional formats and shops will have to find a way of integrating this into their offer. IT will enable shoppers to become more informed – they are likely to research prices, styles and ranges on the Internet before going shopping. There is likely to be more informed and focused shopping and less browsing – requiring shops and shopping centres to be more streamlined and easy to use.

Anchors Remain Important

A good department store remains one of the mainstays and one of the desirable elements of a town centre or shopping centre. In 2001, there were over 600 department stores in the UK. However, they are having to reinvent themselves to respond to younger and more selective markets. Interiors are being modernised and rationalised. Product ranges are reflecting the demands for specialisation; focus is moving to the most wanted products, with fashionware coming to the fore and other product lines being dropped altogether. The presence of anchor stores in a development still remains a crucial factor in attracting other retail tenants to come in.

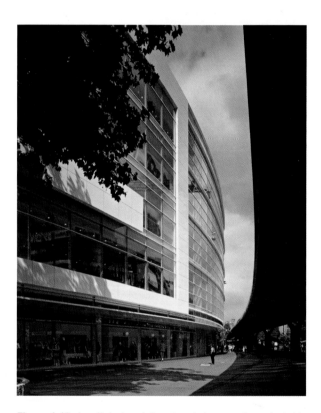

Figure 1.15 A well designed department store remains a desirable element of town centre development, illustrated by Richard Meiers Peek and Cloppenburg Store, Düsseldorf, Germany. *(Source: Arcaid/Richard Bryant)*

Shopfronts Raise their Skirts

With shop units becoming larger, more retailers are taking up mezzanine or first floor space. In response to this trend for double height shops, shopfronts

Figure 1.16 DKNY shopfront – typical of the double height shop fronts frequently seen in the West End, London, UK. *(Source: David Barbour)*

have risen vertically from single-storey to two or more storey heights. This has opened up views into the shops, creating more animation on to the streets and also, by providing public internal spaces in the shops, helping to improve the vertical proportions of the public spaces they address. Shopfronts are now more dramatic, contributing directly to the quality of the streetscape and helping shops provide animated frontages.

The Big Challenges

All these issues facing the retail industry need to be addressed and will have an influence when considering a new shopping facility. Of these issues, there are certain key ones which are already challenging the thinking about the concept and design of a centre, to the point where a new type of facility has emerged. These issues have added to the existing range of shopping formats.

The key issues which will continue to challenge existing assumptions and drive through radical changes are:

1 The maturity of the market: where competition between centres causes them to strive to achieve a difference and capture the public's need to spend.

2 Understanding the customer: where increasingly specialised knowledge enables research to be used to select retailers and create core design values to customise a centre to a location. It is no longer sufficient to roll out a formula.

3 Public sentiment: this has been moving away from internalised shopping centres, towards a wish for more open and permeable environments.

4 Planning background: this has been generating a need for more sustainable shopping environments.

5 The urban agenda: this is encouraging street-based retailing and has caused a change in the type of retail facilities being designed. It is pushing a move towards more mixed-use development, robust and flexible masterplans and managed town centre shopping environments.

All these factors combine to challenge the industry to consider new types of shopping environments and stretch further into new territory – beyond traditional shopping centres into new types of shopping. These include designing street-based retailing in mixed-use environments with all the facilities and amenities of a traditional centre. As the fictional Spock might have said to Captain Kirk: 'It's a shopping centre, Jim, but not as we know it.'

These qualities of reinvention and diversification have influenced both the title and contents of this book. Everyone involved in the formation of shopping facilities will need to be aware of the continual emergence of new types.

In making a step-change away from the established criteria of enclosed shopping centres, combined with the sophisticated knowledge of customer research and the fine tuning of the tenant mix, the time approaches when the maturity of design understanding will allow almost any arrangement to work, so long as it has been thoroughly researched and considered.

Therefore, a design should work so long as it meets these fundamental criteria:

■ it understands and is targeted to meet a local market
■ it meets the requirements of the retailers
■ it provides adequate back-of-house facilities

Figure 1.17 Even an old power station which utilises a well researched retail brief can be converted into a shopping centre, Battersea Power Station, Battersea, London, UK by Sir Nicholas Grimshaw. *(Source: Nicholas Grimshaw/Hayes Davidson)*

- it provides a safe and comfortable public environment
- it complies with planning guidelines and consultative bodies.

New forms of shopping facility will continue to emerge which capture the best of the high street and traditional town centre, while providing levels of retailing and customer comfort with modern efficient servicing and operation.

Whatever new or emerging types of shopping facility eventually come into being, they can only add to the diversity of the existing range. However, each new type will require new skills and technical understanding from those involved in their creation. I see the new urban shopping centre as one which has been added to an existing menu and which, at the moment at least, is actually the dish of the day.

References

British Council of Shopping Centres/Building Design Partnership (2002). *Urban Design of Retail Environments*. BCSC.

British Council of Shopping Centres Report (2001). BCSC.

Department of Environment, Transport and the Regions (1999). *Towards an Urban Renaissance*. DETR.

Grosvenor/British Council of Shopping Centres Report (2002). *Shopping Centre Futures*. BCSC.

Lewis, D. and Bridges, D. (2001). *The Soul of the New Consumer*. Nicolas Brealey Publishing.

Figure 1.18 A glazed diagrid covers the naturally ventilated public space, to form the focus of the Bristol City Centre Expansion, Bristol, UK (2008). *(Source: Chapman Taylor)*

Figure 2.1 Watercolour reconstruction of general life in the Greek Agora, which was intermittently used as a market. *(Source: Mary Evans Picture Library)*

Historical Evolution of Places for Shopping 2

Ancient Times

From the time of selecting goods, from those laid out on a woven trading mat in the Greek *agora*, to choosing with a click of a mouse on a sponsored vinyl mat, the evolution of shopping formats has been long and complex. The background and evolution of shopping formats up to the establishment of the first purpose-planned shopping centre is outlined here.

The different formats of shopping activity have progressed from the earliest civilisations in isolated kingdoms to the interconnected world of today. This journey of evolution has involved a continuous process of change and will continue beyond the formats and guidelines outlined here. The evolutionary process, from the earliest civilisations up to the early part of the 20th century, is summarised in the time-line diagram shown in Appendix 2.1 (page 50), which is organised into the principal periods.

Early Civilisation

From earliest times humankind settled together in groups, probably for reasons of safety and convenience, and at some point began the activities of trading and exchanging agricultural and crafted goods grown or made by others. Early trading activities took place in meeting and gathering spaces.

Although the knowledge and skills of the Egyptians were well-advanced, there is little evidence of where, in what space or building, they carried out their trading activities. For the Greeks, trading took place in the *agora*. This was an open square formed as a meeting-place, often between the ruling palace and the town's principal buildings, and was intermittently used as a market. On market days, goods were laid out on mats or on temporary stalls to allow other activities – such as voting and debate, public displays, sports and parades – to take place outside market days. The earliest trading took place at the hub of the settlement, and so established the integrated relationship between trading and the heart of civilised activity in the centre of towns.

Roman Forums

The major cities of the Roman world also formed open spaces as the centre of civic life. They were used for a variety of purposes and were surrounded by temples, basilicas, bathhouses and state buildings. The activities of religion, law and commerce overspilled into the forum spaces. The citizens came to the forum to worship, do business, play and shop. Shopping was one of a variety of activities which took place both in the buildings and in the forum space.

Rome had two forums, Forum Romanum and Trajan's Forum. The Forum of Trajan, initiated by the emperor in 115 AD and completed by his successor Hadrian by 128 AD, was a vast area, formally arranged as a series of terraced crescent-shaped buildings where the shops were on four levels. These are some of the first recognised defined shop spaces and were provided in a variety of ways from the lowest level upwards. In the crescent-shaped

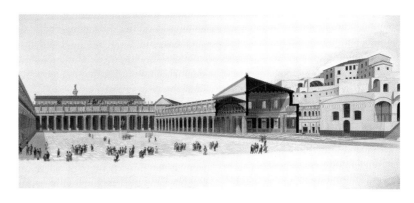

Figure 2.2 Trajan's Forum, Rome – a reconstruction with the Markets of Trajan in the background right. *(Source: AKG)*

Figure 2.3 Reconstruction of the antique Forum Romanum with strong civic architecture and discreet shops. *(Source: AKG)*

colonnade the shops faced directly onto the forum at ground level. Above this sat the Great Hall, forming a two-storey high, vaulted interior hall 33 m long by 9 m wide, lined on each side with shops on both ground and galleried levels. A fourth level of shops arranged in a hemicycle faced onto another terrace. The shops are likely to have been open-fronted with a counter across the front, for display and trading facing onto the public walkway.

Trajan's Forum was a magnificent arrangement of shared-use buildings and is likely to have been one of the first collections of defined shops. They were also unique in being largely under cover and arranged on several levels. Pevsner described Trajan's Forum as having 'about 150 shops on various levels selling wine, grain and oil' (Pevsner, 1976, p. 235). As a shopping venue it has only recently been rivalled and arguably never equalled for its combined civic magnificence.

Medieval to 19th Century

Medieval Market and Town Halls – 11th–16th Centuries

The traditional wisdom used to be that, with the demise of the Roman Empire, western Europe drifted into 500 years or so of dark ages, shopping included. However, trading never ceased and while the large-scale retail environment of the Roman forum was not re-attained until many centuries later, and barter rather than money may have become the normal basis for exchange of goods, the successor kingdoms to the Roman imperium did have markets and ways of obtaining necessary and desirable commodities.

When greater stability and wealth returned to northern Europe under Charlemagne and later the Normans, towns began to prosper again, alongside the castles and abbeys, eventually broadening and developing into trading centres. Markets were held in the towns for trading and led to the formation of shared-use buildings to control this trading and to administer the town. These buildings combined a market hall on the ground floor and town hall above. Under the feudal system, the guilds controlled craftsmanship and also operated from the market hall, frequently leading to the construction of a new hall as craftsmanship prospered.

The market and town halls were the focus of trading and business activity and were located, along with the market square, in the centre of the town. The early market and town hall buildings combined the two uses and were two-storey buildings with a council chamber on the first floor for administering the town, the guilds and the market. The ground floor remained open between the columns and was used as an extension to the market. Trading and the display of goods took place across removable stalls. One of the earliest surviving examples of this combined use building is the Palazzo de Broletto in Como, Italy, inscribed 1215 (Pevsner, 1976, p. 27).

Medieval trading consisted of livestock, agricultural products, craftsman's tools, leatherware and clothing. With growth and prosperity in the towns, the market and town halls grew, leading to the ground floors being walled in, wings being added and courtyards formed to make grand town hall buildings. Some towns developed separate town hall and guild-hall buildings.

Where the market remained within the town hall, the ground floors were arranged into a group of small shops, e.g. Thorn Town Hall, Poland, c1250; Ypres Town Hall, Belgium, c1200 (Pevsner, 1976, p. 29). Thorn Town Hall had ground floor shops for the cloth trade, haberdashers, potters, soap stalls, linen sellers, bakers and cake bakers. These shops faced externally on three sides of the building into the courtyard and also into a covered way beneath the building. In Bruges, which had three separate halls, the Bruges Halles of c1250, separate from the Town Hall and the Cloth Hall, had shops on its ground floor for mercers, spicers, butchers, confectioners, saddlers and cutlers (Pevsner, 1976, p. 236).

Figure 2.4 A typical two-storey medieval market hall with open ground floor trading illustrated by the Old Market Hall, Ledbury, Herefordshire, UK. *(Source: Joe Pie Picture Library)*

Figure 2.5 The ground floor shops influenced the architectural form of the medieval Ypres Town Hall, Belgium. *(Source: AA)*

Figure 2.6 The wealthier medieval cities were able to afford individual halls representing the flourishing trades of the region – illustrated by the separate Cloth Hall, Ypres, Belgium. *(Source: Bildarchiv Foto Marburg)*

These examples are the earliest surviving defined shop spaces in northern Europe. Although they were part of a larger town or guild-hall building, the shops formed the principal uses on the ground floor and faced the street or square. This format of outward facing collections of shops would come to form the basis of shop-lined streets throughout Europe in later centuries.

Another example of a combined market and town hall providing a collection of defined shops can be found at the Ring in Breslau, Germany, dating from 1275 (Geist, 1989, p. 40). Here, the market buildings were attached to the side of the town hall and sat in the middle of the main square faced by surrounding buildings (see Figs. 2.7 and 2.8). Beside the town hall, four parallel linear ways lined with shops on each side provided undercover stalls for different types of trade. Shops also faced externally from the market buildings, along with other separate market structures and stalls. With the four covered ways separated from the town hall, Breslau represents a prime example of a collection of purpose-built shops under cover.

Geist describes each of the market areas in more detail. Of particular note are the four different ways or streets for separate trades:

- The *Tuchaus* (cloth house), a 100 m long three-storey high space lined both sides with 20 shops with storage space above. This space was originally open, although eventually covered.
- The *Reichkrame* (imperial shops), a covered way between 40 small, defined shops.
- The *Schmetterhause* (crafts hall), a two-storey high hall lined with stalls.
- The *Gewandreissergang* (clothes hall), a hall lined each side with single-storey shops.

The Ring market buildings are likely to have been simple vernacular structures with a workaday quality similar to domestic or agricultural buildings. Although attached to the town hall, the Breslau Market buildings are one of the earliest examples of purpose-built single-use market buildings.

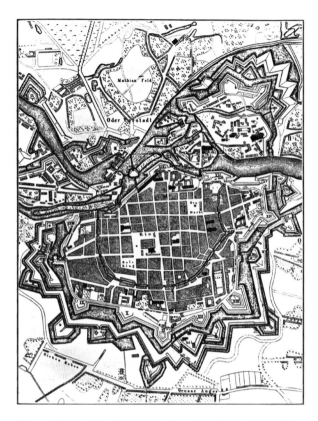

Figure 2.7 A medieval street plan shows The Ring beside the town hall (Rathhaus) in the centre, Breslau, Germany. *(Source: Bildarchiv Foto Marburg)*

In Italy, during the 14th century, the Tuscan town halls of Florence and Sienna moved the markets into separate buildings. Other towns, such as Bologna, Brescia and Padua, maintained the medieval pattern of a combined market and town hall, with the council chambers on the first floors and an open colonnaded market area below.

In England, the market and town halls, which were generally on a similar scale to Europe, followed the medieval pattern.

Although the Netherlands had general purpose market and town halls, by the 15th century it tended to build more individual specialist halls, separating the meat hall from the cloth hall and town hall. This was largely due to its great wealth – illustrated by the three magnificent separate halls in Ghent (Pevsner, 1976, p. 236).

Generally, by the 16th century, across Europe market halls were no longer combined with town or guild uses. New market halls were built as large linear structures covering long nave-like spaces, with side aisles lined with stalls forming collections of shops.

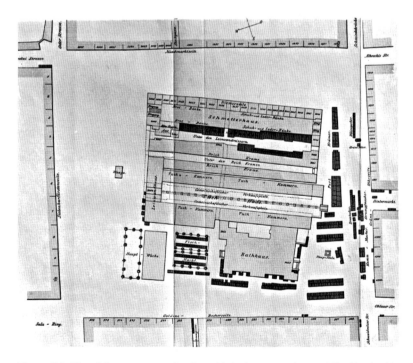

Figure 2.8 Plan of the town square, Breslau, with the four covered ways of The Ring beside the town hall (Rathhaus). *(Source: Bildarchiv Foto Marburg)*

Figure 2.9 The Cloth Hall (1425–1445) Ghent, Belgium. *(Source: Art Directors/Tibor Bognar)*

Eastern Bazaars

While the medieval market and town halls were developing in parallel with eastern bazaars, the European examples outlined above were restrained and austere in comparison with the range of retail formats expressed in the various types of bazaar.

In the bazaars of the East we see significant progress and development in the organisation and arrangement of shops; in the type of retail format; in the use of architectural forms; in the scale of development; and in the self-expression of retail and trading.

Shops in the medieval market and town halls were based around the market square and the shared use of town hall buildings. A collection of shops was formed within the ground floor of a single building, albeit sometimes a large one. The bazaar, on the other hand, took a variety of forms in different architectural arrangements across the cities of North Africa and the Middle East, all expressing the singular use of trading.

The 13th century bazaars in the city of Fez in Morocco illustrate two types: the 'covered street' and the network grid or 'souk'. The covered street bazaar was arranged on a central street lined each side with shops of various sizes, protected from penetrating sunlight by a wooden structure overlaid with grass mats. The shops were raised above the road with a trading counter across an open frontage. Wooden shutters closed off the shops at night. In the second type, as at the Quissariya bazaar, a more intense collection of small shops was formed by a network of small alleyways in a grid. This bazaar represents a type referred to as a 'souk' and is found in many cities of the region.

Istanbul's Grand Bazaar (Turkish *kapaliçarsi* = 'covered market') is one of the largest bazaars, covering a single area of 200000 m² (20 ha) and forming

Figure 2.10 Medinna Bazaar, Morocco – today's Fez retains many of the traditional qualities of the original street bazaars. *(Source: Robert Frerck, Odyssey Productions)*

Figure 2.11 The Grand Bazaar, Istanbul today retains many early characteristics of a network of trading streets. *(Source: Robert Frerck, Odyssey Productions)*

a whole district of the city used primarily for trading. A network of streets, lined each side with booths, forms the general pattern for this collection of shops. There are also two main insertions set into the grid made by two formal masonry buildings, each with major interior spaces formed by domed colonnades. The buildings were surrounded by numerous shops, some with external colonnades and vaulting over the adjacent streets.

Like the markets of medieval Europe, the crafts were regulated. However, they were organised into streets or buildings forming different quarters for leatherware, jewellery and metalworking throughout this major district. In its heyday the scale and variation of goods in the different streets must have been a magnificent sight.

One of the perennial hazards of these historic enclosed shopping spaces is fire, and Kapaliçarsi was damaged by fire to various degrees in 1546, 1618, 1652, 1660, 1695, 1701, 1750, 1791, 1826 and 1954, but has always been repaired after each disaster. It also suffered greatly in the earthquakes of 1766 and 1894.

In addition to the two masonry buildings within the Grand Bazaar, there were other buildings in Istanbul forming bazaars. The Egyptian Bazaar of 1470 was a collection of shops within barrel-vaulted wings which formed interior spaces lined each side with small shops. (A plan shows a part of this bazaar arranged in an L-shaped building.)

The greatest bazaar was built in Isfahan in Persia under Abbas I (1585–1629). This was a formally laid out insertion set uncompromisingly into the organic street pattern. The bazaar was conceived as a forum with the shops laid out as a series of internal architectural spaces based around two large open courtyards. The shops were arranged into various architectural spaces:

- along the sides of the open colonnades facing on to the courtyards
- arranged either side of a 220 m long ogee-arched and domed linear hall
- in a single side of an arched and vaulted aisle attached to the wing of the courtyard
- around octagonal domed spaces arranged at the entrances or corners of the wings.

A commonly illustrated part of this bazaar is the fabric bazaar, formed by a double height vaulted and domed internal space with shops on either side, first floor balconies and an octagonal domed space at the crossing. The shops were arranged between the columns with open fronts and a counter separating the shop from the public walkway. Ornate geometrically patterned wooden screens with first floor

Figure 2.12 Isfahan Bazaar today conveys some of the spatial grandeur of the purpose-built shopping facility in Persia. *(Source: Art Directors/Michael Good)*

balustrades set above the shops had integrated wooden shutters to secure the shops. The vaults and domes were lined with patterned brickwork and small openings in the domes allowed controlled amounts of daylight. The bazaar of Isfahan is a prime early example of architectural forms being used to create humane urban spaces for a large collection of shops.

In the city of Bokhara, now in Uzbekistan, the bazaars adopt the form of linking elements between the major buildings. Here the mosques, baths, *chans*, mausoleums, palaces and formal bazaars, which are separate and individually planned, are linked together by a variety of open and covered shop-lined streets. In some parts the linking street element becomes a vaulted structure through which the thoroughfare passes.

In the eastern bazaars there were major developments in the evolution of shopping formats which were different from those in the European market and town halls. Most notable were the great variety of ways in which the collections of shops were formed, the use of whole covered streets, the increase in scale to form whole city districts, the use of buildings singularly as shops, the formation of retail and trading districts exclusive of other uses, the formation of networks of streets and the confident use of architectural forms to make places. The eastern bazaars were also fundamentally different in that they were generally inward looking, with the shops facing into a covered street or interior space.

The shared-use European market and town halls generally arranged the shops to face outwards on to the squares and streets. As the market halls became separate buildings, in some instances, the shops were also arranged to be inward looking, with the stalls arranged beneath large enclosures.

Exchanges

In late 16th century Europe, with the onset of wider world trade and the evolution of banking, credit, shares and limited companies, another type of trading building emerged following the town hall, market hall and guild-hall. These buildings, known as 'court hall exchanges', originated in Antwerp and Amsterdam and combined simultaneous activities, with open stands selling goods on the first floor and commodity trading stalls on the ground floor.

Between 1566 and 1568 the Royal Exchange was built in London, based on the Antwerp Exchange (this original was destroyed). A two-storey arcaded open courtyard provided two levels of trading, each with corridors lined with leaseable open stalls. Due to its success, other exchanges followed in London. The Exeter Exchange (1676) was a simpler building form on two floors, providing a long room on the

Figure 2.13 A vaulted space between the civic buildings provided a covered space, Bokhara Bazaar, Uzbekistan. *(Source: Art Directors/ Martin Barlow)*

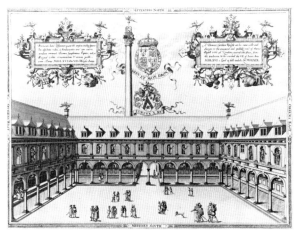

Figure 2.14 Lithograph of the open and colonnaded courtyard with two levels of trading at the Royal Exchange, London, UK (1566). *(Source: Guildhall Library)*

Figure 2.15 Exeter Exchange, London, UK on the site of The Strand Palace Hotel (1676). *(Source: Westminster Archive)*

Marchands in Paris, a similar exchange was formed in the old royal palace, which also sold luxury items. The exchange format, selling luxury items under cover in enclosed spaces extending over two floors, influenced the subsequent shopping formats of arcades and department stores.

Streets of Europe

In Europe, the location of shops gradually diversified from the exclusive domain of the market hall, town hall and guild-hall. Certainly, in Italy during the 16th century, and in northern Europe in the 17th century, trading occupied the ground floor of other premises. Large amounts of the central streets of London and Paris were lined with shops, pubs and coffee shops. Trading was still controlled by the guilds and the shops were organised by type into the same street.

ground floor, with the first floor lined each side with open trading stalls. The unique quality of this building was the collection of stalls in a large interior space with public thoroughfares passing between the lines of stalls. The stalls tended to sell luxury items for the wealthy. In 1773 the first floor was famous for its menagerie and is an early example of shops and leisure complementing one another and attracting visitors with leisure pastimes. At Galerie des

Figure 2.17 Lithograph of the guild controlled Bread Street, London, UK. *(Source: Roger Vaughan Picture Gallery)*

Figure 2.16 Cheapside, London, UK (1638) typifies the urban streetscape of the time with open fronted ground floor shops and living accommodation above. *(Source: Guildhall Library)*

Figure 2.18 Portici Via Roma adopted an urban form in response to the southern European climate, typical of the extensive colonnaded streets of the city of Turin, Italy. *(Source: Archivio Fotografico Tourismo, Torino)*

This organisation is reflected in the naming of certain streets – Milk Street, Bread Street, Cordwainer Street and Rue de la Lingerie. In the larger cities, several streets combined together to form quarters representing a trade or craft – e.g. the jewellers' quarter around Hatton Market in London. Shops are also likely to have lined the ground floors of buildings forming the squares or main streets of other European market towns at a similar time.

The streets in northern European towns, where these early shops were located, were open with some protection provided by individual shop canopies and the projecting gables above. In southern Europe, in order to protect the shops from direct sunlight, the urban form of colonnaded streets was adopted, where the ground floor was inset from the upper floors behind a colonnade. Nearly every street in Turin is laid out in this way.

Figure 2.19 Lithograph of the west view of St Ethelburgh within Bishopsgate, showing the early shopfronts of 1736, London, UK. *(Source: Guildhall Library)*

Figure 2.20 One of the first plate glass shopfronts in England installed at Asprey's, London, UK (c 1860). *(Source: Arcaid/Richard Bryant)*

The early shops had open fronts separated from the street by a counter with the goods displayed on the counter and in the frontage. Trading took place across the counter with little reason for the public to enter the shop. Shops were secured at night by placing removable or sliding wooden shutters across the opening or hinged wooden awnings which were lowered down and locked into place.

It was not until the arrival of glazed shopfronts that shops became areas into which the public walked and with this, the front counter was relocated inside. The first glazed shopfronts appeared from the late 17th century in Holland and from 1700 in France. The early glazed shopfronts were formed by a grid of small panes of glass which reflected the limitation of glazing technology. Glazed shopfronts became widespread in London during the 18th century. Illustrations of Bishopsgate of 1736 show a mixture of glazed and open shop frontages on the ground floor, which were arranged below two and three floors of other premises. Woburn Walk in London, originating from 1822, has close gridded shopfronts on both sides of the street.

The close-gridded, small-paned shopfront remained a common feature of shops until the mid-19th century when, in 1840, advances in glass technology saw the development of plate glass. This allowed glass panes of 2.1–2.4 m by 0.9–1.2 m to be used. This development in glazing opened up visibility to the shop interior. In England in 1845 the removal of duty on glass also assisted the growth of a new generation of more transparent shopfronts. Aspreys in London, 1860, and Benson in Bond Street were some of the earliest plate glass shopfronts. Greater and more daring glazed shopfronts followed.

Market and Fair Buildings

Developing from the single use medieval market halls and 16th century shared use exchange buildings, another building form emerged to continue the evolution of the format of collections of shops. This was the 18th and 19th century market building.

The expanding population of major cities drove the need for more and larger markets. Although the prime use of these markets was to trade livestock and agricultural products, the structures also contained collections of shops. The market structures in Paris at the beginning of the 19th century were based on open courtyards with perimeter arcades lined with stalls and shops. The first floor was used for storage, as illustrated by Marché St Germain of 1813–1816. Later markets were influenced by the grand exhibition buildings and took advantage of advances in iron and glass construction. These market buildings were based on large glazed pavilions and covered avenues, like Halles Centrales of 1853 by Victor Baltard. In London, James Fowler's New Covent Garden Market of 1830 rationalised several messy markets into a single structure, formed from

Figure 2.21 A secondary function of the grand exhibition buildings provided a collection of shops beneath the iron and glass structure of Halles Centralles, Paris, France (c 1853). *(Source: Bibliotheque Nationale de France)*

Figure 2.22 Perimeter shops in the aisles of the ground and first floor galleries of the Hungerford Market, London, UK (1833). *(Source: Guildhall Library)*

two large covered halls with external colonnades containing perimeter shops. Fowler also designed the Hungerford Market of 1833 with a single large hall with perimeter shops in the aisles of the ground and first floor galleries. Colonnading was also a feature around the main halls. Other large market buildings containing collections of small shops were the Padua meat market of 1821 by Japelli and Quincy Market in Boston of 1826 by Alexander Paris.

Italian market buildings tended to be more outward facing with the adoption of the *loggia* architectural form. These markets were more a piece of covered urban space than a building that was entered. Alternatively they adopted an open arcade,

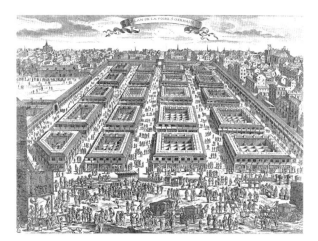

Figure 2.23 A 17th and 18th century fair, set up beyond the city wall to avoid paying taxes, contained shops and leisure pastimes. The Foire, St Germain, Paris, France. *(Source: Bibliotheque Nationale de France)*

facing a street or square, which was lined with stalls and shops.

Another building form to include a collection of shops were the fairs of the 18th century. The Foire St Germain of 1786 was located at the gates of the city of Paris. Although a travelling fair, the shops were organised into a network of pedestrianised open streets with each street representing a type of shop or trade. The fair was famous for its luxury goods and provided entertainment for visitors. It was possible to dance in the marquees, gamble in saloons, visit exhibitions, attend performances in theatres and listen to singers and musicians.

The Foire St Germain was another early example of the compatibility between leisure, shopping and entertainment. (This fair was possible because it occupied a large piece of land outside the city wall.) Purchasing goods from shops and stalls at the fair stopped once the fairs developed into the grand exhibitions that followed.

Observations and comparisons on the evolution of shopping formats from ancient times up to the market and fair buildings of the 19th century are made in Table 2.1.

Table 2.1 Observations on the early historical evolution of shopping

- Early establishment of the physical relationship between shops and the heart of towns
- Early relationships between the activity of shopping with civic and entertainment activities
- Shops originated as a secondary shared use of other building types
- Collections of shops organised into large building structures from early times
- First collections of shops were arranged in buildings with other uses
- First independent shop buildings in western Europe were workaday utilitarian structures (where few examples remain)
- As new formats emerge, collection of shops return to shared use buildings
- Eastern shop formats were more diverse
- Eastern formats first to establish a collection of shops as a single building
- Eastern formats used architecture more confidently to organise shops
- Covered internal solutions were adopted early on
- Protected urban solutions were adopted early on
- Technology made step-change advancements in shop formats
- Trade organisations influenced form and urban quarters
- The early forms established some common principles:
  - a number of shops of similar size aligned together in a linear arrangement, beside a pedestrian thoroughfare
  - two lines of shops arranged either side of a thoroughfare
  - two or more levels of shops
  - the public ways were protected in an internal environment under a masonry, timber or later under an iron and glass roof
  - shops inside a colonnaded arcade
  - gridded networks of covered streets or alleys

First Generation of Planned Shopping

Up to the mid-19th century, the formats for collections of shops were generally haphazard and secondary to other building uses. While there are some notable examples of planned collections of shops, such as the Forum of Trajan and the eastern bazaars of Istanbul and Isfahan, these were exceptions to the various other collections of shops which remained secondary to the prime activities of the town hall, market hall and guild-hall. Even in the exchange buildings and 19th century market buildings, which were built specifically for trading, the collections of shops were secondary to agricultural or commodity trading.

Developing in the 19th century a new generation of specifically planned collections of shops and new types of shops marked a step-change in the evolution of shopping which reached new heights. These new formats mark the beginning of shops becoming recognisable individual pieces of architecture in their own right.

Arcades

Arcades are a highlight in the evolution of shopping. Originating in the late-18th century and extending through to the beginning of the Second World War, nearly 300 naturally lit arcades were built throughout the world. France led the way with the first arcade, the Galeries de Bois, Palais Royal in Paris, built in 1788. This quickly led to several new arcades being formed between the streets in Paris and London.

A comprehensive and authoritative study of arcades is Johann Friedrich Geist's *Arcades – the History of a Building Type*, which traces in detail the social development and evolution of the arcade and includes an extensive illustrated catalogue of all the arcades planned and built (Geist, 1989). Those seeking points of detail and a chronological history of arcades should refer to Geist's book.

The arcade responded specifically to the social and urban planning issues which faced growing and increasingly urbanised cities, first in London and Paris, and later across the globe. In established cities, land for expansion was scarce and developing within existing city blocks intensified land use and utilised under-used rear areas.

The considerable number of new shops aligning each side of an arcade provided the space to display and consume the growing amount of manufactured goods that became available in the 19th century. The street environment in the major cities simultaneously

Figure 2.24 The first European arcade, Galerie de Bois, Paris, France (1788). *(Source: Bibliotheque Nationale de France)*

became increasingly busy, hostile and crowded with horse-drawn vehicles. Society had developed beyond the quality of the available public spaces. The new pedestrianised ways formed by the arcades provided a safe and convenient place, away from the busy roads, which encouraged social promenading.

The arcade was the first European building planned primarily to accommodate a collection of shops. Shops of similar size were arranged on either side of a public thoroughfare connecting two busy existing streets. Early shops in the arcades were open stalls, but quickly became walk-in shops with gridded, small-paned glazed shopfronts. The alignment of the thoroughfare with stalls and shops was an arrangement established in the medieval market building of the Ring in Breslau, the town hall of Thorn and the bazaars of Fez and Isfahan. The unique quality of the arcades was that they were largely naturally lit. This was a feature of the early arcades, which either had top lighting from regular lantern openings in the roof, or were side lit by clerestory windows above the shops. The early arcades were relatively simple and rather narrow, particularly those in Paris which were more like covered alleys and were about 3m wide. Although the interiors were simple, they were unified covered spaces with the

Figure 2.25 Lithograph illustration of Burlington Arcade, London, UK (1819). *(Source: Joe Pie Picture Library)*

wooden shopfronts arranged between regular columns and arches which passed across the arcades. The finishes were painted plasterwork and natural stone floors.

Both the early London and Paris arcades were two storeys high or more and sometimes had apartments or resting rooms above the shops. Two fine examples of the early London arcades are the Royal Opera Arcade of 1818, designed by Nash and Repton, with a single line of shops facing the wall of the original Opera House (now relocated), and the Burlington Arcade of 1819 by Samuel Ware, containing 72 shops aligning a 150m long arcade.

The width of the arcades gradually increased to become more like covered streets. Galerie d'Orleans, which replaced Galerie de Bois in 1830, had an 8.5m wide arcade and was one of the first arcades with a continuous vaulted glass roof along its entire length. The form of the roof over this arcade set the model for many subsequent arcades. These early arcades displayed a mixture of luxury goods, such as confitures, fruit, shoes, gloves, stationery, chocolate, a joiner, a goldsmith, delicatessen, sheet music and toys. The variety of different goods for sale in

Figure 2.26 One of the longer second generation of European arcades, Galerie de St Hubert, Brussels, Belgium (1846). *(Source: Peter Coleman)*

Figure 2.27 The elegant Galeria Vittorio Emmanuelle II, Milan, Italy (1876). *(Source: Peter Coleman)*

the arcade broke away from the guild-controlled, single-product streets and districts.

The glazed covered ways were particularly well suited to the climate of northern Europe. This fit, together with other cities' aspirations to have their own even grander promenading space, led to the emulation of the London and Paris arcades in Milan, Lyon, Bordeaux, Brussels, Liege, Bristol, Glasgow, Newcastle and other European cities between 1820 and 1840.

From the mid-19th century, another generation of arcades emerged which were larger and grander than those of the first half of the century. The development of plate glass in 1840 and the use of iron structures, created possibilities for each successive city to outdo its predecessor. Each new arcade became increasingly grandiose, increasing in width, length, height and organisational complexity.

Galerie de St Hubert, Brussels, 1846, is an arcade based on the proportions of the wider alleys of the old city, where this street was glazed over and organised in two lengths to form approximately 190 m of covered way to become, at the time, the largest arcade. This four-storey arcade also incorporated a mixture of other uses to ensure the thoroughfare was busy throughout the day. Accessed from the arcade were a theatre, a restaurant, club rooms, studios, offices and apartments.

Galeria Vittorio Emmanuelle II, Milan, 1876, designed by Giuseppe Mengoni, became for its time the grandest arcade and reflected a spirit of great enterprise. The arcade formed a cross shape through the block, with a 39 m diameter glazed dome at the intersection, equal to the dome of St Peter's cathedral in Rome.

The Cleveland Arcade, Ohio, 1890 by John Eisenmann and George H Smith, was the largest arcade built in the USA, with over 100 shops on the lower two floors and three levels of offices above. All the floors were accessed from galleries which overlooked the arcade and contributed to the grand quality of this interior.

Figure 2.28 Europe's tallest arcade of the time, Galeria Umberto, Naples, Italy (1891). *(Source: Art Directors)*

Not to be outdone by Milan, the city of Naples built Galeria Umberto I in 1891, another cross arrangement of grand arcades, with a dome at the intersection, which was part of a larger urban renewal plan. Designed by Emmanuelle Rocca, the arcade formed the largest public covered space in Naples. The arcade rises up through six storeys and is the tallest arcade at approximately 26 m to the springing point of the vaulted roof.

The largest and most complex arrangement of arcades are the New Trade Halls, Moscow, 1893 by Aleksandr Pomerantsev. The building occupies a whole city block of 250 m long by 90 m wide, occupying 2.25 ha of surface area alone. Three principal longitudinal arcades are connected by three transverse arcades to form 16 blocks and a network of covered streets. The shops are arranged on three levels providing around 1000 shop units. This arcade was the first in Europe to provide multi-level public access which, when combined with the network of streets, formed a spectacle of movement.

After the Russian Revolution, the New Trade Halls became the state-owned department store, GUM. The grid of covered streets formed a trading quarter aligning Red Square. The scale of this development matches the Grand Bazaar of Istanbul and the bazaar of Isfahan. The building's modernisation in 2004 has restored its overall magnificence to provide a contemporary urban shopping format.

Figure 2.29 Multi-level grand arcades culminated at GUM, New Trade Halls, Moscow, Russia (1893, refurbished 2004). *(Source: BDP)*

Bazaars and Department Stores

Department stores represent a significant milestone in the development of shopping and have had an historical influence on, and a continuing relationship with, collections of shops. The historical significance of the department store on shopping has been the formation of contemporary trading principles, which have been adopted in most shops today. Furthermore the incorporation of innovative construction methods established architectural and interior benchmarks that have influenced subsequent retail design. Department stores were one of the most significant shopping environments (if not the dominant one) for over a century with their scale and grandeur, and only relatively recently have been rivalled and displaced by the advent of the shopping centre in the late-20th century.

Department stores continue to be key components, although no longer essential, in the establishment and success of shopping formats and an understanding of their evolution will assist in the consideration of new developments.

The department store grew out of the *magasins de nouveautés* stores in Paris and the bazaar stores of London, originating in the late-18th century. Magasins de nouveautés were large shops selling fine fabrics, millinery, lingerie, shoes and dresses. These stores operated over several floors, with modest glazed skylights over a central hall or well. They established one of the fundamental trading principles of the department store: fixed prices for goods. By the mid-19th century, Paris had nearly 400 of these stores.

The bazaar stores of London were similar types of store selling a variety of goods, which were displayed in an open area and sometimes from open booths in the store. The bazaar stores traded on several floors, with roof lights over central wells and were often made up from a series of interconnecting rooms. There were 15 bazaar stores in London by 1834, centred on Oxford Street. Bazaar type stores also existed in other major English cities such as Manchester, Newcastle and Liverpool, which later developed into department stores (Kendall Milne, Bainbridges and Hyams respectively).

What marked the main difference between the magasins de nouveautés, bazaars and the department store, was that the latter went on to provide a greater variety of different types of goods for sale which were generally less expensive, being consistently popular merchandise and widely acceptable. The department store was also to become a significantly larger enterprise.

Various definitions have been given to the department store ranging from Paul Göhre's (outlined by Geist, 1989) '… a collection of miscellaneous businesses under one roof and one management. It is limited to the sale of very marketable consistently popular merchandise', to the all-encompassing alleged description by William Whiteley of 'selling everything from pins to elephants' (Pevsner, 1976, p. 267).

The trading principles adopted by the department store, originating from the magasins de nouveautés, were fixed prices, lack of pressure on the shopper, large selection and small profit margins (exploiting the law of greatest exchange). The big difference in the department store was that these principles were now applied to a great range of products, challenging the individual shops lining the streets and in the covered arcades.

The department store also allowed the exchange of goods, offered bargain lines and sold patterns for public use. They established and used capitalist retail principles to appeal and attract a wider social range of shopper. The advent of the department store left its mark on individual shops by encouraging their trade to move towards more specialist and exclusive goods.

The first department store identified by Pevsner was Bon Marché, which opened in Paris in 1852, offering a wide range of goods which were no longer exclusive for the privileged few but appealed to a wider social class (Pevsner, 1976, p. 267). The store was highly successful, allowing the relatively modest original building to be replaced by a new purpose-built store in 1869 and then radically altered and extended again, in a relatively short period of time, in 1873 and again in 1876.

The later extension and alterations to the store were undertaken by the architect LC Boileau and the burgeoning engineer Gustaf Eifel, who together formed one of the first grand interior store spaces around a three storied well, with overlooking galleries, and a large lantern roof light, with the focus of the space being a grand circular staircase. The store interior celebrated the activity of shopping by allowing the participants to overlook other shoppers. The interior, by its grandness and finery of metal balustrading, elegant bridges and flying staircases, seduced the shopper into generating a desire to consume. Grand interior spaces with overlooking galleries and large skylights became a trademark of the Parisian department stores, like the Printemps store of 1883. The architecture and interiors were also influenced by other contemporary buildings, such as the iron and glass exhibition halls and the glass vaulted arcades.

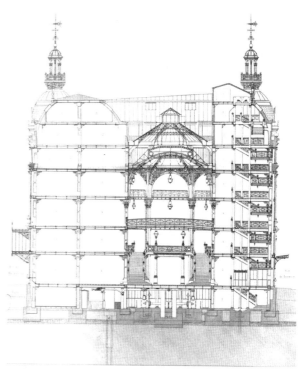

Figure 2.31 The galleried atrium of Le Printemps store, Paris, France (1883). *(Source: British Architectural Library, RIBA)*

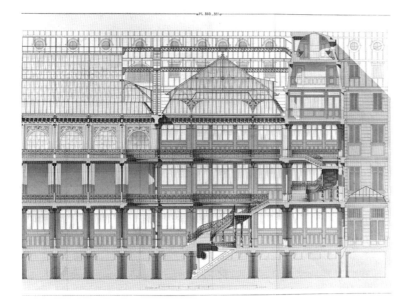

Figure 2.30 The grand, naturally lit interior of the Bon Marché department store, Paris, France (1876). *(Source: British Architectural Library, RIBA)*

The adoption of iron framed buildings allowed the size of shop to increase, to form the identifying large undisturbed trading space of the department store. The iron frame also allowed large floor plates to be commonly formed over four and five storeys and taller in the USA. These new large stores were able to meet the increasing space requirements for accommodating the variety and range of goods displayed for sale.

The early Parisian department stores, although built with iron frames, were clad in stone with two-storey high windows between the columns. The two-storey window element was used for the ground and mezzanine floors and also for the first and second floors. The application and multiple use of the two-storey window element became a recognisable fenestration pattern with the windows to the floor above the fourth storey being above an entablature and arranged in the roof. The Belle-Jardinière store of 1867 designed by Blondel was the first store to establish this pattern of fenestration and was followed by the Printemps store and others.

Figure 2.33 One of first US department stores, A.T. Steward & Co, 1823, enlarged 1843, moved 1859, New York, USA. *(Source: British Architectural Library, RIBA)*

Figure 2.32 Two-storey architectural order to the façade of Belle-Jardiniere, Paris, France (1873). *(Source: British Architectural Library, RIBA)*

Around this time the USA enters the story where, concurrent with the European stores, similar department stores were being established A T Stewart & Co, which started with a dry goods store in New York in 1823, was one of the first department stores, enlarging the store in 1848 and eventually moving into a new store in 1859 between Broadway and 4th Avenue.

The Haughwout & Co store in New York in 1857 was one of the first stores to take advantage of the larger, flexible floor plate achievable with a cast iron frame, with a five-storey building designed by JP Gaynor. Haughwout's store also used a (popular at this time) prefabricated cast iron façade manufactured by Badger. The store is also famous for its incorporation of the first passenger elevator to be used in a department store, installed by Elisha Otis in the large glazed well. Haughwout (a similar store

Figure 2.34 The cast iron façade of Haughwout & Co, New York, USA (1857). *(Source: AA)*

to Asprey and Tiffany) sold elegant goods for the home and is located on the corner of Broadway and Broome Street. Some of its wares were made and stored in a warehouse on the upper floors of the building. Elevators came to be commonly installed in department stores and remained the only assisted vertical circulation movement between floors until the invention of the escalator towards the end of the century. The first elevator installed in a Parisian department store was in 1869.

The department store business flourished in America during the second half of the 19th century, seeing the establishment in New York of Macys in 1858, Bloomingdales in 1872 and Marshal Fields in Chicago in 1865.

The move from cast iron to steel frame construction allowed even larger floorplates and taller buildings to meet the demand for larger buildings on each side of the Atlantic. One of the next generation of larger stores, and one of the finest department store buildings to be built, was Louis Sullivan's design for the Carson Pirie Scott store in Chicago which opened in 1904 (then named Schlesinger and Mayer). This was a 12-storey building expressing the frame, simply clad in terracotta, with glazed windows extending between columns and beams and having the lower two floors clad in decorated cast iron curtain walling.

The department stores not only became larger but, through the inventive use of glazed curtain walling, became increasingly transparent, revealing the grandeur of the interiors and animating the façades. The Hermann Tietz store in Berlin of 1898 by Sehring and Lachmann is one of the most magnificent and daring glazed frontages, extending through four floors with two glazed elements each measuring 27 m long by 17.05 m high.

Equally groundbreaking was the Innovation store of 1901 in Brussels by Victor Horta, which arranged

Figure 2.35 The Carson Pirie Scott Store, an early 12 storey steel frame building by Louis Sullivan, Chicago, USA (1904). *(Source: Architech, Gallery of Architectural Art)*

Figure 2.36 The daring glazed three-storey shop front to the Innovation Store, by Victor Horta, Brussels, Belgium (1901). *(Source: Bildarchiv Foto Marburg)*

Figure 2.37 The impressive façade to the Wertheim Store, Berlin, Germany (1904). *(Source: Bildarchiv Foto Marburg)*

Figure 2.38 The first escalator in a UK store featured in Harrods, London, UK (1896). *(Source: Company Archive, Harrods Ltd, London)*

the whole store frontage in a filigree, metal-framed glazed wall extending through four and five storeys.

From the end of the 19th century and corresponding to the success of the American department store business, Europe saw its own second generation of larger stores which were made achievable by the adoption of steel frame construction. The Wertheim store of 1904 in Berlin by Alfred Messel had a 303 m long façade over five storeys and was one of several similar size stores built in Germany at this time.

The generation of bigger stores was assisted by the invention of the escalator, which aided en-masse vertical movement. Bloomingdales in New York and Harrods in London had, by 1896, installed the first escalator to assist movement between the different floors. It is also worth noting that the retailing business, in the interest of moving its customers, preceded the first escalators on the London Underground by 15 years.

Harrods extended its store again between 1901 and 1905 to form the current terracotta-clad store. This was soon followed by the competing contemporary grand stores for Whiteleys, opening in 1912, designed by Belcher and Joass and the showpiece Oxford Street store for Selfridges in 1908 by Frank Atkinson, assisted by Daniel Burnham (Fig 2.40).

The era for building new department stores in high streets extended up to the early 1930s. The new European stores discarded historical influences and were expressed as Modern architecture. This was evident in two stores designed by Eric Mendelson for Schocken, the Stuttgart store of 1926, with a horizontal emphasis in brick and glass bands,

Figure 2.39 Whiteleys department store, Bayswater, London, UK (contemporary photo). *(Source: BDP)*

Figure 2.40 Daniel Burnham and Frank Atkinsons's stone façade, Selfridges, Oxford Street, London, UK (1908). *(Source: Selfridges Collection)*

Figure 2.42 Early curtain walling used in the UK to the Peter Jones store, Sloane Square, London, UK (1936–38). (*Source: John Lewis Partnership Archive Collection*)

Figure 2.41 Glass and stone curtain wall technology adopted for the Schoken Store, Chemnitz, Germany (1928). *(Source: AA)*

followed by the Chemnitz store of 1928, also with a similar uncompromising emphasis of glass and stone curtain walling.

William Crabtree's building for the Peter Jones store in Sloane Square gave England its first unhindered Modernist department store completed between 1936 and 1938. The use of curtain walling allowed the building to follow freely the curved shape of the streets. (This store completed a phased refurbishment and extension in 2004 designed by architect John McAslam.)

During the heroic new building period from the late 19th to early 20th centuries, the department stores took on the role of extending architectural development in a comparable way to the grand office buildings of the same time. The department stores exploited the following: iron construction to form large open trading spaces; iron and glass to make grand skylight interiors; cast iron for prefabricated façades; steel frames to make larger stores; curtain walling to express skeletal construction; daring glass frontages; and the incorporation of technological inventions to facilitate vertical movement, first with the elevator and secondly with escalators.

Then, from the middle of the 20th century, the department store entered a period of indistinguishable mediocrity, with few notable exceptions. Stores in towns became tired and the new stores, so vital to the success of the shopping centre, became inward looking simple boxes. With increasing competition from stores in shopping centres and other variety stores, the traditional department stores have had to reinvent themselves to survive. Many department stores have closed, but a new generation of department stores is emerging, refocusing on carefully selected brands of merchandising; where interiors are being refreshed and modernised into franchised show pieces; and the buildings are becoming innovative again.

Other Shopping Influences

Chain Stores

Until the advent of the chain store, each town had its own collection of individual and unique shops. The chain store came into being at the end of the 19th century and was facilitated by the development of transport systems – first the railways, then roads, allowing the easy distribution of goods from central warehouses to networks of stores.

The chain store is the fundamental ingredient in a shopping centre and today they make up the majority of shops in a planned collection of shops. Some of the first chain stores were grocers. For example Thomas Lipton opened a grocery store in Glasgow in 1872 and established, within 25 years, nearly 250 stores across the UK. Marks and Spencer's development has been well recorded, but it also originated from a small grocery shop in 1884, growing to have 240 stores by 1960.

Chain stores are not unique to the UK. They developed early and fast in the USA, exemplified by companies like Woolworths, which expanded from its first store in 1879, in Lancaster Pennsylvania, to establish in 30 years, a network of nearly 240 shops across the USA. Woolworths became international by expanding into Europe, opening in Liverpool in 1909, and within 20 years had over 750 stores in England.

Every country has its own national chain stores with some expanding to become international global retailers. Some of these international retailers, along with exciting and successful ranges of merchandise, have set innovative standards of store fit-out and shopfront, establishing themselves as the modern day generators of grand interiors and animators of the high street.

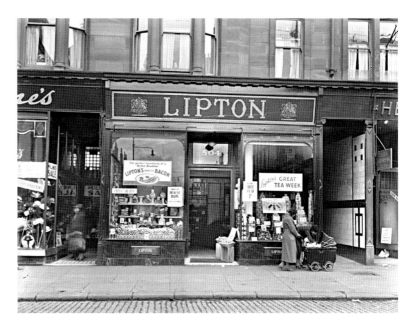

Figure 2.43 One of first chain stores, Thomas Lipton, Glasgow, UK (1872). *(Source: Glasgow City Council)*

Figure 2.44 The early 'Five-and-Dime' store, later to become Woolworths, Lancaster, Pennsylvania, USA (1879). *(Source: Corbis Picture Library)*

Supermarkets

The supermarket is another single shop format which, although not strictly relevant to today's collective shopping environments, has had a radical historic influence on changing retailing and the character of the high street in town centres. The supermarket originated by providing a wide range of foodstuffs, household goods and everyday items under the convenience of one roof and management. Many of the founding principles applied in department stores applied to the supermarket – low margins, wide choice and discount ranges.

Uniquely, the supermarket also established the principle of self-service foodstuffs – supplying packaged and canned foods and establishing the benefits of the principle of providing for the car-borne shopper, which would later influence the suburban malls. These stores catered for the increasing universal ownership of the motor car, located themselves within convenient access to highways and provided large areas of free nearby parking. Its ideal location was on the edge of towns, near and accessible to the major roads and adjacent to large residential populations.

The first supermarket store was King Kullen, which opened in Queens, New York in 1930. Michael Cullen, driven to improve competitiveness, established the principles of supermarket trading. By reducing the number of counters, the number of assistants in the shop was correspondingly reduced. Supermarket food products achieved the target of 80 per cent of all goods being self-service. Store size was increased tenfold from 60 m^2 to 600 m^2, increasing choice and allowing economies of scale. Car parking beside the store allowed more goods to be conveniently taken home. The first King Kullen store was located a few

blocks from the downtown area, with lower rents allowing a larger store and provision of car parking.

The supermarket removed many of the chores from everyday shopping and created one-stop shopping, avoiding traipsing around from shop to shop or stall to stall to obtain the weekly shopping. It quickly established a formula for convenience readily suited to increasingly busy 20th century lifestyles. Supermarket growth and success was facilitated by new road systems, the industrialisation of food processing and packaging, networks of warehouses, and the development of the refrigerator, which allowed large quantities of perishable items to be purchased infrequently.

Supermarkets provided essential perishable goods and therefore came to be related to regular shopping patterns. In the mid-20th century the convenience format and the provision of car parking led to the rapid growth of supermarkets in a symbiotic relationship with the growing suburbs and an increasingly mobile American population.

In the USA, in 1934, there were 94 supermarkets. In two years the number increased to 1200 in 85 cities. By 1950 the total number had increased to 15000, with most of the new stores located in the suburbs.

The spread of supermarkets in Europe came later and adopted more varied formats. In England, for example, the original supermarkets were located in several different types of location – singularly in high streets, collectively as an anchor unit alongside a number of unit shops in small town centre malls, and also collectively arranged with a large number of unit shops to form district centres on the outskirts of towns. It was only more recently that they adopted the stand-alone format surrounded by surface car parking.

The range of goods available in supermarkets has both grown and diversified from foodstuffs to carefully selected consumer durables and fashion items. More product ranges and diversification has led to new larger formats of supermarket emerging such as 'superstores' in England and 'hypermarkets' in Europe. To accommodate the large size of these stores they have been located on the edge of towns. These larger format stores combine economy of scale for the operator and greater attraction of offer to the public, thereby achieving a win-win formula of market forces. For a short period, superstores and hypermarkets spread on to brownfield sites on the edge of towns and cities in most countries across Europe. In mainland Europe, hypermarkets have been used to anchor regional shopping centres.

However, more recently, market forces have not been allowed to progress at will. European countries

Figure 2.45 The first supermarket of King Kullen, Queens, New York, USA (1930). *(Source: King Kullen)*

have implemented various planning legislation to control development, to protect further impact on the countryside and town centres, and restrict unnecessary car journeys, thereby restricting and regulating growth of new supermarkets. Unfortunately, supermarkets had already had a significant impact on the character of the high street before the introduction of controlling planning legislation.

First, through greater competitiveness, the supermarket has replaced individual grocers and reduced the number of butchers and fishmongers on the high street. These shops have been replaced by durable comparison retailers such as fashion shops. Secondly, many town centre supermarkets were allowed to close and have either been redeveloped or also converted into comparison retailers. The effect on the high street has been increasingly to exclude food shops and reduce the variety of shops, focusing high streets more towards comparison shopping. However, specialised pocket-sized food supermarkets have recently begun to return to the high street.

The development and establishment of the supermarket has reinforced and polarised shopping activities into two fundamental types:

1 'Perishable goods' – focused on the supermarket, being essential bulk shopping done at regular intervals, undertaken with the convenience of the car and predominantly away from the town centre.
2 'Consumer durables' – comparison shopping, which has become more of a leisure activity and takes place in town centres or regional malls. It is the design and planning of environments for consumer durables and leisure shopping which we are primarily concerned here.

The Beginning of Shopping Centres

The Suburban Malls

Like many of the planned arrangements of shops, the suburban mall in America took some time to evolve into its recognisable stereotype and to establish itself as the pre-eminent shopping destination. The decline of the town centre main street corresponded with the growth of the suburban mall which, ironically, arose as an alternative solution to the traffic congested and space restricted main street in urban centres.

The meteoric rise of the suburban mall came as more than just a solution to the congested town centres. They also responded to a particular set of social, economic and technological circumstances in the first half of the 20th century. The recognisable form of the suburban mall actually emerged some 30 years after the first example.

Country Club Plaza, Kansas was the first of the suburban shopping centres to be designed and built outside the urban centre and was planned to cater for people arriving by motor car with easy access and plenty of parking.

Jesse Clyde Nichols commissioned the design in 1922 having assembled the land from various run-down plots and swamp land. The masterplan provided large amounts of new residential property whose population, it was intended, would use the new shopping centre. Nichols' vision was based on a Spanish theme, with courtyards and open streets surrounded by stucco and tiled roof buildings. Nichols incorporated many works of art in the form of figurative sculpture, establishing the principle that, by creating a better place, people would take pride in it. Both the downtown and new stores moved into the Plaza, creating a place of style and fashion. The centre also incorporated a cinema which featured the new Hollywood movies. The Plaza was continually altered and expanded to incorporate new stores and attractions, most notably the Plaza Art Fair which became the Mid-West's premier art fair.

Figure 2.46 The forerunner to the suburban shopping centre, Country Club Plaza, Kansas, USA (1922). *(Source: Highwoods Properties)*

By the middle of the 20th century, social and economic circumstances led to a dramatic growth in the number of suburban malls and saw their establishment as the shopping destination of choice. From 1945, when there were only 45 malls across America, they grew over sixty-fold to 2900 in 1958. This rate of growth averages over 200 new suburban shopping centres opening a year!

The causes of the dramatic expansion in the number of suburban malls were:

■ population growth
■ restricted space for expansion in the urban cores
■ universal spread of car ownership
■ traffic congestion in town centres
■ abundance of available and accessible land
■ technological developments in ventilation, air-conditioning systems and lighting.

By the 1950s, the typical American city had become congested with traffic. A sprawling network of highways had grown up on the outskirts of cities, as a result of the universal ownership of the motor car. The highways surrounding major cities linked together the new residential areas and encompassed, between the roads, a patchwork of open pieces of land. These pieces of land sub-divided by highways – eventually to be filled in – were ideal locations for the new suburban shopping centres.

During the 1950s the suburban mall proliferated across the USA to become a recognisable and almost formulaic format. The centre that became the model for the others to follow was Northgate, Seattle, built in 1950.

This shopping centre, designed by John Graham, established the principle of shops being arranged

Figure 2.48 The linear dumb-bell established at Shoppers World, Framingham, Massachusetts, USA (1951). *(Source: Framingham Historical Society)*

either side of a long linear pedestrianised walkway. The street remained open and the walkway passed through each end of the centre. The shops were surrounded by ample surface car parking. The linear street format of Northgate was developed into the classic 'dumb-bell' plan, with anchor shops at each end of the street, in 1951 at Shoppers World, Framingham, Massachusetts, designed by Morris Ketchum. Here a department store and exhibition building were arranged at each end of the street, with shops between the anchors on both sides of the open street.

The suburban shopping centres were usually planned as residential satellites to the cities and combined large amounts of new housing together with the shopping centre, which would itself serve the surrounding population.

Another pioneer who recognised this unique opportunity was the architect Victor Gruen. In 1954 he designed Northland shopping centre, 20 miles outside Detroit's urban core. This centre was arranged differently from the dumb-bell format and was organised as a cluster of shops around a central store, with three pedestrianised streets. With residential development gradually expanding and infilling outwards from the centre of Detroit, Northland became an indistinguishable part of the city conurbation and established itself as a centre of its own.

Victor Gruen's next centre, Southdale, in Edina, Minneapolis, is a true epoch-making landmark in the evolution of shopping environments. Opening in 1956, Southdale was the first fully enclosed, environmentally controlled shopping centre. It was also a multi-level centre with two levels of shops served

Figure 2.47 The linear plan of Northgate, Seattle, USA (1950). *(Source: Museum of History and Industry, Seattle)*

and surrounded by decked parking, providing direct pedestrian access to both levels of the centre. The centre provided over 92936m² (1000000 sq ft) of shops and was the largest centre built to that date. The size of the centre and the extent of the interior space was made possible by the progressive air-conditioning installation which had by then become available.

Victor Gruen's decision to use air-conditioning was not only influenced by the increase in the size of centres but also by the improved environment for shopping that could be achieved. The climatic extremes of Minneapolis could be countered to provide more ideal shopping conditions throughout the year.

Gruen's decision to recommend enclosing and climatising the public areas marked a step-change in the thinking about the design of organised shopping environments, by applying the psychological leverage that customers who feel comfortable will shop longer and spend more. The climate-controlled environment would also attract people to travel further to come and shop in a comfortable place.

This new commercial logic was also attractive to retailers, who also adopted the new air-conditioning systems in their stores. This provided kinder environments to the merchandise, reducing the deteriorating effects of sunlight and dust. Unfortunately, this resulted in stores with less window area and eventually to the blank box enclosures which emphasised the inward looking nature of the suburban mall.

Southdale's enclosed public spaces transformed exterior space into interior space and, in so doing, formed a new type of internal urban space. The enclosed mall was the next step-change from the arcades in the evolution of shopping environments.

Figure 2.50 The first environmentally controlled centre, Southdale, Edina, Minneapolis, USA (1956). *(Source: Minnesota Historical Society)*

As it became increasingly grand in successive centres, the enclosed mall space would also challenge the opulent interiors of the department stores.

Gruen went on to refine the understanding of customer behaviour and its application to the design of shopping centres. His research verified the principle that people will walk further in climatised and protected environments, so stimulating enclosed and larger centres. Victor Gruen designed over 50 shopping centres and has been identified as the inventor of the modern enclosed suburban mall. The continued growth of the suburban mall in America is outlined in Table 2.2.

Table 2.2 The early growth of American mall development

1957	Eastland Regional Shopping Centre – 40 miles east of Detroit. Designed by Victor Gruen
1958	Bergan Mall, Paramms – out-of-town, dumb-bell plan. Designed by John Graham
1959	Midtown Plaza, Rochester – part of a mixed use development. Designed by Victor Gruen
1959	2900 malls in America
1961	Cherry Hill Mall, Cherry Hill. Designed by Victor Gruen
1963	7100 malls in America
1967	South Coast Plaza, Costa Mesa, Orange County. Designed by Victor Gruen
1970	13000 malls in America
1980s	Decade of unparalleled growth with 16000 new centres built
1990s	Prevailing trend to remodel and extend existing centres
2001	45721 Shopping centres in the USA (1182 are enclosed malls with the majority being strip centres)

Figure 2.49 The cluster arrangement of Northland, Detroit, USA (1954). *(Source: Bettman/Corbis)*

Summary from *A Brief History of Shopping Centres*, International Council of Shopping Centres, New York

The suburban mall has gone on to influence the form of many successful regional and super-regional shopping centres throughout the world. The American regional shopping centres influenced the early European out-of-town developments, such as Brent Cross, London 1976 and Parly Deux, Paris 1989, among others. (These examples are reviewed in more detail in a following Chapter.)

Unfortunately, in America many of the less successful malls are now closed or are needing to re-invent themselves. The decline of the suburban mall came about through greater competition from newer and grander centres opening nearby and from cheap construction, which caused the buildings to deteriorate and decline. There is also a growing awareness that suburban malls, with their mono-use and artificial nature, do not address all the functions and activities of a thriving urban lifestyle. (The next phase for suburban malls to re-invent and modify themselves into new types in order to survive is discussed in a following Chapter).

Precincts

The urban issues faced by European cities in the mid-20th century were different from those which led to the suburban expansion in the USA. While it was possible in the USA for population growth to be accommodated in the abundant available land around the edges of its cities, European cities were having to get to grips with rebuilding programmes at the end of the Second World War. The open-air suburban malls in the USA were catalysts for the new residential suburbs, while European cities were repairing town centres, involving mixed-use development.

A common issue on both continents was the growing universal ownership of the motor car, which was causing congestion and traffic-dominated city streets. Many European cities combined the need to rebuild, with the opportunity to apply the principle of separating main traffic routes away from city centre to form pedestrianised precincts.

One of the first and best known examples of the precinct is the Lijnbaan in Rotterdam which opened in 1953, designed by Van den Broek and Bakema. The Lijnbaan was planned just after the opening of the Northgate Shopping Centre in Seattle and ShopperWorld in Framingham, Massachusetts, which both had open-air linear arrangements of shops either side of a pedestrianised thoroughfare.

The Lijnbaan was designed as a pedestrianised linear street, lined with two storey high shops on either side, which extended across several city blocks and was crossed by roads for traffic access. It was part of a mixed-use development, with housing arranged in separate blocks from the shops. The main street of the Lijnbaan was generously wide at 18 m, with canopies on each side providing protection from wet weather. The canopies also crossed over the street at selected positions to form identifiable areas along its length.

The shops are set out on two grids (6.6 m and 8.8 m), creating a variety of shop unit sizes. They are nominally 15 m deep with the shopfronts meandering along the street with 'pop-ins' forming recessed areas to maximise the amount of window display. Although the shopfronts are articulated and offer considerable variety, the street is dominated by the horizontal projecting canopy and the monotonous modular panels of the first floor above the shops.

The Lijnbaan uses a reinforced concrete frame and a system of prefabricated modular cladding and is an uncompromising piece of Modern architecture. The buildings were carefully integrated into the network of city streets and established the principle of separate rear servicing to the shops. After 40 years in existence, and facing competition from modern retail formats, the Lijnbaan was refurbished in 1996 along with the opening of the nearby Beursplein.

The precinct format of purpose-built open-air pedestrianised streets has been applied in many other European cities, either as a linear route or as a network of streets lined with shops on either side. Another notable and comprehensive rebuilding plan following World War II was the central precinct of Coventry in 1955. Gibson's plan, which involved the majority of the city centre, formed an extensive, open-air pedestrianised area. The precinct format, with a 'cross' arrangement of primary pedestrian ways, has the east-west axis aligned with the spire of the cathedral. The layout demonstrates the segregation of pedestrians, service areas, car parks and through vehicular traffic.

Cologne, Germany, was rebuilt utilising the existing street layout, to form an extensive area of pedestrianised streets, with new building blocks inserted into the pattern.

In Stockholm, which introduced a new public transport system, the railways were connected to several new neighbourhood centres arranged around the perimeter of the city. These centres, forming satellites to the city centre, adopted the precinct principle to their layout. The district centres were organised as collections of shops in open-air pedestrianised streets.

Many of the war-damaged cities in the UK were initially less successful than their European

Figure 2.51 The first precinct as Europe rebuilds its town centres after the second world war, The Lijnbann, Rotterdam, The Netherlands (1953). *(Source: Van den Broek and Bakema)*

counterparts in forming attractive pedestrianised shopping areas. Cities like Plymouth, Portsmouth and Bristol were unable to segregate their traffic arteries which, even when rebuilt, continued to pass through the city centre. This often meant that shops were arranged some distance apart on either side of a major traffic thoroughfare. However, in many instances the precincts provided safe, convenient and popular places to shop.

The precinct is a significant development in the evolution of shopping environments as it represents the first purpose-built organised collections of shops to emerge in Europe since the arcades. Prior to this shops were randomly arranged in the streets of towns and cities throughout Europe. Precincts are as significant a step in the evolution of shopping centres as the suburban mall has been in America. The precinct arrangement of shops also established the principle of many shops being leased under single management. By its size and the collective diversity of the retail offer, the precinct was the first collection of single shops to challenge the dominant retail offer of the department store – a position of dominance which the department store had held for

some 100 years. The challenge would eventually be won by the precincts and result, some years later, in the need for the department store to re-invent itself in order to survive.

The precinct is town based and, although these early forms are now considered rather basic, their urban and mixed-use nature are again relevant in the new generation of urban-led shopping environments.

Central Area Redevelopments

Central area redevelopments (CARs) were a more radical solution than the precincts for rebuilding the cities post-1945. They were also often a heroic response to modernising rundown and declining industrialised town centres, which had little or no war damage. This was particularly so in the UK where several towns, having grown rapidly with the early success of industrialisation, were facing, 150 years later, the decline of these same industries, in addition to dilapidated housing which had supported those that worked in the mills, foundries and factories.

Figure 2.52 The seminal UK precinct, Smithford Way – The Precinct, Coventry, UK (1955). *(Source: J Salmon Ltd)*

In addition to dilapidation and the need for regeneration, circumstances in these town centres were exacerbated by traffic congestion, clogging up the streets originally planned for horse-drawn vehicles. The increase in traffic was generated by the growing universal ownership of the motor car and the large number of delivery vehicles supplying the network of chain stores from centralised warehousing. Such severe traffic problems generated radical highway engineering solutions and from the Buchanan Report onwards, highway policies were adopted to separate through traffic with ring roads and to form pedestrianised areas in town centres.

Town councils, faced with decaying buildings and traffic-congested streets in their town centres, welcomed visionary proposals for new ring roads and central area redevelopment. Councils were able to plan town centres and implement new ring road proposals. However, being strapped for cash, councils looked to the private sector to carry out central area redevelopments. Competitive bids and architectural proposals were sought from developers and their consultant teams for various town centre schemes across the UK.

Two of the first such redevelopment schemes in the UK, both opening in 1964, were the Bull Ring in Birmingham and the Elephant and Castle in Southwark, London. In terms of the arrangement and the type of environment they provided, both schemes marked the arrival in the UK of a new shopping type – the enclosed multi-level shopping centre. These two schemes were the forerunners of a generation of town centre shopping formats which, in the following years, would dominate the UK and parts of Europe.

In both these examples, the surrounding highway network had been planned first and put in place before the development proposal. It is evident when examining each scheme that the radical new proposals were compromised by having to fit into and around the roadways, rather than being planned simultaneously.

The Bull Ring in Birmingham was the first purpose-built enclosed shopping centre in the UK. It was a development by the Laing Development Company and designed by in-house architect Sydney Greenwood. The development had some features seen for the first time in Britain: the segregation of vehicular and pedestrian traffic; an enclosed internal environment; shops arranged on several levels around an open court; an artificially lit interior; an air-conditioned environment; integral car parking; basement servicing; and integration with both bus and train public transport. It was also part of a mixed-use development with offices and a banqueting suite which could accommodate 2000 people.

Yet, although the Bull Ring adopted the principles of the enclosed multi-level centre from the USA, applying what suited a simple suburban mall was less appropriate and less successful when converted to a far more complex set of circumstances in a town centre location. The plan layout was complicated by the separation of the site into three parts and the number of levels being stretched to five to suit the level change across the city. The entrance-ways were less than clear and some had to be reached by ramps. Integration with the main shopping areas of the city relied on pedestrian crossings over the major roadways.

Furthermore, the quality of the interior finishes were a stripped down version of their American cousins. The interior was conceived under the design philosophy of being 'atmospheric', allowing the shopfronts to shine out and act as the focus. The rather dark approach to the public spaces was ill-suited to the long hours of darkness of the northern European winter and the common greyness of its skies.

Despite the grand ideas being compromised by the complexity of its setting, the Bull Ring was shopping planned on a grand scale. In scale and ambition, the Bull Ring shops matched the magnificent department stores and furthered the challenge, which had started with precincts, to match the pre-eminence of those stores. The shops in the Bull Ring may have been segregated rather than open counters, the interiors may not yet be so exciting, or the shared shopping experience yet to have reached a level of consciousness achieved when being surrounded on all sides by shoppers, but here were the seeds of a shopping format which, over the next 30 years, would take the interior shopping experience to another level beyond the department store.

Despite its seminal qualities, the Bull Ring could not overcome its fundamental compromises and was demolished between 2000 and 2001, clearing the site again to allow a more integrated new shopping development to open in 2003.

The Elephant and Castle development also opened in 1964, a few months after the Bull Ring. The development site was part of a strategic plan by London County Council, which selected the developer, the Willet Group, from 36 original entries. The proposals for a mixed-use scheme launched the first enclosed shopping centre in London. It is arranged over three floors in a cruciform plan forming a podium block with an office tower above the podium. The building is partly sunk into the ground to form accessible lower and upper ground floors, with a first floor accessed from stairs and escalators. The shops are arranged either side of a wide arcade which was originally planned to have a retractable glazed roof. This was later omitted and replaced by simple glazed roof lights.

The lower ground floor is rather remote from the upper two floors, but has access to the nearby tube station and the below ground car park. Like the Bull Ring, the Elephant and Castle also has basement servicing.

The layout is based on a through-route similar to an arcade, but the premise is compromised by the arcade not being between two busy streets. In fact, the site is completely isolated from its surroundings by major roads on three sides and a railway viaduct on the fourth side, to the extent that an island site is formed.

The island site had been established in the LCC area plan, with the roads being laid out without reference to the development. The Elephant and Castle shopping centre has had to struggle from its inception with the fundamental issue of the site being isolated from its surroundings. However, this may improve in the future with the Elephant and

Figure 2.53 The original Bull Ring established the enclosed shopping centre, Birmingham, UK (1964). *(Source: AA)*

Figure 2.54 First enclosed shopping centre in London open at the Elephant and Castle, UK (1964). *(Source: AA)*

Castle being part of a new masterplan for the area, which should improve the integration of the site with its surroundings.

Blackburn, unlike Birmingham and London, was not war-damaged and therefore had no obvious need to rebuild itself. However, it did exemplify the decline of a mature industrialised town, finding itself in the 1950s with a rundown, decayed and traffic-congested town centre in need of regeneration.

The council executive committee's vision for the central area redevelopment was summed up in its development brochure, in a statement that could be applied to many of Britain's Victorian industrial towns: 'Blackburn is the product of the industrial revolution. It grew up without any apparent sense of planning, with few buildings that can lay claim to real

Figure 2.55 One of the first central area redevelopments in the UK, Blackburn, Lancashire, UK (1964). *(Source: BDP)*

architectural beauty, and with a crowded shopping centre totally inadequate to meet the needs of modern traffic. Drastic change in the way of replanning and rebuilding is inevitable'. The report went on: 'Blackburn is going to have the sense and courage to knock down its whole town centre, replan it, and build in accordance with modern needs and ideas'.

The council, having selected the Laing Development Company in 1961, proceeded with confidence and belief to demolish its existing town centre. The first phase of the new town centre opened in 1964 with the remaining phases completing in 1977.

The new town centre adopted many of the organisational principles of the shops seen at the Bull Ring – segregating shoppers from traffic, forming enclosed shopping facilities, an artificially lit interior, underground vehicular servicing, integration with public transport and being part of a mixed-use development.

To its credit, Blackburn also had significant differences from both the Bull Ring and Elephant and Castle. First, it was planned in a comprehensive manner with the highways and buildings considered in a holistic way. Pedestrian access to the central area was successfully integrated with the surroundings. The shops were arranged on a single level with a network of covered pedestrian ways which were open 24 hours a day. But the car parking, on the roof of the building, prevented natural daylight reaching the public routes below.

Although Blackburn has itself been refurbished since it opened, it was much loved by those who first used it and universally praised both in the press and by its professional peers. Blackburn, like the Bull Ring and Elephant and Castle, set the scene and established the format of many shopping centres that followed.

It is also worth mentioning the influence on the UK's shopping facilities of two like-minded Yorkshiremen – Arnold Hagenbach and Sam Chippendale – who had also studied the shopping developments emerging in the USA in the 1950s. They recognised the importance of providing the convenience of grouping together a collection of comparison shops and of providing the comfort of a climate-controlled and protected environment. They also introduced to the UK the idea of a shopping centre as somewhere you might go for a day out.

Applying their entrepreneurial skills, Hagenbach and Chippendale recognised there were opportunities in mixed-use developments in UK town centres to provide a popular new arrangement of shops. Their version of the new enclosed shopping centres were branded as Arndale Centres.

From 1961, their branded shopping centre was applied in 18 town centre locations across the UK. Many were heralded as regenerating dilapidated sites, while others were straightforward opportunism. Although the first centre in Jarrow was an open-air precinct type of centre, they completed enclosed shopping centres in Bolton, Bradford, Eastbourne, Leeds, Luton, Manchester and Wandsworth.

The typical Arndale Centre was an enclosed centre on one or two levels with artificially lit and ventilated public walkways, which were generally dark, allowing the shops to shine out. These centres were simply built and were often a stripped back version of the American original.

For a while the enclosed shopping centre was popular with the British public. Reflecting this popularity, nearly every major town or city in the UK adopted an enclosed shopping centre, based on the principles first employed at the Bull Ring. Layouts may have been different to suit a particular site and eventually more naturally lit interiors were adopted in the public walkways. The popularity of the enclosed shopping centre continued for 30 years – a level of success not seen since the clamour for arcades in the previous century.

Figure 2.56 One of the many formulaic shopping centres rolled out across the UK, illustrated by The Arndale, Manchester, UK. *(Source: AA)*

However, by the turn of the 20th century a more discerning public had emerged, in parallel with more critical national consultative bodies. With both parties demanding more memorable and integrated shopping environments, the enclosed formulaic shopping centre has become less able to meet these new requirements. Enclosed town centre shopping centres are reviewed in more detail in the following section of the book.

Festival Retailing

A further seminal development in the evolution of shopping centres was the understanding of the retail mix and the influence this has on the feel of the place and on the target audience. Ghirardelli Square in San Francisco, which opened in 1964, was developed by William Roth and his mother, Mrs W P Roth, and designed by Wurster, Bernardi

Figure 2.57 The converted chocolate factory formed a unique setting and established Festival Retailing at Ghirardelli Square, San Francisco, USA (1964). *(Source: Peter Coleman)*

and Emmons together with Lawrence Halpim and Associates. They consciously applied the principle of tuning the mix of accommodation to form the first example of 'festival retailing'. The Roths converted a former chocolate factory to provide a unique setting for novelty shops, various cafés and restaurants. The shops were chosen to provide a distinctive range of merchandising (not found collectively elsewhere) for clothes, jewellery, gifts and ethnic imports (unique one-off products which focused on quality, diversity and speciality). These shops, along with the range of cafés and restaurants, provided an environment specifically targeted towards leisure time use and to act as a destination for tourists.

The Ghirardelli Square setting of re-habited, former factory buildings was carefully selected to utilise the characteristics of the original chocolate works to complement the mix of shops and add to the experience of the place. The existing buildings were carefully combined with terraced spaces to form unique external spaces. This development established the importance of 'placemaking' in forming a unique character and deliberately complementing the selection of shops and cafés. The formation of character from the place and mix was the equivalent of adding colour to an erstwhile 'black and white' retail experience.

Ghirardelli Square was significant in the evolution of shopping environments for reinforcing the following criteria in the planning and design:

■ the significance of the careful selection and tuning the mix of shops
■ the importance of the environment in forming the character and personality of the place
■ establishing complementary catering and leisure activity with shopping
■ providing specific amenities for leisure pastimes.

The conceptual criteria established at Ghirardelli Square would influence many subsequent retail and leisure shopping developments discussed later on.

The design principle encompassed in festival retailing (the conscious use of mix, importance of place and synergy between catering, leisure and shops) added to the earlier real estate-led principles exploited by Victor Gruen (equal footfall, the dynamics of circulation and customer comfort). The founding principles of retail planning were therefore established by the mid-1960s. Some of these very same principles are still relevant in the design of contemporary shopping environments.

References

Geist, J.F. (1989). *Arcades – The History of a Building Type*, 3rd edn. Massachusetts Institute of Technology Press.
Pevsner, N. (1976). *A History of Building Types*. Thames and Hudson. International Council of Shopping Centres (New York). *A Brief History of Shopping Centres*.

Appendix 2.1 Earliest times up to the early 20th century

Period	Date	Example	Point of difference	Retail & general qualities
BC		The Greek Agora	First trading in open space shared with other facilities. Earliest trading spread on rugs on the ground and then on tables and stalls which could all be removed	From earliest civilisations mankind was involved with agriculture and crafts leading to trading. Trading took part in towns in spaces defined by the key civic buildings
1st–5th C		*Roman Forums*		
	110	Forum of Trajan	First shop in a building, in a defined space. First covered shopping space. First multi-level shopping – tiered	Part of the multi-purpose Forum for civic gatherings where a specific part was identified for shopping. Although the area for the shops was a significant part of the Forum, the shops were secondary to the main public functions which were in other parts of the building. The shops were tiered and in masonry vaulted halls. The shops were laid out on their side of the hall and one side of the colonnade
11th–16th C		*Medieval market halls and town halls*		
	1215	Palazzo de Broletto, Como	The shops were part of a building containing other uses	Shops were provided on the ground floor of the European town halls and market halls. These varied from defined shops in colonnades of the grander halls, to stalls between the columns of the open ground floor, simpler market halls. Market halls were adjacent to the markets and used as extensions to them. The upper floors of the market halls were used by the Guilds. Breslan is a particularly interesting example with several market building extensions to the market hall with each one providing a different type of trading. Thorn Town Hall had defined shops
	1240	Bruges Halles, Belgium		
	1275	The Ring, Breslau, Germany		
	1393	Thorn Town Hall, Prussia		
13th–17th C		*Eastern bazaars*		
13th C		The Souks of Fez The Quissariya	First covered gridded network of streets aligned both sides with boutiques	Several different types of Eastern bazaar. All being integral to the city and forming districts. The earliest types were stalls aligning each side of a street and then covering the street with grass mats, e.g. Fez. Another early type
	1461	The Great Bazaar of Istanbul	First formally planned retail district of a town	

Period	Date	Example	Point of difference	Retail & general qualities
	1585–1629	Bazaar of Isfahan Cloth Hall	First masonry building providing a covered hall specifically for shops Urban building elements linking together main buildings	was the grid of covered streets with boutiques on each side of the alley – known as a Souk and representative of many eastern cities. Later version of Bazaar like the Great Bazaar in Istanbul were formally planned with two large domed colonnades. These buildings were surrounded by numerous stalls occupying a total area of 200 000 m² Another grand Bazaar was Isfahan with colonnaded courtyards and a 200 m long vaulted arcade. The cloth hall had domed octagonal spaces along its length
16th–17th C		*London Exchanges*		
	1566–1568	The Royal Exchange, London	First purpose built sole use trading building in England Arranged around a 2 level colonnaded courtyard	Developing out of the Market Halls also influenced by the Antwerp and Amsterdam Exchanges. The buildings were arranged over two floors – markets on the ground floor; open stands and stalls on the first floor. Sometimes arranged with an internal courtyard – Royal Exchange
	1606	The New Exchange, London	First enclosed hall with trading on two floors	The New Exchange was an enclosed hall with trading stalls arranged on both the ground and first floor
	1676 1773	The Exeter Change Menagerie added	First combination of shops and leisure pastimes	The Exeter Change sold luxury goods in a covered hall aligned each side with shops. A menagerie was introduced on the first floor
18th C		*City Streets*		
	1695	Haarlem, Holland	First glazed shopfront. First walk-in shops with internal counters	Prior to this time, shops were open to the streets. First recorded evidence of shops being separate from market halls or exchanges. Shops on the ground floor of premises lining the streets of cities Shops transform from counters at the front to walk-in shops with internal counters Shops organised by trade guilds and arranged by type into the same street-forming quarters.
	1736	Bishopsgate, London	First London shops with glazed fronts.	Bishopsgate had a mixture of glazed and open shopfronts from an illustration of the time
	1788	Galerie de Bois, Palais Royal, Paris	First arcade in Paris	With the scarcity of land and the general hostility of the busy streets in Paris and London as the
	1799	Passage du Claire, Paris		populations grew, arcades became a popular covered haven for the promenading wealthy
19th C	1816–1818	Royal Opera Arcade, London	First arcade in London	The arcades formed protected covered ways through the city blocks and were aligned each side with glazed shops selling luxury goods. Early versions in Paris were narrow of 3–5 m and had residential properties above A series of glazed lanterns provided intermittent natural lighting along the length of the arcade until the glazing systems allowed the first continuous glazed lantern in 1830

Continued

Period	Date	Example	Point of difference	Retail & general qualities
	1830	Galerie de Orlean	First all glazed arcade in Paris	The covered ways were particularly well suited to the climate of northern Europe which, together with other cities' wish for their own promenading spaces, led to the emulation of the Paris and London arcades throughout other European cities during 1820–1840: Milan, Lyon, Bordeaux, Brussels, Liege, Bristol, Glasgow and Newcastle
	1830	*New markets* Covent Garden Market, London		From the late 18th and into the 19th century the populations of Paris and London expanded. The need for improved hygiene created new markets. Some of these also included shops (which were secondary to the market functions)
	1833	Hungerford Market, London		The shops were situated along the sides of the covered markets in lockable stalls located in the aisles and galleries
	1853	Halles Centrales, Paris		Glass and iron construction opened new possibilities for the market halls, possibly the grander example, Les Halles, Paris designed by Boultard, illustrates the construction which would go on to influence subsequent arcades and department stores
19th C	1840	Invention of plate glass	New possibilities for shopfronts with larger panes of glass	The invention of plate glass opened up new possibilities for shopfronts allowing the size of glass pane to increase to 1–2m by 2.1–2.4m
	1846	*Next generation of arcades* Galeries St Hubert, Brussels	The longest arcade	From the middle of the century the next generation of arcades experience a dramatic increase in scale as each successive city aims to outdo its predecessor. The possibilities of the new glass and iron technology in construction assisted these developments. The arcades became increasingly grandiose and monumental increasing in width, height, length and organisational complexity. The forms have progressed from covered ways or alleys to covered streets and glazed cathedrals. The residential is removed from above the shops and is replaced by offices and other public functions like those at Galleries St Hubert in Brussels where a theatre, restaurant and clubrooms are introduced above the shops thereby ensuring a constant flow of people throughout the day
	1865	Galleria Vittorio Emmanuel, Milan	The grandest arcade	
	1890	Cleveland Arcade, Ohio	Largest number of publicly accessed levels	
	1891	Galleria Umberto I, Naples	The tallest arcade	
	1888–93	New Trade Halls (GUM), Moscow	The largest and most complex series of arcades. First network of glazed streets. Established the event of people movement	The ultimate arcade opened in Moscow in 1893 with three longitudinal arcades and three cross spaces arranged on three levels creating 1000 shop units in 16 city blocks. The overall building formed a new quarter opposite the Kremlin and defined one side of Red Square in a building 250m long by 90m wide. (The scale of this development would not be challenged in Northern Europe until the central area redevelopments of the 1960s!)

Period	Date	Example	Point of difference	Retail & general qualities
		Western bazaars		
	1772–1834	Pantheon Bazaar, London	First variety goods store in London	These stores sold a variety of goods in a single building, formed from a collection of rooms and operated on several levels. Roof lights and large openings through the floors allowed daylight to each level
				Trading took place in open floor areas across counters and from sales booths
				The flexibility of cast iron construction eventually allowed large undisturbed floor areas and large openings
	1823	A T Stewart & Co, New York	First variety goods store in New York	
	1824	Belle Jardiniere, Paris	First fixed prices	Concurrent to London's bazaars, Paris also had a series of stores selling a variety of goods – 'magasin de nouveautés' trading millinery, lingerie, dresses, fabric and shoes
	1829	Gallerie de Per, Paris (Bazaar de Bouffles)	First store in Paris built using cast iron	The Bazaars, magasin de nouveautés and drapers' shops were the predecessors to the department store
				These early stores established the trading principles which became fundamental to the department store:
				fixed prices – visible on the goods
				lack of pressure on the customer
				low prices and large selections
19th C	1852	Bon Marché	The first department store	Pevsner identifies the first department store as Bon Marché which was established in Paris in 1852
				This store was aimed at the wider classes and no longer the domain of the wealthy classes
				The store was expanded in 1869 by L C Boileau and Eiffel to create a grand interior
				The principle of the department store was established, i.e. a collection of miscellaneous businesses under one roof and management selling a wide range of goods from 'pins to elephants'
				Exciting and dramatic interiors were incorporated with large openings and galleries overlooking central spaces with hanging staircases and bridges crossing over
				'… buying is converted in the consciousness of the public into a festival'
				Interiors were used to attract and seduce the consumer
	1857	Hauphwout & Co, New York	First cast iron façade to the building of a store	Cast iron is used for the exterior of store buildings first in the USA
			First store with passenger elevator in the USA	The invention of the elevator also facilitates access between different levels. This store was built on 5 levels
	1858	Macy's, New York	First Macy's department store opens	Department stores were developing in America at a similar time to Europe
	1872	Bloomingdales, New York	First Bloomingdale department store	

Continued

Period	Date	Example	Point of difference	Retail & general qualities
		Lipton's Grocery Store, Glasgow	First chain store opened by Liptons	First grocery store of Liptons opens in 1872. By 1898 this had expanded into 245 stores
	1877	Lewis's, Manchester	First Lewis's store opens	
	1879	Woolworth's, Lancaster, Pennsylvania		Woolworth opens a store based on low cost items (everything below 5 cents). By 1909 there were 238 stores across the USA
	1884	Marks & Spencer		First store was a grocer's. They eventually expanded into clothing (and by 1960 had 240 shops)
	1892	Bloomingdale's, New York	First escalator installed in a department store	The first patent for the escalator was in 1892. This was followed quickly by the first installation in a department store
	1895	Harrod's, London	First escalator installed in England	Harrod's established a small store in London in 1849. The store was continuously extended. The current store was not built until 1901–1905 (see below)
	1896–1904	Wertheim Store, Berlin		Stores became grander and demonstrative
	1898	Hermann Tietz Store, Berlin	First extensive use of glass curtain walling on a store in Europe	Glass was used extensively on the façade to create a transparent frontage and reveal the interior drama externally. The glazed area of 26 m long by 17 m high in Berlin was one of the most dramatic and daring
	1899–1904	Carson Pirie Scott, Chicago	First use of a steel frame to construct a store and express it externally	The development of steel and its use in construction allowed even greater flexibility – more floor levels and larger floor plates were possible to meet the demand for bigger stores. Large European stores followed (see below). Carson Pirie Scott store was 12 storeys and expressed the steel frame externally with glazing between the structure which was clad in terracotta and designed by Louis Sullivan
20th C	1900–1901	L'Innovation, Brussels		The Arts and Crafts Movement used glass and metal façades. The store designed by Victor Horta had a 4 storey glazed frontage above the entrance
	1901–1905	Harrods, London	Store extended to its present form	The terracotta clad building was designed by Stevens & Hunt
	1908–1912	Whiteleys, London		Belcher and Joass stone clad store completed
	1908	Selfridges, London		R Frank Atkinson and D H Burnham design the imperialistic Oxford Street showpiece
				The massive department store with six or more floors, 300 m long and 100 m deep now made possible by the use of steel frames
				Although there were some daring glazed shop frontages most of these buildings were clad in stone or terracotta. (The modern expression of the frames was developed in the 20th century – see text)

PART 2

The Contemporary Types of Shopping Centre

Entrance from Chapelfield Plain, Chapelfield, Norwich, UK (2005). *(Source: BDP/David Barbour)*

Overview

3

The historical evolution of planned collections of shops was, until the 1960s, a relatively gradual and haphazard process rather than a sequential or interrelated development. Before the arcades, collections of shops were either unplanned organic parts of town centres or occurred in mixed-use buildings with the shops being secondary to the other uses, i.e. in the town hall or market hall. There were, of course, notable exceptions with the covered shops of the Roman Forums and the Middle Eastern bazaars. These wonderful examples were isolated highlights, like shooting stars which came and went, with little continuing legacy of influence on the subsequent development of collections of shops.

Even with the 19th century arcades, although evolving globally for over a century into ever grander urban arcades, little of significant influence followed their demise. For it was almost another half century before the emergence of the first recognised planned shopping centres – the suburban malls of America and the town centre precincts and central area re-developments in Europe.

The development of festival retailing at Ghirardelli Square, San Francisco, saw the awakening of a level of conscious understanding of the specific ingredients that go together to make up a shopping environment. ('Festival retail' is also generically termed 'speciality retailing' by its departure from the mainstream of 'comparison' and 'consumer' retailing.)

By the mid-1960s, the two archetype categories identified in the previous Chapter were established – 'in-town' and 'out-of-town' – and the science of tuning the mix in 'festival retailing' – representing the understanding of retail function in the formation of shopping environments. While the evolutionary journey of shopping environments has been fragmented and relatively slow up to the1960s, from this formative period onwards, the pace of evolution quickened and the number of different types of retail environment significantly increased. The extensive range of different shopping formats which have established themselves and evolved since the 1960s are examined in Part 2 of the book.

Increased Pace of Evolution

The increased pace in the evolution of shopping centre types can clearly be seen in Appendix 3.1 page 65.

The different types of shopping environments which followed the 1960s, described here in Part 2, have been affected by cross-continental influences and have some common characteristics:

- the increase in size of existing types
- the development of refinement and hybrids of existing types
- the emergence of complete new types.

The new types of shopping centre that have emerged have been driven by greater competition, increased consumer expectations, demand for value and a growing maturity of understanding.

The previous Chapter examined the general evolution of shopping environments from the earliest beginnings up to the time of the first large-scale planned collections of shops in both Europe and America. The following Chapters examine the gamut of different types of collections of shops that have established themselves from the formative 1960s. Before the description of the different types, an explanation is given of how shopping centres have been traditionally categorised and how they have been organised here.

The Evolution of Categorisation

The number of different types of shopping centre is continually evolving in response to changes in commercial climate and physical conditions. As time progresses the number of distinctly different types has increased. The extended menu effect occurs as the earlier original shopping centre types remain while new ones are added. The earlier types do not generally become extinct and come off the menu, but continue to exist in parallel with the new types and develop further examples of their own. The increase is evident by comparing the number of different generic types illustrated in Barry Maitland's book of 1990, *The New Architecture of the Retail Mall*, which identified seven types, compared with the near 20 or so types identified here and shown in Fig. 3.10.

Shopping centres have, with the progress of time, become less generalistic and more specifically tuned to meet the needs and demands of the customer. Research analysis is increasingly used to establish catchment expenditure capacity and the size and mix requirements before the design commences. This is expanded upon further in the explanation of initiating the project in Chapter 8. The criteria used to consider and define shopping centres has therefore become more varied and sophisticated. With this increased sophistication, the categorisation of the different shopping centre types has become more complicated.

It should also be noted that, together with the increased number of different types of shopping, there is not a standard method of categorisation. There have been various earlier criteria used to categorise shopping centres. For example, the different criteria used by Barry Maitland and by the British Council of Shopping Centres are listed in Table 3.1.

A brief explanation of some of the different criteria used in considering shopping centres today is listed below.

Catchment

The size of catchment population is one of the traditional methods used to categorise types of shopping centre, i.e.

- Regional: population in excess of 100 000 people
- District: population in excess of 40 000 people
- Local: population in excess of 10 000 people.

Combined together with the size of population served, the range of different types of goods sold and the type of shops have also been part of a more developed form of this categorisation. For example, 'Regional' centres provide the full range of facilities and retail goods, focusing on fashion and comparison shopping and incorporating one or more anchor stores. 'District' centres offer a reduced range of retail goods but still provide a mixture of convenience and durable goods with a junior department store or variety store as the main unit. 'Local' centres provide food and convenience goods only.

This simplistic method can no longer be used to categorise all the types of shopping centre. However, for some of the simple and small scale shopping developments the terminology of 'District' and 'Local' centres is still relevant. 'Regional' centres have developed and evolved into several new types as we shall see further on.

Table 3.1 Comparison of criteria to categorise shopping centre types

Barry Maitland	BCSC	Criteria in use today
Catchment		Catchment
Location	Location	Location
	Size	Size
Tenant mix (function)	Type of retail goods (function)	Type of retail goods (tenant mix)
Style of retailing		Style of retailing
Physical form		Physical form
		Combination with other uses
		1st or 2nd generation

Maitland (1990) and The BCSC Report (2001).

Location

Following World War II, shopping locations moved from the general exclusivity of town centres into greenfield sites separating 'in-town' shopping from 'out-of-town'. Although America developed out-of-town shopping in advance of Europe, by the end of the 20th century 'out-of-town' shopping was also common throughout Europe and other civilised parts of the world. During the progress of 'out-of-town' shopping, 'in-town' shopping has attempted (with varying degrees of success) to incorporate on smaller, more restricted sites, some of the retailing facilities offered in the larger greenfield locations.

Recently, with restrictions on the use of green-field land, 'brownfield' sites (regenerating land formally built upon) have added a third locational category. These locations tend to be within the conurbation but are not within the town centre. For a while, location came to represent a type of retail offer, with 'in-town' representing comparison shopping and consumer durables moving out of the town centre on to the 'brownfield' locations. The relationship between location and type of retail has become less black and white, with some high street comparison retailers attracted to the cheaper and larger units achievable on the edge of town developments. With high street retailers moving into these brownfield areas, these developments now offer comparison shopping combined with 'lifestyle' consumer durables in edge-of-town and out of town locations.

Figure 3.1 High street retailers move to the retail park with large space accommodation and some lifestyle qualities, The Fort, Birmingham, UK (1997). *(Source: Caroline Field)*

Tenant Mix

Since the mid-1960s, the fundamental retail categories of foodstuffs, consumer durables, comparison and speciality retailing and the relationship between them has become increasingly better understood. With this understanding has come a level of sophistication which has created further distinctions within these types. For example, comparison shopping has become separately targeted towards male and female shoppers and towards different age groups and lifestyles. These are represented in different clothes and price bands.

The tenant mix is specifically geared, through research and analysis, to meet particular customer demands.

Furthermore, catering has similarly progressed from the 'take it or leave it' mentality of basic food courts into coffee bars, cafés, bars, diners, restaurants and eateries targeted towards specific customers' requirements which exist at different times of the day.

In addition to the shops and catering provided in shopping destinations, a complementary range of leisure activities has been added to the larger centres. This has been to attract a wider catchment and to extend the activity of the centre throughout the day and evening. Leisure uses, which are increasingly integral to regional centres, include cinemas, bowling alleys, family entertainment centres, amusements, health clubs, night clubs and entertainment venues. It is not just the larger centres that have incorporated leisure activities, some of the smaller urban centres have understood the synergy and compatibility of leisure uses alongside shops and catering and have formed attractive destinations.

The tenant mix can now involve a mixture of retail, catering and leisure tenants to produce a matrix of different types of centre.

The tenant mix can be interpreted into the design to inform the architecture to represent a different character. For example, festival and tourist attractions can be represented in more frivolous and playful architecture, while upmarket fashion retailing may be more formally represented.

Style of Retailing

Shopping environments are now designed to cater for a specific tenant mix. For example, a centre based largely on quality clothing becomes a 'fashion' centre (Fig. 3.2). Alternatively, selected fashion retailers can be grouped together alongside compatible homeware stores and upmarket catering to represent aspirational living – these centres are called 'lifestyle' centres. The architecture can be designed to complement or respond directly to the same aspirations.

Outlet centres, on the other hand, which sell at a discount the same designer ranges as seen in an upmarket fashion centre, may well wish to convey a different quality representing 'value'. Such differences need to be considered in the design of the architecture and external spaces.

Figure 3.2 A large selection of clothing retailers are grouped together for customer convenience, Fashion Island, Newport Beach, California, USA (1967, 1990). *(Source: Corbis/Robert Landau)*

Physical Form

The physical form of the built environment can differentiate a type of shopping centre. For example, in its simplest interpretation the difference between an open or an enclosed space can make fundamental differences to the qualities of the environment. This is especially important in addressing the 'urban agenda', in order to form open streets with naturally lit and ventilated spaces as opposed to internalised artificially lit and ventilated enclosed spaces. This difference of form is especially important when it is necessary to demonstrate sustainable development in the form of individual buildings rather than monolithic impenetrable blocks.

The physical form of the building can also represent different types of shopping environment, e.g. the direct expression of the larger size of retail units in a retail park. Similarly a department store can be individually expressed either within a group of buildings or on its own in a park setting.

Combination with Other Uses

In addition to the complementary nature of retailing, catering and leisure/entertainment uses, there are other new types of shopping centre arising from the combination of shopping with other building uses in mixed-use developments. Some of these existed before in simpler guises, such as combinations with hotels and offices, while others are emerging as completely new formats.

Shopping combined with major nodes of transport is generating new shopping formats which are responding to the particular circumstances and users of that transport. Shops at railway stations adopt forms that respond to the station spaces and benefit from the high footfall. Station retailing is specifically selected to provide a mixture of daily essentials, small consumer durables suited to short selection time and a range of convenience catering.

Airport retailing, on the other hand, responds to a captive audience of a predictable size. Here the range of retailing is geared to exploit the 'feel good' factor, providing some comparison fashionware, high value durables, leisure goods and a range of catering to be consumed on site.

Figure 3.3 Specifically selected retailing is combined with transport nodes to meet the needs of travellers, The Lawn, Paddington Station, London, UK (1999). *(Source: Peter Coleman)*

New retail types have also grown around the idea of travelling to an attractive destination (setting or climate) both to shop and relax for a few days in comfortable surroundings. These shopping destinations are known as retail resorts. Here the shops offer luxury items and high-end comparison fashion which are complemented by a luxury hotel, health club and potentially a convention centre. The shops are often located at a destination with other leisure facilities such as a ski resort, golf course or gambling destination. The incorporation of the convention centre allows such centres to appeal to both tourists and business users.

Figure 3.4 Combining shopping at a leisure destination complemented by luxurious interiors, illustrated by Park Meadows Retail Resort, Douglas County, Colorado, USA (1996). *(Source: Anthony Belleuschi Architects/Hedrick Blessing)*

Figure 3.5 Shops at Jubilee Place serve a large corporate office development, Canary Wharf, London, UK (2004). *(Source: David Barbour/BDP)*

with residential use incorporates vitality of use throughout the day, night-time use of the buildings, and a measure of passive security arising from the overlooking of the public spaces. These mixed-use developments require the architect to be able to design the civic and residential buildings.

Major office developments can generate shopping environments that are primarily geared to meet the needs of the office population. These shopping areas can be found in central business districts where the shops are selected to meet the daily needs of the office population, with comparison shopping and lifestyle shops that reflect the aspirational levels of these high income workers and where the same quality levels are reflected in the catering offers.

Another distinct type of shopping environment is generated by retail-led regeneration involving mixed development in a town centre. In this instance, the shops may be combined with civic buildings, where the shops will benefit from the synergy of visitors to the town's civic buildings visiting the shops as well.

It is common in such developments for housing to be provided adjacent to the shops. The combination

Figure 3.6 A mixed-use development with residential above the shops, Pentagon Row, Washington DC, USA (2001). *(Source: RTKL)*

Figure 3.7 The form of the urban arcade without heating is as relevant today, Galeria Vittorio Emmanuelle II, Milan, Italy (1876). *(Source: Peter Coleman)*

Figure 3.8 The Lanes, Carlisle, UK was one of the original 'urban' schemes in the early 1980s. *(Source: Martin Charles)*

Figure 3.9 The canopied street of The Beursplein, Rotterdam, The Netherlands, represents the beginning of the current generation of 'urban', open street-based schemes (1996). *(Source: Amstel Multi)*

First or Second Generation

As a measure of the degree of change that has emerged since the mid-1960s, certain shopping types are represented by two separate generations. The first generation illustrating early examples of the type, for example, urban based shopping environments, followed by the emergence more recently, of a completely new urban type.

The Types of Shopping Environment

For the purposes of organising this book, the descriptions of the different types of contemporary shopping centre have been organised into three principal categories with a Chapter devoted to each type:

1 out-of-town – suburban shopping
2 town centre shopping
3 new emerging types of shopping.

The first two categories, defined by location and type of accommodation, had established themselves by the mid-1960s. These categories include seminal examples and evolving refinements of the type. The third category is a 'catch all' to allow for new types of shopping environment which are not developments from the first two principal types.

Sub-categories of the principal categories are used to represent further types of shopping centre that have emerged from the principal categories. The three principal categories and sub-categories can be seen in Fig. 3.10, which is used to structure the following three Chapters.

With continual progress and change, new types of shopping environment will continue to emerge. However, with a mature and sophisticated industry now established, new types are frequently hybrids crossing several categories and these new types do not always naturally fit into any one category. (Where cross-over categories occur, these types have been included in the primary category.)

References

British Council of Shopping Centres (2001). *The BCSC Report*. BCSC.
Maitland, B. (1990). *The New Architecture of the Retail Mall 1990*. Architecture Design and Technology Press.

Contemporary Types of Shopping Centre

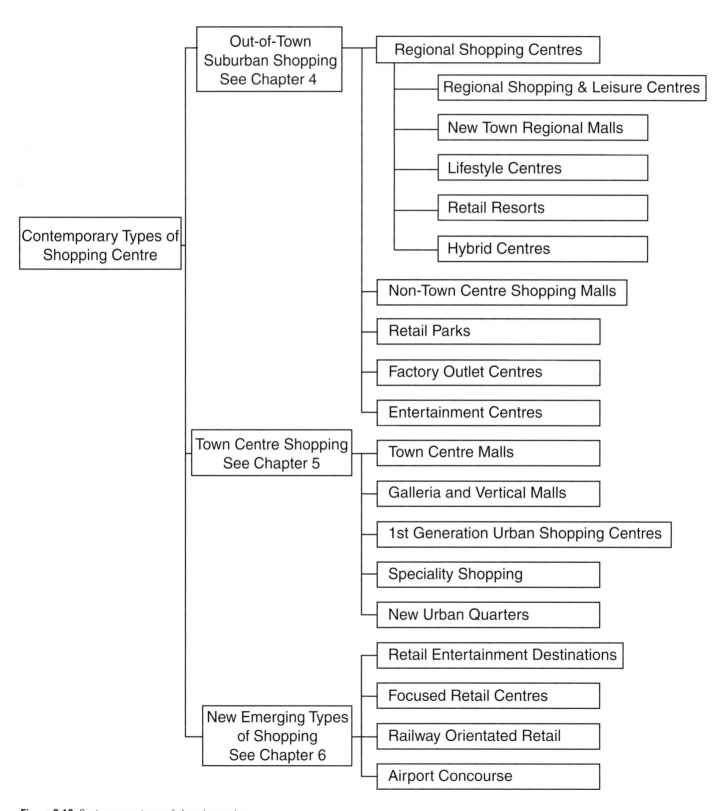

Figure 3.10 Contemporary types of shopping centre.

Appendix 3.1 Shopping centre milestones 20th to 21st century

1900s

- 1901 L'Innovation Store, Brussels, 1908 Selfridges, London
- Department stores expand in major cities of USA and Europe
- Mechanical invention allows the physical size of stores to expand
- New stores built with steel frames allowing larger stores and greater flexibility
- Escalators commonly installed in department stores, for the first time allowing mass vertical movement

1910s

- 1919 sees the first air-conditioned department store in the Abraham and Strauss Store, New York
- Mechanical inventions continue to allow the expansion of shopping environments

1920s

- First unified planned shopping mall opens in 1922 at Country Club Plaza, Kansas City
- Shopping trolleys are introduced in Houston, Texas
- Individual company credit cards introduced

1930s

- Department stores branch out to the suburbs in America
- First self-service supermarket, King Kullen, opens 1930 on Long Island, New York
- Self-service introduced, Los Angeles
- Fluorescent tube brings new lighting opportunities for larger stores

1940s

- Contrasting approaches between Post-War Europe and America
- Both developing new shopping environments in response to growth
- Both responding to circumstances generated by the expanding universal ownership of the motor car
- America generally established the first collection of planned groups of shops, 'The Mall', planned on greenfield land near highways and interconnections (centres in the north are covered, some in the south are left open-air)
- Also, in response to increasing demand and manufacturing, a different type emerged in Europe – town centre based
  Pedestrianised areas of the town/city
  Open-air 'precincts' adopted
- The principal differences between Europe and America:
  Town centre based in the major cities
  Open air
- Abercrombie – policy to protect the countryside. Greenbelt areas established around cities (establishing the Shire counties of London)

America – background
- Abundant land available
- Good road network and access
- Expanding demand and manufacture
- Expanding suburban living
- Shopping centres proliferated and a stereotype emerged

Europe – background
- Re-building bombed cities
- Accommodating increasing urbanised (city) population
- Universal ownership of the motor car
- Congested traffic in high streets

1950s

- Use of escalators worldwide
- America builds a new generation of covered malls, planned for the motor car on the edge of cities
- First dumb-bell plan mall established at Shoppers World, Framingham, Massachusetts in 1951
- First universal credit card established – Diner's Club
- Electrically driven cash registers come into use
- Northland Shopping Centre, Detroit opens in 1954 – the first by Victor Gruen
- Southdale, Edina, Minneapolis, by Victor Gruen, the first enclosed mall, opens in 1956
- Victor Gruen designs over 50 malls from the 1950s through to the 1960s
- Air-conditioning necessary to dissipate heat from the new lighting
- Growth in traffic leads to congestion in town centres of USA and Europe
- Buchanan's policy for separating traffic from pedestrians adopted in Europe

Continued

- Europe rebuilds its bombed cities – establishing pedestrianised areas based on grids or nuclear street patterns
- Growth of traffic leads to pedestrianised open-air type precincts at Lijnbaan Rotterdam in 1951 and The Precincts of Coventry in 1955

1960s

- First WalMart big box value retailing opens in America in 1962 in Arkansas
- Fibre optics allows new lighting possibilities
- Beginning of the roll out of 18 Arndale Centres across England with the first opening in Jarrow in 1961
- Europe continues to rebuild its cities
- Some cities in UK adopt Central Area Redevelopment (CAR) plans with Blackburn, Lancashire opening Phase 1 in 1964
- New town plans prepared in Europe
- Open-air precincts continue
- The American mall reaches the UK but it is adopted differently. In city centre with more constraints – part of mixed-use developments and integral car parks restrict possibility of light from above
- The Bullring, Birmingham opens in 1964 as the first enclosed centre in the UK. It is followed in the same year with opening of the Elephant and Castle, London
- The new enclosed centres in UK are dependent on artificial light
- More economic versions of American centres adopted in the UK, stripped of quality finishes and with parking on top due to more constrained sites, adopting convenience of integral servicing but bland architecture
- First 'speciality retail' centre opens at Ghirardelli Square, San Francisco in 1964
- First suburban enclosed mall in Europe opens at Parly II, Paris in 1969

1970s

- Oil crisis brings temporary halt to commercial development
- Owner occupation development emerges, first with hypermarkets
- European 1st generation of covered enclosed centres in town centres:
    artificially lit
    dark finishes and utilitarian
    internalised – enclosed environments
- USA and Canada commence 2nd generation of covered centres
- First of the big box DIY stores opens in America
- ATMs start to come into use
- Victoria Centre, Nottingham one of the UK's first integrated enclosed two-level town centre malls opens in 1972
- The Galleria, Houston one of the first US town centre malls opens with a fully glazed roof in 1972
- American supermarkets start to use bar codes – UPCs with Marsh's Supermarket, Troy, New York in 1974
- First optical scanners come into use at checkouts in 1975
- La Part Dieu, Lyon opens as one of France's first enclosed town centre malls in 1975
- One of the first US vertically planned town centre malls opens at Water Tower Place Chicago, in 1975, operating on eight levels
- Another integrated town centre mall opens in 1976 at Eldon Square Newcastle becoming at the time the UK's largest town centre mall – $72\,500\,m^2$
- Cash registers allow credit checks, recording of transactions and inventory control
- Festival retailing by Rouse Company starts several urban regeneration projects, with Fanueil Hall, Boston opening in 1976
- First UK suburban mall to adopt US quality of interior finishes and planning principles, opens at Brent Cross, London in 1976
- European shopping centres increase in size with the opening of the new town led regional shopping centre at Milton Keynes in 1979, $140\,898\,m^2$ (breaking 1.5 m ft^2)
- The Eaton Centre, Toronto opens in 1979 with four levels in a glazed galleria as the 'doyen' of town centre schemes and one of the first to use the levels to make two ground floors and achieve integration with underground pedestrian network

1980s

- Speciality retail reaches UK (16 years after USA) with opening of converted Covent Garden in 1980
- Retail parks grow up in suburban locations around town peripheries
- Regional shopping centres in USA increase to larger and larger formats, stretching the standard retail offer and establishing 'super' regional centres
- A new regional shopping centre format emerges with the combination of major leisure and recreational elements with opening of West Edmonton Mall in 1981–1985 – establishes world's largest regional shopping and leisure centre and introduces mini-break retail and leisure destinations
- First regional shopping and leisure centre opens in Europe, incorporating an indoor theme park at the Metro Centre, Gateshead in 1984
- Value and choice influence format to establish large box retailing

- Urban development continues in European towns and cities
- First generation of UK out-of-towns opens, and others start to be planned
- Public opinion influences architecture – backlash against modernism and brutal buildings
- First urban open-air town centre schemes in UK in response to reaction against internalised shopping centres with Coppergate, York opening in 1984
- Pluralism and contextual architecture take hold in UK and USA
- Horton Plaza challenges the mall concept in 1985 with the first of a new generation of urban open-air schemes in the USA, with three levels and individually designed blocks influenced by Italian towns
- St Louis Station railway concourses developed into retail, restaurants and a hotel in 1985
- Themed retailing introduced
- Multi-screen cinemas establish a multiple choice format
- A new format emerges with 'lifestyle' centres providing upscale retailing and fine dining in an external environment – one of first newly planned at Saddle Creek Germantown, Tennessee (1987)
- Railway stations begin to develop their concourses for retail with Union Station, Washington being one of the first in the USA and Victoria Place, London first in the UK, opening in 1988
- Camera surveillance systems introduced
- Covered malls in UK use natural daylight and brighten up
- Retailing formats encouraged by local governments to regenerate regional economies on redundant industrial land

1990s

- Recession cuts major growth of new centres in the pipeline during early period
- Retail entertainment centres emerge in America
- First out-of-town regional shopping centre opens in Ireland at The Square, Tallaght, Dublin in 1990
- One of the first free-standing destination retail entertainment centres opens in 1990 at CoCo Walk, CoConut Grove, Miami, exploiting the synergy between retail, catering and entertainment
- US opens its own regional shopping and leisure centre in Minneapolis with the Mall of America in 1992, becoming one of the most visited attractions and reinforcing mini-break retail and leisure destinations
- Generation of regional out-of-town centres open in the UK – Meadow Hall, Sheffield (1990), Lakeside, Thurrock (1990), White Rose, Leeds (1997), The Mall at Cribbs Causeway (1998), Trafford Centre, Manchester (1998), Braehead, Glasgow (1999)
- Range of retail formats exponentially expands
- Edge of town retail parks spread across Europe
- Airport retailing 'takes off' on both sides of the terminal with World Class Shopping, Heathrow, T4, (1992) and Gatwick South, Gatwick (1995)
- Factory outlet centres introduced selectively across Europe with Clarke's Village, Street (1993) being the UK's first and Troyes Design Outlet Village, Troyes (1995) being France's first
- Big box retailers challenge traditional retail formats for a while, particularly in the USA
- 'Category Killer' retailers emerge in the UK as largest growing format by mid-1990s
- Department stores refocus on selected product areas to re-invent themselves
- Railway station concourses developed for retailing in Europe
- Showpiece stores introduced for singular brands with museum-like displays
- European planning legislation tightens up, preventing further suburban retail and protecting the vitality of towns and the countryside
- In the UK legislation gradually, then finally in 1996 caps out of town centre development with Planning Policy Guidance Note 6 (PPG6)
- Themed interiors based on a synergy with a holiday destination establish another new format of 'retail resorts' with Park Meadow, Denver (1996) being one of the first
- First of the new generation of town centre shopping centres to address the urban agenda completes in 1996 at the Beursplein, Rotterdam in a retail-led mixed-use development, integrating residential and public transport
- The Fort, Birmingham (1997) establishes a retail park with a large proportion of high street retailers bringing comparison retailing in big boxes to a retail park
- Legislation in the UK establishes an 'urban agenda' for sustainable town centre development
- Public opinion turns towards a preference for 'open street' retailing
- Suburban malls are reconsidered – transformed as 'main streets' and opened up
- A failed suburban mall is redeveloped at The Block, Orange County, (1998) into a new retail format of open streets to recreate 'main street' in a retail entertainment centre
- With downtown 'suburbanising' and malls 'urbanising' homogenisation of the shopping experience creeps in
- New urban retail formats emerge in both the USA and Europe

Continued

- 'Shoppertainment', integrating leisure and retailing, is increasingly taken on board in new schemes throughout the world
- Bluewater, Greenhithe establishes a new benchmark for comparison retailing, catering and customer facilities. With research influenced strategy for the regional shopping and leisure centre, it commenced prior to PPG6, with completion in 1999 bringing a full stop to out-of-town regional shopping centres

2000s

- Reacting to the failure of standard mall formats, 'Hybrid Centres' emerge, combining both covered and external space to establish a new retail format
- Planning control and public opinion endorse the need for new urban formats in the USA and Europe
- New urban formats also emerge outside of the USA and Europe
- First generation of new urban formats built and opened
- Further new retail formats emerge
- Sensitivity to terrorist threats to be accommodated
- Sustainability and conservation issues influence design
- The re-built Bull Ring integrated with the city centre opens in 2003 with $11\,000\,m^2$ arranged over three levels, and introduces open and covered streets alongside enclosed shopping

Figure 3.11 The glazed dome and viewing galleries, Victoria Square, Belfast, Northern Ireland, UK (2008). *(Source: BDP)*

Out-of-Town Suburban Shopping

Figure 4.1 Out-of-town suburban shopping.

Out-of-Town Suburban Shopping 4

Establishing the Form

This format of shopping environment covers the different range of planned collections of shops which are outside or on the edge of the town or city centre. The principal type is the regional shopping centre, represented by the suburban mall, and the different forms that have developed and emerged as it has transformed and changed over some 50 years of evolution. The sub-variants of the regional centre are regional shopping and leisure centres, new town malls, lifestyle centres, hybrid centres and retail resorts (Fig. 4.1). Other significant out-of-tow shopping formats, such as non-town centre malls, retail parks, factory outlet centres and entertainment centres, which have either directly or indirectly informed the general evolution of shopping environments, are also described.

The development of the regional shopping centre has had the most significant influence on the form and design of shopping centres in both out-of-town and in-town locations. As well as the direct influence resulting from innovation and progress, the out-of-town regional shopping centre has also had ramifications and an adverse influence on urban shopping.

Out-of-town shopping facilities are often located on redundant manufacturing or industrial sites, unused military sites or similar. Sometimes farmers have cashed in on their newly found proximity to suburban expansion and allowed farmland for retail development and, on rare occasions, even greenfield land has been used. The preferred locations are on the edges of towns, or just outside the conurbations allowing easy access by the local population. With a degree of hindsight, led by concern for the protection of the environment, recent planning controls in different countries of the developed world strictly control development and the land that can be used for shopping development.

Although regional shopping centres have developed and progressed beyond principal recognition, since the emergence of Southdale many of the general characteristics established in its formation are appropriate to nearly all centres of this type:

■ a good retail offer and wide range of different shops
■ general attraction of one or more anchor stores
■ providing a comfortable and secure environment
■ accommodating ease of access and parking for cars
■ planned to maximise pedestrian flow of shoppers past the unit shops between the anchor stores
■ located within easy access of a large resident population.

The traditional criteria, which were once sufficient to define a regional shopping centre, are 'size' and 'catchment'. The latter expressed the size of the immediate population needing to be greater than 100 000 (Maitland, 1990). The physical size benchmark for a regional shopping centre is that it should be greater than $46\,451\,m^2$ ($500\,000\,ft^2$) (BCSC Report, 2001).

Evolution of the Suburban Mall

From the first recognised enclosed regional shopping centre at Southdale, Minneapolis in 1956, the genre has continually progressed and evolved. Chapter 2 illustrated how simple collections of shops surrounded by surface car parking developed into a multi-level enclosed single building type.

Since it established itself in the mid-20th century, the out-of-town regional shopping centre has continually progressed through development and transformed itself into new physical formations and new shopping formats. This progression, and the emergence of completely new forms, have arisen from the continual response to different economic and physical circumstances. The transformation has been furthered by the drive to maintain a competitive edge in the market, creating a spiral of upward change. The suburban mall has come a long way since its simple beginnings at Southdale.

Early development related largely to progressing the physical form, with a second state of development driven by the incorporation of a better understanding of the retail function and the importance of the customer. The suburban mall in its heyday influenced shopping development all over the world, with developers and designers visiting this American example to take home ideas for incorporation into their own projects. More recently, the decline of some of the suburban malls has led to the need to reappraise completely its form and regenerate its appeal. Such questioning has led to new and exciting formats emerging with traditional enclosed malls adopting open-air streets and more urban forms. In fact, the enclosed suburban regional shopping centre has progressed, adapted and transformed itself to the point that the regional format in its simplest form is no longer considered an adequate or relevant approach to new retail development. New forms and hybrids that have emerged from the suburban mall are examined further on.

After the opening of Southdale, the following ten years of development of regional shopping centres saw the consolidation and refinement of the principles which it established:

- enclosing the public spaces
- cooling and heating the environment
- inward looking buildings
- centres conceived as a single building, as opposed to a cluster of separate buildings
- multi-level plan arrangements
- compact and dense plan forms
- simply roofed over streets with clerestory glazing.

The on-going development of the type occurred in various plan formations – 'dumb-bell', 'L-shaped' and 'cruciform' shaped malls – depending on the number of anchor stores being accommodated, be it two, three or four respectively.

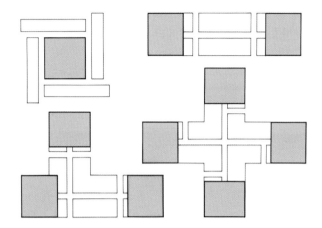

Figure 4.2 Plan diagrams showing the influence of 1, 2, 3 or 4 anchor stores. *(Source: Peter Coleman)*

The third stage of evolution occurred as the centres increased in size from the late 1960s into the 1970s. The increase in size was also accompanied by the centres moving away from long and straight-sided malls, with daylighting from simple clerestory glazing, towards more complex and irregular layouts with the public spaces having more of an interior feel, almost as an extension of the department stores, with modelled ceilings and intermittent daylight.

Woodfield Mall, Schaumburg, Illinois (1971) represents this period providing 190 000 m² (2.1 million ft² of leased space) and adopting a cruciform mall. The malls vary in width along the length, creating local focal points. Another artificially lit centre was Northbrook Court, near Chicago (1976), which adopted a linear sequence of four various shaped courts to accommodate four anchor stores.

Figure 4.3 Interior view of court, Woodfield Mall, Schaumburg, Illinois, USA (1971). *(Source: Taubman Company)*

The fourth identifiable stage in the progress of the form saw the return to largely glazed and naturally lit interior public spaces. This was exemplified by the Galleria, Houston (1970). This falls across several categories of regional shopping centre, as a catalyst for a new central business district, an urban quarter, a galleria and vertical mall. The Galleria, Houston is illustrated in a later Chapter. The Galleria at South Bay (1985) and Westside Pavilion, Los Angeles (1985) are other examples of multi-level schemes with continual glazed roof lights. These examples are also on edge-of-town locations and have a greater intensity of development and incorporate adjacent stacked car parking.

Figure 4.4 The archetype multi-level enclosed shopping centre represented by The Galleria, South Bay, Los Angeles, USA (1985). *(Source: Peter Coleman)*

American Influences on European Centres

While the regional shopping centre type was developing into its second and third stage of evolution in the USA, its influence spread across the Atlantic to establish the first generation of planned out-of-town shopping in Europe. This first wave introduced a move away from town centre dominated facilities and established the idea of out-of-town shopping in Europe. This influence, which began in the mid-1960s, was the beginning of a series of commercially driven retail formats which have continued to be introduced across Europe ever since.

A 20th century grand tour of American shopping centres, and in particular those designed by Victor Gruen, saw developers and architects visiting and studying the US examples. Just as Italy had influenced art and architecture across Europe some 600 years before, the USA represented the shopping Renaissance of the later 20th century.

One of the first applications of the single building enclosed format in Europe was Parly 2, Paris (1969) which was part of several new towns planned around the perimeter of the city. Located to the south west of Paris near Versailles, this shopping centre was planned to serve the new residential population of Le Chesnay. Parly 2 was part of a mixed-use development with 6000 apartments and offices,

Figure 4.5 The American influence brought high quality interior finishes to Parly 2, Paris, France (1969). *(Source: BDP)*

and acted as the nucleus of the new town. The developers, Robert de Balkany and Jean-Louis Solal, had studied the out-of-town shopping examples in America and adopted many of the principles established by Victor Gruen, typified by Southdale. Parly 2 was, however, planned as a two level linear dumb-bell mall with 100 shops and a department store at each end. The interior environment was predominantly artificially lit with little daylight, allowing the shopfronts of a wide-ranging retail offer to establish the drama. The centre provided the convenience of a conditioned environment and was planned to accommodate the growing use of individual transportation, with 3000 parking spaces arranged equally to feed the two different floor levels. Although smaller than the American examples, Parly 2 at 58 000 m² (624 000 ft²) provided a high quality finished internal environment with marble floors, natural wood clad columns, intricate modelled suspended ceilings and copious amounts of artificial planting. A feature court terminates each end of the mall and incorporates a café on the ground floor. Although externally Parly 2 was a bland assembly of rectangular forms, the interiors established new levels of interior design to shopping environments in Europe. At the time, the interiors contained uniquely designed ceilings, plants, seating and mall furniture with an attention to detail which continued the parabolic design motif between the varied elements.

Other regional shopping centres providing similar perimeter new towns to Paris followed Parly 2. These were also influenced by the American examples and were represented by centres such as Belle Epine (1971) and Rosny 2 (1973).

Brent Cross, London was the first out-of-town enclosed regional shopping centre in the UK and was also influenced by Victor Gruen's Southdale. It was conceived at a similar time to its French cousins, in the mid-1960s (planning permission was submitted in 1965) but, owing to a lengthy planning process, the centre eventually opened in 1976. Brent Cross, conceived as North West London's 'West End', revolutionised shopping in the UK with its focus on serving the customer. The centre provided 73 000 m² (790 000 ft²) of wide ranging comparison goods shopping under one roof with the convenience of an enclosed environment, and open six days a week with extended opening hours to 8 pm each weekday evening. It was also planned around providing car access within close proximity of major trunk roads and providing 5600 free parking spaces.

The centre also incorporated one of London's major bus terminuses.

Brent Cross is organised over two levels, arranged in a linear dumb-bell mall (similar to Parly 2) with an additional feature court in the middle. The two anchor department stores are located at each end of the mall with 75 shops set in between, thus utilising the footfall between the main stores. The car parking is equally provided around the centre with access feeding each of the floor levels. The functional plan is allowed to generate an assembly of rectangular forms presenting a bland exterior. The developer, Hammerson, brought a new level of US inspired quality to the enclosed interiors, with marble floors, glass balustrades, individually designed mall furniture and modelled suspended ceilings. Although the interiors were partially naturally lit, the overall lighting effect is predominantly artificial. Brent Cross established a benchmark in UK retail standards for some 20 years. However, developing retail standards overtook it and led to its refurbishment in 1996.

The influence from the USA gradually extended to other European countries beyond France and the UK.

Figure 4.6 Interior view of the original American influenced Brent Cross, London, UK (1976). *(Source: Peter Coleman)*

Regional Shopping Centres

Regional shopping centres in the USA have continued to evolve in response to change and competition from other formats. It is therefore not easy to find a contemporary example representing its purest form. The 1970s saw a return to naturally lit malls followed by an unparalleled period of growth, both in the number of centres and the size, with the establishment of super regional centres greater than $75\,000\,m^2$ (approx $800\,000\,ft^2$) in the 1980s.

Also during the 1970s, catering food courts, along with simple cinemas, were added to the standard format. In the late 1980s the first multi-screen cinemas were included. Eventually the size of catering and leisure added to the regional shopping led to a completely new format emerging which is dealt with under 'regional shopping and leisure centres' described further on.

By the 1990s competition from other types of shopping format, together with a crisis in savings and loans, caused a slowdown in the development of new centres and greater emphasis was given to remodelling and expansion of existing regional shopping

Figure 4.7 The two level central space with catering around the gallery in the single level regional shopping centre, White Rose, Leeds, UK (1997). *(Source: Martine Hamilton)*

centres. Further formats and hybrids have emerged as a result of changing circumstances and competition and these new formats are also described below. However, in the UK, relatively contemporary examples of the out-of-town regional shopping centre format can be found, such as White Rose,

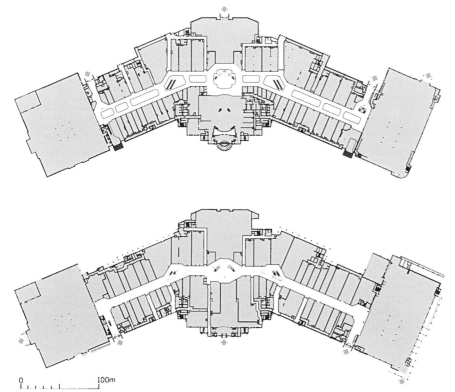

0 ⌶─┴─┴─┴─┴─┴──── 100m

Figure 4.8 The upper and lower ground floor plans, The Mall at Cribbs Causeway, Bristol, UK (1998). *(Source: BDP)*

Leeds (1997) and The Mall at Cribbs Causeway, Bristol (1998) among others.

The Mall at Cribbs Causeway, formed from a joint venture partnership between the Prudential and Jack Baylis, located on the outskirts of Bristol, is a regional shopping centre for the south-west of England. Its size, at 67 500 m² (approx 725 000 ft²), may be on the small size in comparison to US and other European examples, but this centre represents a highly efficient shopping machine and punches above its weight. It has been described as a 'pocket battleship of regional shopping centres' (Architecture Today, 1999). Although it has an adjacent leisure destination with cinemas, leisure facilities and catering, the Mall was designed as a separate and independent entity.

The Mall at Cribbs Causeway, designed by Building Design Partnership, adopts a familiar two level dumb-bell arrangement with the two anchor stores at each end. A variation to the form is the cranking of the mall to form three recognisable lengths of mall, each with its own entrance and the introduction of a feature court at each of the two knuckle points. The cranking of the mall allows each vista to be closed and to lead to a major store. In order to compensate for the relative small size of this centre, three structural grids have been used, 6 m, 7.2 m and 9 m, to achieve different shop sizes and to maximise the number of shops provided. All of the 130 shop units are carefully arranged to allow all to be equally passed by pedestrians and thereby avoid any secondary areas. The car parking is arranged on all sides of the centre with entrances leading along each side and uses the levels to lead to both the lower and upper ground floors. As well as accommodating the car with 7000 car parking spaces and easy access to the adjacent motorway network, the centre has a bus station and coach park. Unloading access is integral to the centre and discreetly located below ground leading from the lower ground floor on the north side and from a basement level on the south side, thereby avoiding any unsightly service yards to the exterior of the building.

The interiors are naturally lit, bright and contemporary using high quality natural materials with patterned granite floors, glass and metal balustrades and perforated metal and plaster ceilings. The continuously glazed roof has been carefully designed to provide 50 per cent shading through utilising fixed perforated metal blinds, which in daytime allow a mixture of direct and filtered light and at night form

Figure 4.9 The central glazed entranceway and upper level food court, The Mall at Cribbs Causeway, Bristol, UK. *(Source: Charlotte Wood)*

Figure 4.10 The extensively glazed public spaces provide naturally lit interiors, The Mall at Cribbs Causeway, Bristol, UK. *(Source: Roger Ball/Image Photo Ltd)*

a surface for up-lighting to avoid the 'black-hole' effect of a fully glass roof. Cross section dimensions of 10 m at the lower floor and 16 m at the upper floor allow good visibility between the two levels. In the middle of the centre at the upper level there is a 1200 seat food area with 15 cafés and restaurants, which overlooks the adjacent countryside and nearby airport runway.

Viewed from the air, the form of the Mall at Cribbs Causeway is typical of the assemblage of rectangular forms resulting from the honest expression of a functional plan surrounded by a sea of cars. Although much of the exterior is bland and inward looking, the crisp detailing of the modular reconstituted stone and metal panelling is animated with large areas of structural glazing. The glazed areas represent the catering area, entrances and windows of the department stores. This centre may not establish much new ground and is not revolutionary, but in evolutionary terms it is a refined and well-mannered example of a regional shopping centre in its purest form.

Regional Shopping and Leisure Centres

A further stage of development occurred in the evolution of regional shopping centres as they entered the 1980s. This was a period of unprecedented growth in the number of new centres being built and in the size of centre being considered. Between 1980 and 1990 more than 16 000 new centres were built (International Council of Shopping Centres). Centres were regularly being built larger than 75 000 m² (800 000 ft²) representing super regional centres and attracting customers beyond the regional catchment. Several of these enlarged centres provided a wide range of retail offer, cafés, restaurants and movie theatres and, as such, represented a standard. With so many new and large centres customers had a choice of venue. Faced with such competition many developers opted for the bigger-is-better approach to gain advantage.

A milestone in the evolution was the incorporation of a major leisure and recreational facility to the standard retail offer, thereby forming a retail and leisure destination. The idea of this approach was to broaden the attraction of the centre and cause as many people as possible to visit it for different reasons. The logic was based on the expectation of coincidental shopping occurring from a visit to the eateries or the leisure and recreational facilities. Also the expectation was that further visits would be made having established at least a relationship and at best a loyalty with a customer.

The Ghermezian brothers recognised the synergy and compatibility between retail and leisure activity in their development of West Edmonton Mall, Alberta (1981–1985), establishing the first retail and leisure destination, attracting both the local catchment and tourists from further afield. West Edmonton Mall was built in three phases and provided a total of 493 000 m² (5.3 million ft²) retail, catering, leisure and recreational facilities. Just under half of the accommodation is for traditional shops and restaurants with the remainder being specifically built to provide leisure and recreational facilities. To accommodate the millions of visitors each year there are 20 000 parking spaces.

West Edmonton Mall is arranged over two levels with a spinal mall and branch malls and food courts along its length. Over 800 shops and six anchor stores are integrated, together with two food courts and all of the leisure and recreational facilities in an enclosed environment forming a city within a city. However, it is the uniquely combined leisure and recreational facilities with the retail environment which set a new benchmark in regional shopping centres.

The leisure and recreational facilities at West Edmonton Mall represent the scale of a standard theme park alone in its own right. In addition to providing the standard add-ons of restaurants and cinemas, the significant feature at Edmonton was the indoor amusement park of 37 100 m² (400 000 ft²), providing 25 different rides and attractions, a full sized ice rink, a miniature golf course, a dolphin lagoon, aquarium, a 2 ha (4 acres) water park for leisure swimming with a wave pool, slides, rapids and whirlpool, an indoor lake with underwater submarine rides and a full size replica of a Columbus caravel. If this wasn't enough, there is also a casino and bingo hall and a themed hotel with 354 bedrooms to accommodate tourists overnight. This mall was the largest built in North America and is currently still the largest shopping centre in the world.

West Edmonton Mall established new standards for regional shopping centres through its wholehearted combining of leisure facilities with the standard retail format. The combination of retail with leisure and recreational facilities has more recently been described as 'retail and entertainment', which has been abridged down to 'shoppertainment'. Designers and developers from around the world have paid homage and visited West Edmonton Mall, which has subsequently led to its influence on many subsequent regional shopping centre

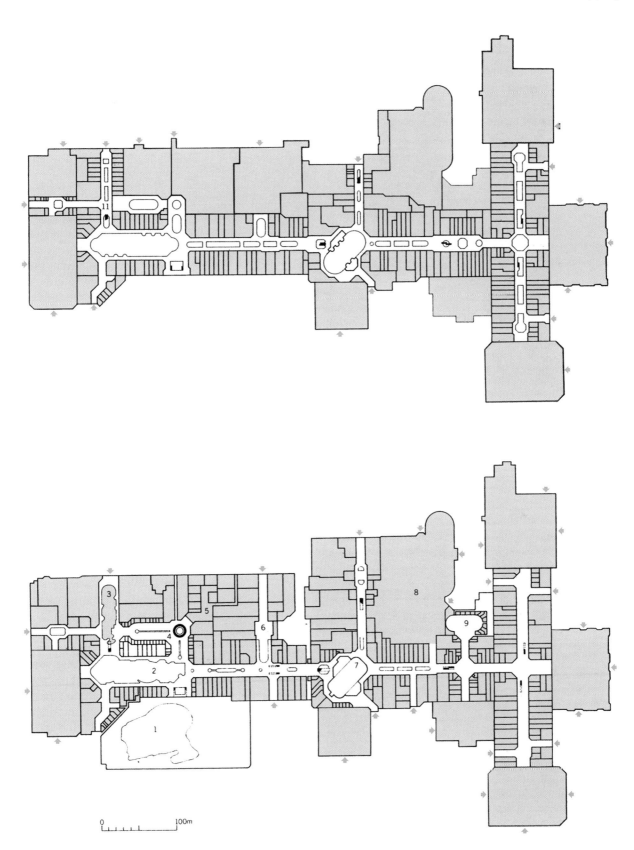

Figure 4.11 The upper and lower ground floor plans, West Edmonton Mall, Alberta, Canada (1981–1985). *(Source: BDP)*

Figure 4.12 The water park at West Edmonton Mall, Alberta, Canada. *(Source: Corbis/Robert Holmes)*

proposals either with similar conviction or in watered down ways.

The Metrocentre, Gateshead (1984–1987), developed by Cameron Hall in three phases, was the first UK regional shopping centre to incorporate major entertainment facilities. Taking advantage of the planning freedom given to the Enterprise Zone status of the former power station wasteland, the developers built a two level combined retail and leisure development of 204 400 m² (2.2 million ft²). Although the Metrocentre was less than half the size of West Edmonton, it incorporated many of its own recreational features. Most notably were a ten-screen cinema, a themed food court, a mini golf course, a games arcade, bowling alley and fantasyland theme park with a roller coaster, Ferris wheels, dodgems and other rides. Metrocentre's entertainment facilities were not as integrated with the overall centre as at the Edmonton Mall, with the Gateshead example separating the leisure elements into identifiable areas in two corners of the figure of eight mall network. However, the Metrocentre was twice the size of any retail development then built in the UK and could claim at the time to be 'the first indoor theme park in Europe'. West Edmonton Mall had both a direct and indirect influence on the Metrocentre whereby Ron McCarthy of McCarthy and Associates, the leisure consultant for the theme park at Edmonton, also advised on the food court and theme park at Gateshead.

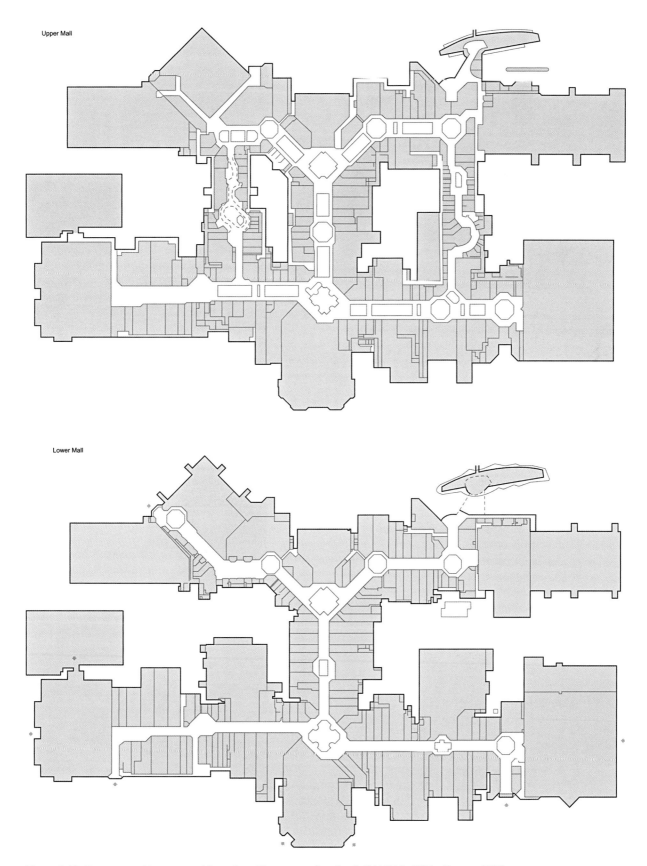

Upper Mall

Lower Mall

Figure 4.13 The upper and lower ground floor plans, Metrocentre, Gateshead, UK (1984–1987). *(Source: BDP)*

Figure 4.14 One of the several node spaces, Town Square 1, Metrocentre, Gateshead, UK. *(Source: Capital Shopping Centres)*

Figure 4.15 Enclosed interior court, Meadowhall, Sheffield, UK (1990). *(Source: Chapman Taylor)*

A further regional shopping centre quickly following to adapt to the new format of incorporating leisure and entertainment was Meadowhall, Sheffield – a development on a former steelworks site by Eddie Healey, which opened in 1990. Edmonton's influence extended to Yorkshire where McCarthy and Associates again acted as the leisure consultant, assisting architects Chapman Taylor and Partners. Meadowhall at 116 000 m² (1.2 million sq ft) was smaller again, being just about half the size of the Metrocentre. Meadowhall, with three department stores and a food superstore, is arranged over two levels in a cranked dumb-bell mall with a significant leisure element accessed from a focal court in the mall. The leisure and catering area is here further separated from the rest of the centre in its own elaborately domed and Mediterranean themed box called the Oasis. Here the leisure and entertainment element provides a 900 seat food court with restaurants, cafés and fast food outlets, a multiplex cinema, family entertainment centre and a television studio.

Edmonton's direct influence continued into the USA when, in 1986, the Ghermezian Brothers, just after completing the third phase of the Edmonton Mall, signed the deal with Bloomington Port Authority jointly to redevelop, along with Melvin Simm Associates, a former sports stadium site into a retail and leisure destination. This development, branded as the Mall of America, gave the USA its first and largest retail and entertainment destination and opened in Bloomington, Minneapolis in 1992.

Figure 4.16 Interior view of the 'Oasis' themed two level catering area, Meadowhall, Sheffield, UK. *(Source: Chapman Taylor)*

Providing 390 000 m² (4.2 million ft²) of accommodation the centre operates over four levels, arranged into four separate malls which are configured in a square shaped circuit with one of the four department stores in the each of the corners. Located in the centre of the perimeter malls is a 28 322 m² (approximately 7 acres) themed leisure park – Knotts Camp Snoopy. The layout is logical and simple to understand, with points of reference between the retail malls and entertainment park reinforcing the legibility of the centre. The leisure and entertainment element is separate from the retail malls but is integral with the form and organisation. The element being positively expressed where the square space is fully glazed over, creating an extensively landscaped and naturally lit covered amusement park. The four malls are each individually themed and have three retail levels and a fourth level providing 49 restaurants and eight night clubs, including a comedy club. The Knotts Camp Snoopy amusement park at the heart of the centre has some 30 different rides which include a water adventure, a roller coaster, a Ferris wheel and nine further restaurants. In addition there is an underwater world with a 100 m long glass tunnel passing through the water with views up to the hammerhead sharks, rays and other fish.

The Mall of America, in addition to its 525 stores and entertainment, has two civic facilities normally found in city centres. The first of these is a chapel offering religious services and wedding ceremonies. The chapel will provide outfitting and the reception catering services if required. The second unique feature is the inclusion of the first college campus within a shopping mall – with 17 separate study areas in the centre.

The Mall of America is an exemplar of the integration of leisure with retail with its very form being the generator of its organisation. Although the leisure is integral to the centre, it is separated from the malls and has its own identifiable area. The centre is totally inward looking and generally presents blank façades to the outside. Despite being described as an 'unalluring, saltine cracker box exterior' (Beets, *The Austin Chronicle*), the Mall of America attracts between 600 00 and 900 000 visitors each week, depending on the season, and is the USA's most visited destination for domestic travellers. Four in ten of the visitors are tourists from outside the two hour drive time, who are encouraged to make two to three day shopping breaks to the retail and leisure destination. Tourists are assisted by the proximity of a local hotel providing over 7000 rooms and the proximity of the Minneapolis St Paul airport which is two miles away. The Mall of America is a highly successful shopping

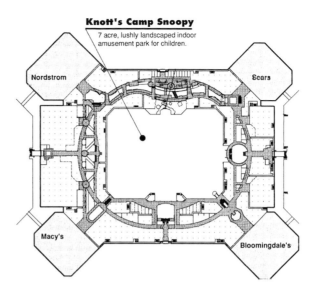

Figure 4.17 Typical upper level floor plan, Mall of America, Bloomington, Minneapolis, USA (1992). *(Source: Jerde)*

Figure 4.18 Camp Snoopy, leisure park at Mall of America, Minneapolis, USA. *(Source: Peter Coleman)*

Figure 4.19 Camp Snoopy, leisure park, Mall of America, Minneapolis, USA. (*Source: Peter Renerts*)

Figure 4.20 A three level intersecting court, Mall of America, Minneapolis, USA. (*Source: Peter Renerts*)

and entertainment machine and has plans to expand the centre beyond the 465 000 m² (5 million ft²) barrier by adding new facilities focusing on life enhancement, entertainment and hospitality.

The Ghermezians were not the only family strongly to influence the regional shopping and leisure centre format. Eddie Healey together with his son Paul went

on in 1991, upon the completion of Meadowhall, to acquire 98 ha of former Thyssen steelworks in Oberhausen, Germany. Applying the legacy of experience of developing a similar redundant steelworks in the UK, the Healeys' (Stadium Group) intention was to build CentrO – a state of the art out-of-town shopping centre together with major leisure facilities. Despite out-of-town retailing being anathema to the German authorities, a combination of Yorkshire nowse and demonstrable experience convinced both the local and regional governments of the ability of a shopping development to regenerate the declining industrial area. The need for economic regeneration of this central Ruhr area also overrode the concerns of the impact of a large new shopping centre on the retail trading in the town of Oberhausen and its other two townships. In order to demonstrate improved integration with the town and townships, major new public transport facilities have been incorporated to connect CentrO with these towns. The former freight railway line was converted into a light railway line and a bus route connecting the town of Oberhausen to CentrO and northern residential suburbs was established. A purpose-built station stands directly outside CentrO in a circular entrance square. A new 12 000 seat multi-purpose stadium, the Arena, was also built, which is accessed from the same entrance square.

The regional shopping and leisure centre is also integrated into a comprehensive mixed-use masterplan containing offices, residential houses and a Rhineland museum.

CentrO opened in 1996 providing shopping and leisure facilities for over 6 million people within half an hour drive time in the centre of the industrial Ruhr district. The shopping element of the centre is arranged in another cranked dumb-bell mall which extends for 400 m and is arranged within 70 000 m² (750 000 ft²) of leasable space (see Fig. 4.22). There are two department stores with one at the eastern end of the mall and the second store located from a T mall which leads from the centre focal court. An internal food court with communal seating, also at the eastern end, sits beneath a large glazed dome and provides culinary specialities from around the globe. This space (sponsored by a major drinks company), the 'Oase', is a similar form to the Oasis at Meadowhall, but at Oberhausen the food court is an integral part of the mall and is arranged at the end adjacent to the entrance space leading to the multi-screen cinemas, external catering and the theme park (see Fig. 4.23).

Running parallel to the CentrO mall is an external walkway, the Promenade, with 30 or so separate and individual bars and restaurants (see Fig. 4.24). These can be separately accessed or connected from either end of the mall and through the centre. The Promenade is expressed as a series of individual buildings along a canal side. The artificial canal runs along the length of the Promenade with bridges leading to an 8 ha theme and amusement park with rides, children's activities and an adventure island.

The shopping facilities at Oberhausen are generally similar to those provided at Meadowhall. Where Oberhausen raises the bar and progresses the format is in the additional catering and leisure facilities, which are both more extensive and integrally planned with the centre. Oberhausen has the internal food court and cinemas and then adds the waterside external catering and the significant theme park attracting adults and children of all ages.

These additional facilities along with the Arena and museum offer more attractions and reasons to visit the centre. Although the centre is primarily providing shopping facilities, by its incorporation of significant catering and leisure facilities, it is consciously building on the synergy and complementary nature of these three uses. This is a clear example of the sum of the parts being greater than the individual pieces. Oberhausen comprehensively and holistically took on board other uses and provided an integrated mixed-use masterplan. The shopping element at its core occupies less than half the site. The completion of Oberhausen marked the point where the European mainland recognised that, in order to achieve a successful centre, it is necessary to provide more than just shopping facilities and a bold gesture to incorporating catering and leisure.

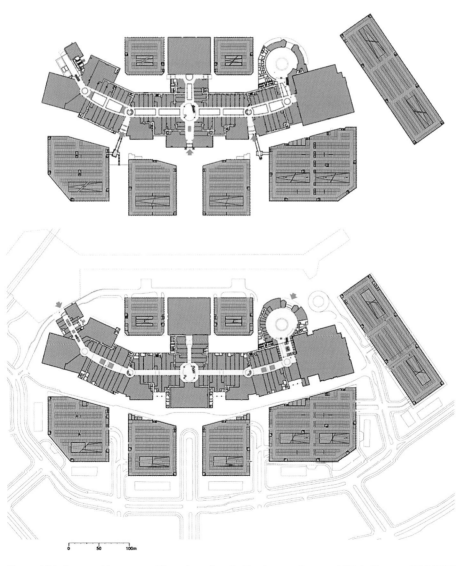

0   50   100m

Figure 4.21 Upper and lower ground floor plans, CentrO, Obserhausen, Germany (1991). *(Source: RTKL/BDP)*

Figure 4.22 The two level naturally lit enclosed interior to CentrO, Oberhausen, Germany. *(Source: Peter Coleman)*

Figure 4.23 The 'Oase' food court, CentrO, Oberhausen with a similar form to Meadowhall, UK. *(Source: Peter Coleman)*

Figure 4.24 The separate external catering with individual restaurants forms the Promenade along the canal, CentrO, Oberhausen, Germany. *(Source: Peter Coleman)*

Another exemplary type of a regional shopping and leisure centre is Bluewater at Greenhithe, Kent. Described by the ICSC as 'Europe's most innovative retail and leisure destination …[it] has changed the face of retailing since it opened in March 1999'. This benchmark was only achieved by a conscious decision to raise the bar during its development. Bluewater was originally conceived with several contemporaries but emerged some ten years later well ahead of the pack.

The first planning permission for regenerating the former cement works in a quarry in Kent was achieved in the same year as the opening of Meadowhall in 1990. At the same time as CentrO, Oberhausen was laying its foundation stone in 1994 a new developer Lend Lease took over the project. This occurred at the time when the UK was coming out of a recession and the government was beginning to restrict out-of-town retail development. Lend Lease was quick to realise the potential value of Bluewater being likely to be one of the last regional shopping and leisure centres to have planning permission. A considered assessment which turned into reality with the government's planning guidance (PPG 6) coming into effect in 1996, slamming the door firmly shut on all further major out-of-town development in the UK. Lend Lease was also soon to realise that with competition and a mature retail market providing more of the same shopping facilities, no matter how well executed, would not be good enough to make the difference and make Bluewater a consumer destination of choice for an increasingly demanding public or to attract the major anchor tenants.

Lend Lease, driven by necessity and a wish to demonstrate being a global company, went about a research exercise to gain a better understanding of consumer requirements and reappraise what future shopping centres should be. The research study involved some 20 000 responses to questions such as:

- what should shopping centres be?
- what do consumers want?
- what will they want in ten years time?
- what is good and bad in existing centres?

The survey concluded that, in addition to providing the best choice of shops and available retail offer, the following issues should also be provided:

- a total experience of being cared for from arrival through to departure
- facilities that have sufficient variety to cater for a range of shopping, catering and leisure activities for a full day out
- creating the right atmosphere and environment
- a choice of different restaurants and catering
- a feeling of safety and security
- a level of comfort
- good access to various modes of transport.

Many of these points were not new to shopping centre planning. However, Lend Lease was probably the first to address them all simultaneously and then to use them to influence its decision-making in the design process.

From 1997 onwards, Joseph Pine II and James Gilmore brought to light the realisation of a change taking place in consumer expectations. They highlighted a three-stage transition in shopping which had occurred over 50 years, from buying a product, to delivering a service and then staging an experience. Pine and Gilmore demonstrate in their book 'The Experience Economy' (Pine and Gilmore, 1999) how each stage moving forward improves both competitive position and the ability to achieve a more premium price. Lend Lease was cognisant of Pine and Gilmore's findings and recognised the value of providing an appropriate experience when visiting a shopping centre.

The ability to provide the shopping visitor with a memorable experience influenced the developers' design brief and decisions in providing better levels of customer facilities (toilets, washrooms, resting facilities etc.) and the quality of the external and public spaces. Lend Lease's commitment to providing an environmental/spatial experience led to the selection of Eric Khune as concept architect to bring the civic and cultural qualities to the internal and external architecture and the public realm.

The research led approach and feedback from the public influenced the brief making process requiring the design team to address the following issues:

- redefining both the range and quality of retail offer
- developing new retail and leisure experiences
- the integration of internal and external environments
- operating a 'host' and 'guest' approach
- how to attract the best of British and international retailers, non-mall retailers and caterers
- how to make the building innovative
- how the building could embrace the external countryside.

In addition to influencing the briefing process, Lend Lease also used the research to influence the team's working process. For example, the team was required to understand the answers to the above briefing issues, to use them and ensure the project achieved them. The requirement to provide innovative shops and attract new retailers was correspondingly met by the developer committing resources to facilitate and work with the retailers' teams to help achieve new standards of shop fitting.

Compared with some of the larger out-of-town regional shopping and leisure centres in Europe, Bluewater proves that size isn't everything once the size reaches a point of critical mass. The schedule of accommodation is relatively modest with 140 000 m^2 (approx 1 500 000 ft^2) of retailing and catering along with 13 000 m^2 (approx 142 000 ft^2) of leisure facilities. The space provides 320 shops, three department stores, 45 cafés and restaurants, 13 cinemas and 13 000 car parking spaces on a 100 ha site. As Greenhithe, Kent is located next to a motorway with new connections to the motorway network, Bluewater has a catchment population of over 10 million people within a one hour drive time.

The centre is arranged as three malls forming a triangle with a department store in each of the corners. The unique layout is arranged over two levels with the car parks feeding equally into both of the levels. The triangular plan forms a circuit and avoids the up and down gun barrel of the traditional dumb-bell format. The layout has the advantage of compactness but does require below ground tunnel access to the central service area.

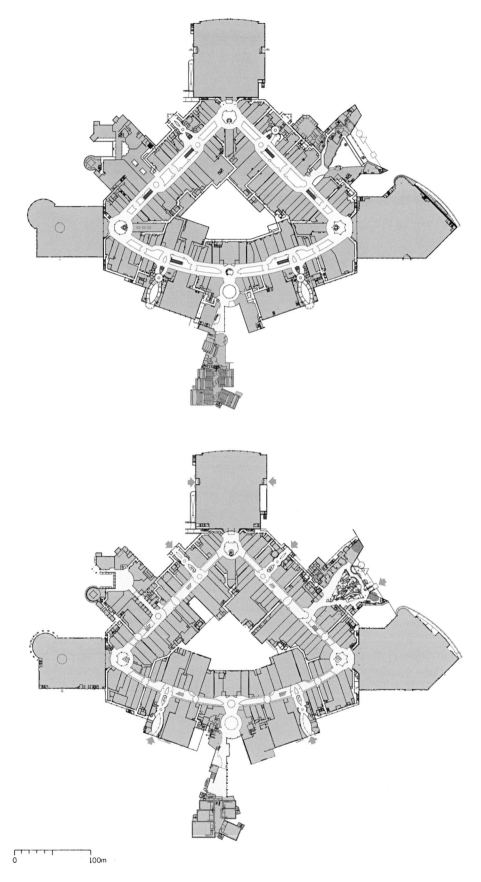

Figure 4.25 Upper and lower ground floor plans, Bluewater, Greenhithe, Kent, UK (1999). *(Source: Benoy/BDP)*

0   100m

Figure 4.26 Thames Walk celebrating the journey of the River Thames, Bluewater, Kent, UK. *(Source: Lend Lease)*

Figure 4.27 The Guildhall Mall with guilds and crafts celebrated in the bulkhead mouldings, Bluewater, Kent, UK. *(Source: Lend Lease)*

Figure 4.28 The Rose Gallery with its delicate metalwork, Bluewater, Kent, UK. *(Source: Lend Lease)*

Each of the three malls has its own distinct identity and character. At the junction of the malls a knuckle space forms a point of punctuation in the circuit and a recognisable entrance to each of the department stores. Each of the three malls is entered midway along its length by a 'welcome hall'. Three separate and identifiable catering areas reinforce each of the malls. The east mall, the Rose Gallery, has a landscape theme, which is principally aimed to appeal to families with high street multiple retailers. The catering is correspondingly targeted to family needs in a food court with communal seating, arranged in a large glazed 'winter garden', inspired by the Palm House at Kew. Fast food outlets arranged around the perimeter provide for 750 seats set among the tropical plants. A themed playground and discovery trail are also provided amidst the botanical garden. The west mall, the Guild Hall, is themed on the trade guilds of England, represented by high level sculptural motifs. The upmarket and aspirational retailers are focused in this more urban mall. The catering is accessed by a traditional arcade with an external piazza as a setting for high quality cafés and restaurants on three of its sides. The lakeside terrace forms the fourth side of the piazza with views extending out across the lake. The catering area forms a link with the outside and provides the opportunity to get away from the mall environment. The third mall is the south mall, which is curved and called the Thames Walk. The interior of this space is themed on associations with the river Thames with the river path depicted in the stone floor. The retailers in this mall are aimed at media, entertainment and other complementary uses with highly animated and expressive shopfronts reinforcing the entertainment quality. The catering area leads

Figure 4.29 The Wintergarden catering area overlooking the lake, Bluewater, Kent, UK. *(Source: Lend Lease)*

towards the cinemas and the cafés and restaurants provide catering suited to eating before and after the cinema. The catering relates to an external 'water circus' with programmed fountains, pools and cascades reinforcing a lively evening experience.

The knuckle spaces at the junctions of the malls form a forecourt to each of the department stores and each space is identifiable by its own astrological themed ceiling and central feature. Within each

Figure 4.30 The water circus beyond the multi-screen cinemas, Bluewater, Kent, UK. *(Source: Lend Lease)*

Figure 4.31 Escalator-free knuckle space, The Sun Court, Bluewater, Kent, UK. *(Source: Lend Lease)*

knuckle space are seats, coffee shop and stairs connecting the levels.

Unique to Bluewater are the welcome halls which enter each of the malls from the car parks. These are arranged to meet customers' needs on arrival and departure and incorporate services such as information desks, lockers, drinking fountains, coffee bars, cash machines, post boxes, telephones and high quality washrooms more akin to a five star hotel lobby. To assist recognising the arrival point of each welcome hall a significant artwork is located in each of the malls. The welcome halls have individual entrances in the car parks and are finished and animated to correspond to the adjacent mall and avoid the feel of being in a secondary mall.

Figure 4.32 A griffin artwork identifies the location of the welcome hall in the Guildhall Mall, Bluewater, Kent, UK. *(Source: Lend Lease)*

Bluewater is not the largest regional shopping and leisure centre in Europe, but it is sufficiently big to provide a wide range of carefully considered retail, catering and leisure facilities. It has graduated from the bigger-and-better philosophy to smarter and best and raised the consciousness of understanding how shopping environments work.

As the last planning permission for a generation, Bluewater recognised it was the last contender competing in the event and decided to raise the bar to a height above any of the previous participants. Making certain by its successful opening that it not only won the event but established a level of quality and understanding of the type of shopping format that others would not have the opportunity to challenge for some considerable time.

Bluewater claims to be the most exciting retail and leisure destination in Europe. This may for the moment be the case. It is a great achievement and the developer should be congratulated for rising to the challenge and making the most of the opportunity of being at the right place at the right time. Bluewater is a significant benchmark in both the development of regional shopping and leisure centres and in the development of shopping environments. Bluewater will represent the zenith of this format for sometime, but by the nature of change and progress it too will eventually be bettered.

The regional shopping and leisure centres illustrated so far consist of the three key ingredients of shopping, catering and leisure accommodation. Common to this format of retail environment the shopping component remains the dominant and primary element even where the leisure element is a comparable size to the shops. The catering and leisure elements are added to attract a wider age range of visitors and provide more reasons to extend the stay of the shopping trip.

The Gateway Theatre of Shopping in Durban (2002) is a fine example of this type of shopping format opening in the developing world of South Africa and was the largest of its type in the country when

Figure 4.33 Aerial photo of Gateway Theatre of Shopping showing the Boulevard facing towards the next phase of the new town development, Umlanga, Durban, SA (2001). *(Source: RTKL)*

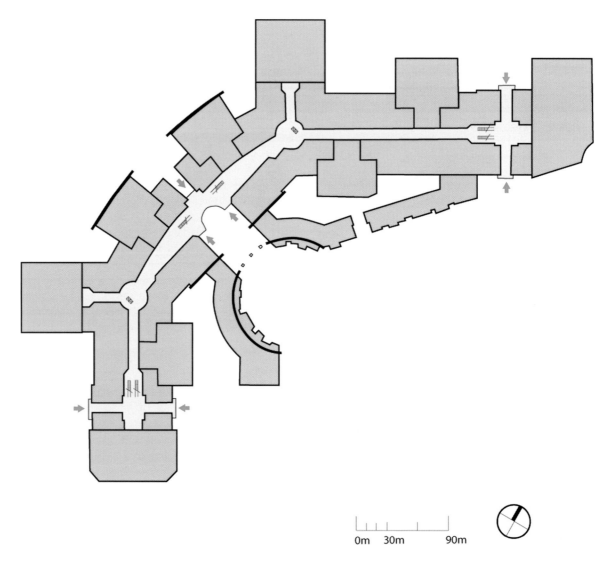

0m   30m   90m

Figure 4.34 The lower ground floor plan, Gateway Theatre of Shopping, Umlanga, Durban, SA. *(Source: RTKL/BDP)*

it opened. Developed by Marcland Developments for Old Mutual Properties, Gateway is planned as a catalyst for the new town of Umlanga, allowing for the northward growth of the conurbation of Durban. The Gateway centre therefore falls across two of the categories of shopping format – 'the new town regional centres' and the 'regional shopping and leisure centre'. It is described here under the latter category.

Gateway is a world-class development with 120 000 m² (approx 1.3 million ft²) of accommodation with a wide range of retail shops and a variety of leisure and entertainment facilities, providing activities which extend from the daytime into the evening. The 350 shops include local specialists, national chains and international brands together with a large number of themed and family restaurants.

Figure 4.35 The outward facing cresent shaped entranceway, Gateway Theatre of Shopping, Umlanga, Durban, SA. *(Source: Peter Coleman)*

Figure 4.36 The cafes lining the entrance square, Gateway Theatre of Shopping, Umlanga, Durban, SA. *(Source: RTKL)*

The centre is able to attract a wide age range of the population and tourists with a catchment population of 3 million visitors within half an hour driving time. Gateway is arranged with an outward facing crescent shaped entranceway and a boulevard lined with individual catering buildings. The entranceway and boulevard form the armature for the planned town centre of Umlanga. The animated exterior frontage is intended to encourage complementary street frontages to be added adjacent to the centre in future. Behind the entry crescent, the central piazza forms another external space with cafés, bars and restaurants which lead past a water cascade to the central entrance.

Gateway is planned as a two level centre arranged in a cranked dumb-bell plan with a single department store and a youth themed retail and entertainment zone anchoring each end. A partial third level, an eighteen multi-screen cinema, is accommodated above the central entrance. Circular knuckle spaces with domed roofs are used to change direction in the mall. The interiors are formed by a series of large naturally lit market hall spaces which have the feel of glazed streets.

Figure 4.37 The wide interior with clerestory natural light, Gateway Theatre of Shopping, Umlanga, Durban, SA. *(Source: RTKL)*

Gateway is well endowed with state of the art leisure and entertainment facilities which are distributed in various locations about the centre. Complementing the external cafés and restaurants, a 600 seat first floor food court provides fast food adjacent to the cinemas. Also located in the centre of the scheme is a $12\,000\,m^2$ (approx $130\,000\,ft^2$) family entertainment centre with a jungle themed indoor amusement area with gaming machines, electronic simulators and ten pin bowling lanes. A science centre with interactive areas and displays allows children of various ages to be in a secure and supervised space and left to discover the principles of science.

The eastern end of the mall is anchored by Expo Explore, a series of youth themed lifestyle shops based on extreme sports, which surround and form an enclosed multi-level events space. In the centre of the space is a 24 m high climbing rock which forms a focus to a pulsating audio and light show. The large volume space is used for fashion shows, product launches and parties and successfully attracts a youth market. Adjacent to the multipurpose space is a combined retailing and teaching area relating to external sporting activities such as

Figure 4.39 The Wavehouse water board surfing, Gateway Theatre of Shopping, Umlanga, Durban, SA. *(Source: Peter Coleman)*

climbing, scuba diving and camping. This mixture of specialist retailing with training possibilities for similar leisure activities is an innovative facility within a shopping centre. The inclusion of teaching space provides an engaging experience with the public and goes towards meeting the increasing need for shopping facilities to provide a memorable experience as well as merchandising. Also complementing the leisure lifestyle activities and shops of this area is a specialist travel agent which can assist in the organisation of adventure travel and activity holidays.

Beyond the internal youth events space and activity shops is an external area for board sport leisure facilities. These cover different types of sports on boards, from a skateboard park to a water surfing wave machine. The Wavehouse, with an artificial standing wave machine forces water into waves which allows both beginners and experts to surf and practise their skills under specialist organisation all year round. The artificial wave machine and the performance of the participators provide a lively spectacle. This opportunity is used to create bars and cafés which overlook the Wavehouse.

Figure 4.38 The climbing wall inside the Expo Explore entertainment and leisure area, Gateway Theatre of Shopping, Umlanga, Durban, SA. *(Source: RTKL)*

The leisure facilities are also complemented by a separately accessed Imax and arts cinema, a live theatre, club and an external four-wheel vehicle drive course. A series of internal and external water features has also been incorporated at Gateway, the most spectacular being the programmed fountain which runs across the entrance crescent and allows the space to be both an urban piazza and features a dramatic 25 m long wave effect in front of the entranceway.

Figure 4.40 The water feature at the entrance runs across the urban piazza, Gateway Theatre of Shopping, Umlanga, Durban, SA. *(Source: RTKL)*

The Gateway centre has understood shoppertainment by providing a wide range of leisure attractions and facilities to complement the shops and attract as many visitors as possible to the centre. The distribution of the leisure facilities throughout the centre has been carefully organised with appropriately themed retailing to create a special synergy between the shops, catering and retailing. These identifiable areas form distinctively different parts of the large centre and help with the orientation and legibility of the centre. For example, the cinemas and family and entertainment centre relate to the food court and external family catering in the palm court. The North Mall has the youth lifestyle shops, the outside leisure activities and the multi-use space.

Gateway has recognised the importance of the youth market and how this generation can influence and determine where a family goes to shop. It has gone out of its way to provide the right shops with the brands and the leisure activities which will attract

a range of young people and their corresponding families to the centre.

The trend for regional retail and leisure centres has extended across Europe. This is particularly so in those countries which have relatively recently enjoyed democratic politics like Spain and Portugal, and which had largely missed out on the first generation of regional shopping centres. The economies of both Iberian countries have rapidly grown following their liberation and have also readily grasped the latest retailing trends. In Spain, for example, which has been keen to catch up with retail and leisure destinations, several new regional retail and leisure centres have recently opened. Two of these, Tres Aguas, Alcorcon (2002) and Xanadu (2003), opened on the perimeter of Madrid, serving both the immediate expanding new residential districts as well as attracting visitors from the wider catchment of the city.

Both centres have significant leisure and entertainment facilities alongside regional shopping facilities. Each centre has multi-screen cinemas, family entertainment centres, health clubs as well as a wide range of cafés, bars and restaurants.

Tres Aguas, designed by Building Design Partnership, is arranged around an open air, landscaped, circular plaza space which forms the entranceway to both the shop and leisure areas and links the two elements together.

Figure 4.41 The open air entrance piazza between the shopping and leisure facilities, Tres Aguas, Alcorcon, Madrid, Spain (2002). *(Source: David Barbour)*

Figure 4.42 The entranceway to the Family Entertainment Centre, Tres Aguas, Alcorcon, Madrid, Spain. *(Source: Jeremy Sweet/ BDP)*

Xanadu, designed by Chapman Taylor, provides a spectacular covered leisure area which uses dramatic tensile fabric roofs to form a major indoor sports and entertainment facility. Located on one side of the tented space is Europe's largest indoor real snow ski slope – the Parque de Nieve. The ski

Figure 4.43 The influential form of the indoor ski slope incorporated into Xanadu, Madrid, Spain (2003). *(Source: Mills Corporation)*

slope is expressed in a wing-like metal structure where the slopes are overlooked by some of the bars and restaurants. Xanadu, developed by the Mills Corporation from America, represents, by its scale and range of leisure and entertainment facilities, another milestone in the development of regional shopping and leisure centres.

Figure 4.44 The tented leisure and entertainment area, Xanadu, Madrid, Spain. *(Source: Mills Corporation)*

New Town Regional Malls

The new town regional mall shopping format is another sub-category of the regional shopping centre. They are planned as part of a new town, usually outside of an existing framework on a greenfield or brownfield site where the shopping centre will act as the catalyst for the following new town developments. These centres when first planned and opened often stand on their own until the surrounding residential, cultural and workplace buildings are completed. The format differs from that of the regional shopping centre, which utilises an existing residential population, by the centre's adjacent proximity and immediacy to the primary road network to capture visitors within the half an hour drive time. The new town regional mall is planned as a completely new facility together with a new residential population which will form a large part of its catchment, alongside a new local road network.

Mention was made earlier as to examples of new town regional malls which cut across two of the categories of different types of shopping environments. Parly 2, which was one of the first European examples of a regional shopping centre, was planned as part of the new town on the perimeter of Paris (1969) and Gateway, Durban (2001) was planned as the catalyst for the new town of Umlanga. Some other examples and characteristics of new town regional malls are examined below.

The new town regional mall represents a transitional stage between two other shopping environment formats – the regional shopping centre and the town centre malls. The stage of its development determines which of these two types the new town regional mall is closer to. For example, the new town regional mall in its immature raw stage, when there is little of the other planned development complete, has little to differentiate it from an out-of-town regional shopping centre. At the other end of its development, in its mature stage when all the surrounding development and residential population is in place, the format is close to a town centre mall. New town regional malls have unique qualities which clearly differentiate them from the purely functional shopping machines represented by the regional shopping centres. By being part of a larger masterplan, the form and layout of the centre is often influenced by the holistic vision of the new town.

Central Milton Keynes is an interesting example of a new town regional mall. On its opening in 1979 opinions representing the extremes of view were well documented. In view of its seminal nature in the development of the UK new towns and its on going metamorphosis and transformation from ugly duckling into beautiful swan it is worthy of further consideration here.

Central Milton Keynes was one of a generation of UK new towns, along with Runcorn, Irvine and Cumbernauld, planned as complete new towns. Milton Keynes was one of the last to be completed and grandest in being planned for a new population of 250 000. On its opening it was also the biggest shopping centre in the UK providing 101 000 m^2 (approx 1.1 million ft^2) of lettable floor space. Milton Keynes was planned for ease of movement of the car with Central Milton Keynes being integral to the generous network of roads and roundabouts which the city was planned around. The heroic planning of the city located different activities into separate zones with the shopping centre being the first of the commercial buildings located on a strategic high point in the centre of the city. The shopping centre plan is influenced by the planning of the city and is arranged as a gridded network of pedestrian ways, surrounded by surface car parking, set between the new roadways in a parkland setting. In summary, the antithesis of an urban city.

Despite Central Milton Keynes's urban shortcomings the centre is uniquely planned and established several benchmark qualities in UK shopping centres. The centre is arranged around a gridded network of generously proportioned day-lit pedestrian ways. Running the 800 m length of the centre are two parallel arcades which are crossed at regular intervals by secondary malls. The shopping is divided into three bands with the middle band used for the large space users and primary public spaces and the outer bands housing the smaller unit shops. The lattice network of public ways

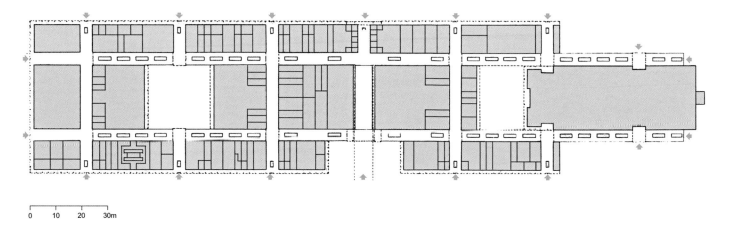

0   10   20   30m

Figure 4.45 Ground floor plan, Central Milton Keynes, Milton Keynes, UK (1979). *(Source: MKDC/BDP)*

extends the rational qualities of the city planning into the centre itself.

Another unique quality of Central Milton Keynes is that it is all arranged at a single mall level, although the larger shops are multi-level. The mall spaces also remain open to the outside air. Along with the natural daylighting and the double height circulation spaces there is a relaxed and spacious atmosphere to the interiors.

Figure 4.46 The spacious qualities of the original interior street to Central Milton Keynes, UK. *(Source: Richard Bryant/David Lock Associates)*

The surface car parking surrounding the centre is set in generously planted boulevards and provides 2000 spaces but detaches the centre from its surroundings. Vehicular servicing to the shops is separated from public view by being arranged at roof level, although where these routes cross the malls the spaces are reduced in height.

The centre set new benchmarks for both its interior and exterior architecture. In addition to the spaciousness of the interiors, they also set quality standards by the extensive use of natural stone on the floors and walls. The exterior modular cladding formed a neat container repeating a well designed element endlessly along the façades and was considered highly controlled and ordered by comparison with the incongruous exterior of its peer at Brent Cross.

While a few purists thought Central Milton Keynes as beautiful and a lesson in control, the popular view, and impression borne out over time, was that the centre lacked vitality (through its single use), had little local identity (by all being uniform), and prevented spontaneity (by being too purposeful and controlled). In an attempt to address the long-term success of the centre, extensive alterations and extensions were made in 1999 and a long-term vision to extend further and alter the centre has been prepared for completion by 2016.

Midsummer Place brought individuality and a new identity to Milton Keynes on its opening in 1999. A 40 000 m² (approx 430 000 ft²) extension introduced a new expressive stone clad department store and 54 new shops in an individually designed public space. Furthermore, the rectangular grid was broken by the careful insertion of a circular natural stone clad courtyard around an existing tree. The long-term vision for 2016 will continue to enhance and improve the centre. New leisure, catering and residential uses will be added to move away from the single use, attract visitors and extend the use of a building throughout the day and evening. Over 200 new residential homes will bring added vitality to the central area. Further alterations and extensions will add another 100 shops, cafés, bars and restaurants as well as additional public spaces. The existing open air Queens Court will have a retractable glass roof allowing the space to be used for sitting out at café and restaurant tables in all seasons and throughout

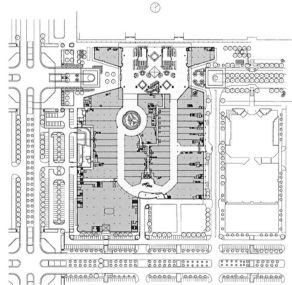

Figure 4.47 Plan of the Midsummer Place extension to Central Milton Keynes, UK (1999). *(Source: GMW)*

Figure 4.48 The new circular courtyard to Midsummer Place, Central Milton Keynes, UK. *(Source: Peter Cook)*

Figure 4.49 Illustration of the proposed retractable roof Queens Court, Central Milton Keynes, UK *(Allies & Morrison Archts)*. *(Source: Allies & Morrison/ Miller Hare)*

the day and evening. The car parking will also be extended to provide 2400 more spaces and public transport access will be improved by the addition of bus stops and interchange facilities for passengers.

A different type of town centre regional mall is illustrated by the Vasco da Gama centre in Lisbon (designed by Building Design Partnership with Jose Quintela). This new town example was planned to allow for the expansion of the existing urban conurbation of Lisbon onto a disused oil refinery and thereby regenerating the dockside area. The masterplan for the dockside and part of the municipality of Loures was aimed to create a vibrant mixed-use area with housing, offices, shops and leisure uses set within a high quality urban environment. The masterplan was given a great impetus by a large part of the new town being used for the 1998 World Exposition – this was adapted and the remainder of the area developed for completion by 2009.

The Vasco da Gama centre (1999) is strategically located in the masterplan beside the new railway and metro station. During the Expo the centre was used as the entranceway into the Exposition from the station. After the Expo the shopping centre was completed retaining the strategic and direct connections with the station.

Figure 4.50 The connecting Calatrava-designed bridges leading from the station, Vasco da Gama, Lisbon, Portugal (1999). *(Source: Rui Morais de Sousa)*

The centre is planned over three public levels with direct connections leading from the station at level 1 below the road and at level 3 via steel bridges designed by Santiago Calatrava. A partial fourth level overlooks the waterside and provides a decked terrace for catering and bars. The plan is arranged as a circuit with two contrasting different parallel malls. The smaller mall is a single level artificially lit arcade with a light feature in the ceiling and a train running along the ceiling at the lower level. The larger parallel mall is a grand three level galleried space with a fully glazed roof, which has water passing over its surface to assist with cooling. Crossing diagonally along the length of this space are glass floored steel bridges which encourage pedestrian movement between each side of the mall. The glazed roof runs the full length of the building and formally represents the axial relationship in the masterplan from the station to the ponds which lead down to the river Tagus waterfront. The galleried mall in the centre is more like a traditional arcade passing through a block connecting two busy streets. In this case the arcade connects the arrival street with the main pedestrianised spine which runs the

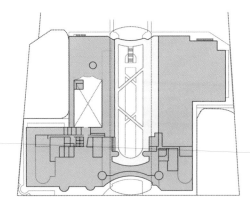

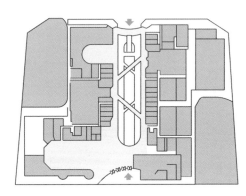

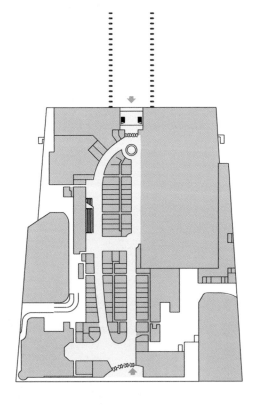

Figure 4.51 Upper, lower and first floor plans, Vasco da Gama, Lisbon, Portugal. *(Source: BDP)*

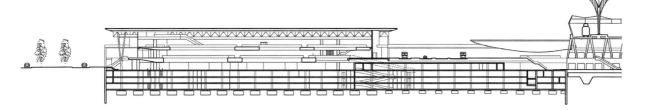

0   100m

Figure 4.52 Longitudinal cross-section through the mall, linking with the adjacent station, Vasco da Gama, Lisbon, Portugal. *(Source: BDP)*

Figure 4.53 The three level galleried space, with glazed bridges and patterned terrazzo floor, Vasco da Gama, Lisbon, Portugal. *(Source: Rui Morais de Sousa)*

length of the Park of Nations and unites all of the waterfront area.

The Vasco da Gama centre provides 47 600 m² (approx 512 000 ft²) of lettable shop, catering and leisure accommodation. The majority of space is let to comparison retailing occupied by national and international retailers. A hypermarket anchors the centre at the lowest level and there is a multi-screen cinema. A special feature of the centre is the

Figure 4.54 The decked waterfront catering overlooking the Parque das Nacoes, Vasco da Gama, Lisbon, Portugal. *(Source: Rui Morais de Sousa/BDP)*

waterfront catering, used by the cafés and restaurants, which extend externally on two levels of decked terracing overlooking the urban park and river Tagus. The interiors are contemporary with steel and glass balustrades and terrazzo floors which incorporate water themed motifs. As well as the train and metro station, access to the centre is encouraged by car with 2560 spaces provided in three levels directly beneath the centre.

Sitting above the centre on either side of the entry axis are two 24-storey apartment towers. The sculptural shape of the towers is inspired by the shape of a crab's claw and reinforces the nautical theme of the overall masterplan.

The Vasco da Gama centre sits in the centre of a new residential district with 10 000 new homes, largely provided for those who work in the adjacent offices, corporate headquarters, exhibition halls and government buildings. In addition, hotels, an aquarium, sports stadium, marina, local shops, cafés, restaurants and bars make up a vibrant new urban area of Lisbon. The high quality public realm spaces, which commenced with the Expo, continue and are extended throughout the new district. A magnificent bridge extends from the new town across the Tagus linking the area to the national motorway network and extending beyond to the south of Portugal.

Figure 4.55 The Sao Gabriel 24-storey tower of apartments above Vasco da Gama, Lisbon, Portugal. *(Source: Rui Morais de Sousa/BDP)*

Reinvention of the Regional Shopping Centre

The next three types of shopping environment are further sub-categories of the regional shopping centre and are the result of the base format having to reinvent itself. Lifestyle centres, hybrid centres and retail resorts, which have all developed in North America, each exemplify how the regional shopping centre has adapted as its popularity and usage has declined.

During the 1980s the standard offer at the regional shopping centre, with some additional leisure and catering facilities, sufficed to meet public expectations and was generally unquestioned. The world recession of the early 1990s naturally slowed down shopping expenditure and marked a turning point in public attitude. On return to economic stability in the mid-1990s the retail industry faced a more discerning and questioning public. Suddenly malls were declining in popularity and use. The problem was most noticeable in North America, with its heavy reliance on regional shopping centres. The wheel had finally come off the wagon and developers and designers had no choice but to re-examine what shoppers required in order to attract them back and to encourage them to spend.

The dead mall in 1997

Figure 4.56 A defunct American mall which is being urbanised illustrated by Winterpark, Florida, USA. *(Source: Dover, Kohl & Partners)*

The decline in popularity and usage of the standard regional shopping centre and mall was caused by a variety of reasons coming together simultaneously:

- the massive building programme in the USA in the 1980s resulted in the country being over-supplied with shopping facilities

- the over-supply was exacerbated by the overestimation of buying power and the immediate recession
- the regional shopping centre was faced with greater competition from alternative retailing formats, including highly formed and specialised power retailers who were attracted to retail parks (described below), discount retailing available at factory outlet centres (see below) and the availability of home shopping from catalogues and then through the Internet – e-commerce
- society's and shoppers' expectations had moved on from just purchasing products to looking for an experience in the process of shopping
- the public had become more discerning and knowledgeable and expected a uniqueness and individualistic environment rather than simply more of the same institutional centre
- finally, faced with an over-supply and a choice between malls the shopper would naturally select the bigger, newest or the one with a wider range of attractions with leisure facilities as well as a good retail offer.

By the mid-1990s North America saw for the first time a string of older and smaller regional shopping centres start to fail with some closing down completely. Many existing shopping centres had to undertake extensive renovation and alteration programmes to survive. New centres being planned had, through economic necessity, to become more inventive and focused towards customers' needs. Such was the extent of the problem in North America that some interesting new formats emerged.

The problem of failing centres has been less obvious in Europe, largely due to it not being so dependent on the out-of-town regional shopping centre format or having over-supplied to the same degree. However, those involved with new centres, in both out-of-town and town centre locations, have had to address similar issues of greater competition, more choice, higher customer expectations and a more discerning customer. Furthermore, the European situation was further differentiated by greater planning restrictions on out-of-town development. This forced those involved with development to address the issues of greater competition and a more discerning customer through evolving new shopping formats in town centre locations (types that are discussed later).

Out of economic necessity regional shopping centres have had to evolve and become more inventive and focused.

Lifestyle Centres

Regional shopping centres were generalist and catered for all ages and consumer groups. In the light of the potential demise of this format, lifestyle centres are targeted at a specific sector of the market – the young urban professional, with a tendency towards upmarket retailing, providing shops and facilities for those with ambition and the desire to succeed. In times of insecurity this is a market sector more likely to succeed than others. Lifestyle centres are composed of selective elements found at the mall but arranged in an external and attractive environment. As such they attract those customers from the mall and those who would not normally select the mall for shopping. Lifestyle centres are made up from a carefully selected mix of aspirational retailers. These retailers are a mixture of comparison fashion brands, leisure and sportsware, which reflect a hobby or interest, and household goods providing good quality furniture and houseware. All the shops contain certain products which the shopper would aspire to and reflect their ideals. Combined with these retailers there will be a variety of cafés and restaurants allowing a visit to the centre to be combined with a relaxed refreshment or a meal.

Ease of access and proximity of car parking are an important facility in these centres. It is usual for the parking to be well distributed and close to specific shops. This allows easy and recognisable access to particular shops, allowing the customer the convenience of parking close to chosen shops without having to walk past shops in which they have no interest. One advantage of the external environment, arranged at single level streets, is that the shops can be given an individual identity which allows for variety and helps with orientation at the larger centre.

Lifestyle centres were originally conceived without an anchor store. The retailers chosen are selected because they can deliver and, being aimed at a specific customer band, tend to generate a greater synergy from the collective gathering.

The typical size of the centres varies from anything between 18 500 m^2 (approx 200 00 ft^2) to 46 500 m^2 (approx 500 000 ft^2). (According to categorisation by size, lifestyle centres are not generally large enough to qualify as regional centres but are included here to illustrate the evolution of the format.) Some exponents cite the Country Club Plaza, Kansas City (1922) as the very first lifestyle centre

(see previous Chapter). Its open streets and architectural style, based on Spanish vernacular tradition, and perimeter parking does indeed meet much of the current characteristics of this format. It was not consciously formed to be this particular type and represents it by coincidence. One of the first centres specifically developed as a lifestyle centre was by Poag and McEwan at Saddle Creek, Germantown, Tennessee (1987). It was small, only 13 300 m^2 (approx 143 000 ft^2) providing 45 shop units. Saddle Creek is typical of the form adopted by many subsequent centres, based around a single level open street with the shops expressed in individual buildings with a variety of height and different architectural character. There were other centres developed prior to Saddle Creek which have similar characteristics, but it was Poag and McEwan who first identified the terminology and focused attention on this particular format.

Figure 4.57 An open street retail environment with carefully selected, identifiable individual stores, Saddle Creek, Germantown, Tennessee, USA (1987). *(Source: Shops of Saddleback)*

A later example at the Summit, Birmingham, Alabama (1997) is considerably larger at 70 600 m^2 (approx 760 000 ft^2) and provides 76 shop units along with a department store. A more recent example of this type of shopping environment at the Grove, Los Angeles (2002) also adapts the original format by including a small department store (Nordstrom) in a total development of 53 500 m^2 (approx 575 000 ft^2). The Grove, developed by

Figure 4.58 Well landscaped open air shopping at The Summit, Birmingham, Alabama, USA (1997). *(Source: Bayer Properties Inc)*

Figure 4.59 A 'main street' shopping environment, The Grove, Los Angeles, California, USA (2002). *(Source: Corbis/Robert Landau)*

Carnso Affiliated Holdings (with architects Elkus Manfredi of Boston and Langdon Wilson of Los Angeles), is based on a main street. The main street forms the spine with a town square and a recognisable farmers' market at each end. A variety of external spaces provides an attractive open-air pedestrian environment, with well landscaped and finished promenades, streets and a square with a fountain. Cafés overlook the square providing a relaxing space to take a break and enjoy the water feature and mature trees.

The architectural forms adopted at the Grove addressed the urban design issues of making a new piece of town from scratch. Key corners were identified to address selected vistas and have vertical features. Identifiable individual buildings relate to specific spaces forming a sense of place to different areas. The urban grain of the buildings has an overriding vertical quality with two and three storey buildings defining the streets and spaces. The upper levels are occupied and animated by the tenants taking the larger space on the first and second floors. The architecture creates individual buildings and is varied in style. The building styles are largely historical but are well articulated and convincing. Individual buildings are formed from a wide-ranging set of styles, which extend from art deco, Spanish vernacular and a kind of imperial colonial. The Grove exemplifies the particular attention paid to the external architecture and the external spaces, with carefully selected street furniture and urban works of art, in this new form of shopping environment.

Retail Resorts

In the mid-1990s the ICSC identified that shoppers in the USA were spending less time and money at the mall. This trend, along with the issues of increasing competition and more discerning customers discussed previously, challenged the retail development industry to find ways of attracting the customer back to shopping centres. Furthermore, apart from this general challenge to the industry, individual developers were faced with how to make their centre the destination of choice in preference to another centre. Part of the response was to cosset and demonstrate greater care of the customer by providing greater luxury and comfort in the public areas. This was in addition to providing the right range of retail and leisure facilities along with easy access by car. Trizechahn full-heartedly addressed the issue by blending retail with relaxation in its Park Meadows shopping centre in Littleton, Denver, Colorado, and established the term 'retail resort' on its opening in 1996.

Park Meadows is fundamentally a regional shopping centre with a difference, where all of the public interiors emulate the spirit of recreation in Colorado. For example, Anthony Belluschi has designed all of the interiors to resemble the warmth and richness of a mountain lodge hotel. Set within the backdrop of the Rocky Mountains, Park Meadows is appropriately and logically located to respond in this fashion and in so doing creates a unique sense of place with a synergy to this particular location. By responding in this way, the centre is both more comfortable and has its own identity, differentiating Park Meadows from the other regional shopping centres such as Southglen Mall and Cherry Creek nearby.

Park Meadows is laid out in a conventional two level dumb-bell plan between anchor stores at either end with three mini anchors interspersed along its length. The centre has 100 units for speciality retailers of which 16 of these are large format stores: 550 – 3000 m^2 (approx 6000 – 32 000 ft^2). These larger store units allow the centre to accommodate the specialist retailers normally located outside a centre. In providing these larger stores, Park Meadows offers the customer the convenience of a wider choice under one roof, which might otherwise involve three or four different trips. This conscious decision to bring more levels or different types of retail into one destination builds on the founding principle of improving customer convenience associated with the traditional mall.

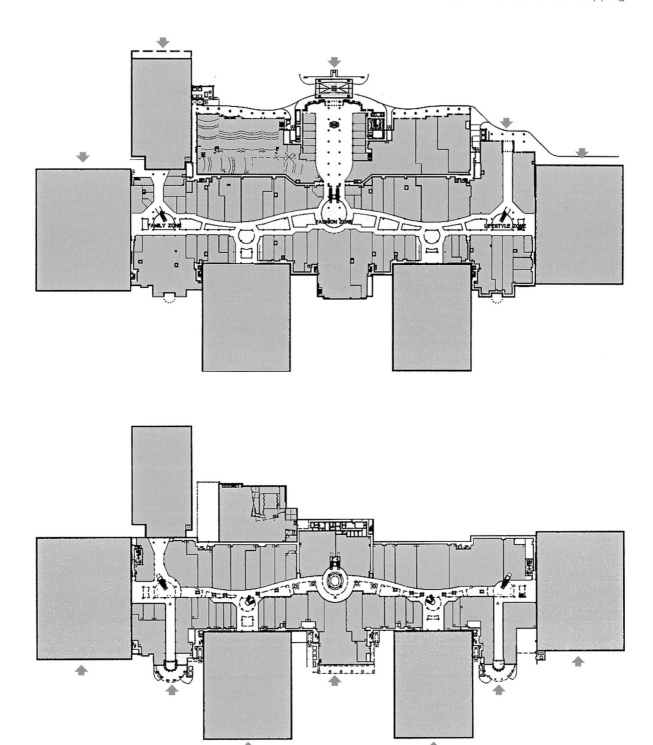

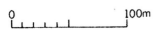

0   100m

Figure 4.60 Upper and lower level floor plans, Park Meadows, Littleton, Denver, Colorado, USA (1996). *(Source: Anthony Belluschi/BDP)*

Figure 4.61 The mountain lodge interiors with warm timber linings and stone floors, Park Meadows, Littleton, Denver, Colorado, USA. *(Source: Anthony Belluschi)*

cascading waterfall which passes over a massive natural rock; the Challet Court marks the fashion zone which incorporates luxurious furnishings, woollen rugs, hand crafted leather chairs and sofas placed around a fireplace; the Centennial Ranch Court is located in the family zone which is a relatively playful setting featuring hanging mobiles of natural wild life; and the Grand Dining Hall represents the food and entertainment zone, which is celebrated in a double height nave-like space with natural light filtering in from the clerestory windows onto the timber structure and ceilings. The Grand Dining Hall accommodates 700 diners at wooden tables with matching ladder-back chairs which all emphasise the warmth and richness of the space. A grand stone fireplace towers some 20 m high at the end of the hall.

Along the length of Park Meadows mall are courts which widen out to form spaces of punctuation and relate to the intersection points with the side malls. The shops in the centre have been grouped together into four zones of similar types of offer: lifestyle, fashion, family and food and entertainment. A different identity has been given to each of these zones. The Majestic Court represents the chief characteristic of the lifestyle zone with warm timber surfaces and a

Figure 4.62 One of the luxuriously finished court spaces, Park Meadows, Littleton, Denver, Colorado, USA. *(Source: Anthony Belluschi)*

Figure 4.63 The Grand Dining Hall, focused around the 20 m high stone fireplace, Park Meadows, Littleton, Denver, Colorado, USA. *(Source: Anthony Belluschi)*

Although Park Meadows is a conventional layout with the same intensified retail mechanisms, it is the use of its interior design and architecture which marks the point of difference with other regional centres and signifies a different type of shopping format. The extensive use of warm natural materials such as the timber structure, Douglas Fir ceilings, hardwood and stone floors, together with the luxurious lounge furnishings set around the fireplaces, make the centre feel more like a lodge hotel or gentleman's club than an institutional shopping centre.

The exterior architecture reinforces the characteristics of a large park lodge and exploits the setting with the Rocky Mountains forming the backdrop. The individual identity of Park Meadows is reinforced by natural stone and timber clad façades sitting beneath pitched and stepped copper roofs which are scaled by large clerestory windows and dozens of dormer windows. The large clerestory windows allow views into the interior spaces, revealing the timber structure and stone fireplaces and reinforces the whole identity of the place.

Figure 4.64 The mountain park lodge is extended to the architectural form, with stepped roofs and dormer windows, Park Meadows, Littleton, Denver, Colorado, USA. *(Source: Anthony Belluschi)*

The club-like comfortable interiors seem to appeal to a wide consumer group, with the mature and affluent customers attracted to reading a paper and taking a coffee around the fireplace, while a family enjoy some quality time and have an entertaining experience passing through the unique interiors. Park Meadows may be a blatant way of drawing a wide audience into a shopping centre, but it appears to succeed in attracting customers beyond the

mainstay of the housewife, luring families and the young and old alike.

Another regional shopping centre which also illustrates the principles of a retail resort is Flat Iron Crossing, Broomfield, Colorado (2000). This centre also addresses the trend of providing wide-ranging retail facilities within comfortable and unique interior spaces. Considering that Broomfield and Littleton are both suburbs of Denver, it was a challenge and a bold move for developer Westcor and architect Callison to establish something equally unique within such proximity of Park Meadows. Needless to say, many of the principles and qualities of the former centre have been adopted in its younger cousin.

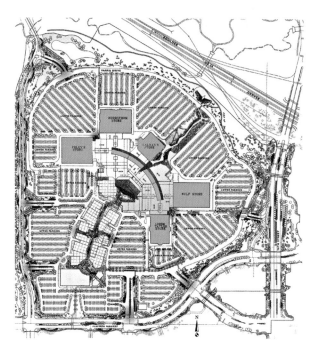

Figure 4.65 Site plan, Flat Iron Crossing, Broomfield, Colorado, USA (2000). *(Source: Callison)*

Flat Iron Crossing has a more inventive plan than Park Meadows, with both an enclosed mall and external street formed from two interconnecting arcs. (These are described separately further on under hybrid centres.) The interior and exterior architecture does, however, adopt more contemporary forms in this later example. Flat Iron Crossing makes extensive use of warm natural materials with an exposed timber roof structure and ceilings stone columns and natural stone floors with inset areas of hardwood. Comfort and luxury are emphasised by localised relaxation areas with upholstered armchairs and woollen rugs. A fire pit with a conical hood and metal flue forms a focus in the food area. The form of the spaces at

Broomfield is less formal and more organic, where the geometries of the plan and section have been allowed to generate the spatial shapes. Again much use is made of gentle clerestory lighting allowing the space to be lit by natural light, reflecting from the warm timber surfaces in the daytime and, at night time, artificial lighting glows on the same timber surface.

of the Rocky Mountains. The building here resembles a contemporary mountain lodge. The building has an articulated roofline which rests beneath the mountain skyline. The sheet metal roofs are articulated by butterfly roofs to the entranceway, overhanging clerestory glazing and the expression of individual buildings representing the main stores. Individual buildings are identified by a different cladding material which varies from brick, stone and render with fully glazed entranceways.

Figure 4.66 Customers provided with comfortable and luxurious interiors, Flat Iron Crossing, Broomfield, Colorado, USA. *(Source: Callison/Chris Eden)*

Figure 4.68 Flat Iron Crossing is designed to represent a contemporary mountain lodge at the foot of the Rocky Mountains, Broomfield, Colorado, USA. *(Source: Callison/Chris Eden)*

Figure 4.67 Clerestory lighting gently illuminates the informal interiors, Flat Iron Crossing, Broomfield, Colorado, USA. *(Source: Callison/Chris Eden)*

The exterior architecture at Flat Iron Crossing succeeds in forming an individual identity and reinforces the unique response to its setting at the foot

Flat Iron Crossing has its own unique identity which, although similar to Park Meadows and a modest version of it, is distinctly different by its confident expression of more informal contemporary buildings and interior spaces. Both centres convey a relaxed and informal luxury which respond to the lifestyle and cultural aspirations of the Denver consumer. The two centres also uniquely respond in appropriate ways to the scale and imposing nature of the Colorado mountain landscape, the elder cousin by over scaling the forms of its indigenous buildings with the younger confidently interpreting the scale to develop its own architecture.

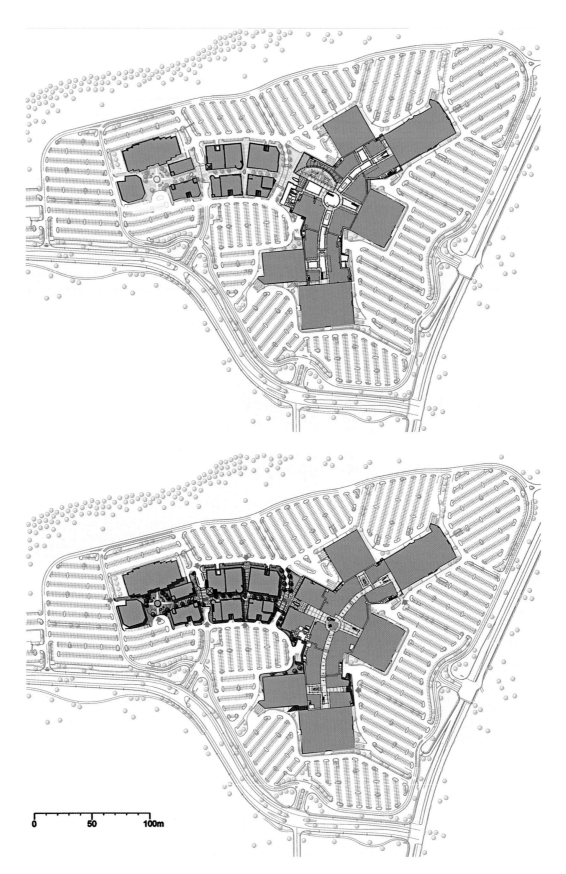

Figure 4.69 Upper and lower ground floor plans, The Streets of Southpoint, Durham, North Carolina, USA (2002). *(Source: RTKL)*

Hybrid Centres

This format of shopping environment is another sub-category of the regional shopping centre. Hybrid centres provide largely the same collection of retail and leisure facilities but in a different physical form. In form these centres are a deliberate combination of both an enclosed and open-air shopping environment. They have been described as representing and bringing together the best of both worlds.

Hybrid centres are another outcome of developers in North America positively addressing the decline in popularity of the stereotyped mall. They represent a way of developers providing all things to all people. The combined environments in a single centre give the customer the convenience of providing a wide-ranging retail offer under the protection of enclosure along with the natural ambience and visually richer environment of the external street. Furthermore, the street environment can be given an identity and more readily achieve symbolic and personal association qualities which, by regular use of the external spaces over a relatively short period of time, would certainly be achieved. The external street environment naturally lends itself to be used to accommodate the lifestyle and leisure related shops, along with the individual restaurants and leisure and entertainment elements of cinemas, clubs and theatres. The external street also allows retailers, caterers and leisure tenants, who would not normally be attracted inside a shopping centre or able to afford its higher rents, to be engaged into the centre. The hybrid centre, like the lifestyle centre, in having an external environment, attracts customers who would not normally use the mall and thereby increases the potential catchment.

An important quality of hybrid centres is their holistic nature and a tendency to incorporate all of the peripheral retail offers found around the outskirts of a regional shopping centre, such as big box retailers and parking lot eateries and provide them in an improved environment under a single brand. This has required a more encompassing masterplan approach, but has provided the developer with the opportunity to offer a wider range of retail attractions. It appeals to the consumer by providing the convenience of dropping off the dry cleaning, having lunch then buying a new shirt all in one trip, rather than several car journeys. The hybrid centre has brought together the once random collection of the enclosed mall, the restaurant out-parcels, the multi-screen cinemas, and big box retailers and considered them

together in a single masterplan. In so doing it has improved the environmental form for the customer and expanded the attraction of the retail offer.

There are, however, practical challenges to hybrid centres in that they need to be of a sufficient size to provide all of the facilities and for this reason tend to be larger than 93 000 m^2 (approx 1 million ft^2). The consequences of the likely size issue requires the demand for such a centre to be carefully verified, while also solving the problem of finding a suitably large site in an appropriate location. While developing a complete new hybrid centre from fresh will be restricted by these issues, the format is also potentially achievable though the adaptation of existing enclosed centres which have sufficient available land. The opportunity of adapting existing centres into hybrid centres is reviewed later on.

Despite the challenges of demand and suitable location, by the end of the 1990s several development companies had completed new purpose-built

Figure 4.70 The open-air Main Street with individual buildings and well detailed street furniture, The Streets of Southport, North Carolina, USA. *(Source: RTKL)*

Figure 4.72 The entrance space canopy extending from inside to out, The Streets of Southpoint, North Carolina, USA. *(Source: RTKL)*

Figure 4.71 The entrance passing from the open street into the enclosed centre, The Streets of Southport, North Carolina, USA. *(Source: RTKL)*

hybrid centres in the USA. Simon Property Group, in a joint venture with Ben Carter, completed the first purpose-built hybrid centre with the opening of Mall of Georgia, Buford in 1999. More recently complete, the Streets of Southpoint, Durham, North Carolina (2002) represents another typical purpose-built example of this format. Originally developed by Urban Shopping Centres, and purchased by the Rouse Company, this hybrid centre provides 120 800 m² (approx 1.3 million ft²) of regional shopping and leisure centre accommodation. Architect RTKL Associates of Dallas has combined a two level enclosed mall seamlessly with an external street in a T-shaped layout made up by the intersection of two gentle curves. The leg of the T is the outside street, which extends from a cinema entrance plaza, past a series of individual building blocks, up to another entrance space at the mid-point of the enclosed mall. The open street, Main Street, is crossed by cars in two locations giving an authentic town feel. The entrance into the enclosed interior space appears as another block at the end of the open street. The entrance space, with the building façades and canopy continuing from outside to inside, is almost continuous with the only separation being a four storey high glazed screen between the two environments. Southpoint Street is a two level interior street arranged in a gently curved dumb-bell formation with anchor stores at each end and three other department stores interspersed along its length.

RTKL's design carefully blurs the distinction between the exterior and interior shopping environments. The open-air Main Street has been urban

design led to form individual buildings in a variety of stone and brick architecture. Shops are represented in individual buildings, which are further articulated by clock towers, circular domes and a variable cornice line which reinforces the vertical grain to the street. The street environment has been carefully considered with patterned hard surfaces, purpose designed street furniture, lamp-posts and discreet landscaping. Moving inside, the urban quality and variety is also continued into the internal shops, which are also individually expressed at both levels of the enclosed space. The use of external quality materials, with a mixture of stone and brick for the shopfronts, limestone paving and the same lamp-posts continue the character of the external street inside.

To assist achieving internal variety to each shop, the shopfronts have been encouraged to extend beyond the normal uniform goalposts. For example, the lower level shops have been allowed to design up to the handrail of the balustrading above, thereby nearly doubling the normal vertical influence from 3.5 m to 6 m. This flexible approach has greatly assisted achieving variety and a vertical scale to the lower level shops. Projections and set backs have also been encouraged and help to achieve a visual richness akin to a traditional street.

The upper level shops are naturally taller and feature mezzanines, and here again the shopfront design has been allowed to extend up to the cornice. The individual design of each shop has resulted in a variable cornice line and the feeling of an internal two level street. A continuous clerestory window, which is set back from the shopfronts, allows natural daylight to emphasise the variable cornice line. An articulated ceiling of draped planes extends beyond the cornice line and resembles the canvas drapes above a Middle Eastern street market.

Figure 4.73 Individual shopfronts continue external materials up to the gallery balustrading, avoiding the traditional horizontal character, The Streets of Southpoint, Durham, North Carolina, USA (2002). *(Source: RTKL)*

Integration between the open-air and enclosed environments succeeds because, in both streets, a townscape has been generated by allowing the expression of individual shops. The integration of over 100 individual shop units into the two level Southpoint Street has not occurred without a good deal of collaboration between the developer's team and the shop designers. The successful result has involved the developer preparing a brochure of shopfront illustrations prior to letting and the provision of a dedicated on site team of design coordinators to work with the shop designers during construction.

The Streets of Southpoint is one of the first purpose-built two level hybrid centres to achieve seamless integration of the two environments, and is a fine example of achieving a balance between

integration, while also allowing each to have its own separate identity.

Flat Iron Crossing, already featured, is another example of a hybrid centre providing regional shopping and leisure facilities in a combination of an open-air street and an enclosed two level mall. This centre also has the qualities of a retail resort and is referred to in that section.

The plan layout of Flat Iron Crossing is similar to the Streets of Southpoint. Both centres have adopted a 'T'-shaped plan which is formed from two intersecting curved arcs where the leg forms the external street and the crossbar is a two level enclosed mall. The crossbar at Flat Iron, however, joins the open street on the concave side of the curve. The internal mall is a two level, curved dumb-bell with anchor

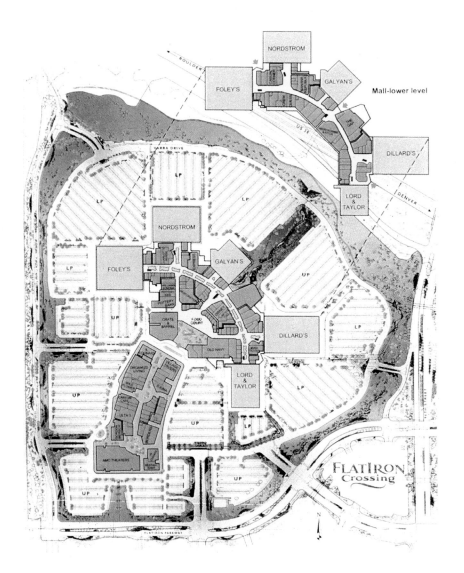

Figure 4.74 Upper and lower level mall plans, Flat Iron Crossing, Broomfield, Colorado, USA (2000). *(Source: Callison)*

Figure 4.75 The transition from external to interior spaces is encouraged by the projecting canopy and large doorway, Flat Iron Crossing, Broomfield, Colorado, USA. *(Source: Callison/Chris Eden)*

stores at each end with three other department stores interspersed along its length. Although both open-air streets meet the enclosed mall midway along its length, the Flat Iron entry space is more constrained and enclosed by joining on the concave side of the curve. However, the transition between the outside and internal spaces from the entrance plaza is continuous, which is achieved by the building façades and roof canopy passing from the outside and through into the interior. A three storey glass wall separates the two environments with a garage type glazed roller door framing a large entranceway.

The external street at Flat Iron accommodates a mixture of aspirational retailers, individual restaurants and entertainment facilities. The design of the street also adopts urban design principles with separate shops expressed in individual buildings. The form of the street has been carefully considered, using a variety of architectural forms and materials. A strong local vernacular has been established to the buildings with a limited palette of materials consisting of stone, render and timber. Vertical elements are positioned at strategic corners; first floor balconies animate the upper levels and various expressive timber roof elements, pergolas, projecting eaves and individual roofs achieve a varied skyline.

The street and sequence of spaces are more informal, which suit the general grand scale and openness of the Colorado countryside. The public realm in the street has been carefully thought through, with stone paving and stone forming the base to the feature lighting, seating, plant containers and water features. There is also continuity in the use of materials between the external and interior spaces, where

Figure 4.77 Open street shopping with individual buildings and the adoption of urban design at Flat Iron Crossing, Broomfield, Colorado, USA. *(Source: Callison/Chris Eden)*

the stone column bases, stone floors and expressive timber roof structure are continued inside.

Flat Iron Crossing is less successful in achieving a seamless transition between the internal and external shopping environments. Although some attempt has been made to express some of the internal shops, with pop outs and individual frontages, the overriding impression of the interior shops is one of uniformity and of being dominated by the horizontal emphasis of the mall architecture.

Flat Iron Crossing does have its own interior quality and relies on the informal luxury of its public spaces to create the atmosphere of the contemporary lodge (discussed under retail resorts earlier in this Chapter).

The term hybrid centre can also be applied to other centres which, in the initial planning, consciously combine both external and internal environments. For example the Gateway Theatre of Shopping, Durban (referred to under regional shopping and leisure centres), which has both an enclosed mall environment together with external facing individual buildings of the Boulevard and entrance piazza restaurants, could also represent this format. However, in the Gateway the external spaces are incomplete until the Umlanga new town is further developed. With the completion of the corresponding other side of the street to the Boulevard, the Gateway centre will also fully represent a hybrid centre.

Hybrid centres are not limited for consideration to new shopping developments. At a time of moving into the 21st century, with 7 per cent of America's 2800 malls dead or languishing and a further

Figure 4.76 Enclosed interior shopping in a two level curved mall at Flat Iron Crossing, Broomfield, Colorado, USA. *(Source: Callison/Chris Eden)*

12 per cent showing signs of similar decline, many anchors are having to consider options of how to improve their offer and become more attractive to a wider customer base (Price Waterhouse, 1999). The potential of being able to add an exciting new open air street, with new shops and restaurants in an attractive main street type of environment to a flagging mall is a natural solution for owners faced with this problem.

The hybrid extension can add a variety of different types of accommodation to complement those of the existing centre and so transform it into another format. The extension may add the same accommodation found in the new hybrid centres discussed above – a mixture of synergetic retailing, catering and entertainment/leisure facilities. Westfield, for example, is expanding several of its enclosed malls to include open-air villages with this type of accommodation. Alternatively, the extension may add an open-air lifestyle centre element to the mall. In this instance (as described above), the accommodation will predominantly provide new shops for aspirational retailers with some individual restaurants also being added.

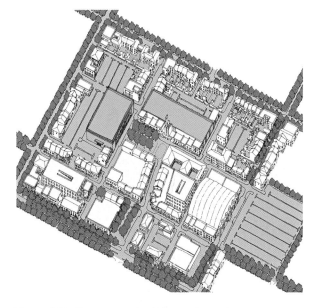

Figure 4.79 The metamorphosis from mall to main street proposed for Eastgate Mall, Chattanooga, Tennessee, USA. *(Source: Dover, Kohl & Partners)*

Figure 4.78 A Westfield Village open street type environment added to an existing mall, Santa Anita, Arcadia, California, USA. *(Source: Westfield)*

Hybrid opportunities are not restricted to extensions. In the ailing malls with failed tenancies, parts of the existing centre can be removed to make way for an open-air based extension or to assist with the integration of the urban element with the existing internalised interior environment. The Eastgate Mall, Chattanooga, Tennessee (1963) has prepared a long-term masterplan for the redevelopment of the centre. In the first phase a town square with residential accommodation is formed in front of the centre and, on the other side, a new main street with open-air retailing is also added. To connect these two new elements a new street is also cut

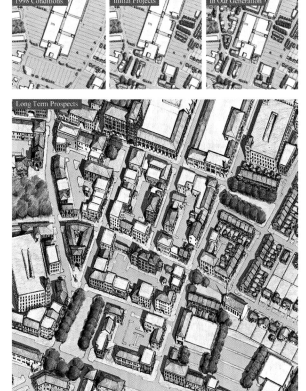

Figure 4.80 A defunct mall which has been radically altered and surrounded by an urban setting, Winter Park Village, Winter Park, Florida, USA. *(Source: Dover, Kohl & Partners)*

through the existing mall, thereby integrating the new areas with the existing centre. It should be noted that the integration of a new open-air street element along with an existing enclosed interior environment is more challenging than building both parts from new. It will be very difficult to achieve a seamless transition between the old and new elements because the differences between the two retail environments are so great.

Urbanising the mall is not restricted to America. In the mature retail parts of the European market, particularly where planning constrains further large-scale out-of-town expansion, the potential to expand with an urban open-air format will also be attractive. Developers Hammerson and Standard Life have prepared a masterplan for the Brent Cross shopping centre in north-west London to extend the centre with a network of open-air streets that connect to the existing malls. The new Brent Cross will be part of a mixed-use development with 500 new homes and the addition of some 50 000 m² (approx 538 000 ft²) of new retail, catering and leisure accommodation.

On the simple basis that consumers find well designed urban environments both attractive and convenient, and that these environments also give retailers the best opportunity for individual expression,

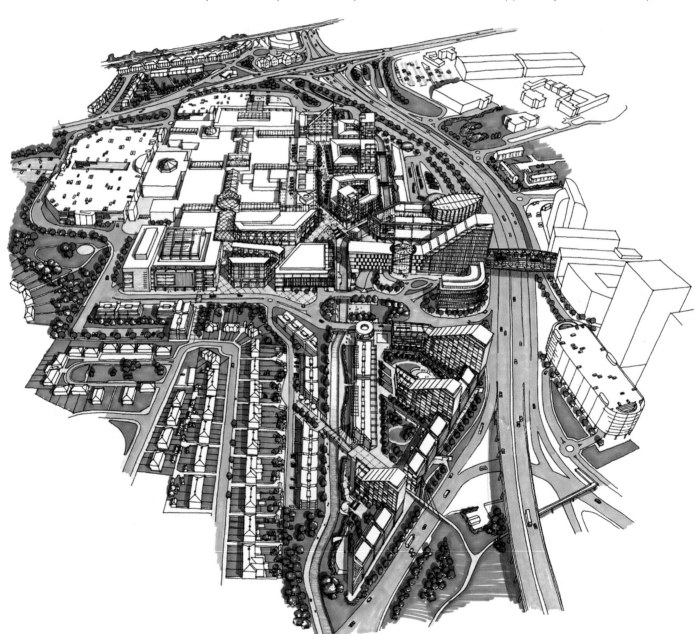

Figure 4.81 The New Brent Cross – Before and after aerial view of the Masterplan, Brent Cross, London, UK (planned 2010–2012). *(Source: BDP)*

it is likely that hybrid centres will be an attractive future format and likely to be considered wherever a shopping environment is being planned. The hybrid centre format may be the next stage before returning to the full open-air centres of the past.

Non-Town-Centre Shopping Malls

This type of shopping environment may not be universally recognised, but it is commonly found in Europe. The term is one identified by the British Council of Shopping Centres and is defined by criteria of size, location and retail offer (BCSC, 2001). This format's size ranges from 27 800 m² to 46 500 m² (approx 300 000 to 500 000 ft²) and represents a smaller version of a regional shopping centre. These places for shopping are located outside the town centre but within the urban areas of the conurbation and are readily accessible to the residential population within half an hour's drive time. These pocket battleship versions of regional shopping centres tend to have a simpler layout and are often arranged on a single level, although some land restrictions have generated multi-level schemes. The centre is often anchored by a hypermarket or large supermarket. In addition to the convenience retailing of the supermarket, a wide range of other retailing is provided. The range consists of both comparison and bulky goods retailing, with the comparison retailing being accommodated by national high street multiples and sometimes a national variety store. Although these centres are not aimed at a day out experience, customers are encouraged to extend their visit by the provision of catering. The form of catering is commonly a café or fast food in a food court with communal seating. The catering can also be supplemented by one or two restaurants.

Corresponding with the expansion of towns and cities, with the trend of depopulation of the countryside, the end of the 20th century saw the growth of hypermarkets and supermarkets. As well as this expansion being met in stand alone stores, developers and foodstores seized the opportunity to combine together some comparison retailing with a hypermarket. These combinations were accommodated in simple enclosed malls which ran parallel with the checkouts and the area for the service shops. A period in the early 1990s saw the establishment of many of these hypermarket led malls on the edge of several European cities.

The negative impact of hypermarket-led malls on town centres was quickly realised with the planning legislation restraints quickly following on out-of-town development and control of licences. Consequently, by the end of the 1990s there were relatively few new examples of this format being opened in the mature markets of Europe.

A non-town centre shopping mall example specific to the UK which typifies this format is the Gyle Centre, Edinburgh (1993). This development was instigated by a three-way joint venture involving the district council, a food store (Safeway) and a variety store (Marks and Spencer). It is located at South Gyle on the western outskirts of Edinburgh and has a catchment population of one million living within a half an hour drive time. The centre provides a total of 27 000 m² (approx 290 500 ft²) of lettable accommodation in a single level dumb-bell mall with the foodstore and variety store anchors at each end. The anchor stores occupy over two thirds of the accommodation with the remaining 11 000 m² (approx 118 300 ft²) providing 65 shops and catering units arranged between the anchor stores. Three entranceways lead from the surface car parks with 2700 spaces. An entrance is adjacent to each of the anchor stores with a central entrance leading from a bus drop off. A 500 seat food court with an additional 100 seat licensed bistro arranged at first floor level overlooks the central entrance space. The centre is also well provided with public facilities in terms

Figure 4.82 The food court over the entrance at a non-town centre shopping mall on the edge of the city, The Gyle, Edinburgh, UK, (1993). *(Source: Paul Harmer)*

of toilets, crèche and baby changing facilities. Gyle Centre is an efficient and convenient place to shop for certain retail items. In an age where a wider retail offer is the norm, with higher expectations for catering and leisure facilities, the centre is now considering proposals for expansion. The existing centre lacks individual character and has an institutional demeanour. Hopefully the expansion and alteration plans will address the issue of personality.

Another and different example of this shopping format is Guimaraes Shopping (1995) in northern Portugal. Sonae Imobiliari, one of Portugal's leading property companies, led the development, which is anchored by a hypermarket (Continente) and is located on the edge of the historic town of Guimaraes. This pocket battleship is more complex than the Gyle centre because of the more constrained site and the additional requirements of the town council. Guimaraes Shopping provides 24 500 m² (264 000 ft²) of lettable space in a compact arrangement. There are two enclosed mall levels with the hypermarket at the lower level, with three floors of parking (1800 spaces) sitting above it. The upper mall leads directly to the first of the car parking levels. The 85 shop units are arranged in the two enclosed mall levels which sit above each other and which run parallel to the hypermarket checkouts. The lower mall level connects with the hypermarket at two points. A 400 seat food court at the end of the upper mall overlooks the fountain piazza, which also forms the roof deck to the bus station which enters into the lower mall. Shop units are considerably smaller in Portugal than those in the UK and America with the units at Guimaraes Shopping ranging from 32 to 100 m² (approx 350 to 1100 ft²).

The building is made up of three architectural elements. The mall and unit shops form a yellow granite building which is animated with windows and faces the main road. The second element is the car park and hypermarket, which is largely set into the rising ground. The top level of the car park is directly accessed from the surrounding perimeter access road. The third element is the oval piazza which sits above the bus station and forms the setting to an existing town building. All three elements come together in an intriguing solution which fills the entity of the site. Guimaraes Shopping, despite representing an out-of-town centre, is more like the type of solution found in many urban shopping centres. It illustrates the lengths developments of this nature are required to go through in the land-short European countries.

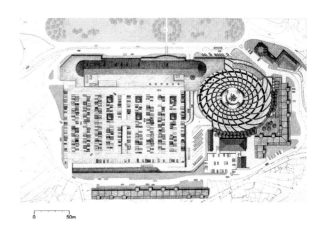

Figure 4.84 Roof plan showing the three elements of Guimaraes Shopping, Guimaraes, Portugal. *(Source: HOK)*

Figure 4.83 Design model for Guimaraes Shopping showing the car park above the centre and the piazza above the bus station, Guimaraes, Portugal (1995). *(Source: HOK)*

Figure 4.85 Enclosed two levels arranged one above the other at Guimaraes Shopping, Guimaraes, Portugal. *(Source: HOK)*

Retail Parks

Another out-of-town shopping environment which has also had a significant impact on both regional shopping centres and town centre retailing is the retail park. Retail parks are formed from a collection of medium to large size single span sheds. Sheds or unit range in size from 500 to 2500 m² (5000 to 25 000 ft²) and are sometimes referred to as 'big box retailing' or 'retail warehouse park'. The format provides three or more units in an open-air environment with shared surface parking and access. The units are typically arranged together in a line, a concave 'L' shape or arch which faces the approaching access road. A significant amount of car parking is provided, which is usually laid out between the access road and the front of the units. Shop entrances are commonly aligned to face the surface car parking and approach road.

Retail parks can accommodate a wide range of different tenants. The format has evolved from its inception in the early 1970s – where a simple group of warehouses housed bulky good retailers – up to contemporary arrangements which incorporate a wide ranging retail offer alongside leisure facilities. Some of the later more comprehensive retail parks incorporate bulky goods, high street retailers, multi-screen cinemas and restaurants, which provide a diverse retail attraction appealing to a wider area than the immediate local catchment. In these cases the retail park can potentially challenge, in a simple open-air environment with little pretence at creating a place, both the more complex regional shopping centre and town centre shopping.

Figure 4.86 High Street retailers in a retail park with two level decked parking, Castlepoint, Bournemouth, UK (2003). *(Source: Peter Coleman)*

Figure 4.87 Terracotta and metal modular clad boxes face the car park to form the Retail Park, Crown Point North, Denton, UK (2004). *(Source: Daniel Hopkinson/BDP)*

Figure 4.88 A simple vocabulary of metal canopies and entrances are layered on to the trading boxes at the Retail Park, Crown Point North, Denton, UK. *(Source: Daniel Hopkinson/BDP)*

Retail parks are usually located on edge-of-town sites. In these locations, the retail park retains an identity with the town centre retailing and have ready access to the immediate conurbation.

Retail parks originated from a need which arose from a large proportion of existing town centre accommodation being the wrong size, poorly configured or constrained and therefore unable to meet the needs of modern day volume retailing. To illustrate the point of the dated nature of town centre retail space, Mark Teal, in his report of 1997, summarised that half of the UK town centre floor space was accommodated in premises built before 1937 (Teal, 1997). With value driving competition and planned growth, retailers' only option of accommodating the needs for more space of the right type was to seek new premises in the out-of-town retail options of either the regional shopping centre or the retail park.

Non-town-centre retailing in its original guise came from retailers moving into converted garages and warehouses. These premises, though compromised to some degree, met the need for large areas of floor space in simple flexible structures. The first purpose-built retail warehouse premises were established in the 1970s. The types of retailer that were permitted to move into these premises were seen as those involved in new forms of retailing with no equivalent and thus would not detract from the town centre. For example, the earliest retail parks accommodated DIY stores and gardening goods. These were quickly added to with carpet and furniture stores which were permitted through the argument of not being readily housed within the constraints of the town centre. These first generation stores were accommodated in relatively large units of 2500 m² (approx 25 000 ft²).

In the early 1980s pressure came from electrical retailers also to be allowed to locate in the retail parks. Through the persuasive argument of needing more space to house bulky white goods, these retailers became acceptable tenants and conveniently provided other electrical items from the same premises. The electrical retailers required less space than the DIY stores and introduced a smaller unit size of 1000 to 1500 m² (approx 10 000 to 15 000 ft²) into the mix. In an age of increasing appliances and gadgets, along with insatiable DIY trends, the demand for space in retail parks was immense. The demand saw a spread of retail parks spring up on the edges of towns throughout the UK. Clifford Guy, in his paper for the Town Planning Review, identified that within 15 years from the first retail park opening in 1981, a further 385 opened with yet more in the pipeline (Guy, 1998).

With growing consumer demand, pressure continued on high street retailers for larger stores and more space. Another wave of decentralisation was driven by the constraints of old property and shortage of space. Within ten years the typical product range available at a retail park expanded further, with high street stores relocating into larger premises and new large volume single category retailers to provide toys, children's wear, home furnishings, kitchen goods, office stationery and pet merchandising in addition to the bulky goods line up. In a small number of selective retail parks even some comparison retailers expanded on to the retail park to provide chemists, clothing and footwear goods. With the representation of traditional high street retailers the retail park transformed itself from a complementary retail facility, limited to bulky goods, into an organism competing directly with the high street. Fosse Park, Leicestershire (1989) is a typical example of a UK retail park which provides comparison retailers from the high street in simple large premises alongside the large box bulky retailers.

A further development of the retail park saw the introduction of leisure facilities such as cinemas, ten-pin bowling, family entertainment centres and restaurants being combined with the retail outlets. With the combination of retail and leisure facilities the retail park further detracted use away from the town centre. Furthermore, in this format, despite it being open air, the retail park is also able to compete directly with the regional shopping and leisure facilities.

Over a period of 20 years the constraints of many European town centres, along with imprecise planning restrictions, allowed a rational new retail format to establish itself on the edge of many major towns and cities. Subsequently and in a reactive way planning policies have generally been identified to restrict further off centre development. Certainly, in the UK, planning policy introduced in the mid-1990s has generally restricted further off centre retail development. In America, the culmination of the retail park format are the huge agglomerations of free standing large stores selling almost everything that is available in a conventional mall. The standard marker of these arrangements is the simplicity of the environment and the stores offering the goods at lower prices. Furthermore, frequently through size and volume, these stores are also able to offer a wider range of goods.

Figure 4.89 Strong environmental graphics and simple architecture characterise 'power centres', The Market Place, Irvine, California, USA. *(Source: Irvine Company)*

Figure 4.90 A careful selection of category killers, typify 'power centres', The Market Place, Irvine, California, USA. *(Source: Peter Coleman)*

These centres with a collection of category killers are sometimes referred to as 'power centres'. An example of the type is La Brea, California. The 'power centres', and others like it across America, have become serious competition to the regional shopping centres and have partly caused the decline of many malls. The decline has been sufficiently severe to close many malls, with others having to refocus and provide something new or become more client focused. These new formats, coming out of the need for reinvention, such as Lifestyle Centres, Retail Resorts and Hybrid Centres, have been discussed above.

Illustrating the continual dynamics of retail and reaction to the UK planning restrictions, further new retail formats have emerged. These have taken the form of retail park type open-air facilities located beside existing town centres or incorporated in new town centre development adjacent to prime comparison retailing. An example of the type integrated with an existing town centre is The Brewery, Romford (2002).

The Brewery is built on the site of a former brewery located immediately behind the high street, with pedestrian connections leading directly to it. The scheme is part of a mixed-use development incorporating retail, leisure and residential accommodation and was part of the town centre regeneration. The Brewery provides 56 000 m^2 (approx 600 000 ft^2) of retail and leisure space in an open-air, generally single level, 'L'-shaped arrangement with the parking laid out in front. The accommodation includes a supermarket, a sixteen screen cinema, a food court, bowling alley, family entertainment centre and 1250 car parking spaces in stacked and surface parking. The housing element completes the small scale urban edges and defines a street leading to the centre. Furthermore, there is a petrol filling station and a new bus terminus addresses access by public transport. The centre piece, which enforces the centre's legibility, is the careful retention of the brewery chimney around which is a spiral tube leading to the stacked car park. Integration with the existing streets brought a new lease of life and provides more specialist individual stores and cafés.

The accommodation is arranged in simple big box, contemporarily clad, buildings designed by Chetwood Associates. Set against the modular buildings are a series of expressive entrance features and canopies, which act more as markers than weather protection, and which take the form of butterflies. The animated canopies are formed from steel structures and metal roofs. These elements give the simple development a personality and identifiable characteristic.

The Brewery takes an out-of-town format and locates it in a town centre. In so doing it forms another hybrid and illustrates the cross-over between categories.

Figure 4.91 The car park entry ramp is wrapped around the retained chimney, The Brewery, Romford, UK (2002). *(Source: Chetwood Associates)*

Figure 4.92 The expressive 'butterfly' entry structures, The Brewery, Romford, UK. *(Source: Chetwood Associates)*

Another example of the combination of the out-of-town retail park in a town centre is the proposed Union Square, Aberdeen, designed by Building Design Partnership (see Fig. 4.93). In this example, the retail park (big box) type accommodation forms an external element in a new town centre shopping and leisure development which combines together with a two level enclosed retail environment. It is likely, with the constraint on edge-of-town and out-of-town development, that the introduction of retail park type shopping, either on its own or combined with other retail formats, will generate further combinations of retail park and town centre shopping.

Figure 4.93 An open retail park combined with a two level enclosed shopping facility combine to form an interesting town centre format, Union Square, Aberdeen, UK (Planned 2007). *(Source: BDP)*

Factory Outlet Centres

Factory outlet centres are shopping environments specifically formed to sell end of line goods at a reduced price. They are sometimes referred to as 'designer outlet centres' and generally sell fashion-ware and household items from recognisable brands. The shop units in these centres can be occupied by manufacturers, retailers and department stores who use the format to clear end of line goods. As such they are, in a way, a convenient permanent clearance sale which allows the main store to focus on new lines. The format is categorised by the British Council of Shopping Centres as a centre where the majority of retailers sell branded merchandise at discount prices. Factory outlet centres are formed from collections of shops which are larger than 4600 m² (approx 50 000 ft²) of lettable accommodation.

The attraction of discount shopping has existed for a long time and extends back to the earliest market trading shopping formats identified earlier. The popularity of closing down and end of season sales are notoriously known and attract large numbers of customers. The hardship which customers are prepared to endure in the queues and the discomfort of the squabbling crowd demonstrate the attraction of a bargain. However, traditional bargain hunting environments come at a price of compromising convenience and the quality of experience, and little opportunity for comparison and trying. So, although popular, a significant compromise to the experience was associated with the bargain. Traditional bargain shopping environments would of course be unacceptable as a regular experience and wouldn't attract all social types. In order to be widely attractive developers and retailers needed a format which would offer a bargain with style.

Various developers reached a similar solution of the factory outlet centre. The Mills Corporation in America and BAA McArthur Glen in Europe, respectively, recognised the opportunity of providing discount shopping with panache. Both these companies saw that the solution lay in providing purpose-built environments with the convenience of choice and the comfort of a protected environment and the ability to make comparisons between different shops. (In short, a collection of shops similar to a high street or regional mall.) These purpose-built facilities give the customer the choice of shopping when they wish rather than having to go at the specific sales time.

Factory outlet centres tend to be visited three or four times a year by their customers. This is significantly fewer visits than would be expected at a regional shopping centre or town centre mall. To compensate for the less frequent visits factory outlet centres must attract visitors from a wider catchment area to make up their visitor numbers. They are therefore generally located to relate to a catchment area of one to two hours drive time. In attracting visitors from further afield they need to offer customer facilities which can accommodate a day out visit such as catering and amenities. As well as meeting the needs of a day out shopping visit they are also considered as tourist destinations. On both these counts the centre benefits from offering eating and leisure facilities and providing a variety of experiences for a day out visit.

The factory outlet format originated in the late 1980s and grew substantially in the USA and Europe during the 1990s, following the recession when traditional retail formats were challenged or starting to decline. Although factory outlets challenge traditional retail formats by offering an alternative for capturing disposable income, the high street and mall shops remain the prime destination for selling new product lines. Retailers and manufacturers both support the outlet centres as a means of clearing products. As such, in theory, both locations offer complementary retail products and are not in direct competition with one another. This argument has also been promoted by the developers and accepted by the controlling authorities.

Factory outlet centres are accommodated in a variety of different types of environment. Early versions are seen in single use out-of-town retail and leisure developments, while more recent examples have been adapted in mixed-use developments. Some early European examples can be found in the careful adaptation of existing buildings, such as Clarks Village, Street, Somerset (1993) and The Great Western, Swindon (1999). Clarks Village was the first outlet centre to open in the UK. The centre made use of the existing shoe manufacturing and warehouse buildings to form an open-air village like environment. This centre is connected to the existing high street of Street and is therefore strictly not an out-of-town centre. Clarks Village modestly established the principle of factory outlet retailing and indicated that the format would be successful elsewhere in Europe. Following in 1995 further purpose-built factory outlet centres opened such as Cheshire Oaks near Ellesmere Port and Bicester Village, Oxfordshire. The former, developed by BAA McArthur Glen, was the first of several centres this company would go on to complete across Europe – Troyes Designer Outlet Village, Troyes, France (1995) and Designer Outlet Village, Ashford, Kent (2000).

Bicester Village, Oxfordshire is strategically located midway between London and Oxford and, designed by Lyons, Sleaman and Hoare, forms an open-air environment of 18 000 m² (approx 196 000 ft²) with 93 shops, cafés and restaurants. The pedestrianised streets are lined by individual clapboard fronted buildings, which resemble a traditional New England street lined with cobblestones and landscaping. The streets are characterised by the two-storey buildings with pitched roofs, which require the shops to occupy double storey high units. The pavements have covered walkways with pitched roofs formed by open colonnades.

Another and more imaginative example of a factory outlet centre utilising existing buildings is the Great Western, Swindon (1999), designed by Rawls and Co. This centre has sensitively converted the former engine manufacturing sheds of the Great Western Railway. It is organised on a single level in a network of covered streets and provides 103 shops and cafés in 19 300 m² (approx 208 000 ft²) of lettable space, making one of the largest factory outlet centres in Europe. The shops sit within the umbrella of the large span steel roofs and, by the careful introduction of new roof lights, the robust building provides double height naturally lit public spaces between the shops. The industrial quality of the space is further emphasised by the incorporation of original steam engines and railway artefacts into the public spaces.

The Great Western is unusual to Europe by being an enclosed centre where most other examples are

Figure 4.95 The large space of the converted railway workshop forms a designer outlet centre, Great Western, Swindon, UK (1999). *(Source: McArthur Glen/Michael Hart)*

Figure 4.94 A traditional New England street is adopted for the identity of Bicester Village, Oxford, UK (1995). *(Source: Lyons, Sleaman, Hoare)*

open-air village formats. The shopfronts are a contemporary design with steel surrounds and coordinated shop signage. The interior space is simply finished with ceramic tiled floors and takes its character from the industrial nature of the former railway sheds.

Since the late 1980s, in response to the decline of the traditional regional shopping centre, The Mills Corporation has revolutionised and reinvented the format by transforming the standard retail offer shop units from traditional shops into brand outlet stores. In so doing, the Mills Corporation has formed massive designer outlets of a similar scale to the regional shopping and leisure centres found elsewhere in America.

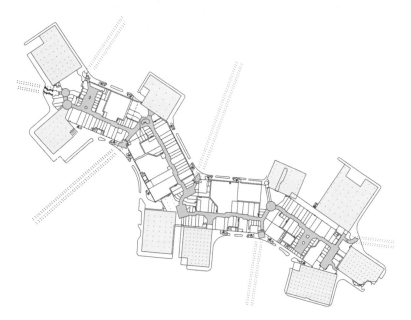

Figure 4.96 A mega mall forms a factory outlet at Sawgrass Mills, Fort Launderdale, Florida, USA (1990–1999). *(Source: Arquitectonia)*

Figure 4.97 The enclosed mall, Sawgrass Mills, Fort Launderdale, Florida, USA. *(Source: Patricia Fisher/Mills International)*

Sawgrass Mills, Fort Launderdale, Florida (1990) (with two subsequent extensions in 1995 and 1999), provides over 400 shops, cafés and restaurants in 176 500 m² (approx 1.9 million ft²) of accommodation. The traditional anchor stores have been replaced by ten outlet shops for the major stores. The centre is arranged on a long linear single level enclosed dumb-bell mall. The plan is made up of four separate lengths of mall with a change of direction identifying each length of the mall. Feature courts occur between the change of direction of the malls. The 1995 extension added a parallel mall (Verandah on Main Street) to one of the central lengths of mall and thereby formed a circuit in the middle length of the centre and added 30 new outlet stores. The 1999 extension added a further arm to the new circuit to form the Oasis, with additional shops, al fresco dining and a multi-screen cinema complex. The resultant plan is rather confused and over-reliant on imposed themes to enable customers to identify their location. Sawgrass Mills may be a factory outlet centre by its retailing being discounted brand stores, but by its very size it is the equivalent of a regional shopping and leisure centre. The Mills Corporation operates some fifteen similar scale centres of this type across America.

An interesting UK development of this format of shopping environment can be seen at Gunwharf Quays, Portsmouth (2001), where the factory outlet centre is the retail component of a major mixed-use development. Gunwharf Quays regenerates a brownfield site in the redundant naval docks. The retail led masterplan for the development comprises waterside residential apartments, offices, a hotel, leisure uses, catering and the discount brand stores. The existing listed buildings have been incorporated into the scheme with the Vulcan Building being converted into residential apartments and commercial uses and the Vernon Building (the former custom house) transformed into a pub. The Berkeley Group have developed 65 shop units in 17 000 m² (approx 180 000 ft²) of accommodation together with a further 20 waterside restaurants and cafés of 8100 m² (approx 87 000 ft²). The scheme, designed by Geoffrey Reid Associates, is arranged around the waterside in an open-air environment. The combination of uses and settings builds on the synergy between the different uses, making the total greater than the individual parts. The centre creates a daytime shopping destination and a place for evening leisure activity. The format of this centre is interesting in that it is one of the first to replace traditional retailing with factory outlet retailing as the generator for a retail led regeneration project.

Figure 4.98 A waterside mixed use development with a factory outlet centre, and cafés at Gunwharf Quays, Portsmouth, UK (2001). *(Source: Reid Architecture)*

Figure 4.99 The waterside acts as an evening destination, Gunwharf Quays, Portsmouth, UK. *(Source: Reid Architecture)*

Figure 4.101 The protected fabric covered walkways, Designer Outlet Village, Ashford, Kent, UK. *(Source: Peter Coleman)*

Another example of discount brand shops making up the retail element of a mixed-use development can be found at the Lowry Designer Outlet Mall, Salford Quays, Salford (2001). This is a canal side regeneration project combining residential, offices, shopping and leisure facilities. The shops are arranged in a two level enclosed internal environment which form the podium to the residential tower which sits above.

A more contemporary designed example of a purpose-built open-air factory outlet centre is

Figure 4.100 Tented structures used to establish a unique identity and form, Designer Outlet Village, Ashford, Kent, UK (2000). *(Source: Peter Coleman)*

Figure 4.102 The glass enclosed catering area, Designer Outlet Village, Ashford, Kent, UK. *(Source: Peter Coleman)*

represented by the Designer Outlet Village, Ashford, Kent (2000), which provides 19 000 m² (approx. 210 000 ft²) of accommodation. Designed by the Richard Rogers Partnership, the centre is given a unique identity by the use of oversailing fabric roofs. The centre is arranged in an oval circuit with the car parking arranged in the middle, with views to the surrounding shops. The tented skyline resembles a large Middle East caravan with the oversailing fabric roofs protecting the walkways and passing above the simple metal clad structures which enclose the shops. The pedestrian walkways are raised up and separated from the car parking by a landscaped perimeter to the car park. A glass enclosure beneath the fabric roof forms a catering area for fast food and refreshments at one end of the circuit.

Located in the southern hemisphere, Waterfront City, Melbourne (planned opening 2006), a development by Lewing and designed by Building Design Partnership with local architects Hassell, is another mixed-use development incorporating a mixture of factory outlet and traditional international and national shops. The shops are arranged in a network of open-air streets which integrate into the Victoria Dock masterplan. Two primary streets run north-south through the development connecting the waterfront with the leisure area which is focused on the Melbourne Eye. These two parallel streets are open to the air with canopies providing shading. The streets are on two levels which are lined with shops and have residential apartments in two to four storey buildings arranged above the shops (see Fig. 4.104). The development provides an overall total of 83 000 m² (approx 893 500 ft²) for a three-phased development of retail, café and restaurant accommodation. The catering is focused to overlook the waterfront and leisure area.

Factory outlet centres and the forms they adopt are constantly evolving. Originating from single use villages or mall arrangements, as these later examples illustrate, they can be (planning permitted) incorporated together with other uses just as flexibly as traditional retail arrangements. Although they have been categorised under out-of-town suburban shopping, they can be just as flexible as a catalyst for regeneration in town centre examples.

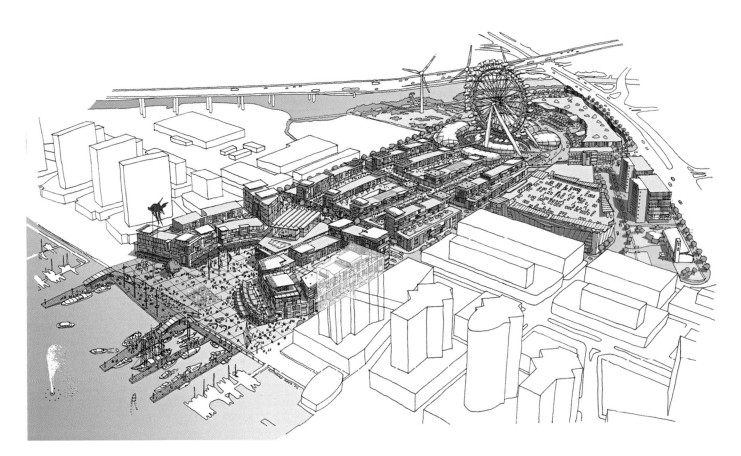

Figure 4.103 A factory outlet centre incorporated into a mixed-use development, Waterfront City, Melbourne, Australia (Planned 2006). *(Source: Richard Rees/BDP)*

Figure 4.104 The residential apartments above the designer outlet shops, Waterfront City, Melbourne, Australia (Planned 2006). *(Source: Hassell)*

Entertainment Centres

The out-of-town shopping environments examined so far have been led and organised around the primary demand for providing retailing. Some of the formats have included significant leisure and catering elements, but they have been clearly included as a secondary component to the function of retailing. Coincident with the greater demand on available leisure time and a general expectation of a bang for buck, a new format emerged in the 1990s. This new format is separate from the retail developments incorporating leisure elements and are represented by developments which are principally led by the provision of leisure and entertainment facilities. In these leisure led formats the shopping element is included as a complementary element to the leisure, thereby again making the total experience greater than the sum of the parts. The new format also often includes catering facilities and builds on the synergy between the three ingredients of leisure, catering and shopping.

The shopping environment format examined here is led by the provision of leisure and entertainment facilities and they are referred to as 'entertainment centres'. The shop tenants in these examples are restricted to specific types which tend to be specialist shops that are recreational focused rather than comparison fashion retailers. The purchasing is generally impulse-driven which is more dependent on the 'feel good' factor derived from experiencing the place or participating in the entertainment activities.

The leisure facilities are likely to be wide ranging to appeal to a diverse and targeted audience. The audience is also likely to vary at different times of the day. For example, the audience to be provided for will range from business people requiring a relaxing lunch, to thirty-something professionals looking for a memorable evening experience, to providing quality time recreation for families at weekends, to days out for tourists and to meeting the credibility demands of generation x and y.

Entertainment centres require a sufficiently sized attraction to guarantee a level of attention to the centre. This fundamental requirement is similar to the role played by the department store in the traditional centre, of ensuring sufficient visitors to encourage the occupation of the small units which accompany the anchor. The anchor role in an entertainment centre is often met by a multi-screen cinema (of at least ten screens). The anchor role can also be met by a significant recreational sporting activity such as indoor skiing. Occasionally a group of focused recreational activities can also combine together to form a critical mass of activity. For example, the combination of activity and different board sports illustrated earlier on at the Gateway Centre in Durban. In certain cases a large casino can even fill this role.

One of the first examples of a free-standing entertainment centre is Irvine Spectrum, Irvine, California (1995), which was originally formed around a large multi-screen cinema complex with twenty-one screens including an IMAX cinema. Irvine Spectrum was the first entertainment led centre of this format in America (Urban Land Institute, 1996). On its opening the centre was made up from three key ingredients – leisure facilities (the cinemas and interactive multi-media), catering (trend setting national restaurants) and speciality retailing (shops focused on entertainment or recreational activity). Two thirds of the total accommodation of 24 000 m² (approx 260 000 ft²) consists of the leisure activities. The remaining lettable space is broadly equally divided between the catering and retail uses which illustrates that the collection of shops plays a supporting role at this centre. The first phase of

Irvine Spectrum, designed by architects RTKL, is an example of a format orientated around entertainment instead of shopping and works on the basis of a synergistic experience formed from the total mix of entertainment, food, people watching and shopping. Unfortunately, subsequent extensions to the centre, which are described further on, have added more traditional shops, department stores and restaurants, thus diminishing the clarity of the formative first three years.

Irvine Spectrum was part of a masterplan for a new business and residential community for Irvine, Orange County, where the current site was zoned for a shopping centre. The zonal plan evolved from the consideration of providing restaurant and dining facilities for the new 36 000 employees in the adjacent business community. Final considerations of needing to extend activity into the evening, forming a focus and gathering place for the residential community and anchoring the development were also incorporated before the brief was finalised and the project realised.

The chosen site for Irvine Spectrum is ideally located at the convergence of two major freeways, making it easily accessible and having outstanding visibility from the 500 000 vehicles which pass daily. The boldness and success of the centre is supported by its excellent catchment. The location is able to attract visitors from both the local population of 2.4 million residents within a twenty minute drive time and the wider conurbation of Los Angeles and San Diego which are within a 40 minute journey time.

Entertainment centres are heavily dependent on providing large numbers of on-site car parking. This is generated by the daily cinema programme forming two or three waves of traffic. Irvine Spectrum's initial phase provided a total of over 4300 car parking spaces with some 2300 immediately on site and a further 2000 spaces provided off site by the ingenious use of a valet parking facility.

The entertainment centre at Irvine Spectrum is formally arranged within a cluster of individual buildings radiating from the large cinema building. The single level layout forms a series of pedestrian circuits which lead from a central plaza in front of the cinema to a mixture of outdoor and covered spaces. The central plaza acts as a gathering space and point of orientation. A series of more intimate spaces lead from the central plaza and take the form of passages which lead to a tented food court. The centre is planned with spaces which are defined by Moroccan styled buildings and extensive landscaping with palm and olive trees. The buildings and spaces, inspired by the Alhambra and Southern Spain, create a colourful and visually rich environment

with tiled buildings, patterned paving and the cooling effect from many water features. The open nature of the streets are appropriate to the Mediterranean climate where additional shading is provided by timber pergolas and fabric awnings to moderate the high summer sun.

Figure 4.105 A Moroccan styled passage adopted for the entertainment centre, Irvine Spectrum, Irvine, California, USA (1995). *(Source: RTKL)*

Figure 4.106 The tented food court, Irvine Spectrum, Irvine, California, USA. *(Source: RTKL)*

The adoption of Moroccan styled buildings is a populist approach to forming a sense of place and establishing an identity. Beyond the themed buildings the designers have applied solid urban design principles to form local identity and orientate customers, with vertical elements addressing key views and spaces defined and differentiated by

Figure 4.107 The gated entranceway to the open street, Irvine Spectrum, Irvine, California, USA. *(Source: RTKL)*

Figure 4.108 The night time street of Irvine Spectrum, Irvine, California, USA. *(Source: RTKL)*

entrance gateways. The buildings are appropriately scaled to address the adjacent spaces, whereby the cinema building is expressed as a grand palace with towers and a decorative cornice, while the remaining buildings housing the shops and restaurants are more modestly scaled and define the more intimate paseos. Donald Bron, chairman of developer The Irvine Company, aptly summarises the nature of the Irvine Spectrum entertainment centre, 'a destination resort for those in search of a smile – a place that demands that you leave your cares in the parking lot' (Urban Land Institute, 1996).

Since the opening of the entertainment centre in 1995, Irvine Spectrum has subsequently been extended in two significant further phases. Phase 2, also designed by RTKL, added a further 23 000 m^2 (approx. 250 000 ft^2) to provide 50 additional shops and restaurants. A linear arm leading from the central plaza forms another open air paseo which leads past three individual courtyards before arriving at Dave and Busters store. Phase 3 was added in 2002, providing a further 30 000 m^2 (approx 330 000 ft^2) for 60 additional shops and restaurants and a new anchor store. This extension was formed from two parallel paseos which lead between two large spaces. In each of these large spaces is a new entertainment facility. A carousel with antique horses leads from Phase II to the Giant Wheel which forms the focus of the latest space. This space is planned for a further extension which will lead to two new anchor stores due to open in 2005 and 2006 and each consisting of 11 000 m^2 (approx 125 000 ft^2) and 12 500 m^2 (approx 135 000 ft^2) respectively. Further car parking will be provided by two new multi-storey car parks being built.

On the eventual completion of the planned new anchor stores, Irvine Spectrum will have evolved from an entertainment centre into a full blown regional shopping and leisure centre with over 100 000 m^2 (approx 1 million ft^2) of accommodation with four anchor stores. Unfortunately, its metamorphosis will no longer represent the unique format from which it originated.

Another example of an entertainment centre which is anchored by a large multi-screen cinema is Star City, Birmingham (2000) which has a total of 37 000 m^2 (approx 400 000 ft^2) of accommodation providing a mixture of leisure, catering and shopping facilities. Star City is deliberately located beside a major motorway, giving the centre excellent presence with access from two motorways serving a greater catchment of 6 million within a 60 minute car journey. The majority of facilities are for leisure and entertainment activity with a multi-screen cinema complex with 30 theatres providing 5823 seats, night clubs, a casino, 22 lane bowling alley and a health club with gymnasia, swimming pools and health spas. A wide range of restaurants and bars provide different catering facilities for the various users of the centre. A small number of shops provide a supporting role to the leisure activities and these are focused on recreation, branded discount fashionware and fashion accessories. On arrival customers are able to park in the 3000 space surface car park.

The facilities, designed by the Jerde Partnership, are arranged in a linear series of buildings along a one sided promenade which faces the approach road and surface car parking laid out in front of the centre. The accommodation is reached from a mixture of open-air walkways and an enclosed atrium space. The architecture along the promenade is made up of a series of individual buildings which represent the different activities. Three-dimensional graphics layered onto the buildings form signage, lighting, gantries and vertical markers which make up a playful and colourful setting (see Fig. 4.110).

In addition to the pedestrian promenade, a central atrium space provides a vibrant enclosed environment which is equipped for audio, video and

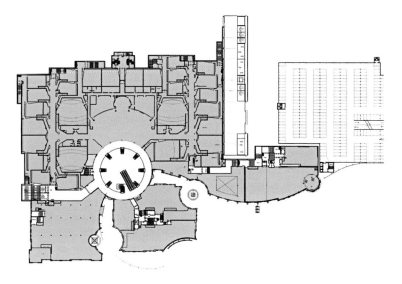

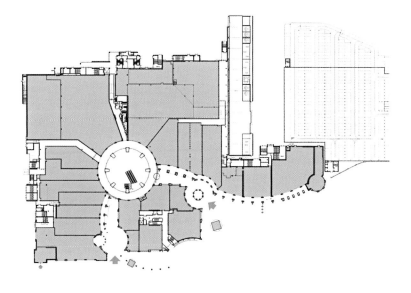

0   100m

Figure 4.109 Upper and lower ground floor plans, Star City, Birmingham, UK (2000). *(Source: Reid Architecture/BDP)*

Figure 4.110 Three-dimensional graphics characterise the entertainment centre along The Promenade, Star City, Birmingham, UK (2000). *(Source: bpl photo/Jonathan Berg)*

Figure 4.111 The central atrium space, Star City, Birmingham, UK. *(Source: Reid Architecture)*

lighting shows. The atrium space can be transformed into a public theatre advertising the centre or used for events and shows. The choreographed lighting is projected on to the floor and a fabric canopy draped beneath the skylight. Hanging within the space are six video screens, each measuring 6 × 4 m (approx 18 × 12 ft), which show film and music trailers or computer generated imagery.

Entertainment centres can also be anchored by activity sports as illustrated by the Xscape, Milton Keynes (2002), an interesting variation to the leisure, catering and shopping mix, which makes up the 51 000 m^2 (approx 550 000 ft^2) of accommodation at this centre. At Xscape, the leisure components are similar to those found at Star City, with the unique addition of real indoor snow ski slopes occupying 10 000 m^2 (approx 107 000 ft^2) of the space. The ski slopes provide three pistes ranging in length from 130 to 170 m (approx 420 to 550 ft) with a 35 m (approx 105 ft) descent for different grades of accomplishment. In addition to the ski lifts, there is also a travelator to encourage beginners as well as experienced skiers. Activity on the snow is not limited to skiing with snow boarding and tobogganing equally encouraged, thereby providing a wide range of snow experiences. A further activity sport is provided at Xscape with a 15 m (approx 48 ft) high climbing wall which is under cover and passes between the two main floor levels engaging both of the public areas.

The catering and shopping elements at Xscape are more significant than those at Star City, with a large number of restaurants and bars providing for a wide range of tastes. Similarly, a more extensive range of shops is accommodated than at its Midlands neighbour with some 14 units providing recreation focused and extreme sport retailing.

All of the facilities are housed within a single iconic building form, designed by architects Faulkner Brown, which takes the form of a steel clad spaceship that has landed in central Milton Keynes. A good local road network provides easy access to the nearby motorway, which makes the centre easily accessible to a large catchment. A surface car park surrounding the building provides 1200 parking spaces. The centre is entered through a dramatic parabolic shaped glass wall which is 44 m (approx 143 ft) high at the gable. The ski box and cinemas are subsumed within the spaceship form with the cinemas arranged beneath the slope of the ski slope.

Figure 4.112 The 'armadillo' enclosure to the indoor, real snow, ski slope, Xscape, Milton Keynes, UK (2002). *(Source: Faulkner Brown)*

Figure 4.113 Inside the indoor ski slope, Xscape, Milton Keynes, UK. *(Source: Faulkner Brown)*

An enclosed internal street leads past the catering and shop units to the snow centre, family entertainment centre, 10 pin bowling alley and climbing wall entrances on the ground floor. Stairs, escalators and lifts lead from the street up to the first floor which accesses the cinemas, nightclub and upper level of the family entertainment centre. The health club, which is also at the first floor, has its fitness suite overlooking the ski slopes. The encompassing cocoon of Xscape has solved the challenge of thermal insulation to provide suitable conditions for real snow inside the ski box and acoustic insulation separating the cinemas from the other uses.

Xscape was the first of its kind in the UK, providing a major indoor ski slope alongside other leisure and shopping facilities. A second similar centre by the same developers, opened in Castelford, 2003.

References

Architecture Today (1999). **94**, January.

British Council of Shopping Centres (BCSC) (2001). Report prepared by Experian Micromarket Division.

British Council of Shopping Centres (BCSC) (2001). Report BCSC.

Beets, G. *The Austin Chronicle*, **17** (46).

Guy, C. (1998). *Town Planning Review*, **69** (3), 291–309.

International Council of Shopping Centres, New York. *A Brief History of Shopping Centres*. ICSC.

Maitland, B. (1990). *The New Architecture of the Retail Mall*. Architecture Design and Technology Press.

Pine, J. and Gilmore, J. (1999). *The Experience Economy*. Harvard Business School Press.

Price Waterhouse (1999). *Study for Bodzins Urban Congress*, New York.

Teal, M. (1997). Big Box Retailing. *Estates Gazette*, no. 9745, November 8.

Urban Land Institute (1996). Project Reference File.

Figure 4.114 The strong form of the enclosed ski slope adds leisure uses to the shopping, Braehead, Glasgow, Scotland (2006). *(Source: Faulkner Brown)*

Town Centre Shopping

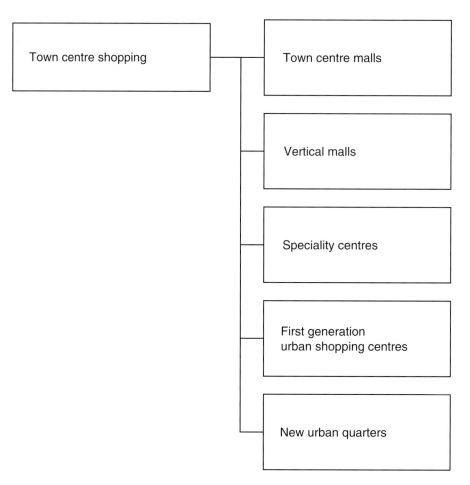

Figure 5.1 Town centre shopping.

Town Centre Shopping 5

The Big Issues

The different types of town centre shopping, which are located in the urban centre of towns or cities and listed in Fig. 5.1, are examined here. Before reviewing the different types of town centre shopping the Chapter continues to expand some of the big issues facing town centre shopping design identified in the opening Chapter. These include the public sentiment moving away from internalised shopping environments, planning control requiring more sustainable development, the urban agenda encouraging more open street based retailing and the combined effect of these issues.

Town centre shopping involves collections of shops, which can make up a significant portion of a town or city centre and in some instances represent the very heart. This type of shopping also has an influence on both the commercial well-being and the environmental quality of the urban centre. Because of the interrelationship between the urban centre and its shopping, it is necessary for those involved in the design of shopping facilities in these locations to have a wider understanding of the role of the town centre. For example, town centres are more than just areas of real estate; town centres will have both a social and personal interrelationship with those who use them. Individuals associate town centres with their home and have personal memories relating to particular places. Those involved with influencing the form of our towns and cities should therefore understand the qualities that a town centre incorporates and the roles it plays.

The formation of successful town centre shopping requires more skills than just providing accommodation for shops to trade from. It requires the ability to make urban places: locations which can range from places to walk in, to meet friends, watch people, participate in social events, and mark the new year; as well as conveniently allowing movement from one shop to another. Town centre shopping also involves the integration of the built form, not just with other buildings, but with the sensitive historic fabric, requiring appropriately scaled buildings.

As noted in Chapter 4, Mark Teale claimed that, with half the current town centre building stock in the UK being built before 1939, existing building stock is unable to meet the needs of modern volume retailers (Teale, 1997). Similar pressures exist elsewhere in Europe with facilities in town centres needing modernisation to provide shops of the right size and arrangement. Therefore, the demand for appropriate town centre accommodation is likely to continue for some time.

In addition to the general need to modernise, the past 25 years have seen the changing face of the European high street. Decentralisation, involving the removal of bulk retailing and perishable goods to retail parks and supermarkets respectively, has caused town centre retailing to become more focused towards comparison fashion, fashion accessories, personal adornment and recreational retailing. Town centres have also to compete with the ever increasing rate of the out-of-town and other shopping formats identified previously.

One could be excused for gaining the impression that overcoming this doom-list of challenges is insurmountable. In fact, despite all these challenges, the future of the town centre is assured, so long as it manages to address them. In the age of the experiential society, the town centre is aptly equipped to offer a unique experience by combining civic and cultural activities alongside shopping.

Town centres have the inherent advantages of commerce, culture and civic qualities which, when combined together, can provide a unique experience. The natural synergy between these qualities can also generate a variety of different experiences for

Figure 5.2 Historical town centre high streets provide civic, cultural and commercial activities, Chester, UK. *(Source: Peter Coleman)*

each visit to a town centre. With such a wide range of reasons to visit the town centre, it doesn't have to resort to devices to encourage customers. Town centres are therefore potentially better equipped to meet the needs of the contemporary customer than the various out-of-town retail formats. That is, of course, provided the town centre has the right retail accommodation, is accessible, and has worked to combine its commercial and civic qualities to make the total greater than the sum of the individual parts.

With some type of planning constraint on most forms of out-of-town retail development across Europe, town centre retailing is likely to be the only permitted form of shopping development for some time. Even in the USA the tide is turning away from the exclusive favour of the suburban mall. There is

Figure 5.3 High end fashion retailers finding downtown Manhattan attractive again, New York, USA. *(Source: Adrian Price/BDP)*

a gradual realisation that 'main street' has more of an authentic experience to offer than 'mall street'. The swing towards the more unique, along with a growing urban consciousness, is seeing a series of regenerated downtown retail areas. More American retailers are moving back to the downtown with exciting new retail offers.

So the future of the town centre, after years of decline and increasing competition, looks potentially very bright, partly due to the simultaneous forces of public preference and the planning authorities' support for development. Provided town centre shopping can address the physical constraints of the urban fabric and work alongside the town authorities to combine a unique urban experience, an exciting new generation of town centre shopping will emerge.

Evolution of Town Centre Shopping

From their origins in the early 1960s, through to the end of the 20th century enclosed town centre malls have largely been adopted, without question, as the accepted format of new town centre shopping development throughout the world. Technological progress, competition and expanding economies have allowed them to become more ambitious and complex over time.

With increasing demand for new facilities and constraints from available land, a new and denser retail format emerged in the mid-1970s. These dense developments saw the number of public levels extend beyond three to establish 'vertical malls', with four or more publicly accessible levels. The format and examples of vertical malls are explored separately later.

The 1980s saw the European philosophy for town centre mall interior spaces change from subdued dark interiors, dependent on artificial light and focused on the shop displays to brighter and largely naturally lit interiors, with lighter floor and ceiling finishes. Grand public spaces were also formed.

Many of these changes and the progress made in town centre shopping up to the end of the 1980s have been explored in earlier books by Nadine Beddington, *Shopping Centres, Retail Development, Design and Management* and Barry Maitland *The New Architecture of the Retail Mall*.

A common quality of town centre malls up to this time was the overridingly artificial nature of the enclosed internal environments which were reliant on mechanical venting, heating and cooling. Furthermore, the common characteristic of the brighter public spaces was the dependence on applied interior decoration rather than an expression of the architecture. A few centres had a more urban quality and some naturally lit centres utilised roof glazing to combine natural ventilation.

With the continued growth and expansion of town centre malls, a growing perception of uniformity crept in to the public's mind. Initially in Europe and later in America, public opinion, for the first time, questioned the universal acceptance of the enclosed shopping centre format in a town centre. Opinion demanded the creation of more unique places for shopping, which specifically related to the characteristics of the locality. For a short while, in Europe at least, this reaction caused a trend in favour of more urban and open-air shopping environments. The trend moved away from the interior design led shopping environments towards unheated covered streets and open squares. Although the artificial nature of the town centre mall fell out of public favour for a while, by the early 1990s a newer and grander generation of enclosed centres had opened in some European cities.

Throughout the 1990s, enclosed monolithic town centre malls continued to establish themselves in European cities, long after planning guidance had identified them as inappropriate development. This occurred as permissions were granted while further planning control was coming into effect. Furthermore, the time to build out the large and complex schemes saw several enclosed centres open after development control had supposedly closed the door on this type of shopping environment. In the UK in the mid-1990s, for example, a further generation of bigger and more refined enclosed centres were granted planning permission at precisely the time when the new planning guidance against this type of retail development was coming into effect. A dichotomy emerged in the UK. As the Millennium closed, a planning system established itself which was against monolithic town centre malls, while at the same time a series of town centre malls, representing the best in their class, were built out and consequently opened. Examples include The Oracle, Reading (1999), WestQuay, Southampton (2000), Touchwood, Solihull (2001), Festival Place, Basingstoke, (2002) and The Bullring, Birmingham (2003).

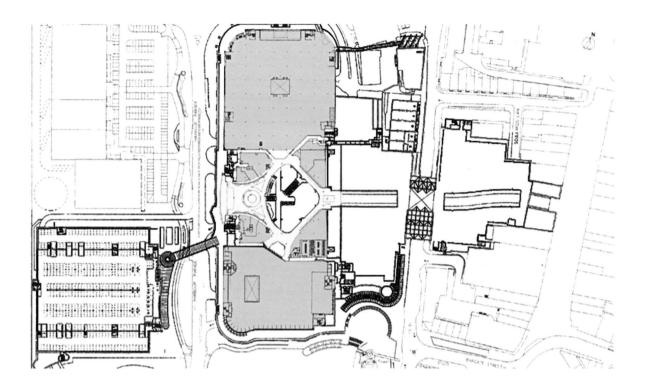

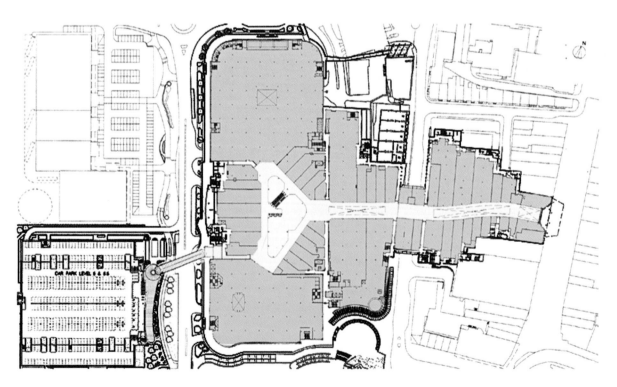

Figure 5.4 Upper and lower ground floor plans, WestQuay, Southampton, UK (2000). *(Source: BDP)*

Figure 5.5 The seven-storey central square typifies the bigger and more refined enclosed shopping centre of the late 1990s, WestQuay, Southampton, UK (2000). *(Source: Charlotte Wood/BDP)*

In 1999, to help police its planning policy, the UK introduced a strategic consultative body with real teeth to monitor compliance of major town centre development with planning guidance. This body, the Commission for Architecture and the Built Environment (CABE), produced its own design guidelines to amplify and reinforce this planning guidance (*By Design – Urban Design in the Planning Systems; Towards Better Practice*). By the end of the Millennium, the general planning strategy for more sustainable town centre development had been adopted in the UK and was generally similarly held in Western Europe.

Sustainable planning control has caused a fundamental change in the design thinking of town centre shopping. The planning guidelines generally encourage:

- mixed-use development
- integration with the existing urban setting
- individual high quality buildings
- equal attention given to the quality of the public space between buildings
- access to be available via several means of public transport.

Such policies effectively made the consideration of monolithic and enclosed town centre malls an inappropriate format for future new town centre shopping, certainly at least for the foreseeable future.

The challenge to those involved with retail development is how to meet the requirements of the

Figure 5.6 A two level daylit, enclosed town centre mall typified by Festival Place, Basingstoke, UK (2003). *(Source: Peter Coleman)*

urban agenda while retaining the benefits of convenience, comfort and security provided by the town centre malls. In other words, avoiding throwing the baby out with the bath water.

With the vogue for more urban street-like shopping environments, the design philosophy for town centre shopping appears to have moved full circle, returning once again to favour open pedestrianised streets. In the last half-century, shopping formats have evolved from the open precincts of the 1950s, to the universal adoption of enclosed centres, returning once again to favour more open natural shopping environments. The difference between the early precincts and the new format is the availability and affordability of modern construction technology and the expectation of high quality architecture and external spaces. The new format is different from the traditional high street as it involves the simultaneous formation of several streets, together with the surrounding buildings, and means they are planned as one to form a total shopping environment, which is an integral piece of the town centre. These new homogeneously planned shopping environments take the form of town or city quarters. Whole areas

of shops are considered at one time and differ from the random inclusion of individual shops, which were fitted into the historic high street in a piecemeal fashion. The nature and challenge of the new open street format, along with examples of the 'New Urban Quarters', are reviewed in more detail later.

American Origins

The first forms of shopping illustrated the integral relationship between shops and the fabric of a town and its administration in the combined market hall buildings. Earlier exploration revealed that all shopping formats were originally located in the town centre, from the time of the earliest civilisations right up to the 1920s in the USA, and as late as the 1960s in Europe. Until these points of departure, shops were the very urban fabric of a town or city, lining the main streets and principal spaces, forming landmark buildings, connecting streets through urban blocks with arcades and making up the ground floor of street after street of buildings with employment or living space above.

The first European examples of planned town centre shopping are found in the post-war open precincts and the early enclosed centres in the UK. The actual first claimant to being an enclosed centre in a downtown area was Midtown Plaza, Rochester, New York (1962) (see Fig. 5.7). It was designed by Victor Gruen, who, in so doing, extended his seminal influence upon shopping centre design from the out-of-town malls to the early enclosed town centre format.

Midtown Plaza was a catalyst for the regeneration of the downtown area. The centre, in addition to

Figure 5.7 One of the first enclosed town centre schemes in the USA with a multi-level interior space Midtown Plaza, Rochester, New York, USA (1962). *(Source: Rochester Public Library)*

re-accommodating existing stores, provided additional new small shops in a 90 000 m² (960 000 ft²) development, plus an 18-storey office and hotel tower. Gruen arranged the plan on two levels around a large rectangular galleried space, in a similar way to the covered courtyard and cluster of shops at Southdale. Midtown Plaza extended the cluster arrangement with short malls leading from the corners of the ground floor, in a pinwheel fashion, to the adjacent streets. Reflecting the higher land values of a downtown location, the centre illustrates the need for a greater density of development by organising the 2000 car parking spaces and part of the servicing into the basement levels below the centre. Following the centre's successful completion, further commercial development was attracted back to the central area of Rochester.

Another dense city centre development, which established a new benchmark for the town centre retail format, was the Galleria, Houston (1970) designed by Hellmuth, Obata and Kassabaum (HOK) for the developer Gerald Hines. The development occupies a key site adjacent to the West Loop Freeway on what was an expanding fringe of the downtown western edge of the city. The site was assembled from six land parcels to form a new rectangular block. The mixed-use development exploited the opportunity created by an absence of zoning controls, to provide a shopping galleria, two office towers, a 404 bedroom hotel, and a university club and acted as a catalyst for the regeneration of this part of the city.

The original Galleria (Phase 1) provided 56 000 m² (600 000 ft²) of shopping space over three levels. The Galleria building is integral to the office, hotel and club elements. A simple linear space covered by a continuous barrel vault led originally to a single department store at one end with the potential for another store to be added at the opposite end. The simple dumb-bell plan has subsequently been extended in two further phases into a cross-shaped arrangement which crosses a roadway with a T-shaped building. Phase 3 (2003) extended the Galleria into a centre with over 300 shops, six department stores and 200 000 m² (2 million ft²) of shopping and restaurant accommodation.

Phase 1 of the Galleria has a full size ice rink at its lowest level, which is overlooked from the cantilevered balconies of the two shopping levels above. Banks of escalators and stairs run at each end of the ice rink and connect vertically between the three levels of the linear space. The lowest level is set into the ground making the street entrances arrive at the middle level. The third level is fed by

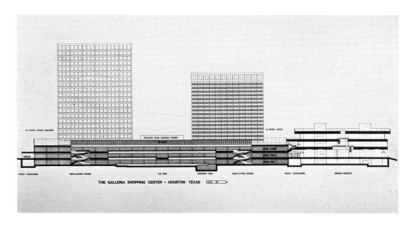

Figure 5.8 Cross section through The Galleria, Houston, USA. *(Source: HOK)*

the parking garages which lead into this level on both sides of the centre. The centre has an integrated service area located at the lowest level which leads to the levels above by service cores. The barrel vaulted public space is naturally lit in daytime, which differed from the dark and largely artificially-lit contemporary centres in both America and Europe at that time.

Figure 5.9 A three-storey galleria forms the central shopping space above the ice rink, The Galleria, Houston, USA (1970). *(Source: HOK)*

The Galleria Phase 1 represented a landmark in shopping environments by establishing bright naturally lit interiors. This occurred as a long-term result of the early 1970s energy crisis, which eventually caused other later planned centres also to adopt more naturally lit interiors.

The Galleria, Houston was a significant shopping development for several reasons. First, it addressed the issue of needing to be a dense development both by incorporating a mixture of uses and also by extending the shopping facilities over three levels. As one of the early city centre schemes in America it became one of the first centres effectively to become a hub of urban life, establishing itself as the place to go, to see and to be seen. Finally, the bright day-lit interiors were also ahead of their time and the centre went on to influence a generation of centres that followed in America and Europe.

Early European Town Centre Shopping

The Bullring, Birmingham and the Elephant and Castle, London described earlier, were not successful examples of early town centre malls. These UK developments from the 1960s were flawed by their lack of integration with their surroundings. In both examples, the surrounding context had been formed by ambitious new highways, planned in isolation of the shopping centre. Consequently, in both cases, the

centres were isolated from the surrounding context. The subsequent generation of utilitarian and inward looking Arndale Centres were rolled out across several English cities. In 1965, the Grosvenor Estate developed one of the first naturally lit, integrated enclosed centres in the established city centre of Chester. Here, a simple single level mall connected a backlands site to the prime retail frontage of Chester. Further town centre development continued the principle of the enclosed pedestrian shopping environment separated from the busy open streets by traffic. These centres established the successful format of the town centre mall in Europe by the early 1970s.

The development company, Capital and Counties Property Company, pioneered two early successful town centre malls in the UK with the Victoria Centre, Nottingham and Eldon Square, Newcastle.

The Victoria Centre, Nottingham (1972), developed on the site of a former railway station, is a mixed-use development with residential flats and offices located above the centre. It provides 95 shops in 58 000 m² (622 000 ft²) linking two of the city centre principal streets. The two-level centre was one of the first to integrate with the different levels across the city to form two ground floor levels. A simple linear plan forms a pedestrian link connecting two sides of the city. The linear plan is arranged as a dumb-bell with a department store anchoring both levels at one end, and a food store and bus station anchoring levels one and two respectively at the other. A two-level public market connects to both levels in the middle of the plan. Car parking, vehicular servicing and storage are arranged beneath the shopping levels.

The interior public spaces, designed by the architect Arthur Swift and Partners, had dark finishes and were reliant on artificial lighting (see Fig. 5.11). The interior spaces represented a common school of thought at the time – allowing the shop units to be the focus of the interior. This approach resulted in rather dark and uninviting public spaces, which with the benefit of hindsight, have now been recognised as an inappropriate shopping environment. Today, other than the basic layout, little remains of the original interior. The centre was refurbished in 1988, extended in 1997 and, in 2000, the remainder of the centre was refurbished again to match the extension.

Eldon Square, Newcastle (1976) is a more complex and challenging example of a town centre mall. This example illustrates some of the typical issues faced by integrating a major mixed-use development into an urban context. The site was made up from several city blocks set within an irregular framework of streets and sensitive existing buildings.

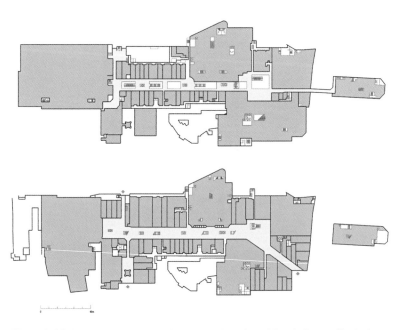

Figure 5.10 The original upper and lower level floor plans, Victoria Centre, Nottingham, UK (1972). *(Source: Capital Shopping Centres)*

Figure 5.11 One of the early UK enclosed town centre schemes; the original artificially lit two level shopping interior, Victoria Centre, Nottingham, UK (1972) (Refurbished 1997). *(Source. Capital Shopping Centres/Haskol)*

Figure 5.12 An artificially lit interior with feature ceiling, focusing upon the shopfronts, Eldon Square, Newcastle, UK (1976). *(Source: Chapman Taylor)*

Figure 5.13 The subdued introduction of natural daylight above the concourse, Eldon Square, Newcastle, UK. *(Source: Capital Shopping Centres/Newcastle City Council)*

The development was required to comply with specific planning constraints, determined by the local authority, in order to integrate the development into a sensitive context.

The level change across the city has been used by architect Chapman Taylor to generate a two level centre with effectively two ground floors. Forming a pedestrian route between the existing streets has given the layout an F-shaped plan. Responding to the levels of the streets, the malls are also sloped to fit in with the city. This was the first example of sloping the public spaces in a town centre mall and involved the careful alignment of the shop floors to allow access. A major bus station and servicing have been integrated below the centre.

Eldon Square is part of a mixed-use development, which incorporates offices, city sports and a recreational centre above the shops. Two stacked car parks provide car parking on each of the main sides of the centre. The centre provides 90 000 m² (968 000 ft²) in 110 shop units, a department store, six large shop units and a two-storey market.

The original interiors were a mixture of naturally and artificially lit spaces, where the interior design of the straight malls were part of the dark school retaining the focus on the shopfronts. At strategic locations, where two malls meet, at entranceways or the connecting spaces between the levels, natural light from roof lights is introduced into courts and squares (referred to as concourses) to punctuate the public spaces. To assist orientation within the long and complex mall network, there are points allowing views to the outside. These points of contact with the city occur mainly at the entranceways.

Eldon Square was extended and refurbished in 1985 and connected to the Eldon Gardens Centre via another bridge across Percy Street. Plans are in progress for a further major extension to the centre which is due for phased completion between 2006 and 2009.

The integration of such a large development, while retaining selected qualities of the urban fabric, was a challenging undertaking and completed with considerable skill. The mass of the monolithic development has been broken down into separate elements, although they remain part of a single built form. A sensitive architectural treatment has been applied adjacent to the retained historical buildings in Eldon Square. Natural materials were used on the majority of the buildings, with mirror glass used to highlight the entrances being the exception. The retention of a key existing street (Blacket Street) resulted in the centre being separated into two halves, with the only connection being a pedestrian bridge across the street. The separation of the centre into two parts compromises the layout and the bridge element highlights the separation between the internal shopping and the urban street environment of the city centre. These two compromises illustrate a fundamental weakness of the enclosed town centre mall. This weakness is exacerbated when the philosophy of providing a continuous protected internal shopping environment is applied uncompromisingly to an urban context.

Figure 5.14 Brick façade facing onto Eldon Gardens, Newcastle, UK. *(Source: Chapman Taylor)*

Eldon Square is not unique in illustrating the problems arising from the monolithic shopping centre being applied to the town centre. However, its urban shortcomings were largely overridden by its overall success in regenerating the commercial centre of Newcastle.

The commercial success and attractiveness to the public of providing a protected and comfortable shopping environment has resulted in the enclosed shopping centre format being adopted in most UK town centres and, to a lesser degree, in Europe. Following the arrival of the town centre mall in the early 1970s, the format has been applied almost unquestioningly for a period of some 25 years.

Further Developments

One of the first town centre malls in mainland Europe was developed in France and was instigated by the city of Lyon along with a consortium of owners (notably La Société des Centres Commerciaux and the Credit Lyonnais Bank). The extensive site in the city centre was a former military academy. The site was purchased from the defence ministry by the city of Lyon with the intention of promoting a mixed-use development which would strengthen the downtown area and reinforce the city's economic activity.

La Part Dieu shopping centre opened in 1975 and was part of a mixed-use development which incorporated a hotel, offices and apartments (see Figs. 5.15 and 5.16). It provided 250 shop and restaurant units in 110 000 m^2 (1 200 000 ft^2) of retail accommodation. At its opening it represented the largest enclosed shopping environment in Europe. The centre is arranged with three principal levels that are interconnected along a dumb-bell arrangement, with a department store at each end of the mall. A court at each end of the linear space, alongside a central court, punctuate the public areas and receive the side malls. The upper floors form galleries which overlook the space.

La Part Dieu's level 1 is set into the ground (as at the Galleria, Houston). The main entrance terraces relate to the surrounding streets and lead into level 2. The third level is fed from the car parks above, which are in a stack to the side. A bridge also connects this level to the adjacent railway station. The basement level, aligned with small shops, forms a fourth public level and leads to the Metro station located beneath the centre. There is additional parking in the basement which, together with the stack and rooftop parking, provides 4500 spaces. Buses and trams also arrive at the centre making it easily accessible by both public and private transport.

The original interior spaces of La Part Dieu followed the approach of focusing attention on the shopfronts with dark finishes and a reliance on artificial lighting. The centre was refurbished in 2001 and natural light introduced by punctuating holes through the rooftop parking and replacing the floor and ceiling finishes with lighter materials. The centre remains a successful urban destination, attracting 100 000 visitors per day and is integral to the economic success of the city centre.

A town centre mall that attempted to break the stereotype of the uniform enclosed shopping centre type is EuraLille, Lille, France (1994). Designed by Jean Nouvel, the centre adopted a rationalistic approach to both its external architecture and its interiors. The end result is that EuraLille appears uncompromisingly modernistic and forms a landmark building (see Fig. 5.19).

The statement building was made possible by the site being located just outside the historic town and its design being unfettered by the considerations of integration and sensitive constraints. EuraLille is

Figure 5.15 An early European inward looking enclosed shopping centre, La Part Dieu, Lyon, France (1975). *(Source: BDP)*

Figure 5.16 One of the few daylit spaces in the original enclosed interior, La Part Dieu, Lyon, France. *(Source: BDP)*

also part of a grand masterplan, prepared by Rem Koolhaas, which extends the town from the original railway station up to the new Eurostar station and exhibition centre to the north of the city.

EuraLille is in part a mixed-use development, conceived as a single design, with new housing taking the form of towers on the perimeter of two sides of the building. The $69\,300\,\text{m}^2$ ($746\,000\,\text{ft}^2$) centre is anchored by a large two-level hypermarket of $24\,000\,\text{m}^2$ ($258\,000\,\text{ft}^2$). There are 124 shop and restaurant units arranged on two principal mall levels, with a lower partial third level which provides a catering area overlooking a piazza and leads to the new railway station. The car parking is discreetly provided beneath the shopping levels in two parking decks, which are connected to the centre and the hypermarket by travelators.

The public circulation spaces organise the malls into a triangular-shaped circuit, where the apex leads from the main entrance towards the hypermarket. A further cross route subdivides the triangle and forms a mall as an axis leading to the station piazza. The malls are a mixture of three, two and single storey height spaces. Most of the public spaces have natural daylight with only the single storey malls reliant on artificial light.

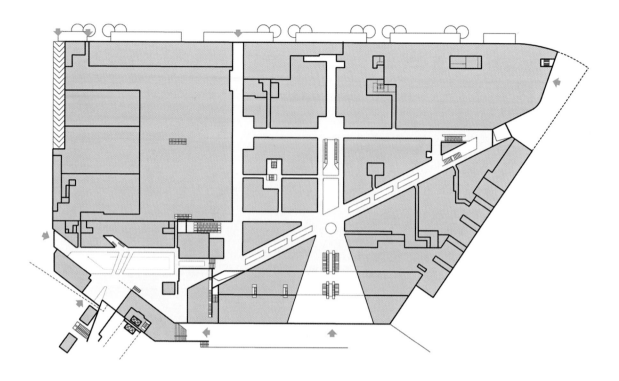

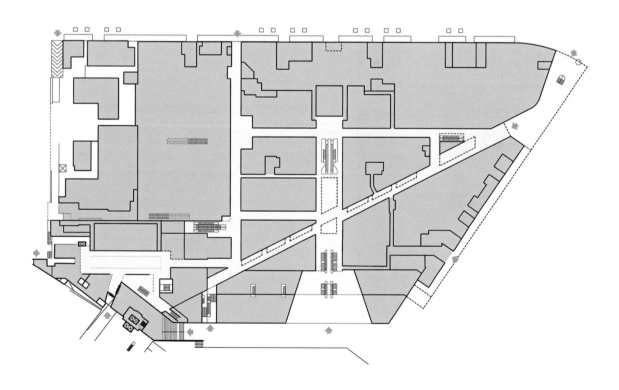

0 ⊢—┴—┴—┴—┴—┴—┴—┴—┴—┤ 100m

Figure 5.17 Upper and lower level plans, Euralille, Lille, France (1994). *(Source: Jean Nouvelle/BDP)*

Figure 5.18 Double height mall, with some daylight, leading towards the hypermarket, Euralille, Lille, France. *(Source: AJN Architect)*

The dominant feature of the design is the large, gently sloping roof which sits above the rooftop plant and descends down from the south to the north elevation. The roof conceals, beneath a metal grid which floats above the structural decking, all the mechanical plant from the view of the tenants in the towers above. A similar metal gridded suspended ceiling sits beneath the structural

Figure 5.19 The unifying ceiling following the roof floating over the shops and public spaces, Euralille, Lille, France. *(Source: AJN Architect)*

trusses, allowing the roof to appear from the inside to float above the shops and public spaces. The two principal mall levels sit beneath the sloping roof and correspondingly step down towards the piazza on a lower level on the north elevation. This creates the dramatic spatial effect of stepped terraces, which form a multi-level catering space leading out on to the piazza.

The main entranceway faces the old town and is dramatically expressed by the roof cantilevering out from the building to form a four-storey covered, open space (Fig. 5.20). The roof continues from outside to inside moving from porte cochure to two-level entrance space, thus encouraging people to move into the centre. Once inside the centre, the gently sloping underside to the roof floats above the entranceway and leads onwards into the two double height malls. The floating roof slopes from the apex of the four-storey entranceway on the south elevation down to the two-storey piazza on the north elevation. The roof forms the unifying element to the architecture and all the main public interior spaces.

A grilled metal ceiling conceals the steel roof structures and allows indirect daylight to filter through to the public spaces below. Artificial lights in the grilled ceiling supplement the lighting. The grille creates a generally dark feeling and, by hovering above the public spaces, tends to dominate the quality of the interiors.

The remaining interior finishes, designed by Daniel Poissonet, are generally a light grey neutral monochrome with selected splashes of red. The grey tile floors have highlights formed in red tiles. The shopfronts are surrounded by metal goal posts with modular cladding in metal and glass making up the upper storey. Selective red panels break up the modular cladding above the shops and continue the geometric patterns from the external elevations. Glass balustrades with steel handrails, along with a grey channel and grey clad spandrel panel, line the openings in the floors. A small red motif in the channel highlights the floor edges. Circular columns are clad in a polished metallic lining which has a dichromatic effect, adding another controlled colour. The finishes have a rather hard and cool effect on the spaces but, in turn, relate to the exterior architecture. Even though the architecture and interiors have involved two designers, they do appear to be from a single hand with continuity from outside to inside.

EuraLille is a rather unique town centre mall which demonstrates a singular architectural idea. It represents a rational architectural statement of which there are relatively few shopping centre examples.

Figure 5.20 The cantilevered entranceway facing towards the old town, Euralille, Lille, France. *(Source: AJN Architect)*

Judgement as to the appropriateness of the cool and modernistic interiors is a matter of personal taste. EuraLille has certainly given Lille a unique and individual shopping environment and a modern extension to the old town centre.

Town Centre Malls

This format of shopping is largely represented by the enclosed town shopping facility illustrated earlier in the base form and represented here by some of the most evolved examples of the type. More recent urban evolutions of the type are illustrated towards the end of this Chapter.

The Millennium ended with the completion of The Oracle, Reading (1999/2000), a significant town centre mall developed by Hammerson. This centre is one of those enclosed shopping environments where planning permission was obtained

in the mid-1990s, and completed after planning guidance turned away from this format in favour of more integrated and sustainable development. At its completion, the Oracle and its immediate peers represented the benchmark of progress achieved with enclosed town centre shopping environments.

The Oracle is located in the heart of the town centre of Reading, with both a direct connection to the pedestrianised high street and a second linkage via a connecting street. A large portion of the development runs parallel to the high street, separated by a road and on land assembled from a former cleared site, furniture store, multi-storey car park and bus garage.

The Oracle makes clever use of the levels to form a two-level enclosed centre, with a further lower third level forming open-air promenades on each side of the river. A pedestrian route is formed through the centre, linking the high street with the river. The L-shaped pedestrian route organises the plan from the high street leading to an anchor department store with a second department store arranged midway at the knuckle. The enclosed pedestrian route is arranged at two levels between the two anchor stores to form a dumb-bell arrangement. Leading off from the knuckle space at the upper ground floor level, a single level mall leads to the High Street.

The two-level enclosed interior accommodates 80 shop units and two department stores totalling 65 500 m^2 (700 000 ft^2). Cafés, restaurants and bars are spread on either side of the river to form an attractive multi-level waterside environment. A feature bridge leads to a separate ten-screen cinema complex on the other side of the river. Also on the opposite side of the river a separate multi-level car park structure, animated with ground floor shops and studios, feeds customers to the centre from the riverfront via the bridge.

Figure 5.21 The controlled two level enclosed interior, The Oracle, Reading, UK (1999–2000). *(Source: Hammerson)*

Figure 5.22 Catering activity lining the frontage on each side of the river, The Oracle, Reading, UK. *(Source: Hammerson)*

Architect Haskoll organised the centre into three architectural elements. The car park and cinema form two blocks arranged on one side of the river, with the third block, the enclosed centre, on the other side of the river leading to the High Street. The third block with the enclosed shopping centre is by far the largest, and although architecturally made up from different elements, represents a single monolithic building in the town centre. The interiors provide a tempered environment with mechanical heating and cooling. A glazed barrel vault, extending the length of the two-storey mall, with roof lights to the other mall, provide largely naturally lit interiors during the daytime. The two-level mall is a lofty space with single-storey shops to the ground floor and double-storey shops on the upper ground floor. The interiors are robust and contemporary with hard wearing natural materials formed from two tone granite floors,

glass balustrades, timber handrails and panelled plaster wall linings above the shops (see Fig. 5.23).

The assembly of land and relocation of one of the department stores into the development resulted in a phased development. Phase 1 was the main two-level mall between the anchor stores, Phase 2 the cinema block and Phase 3 the formation of the link to the high street with the single-level mall.

The Oracle is a successful town centre mall improving the commercial use of the town centre and significantly improving the national trading position of this Thames Valley town. Although largely an enclosed shopping environment, the leisure and catering uses focused on the river have regenerated the riverside and made a new public destination on the waterfront for day and evening use (see Fig. 5.24). In recognition of its success, The Oracle has won both UK and European industry awards.

Figure 5.23 Hard-wearing interior finishes to the interior, The Oracle, Reading, UK. *(Source: Hammerson)*

Figure 5.24 Restaurants line the ground floor of the car park facing the river, The Oracle, Reading, UK. *(Source: Hammerson)*

Birmingham, England's second city, earlier represented a milestone shopping environment with the original Bull Ring (1964), which started the generation of enclosed town centre shopping facilities in the UK and Europe. Within 40 years of the original, the city, known as 'the city of a thousand trades', redeveloped the same site to craft another leading edge shopping environment by completing the new Bullring (2003). The new Bullring corrects many of the past mistakes and, with the planning door firmly closed on future enclosed shopping environments, represents one of the last enclosed town centre shopping environments in the UK. Birmingham, home of the first of the original enclosed shopping centres and then, in its redevelopment home of one of the last of a recent generation of enclosed town centre shopping, reinforces its significance in the evolution of shopping environments.

New Bullring joint developer, Hammerson, had already undertaken two major town centre malls with the Oracle, Reading and WestQuay, Southampton (2000). It was able, with the formation of the Birmingham Alliance involving Land Securities and Henderson Global Investment, to refine the type by completing the third major centre within four years at the Bullring. The increase in scale over its predecessors and continual refinement of the type makes the Bullring one of the finest enclosed town centre mall examples.

Although the Bullring is an enclosed shopping environment, which generally is not an acceptable form for new development at the start of the 21st century, the timing of the centre's completion led to it incorporating some of the urban qualities required in recent planning guidance – such as integration with the surrounding urban fabric and more outward facing open-air shopping. The Bullring therefore has a foot in both camps, with large areas of enclosed shopping and the inclusion of some open-air shopping spaces.

The Bullring reconnects a retail quarter to the heart of the existing city centre, extending the retail core from New Street and High Street (Fig. 5.25). Masterplanned by architect Benoy, the scheme is arranged with three axes which lead from the existing city centre to form pedestrian routes through the new neighbourhood. Two of these routes are natural extensions from the existing street pattern and become enclosed covered streets. The third axis forms an open-air street which passes between the two covered streets and separates the quarter into two blocks on each side of the street. The open street leads on from the city and reconnects the church and market area.

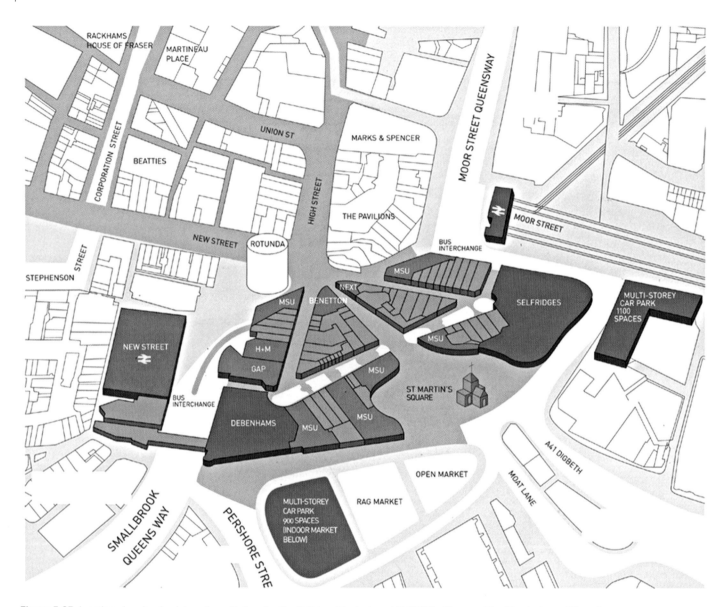

Figure 5.25 Location plan showing integration with the city, The Bullring, Birmingham, UK (2003). *(Source: The Birmingham Alliance)*

The two new covered streets leading from the city are, in turn, connected by a third, enclosed street to form a triangle of covered ways. With the connection to the city forming one corner of the triangle, the other two corners are used to locate each of the new department stores. The two new department stores, at the end of the extended existing streets, form a wishbone arrangement with the existing retail area. The triangular arrangement establishes a strong synergy between the city and the two new department stores.

The significant level change of 19.5 m (63 ft) across the site is used to form three main publicly accessible shopping levels: upper (level 3), middle (level 2) and lower (level 1). Each of the three levels has a relationship with the external ground, which is used to form an entranceway to each floor. Each level also has an individual layout of pedestrian routes and therefore its own identity. The upper level forms two separate V-shaped wings; the middle level forms the direct link between the two department stores, but is separated by the open street; and the lower level completes the dumb-bell link between the two department stores.

Connecting naturally between all three vertical levels is the new open-air street which slopes down

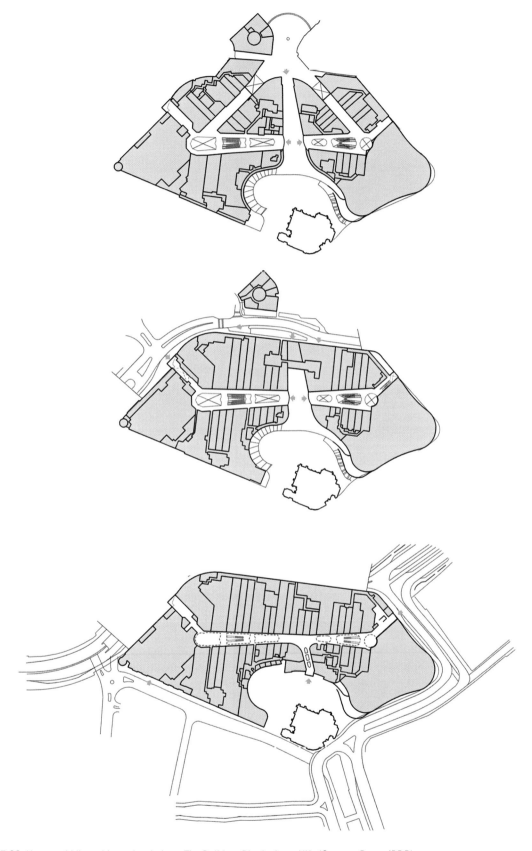

Figure 5.26 Upper, middle and lower level plans, The Bullring, Birmingham, UK. *(Source: Benoy/BDP)*

Figure 5.27 The open sloping street which leads to St Martin's Square, The Bullring, Birmingham, UK. *(Source: Ravi Deepres/Hammerson)*

Figure 5.28 St Martin's Square looking towards Selfridges, The Bullring, Birmingham, UK. *(Source: Michael Betts/Hammerson)*

to the middle level, and steps down to the lower level and St Martin's Square around the church. The escalators, which connect between the three enclosed levels, are located on each side of the dumb-bell mall between the two department stores.

The Bullring is much more than an enclosed town centre mall. The masterplan incorporates a series of open-air external spaces which overlay and relate to each of the three enclosed levels. The external spaces integrate the new quarter with the urban structure of the city, form new public spaces to reinforce the legibility of the city and structure the massing of the new development.

A new square forms the connection with the city and the entry space into the new quarter. From the new entrance space, a new pedestrianised open-air street leads to the church. The new street allows the spire to be visible from the entrance and thereby reinforces the legibility and connection between the city and its historic buildings.

A new multi-level public piazza is formed around the church and becomes a destination space with cafés, bars and restaurants at the end of the new street. The two new spaces individually relate to each of the upper and lower levels of the centre. The sloping street connects these two new public spaces and forms an entrance to the middle level. The new squares and open street thereby relate to each part of the enclosed centre while simultaneously integrating it with existing parts of the city. The open street also allows the new quarter and connections to parts of the city to remain accessible 24 hours a day.

With three publicly accessible main floors, and with the upper and lower floors having additional mezzanine space, the Bullring is a denser town centre mall than its peers in Reading and Southampton. The centre occupies 10.5 ha (26 acres) and provides 110 000 m^2 (1.2 million ft^2) of accommodation with 146 shops and two department stores.

The triangular layout is an organisational diagram where none of the three levels individually forms the overall pattern. The triangle is formed by the combination of the three levels layered upon each other. The upper and middle levels consist of two separate wings symmetrically arranged with an implied relationship on either side of the new open street. It is only at the lower level that the two sides are directly connected by the dumb-bell mall between the two department stores. The dumb-bell mall connects vertically between the three levels and physically pulls the arrangement together. Knuckle spaces at the end of the mall receive the different routes and provide entranceways to each of the department stores.

Pedestrian flows are evenly distributed between the three levels. This is achieved by the level change across the site being used to provide an effective ground floor entrance to each level. The upper level has entranceways which relate to the retail areas of the existing city; the middle level is entered mid-way from the open street and has entranceways on each side relating to the two railway stations on either side of the development. The lower level, which is organisationally the strongest, relates to the destination piazza and is fed from the car park with 1000 spaces below the centre.

Figure 5.29 The three level naturally lit enclosd space looking from Debenhams, The Bullring, Birmingham, UK. *(Source: Chapman Taylor)*

The layout is used to organise the different types of tenant into focused areas with similar and compatible types of retailing. In this case the three levels have been used to reinforce three different types of retailing:

- lower level: high street retailers and catering
- middle level: young fashion and lifestyle
- upper level: more aspirational.

The two department stores are each focused towards a different quality level of retailing, one being more upmarket, the other appealing more to the mainstream. The qualitative differences represented on each side of the centre by the department stores have been used to reinforce corresponding groupings of shop units. For example, the covered street leading to the upmarket department store has grouped together more upmarket aspirational retailers, while the corresponding covered street on the same level has mainstream fashion retailers leading up to the mainstream department store. Similar linked groupings of mainstream and upmarket retailers have been made with the respective department stores on the middle level and the young fashion and lifestyle retailers.

The massive scale of the Bullring presents a significant architectural challenge and demonstrates how to integrate successfully such a large development into the fabric of the existing city. The architectural solution, conceived by the architect Benoy, with detailed design by architect Chapman Taylor, attempts to scale the mega-structure by expressing individual elements in different architectural forms.

The challenge of achieving a variety of architecture has been partly addressed by the introduction of a separate architect, Future Systems, to design the Selfridges department store. Future Systems have created a radical solution by adopting an organic

Figure 5.30 Aerial view above St Martin's Square, The Bullring, Birmingham, UK. *(Source: Hammerson)*

form made from a concrete shell, over-clad with insulation, blue paint and aluminium discs. The end result is radically different from the remainder of the centre with an iconic solution which has little response to its context or surrounding neighbours. The challenge of integration has been assisted by the retention of some existing key buildings which have their own architectural identity, such as the circular tower to the Rotunda and the historic St Martins Church.

The use of different architectural expression in the remainder of the Bullring's mega-structure achieves varied degrees of success. Where the different functions are clearly identifiable, the different parts of the building have been convincingly expressed in different architectural forms. For example, the second department store is clearly expressed as a separate building, the covered streets are expressed as planar glass façades and the buildings, bridging over the railway lines, confidently expose the bowstring trusses from which the building structures are suspended.

The less successful façades are those where a different architectural expression has been applied to similar functions – such as making the unit shops on either side of the middle level entrance arbitrarily adopt different architectural forms. In this instance the upper side of the street expresses the three-storey shops with an ordered polychromatic stone clad structure with glazed infill panels, whereas the lower side of the street adopts a style of stripped classicism using light coloured brick façades with punched hole windows and stepped back upper floors with an overriding horizontal cornice. The architecture of the brick buildings is extended around both sides of the piazza to define the public space to the church. Here the façades continue the overriding horizontal quality found in the more intimate street. Rather than allow the horizontal architecture to be confidently expressed, verticality has been arbitrarily introduced by extending the brick elements upwards to form an additional floor, or by replacing the colonnade of open shopfronts by bringing the façade down to the ground.

The shopping environment at the Bullring is predominantly that of an enclosed centre. However, the shopping experience is more than an internalised town centre mall. The clear organisation of the plan means the internal spaces have an integral relationship with both the new external street and squares and the existing streets of the city. Although the majority of shops are accessed from inside, the edges which face the new street and square are animated, with outward facing shops and cafés.

On entering the Bullring from the city centre, there is a gradual transition from pedestrianised open-air spaces to the enclosed spaces of the centre. Single-level covered streets lead from the new entrance square up to the knuckle spaces in front of each of the two department stores. From the upper level of the knuckle space the streets change direction and scale as the enclosed street becomes a three-level mall connecting between the two department stores. Although the space from the knuckle is three levels, the dumb-bell mall is bisected by the external street, with only the lower level continuously connecting beneath it. The upper levels are stopped off on either side of the street and continuous passage on the middle level involves having to go outside to cross the street and re-enter the building on the other side.

The enclosed spaces of the Bullring are treated like covered internal streets by the use of simple planes of clear glass passing across the space above the shops. The 'sky plane' glazed roof is formed from planar glazing suspended from external, primary steel trusses. The minimal roof enclosure maximises contact with the external environment. This type of roof in a shopping environment is a marked departure from the various vaulted roofs which normally enclose public spaces and, as such, marks a step towards covered streets representing the urban agenda. The resulting interior spaces are bright and predominantly naturally lit in daylight hours. The interiors are, however, mechanically heated and cooled to temper the environment (see Fig. 5.31).

The character of the covered street is less successful beneath the glass roof, where the sheer size of the shop interior overrides the character of the space. The covered street attempts to develop an expression of individuality by introducing a variety of external materials, in different designs, to the shop surrounds. The shop surrounds, although using external materials, such as brick, stone, glass and metal, struggle to be convincing as individual external buildings. The treatment of the shops and the feel of covered streets are more successful in the single level spaces. In the three-level space, the shops and character are dominated by the overridingly strong horizontal lines of the overhanging galleries. Unfortunately, the inherent form of the building overrides the worthy efforts of the developer and consultants to treat the shops as external buildings in a covered street.

Accepting that the feel of covered streets fades below the roofline, the public spaces are actually grand interior spaces. The interiors are clean lined and contemporary using natural materials with a robust attention to detail. Apart from the shop surrounds, the materials selected for the remainder

Figure 5.31 The glazed sky plane roof floats over the upper level street, The Bullring, Birmingham, UK. (*Source: Michael Betts/Hammerson*)

of the public spaces are restrained with natural stone (limestone) floors, plaster ceilings and metal balustrades. The detailing to the gallery edges on the two sides of the separated primary mall is varied to reinforce local identity and reflect the qualitative difference to the tenant selection. For instance, the gallery edges on the Selfridges side are curved and correspond to the organic store, while on the other side the gallery edges are angular and clean lined (see Fig. 5.33). Similarly the stick-like, angled supporting columns are treated differently, with a metallic finish on one side and an earth-like feel corresponding to the other side.

Figure 5.32 The Selfridges mall with the softer characteristic, The Bullring, Birmingham, UK. (*Source: Peter Coleman*)

Figure 5.33 The Debenhams mall with more angular edges, The Bullring, Birmingham, UK. *(Source: Peter Coleman)*

Considerable attention and effort has been given to extend the quality achieved in the public spaces into the 146 individual shop fit outs. To enable this, the developer (the Birmingham Alliance) dedicated a separate team, referred to as the 'design guardians', for this task in a similar way to Bluewater. The design guardians first prepared vision guidelines and worked closely with the tenant teams to encourage the most appropriate designs for a particular location. This team then continued to coordinate the site work during the shop fit out. The attention to detail given to the public spaces extends throughout all the areas the public experiences from arrival to departure. Contemporary artists have integrated elements of art into the public realm, which range from tall stainless steel totems at the entrance square and a tactile bronze bull and coloured glass cubes incorporated into the water feature in the church piazza.

Of particular interest are the washroom areas which were individually designed by Amalgam, with the objective of providing luxury hotel standards. The facilities provided in the washroom areas have moved on from municipal standards to those of a swish hotel. The washroom areas are identified and celebrated by the use of tiled entrance murals, with entry encouraged by the removal of doors and corridors. The washroom interiors incorporate specially designed family rooms, photography-lined panelling behind urinals, individually designed cubicles, grooming areas with back illuminated mirrors, and other specially designed features normally only encountered in upmarket designer restaurants (see also Chapter 10).

The Bullring represents the largest city centre development then undertaken in Europe. Its size is, however, representative of the scale of retail-led regeneration projects currently being considered.

Figure 5.34 The dramatic and high quality of shopfront and fitting which typify the enclosed interior to The Bullring, Birmingham, UK. *(Source: Davi Deepres/Hammerson)*

Figure 5.35 Luxurious and easy to use toilet facilities, designed by Amalgam, typify ever improving customer facilities in contemporary shopping environments, The Bullring, Birmingham, UK. *(Source: Peter Coleman)*

The combination of the enclosed interiors and the early urban qualities are the outcome of a project completed in a time of transition. For example, the creative thinking and core values of the design were fixed before the establishment of the urban agenda.

In this respect, the Bullring represents a type of town centre development which would generally not be acceptable today. However, it is clear that the formative urban guidelines had a significant influence on the project, if not to the extent of changing its enclosed status.

The urban qualities that the scheme incorporates, and which would be considered acceptable qualities for current retail development, make an impressive list:

- the repair of the city fabric by the complete removal of the heroic 1960s mistakes of infrastructure and development
- the integration with the urban structure to connect the church and market with the city
- the connectivity and extension of the existing street network
- the formation of external streets and spaces which are integral to the layout of the centre
- the civic place making
- the integration with the railway modes of transport
- the introduction of a variety of architectural treatments by involving more than one architect.

The new Bullring is much more than the end of the line of the enclosed town centre mall. By incorporating the urban qualities listed above it has a foothold on the future generation of urban town centre shopping environments. The Bullring is a point of transition representing both the best of development that is no longer permissible and incorporating many urban qualities which are encouraged in current town centre retail development. The Bullring balances a representation of the past and a recognition of the shopping environments of the future. It is a hybrid with potentially the best of both worlds.

Galleria and Vertical Malls

The evolution of town centre shopping encompasses the development of the quality of the interior space. The demand for town centre malls and the constraint of available land in dense urban centres has resulted in radical solutions in order to accommodate them. With these new solutions a new format of shopping environment emerged.

Town centre malls, by their very location involve higher land values than the equivalent land on the perimeter of a town. Brownfield sites often have the added cost of needing to clear existing structures. Land assembly and site preparation costs are therefore greater in town centre locations. Consequently, any development on town centre land has to maximise land usage. This is likely to result in a greater density in order to compensate for the increased land value and development cost. This general economic principle applies to land for shopping centres as for any other use. The greater the density of development, the greater the rental income and capital value of the development. The density needs to be carefully balanced with the build cost and demand, and doesn't necessarily increase rental and capital value *ad infinitum*. This economic issue is discussed in greater detail in a later Chapter.

In the town centre mall examples of the Galleria, Houston and the Bullring, Birmingham, we have already seen the number of shopping levels increase from two to three, together with the inclusion of other commercial aspects in order to maximise development value. In cities with particularly high land values, it has been necessary for the town centre mall to increase the number of publicly

Figure 5.36 High quality finished multiple level shopping at The Shops at Columbus Circle, Colombus Circle, New York, USA (2004) SOM. *(Source: Adrian Price)*

accessible trading levels to four or more levels. In extreme examples the number of levels has been increased to as many as nine floors. Shopping facilities which adopt more than three floor levels are referred to as 'vertical malls'. Vertical malls first came into being in the mid-1970s and have since been developed in cities across the world such as New York, Chicago, San Francisco, Hong Kong, Singapore and Tokyo.

The joint venture between the development company, Urban Investment Development, and the retailer, Marshal Field, to build Water Tower Place, Chicago (1979) led to the formation of one of the first vertical shopping malls in America. Water Tower Place is a large high-rise mixed-use development designed by architects Loebl Schlossman and CF Murphy Associates. It comprises a 74 storey complex with 22 floors of hotel, 44 floors of luxury condominiums with offices, and shopping in the ten-level podium which forms the base of the tower. Architect Warren Platner Associates addressed the challenge of designing 67 750 m² (729 000 ft²) of retail space into the first eight floors of the podium element of the landmark building. The development acted as a catalyst for this part of North Michigan Avenue to attract top brand and famous retailers, transforming the street into a world-class shopping area.

Other vertical malls have subsequently been developed in North Michigan Avenue, reinforcing the area as a premier shopping destination and earning the title of the 'magnificent mile'. The surrounding district is one of the most affluent areas and sits parallel to the Lake Michigan shoreline among several of Chicago's landmark skyscrapers.

The arrangement of the shopping at Water Tower Place is a one-off solution which straightforwardly addresses the issue of getting the customers up among the shops. With the two department stores occupying the first two levels, the centre is arranged so that the first public space with shops begins two floors above street level. The entrance confidently addresses the need to attract customers and raise them upwards. It is a grand entrance concourse with escalators rising up through a cascading garden of plants and fountains. The entrance concourse emerges into a high quality atrium space which leads to the remaining six shopping levels.

Once inside the enclosed emporium there are over 100 small and medium sized shops and restaurants which are fitted in and around the two department stores. These two stores occupy half the accommodation and have been located on all the retail levels. The extent of the anchor stores illustrates the degree to which the unit shops have had to be shaped into the centre. With an entrance from each floor of the atrium, the department stores anchor all six levels of the atrium.

Figure 5.38 The six level Grand Atrium, Water Tower Place, Chicago, USA. *(Source: Index Stock Imagery/Ralph Krubner)*

Figure 5.37 Entrance space leading customers up to the shopping two levels above street level, Water Tower, Chicago, USA (1979). *(Source: Peter Coleman)*

The centre layout varies on each of the six retail floors, with the only constant being the central atrium and surrounding space, which is identified as the 'Grand Atrium'. From the Grand Atrium, single-level shopping arms radiate out from each floor. These shopping arms are dead ends, although some have floor openings forming secondary atriums which extend between two or three floor levels. The only means of vertical circulation is through the Grand Atrium, which has elevators and a bank of escalators connecting all the floor levels. The Grand Atrium also connects to the street level motor concourse which receives customers being dropped off by car or taxi. The motor concourse in turn connects to the below ground parking levels which provide 650 on site parking spaces. There is also direct access from the hotel into the shopping area. Separate street entrances provide individual access to the hotel, offices, condominiums and theatre.

Water Tower Place provides an interesting choice of eateries and catering which are arranged on the mezzanine floor, accessed from the Grand Atrium. This area has become a sought after destination in the retail area of the city. A wide choice of cosmopolitan food is available in a street market atmosphere which celebrates freshly cooked food and the social activity of eating.

The shopping environment at Water Tower Place is in an enclosed interior which is artificially lit and focused on the shops. The Grand Atrium and richly furnished interior alleviate it from being overly oppressive. To assist with this, the interior structure is minimal with cantilevered galleries encouraging views between the different floor levels. Tapered beams, which have been left exposed beneath a thin edged floor slab, structurally support the galleries. Above the floor, the galleries are edged by a glass balustrade with a polished chrome handrail to match the shaft of the elevators which rise through the atrium.

The architectural form of the podium is conceived as part of the high-rise building and is subservient to it by providing a controlled and ordered base to the tower. The podium element continues the simple form of the tower with a stone clad expression of the beam and column structural frame. Replacing the infill windows, which are used in the tower, with a polychromatic stone infill panel in the base of the building, the podium presents a generally unanimated edge to the streets. A double height colonnade to the base of the podium forms both a protected entrance space to the centre and department stores, as well as animating the pavement level with shop fronts.

Figure 5.39 The shops in the podium to the tower, Water Tower Place, Chicago, USA. *(Source: Peter Pearson/eStock Photo)*

The Eaton Centre, Toronto (1977–1979) is strictly not a vertical mall and would more accurately be categorised as a modern day arcade or galleria. By having more than three publicly accessible trading levels with a part fourth level (providing restaurants and space for artists and artisans), it is included in the category here with vertical malls. More importantly and overriding the academic criteria, the sheer magnificence of the multi-levelled urban space, with its public shopping galleries overlooking offices, restaurants and the Eaton's department store, make it worthy of inclusion here. Despite its age and its emulation by many subsequent centres, it is still deserving of Nadine Beddington's description as 'the doyen of urban shopping centres' (Beddington, 1981, p. 209).

The Eaton Centre is located in the prime area of downtown Toronto. The centre sits beside the financial district and civic quarter with government and city buildings, theatres and university buildings. The shopping element forms over two-thirds of a larger mixed-use development totalling 300 000 m² (3.2 million ft²) of retail, offices, parking and connections to public transport infrastructure. The project, instigated by the development company Cadilac Fairview, and designed by architects Zeidler Associates and Bregman and Hamann, in essence came about by the removal and rebuilding of the Eaton's department store to a location further up the street. This allowed the introduction of a new covered shopping route to be inserted between two of the world's largest department stores – Eaton's and Simpsons – each with nearly one million square feet of accommodation.

The Eaton Centre is one of the largest town centre shopping developments in Canada, with 145 000 m² (1 960 000 ft²) of retailing and catering space, (in addition to the Eaton's department store), and is arranged over three main trading levels with a part fourth level at the north end. The arrangement utilises the 5.5 m (19 ft) level change across the site to form two natural ground floor levels, each with its own street entrance. The third level is a basement which directly connects the two locations into the city subway network. Parking garages with 1650 car spaces are placed above the shopping accommodation and connect customers to the third and fourth levels. The layout ensures all floors have fundamentally strong pedestrian flows passing through, with specific reasons for people to use them.

The plan of the galleria is more than a simple north-south, gun-barrel dumb-bell between the two powerful anchor stores, with the layout responding

to the surrounding urban grain by introducing east-west cross routes. The routes have been generated by the extension of the existing street pattern beside the City Hall and a second extended linkage from the space around the historic church. These two pedestrian ways break down the large mass of the galleria and subdivide the plan into five separate blocks. Further orientation and identity is given to the galleria by each end having a different relationship with the department store. The Eaton's store closes the space and has direct access from all four levels of the galleria. Contrasting with this, the Simpsons end of the space is open, with a full-height glass façade resulting from the fact that the store is on the other side of the street. Entering Simpsons requires going outside and crossing the street at ground floor or using the direct connection from the upper-level bridge or the basement subway.

Although the glass vaulted roof gives the Eaton Centre a strong overriding identity, the centre also achieves the unique quality of diversity of spatial experience when using each of the different levels. Each level, for example, is distinctly different and not simply a stacked version of the preceding one so often found in gallerias. The arrival points to the cross routes are used to introduce asymmetry into the plan. The length of the mall is also treated in two halves, with the form alternating between being open to the roof or enclosed, and being narrow or wide.

The basement level is the most intimate of the levels with a largely artificially lit single storey space. The subterranean experience is punctuated by three large light wells, the central void facilitating a dramatic

Figure 5.40 The galleria interior looking towards the Eaton's store showing the three principal levels and the variety of the layout along its length, Eaton Centre, Toronto, Canada (1977–1979). *(Source: Zeidler/Grinnel)*

Figure 5.41 The basement level fountain projecting upwards through the space, Eaton Centre, Toronto, Canada. *(Source: Zeidler/Grinnel Partnership)*

water fountain which shoots into the levels above. Above the basement, the lower ground floor is a brighter and larger space which is divided into two halves. The southern length is narrow and enjoys the natural light and height of the vaulted roof. While the northern length is wider and formed into two galleries which overlook the basement shops, this length of mall passes beneath the floor of the level above and is a more contained space.

The two different characters at each end of the mall are further punctuated by major floor openings which allow views down to the basement. These openings occur where the entrances arrive from the side. The third level (upper ground floor) sits totally beneath the glazed roof with spacious views along its length. This floor is also divided into two lengths with the southern end formed from two galleries which overlook the floor below. The northern end differs by narrowing down and has a solid floor with the views being restricted upwards or lengthways. The escalators are located at the side entrances positioned at three points along the mall. The individuality that has been applied to different areas and different floors helps with orientation for the visitor and divides the large centre into a sequence of understandable experiences.

Figure 5.42 The galleria interior looking towards Simpsons and street entrance with offices overlooking the space, Eaton Centre, Toronto, Canada. *(Source: Zeidler/Grinnel Partnership)*

Although the individual areas of the Eaton Centre have been carefully scaled, it is the drama of the overall experience of the multi-levelled shopping space which leaves the lasting memory. This enclosed shopping centre has the vertical scale and visual interest comparable to the Galleria in Milan and transforms into being more like a covered urban street. The street-like qualities have been formed by the careful incorporation of a series of elements which come together to animate the space. The internal animation is formed by the combination of:

- the overlooking of the multi-level shopping walkways
- the variety of character to the pedestrian ways
- the suspended bridges which cross the space
- the balconies that activate the car park
- the various escalators that move people between levels
- the glazed elevators moving vertically in the space
- the exposed ventilation ducts
- the office building which passes through the space and overlooks it
- the water fountains
- the trees that grow in the middle of it
- being able to see people actively shopping in the space
- engaging with all these ingredients.

The opening of the first phase of the Eaton Centre in 1977, and its following phased completion in 1979, formed a new type of enclosed shopping environment. It is commercially successful, providing critical mass and the right retail mix in a downtown location. Despite its large size, it has been appropriately integrated into the urban context. This has been achieved by the incorporation of a mixture of uses and by utilising the office accommodation to form tower elements to vary the mass. Furthermore, the subdivision of the layout into individual blocks, generated by responding to the surrounding grain has assisted this fit. Although the centre is inward looking, care has been taken to activate the outside edges of the building with commercial uses and shops which animate the streets.

The planning of the centre has incorporated a variety of modes of transport access:
- accommodating pedestrians from the streets and protected underground network
- forming linkages with the metro from the subway and making provision for trams in the streets
- on site garages cater for customers arriving by car and service vehicles are integrated beneath the shopping centre.

Despite its age, the Eaton Centre, with its fully glazed galleria, which is 28 m (90 ft) high and 275 m

(890 ft) long, forms an exemplary urban shopping environment – a modern day arcade.

A European example of an enclosed shopping facility in a dense high volume city centre is Sevens, Düsseldorf (2001), designed by the architect Rhode, Kellermann, Wawrowsksy, (RKW). Sevens is a shopping environment housed in a contemporary galleria with seven daylit levels, and can also be categorised as a vertical mall. This urban shopping example forms a dramatic public space directly on to the

Figure 5.43 The dramatic general view on arrival from Konigsallee, with the seven level space opening up, Sevens, Düsseldorf, Germany (2001). *(Source: RKW/H G Esch)*

Konigsallee, which is the prime fashion pitch in the city. The Konigsallee is a single-sided promenading boulevard lined along its length with fashion emporiums, designer shops and shopping centres (see Figs. 5.50 and 5.51). Stepping off the promenade midway along the street, the customer arrives at the second level of the centre and is presented with a seven-level atrium space inviting entry inside. Looking upwards there are five curved gallery edges framed from the sickle-shaped atrium which leads to the glass elevators at the back. Looking down from the entry level with the cafés, restaurants and delicatessens arranged on the level below, it is like looking onto a giant laid up table.

The seven levels of the Sevens development are organised with the catering and retail food on level 1, with three floors of unit shop retailing occupying levels 2, 3 and 4, and the department store occupying the top three floors – levels 5, 6 and 7. An interesting quality of the Sevens shopping arrangement is the themed approach to shops on specific floors, similar to that used at the Bull Ring. For instance, the lower floors have different but related shops arranged into themes, such as 'designer', 'lifestyle', 'sport' and 'multimedia'. The department store shares the same atrium and glazed roof with the shops and is open to the atrium. Located beneath the lowest level of the atrium is a parking garage which is accessed by the main feature lifts. The atrium lifts extend down to the parking and are arranged in an extended shaft which allows atrium daylight to reach the garage levels. This is especially inviting when arriving by car, where the presence of daylight makes the atrium above immediately apparent.

The sickle-shaped atrium opening is formed from one straight side and one gentle curve which meet at a point facing the street entrance. The galleried levels generally repeat the sickle-shape opening all the way up the building. The similarly shaped roof light is a fully glazed mono pitch steel structure which extends across the void of the atrium and forms a prow up to the front edge of the building. Although the roof light allows the atrium to be largely naturally lit, the interior environment is tempered with mechanical venting, heating and cooling.

The seven level shaped atrium forms a unique urban space in the city and has become a place to see and to be seen – a theatre for shopping. Sevens has an animated interior which reveals itself on arrival from the street. The animated interior is on a smaller scale to that of the Eaton Centre, but is a contemporary equivalent of the exciting interiors presented in the French department stores of the 19th century, such as those of the Bon Marché. The animated

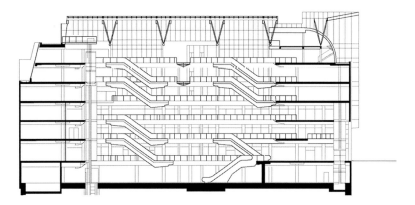

Figure 5.44 Section through the multi-level space, Sevens, Düsseldorf, Germany. *(Source: RKW)*

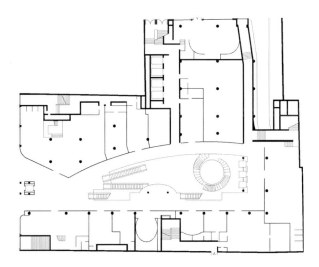

Figure 5.45 Level 2, ground floor plan, Sevens, Düsseldorf, Germany. *(Source: RKW)*

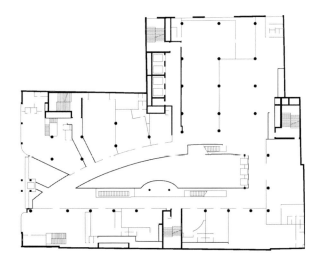

Figure 5.46 Level 3, Sevens, Düsseldorf, Germany. *(Source: RKW)*

Figure 5.47 The interior space looking up towards the roof light with the feature screen, Sevens, Düsseldorf, Germany. *(Source: RKW/H Esch)*

Figure 5.49 Overlooking the immacutely detailed café counter to the lower ground floor, Sevens, Düsseldorf, Germany. *(Source: RKW/H G Esch)*

Figure 5.48 The catering area on the mid-level lily pad with the stair wrapped around it, Sevens, Düsseldorf, Germany. *(Source: RKW/H G Esch)*

interior of Sevens is formed from the combination of these elements:

- the repeated layers of cantilevered galleries
- the finely detailed escalators hung from the galleries
- the glass lifts
- the video presentation in the blip-shaped sphere
- the elegant bridges at the topmost floors
- and, most importantly, all these elements are carefully combined to allow unhindered views across the space to the different shops and cafés.

The catering area, located on the lowest floor, allows food to be eaten on the premises or taken home. This area is a lesson in product design with each of the different restaurants, cafés, bars and shops individually designed and finely detailed. Recognition has been given to the importance of the view from above when designing the counters, seating and features. A circular, glass-floored landing positioned between the levels forms an intermediate lily-pad floor with café seating. A feature staircase wraps around the lily pad descending to the catering floor.

The drama and elegance of the Sevens interior is achieved by fine detailing, where all the parts of the animated inside combine carefully together. The most frequent element, the gallery edge, which is repeated on each floor, is made from a shaped metal nosing to form a precise boat-edged opening. Above the finely edged opening, a glass balustrade and metal handrail continue the minimal edge to the galleries. A blue cathode light on the gallery edge, together with continuous general up-lighting on to the shaped ceiling, emphasise the shaped atrium space. The simple effect of perspective allows the repeated gallery edge to add drama to the prow which points towards the entrance.

The prow form to the atrium and glazed atrium roof are effectively expressed on to the main street façade as a continuous prow above the entranceway. The full height glass prow forms a symbolic vertical marker to the stone façade facing the boulevard of Konigsallee. The marker signifies the existence of the atrium space located behind the street façade. The façade also has a three-storey, double curveshaped bay window which projects and recedes into the stone wall. In addition to the prow and bay

sculptural windows, there are other windows which activate the street façade, such as the double height, glazed shopfronts and glazed entrance which face onto the pavement. There are also window openings on both sides of the entrance to levels 4, 5 and 6. With all these different window elements, the Konigsalle façade is well animated with views into the different shops and the entranceway. The drama of the atrium space is concealed behind a stone lift shaft and the point of the glass prow; the real impact of the atrium space only revealing itself on entering the building.

The exterior and interior architecture achieve a high level of quality with great attention paid to detail and both using high quality materials. Although the exterior architecture responds to the function of the interior space, it has its own characteristics and responds to the street with an animated masonry building. This architectural treatment stops on entering inside which is treated as a separate piece of interior design. The interior finishes and details have a rather cool and hard-edged feel to them which is emphasised by the lighting. The interior environment is sophisticated, urban and represents its own space, which is a haven from the bustle of the street. The interior space is a piece of place making and has become a destination in the city.

The Konigsallee building is a landmark, conveying the brand in a significant street and inviting the inquisitive to explore further. The exterior form is a

Figure 5.50 The Konigsalle façade, Sevens, Düsseldorf, Germany. *(Source: RKW/H G Esch)*

Figure 5.51 The illuminated façade to Konigsalle, Sevens, Düsseldorf, Germany. *(Source: RKW/H G Esch)*

Figure 5.52 Seven levels of shopping at Zeil Gallery, Frankfurt, Germany. *(Source: Peter Coleman)*

neutral and well-mannered container. On the other hand, contrasting with the façade, the interior forms the drama, opens itself to full view and forms a new place in the city. The Sevens interior is a successful enclosed shopping environment.

Although it may not be urban inside, the overall form of development sits comfortably within this area of the city without dominating it. In respect of its fit and integration within the city, it can be considered an urban development. The density of this form of enclosed environment has made it containable within a part of a city block. It demonstrates that it is possible to form an enclosed shopping environment, provided it is of a suitable size and of sufficient density to be containable and not to dominate the city. When Sevens closes, the rest of the street and surrounding area continue to be accessible. It illustrates that the vertical mall shopping format is an appropriate urban form for retail development.

Sevens is a gem and a fine example of an enclosed shopping environment. It is also an exemplar urban shopping environment for consideration in other city locations.

Speciality Shopping

Shopping formats based on carefully tuning the tenant mix and combining catering to form retail facilities focused towards leisure activity and the attraction of tourists were identified in a previous Chapter (see Chapter 2: Festival retailing). Speciality shopping extends the qualities of the 19th century arcades and the principles established at Ghirardelli Square, to form specifically targeted collections of shops in unique environments which reinforce the character of the shops.

Speciality shopping proliferated in North America in the 1970s and crossed the Atlantic to emerge in Europe during the mid-1980s. John Milligan aptly described speciality shopping as '...the concentration of fun shopping in identifiable centres' (Milligan, 1986).

As it emerged, speciality shopping developed beyond shopping limited to a wealthy elite to attract a wider audience of customers with greater disposable income and a disposition to express their identity with stylish branded goods. The demographic change, together with a groundswell of public opinion for more individualistic shopping facilities, opened the door for shopping formats which were unique from the standard shopping centre. The wish for greater individuality and the charm of the bazaar led to early exemplar developments in the USA and Europe, with Faneuil Hall, Boston (1976) and Covent Garden, London (1980).

Figure 5.53 Early example of speciality shopping, Faneuil Hall, Boston, USA (1976). *(Source: Peter Coleman)*

Figure 5.54 Early speciality shopping Covent Garden, London, UK (1980). *(Source: David Barbour)*

Retailers responded to the demographic change of customers having greater disposable incomes by providing stores with more specifically focused merchandising and concentrated narrow ranges of goods. Recognising the opportunity and seeing customers with less time to search out the goods, landlords collected together suitable retailers to form the speciality centres.

A fundamental quality of speciality shopping centres is to offer a range of merchandise and level of service not available in a conventional centre. They are more than a collection of speciality retailers where the character of the shopping environment is required to reflect the nature of the shops. The whole place will have a coherent quality where each element and component will be selected to contribute to the character of the place. A speciality centre needs to be able to draw crowds for pleasure and recreation as well as to buy.

In view of the significance of the character of the shopping environment in speciality centres, design is a fundamental component in determining the nature of the place. Contemporary designs need to form a unique quality in order to establish a sense of place. The character of place can be assisted by the appropriate use of location, especially if this can be exploited, such as a waterside. Successful examples of waterside locations combining with contemporary buildings can be seen at Harbor Place, Baltimore, Maryland and South Street Seaport, New York. The reuse of historic or disused industrial buildings can lend itself to readily establishing a unique character. The Faneuil Hall and Covent Garden examples along with Jacksons' Brewery, New Orleans and Princes Square, Glasgow, illustrate the success of working with the character of existing buildings. More than with other retail formats, the environment of speciality shopping centres needs to form a showcase for the retailers which reinforces the merchandising.

Figure 5.55 Contemporary buildings provide shopping facilities beside the waterside, The Gallery at Harbor Place, Baltimore, Maryland, USA (1987). *(Source: Zeidler Partnership)*

Figure 5.56 Open streets and converted buildings at South Street Seaport, New York, USA. *(Source: Peter Coleman)*

Another characteristic of speciality centres is that they tend to be smaller than conventional comparison shopping formats. The typical size of a speciality centre ranges from 5580 to 11 150 m² (60 000–120 000 ft²). The retailers who occupy these centres also tend to require smaller premises which range from 50 to 150 m² (500–1 600 ft²). It is important to note that generally there are only a limited number of individual retailers, which restricts the opportunities for speciality shopping centres. This is especially the case in the UK, despite the number of multiple retailers who are diversifying into specialist markets. Speciality shopping centres tend to suit the following catchment areas:

- a high concentration of upper income
- a concentration of a particular demographic group
- a large daytime working population
- the availability of tourists.

The layout of speciality shopping centres tends to be simple and easy for the visitor to understand. The physical size of the public spaces can generally be more intimate. There is, however, still the requirement to provide a large space which can accommodate large social gatherings and to act as a focus for the centre. These focal spaces can be external to the buildings and part of the public realm, as demonstrated by the square in front of St Paul's Church, Covent Garden, London.

Mention has been made of the importance of the design to the success of speciality centres. This extends to all aspects and components of the building, both interior and exterior public realm. Coordination of all the elements will be required in order to reinforce the cohesive quality of the place. This will involve the careful design of the lighting, signage, shopfronts and furniture.

Although there are few recent UK examples of speciality shopping centres, a well executed recent example can be seen in the Royal Exchange, City of London (2004). Speciality shopping has been introduced to the ground floor interior of the building, returning the space for public use during the day and evening time.

The Royal Exchange forms 1450 m² (15 600 ft²) of luxury retail space in the former courtyard of the

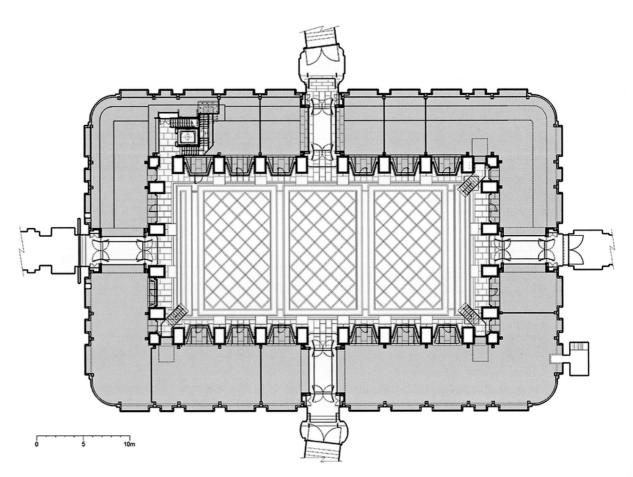

Figure 5.57 Ground floor plan of shops inserted into the ambulatory, Royal Exchange, London, UK (2004). *(Source: Fitzroy Robinson)*

London International Finance Futures Exchange (LIFFE). The Grade I Listed building originates from 1844 and was renovated and extended. A new glazed and panelled roof was introduced in 1991 enclosing the courtyard. The architects, Fitzroy Robinson, extended their involvement with the building by removing the temporary LIFFE enclosure, which occupied the courtyard space, to convert the space to form speciality retailing facilities.

Elegant retail units are set within the fabric of the existing ambulatory to face the covered courtyard space. The new shops occupy the four quadrants of the ambulatory, which is separated by the four main street entrances, and provide space for high

Figure 5.58 The covered interior of the trading floor with shops added into the ambulatory and central café, Royal Exchange, London, UK. *(Source: Fitzroy Robinson/Peter Cook)*

value retailers such as jewellers and designer fashion shops. The courtyard shops add to the original street-facing shops to complete the mixed-use building, which has offices above. The courtyard floor has been repaved with marble tiles to provide access to the shops and café space. A central servery with loose fitting tables and chairs occupies the centre of the space.

New steel and glass stairs have been inserted into each corner of the Royal Exchange courtyard to provide access to a mezzanine level above the shops. The mezzanine forms a continuous circuit, which provides an upper floor to some of the shops and restaurant space overlooking the long sides of the courtyard. The mezzanine floor floats between the columns of the colonnade and is set back from the

Figure 5.59 Restaurant on the mezzanine level with retained frescoes on the left, Royal Exchange, London, UK. *(Source: Fitzroy Robinson/Peter Cook)*

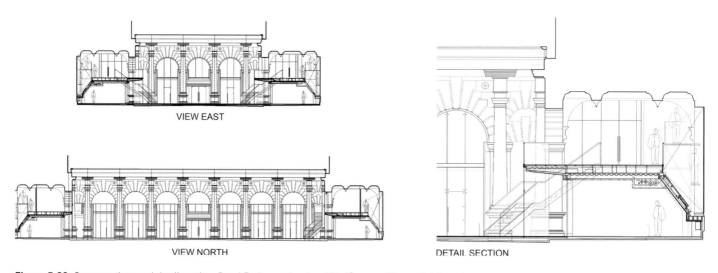

VIEW EAST

VIEW NORTH

DETAIL SECTION

Figure 5.60 Cross sections and detail section, Royal Exchange, London, UK. *(Source: Fitzroy Robinson)*

rear wall to reveal the original fresco paintings. The ground floor shops are contained by the careful raking back of the rear enclosure to a point beneath the paintings.

The steel and glass shopfronts are inserted between the historic columns with a series of 'pop outs' which maximise visibility to the shops, while accommodating the wishes of the conservationists. The minimal quality of the shop enclosures sublimate their presence, allowing the grand proportions of the courtyard to dominate. The lightness of the shopfronts also allows good visibility to the high quality shop merchandise and contact with the diners on the mezzanine.

The Royal Exchange retailing is aimed at the large daytime working population of the City of London, which also has a high proportion of upper income workers suited to speciality shopping. It is a sensitive and elegant contemporary example of introducing retail and catering facilities to give new life to an historic building and in so doing, has returned a covered space back to the public.

Figure 5.61 Glass and steel shopfronts set between the columns of the colonnade, Royal Exchange, London, UK. *(Source: Fitzroy Robinson/Peter Cook)*

The First Generation of Urban Shopping Centres

The examples reviewed here illustrate a generation of shopping centres developed in the mid-to late 1980s, which responded to the prevalent opinion opposed to the proliferation of uniform, interior design-based, enclosed centres. The reactionary examples shown here have the following design characteristics in common with the current generation of urban projects: design with a more individual response to the locality; a more architectural or urban character; providing a more natural internal environment; questioning the enclosure of the public space; and return to open-air environments.

It is important to note that these urban examples were adopted when the opportunity still remained to choose between enclosing, covering or leaving the space open. Here they are reviewed separately from the subsequent generation of shopping facilities which are now required by planning guidance to provide more urban public spaces. The shopping environments prepared under the contemporary directive for urban shopping are reviewed in the final part of this Chapter.

It took an enlightened developer, the Hahn Company, and Californian architect John Jerde, to change the tide of 30 years of shopping centre development which had been driven by function and convenience. The ground breaking Horton Plaza, San Diego (1985), inspired by Italian hill towns, was the product of this pairing which came together to form a shopping environment from the design of a piece of urban city fabric. This project redefined the rule-book of retail design in more ways than one. Horton Plaza challenged the precept of centres having to be enclosed and fitting into a single building. It also focused on the importance given to the consideration of the total shopping experience – viewing customers as citizens as well as consumers. Furthermore, it made good use of the local climate and indigenous architecture to confidently form an open-air environment bespoke to San Diego. The obvious simplicity of these ideas rejuvenated the career of John Jerde who, from this initial work, has gone on to become one of the world's leading retail architects.

Horton Plaza is located in an historic district of San Diego which, prior to the development, had declined to become a disreputable area, with both the resident population and shopping accommodation migrating

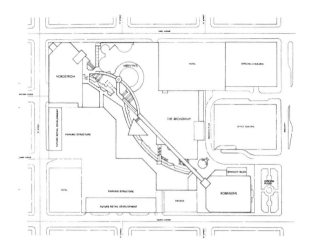

Figure 5.62 An early urban design led example with open multi-level streets, individual buildings and integration with the grid of city blocks, Horton Plaza, San Diego, California, USA (1985). *(Source: Jerde)*

to the suburbs of the city. Ernest Hahn recognised the opportunity and purchased the six block site between the historic district and the waterfront. Hahn and Jerde regenerated a new quarter in the city to form a 140 000 m² (1.5 million ft²) mixed-use development with retail, restaurants, cinemas, offices, hotel and a theatre. The new quarter has become a catalyst for the regeneration of the surrounding districts with private housing, employment, a convention centre, a light railway system and waterfront development all being developed since the opening of Horton Plaza.

From the outset, the design approach to Horton Plaza acknowledged that the layout would be based on a series of individually expressed buildings which

would come together to form a piece of urban fabric and a new district, thus forming a piece of city within the city. Such a concept involved the formation of an open-air shopping environment with a variety of shaded and covered walkways.

With the urban principles in place, the actual layout is formed by covering the site between the main streets with buildings and then cutting a diagonal route from one corner to another. The diagonal forms the route from the downtown to the waterfront district. The diagonal runs from the main entrance on Broadway across to two of the department stores in the opposite corner. There are also other department stores ranged along the street.

The simple diagonal is developed into an elaborate armature along which all the architectural elements are arranged. One of the layers of elaboration added to the street is the double curve and terracing which forms a varied multi-level route. The experience of passing along the street then alternates between narrow and wide as well as covered and open. The widening is formed on one side by the introduction of a curve at each end of the street. The curves are arranged to alternate on different sides of the street with an overlap in the centre. Layered on to the plan are a series of architectural insertions: a triangular tower, stairways, view arches, bridges and arcades, which form local incidence and identity. The street presents a series of animated views, inviting exploration and movement from one area to another.

Even with the series of architectural events arranged along the street, the journey through the new district can earnestly be completed while remaining in the terraced street. Alternatively, taken at a more leisurely pace, the journey can involve engaging with one of the insertions or buildings *en route,* which encourages a diversion and a rejoining of the street further on.

The shops are generally laid out on three levels with open or colonnaded galleries passing above the street at first and second floor levels. Bridges cross the street connecting the buildings at selected positions and encouraging the journey through the neighbourhood at a variety of levels.

The individual design of the six building blocks has brought variety and spontaneity to the district. The six individual buildings, along with the various architectural insertions to the street, create a visually rich and elaborate environment. It is hard to find one view of Horton Plaza that represents the whole complex. The lasting impression is the richness of the place, formed from a collage of images representing the variety of architecture and spaces.

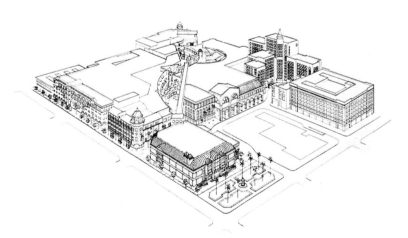

Figure 5.63 The three level armature forms the public space through the city blocks, Horton Plaza, San Diego, California, USA. *(Source: Jerde)*

The architectural language is based on a re-interpretation of that found elsewhere in the city. The individual language of each building is relatively straightforward, with painted stucco being commonly used in a variety of different colours. The triangular tower is finished in contrasting bands of stone which emphasises the insertion made in the street and the point of focus. The individual response made to the local architecture, together with the open street environment, suits the local climate and makes Horton Plaza a bespoke and appropriate solution for San Diego.

The diagonal armature of Horton Plaza weaves together the individual architecture and the various incidents to form a complex sequence of spaces and makes a stunning journey through the district. This street, as well as connecting the historic downtown with the waterfront, has become a place in its own right in the city. The diagonal armature originating as a framework for the architectural elements has also become a framework for the public life of the city.

Horton Plaza is a ground breaking and seminal shopping environment. Even if the architectural treatment is questionable (and this is a subjective issue), there are still many innovative qualities to this centre which have a relevance to contemporary issues. The consideration of providing an experience and assuming the visitor to be a citizen are factors to consider in the design of centres today. Also relevant is the big issue of creating shopping environments as a piece of the city or urban quarter, which Horton Plaza addressed 30 years ago and which is one of the biggest challenges facing designers today. John Jerde must be congratulated for getting to grips with this issue as long ago as 1975 when the concept began.

While Horton Plaza is an example of a new piece of city formed into an urban shopping environment, the next example examines the reuse and the conversion of existing buildings and spaces to provide a ready urban format. Covent Garden, London was mentioned earlier to illustrate the reuse of the former market buildings as a speciality retail format (sometimes referred to as festival retailing), but it could equally have been reviewed here representing an early type of urban shopping centre. Some other examples of reusing existing buildings as an urban shopping facility are reviewed here.

Princes Square, Glasgow (1987), developed by Guardian Royal Exchange with Teesland Development and designed by architect Hugh Martin and Partners, shows how the covering of a courtyard and the conversion of a group of existing 19th century Victorian buildings can become an urban

Figure 5.64 Polychromatic marble clad individual building, Horton Plaza, San Diego, California, USA. *(Source: Peter Coleman)*

Figure 5.65 A variety of architecture on either side of the street, Horton Plaza, San Diego, California, USA. *(Source: Stephen Simpson/Jerde)*

Figure 5.66 The covered courtyard space with the retained façade and gallery insertions, Princes Square, Glasgow, UK (1987). *(Source: Peter Coleman)*

Figure 5.67 The supporting roof structure and topmost catering level, Princes Square, Glasgow, UK. *(Source: Peter Coleman)*

shopping facility. The original merchant buildings front on to the pedestrianised Buchanan Street, which is the prime retail area of the city. The conversion of these buildings and the roofing over of the courtyard provides 7000 m² (75 000 ft²) of leasable retail space with 68 small to medium sized shop units arranged in four galleried levels fitted into the courtyard. Three levels are primarily used for shops with the fourth and top level providing catering, cafés and restaurants. Seating around the gallery edges overlooks the atrium space and makes use of the additional height at this level.

Entry into Princes Square is from Buchanan Street and made through three entranceways which pass through the retained and restored existing buildings. Two of the entrances lead directly to the second level with the third, central entrance, taking visitors direct to the top floor of the atrium via a double length escalator. This entry arrangement has been made to distribute footfall to the topmost floor and to ensure all the floors are circulated and equally used.

On entering into the covered courtyard from street level, the visitor is presented with an animated space. With escalators immediately beside, the view overlooks the patterned floor of the level below, across the space to the feature stairway and lifts, and upwards through the atrium to the two gallery levels above. The enclosed space has been formed from the reuse of the 19th century textile merchants' courtyard. The four-storey sandstone façades have been retained with the space behind them on three sides being rebuilt to provide modern retail accommodation. The lower level has been formed by the excavation and lowering of the courtyard floor. The enlarged volume has then been covered by a glazed roof on a decorative steel structure. In addition to the formation of new shopping facilities, the enclosed space uses its lowest floor for events, promotions and functions and has become a recognisable place in the city.

The interior additions to the urban space are exuberant and finely detailed. The retained sandstone walls form a neutral backdrop to the overtly rich insertions. There are four principal components to these additions which have been layered onto the existing buildings: the supporting steel structure to the new galleries and enclosing roof; the elements of vertical movement; the gallery floor and edges; and finally, the fittings and lighting.

An elegant expressed tubular steel structure, with trefoil columns, rises through the space, supporting each of the gallery floors and the enclosing glass roof. The columns are continuous with the roof structure and branch out at the top to cross the space and brace back to the façades. The major roof steels are gently arched across the space and fully arched between the columns and the façades. A simple secondary framework supports the glass roof from the arched roof.

The four public levels are well connected by the generous provision of different means of vertical circulation; a La Scala-shaped feature staircase with intermediate landings connects the lower three shopping levels, a separate bank of up and down escalators on the opposite side connects all levels, as well as two brass and glass feature lifts. All these elements are arranged around the gallery edges and, like Düsseldorf's Sevens, animate the space.

elaborate as the floors move up the building. The lowest balustrades are a combination of simple glass panels supported by wrought ironwork. By the fourth level, the balustrades are solely made from decorative wrought ironwork in an organic pattern. An oak handrail tops the balustrading on all floors, following the curvaceous layout of the galleries and flowing down the staircase. The floors to the galleries are finished with tiles laid to a pattern.

The final layers of insertion involved with the conversion of the courtyard are the fittings and lighting. The light fittings to Princes Square have been treated as a decorative feature and add to the visual richness of the space. Decorative lights formed from glass spheres are supported on wrought iron brackets fixed around the gallery edges. Similar feature lights on iron columns form standard lights on the landings to the stairs. Additional special effect lighting is contained in metal cages hung from the roof. To simplify the roof structure, ornate metal infill panels are placed above the shorter building parapets to allow the roof to spring from a constant height.

The crafted metalwork theme is continued externally on to the street façade where a magnificent

Figure 5.68 The La Scala staircase and limed oak linings, Princes Square, Glasgow, UK. *(Source: Peter Coleman)*

Contrasting with the white vertical structure, the horizontal elements are all finished in a limed oak which complements the sandstone courtyard walls. The three gallery edges and escalator sides are clad with continuous moulded oak panelling which reduces the apparent thickness of the floors. For consistency, the feature stair strings and landing are also finished in oak. The galleries are also edged by balustrading which progressively becomes more

Figure 5.69 The Buchanan Street entrance canopy and peacock metalwork, Princes Square, Glasgow, UK. *(Source: Peter Coleman)*

peacock sits on the stone parapet over the central entrance. A curvaceous glazed canopy, which is hung from the stonework with metal brackets, has been applied to the existing façade to mark the entrance. Similar metalwork motifs adorn the smaller canopies above the other two street entrances.

Princes Square was one of the first generation of urban shopping environments in the UK that addressed the public's antipathy towards enclosed internalised shopping centres. It has transformed a courtyard, once used by local textile merchants, into an enclosed space occupied by national and international retailers trading their wares and giving new life to the existing buildings. Despite the length of time since completion and its coverage in Nadine Beddington's original book, it remains a popular and successful centre.

Figure 5.70 Axonometric of the new glass roof inserted over Queen Victoria Street, Leeds, UK. *(Source: Ian Latham)*

When analysing the quality of the enclosed space, the effect may have been slightly compromised by the approach taken towards the application of interior design elements. The original stone buildings are almost lost in the different insertions applied in converting the space and only become recognisable at the topmost level. Although the interior space is visually rich and vibrant, it would have benefited from more restraint and control. While each of the interior elements is acceptable on its own, the combination of so many expressive elements detracts from the space formed by the original buildings and the shops themselves. However, despite this critical observation, the spirit of the converted external space manages to override the excesses of the enclosed interior.

Princes Square is a covered urban shopping environment which is accessed from the prime shopping street in the city. Its scale and form are exemplary and relevant to the current urban agenda, which is encouraging the adoption and creation of urban forms of shopping development.

By the end of the 1980s, Leeds had its fair share of enclosed internalised shopping environments. In response to the public antipathy towards uniform shopping malls, the property owner, Prudential, and architect Ian Latham decided to form a more natural shopping environment from an existing turn-of-the-century arcade and an adjacent parallel street. The Victoria Quarter, Leeds (1990) is another example of taking existing buildings and transforming them into a contemporary urban shopping environment.

A common quality of the Victoria Quarter and Princes Square, Glasgow is the glazing over of an existing space between buildings to form a protected and naturally lit place for shopping. Princes Square is the more radical concept by its creation of four galleried levels of shopping facilities where there were none before. In contrast, the Victoria Quarter less ambitiously rejuvenates a single level to form some 90 shops in a combination of sensitive refurbishment and creative additions. The covered street makes a step-change to the shopping environment, forming a new quarter with its own identity. The Leeds example is also a more coherent design with more complementary qualities between the insertions and existing fabric. The Victoria Quarter demonstrates greater integration with the surrounding fabric of the city and a model example, through its use of existing urban streets, for other contemporary natural shopping environments.

The Victoria Quarter is located on the eastern side of the city and sits between the traditional office district and the market neighbourhood. It is part of a network of city streets and is contained between two main streets, Briggate and Vicar Lane. Briggate leads to the principal shopping areas and is a prime shopping street.

The Victoria Quarter was formed from the refurbishment of the County Arcade and the covering over of the adjacent parallel Queen Victoria Street, with the recognition that the refurbishment of the County Arcade would not be sufficient in itself to form a quarter and that it would be necessary to combine another street to form a sense of place. Cross Arcade, another arcade perpendicular to the two covered ways, connects them and leads to an entrance on a third parallel open street. The combination of surrounding streets, arcades and covered streets forms a network of shopping spaces.

Figure 5.71 The restored County Arcade, The Victoria Quarter, Leeds, UK (1990). *(Source: Ian Latham)*

The Victoria Quarter benefits from the richly decorated Victorian architecture of the buildings that line the streets and form the arcades. The three and four-storey buildings are ornate, red brick façades decorated with terracotta. The arcades are typically two storey with decorative féance façades above the projecting shopfronts. The network of routes is contained between two to four storey buildings with the shops trading on the ground and first floor and using the basement and upper floors for storage.

The combination of the strong architectural identity and the encouragement of a series of pedestrian circuits has helped to make the Victoria Quarter a destination rather than just a route through to the main streets. The identity has been formed by focusing on smaller speciality shops, with high fashion and branded retailers. The subsequent opening of a new Harvey Nichols store facing on to Briggate and Queen Victoria Street has further endorsed this upmarket identity. This store also connects directly into the covered street and has complemented the smaller shops, influencing the claim that the quarter is becoming 'the Knightsbridge of the north'.

The shopping facilities in the Victoria Quarter are formed in the two principal covered spaces. The County Arcade was formed from the careful restoration of the Frank Matcham design, using photographs and original drawings. The refurbishment required the removal of unsympathetic alterations – aluminium shopfronts, plastic fascias, signs, light fittings and reforming the ordered decorative interior. The restoration involved refitting the mahogany shopfronts and the pilaster surrounds, renewing the floor with terrazzo and mosaic patterns, installing new light fittings and redecorating the interior with authentic colours. The féance decoration to the walls and the windows above the shops were repaired to animate the upper floor of the arcade. The arched roof was repaired and reglazed with clear glass, allowing the space to be naturally lit.

The second covered space was formed by pedestrianising Queen Victoria Street and covering over the three-storey brick and terracotta buildings with a new glass roof, supported on an independent steel structure inserted into the street. The steel structure is formed from four steel tubes welded together to make up the columns, supporting lattice steel trusses which, in turn, support a simple pitched glazed roof. The inserted column structure forms a nave with side aisles in the street, where the aisles pass in front of the shops on either side. The central nave is used for activity and enjoyment, with seating, planting, tables and chairs for use by the restaurant. The new glass roof is made of three lengths with two-storey high spaces at the entranceways on to the streets and the central portion raised to form a three-storey space. The taller roof has a continuous raised central portion with vertical clerestories. The vertical elements of the roof are used for louvres and ventilation of the space. The taller portion of roof oversails the existing façades, while

Figure 5.72 The new steel and glass roof insertion to Queen Victoria Street, Leeds, UK. *(Source: Peter Coleman)*

the two entrance portions are contained within the brick façades of the buildings.

The character of the street comes from the Victorian brick and terracotta decorated façades which have been cleaned. The shopfronts and signage have been replaced in hardwood to match those in the arcade. The first floor is animated by the double height, ground floor window order which continues above the shopfronts and allows these windows to be dressed as part of the shop. This achieves a contemporary effect, with the appearance of a double height shopfront. Complementing the articulated existing architecture is a stained glass roof created by the artist Brian Clark.

The glass artwork is an integral part of the glass enclosure and runs the length of the central portion of the roof, to form one of the largest secular commissioned coloured glass windows in the world. The vivid colours of blue, green and orange in the roof complement the ornate red brick and

terracotta façades and give Queen Victoria Street a unique character which is distinct from the County Arcade. The floor finishes in the arcade and street are unified by the use of a matching terrazzo.

In addition to the sumptuous architecture, the identity of the quarter has also been reinforced by the commissioning of craftwork for functional items such as seats, litter bins, light fittings and gates which contribute to the character of the space. These works are both sympathetic and contemporary and remain within the ornate ethos of the Matcham architecture.

The Victorian Quarter is a destination with its own identity in the city. The identity has been formed by the focus on upmarket fashion retailing and the complementary nature of the rich architecture. Here, the total result is certainly greater than the sum of the individual parts. The regeneration of the quarter has had a ripple effect on the surrounding streets which have also been subsequently rejuvenated. The network of streets which make up the quarter is well integrated with the surrounding streets and is an integral and distinctive part of the rejuvenated city centre of Leeds.

New Urban Quarters

This format of shopping represents the trend towards new urbanism. They are located in town centres and adopt urban design principles rather than being monolithic, stand-alone buildings. New urban quarters are planned shopping environments, formed from making pieces of the town centre and involve open or covered streets which are integrated with the surrounding urban context. They have invisible thresholds and are unlikely to have doorways.

New urban quarters address the planning requirements for sustainable development that are now applicable to most European cities. These principles are also universally appropriate to the regeneration of downtown areas elsewhere. The format addresses the public requirement for providing more individual and unique shopping facilities.

New urban quarters are frequently regeneration-led, involving mixed-use development which is economically driven by the requirements for retail growth and expansion. (Retail entertainment centres, which are similarly, but equally driven, by the three elements of leisure, catering and retail requirements, are reviewed separately further on.)

Following closely from the first generation of urban shopping (which addressed the public antipathy towards uniform enclosed shopping centres), the new urban quarters are a post-mid-1990s phenomenon. This coincided with European planning guidance requiring more sustainable development and is likely to remain a relevant shopping format for the foreseeable future. Although there are some good American examples, namely Pentagon Row, Washington (2001) developed by Federal Realty and designed by RTKL, the format is illustrated here by a lineage of European projects. The following examples illustrate both built projects and some of the more challenging examples in the pipeline.

Figure 5.73 Mixed use urban development with city living above the shops, Pentagon Row, Washington DC, USA (2001). *(Source: RTKL)*

Rotterdam

An earlier reference was made to the city of Rotterdam for its seminal pedestrianised precinct, the Lijnbaan, built in 1951. After some 40 years, and following decentralisation to the suburbs, the city found its precincts and heroic roadways in the city centre an unsatisfactory urban environment. The city was determined to rectify its simplistic post-war rebuilding and infrastructure, in order to create a more cohesive city centre. Working with Dutch developer, Multi Development Corporation (MDC now AM), they instigated a retail-led mixed-use regeneration project. Their approach represented a radical departure from the enclosed monolithic shopping centre by adopting urban design principles to form a piece of city into an open-air type of shopping environment. The Beursplein, Rotterdam (1996) development is one of the first European examples to apply the principles of new urbanism to create a shopping facility.

MDC invited architect Jerde Partnership International (JPI – renowned for its use of urban forms to make shopping environments and Horton Plaza illustrated above) to join local architects T+T Design and De Architecturen Cie to design the 60 000 m² (650 000 ft²) mixed-use development in the centre of Rotterdam for 95 shops, 112 residential apartments, 450 car parking spaces, the expansion of the Beurs metro station and the formation of the public realm to unite the city centre.

The challenge of the Beursplein was the question of how to use its pivotal position to reconnect the Lijnbaan precinct and Hoogstraat markets, which had been separated by the major traffic through road – the Coolsingel. This pivotal neighbourhood also contained several department stores, major banks and the city hall, which had become fragmented insular buildings sitting on either side of the Coolsingel. The simple solution forms two largely pedestrianised open plazas, connected by a subterranean open street which passes beneath the separating roadway to form a 300 m (975 ft) long promenade. The public realm of the promenade connects the Lijnbaan and Hoogstraat districts, effectively extending the city centre into one large, pedestrian-friendly environment.

The promenade adopts the form of the double curve (seen before at Horton Plaza). It is separated by a circular concourse below the roadway which, in turn, leads to the Beurs metro station entrance. Footfall to the district is ensured by its central position and the 70 000 daily passengers passing through the metro station.

The plaza forms a two-level public space, with shops on each side of the promenade (lower ground floor level) and a mixture of shops, department stores, banks and the city hall aligning the plaza at grade level (upper ground floor level) above. The promenade shops sit beneath the paved surface of the plaza, with the plaza shop units above forming the ground floor of the various surrounding buildings. The curve on one side of the street forms a natural amphitheatre of shopping and allows the majority of shops to be visible from the ends of the street. The promenade is accessed from its two ends primarily by sloping ramps and steps, which maintain continuity with the adjacent spaces and keep an urban quality between the levels. There are additional escalators and lifts located towards the centre, on one side of the plaza, which are carefully treated as glass and steel insertions. Another insertion into the plaza space is a cantilevered steel structure which supports a glass canopy above the two alternating curved sides of the street. The canopy sits above the plaza level and offers a degree of protection to both levels of the street.

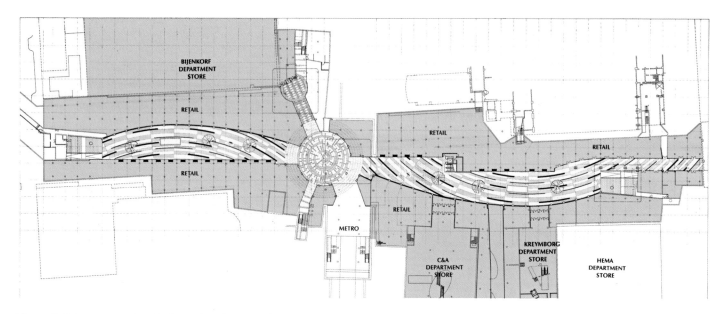

Figure 5.74 Lower street plan, The Beursplein, Rotterdam, The Netherlands (1996). *(Source: Jerde)*

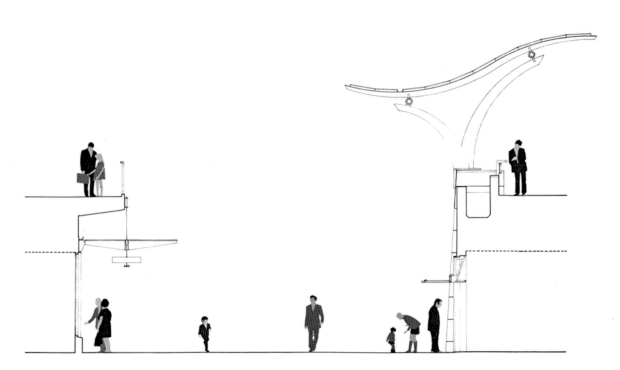

Figure 5.75 Section through the two level street and canopy, The Beursplein, Rotterdam, The Netherlands. *(Source: Jerde)*

Figure 5.76 The open two level plaza with the protective glass and steel canopy, Beursplein, Rotterdam, The Netherlands. *(Source: AM Development/Tom de Rooij Fotografie)*

In addition to the open street shopping, a separate new enclosed shopping area is provided on the Hoogstraat side of the Beursplein, which connects across the block to a parallel street. The enclosed area contains three levels of shops with two public levels. The first of the publicly accessible levels is entered directly from the plaza, with escalators leading up to the first floor. The lower level is accessed through the shops which face on to the promenade level. The covered space, which passes through the block, is characterised by a hull-shaped timber structure which sits dramatically above the public route.

In the open promenade, the two sides of the street are treated individually. The curved side of the street is formed from stone with the shops

Figure 5.77 The escalator and glass lift insertions treated as separate elements within the street, The Beursplein, Rotterdam, The Netherlands. *(Source: Peter Coleman)*

Figure 5.78 The Hoogstraat enclosed shopping element formed within the block to one side, Beursplein, Rotterdam, The Netherlands. *(Source: Peter Coleman)*

Figure 5.79 The curved side of the street is individually treated in stone, The Beursplein, Rotterdam, The Netherlands. *(Source: Peter Coleman)*

Figure 5.80 Unifying canopy connecting the two sides of the street, Beursplein, Rotterdam, The Netherlands. *(Source: AM Development/Avec Fotografie)*

inserted between projecting buttresses. The straight side of the street contrasts with the robustness of the stone, the shops set between simple metal and glass surrounds. Each side of the street responds to the history of the city – the stone relating to the former protective walls of the historic city, and the steel and glass on the straight side reflecting the linear nature of the rebuilt post-war era.

The promenade is treated as an external space, using good quality natural materials and is paved with a radial patterned limestone to form a generous street of varying width. The space is animated on each side of the Coolsingel by plane trees and a programmed water fountain which projects controlled amounts of water through flush metal grills in the paving, to delight children and adults alike. On the Lijnbaan side trams successfully share the paved surface of the upper level plaza with pedestrians, and provide additional public access to the area. Also on the Lijnbaan side of the plaza, a café enclosure sits beneath the canopy and overlooks the passing public on the promenade.

The Beursplein has been a catalyst for further urban repair, with one of the department stores completing a full upgrade and refurbishment. The Vroom and Deesmaan store, which anchors the eastern end of the district, connects directly to both the promenade and plaza levels of the public space. The store has a new entrance façade and created a circular feature roof facing onto the plaza. The food hall and eateries are located on the top floor of the store, with dining areas and terraces overlooking the public spaces of the Beursplein.

The architecture of the Beursplein is characterised by the high quality of the public realm and the area's integration within the surrounding city rather than by any particular building. If there is one identifiable form to the new quarter, it is the double-curved, glazed canopy which extends along both sides of the thoroughfare and unifies the two parts.

The Beursplein forms an urban framework for individual buildings, bringing together the Marcel Breuer-designed Bijenkorf store, the Vroom and Dreesmaan store, the Beursplein Mall, the city hall and the new C & A store. It engages the once isolated buildings, allowing them to define and relate to the public spaces. The Beursplein successfully unites the separated districts into a unified city centre. The new quarter sensitively repairs the fragmented districts and urban fabric of the city and realistically connects two separate areas, while retaining key infrastructure and access to the city centre. Rotterdam once again has a sustainable city centre with an integral and vital core, which provides a place to live, work, relax and shop.

Nijmegen

In a smaller Dutch city, Marienburg, Nijmegen (2000), another new urban quarter can be found. This joint venture development by ING Real Estate and Nijmegen Town Council was masterplanned by the architect Sjoerd Soeters. The Marienburg urban quarter, like the Beursplein, is another example of a city having to right post-war reconstruction which left the city with little urban cohesion and focused on providing for the motor car with oversized roads. Marienburg returns the central area for the priority use of pedestrians and re-establishes vitality by the reintroduction of a variety of activities in the city centre. It also addresses the requirement of providing additional contemporary retail accommodation to reinforce the city centre retail offer and to prevent local shoppers from travelling to other nearby competing towns.

Marienburg is located in the historic heart of the city between the two main shopping streets of Burchstraat and Zeikerstraat. The role of the masterplan was to find a way to connect these streets which had been separated by a series of large, free-standing office blocks with extensive open spaces between them. Sjoerd Soeter's objective was to recreate the density of buildings and intimacy of public spaces that existed in pre-war Nijmegen. His adopted approach was to look at the area once again as being a solid urban mass, and forming streets and squares by carving them out of the solid urban mass. The reality of this simplistic approach to the recreation of the urban mass involved demolishing one complete block and relocating the social services; extending and grafting onto the retained existing buildings to form suitably shaped blocks to define the streets and spaces; cutting through and carefully removing some existing buildings to allow desired routes to be formed; and building new blocks to complete the definition of public spaces.

Figure 5.81 Children engage with a playful water feature, The Beursplein, Rotterdam, The Netherlands. *(Source: BDP)*

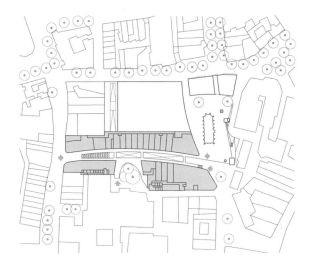

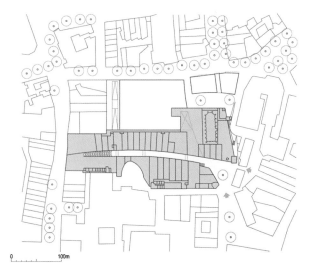

Figure 5.82 Upper and lower ground floor plans, Marienburg, Nijmegen, The Netherlands (2000). *(Source: Soeters/BDP)*

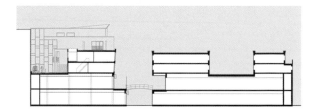

Figure 5.83 Cross section through the two level street with housing above the shops, Marienburg, Nijmegen, The Netherlands. *(Source: Sjaak Henselmans)*

The shopping area of Marienburg is focused on a new two-level street, Marienstraat, which connects the Burchstraat and Zeikerstraat. The formation of Marienstraat establishes an extended retail circuit in the city centre, which is focused on open streets

and a neighbourhood of high quality pedestrian environments. Marienstraat is a gently curving open-air street leading directly from the Burchstraat, with private apartments located above the two shopping levels, which are separately accessed from the rear court.

The layout uses level changes across the city to form two natural ground floor levels. Each level relates to a different level of the prime retail streets. The upper ground level relates to the higher Burchstraat, together with the raised level of the reshaped Marienburg Square around the church. This is enclosed by the new civic buildings of the archive collection, the library, social services offices, theatre and cinema building. The lower ground floor level corresponds to the lower Zeikerstraat and the streets that lead to it. Another square defines an existing high point in the city outside the original social services offices. This small square is midway along the street and is accessed from the west side of the upper level. The square retains a mature tree

Figure 5.84 The two level open street with residential above, Marienburg, Nijmegen, The Netherlands. *(Source: Vera Yanovshtchinsky)*

and is used for external seating by an adjacent café overlooking Marienstraat.

The lower ground level of Marienstraat forms a continuous run of unit shops on each side of the street. The upper ground level is formed by two galleries which sit directly above the shops below and form another run of unit shops along each side of the street. The gallery shops are continuous up to Marienburg Square on the east side, with the shops separated by the café square on the west side. The larger shop units are located at the end of the street at both levels to assist the dynamics of pedestrian movement along the street. The shops are extended below Marienburg Square to maximise the amount of retail space. Most of the shops are serviced from an internal service corridor at the rear which leads from a below ground service yard.

Figure 5.86 The upper level square on the west side signifying the city high point and formed around an existing tree, Marienburg, Nijmegen, The Netherlands. *(Source: Peter Coleman)*

Figure 5.85 Marienburg Square, incorporating the level change and existing church, Marienburg, Nijmegen, The Netherlands. *(Source: Sjaak Henselmans)*

Access to the two ground levels is generally dealt with in a natural and urban manner, which is essential for the integration of the two level street with the city, where each of the existing prime retail streets corresponds to the two street levels of Marienstraat. At the northern end Burchstraat leads directly on to the galleries, with a gentle ramp sloping down to the lower street level. At the southern end, one side of the gallery leads into Marienburg Square, with a dogleg stair and ramp connecting down to the lower level. The western gallery level descends via escalators, which are tucked beneath the overhang of the projecting building above. The lower level of Marienstraat connects to the lower level of the square and also leads directly on to Zeikerstraat. An elegant, glazed lift enclosure sits independently in the square and connects between the two levels.

Gently arched metal bridges cross Marienstraat and connect between the galleries on each side of the street. The street is simply finished with brick paving to the lower level and stone paving slabs lining the galleries and continuing into the church square.

To capture the variety of architecture which had characterised the city over the years, the masterplan allowed for three different architects to design the blocks. A different architect has designed each side of the street to Marienstraat. Architect Vera Yanovshtchinsky has designed the concave east side in a restrained modernist fashion. The base to the lower ground floor shops is framed in an exposed concrete structure with blue brick surrounds. The upper level shops and residential apartments are formed in a continuous red brick wall which is articulated by the regular shop openings and a repeated fenestration of windows to the apartments (see Fig. 5.87). The ends of the street are defined by separate, four-storey, blue brick buildings which

Figure 5.87 The two level street with galleries and a gentle ramp leading down from Burchstraat, Marienburg, Nijmegen, The Netherlands. *(Source: Sjaak Henselmans)*

have expressive horizontal windows to the sloping corners of the block. An element of surprise is introduced into the façade by the slight inclination of the red brick wall which varies along the length of the street, moving from the vertical in the centre to an incline at the ends of the street. The inclined façade reinforces the sense of enclosure to the street and counters the effect of perspective.

The convex side of the Marienstraat, designed by architect Molenaar and Von Winden, is a more contextual solution (see Fig. 5.89). The lower level

shops have brown brick surrounds and ornate metal lamp standards to the gallery edge. The residential apartments above the shops project out over the gallery in a series of brown and white patterned brick elements. Additional interest is given to this side of the street by the varying extent of the overhang to the apartments over the gallery. The projection is least at the north end of the street and increases to overhang the gallery fully by the midpoint; thereby creating the effect of a colonnade on the west side of the street, contrasting with the open street on the east side. The metal balustrading and light fittings are also correspondingly different on each side of the street, emphasising the identity of each side.

The remaining civic and public buildings define Marienburg Square around the existing church. These buildings have been designed by Soeters van Eldonk Ponec Architecten and house the archives, social services, library, theatre and cinemas in individually expressed different coloured brick buildings.

A characteristic of the Marienburg development is the different buildings which define the intimate spaces and provide ever-changing interest as the pedestrian moves from one public space to another. The Marienburg quarter is well integrated with the surrounding neighbourhoods of the city. It has successfully repaired the urban fabric and extended both the public realm and retail core of the city. The urban design-based masterplan has succeeded in creating a new retail facility and established a neighbourhood of pedestrian-friendly contemporary

Figure 5.89 Molenaar and Von Winden's design with patterned brickwork for the west side of the street, Marienburg, Nijmegen, The Netherlands. *(Source: Sjaak Henselmans)*

Figure 5.88 Vera Yanovshtchinsky's design to the east side of the street with the sloping brick façade, Marienburg, Nijmegen, The Netherlands. *(Source: Sjaak Henselmans)*

narrow streets and squares. Marienburg is an intimate example of the principle of new urbanism and the formation of a shopping environment in a new urban quarter.

Manchester

The regeneration of the North West Quarter, Manchester (1996–2007) is an example of a major city consciously regenerating its city centre retail facilities in partnership with private companies. This quarter's regeneration is, however, part of a comprehensive regeneration strategy for the greater area of the city. As a part of this larger plan, the city authority recognised in the early 1990s the need, both environmental and economic, of regenerating its city centre retail facilities. The North West Quarter has undergone a transformation to become a destination of choice, offering a leading range of varied retail and leisure facilities (see Table 5.1, p. 205). The quarter is made up of several individual shopping facilities which interact together, representing a significant part of the city centre shopping. Manchester's North West Quarter is an exemplary urban example and illustrates the complexity and lengthy process involved with such projects. This multiple example, which is a collection of separate developments, commenced in the early 1990s and will largely be completed towards the end of 2006.

Manchester initiated its comprehensive regeneration in the early 1990s, recognising from the way Barcelona revitalised itself for the 1992 Olympics, the kickstart effect to regeneration of hosting a major sports event. Not deterred by failing in selection for the 2000 Olympic Games, the city was successful with its bid for the 2002 Commonwealth Games and, in preparation, began a series of regeneration projects around the greater city.

The programme was accelerated by the city's vigorous response to the terrorist bomb detonated in the city's prime shopping area in June 1996. The damage was extensive, ripping the heart from the city centre, devastating 45 000 m^2 (480 000 ft^2) of retail space and damaging historic buildings and undistinguished 1960s buildings alike. The catastrophe focused attention on the city centre, acting as a further catalyst for its regeneration. From adversity came the opportunity to rectify several of the post-war mistakes; the mono-use zoning; the unfounded traffic planning; and the opportunity to remove mediocre buildings and extend the retail facilities, reconnecting isolated parts of the city.

The Manchester Millennium Commission formed immediately after the bomb was given four years effectively to steer the rebuilding and transformation of the city centre for the commencement of the new millennium. The process of regenerating the North West Quarter began with a design competition for a robust masterplan, which was won by a team led by planner and urban designer EDAW.

The North West Quarter Masterplan: focused on regenerating the North West Quarter of the city centre. The proposals readily grasped the opportunity of both repairing the bomb damage and the erosion of the urban fabric. The plan illustrated reforming pieces of the city to address three primary objectives: extend the retail facilities; improve the quality of the public spaces; and introduce vitality by incorporating a mixture of uses. As such the proposal represented a retail-led regeneration project which would, on completion, replace the devastated retail space and increase it by the same amount again, introducing city living and new civic facilities.

The EDAW masterplan addressed the requirements of the urban agenda and allowed for its implementation by a variety of private developers and public grant funding, each with its own design team. The Millennium Commission monitored the implementation of the masterplan and coordinated the interfaces. The plan represents the first major retail project in the UK to demonstrate the reality of new urbanism.

In view of the seminal nature of Manchester's North West Quarter for new urban retail facilities, the masterplan principles are worth further examination. The masterplan can be separated into general principles and overall proposals. The general principles were:

- creating a public realm of streets and spaces that people want to use and readily understand
- including mixed-use development
- good quality architecture with the opportunity for selective iconic buildings
- buildings with active frontages.

These general principles are common to many projects currently being undertaken in the formation of urban quarters. The overall proposals of the masterplan are outlined in Table 5.1.

The masterplan for Manchester's North West Quarter is almost a city centre retail scheme in its own right. Alone it represents a good proportion of the city's overall retail facilities. The proposal is a masterplan of smaller masterplans rather than of building blocks. For instance several blocks contain various elements or different phases of work such as the Arndale Centre's phased refurbishment and extension; New Cathedral Street's different buildings; and the subsequent alteration to the new Marks and Spencer store.

To summarise, the overall retail provision of the North West Quarter will provide: four destination stores (where once there was one); between the various retail elements there will be over 100 new retail units, which will provide accommodation to meet the needs of contemporary retailers, and which will give a net gain of retail space equal again to the amount lost in the devastation; the new pedestrian street through the Shambles block will provide a continuous shopping circuit from King Street and St Anne's Square in the south, all the way up to the Triangle and Exchange Square in the north; additional new leisure and entertainment facilities have been incorporated into the city centre with a 20-screen and Imax cinema complex, along with complementary cafés, bars and restaurants; Manchester's western edge retail facilities will be extended up to and including Deansgate.

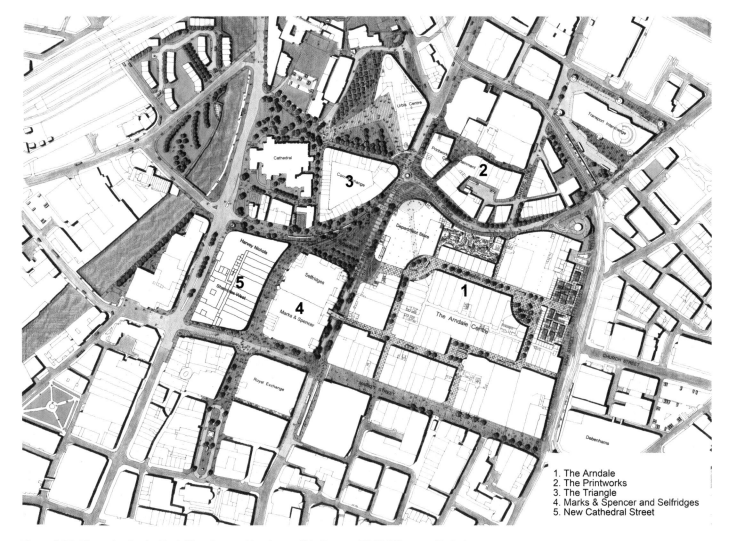

Figure 5.90 Masterplan for the North West Quarter, Manchester, UK. *(Source: EDAW/Chapman Taylor)*

1. The Arndale
2. The Printworks
3. The Triangle
4. Marks & Spencer and Selfridges
5. New Cathedral Street

The masterplan contains different types of retail format which can be equally divided into shops which are accessed from an enclosed interior environment and shopping directly accessed from the street. Commencing with the former, the masterplan's eastern edge incorporates the Arndale Centre (1975), (the flagship of Hagenbach and Chippendale's empire of first generation, UK enclosed shopping centres). The centre is undertaking a series of phased improvements, starting with the internal refurbishment of the existing centre.

Arndale, Manchester (2000–2007): (separate from the internal face-lift and the western façade extensions in 2000) a major two-level 30 000 m² (323 000 ft²) extension is underway to the north, instigated by the Prudential Property Fund and designed by architect Chapman Taylor, is due for phased completion in 2006–2007. The proposal will connect the remote northern part of the centre and involves the closure of a road (currently bridged) and making better use of the spaces occupied by the

Figure 5.91 Plan of the extended Arndale, Manchester, UK (planned 2006–2007). *(Source: Chapman Taylor)*

Figure 5.92 The new Next store in the extended Arndale, Manchester, UK. *(Source: Chapman Taylor)*

Figure 5.93 The internal street to the retail entertainment destination, The Printworks, Manchester, UK (2000). *(Source: RTKL)*

disused bus station and declining market. The new works will extend the existing internal malls at both levels to form a simple, largely naturally lit, pedestrian circuit in contemporary, naturally lit interiors. One of the destination department stores will be incorporated into the north-west corner of the Arndale to provide a four-level store of 15 000 m² (161 000 ft²). The northern extension will continue outward facing shopfronts and animated façades from the west elevation around to the north-west elevation. The completed extension will form a total Arndale Centre of 130 000 m² (1.4 million ft²) of contemporary retail accommodation for mainstream multiple retailers and cafés.

The Printworks (2000): developed by Richardsons Developments and designed by architect RTKL, is a new 55 000 m² (592 000 ft²) entertainment and leisure complex built behind the retained neo-classical façade of the former Daily Mirror newspaper works, originally known as the Chronicle building. (This format is discussed further in the following Chapter.) The façade is now overlaid with a filigree of powerful illuminated graphics displaying the internal activities and tenants, along with a large video screen over the entranceway. The exterior faces on to the new public space of Exchange Square. A new pedestrian route leads from Exchange Square diagonally through the block to an adjacent street (see Fig. 5.93). The route is formed internally through the block by an artificial street, lined with a collage of locally inspired façades and a 'projected sky' ceiling. The interior is more of a theatre set which leads to the 20-screen multiplex and Imax theatre, a health club and a variety of themed bars and restaurants. On its opening the Printworks formed the largest licensed premises in the UK. The Printworks is a night-time destination and during the day the interior street remains an artificial edifice.

The Triangle (2000): internally accessed shops have been formed in the former bidding hall of the historic and listed Corn Exchange (rebuilt 1897–1903), which has been renamed the Triangle by developer Frogmore Estates (designed by The Ratcliff Partnership and Benoy). The three-sided interior hall of the original exchange has been formed into a three-levelled, galleried space providing 35 unit shops around the perimeter (see Fig. 5.94). The shops are generally occupied by upmarket branded fashion and lifestyle home accessory stores.

The hall has been sensitively converted and is naturally lit from the restored, central, domed roof and surrounding perimeter glazed sky lights. The three sides of original balconies have been widened in width to allow appropriate pedestrian movement at each level. An elegant metal and glass floor has been added on the gallery which, in turn, supports a matching balustrade and metal handrail. The gallery edge treatment assists light to percolate through the space down to the lowest level. The interior has a bright contemporary character which allows the

Figure 5.94 Multi-level shopping formed within the original Corn Exchange building, The Triangle, Manchester, UK (2000). *(Source: Peter Coleman)*

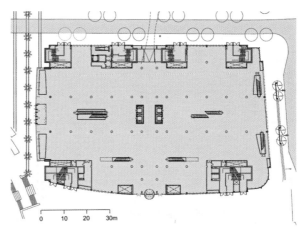

Figure 5.95 Cores located on the perimeter leave large uninterrupted floor plates and active frontages to the north and south façades, The Marks & Spencer and Selfridges building, Manchester, UK (1999–2000). *(Source: BDP)*

shopfronts to dominate and to be readily seen. Movement between the levels is provided by a delicate metal and glass spiral staircase which has been inserted into one corner and surrounds the glazed lift enclosure, extending vertically through the three floor levels. A further bank of escalators connects between the different levels. The original entranceway to the Exchange is used as the main entrance from Exchange Square and leads from the entrance lobby to the mid-level. In 2004 new owners introduced a further entrance directly on to Exchange Square by the removal of the shops from one elevational bay. The ground floor shops have dressed the windows facing the streets and, although the Triangle is an internal, closed shopping facility, it appears to face outwards.

The second broad category of new shopping to be found in Manchester's North West Quarter is the shops that are directly accessed from the street. These shops include the new destination stores and the New Cathedral Street shopping development (on the Shambles west block) designed, in recognition of the urban agenda, to face externally on to the streets.

Marks & Spencer and Selfridges Stores (1999–2002): following the near destruction of the original Marks and Spencer store in 1996, architect Building Design Partnership (BDP) was commissioned to design a new flagship store on the reformed Shambles east block, incorporating the adjacent office building to form a plot of sufficient size. The 23 250 m² (250 000 ft²) store (1999) was arranged over five trading levels with integral vehicle servicing to the lowest floor and car parking below in the basement. The rational design organised all the service functions on to the perimeters of the east and west sides of the building, forming large uninterrupted floor plates. The floor plates extend the length of the building, leaving the entire north and south elevations to become giant shop windows which extend the full height and width of the building. These structurally glazed windows form dramatic animated façades allowing views both into the store from the streets, and outwards to the adjacent historic buildings – establishing orientation inside the large store.

Marks and Spencer's occupation left the top floor fallow to allow for future expansion. Following the opening of the store and the company's corporate reorganisation, the decision was made to subdivide the store in order to accommodate another destination store inside the original building. This involved Marks and Spencer retracting into 11 150 m² (120 000 ft²) and occupying all the floors in the southern half of the building. This left the remaining northern half of the building overlooking Exchange Square, to provide a similar size store for Selfridges, which opened in September 2002 (Fig. 5.96).

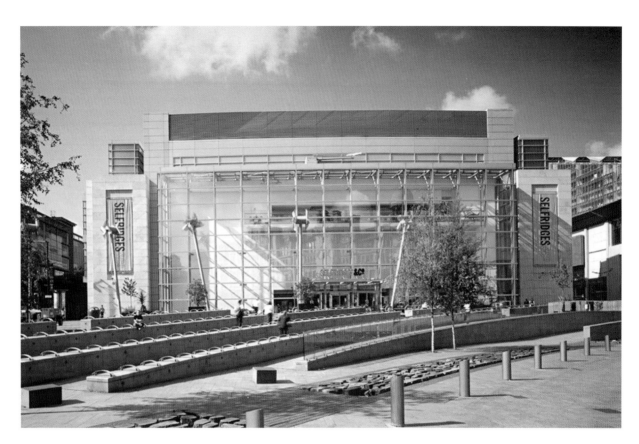

Figure 5.96 The continuous glazed façade on the north elevation provides an active frontage to Exchange Square, Selfridges, formally the Marks & Spencer frontage, Manchester, UK (1999–2000). *(Source: Daniel Hopkinson)*

Figure 5.97 The minimalist white interior by Stanton Williams to one of the four individually designed floors to Selfridges, Manchester, UK (2002). *(Source: Martine Hamilton Knight)*

Selfridges commissioned architect Stanton Williams to reorganise the interior to form the new store trading over four levels. Each floor is individually designed to form its own identity within the building. This approach was similarly applied to their subsequent new store in Birmingham referred to earlier. The new store was achieved by internal reorganisation of the building with only minor external alterations to the award winning building. Unfortunately, shop-fitting requirement, for inward looking departments, has closed off the views from the large window to the Cathedral and Corn Exchange and into the store from the urban space.

An internal, double height atrium has been formed in the centre of the building as a calming space which separates the two stores. The atrium forms an internal street which connects across the block to the adjacent parallel streets and forms an enclosed arcade-like entrance space. Elevators adjacent to the atrium lead to the different levels and the basement car park. A glazed diagrid bridge (designed

Figure 5.98 The entrance atrium formed between the two department stores which occupy the original building, Manchester, UK. *(Source: David Barbour)*

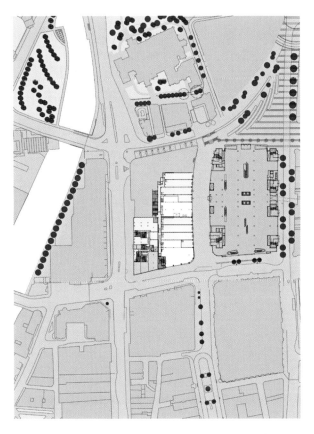

Figure 5.99 Street level plan with shops facing on to New Cathedral Street, Manchester, UK (2003). *(Source: BDP)*

by Hodder Associates) connects directly from the upper level of the neighbouring Arndale centre into the first floor of the atrium, providing access to the first floor of the stores.

New Cathedral Street (2003): the mixed-use development of the Shambles west block New Cathedral Street was developed by Prudential and master-planned by architect BDP with three main elements: a new destination store; new unit shops; and a residential block for luxury apartments. Crosby Homes became the developer for the residential block and appointed architect Ian Simpson to design the corner block, with a two-storey podium and a fourteen-storey tower of apartments. Prudential built out the remainder of the New Cathedral Street block to provide 14 400 m^2 (155 000 ft^2) of retail accommodation for ten shops facing on to the new street, and a four-level destination store for Harvey Nichols of 8800 m^2 (94 500 ft^2) overlooking the Cathedral and Exchange Square.

The new shops and destination store form a three-storey building facing on to the new pedestrian street, which connects the niche retailing of King Street with the new retail and entertainment facilities around Exchange Square. The other side of the street is defined by the Marks and Spencer and Selfridges building. The new shops accommodate a variety of upmarket retailers, which range in size from 200 m^2 (2100 ft^2) to 3800 m^2 (32 000 ft^2), occupying one to four levels of the building. The shops lead along to the new Harvey Nichols store at

Figure 5.100 The three storey building with shops facing on to New Cathedral Street, Manchester, UK. *(Source: David Barbour)*

Figure 5.101 The Harvey Nichols store with corner tower, New Cathedral Street, Manchester, UK. *(Source: David Barbour)*

Figure 5.102 The glazed corner to Zara addresses the approaching street with residential apartments behind, New Cathedral Street, Manchester, UK. *(Source: David Barbour)*

the end of the street. All the new shops have integral servicing in a basement service yard which leads, via lifts, to a service corridor at the rear of the units. Access to the service yard is shared with service vehicles for the adjacent destination stores.

The design of the New Cathedral Street building continues the local tradition of major stores occupying stone pavilions. The three-storey façades face outwards on to the streets and are animated with windows and shopfronts. The street elevations are clad in natural stone with a mixture of two and three-storey shopfronts set in metal surrounds with terracotta rain screen walling projecting from the upper levels. The principal façade to New Cathedral Street follows a gentle curve to form a natural retailing amphitheatre where all the shops are visible on entering the street. A projecting zinc cornice caps the building and follows the curve of the street to emphasise the containment of the space.

The Harvey Nichols store has its own identity within the block and is expressed as a separate stone and glass building at the end of the street. The store's restaurant is located on the fourth level with a panoramic window overlooking the street and Exchange Square from the corner tower. Each corner of the building is articulated with a vertical, glazed tower which responds to the towers on the adjacent historic buildings. The glazed corners address the views of the approaching streets and are individually treated to assist orientation. The rooftop plant is contained within a louvred metal enclosure to present a tidy outlook from the overlooking apartments.

The No. 1 Deansgate apartments are arranged in the glass tower which sits on expressed steel piloti above the glass-clad podium of shops. A separate street entrance from Deansgate leads to an entrance vestibule which sits above the podium, amidst the piloti which support the tower. Two separate cores lead from the vestibule to the 80 luxury apartments. The apartments are housed within a striking double-skin, glass wall separated by a 1.2 m buffer zone. The inner skin is double glazed and contains adjustable blinds for privacy, while the outer skin is formed from large glazed louvres which can be opened for ventilation. The buffer zone contains a continuous balcony, which can be used by each of the apartments, with privacy provided by a vertical glass screen which corresponds to each flat. The apartments all have dramatic views across the roofscape of the city.

The inclusion of the residential tower into the mixed-use development has succeeded in bringing luxury city living into what was a declining district.

Table 5.1 Masterplan proposals for Manchester's north west quarter

- Removing inward looking and windswept Shambles Square and the poor quality 1960s surrounding buildings
- Dismantling and relocating two historic pubs on to an adjacent street (Cathedral Street)
- Subdividing the oversized block to form two city blocks with outward facing buildings
- Forming a new pedestrian street connecting St Anne's Church to Manchester Cathedral (New Cathedral Street) and reconnecting the area up to Victoria Station with the city centre
- Allocating the entirety of one of the new city blocks for a new flagship store to re-accommodate Marks and Spencer
- Assigning the west block of the new city blocks to a mixed-use development consisting of a new destination department store, additional shops for upmarket retailers and residential apartments above the shops
- Animating the inward looking Arndale shopping centre by extending the western façade of the building to form new shopfrontages facing on to the street
- Connecting the two parts of the Arndale shopping centre by the closure of the under passing street, forming a winter garden entranceway on the former street junction and
- extending the enclosed ways into a new circuit within the extended centre
- Forming a new iconic public building to house exhibitions and museum displays
- Retaining and repairing the listed buildings (Corn Exchange and Royal Exchange)
- Developing a new entertainment, leisure and retail facility behind the existing façade of the former Daily Mirror building (The Printworks)
- Establishing a network of streets which connect with the existing surrounding city centre streets
- Establishing pedestrian priority to as many streets as possible, restricting vehicle access to the core area to public transport and service vehicles
- Removing traffic from Hanging Ditch to form a new urban space for the retail and entertainment district and establishing the setting of the existing and new buildings
- Transforming a surface car park into a new city centre park, engaging with the surrounding existing buildings and the new public building to reconnect the area with Victoria Station (Cathedral Gardens)

Figure 5.103 The double skin glass façade to the residential apartments, No. 1 Deansgate, Manchester, UK. *(Source: Adam Wilson)*

The completed mixed-use development has transformed the area into an integral part of fashionable Manchester.

The transformation of the North West Quarter has led to a series of ripple effect improvements to other retail areas of the city centre. All these have provided Manchester with a wide variety of types of shopping and helped to reinforce the city centre as a destination of choice in the region's regeneration.

Projects in the Pipeline

As well as the built examples of new urban quarters, some of the most inventive and challenging proposals are currently in the pipeline and yet to be realised. This is well illustrated in the UK where there are a series of retail-led regeneration schemes, (addressing the urban agenda), which will be completed from 2005 to 2010. Some of these are identified in Table 5.2 (see also Figs. 5.103–5.105).

Some example urban quarter developments currently in the pipeline are now reviewed in more detail.

Figure 5.104 The proposed Performing Arts Centre, in the mixed-use development, Northgate, Chester, UK (planned 2008). *(Source: Chapman Taylor/Hopkins Architects)*

Table 5.2 UK town centre projects in the pipeline

2005	Chapelfield	Norwich
2006	Drake Circus	Plymouth
2007	Eagle Centre	Derby
	St Stephen's	Kingston upon Hull
	Princesshay	Exeter
	Victoria Square	Belfast
2008	Broadmead	Bristol
	New Shires	Leicester
	Northgate	Chester
	Paradise Street	Liverpool
	St David's 2	Cardiff
	Westgate	Oxford
2009	Pinstone Street Phase 1	Sheffield
	(Phase 2 – 2011)	

The completion dates are expected dates. Source: 'Centre Retailing' Estates Gazette 2004 (and direct knowledge from involvement with Liverpool and Sheffield projects)

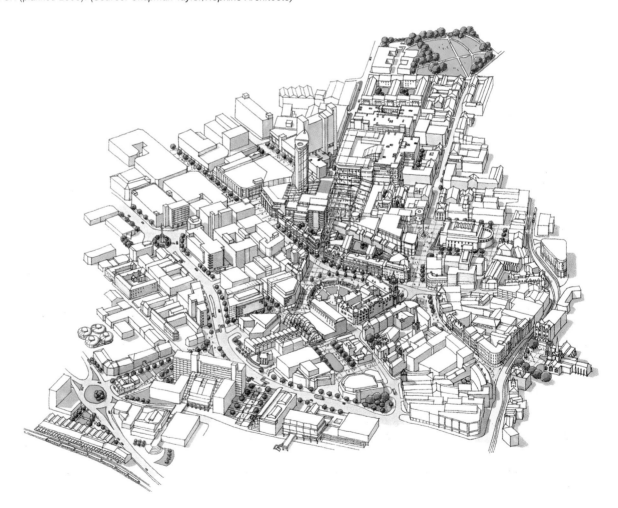

Figure 5.105 Aerial view from the east illustrates the integration of the mixed-use retail-led regeneration scheme in the heart of the city, the New Retail Quarter, Sheffield, UK (planned 2009–2011). *(Source: BDP)*

Victoria Square, Belfast

The inventive Dutch developer, AM, previously responsible for the seminal Beursplein project, is extending its portfolio to the UK for the first time with another innovative mixed-use development, with proposals for Victoria Square, Belfast (2007 expected completion), designed by architects Building Design Partnership (BDP) and T+T Design. This project's timely planning permission in 2003 for the extension of the city centre retail core, coincides with the recent greater stability in the once troubled Province.

The proposal is located between the prime retail of Donegal Place and the regenerated Laganside and represents the opportunity to connect the city centre with the river, simultaneously regenerating the declining district in between. A declining shopping centre, surface car park and government offices currently occupy the site. These are adjacent to a

relatively busy high street, Ann Street, with several decorated Victorian brick buildings contained within the district. The mixed-use proposal for over 60 000 m² (646 000 ft²) of shops, catering, health club and cinemas, with additional residential apartments, is part of an overall masterplan for the neighbourhood.

The masterplan repairs and completes the urban mass to form a complete block between the surrounding perimeter streets, Ann Street to Chichester Street and Montgomery Street to Victoria Street. Pedestrian streets are cut through the block connecting the new quarter with the adjacent city in a manner similar to Soeters' approach to the masterplan for Marienburg, Nijmegen. A route is formed through the block connecting Donegal Place to Victoria Street and on to the river Lagan. The primary street forms a simple circuit with the high street by returning the route, which commences from the end of Ann Street, to break through the Ann Street frontage further along

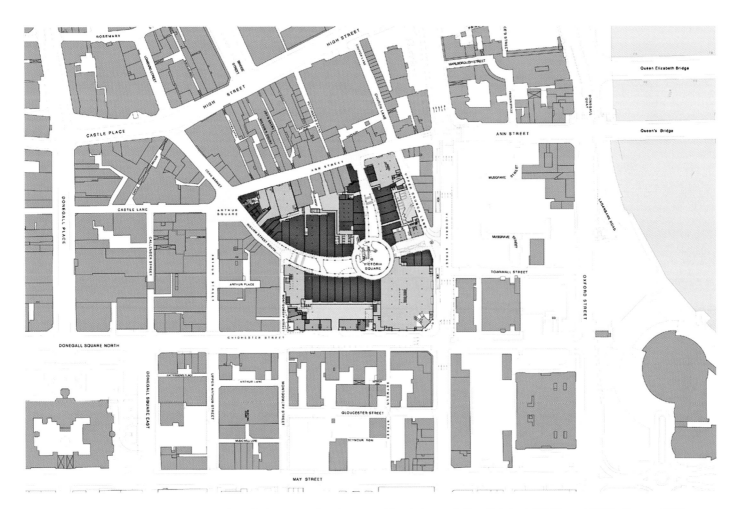

Figure 5.106 Ground level plan shows integration with the surrounding city streets, Victoria Square, Belfast, N. Ireland, UK (Planned 2007). *(Source: BDP)*

Figure 5.107 The entrance to the two level galleried street with a simple glass roof and natural ventilation, Victoria Square, Belfast, N. Ireland, UK. *(Source: BDP/Peter Hutton)*

Figure 5.108 The domed destination space with catering on various levels overlooking the city, Victoria Square, Belfast, N. Ireland, UK. *(Source: BDP/Peter Hutton)*

the street. A circular rotunda provides a focus at the intersection. A new department store building, providing 18 000 m² (194 000 ft²) of accommodation on four levels, defines the main external corner of the block and anchors the intersection of new streets. The new street cutting through the block is a two-level pedestrian street, covered by a simple glass roof passing between the buildings on either side.

Victoria Square forms an urban neighbourhood made up of a series of individual buildings aligning the streets. The covered streets are treated as external spaces defined by the buildings on either side. The covered ways are naturally ventilated and untempered with permanent access maintained throughout the day keeping the neighbourhood integral with the city.

The two-level street is physically formed by lowering the lower ground floor by 3.5 m from grade level of the surrounding streets and raising the upper ground floor by 1.5 m (from grade) to form a full storey height. Access from the street to the changed new street levels is made in an urban way by the use of sloping ramps and steps. Mechanical escalators and lifts in the rotunda connect between the levels.

In addition to the new destination department store, there are some 70 new shops provided between the two public street levels. The lower ground floor level is lined on both sides with continuous rows of single-storey shops. The upper ground level is formed by a gallery on each side of the street with double height shops lining the sides. The galleries move between covered colonnades, beneath buildings and open walkways with the sky above. The shop units are arranged according to shopping centre science with larger units placed at the ends of the street, like book ends, to facilitate pedestrian movement past the frontages of the standard size shops. A third level of retail space forms a first floor, accessed through the shop units, providing double height shop units at the upper ground floor level. Also located at the first floor is a two-level catering terrace, with individual cafés and restaurants, which is accessed from the rotunda.

The rotunda at the intersection of streets is a focus for the neighbourhood and a new covered public space for the city. The rotunda roof is formed by a Fabergé egg-shaped, glazed roof which sits above five lily-pad-shaped decks which form cafés and viewing decks over the city roofscape from the top two levels. A second floor level, also accessed from the rotunda, accommodates the second level of the food terrace, the health club and cinema complex, all contained in the buildings overlooking the street.

All the shops have the facility for delivery of goods via a rear service corridor which leads from two separate service yards with direct street access. There is also basement parking below the lower ground floor level providing 1000 parking spaces with direct access to the rotunda and department store.

Victoria Square is a mixed-use development which will also provide 87 apartments in three different buildings within the masterplan. There are three levels of residential apartments directly above the shops in the main entry street from the city (William Street). A second linear block faces onto the main street, Chichester Street, with five storeys of apartments above the street level restaurants. In the same street, an eleven storey tower block, located directly on a street corner, provides the third element of residential accommodation. A long-established public house will be re-accommodated into new facilities behind the façade of a retained building.

The architectural approach to Victoria Square adopts a contextual solution which responds to the urban context of each street, with a series of individually expressed stone and brick buildings that continue the variety of architecture found in the city. Several existing buildings and façades worthy of retention are incorporated into the neighbourhood and given new uses and life. Some of these buildings form street corners and set the urban context for the new buildings in the street. The Masonic Hall, a robust four-storey brick building with paired arched windows, sets the scene for the new brick buildings in the entry from William Street. Another retained five-storey ornate brick façade defines the street which leaves the neighbourhood on the way to the river.

Individual buildings are established by the expression of the different uses: the residential apartments, department store and large stores are expressed as separate buildings. Further variety is added to the new street with a different approach to each side – one side formed from stone and the other defined by brick buildings. The department store forms a stone pavilion on the main corner with a three-storey façade with outward facing shopfronts and windows to the upper floors. A set back fourth floor, with an expressed structure, supports a floating roof capping this building.

Paradise Street, Liverpool

The Paradise Street Development Area (Paradise Street), Liverpool is another major new urban quarter which is in the pipeline for future shopping development with an expected completion in 2008. The scale of this retail-led regeneration project significantly raises the bar in the extent of regeneration involved and is substantially larger than the Victoria Square example. The regeneration involved with Paradise Street represents a significant portion of the overall city centre of Liverpool, rather than just an important part, and its relative importance to the city is more comparable with the North West Urban Quarter of Manchester described earlier.

As with Victoria Square, Paradise Street is located in the heart of the city. It involves an underperforming area, which has been left under-used from 20th century war damage. Paradise Street involves some 13 ha (32 acres) of city centre land whose rehabilitation is significant both to the regeneration of the city and surrounding region. The scale and comprehensive nature of mixed-use development will bring economic, commercial, transport and social benefits to the area.

The need for regeneration of the region has long been recognised and is reflected by the formation in 1998 of one of the first urban regeneration companies to steer and coordinate redevelopment in the city. Following the establishment of strategic planning policies for the regeneration of the city centre, a competition was held to select a developer and consultant team to become the city's

Figure 5.109 Arthur Square entrance showing the scale of the new buildings beside the Masonic Hall on the left, Victoria Square, Belfast, N. Ireland, UK. *(Source: BDP/Peter Hutton)*

development and investment partner. The Grosvenor Henderson team was selected in 2000 and committed to prepare an urban design-led masterplan for the Paradise Street Development Area. Since selection, the developer, Grosvenor, is proceeding on its own with the development. Planning applications were submitted in early 2001, following extensive consultations with both the public and national consultees and, with the completion of two public inquiries, planning permission was obtained in 2002. (A further planning application was submitted in 2004 – see www.liverpoolpsda.co.uk for further information.)

The local commitment to the development was given further impetus by the city's selection in 2003 as European City of Culture for 2008, which coincides with the project's completion and has given a great incentive to the target date.

The scale of Paradise Street has involved the preparation of a comprehensive masterplan for the

area. The size of the development has also led to the formation of several integrated places within the city centre rather than one large development. The masterplan, prepared by architect BDP, is one of the first in the UK to address the issues of the urban agenda on a large scale in the formation of new shopping facilities as part of a comprehensive mixed-use town centre development. The innovative approach of the masterplan adopts an urban design-led layout, based largely on existing street patterns, to form a shopping environment based on open streets and spaces. The streets will be defined by individual buildings which will be designed by several different architects. The building designs will be based on compliance with the masterplan principles, together with a building brief for each building.

In order to make a new departure in the perception of Liverpool's city centre, the masterplan incorporates a rich and varied range of different accommodation

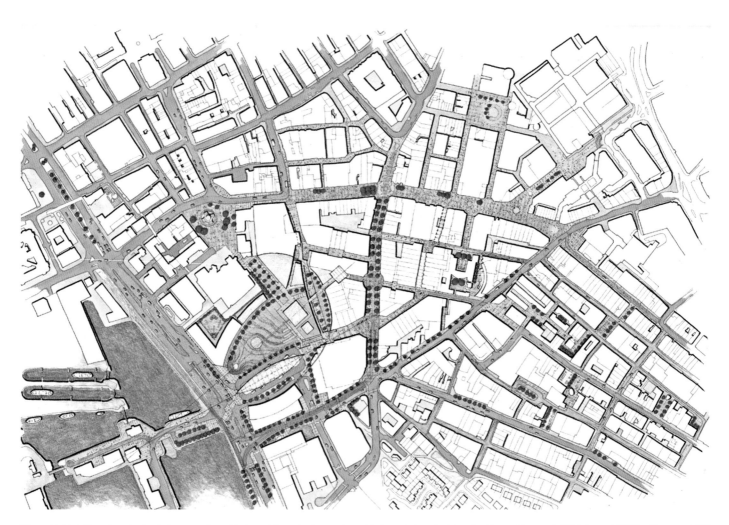

Figure 5.110 The urban design led masterplan with the public realm integrating with the existing city, Paradise Street, Liverpool, UK (planned 2008). *(Source: BDP)*

and facilities. The new accommodation will replenish the loss of scale and activity in the area providing new shopping, leisure, living and working facilities in the city centre. The 140 000 m² (1.5 million ft²) of retail space will provide a range of retail facilities with street level access including department stores, medium size stores, unit shops, speciality, local and regional shops, cafés, bars and restaurants and space for market retailers.

The Paradise Street masterplan covers a triangular-shaped area which extends from the principal shopping area of Lord Street and Church Street in the north, to the historical and cultural quarter of Hanover Street in the east, and extends across to the dockside waterfront of The Strand to the west. Dividing the area and connecting with the northern part of the city, Paradise Street forms a central spine to the masterplan. The masterplan incorporates two fundamental urban forms which correspond to the two areas either side of Paradise Street. The west side is formed from a newly made, urban fabric

of large scale, contemporary mixed-use buildings (which define the Park, South John Street and the west side of Paradise Street). The urban form on the east side sits within the finely grained existing fabric of retained historic buildings and the mixture of creative new infill buildings.

The layout for the new shops will form a network of open-air streets which ensures all the development area remains a public place. The network of streets is based on reinforcing the existing arrangement, with the formation of some new streets connecting to important parts of the city. The approach of largely adopting the existing street pattern, along with reforming desire lines, assists the integration and continuity of the new with the existing city. Furthermore, the network of combined streets encourages a series of pedestrian circuits which extend between the existing and newly regenerated parts of the city, thereby integrating the two parts together, providing choice and variety in the use of the city centre.

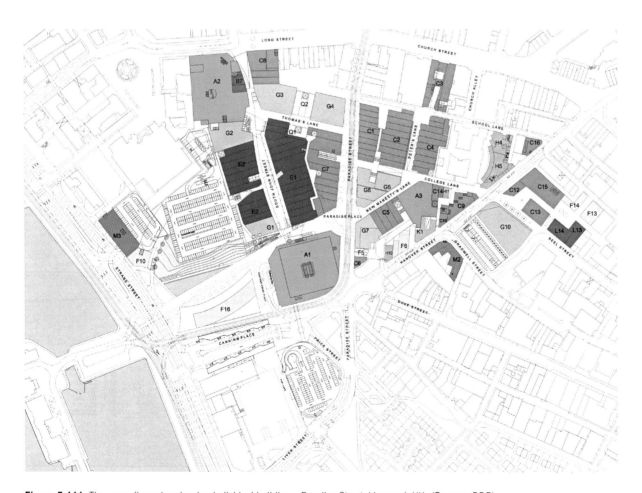

Figure 5.111 The upper floor plan showing individual buildings, Paradise Street, Liverpool, UK. *(Source: BDP)*

In recognition of the size of the Paradise Street regeneration area, the masterplan establishes a series of different, but overlapping quarters. Each quarter will have its own physical characteristics, atmosphere and principal uses. The quarters will form a series of interacting districts, creating a vibrant part of the city centre. The scale and nature of the streets, both old and new, is the main generator for the character of five different quarters. The form of street varies, for instance, from the grand scale of Paradise Street and South John Street to the narrower streets of College Lane and Peter's Lane, and the even further finely grained passageways linking School Lane and College Lane to Hanover Street. The masterplan defines the form, nature of uses and the overall atmosphere for each of the five quarters.

Figure 5.114 The proposed new arcade through the Church Street building in the Peter's Lane quarter, Paradise Street, Liverpool, UK. *(Source: BDP)*

Figure 5.112 The five individual quarters within the Masterplan, Paradise Street, Liverpool, UK. *(Source: BDP)*

The Paradise Street Quarters

The Hanover Street quarter: combines several historic buildings together with creative new infill buildings. It is finely grained and acts as an interface between

Figure 5.113 The street elevation to the Hanover Street quarter, showing the individual buildings adjacent to Bluecoat Chambers, Paradise Street, Liverpool, UK. *(Source: BDP)*

the smaller scale retained fabric and the new interventions. The character is to be informal and vibrant, with ground floor speciality and market type retailing, residential and live/work accommodation above the shops.

The Peter Lane quarter: is represented by a network of pedestrianised streets and smaller passageways formed by a similar mixture of retained and new infill buildings. The area forms the main connection with the existing prime shopping street and is intended to be busy, containing the prime shopping and facilities for evening activity. Double height shops line the streets with restaurants and bars. Residential apartments will be located above the shops.

Paradise Street: will be a point of arrival and connects routes to other parts of the city. The street will be formed into a grand tree-lined boulevard with pedestrian sidewalks and tram stops. The boulevard will be lined with buildings four-to-eight storeys high and will be busy and vibrant, leading to the other quarters on each side. Street level shopping will be formed by double height shops, with residential uses above on the east side, and leisure uses above on the west side of the street. One of the new four-level department stores defines the southern corner on the west side of the street.

The South John Street quarter: will be the focus of retailing activity, formed from a two-level, galleried, open-air street with a new department store at each end. The galleried space will be defined by large scale permeable buildings which will connect to Paradise Street and the park on either side. The principal retail destination will remain open-air with some protection given by a mixture of canopies and colonnades. The upper ground floor leads directly from the existing prime shopping in Lord Street and forms a gallery of double height shops on each side of the street. The lower ground floor is lined with single-level shops and connects to Paradise Street

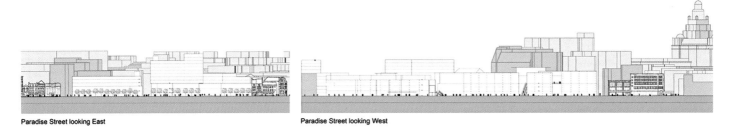

Paradise Street looking East

Paradise Street looking West

Figure 5.115 The tree lined focal street with trams showing the block massing to Paradise Street looking east, Paradise Street, Liverpool, UK. *(Source: BDP)*

Figure 5.116 The two level open street with a canopy providing shelter in the St John Street quarter, Paradise Street, Liverpool, UK. *(Source: BDP)*

and the adjacent bus interchange. The new car park below the Park leads to both ground floor levels. Catering and leisure facilities form a first floor gallery set back on the east side of the street, with views across the Park to the waterside.

The Pool and the Park: form the final quarter connecting the city with the waterfront. The Park is composed as a large urban set piece with the reformed Chavasse Park sloping up from the waterfront, concealing the car parking beneath. The Park

Figure 5.117 The landscape public space above the car parking in The Pool and the Park quarter, Paradise Street, Liverpool, UK. *(Source: BDP/Cesar Pelli)*

will be defined on three sides by a series of pavilion buildings which individually accommodate a hotel, residential apartments and a cultural facility. The bus station and one of the department stores engage with the Park. The Park will incorporate a water feature to commemorate the original commercial dock formerly located here.

Paradise Street is one of the first of several current retail-led regeneration schemes that has adopted a masterplan approach to meet the requirements for more sustainable town centre development. The masterplan is based on the involvement of other architects to design individual buildings and achieve architectural variety more closely resembling the natural collage obtained over time in the historical evolution of a city. This raises issues of collaboration and coordination which the masterplanner will need to consider, especially in the procurement stages of the project.

In view of the increasing relevance and likely continued adoption of the masterplan approach to other future major town centre shopping environments, the principles of the Paradise Street masterplan are outlined in Table 5.3. The masterplan prepared for this project has involved three principal levels of information being established by the masterplanner, for use by each individual designer.

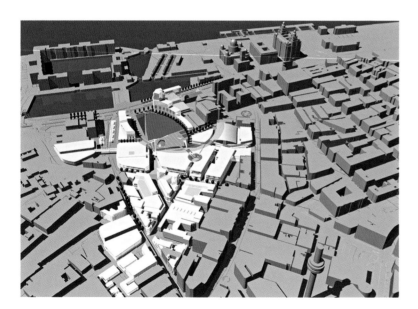

Figure 5.118 Aerial view of the overall masterplan and block massing set within the city, Paradise Street, Liverpool, UK. *(Source: BDP)*

Table 5.3 Paradise Street, Liverpool: principles

1. The Masterplan

Level 1 information in the masterplan establishes the overall layout for the development site, defining the setting out for the streets, spaces and building blocks to include the urban massing of the buildings. The masterplan determines the different uses, the location and area of accommodation for each use. It will also set the primary floor levels of the buildings and spaces to define the cross-sections. Pedestrian routes to and through the site are determined along with the interrelationship with the surrounding parts of the city.

Strategies are also established and defined for:

- the different modes of public transport, including buses, trams, trains and taxis
- car access and means of parking
- bicycle routes and facilities
- means of access for vehicular deliveries and distribution between the different elements
- access for fire-fighting vehicles
- phasing of construction

The overall strategy establishes the hierarchy and character of buildings, including consideration of views to other key existing buildings and the visual impact of the new buildings on the surroundings.

Table 5.3 Paradise Street, Liverpool: principles—cont'd

The masterplan also determines an overall strategy for the public realm which considers the interrelationship between spaces and new buildings and between spaces and existing buildings. The nature, character, uses and hierarchy between spaces is also defined. The overall finished level of the spaces is determined and the means of vertical movement between the different levels established.

2. The Quarters

Level 2 information defines the brief and characteristics of the different quarters within the masterplan.

The masterplan establishes the character and overall nature of the quarters. This part determines the interrelationship between the different buildings and spaces adjacent to and within the quarter. These aspects of the quarter are established:
- the different uses
- the massing and building uses at the different levels of the building
- key views to and from the buildings
- the character and quality of the key buildings and spaces
- the setting out of the building blocks, streets and spaces
- the building levels, massing and profiles

3. Buildings

Level 3 information determines the requirements for each of the individual buildings. In the Paradise Street example, this involved 22 individual building briefs. This establishes the uses and areas to be accommodated into each building, the massing profile and character of the building. These briefs are given to the individual building designer before the commencement of outline design.

References

Beddington, N. (1981). *Shopping Centres, Retail Development, Design and Management.* Butterworth.

Department of the Environment, Transport and Regions and Commission for Architecture and the Built Environment (2000). *By Design – Urban Design in the Planning Systems; Towards Better Practice.* Thomas Telford.

DI Design and Development Consultants (1986). *Speciality Shopping Centres.* Jones Lang Wootton. p 5.

Maitland, B. (1990). *The New Architecture of the Retail Mall.* Architecture, Design and Technology Press. pp 20-25.

Milligan, J. (1986). *Speciality Shopping Centres.*

Teale, M. (1997). Big Box Retailing. *Shopping Centres Progress.* BCSC, Estates Gazette.

Figure 5.119 Partially covered two level South John Street, Paradise Street, Liverpool, UK (2008). *(Source: BDP)*

Emerging Types of Shopping

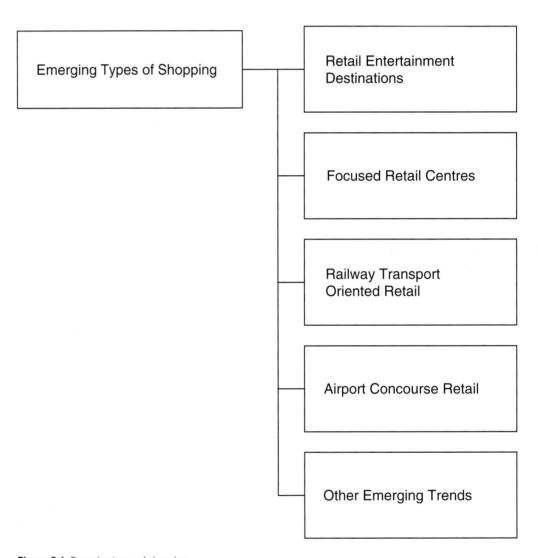

Figure 6.1 Emerging types of shopping.

Emerging Types of Shopping

6

This Chapter serves as a catch-all for other types of planned shopping facilities, listed in Fig. 6.1, encompassing the following broad issues: shopping formats falling outside the categories identified thus far; types having evolved following a more sophisticated understanding of social behaviour; and opportunistic formats developing as a secondary function from the presence of large numbers of people.

Retail Entertainment Destinations

The coincidence of public opinion becoming bored with traditional malls, social behaviour expecting more sophisticated facilities, and government encouragement, has led to the emergence of a new retail format in America – the retail entertainment destination. Although principally located in urban downtown situations, these shopping facilities can also be found in densely populated suburban locations. The regenerating effect on urban locations means retail entertainment destinations have many similarities with the new urban quarters referred to in the previous Chapter. Retail entertainment destinations are considered separately here because they are not exclusively located in town centres.

Other distinguishing qualities of retail entertainment destinations are the importance given to the inclusion of entertainment (leisure) facilities and their independence from traditional department store anchors. Retail entertainment destinations have previously been referred to as 'urban entertainment centres' and the evolving terminology reflects a greater understanding and maturing of the type. For instance, the first edition of *Developing Retail Entertainment Destinations* (Beyard et al., 2001) was titled *Developing Urban Entertainment Centres* (Beyard, 1998).

Retail entertainment destinations are a progression from festival and speciality retailing, referred to earlier, which established many of the retail principles upon which retail entertainment destinations are based – tuning the mix of merchandise, the importance of the environment in forming the character of the place and the complementary nature of catering and retail. However, other than the leisure pastime involved in festival and speciality retail there were few specific facilities for entertainment. The step forward made by retail entertainment destinations has been the specific inclusion of entertainment facilities and their equal importance to the retail and catering components. The entertainment facilities range from cinemas, special format theatres, game based attractions, sports and live performance venues.

The inclusion of entertainment facilities with retailing is not unique. The regional shopping and leisure centres discussed in Chapter 4 illustrate this point. The bolting on of entertainment facilities to a traditional shopping centre has also been described as 'shoppertainment'. Unfortunately, the same format has been applied to retail entertainment destinations and because of 'shoppertainment's' loose application, it is not referred to further here.

However, what makes retail entertainment destinations specific and different is the incorporation of entertainment with equal billing to retail and catering, rather than just as an add-on to the dominant shopping element. In addition, the new format often avoids the dependence on the traditional department store anchor. Furthermore, by careful shop selection, the synergy between the three elements of retail, catering and entertainment can be emphasised. For example, the retailing is often more leisure focused with books, music, sports and outdoor activity shops. The restaurants are also often selected to reinforce a film or sports theme. The inclusion of the three main components and their individual make up are carefully conceived to ensure the sum of the parts is greater than the total of the individual pieces.

Many of the qualities that are being incorporated into retail entertainment destinations reflect the general issues being addressed in American shopping centres. These common issues are: adapting to remain attractive in the face of competition from other retail formats; changing to meet increased public expectations; and incorporating new trends in retailing. The issues that set the background for retail entertainment destinations are reviewed below.

Competition has arisen from an oversupply of traditional malls and alternative forms of retailing, such as power retailers, retail warehouses and e-commerce. The public's expectations have increased and, for a centre to remain an attractive destination when competing against other centres, it is necessary for it to incorporate both entertainment and a wide range of catering facilities. The standard mall is not sufficiently attractive and needs to overcome a general antipathy towards it. Shopping facilities are required to provide environments where people want to be. With the rediscovery of main street-type environments, there is an increasing wish for this type of open-air pedestrian friendly place. New shop tenants are incorporating retailing trends developed towards entertainment of the customer and reflect the general move towards

Figure 6.2 A vibrant main street environment with catering and recreational uses forms a retail entertainment destination, Universal City Walk, Los Angeles, USA (1993). *(Source: Jerde/Stephen Simpson)*

more experimental shops where goods are fun, exciting, social, interactive and educational. In addition to the drama of the new shops, retailers are responding to lifestyle profiles and becoming more specific with their products to reflect how individuals identify themselves. Shops are also acting as indirect fashion consultants to meet customer aspirations.

By being considered and developed as new facilities, retail entertainment destinations can incorporate all these trends and issues in a new bundle of specifically assembled facilities, offered in an attractive open-air, pedestrian friendly environment. The old style shopping mall seems dull by comparison. New collections of retail and entertainment facilities, when creatively executed, capture the interest of the jaded customer.

Against this background of change, municipal governments have recognised the economic benefit of regenerating downtown areas. Consequently, municipalities in the USA have encouraged retail entertainment districts by offering incentives ranging from cash contributions, financial aid, tax abatements, zoning and building code variations, along with the completion of infrastructure. It is therefore not surprising that this has led to a growing number of retail entertainment destinations emerging across America.

The Urban Land Institute (ULI) defines the three main elements of a retail entertainment as the 'trinity of synergy', providing a combination of entertainment, dining and retail facilities within a pedestrian orientated multi-use environment (Beyard et al., 2001, p. 30). The entertainment element will consist of at least one of the major attractions outlined above and,

if limited to one, it is often a cinema complex. Different types of dining facility, ranging from small cafés to several major themed restaurants of 600 m² (6500 ft²) and above, are provided which meet the diverse needs of a wide age and social range. The retailing tends to be entertainment orientated with shops accommodating books, media, music and outdoor activity clothing retailers. It may also incorporate some carefully selected lifestyle retailers with homeware and aspirational fashion shops.

The facilities are arranged in accommodation which addresses a street or public space. The shops can sometimes be accommodated in modified existing historic buildings, providing the structure and floor-plate are suitable. Otherwise, historic façades can be retained and new structures built behind. Alternatively, suitable new buildings are formed to provide outward facing shops on to the street.

The public spaces are activated during the day by customers and local workers using the dining facilities. Later, the entertainment and dining facilities become the main activities, complemented by the shops in the early evening. By the late evening, the entertainment and club facilities are principally in use. These different uses act independently, but are frequently complementary to one another. There is a greater emphasis on evening and night-time activity than in a traditional shopping centre. Retail entertainment destinations are often part of a mixed-use development combining residential and office accommodation alongside the three main uses. The combination of other uses provides additional activity in the streets at different times of day.

Retail entertainment destinations are frequently found in downtown districts, but are not restricted to town centre locations. They are also located in densely populated suburban areas which are able to generate the high levels of usage and frequency of return visit required for success of this format. There are two principal reasons why retail entertainment destinations require higher visitation levels than traditional shopping centres. The first is that the new format will have higher construction and running costs for the same amount of accommodation. Secondly, the rental levels for catering and entertainment facilities are less than those for shops which, in this format, make up a smaller portion of the total.

The characteristic qualities of a retail entertainment destination are generated by a mixture of uses adopted in a medium density form. For example, street-facing facilities, together with an eclectic choice of amenities, providing vitality to a pedestrian friendly environment.

Figure 6.3 A mixture of shops, catering and cinemas form an urban multi-level retail entertainment destination, Denver Pavilions, Denver, Colorado, USA (1998). *(Source: Entertainment Development Group/Stan Obert)*

Figure 6.4 The regeneration of an urban quarter forms a retail entertainment destination in downtown Old Pasadena, Pasadena, USA (1983–2005). *(Source: Corbis/Robert Landau)*

Retail entertainment destinations are a popular phenomenon because they readily address the convergence of retail trends outlined above and are popular with a variety of different interest groups. First, they are a popular format with the public as they address the trends in both retail and leisure facilities; meeting consumer demand for more immediate recreational facilities; providing retail facilities which address lifestyle aspirations and, by being closer to homes, are readily accessible. Their popularity and accessibility ensure they are frequently enjoyed and thus perpetuate their own success. They are also keenly supported and instigated by a variety of interests; developers, for example, favour the format as a new way of successfully competing against the value orientated retail formats; entertainment companies are eager sponsors as they seek opportunities to supply the demand for leisure facilities; and municipalities recognise these developments as potential catalysts for the regeneration of

downtown areas and are keen to support them by offering a range of incentives.

The ULI has identified three fundamental types of retail entertainment destination:

- free-standing destinations
- retail entertainment districts
- shopping centres infused with entertainment amenities.

The first two types are examined in more detail here, along with a review of typical examples of each type. The third type has largely been examined in an earlier Chapter when reviewing regional shopping and leisure centres.

A more comprehensive explanation of the qualities and issues involved with retail entertainment destinations, together with numerous example case studies, can be found in ULI's book *Developing Retail Entertainment Destinations* (Beyard et al., 2001).

Free-Standing Destinations

Free-standing destinations can be situated in urban or highly populated suburban location. These developments can be implemented independently by private companies and, when completed, form cohesive managed properties. They represent the new generation of leisure development. Typical examples are Irvine Spectrum Centre, Irvine (1995), reviewed under Entertainment Centres earlier on; The Printworks, Manchester (2000) reviewed under New Urban Quarters; Universal City Walk, Los Angeles (1993) and The Block at Orange, Orange (1998).

The Block at Orange, Orange County, California (1998) is an example of a free-standing retail entertainment destination located in the densely populated suburbs of Orange County to the south of Los Angeles. Situated near the convergence of several freeways, the complex is readily accessible to 1.8 million people who live within a ten mile drive. The location benefits from offices and other businesses which surround the complex and provide a built-in daytime market.

The Block at Orange occupies the site of a former traditional enclosed shopping centre which closed in 1994. Developer Mills Corporation studied ways of reusing the original structure (which was only enclosed in the early 1980s) with its traditional department store anchors, but concluded it to be inappropriate and incapable of establishing the new brand they intended.

Consequently the site was redeveloped, but the new site planning retained a vestige of the former mall, with the new complex similarly being located

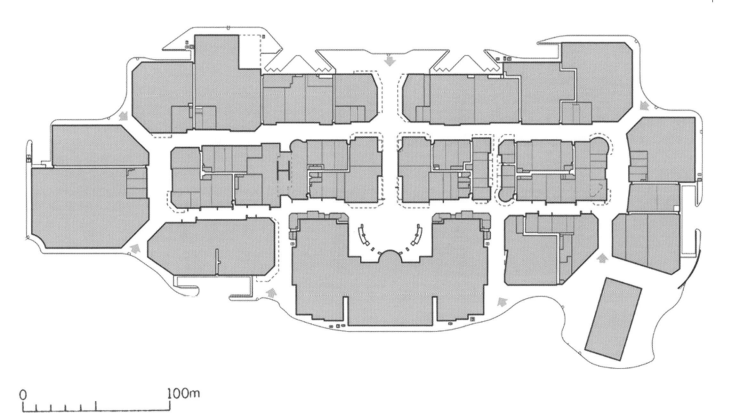

0 _____ 100m

Figure 6.5 Ground floor layout, The Block at Orange, Orange County, California, USA (1998). *(Source: Mills Corporation)*

in the centre of the site, surrounded by surface car parking and bounded by a ring road. The new arrangement adopts an urban form, consisting of nine separate buildings defining a network of open-air streets and spaces. The streets form a circuit of pedestrian ways with major and minor streets. The two principal streets run lengthways and are approximately 370 m (1200 ft) long, connecting all of the accommodation. Each street, designed by architects D'Agostino, Izzo, Quirk of Somerville, Massachusetts, has its own identity and ambience, and they form 'the Boulevard' and 'the Strip'.

The Boulevard at 15.4 m (50 ft) is the wider of the two streets and has a more relaxed atmosphere with spreading canopy trees, benches for taking a pause and historically styled lamp posts. The Strip, by deliberate contrast, is more vibrant and high energy, being narrower at 9.25 m (30 ft) wide. The trees and lighting standards in this street have a greater vertical emphasis and there is less seating. The Boulevard and the Strip are connected at each end and also by two further cross streets. Seven entranceways from the surrounding car parking connect to the streets from each of the corners and along the length of the complex.

Figure 6.6 The relaxed character of 'The Boulevard', The Block at Orange, Orange County, California, USA. *(Source: Mills Corporation)*

Figure 6.7 The contrasting quality of the more vibrant street to 'The Strip', The Block at Orange, Orange County, California, USA. *(Source: Mills Corporation)*

Anchoring the Block is a 30-screen cinema complex located midway along the Strip which terminates the primary cross street with a square-shaped open space – the Plaza. The Plaza is formed by the U-shaped cinema block and forms the focal point of the public spaces. Two large themed restaurants complete the enclosure of the Plaza. The main cross street continues from the Plaza and is lined by four other full service restaurants. The other interconnecting cross street forms another, different, type of dining environment with fast food outlets lining the street in an open-air food court type of facility.

Figure 6.8 'The Plaza' public space anchored by multi-screen cinemas and themed restaurants, The Block at Orange, Orange County, California, USA. *(Source: Mills Corporation)*

The remaining accommodation is arranged with the larger entertainment and retail units located around the perimeter of the complex and the smaller units grouped into the central island blocks.

The buildings that make up the Block are deliberately modest and understated to allow the signage and lighting to create the atmosphere of the place. The large footprint of each block is sub-divided by a variable roofline and a plan profile with projections and set-backs which express the individual tenants and provide variety and incident along the length of the street. The buildings are mostly one level, with some two-level frontages, and are finished in stucco painted a variety of pastel shades. Brightly coloured, pitched, metal awnings add a further layer of visual interest to the buildings.

Figure 6.9 An architecture from simple buildings with character derived from environmental graphics, The Block at Orange, Orange County, California, USA. *(Source: Mills Corporation)*

The Mills Corporation's architectural brief allowed the signage to set the character, with the buildings forming a backdrop for the graphic insertions and street furniture. The philosophy is based on the signage being readily changeable and updated, thereby keeping the feel fresh and vibrant. To achieve this effect, the Block has adopted a variety of different types of signage, with a hierarchy for each type, conveying a separate type of message. The primary signage is immediately apparent on arrival at the development where, in the car park, large vertical signboards (designed by Communication Arts of Boulder, Colorado) called 'stylons' dramatically tower above the buildings. The stylons vary in height with the tallest standing up to 28m (90ft) high. The stylons are also used within the centre establishing a memorable visual landmark which represents

Figure 6.10 Presence from bold vertical signage 'stylons', The Block at Orange, Orange County, California, USA. *(Source: Mills Corporation)*

Figure 6.12 Characterful way-finding street totems, The Block at Orange, Orange County, California, USA. *(Source: Mills Corporation)*

Figure 6.11 Billboard signage on the buildings, The Block at Orange, Orange County, California, USA. *(Source: Mills Corporation)*

the development. Utilising the latest digital printing these vertical signboards are used both to promote the centre and to provide a large visual display. Large horizontal billboards are the next layer in the signage hierarchy. These billboards adopt an urban tradition, deliberately creating further visual interest and are used for traditional advertising. The billboards are integrated with the buildings, positioned either above or on the façades. More functional, way-finding signs, standing in the streets, are the third signage level. These totems are formed from a vibrant and playful collage of letters representing the centre and sit above the informative street directions.

Reflecting the importance of the signage to the character of the complex, a comprehensive signage package was submitted to the city of Orange for approval. This process needed the municipality's cooperation and required the altering of certain codes to accommodate the dramatic signage approach.

Complementing the signage and reinforcing the urban imagery of the Block is an equally dramatic lighting scheme, designed by Francis Krahe and Associates of Laguna Beach, California. The lighting scheme includes illumination of both the buildings and the spaces. The street lighting is provided by a range of different lighting masts which correspond to the character of the particular street. The lighting masts range from fully glazed, double spheres capping vertical masts, scaled down, highway type standards which cantilever from metal masts, and smaller, more historic, vertical lighting masts. The principal cross street leading to the cinema has additional feature lighting to emphasise the drama of the route. This feature lighting is formed by vertical light bars hung from cables which are suspended between the light masts and buildings.

Figure 6.13 Vertical light bars hung from cables, The Block at Orange, Orange County, California, USA. *(Source: Mills Corporation)*

The tenant mix, which makes up 72000 m² (775000 ft²) GLA retail entertainment destination at the Block at Orange, is typical of the three principal types involved in this format – entertainment, catering and retail. The entertainment and catering, at 30700 m² (330000 ft²) and 9250 m² (99500 ft²) respectively, make up the majority of the accommodation. The principal tenants are a 6066-seat, 30-screen cinema complex, a 5575 m² (60000 ft²) adult sports and games venue; a skateboard and roller-blading facility of 4275 m² (46000 ft²) for teenagers and younger children; a watersports shop of 2370 m² (25500 ft²); and a slightly smaller Hawaiian goods store. The other retailing accommodation provides major stores for leisure related goods such as books, games, music, media and a variety of aspirational clothing retailers. The dining facilities are provided by a variety of large restaurants, with both internal and external seating, and fast food outlets catering for different markets and times of the day.

The tenants at the Block at Orange have been selected to respond to a wide range of demographic interests. The mix of different uses complement and support each of the primary types. During the day, for example, the dining facilities rely on the large adjacent population. In the evenings, the cinema complex generates the use of the different restaurants. The late night opening of the retail shops reinforces the restaurant sales and the use of the restaurants correspondingly supports the shops. Although the different uses operate independently, the interdependence and mutual support of the three principal components of entertainment, dining and retail demonstrate the 'trinity of synergy' that exists between them. The workings of the mix illustrate the greater importance given to evening trade in this format of shopping, compared to a traditional shopping centre.

In 2000 the Block at Orange was extended to incorporate additional tenants, including new entertainment facilities – a night club, a health club and a bowling alley. Additional dining was provided by the inclusion of a pub, and new retailing by a new music store and several smaller shops.

Retail Entertainment Districts

Retail entertainment districts are integrated within the urban fabric of a downtown area. Depending on the scale of development, they can involve the revitalisation of several city blocks and, in these instances, are likely to involve a public and private partnership. The larger projects are likely to involve several private companies working together with the municipality. The retail entertainment districts of this format are often on sites in blighted city centre areas. A typical example of this type is represented by Old Pasadena, Pasadena (1983–2005), and Denver Pavilions, Denver (1998) described below.

Denver Pavilions, Denver, Colorado (1998) is an example retail entertainment district. With 33 000 m² (347 000 ft²) of lettable space, it is a medium size retail entertainment destination, forming a small district in the downtown financial area of the city. This development of retail, catering and entertainment occupies two city blocks which were formally used as surface parking lots, serving nearby offices. The site benefits from facing onto 16th Street Mall, which acts as the urban spine of the city, connecting between lower downtown and the city centre. It is also close to the main convention centre and benefits from the natural synergy between the civic and commercial amenities in this district of the city.

Bill Denton of Entertainment Development Group (EDG) chose Denver to complete his company's first development, having realised the city's commitment to the downtown area and recognising the benefit of having a large number of in-town workers and a significant local residential population close to the city centre. Denton also recognised that Denver would benefit from not having another significant downtown area competing for the catchment population within a radius of 500 miles.

Although Denver Pavilions may have been EDG's first development, the company's skills were put to the test and aptly demonstrated in the process it had to navigate in order to get the project underway and completed. The project involved the formation of a public/private partnership (involving the municipal redevelopment authority, the fund, the joint venture development companies and the construction company) to put up equity for the development. Land acquisitions involved negotiating with a reluctant owner, who was coerced by the rear of the site being given over for his separate office, hotel and residential development. In addition, the majority of key tenants had to be convinced to commit well in advance of completion in order to release the funding for the project. Despite the various challenges, the project was completed in a relatively short time frame – commencement of planning in 1994 and opening in November 1998.

The key to the success of this project was the securing of a flagship entertainment anchor in the form of a recognisable multi-screen operator. With this commitment in place, EDG was able to search for some major brand retailers. Utilising the strong mix of professional sports based in Denver (football, basketball, baseball and hockey), EDG convinced Nike Town to open. With the strength of Nike, other major aspirational, leisure and lifestyle retailers followed suit and signed up. Having established the key entertainment and retailers, the next key component was finding recognisable complementary themed restaurants. The Hard Rock Café and several other restaurants engaged to join the development, thereby forming the tripartite framework for the remaining tenants to complete. The 70 per cent pre-letting was thereby achieved and the funding released for the project to proceed.

The street and building layout of Denver Pavilions is arranged as an integral part of downtown Denver, extending the scale and pattern of the local street grid. The development is formed by four individual buildings which define the streets and spaces with three and four-storey high blocks (see Fig. 6.14). A network of open streets has been formed, incorporating the existing street framework. The scheme faces on to the main street, the urban spine of 16th Street Mall. The original two city blocks are subdivided by a new street which leads from, and then connects back to, 16th Street Mall, crossing the other original street, Glenarm Place, which has

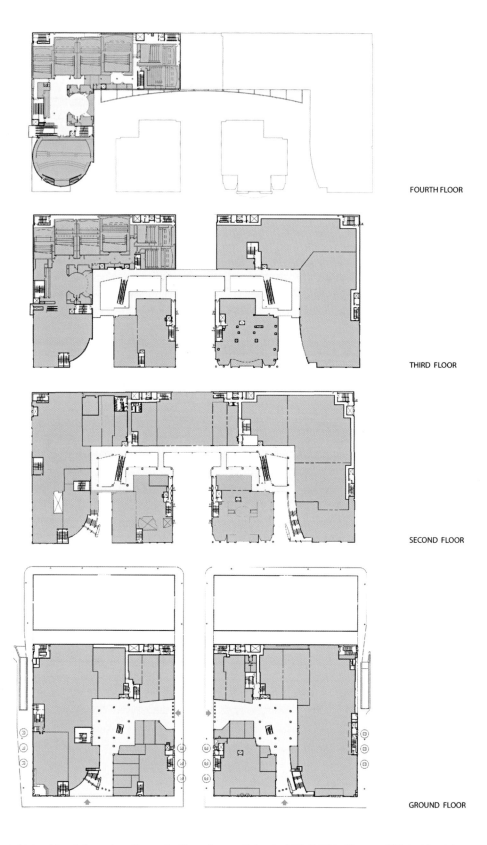

FOURTH FLOOR

THIRD FLOOR

SECOND FLOOR

GROUND FLOOR

0   25   50
Scale: 1" = 50'-0"   Proj. North

Figure 6.14 Ground, second, third and fourth floor plans, Denver Pavilions, Denver, Colorado, USA (1998). *(Source: ELS Architects)*

been made pedestrian friendly. The network of pedestrian walkways provides multiple entrance-ways from the main street and extends the primary frontages from 16th Street Mall into the centre of the blocks.

Retail shops and restaurants occupy the first two floors of Denver Pavilions. The third level is occupied by large night clubs and themed cafés which form the entranceway to the 15-screen cinema which, in turn, occupies the fourth level of the larger blocks at the rear. A grand stone staircase leads down on to the main street from the cinema entrance. Escalators also lead up to the cinemas. Underground parking garages provide 800 car parking spaces on site. The car parking is supplemented for shoppers and cinema users by use of the adjacent 8000 office car parking spaces which are available outside of working hours and are within a few blocks.

including stone, coloured concrete, painted render, metal and glass. The street frontages are animated by a variety of different sized, grey, metal framed shop windows. Double and single height shop fronts, together with strategically positioned double height, upper floor windows, create impact on 16th Street Mall. Individual tenant brand imaging has been carefully coordinated on the façades and adds another layer of vitality to the buildings.

Figure 6.16 One of the individual buildings with active frontages aligning 16th Street Mall, Denver Pavilions, Denver, Colorado, USA. *(Source: Entertainment Development Group/Stan Obert)*

Figure 6.15 Four levels of shops, catering, leisure and cinemas form urban blocks, Denver Pavilions, Denver, USA. *(Source: Entertainment Development Group/Stan Obert)*

The four building blocks that make up Denver Pavilions, designed by ELS Architects of Berkeley, California, are treated as four individual buildings, each with their own architectural treatment. The elegant and restrained buildings are arranged as either red or white pavilions, establishing a variety of architecture for the neighbourhood. A simple palette of natural materials has been used to clad the buildings,

A striking 110 m long and 12 m high (365 ft by 40 ft) light wall runs above and between the two rear blocks and displays 'Denver Pavilions' in large lettering, which can be read from 16th Street Mall and the approaching streets. The lighting filters through perforated metal panels and is programmed to change colour during the evening. The light wall forms a memorable backdrop and announces the new district to the main street. Combined with the urban architecture, the signage plays a major part in forming the character of the place in the new district. It may not be as comprehensive an approach as the Block at Orange, but it does illustrate the importance of good signage design and the contribution it makes to this type of shopping format.

Figure 6.17 Strong three dimensional graphics and the light wall, Denver, Colorado, USA. *(Source: Entertainment Development Group/Stan Obert)*

Denver Pavilions works as a retail and entertainment destination in its own right and is contributing to the success of the other businesses along 16th Street Mall, which have noticed a significant increase in traffic. EDG's early analysis of Denver has proven correct, with the urban entertainment centre benefiting from the strong downtown and city centre residential population. The strong disposition of suburban residents has contributed to the high visitor levels to the complex.

Focused Retail Centres

Focused retail centres, sometimes referred to as themed retail centres, are a shopping environment where all the retailers collected together in a single centre sell goods or services of a similar type, such as fashionware, sportsware or houseware. The evolution of this particular shopping facility reflects an amalgam of both social and retail trends.

The idea of themed collections of shops is not new in itself, as several major centres have certain zones, or a particular floor, with similar types of retailers grouped together, as in the Bullring, Birmingham, where each mall level has a different retailing theme. What is unique to focused retail centres is that the whole centre or collection of shops is focused on a single type of product. In theory, the type can be open-air or enclosed. It is likely to be located on the edge of an urban centre, as the tenants are likely to be unable to pay the prime rental levels associated with town centre locations.

Focused retailing has emerged in order to provide customers with the convenience of a readily available, wide choice of similar products in a single place, without having to walk extensive distances or search around shops in the process of comparison retailing. The type has emerged as a response to the needs of an increasingly busy, time pressured society which can readily benefit from the time saving convenience of similar shops grouped together.

A particular type of themed retailing, created in recognition of the high proportion of income directed towards the home, is home furnishings, which can be seen in the Dutch example at Villa Arena, near Amsterdam (2001) reviewed below.

Villa Arena is a focused retail centre based on home furnishings in a single-themed mall, on the scale of a regional shopping centre, with 75 000 m^2 (807 000 ft^2) of retail accommodation. It provides everything connected with the home, (furniture, furnishings, finishes, appliances and home related services) all together under one roof. Developed by a joint consortium of Ballast Needam, Bam, NBM Vastgoed and ING Real Estate, this unique retail offer is aimed at providing convenience, pleasure and value. It is located on the outskirts of the city, adjacent to Amsterdam Arena Stadium, the Ajax football stadium.

Villa Arena is an enclosed centre and provides four levels of shops, cafés and offices within the building. Internally, its public environment could be a traditional shopping centre. The home furnishing focused shops are arranged around a day-lit atrium

Figure 6.18 Four levels of shops and facilities focused on homewares, Villa Arena, Amsterdam, The Netherlands (2001). *(Source: Benthan Cronwell)*

with 2500 parking spaces on two decks above and in a basement.

Villa Arena brings together under one roof, in an attractive enclosed environment, the ad hoc rag-bag of DIY stores, furniture stores, carpet warehouses, and appliance shops usually found on retail parks and peripheral town centre areas. The focused centre makes a step-change from the poor quality, open-air environment normally associated with such individual stores, providing catering and public facilities to make the visit to this centre a pleasurable experience. These facilities raise the quality of experience associated with an out-of-town retail park to those of a traditional shopping centre. In so doing, they reflect the general condition of society's rising expectations.

The specialist nature of Villa Arena is aimed at a large catchment area, catering for day out excursions with the provision of restaurants and a children's nursery. There is even a small entertainment provision in the centre in the form of a 'home of

the future', which includes thinking installations and smart appliances. Part of the centre's innovative thinking is the inclusion of an educational facility, represented by the demonstration square, which is used for informative exhibitions, training demonstrations and presentations. This facility is aimed at educating customers, offering help and advice on purchases and generally making purchases more useable. The objective of the educational facility is to make the experience of Villa Arena beneficial and to attract further use of the centre. In addition to the shops, there is 4000 m² (43 000 ft²) of space for home-related service providers such as insurers, interior designers and mortgage advisers, thus allowing services to be provided as well as products purchased.

The architect, Benthan Cronwell, has arranged the centre around a multi-level atrium which is naturally lit by a fully glazed, ETFE inflated air cushion roof. This central feature space collects visitors arriving from the roof car parking and those

Figure 6.19 Naturally lit atrium space with air cushion roof and cantilevered escalators, Villa Arena, Amsterdam, The Netherlands. *(Source: Benthan Cronwell)*

Figure 6.20 Interior with successive floor levels producing galleries with variable overhangs and setbacks and an unusual terracing effect, Villa Arena, Amsterdam, The Netherlands. *(Source: Benthan Cronwell)*

entering from the boulevard at ground floor level. Vertical movement between the four public floor levels, is celebrated by cantilevered escalators which project out from the gallery into the atrium.

The atrium is angled in plan, with each successive floor being slightly twisted from the one below, giving the galleries variable overhangs and set-backs. The twisted galleries form a variety of internal spaces around the atrium, which vary from covered walkways to open terraces. The open terraces, from above, provide views on to occupied areas and emphasise the stepping of the accommodation. The variable galleries provide greater visual interest and give a distinctive quality to the interior space, avoiding the monotony and predictability of stacked parallel floors. Further animation is layered on the atrium by the cascading escalators, lifts and angled walkways crossing the space. A copper finished, tube shaped, feature restaurant sits above the atrium floor on pairs of metal stilts.

The interior, designed in collaboration with interior designers Virgile and Stone, is contemporary and clean edged, using a variety of simply detailed, natural materials. Glass balustrades are arranged in front of higher, metal supported timber handrails; steel roof trusses are left exposed in the space; iroko seats and kiosks sit on the stone floors. The gallery edges around the atrium are finished, beneath the glazed balustrading, with a finely detailed metal edging which avoids the bulkheads dominating the space.

The exterior of the building is contemporary and a straightforward expression of the inward looking shops. The simple box-like form is clad in polished concrete and vertical aluminium slats. The simple building sits comfortably and unassumingly in the robust outer city context amidst the functional stadium building and high rise-office buildings.

Figure 6.22 Entry to car park ramp showing simple exterior architecture to Villa Arena, Amsterdam, The Netherlands. *(Source: Benthan Cronwell)*

The bringing together of similar retailers into a single building is a move forwards in the evolution of themed shopping and its holistic approach to gathering otherwise piecemeal, edge-of-town, retailers is a welcome shift forward. However, the particular form of this centre, with its large inward looking box, may not be appropriate in some town centre locations. Hopefully, alternative ways of housing this innovative type of shopping environment can readily accommodate the principal of a focused shopping centre and allow this format to be readily progressed elsewhere.

Figure 6.21 The free standing copper restaurant standing on stilts in the atrium, Villa Arena, Amsterdam, The Netherlands. *(Source: Benthan Cronwell)*

Railway Transport Oriented Retail

The shopping environments emerging at transport hubs are not surprisingly secondary to the primary function of the railway station building. The shopping formats described here have taken advantage of the large number of pedestrians passing daily through railway stations. This form of shopping highlights one of the fundamental principles of shopping – where there are high volumes of pedestrian foot fall, shopping facilities are likely to succeed.

Figure 6.23 A sensitive glass and steel extension forms shops and catering, The Lawn, Paddington Station, London, UK (1999). *(Source: Peter Coleman)*

The first type of railway oriented retail facilities is found at the major city railway stations which act as 'destination stations'. Destination stations are located in cities which act as centres of employment for large, surrounding commuting populations who arrive in the city and pass through the station on the daily journey to and from work. In these instances, the stations are destinations for a large conurbation; the station buildings are generally large and significant and can accommodate the retail facilities within the station building. The second type of railway transport oriented retail facility is that of the local 'neighbourhood stations'. These local stations serve a community that commutes from the local station to the destination station and provide more of a community focus. Shopping environments found at neighbourhood stations are described later.

Destination Stations

The trend for station retailing took off in the late 1980s in both Europe and America. With most railway buildings formed half a century ago or earlier, the retail facilities tend to be accommodated within existing buildings, often involving the alteration and conversion of grand 19th and 20th century buildings. The retail facilities tend to be accommodated within the station concourse, which also serves as the passenger waiting and arrival space. The concourse is separate from the train shed and embarking platforms. The extent of retail facilities is therefore often constrained by the physical size of the existing buildings and the need to retain the main function of movement to and from the trains, passenger information and ticketing facilities.

As well as the grand railway sheds, some of the older city stations have monumental, day-lit concourse spaces which, when sensitively converted and altered with new insertions and independent kiosks, can make splendid shopping environments. One such example is Union Station, Washington, DC (1907) with its grand vaulted concourse space, originally designed by Daniel H Burnham, which was sensitively converted by architect Benjamin Thompson Associates in 1988. An unobtrusive vocabulary has been adopted, allowing the insertion of a mezzanine floor and independent glass and steel kiosks, which both sit within the vaulted space to provide shops and catering facilities. A similar approach was applied by Arup Associates in its design for the insertions added into the concourse of Liverpool Street Station, London. Here, steel and glass insertions form a mezzanine floor and independent kiosks within the grand Victorian station concourse.

One of the earliest UK examples where working within the size and architectural constraints of the historical concourse space was overcome, is Victoria Place, Victoria Station, London, (1987) which provides 7435 m² (80 000 ft²) of lettable retail facilities. These facilities, designed by Chapman Taylor and Partners, have been ingeniously inserted above the train platforms by the introduction of a deck structure supported from the existing columns. Twenty-one shop units were originally provided in a new two-sided mall, accessed from escalators that lead up from the main concourse level. A further partial mezzanine level was also inserted to provide additional catering facilities, accommodating restaurants and cafés. Since its completion, a further series of alterations has been completed to make improvements and provide additional space. The formation of the Victoria Place retail facilities by

Figure 6.24 Shops inserted into the concourse space of Union Station, Washington, DC, USA (1988). *(Source: Anthony Baker Artwork)*

Figure 6.25 An elegant glass and steel insertion form shops within the Victorian Concourse, Liverpool Street Station, London, UK. *(Source: Peter Coleman)*

Figure 6.26 Shops added above the tracks, Victoria Place, Victoria Station, London, UK (1987). *(Source: Chapman Taylor)*

Figure 6.27 Catering and shop facilities arranged over three levels, The Lawn, Paddington Station, London, UK (1999). *(Source: Peter Coleman)*

decking over the platforms and train tracks has, at the expense of freeing up the shopping facilities, partially compromised the quality of the travel experience from this station.

Another interesting UK example of retail facilities within a destination station can be found at 'The Lawn', Paddington Station, London (1999). Here, the grandeur of Isambard Kingdom Brunel's magnificent railway sheds and glass and steel concourse has been restored, with new retail facilities inserted to form 'The Lawn'. Designed by architect Nicolas Grimshaw and Associates, 'The Lawn' provides 2800 m² (30 000 ft²) of retail facilities, carefully inserted behind the restored glass and cast iron screen of the former concourse. The facilities accommodate a supermarket, shops and cafés. A partial mezzanine has been inserted beneath new glazed roof lights which provide natural daylight to the double height space. The mezzanine structure encloses the new shops at station level and forms a first floor gallery of cafés and restaurants overlooking the grand railway shed and platforms.

Network Rail (formerly Railtrack) completed the gateway building for the 2002 Manchester Commonwealth Games with the new entrance concourse and restoration of the train shed, transforming Piccadilly Station, Manchester (2002) into an exemplary railway station with retail facilities. The new retail facilities, situated beyond the iron and glass train shed and separated from it by a fully glazed screen, are located in the new entrance concourse building designed by architect BDP. The new building forms a double height, fully glazed space provided by an ETFE cushion inflated roof, supported on a light-weight steel structure. Located in the entrance concourse is 4200 m² (45 000 ft²) of lettable accommodation, which is arranged on two levels.

The Piccadilly Station retail layout was influenced by careful analysis of the likely passenger usage of the station. The analysis revealed an average dwell time of 13 minutes by the 50 000 daily passengers. This led to the separation of the retail facilities into three broad types, each part being positioned to be most convenient to the passengers likely to use it. For example, the 'grab and go' retailing is located at the concourse level and is immediately accessible from the train platforms. The standard and leisure shop units are located in a separate pedestrian route, situated away from the congested areas leading to the platforms. The third category – catering (separated from the fast food, located at concourse level) – provides quality cafés, bars and restaurants located at the upper concourse level. The upper level provides a more relaxed environment

Figure 6.28 Two levels of shops and catering in the new entrance concourse, Piccadilly Station, Manchester, UK (2002). *(Source: David Barbour/BDP)*

and allows views both internally across the concourse to the train shed, and externally to the city beyond. Strategically placed escalators, lifts and stairs lead up from the concourse at each end of the first floor gallery.

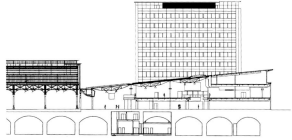

Figure 6.30 Typical cross section through the concourse and train shed, Piccadilly Station, Manchester, UK. *(Source: BDP)*

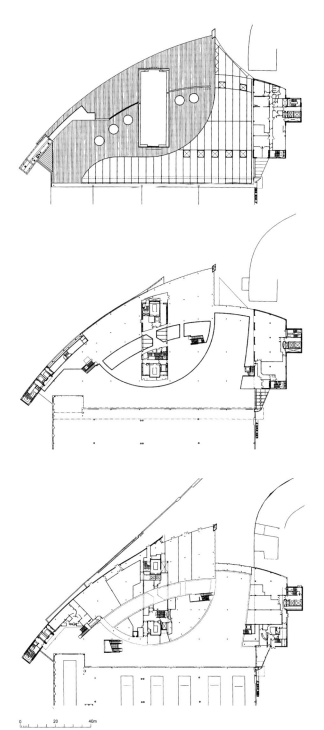

Figure 6.29 Ground, first floor and roof plans, Piccadilly Station, Manchester, UK. *(Source: BDP)*

The main concourse accommodates 23 shop units, the majority being less than 50 m² (530 ft²). An additional six mobile, glazed units sit within the concourse space beneath the glazed roof. The main passenger ticketing area is located directly off the concourse area and faces the train platforms and travel information screens, which are freestanding in the concourse. Additional storage space is located beneath the station concourse and is served by an integral vehicular service yard. Service lifts connect from the service yard to the storage areas and concourse level shops.

The combined Piccadilly Station concourse facilities are planned with the objective of enhancing the passenger experience. Although the concourse feels like a shopping space, it is also planned to allow the operational aspects of the station to remain paramount. The retail facilities are arranged with the orientation of the passenger and legibility of the station in mind. On arrival into the station the concourse is kept clear, allowing views through to the platforms and, conversely, out to the city beyond. Critical passenger facilities, such as the travel centre, information point and destination timetable, occupy key points in the concourse and are visible from the strategic points of entry. The legibility of the station has largely been retained by locating the retail facilities to one side of the congested passenger activities. A separate pedestrian route, lined on both sides by shops, accommodates the majority of shops and leads between the main entrance and second entranceway to the taxi and car drop off area. Although most of the shop units are small, the layout accommodates some deeper units and provides larger units for a food store and a stationer, one at each end of the street, to act like anchors.

The formation of the new entrance concourse at Piccadilly Station involved the removal of all the former 1960s concourse structures. The taxi and car drop off area has also been reorganised in an unused

Figure 6.31 Separate from the concourse a mall provides additional shopping, Piccadilly Station, Manchester, UK. *(Source: Peter Coleman)*

Figure 6.32 The catering gallery overlooking the concourse, Piccadilly Station, Manchester, UK. *(Source: Peter Coleman)*

Figure 6.33 Shopping within the railway concourse, Piccadilly Station, Manchester, UK (2002). *(Source: BDP/David Balbour).*

undercroft area, with direct road access beneath the station. This reorganisation has left the original front entrance ramp for the sole use of pedestrians. Complementing the new concourse, the Victorian train shed has been restored and the retained 1960s office building has also been reclad.

Piccadilly Station's new concourse is a contemporary design, confidently expressing the building technology of the elegant steel structure and inflated cushion, glazed roof used to form it. The concourse forms a lofty day-lit space which serves as the hub of the station. The two-level shopping area takes advantage of the height created beneath the mono-pitch roof, which slopes, in a single gesture, from the entrance down towards the train shed. The catering, located on the galleries, sits beneath the encompassing roof and feels like an upper terrace to the concourse, rather than a separate area. The layout of the shopping facilities allows the station to function, while maximising pedestrian flows in front of the shops and between key parts of the station.

With the number of passengers passing through Piccadilly Station and its extended opening hours as a public space, the interior has adopted a robust palette of materials. Monochrome terrazzo tiles have been used on the floors, with glass balustrades and steel handrails lining the gallery edges. Modular panels of metal and glass enclose the upper parts of the first floor level shops. A splash of colour has been introduced into the controlled interior by the insertion of an organically shaped plant enclosure, which is finished in red painted plaster, beneath the overriding roof.

In order to achieve a balance between an economical solution and an acceptable internal environment in the large concourse space, thermal modelling techniques were used to predict the internal conditions in both summer and winter. As a result of this environmental analysis, natural ventilation systems and a reflective middle layer in the roof are used to reduce heat gain during the summer. An underfloor heating system has been installed in the upper concourse level floor to produce a comfortable catering environment in the winter. The inflated cushion ETFE roof has good thermal insulation qualities and performs well acoustically in the predominantly hard-finished space.

The combination of the new concourse space and shopping facilities contained within Piccadilly Station gives an air of excitement and once again establishes a sense of glamour associated with travel. Alongside the activity of the railway station is an inseparable shopping facility serving both travelling passengers and, to a lesser degree, local residents.

What was once just a rather dreary railway station, has been transformed into a shopping venue which happens to have 1200 trains moving in and out of it every day. The opportunity exists to apply the similar levels of quality and customer facilities achieved in Manchester's Piccadilly Station, to other languishing stations in the UK.

Neighbourhood Stations

The second type of railway transport oriented retail facilities is that developed around railway stations from which passengers originate. These tend to be retail facilities specifically developed at stations that have a sizeable residential population within commuting distance of a major city. These stations are located on the periphery to major conurbations, whose business districts generate large numbers of workers commuting daily to their place of work. As such the retail facilities provided at these stations relate more closely to the local residential population and also act as a neighbourhood hub. The retail facilities found at neighbourhood stations are distinctly different from those found at the destination type of station. The neighbourhood station will witness a larger dwell time by its visitors and, by serving more of a community focus, will provide a mixture of facilities including aspirational shops, catering and entertainment facilities. The retail facilities at neighbourhood stations will be both for the convenience and for the leisure requirements of the local population.

Mockingbird Station, Dallas, Texas (2002) is one of the first purpose-designed and built examples of a neighbourhood station retail facility. Mockingbird Station is part of a mixed-use development, developed jointly by UC Urban of Texas and Simpson Property Group, with RTKL as design architect and Selzer Associates as project architect. This satellite development is linked directly to the Dallas Area Rapid Transit (DART) which connects, in an eight minute journey, to the central business area of the city. The development is the first mixed-use project in Texas specifically built together with a light-rail station (Boroski and Arrington, 2002). This urban village contains 211 upmarket loft type apartments, 13 000 m² (140 000 ft²) of office space, as well as the 16 700 m² (180 000 ft²) of space for shops, theatres and restaurants. The station also serves as a major bus transfer centre. The shops, entertainment and catering facilities are a mixture of destination and convenience facilities serving a predominantly upscale market.

Figure 6.34 An open street environment provides shops and leisure facilities to the local neighbourhood in a mixed use development, Mockingbird Station, Dallas, Texas, USA (2002). *(Source: RTKL)*

Mockingbird Station is just 6.4 km (4 miles) north of central Dallas and serves both a new fashionable residential population alongside an established upmarket residential area. The station is also near to a 32 000 seat stadium and the Southern Methodist University, with a shuttle link to the campus. Furthermore, the station is conveniently close to two recreational facilities – a hike and bike trail and a lakeside water sports centre. These recreational and civic facilities, alongside the residential community, provide an additional draw for visitors to use the station.

The Mockingbird Station development is formed from several individual buildings which define external streets and spaces. These public spaces are landscaped and form an open-air environment for the shops and restaurants, which face outwards on to the streets. A grand staircase links the cinema to the shops, offices and apartments. A public plaza in front of the cinema connects between the staircase and the adjacent station via an interconnecting bridge. Two separate existing buildings have been converted into individual office and residential buildings. The residential accommodation

has been formed from a former factory building which has been extended by a four and five-level rooftop extension to provide loft type apartments. New buildings and the use of the ground floor of the converted buildings accommodate some 90 shop and restaurant units. A new underground car park structure has been built providing 1150 parking spaces for residents, workers and customers. This new car park has allowed part of the former above ground car park to be converted into a medium sized store of 3250 m² (35 000 ft²). One of the new individual buildings houses an eight-screen cinema complex in a distinctive metal and glass building.

Figure 6.35 A grand staircase leads up to the cinema entrance, Mockingbird Station, Dallas, Texas, USA. *(Source: RTKL)*

Figure 6.36 Apartments above the shops provide urban density to the blocks and open streets, Mockingbird Station, Dallas, Texas, USA. *(Source: RTKL)*

Figure 6.37 The entrance canopy covers the public space and entrance piazza, Salamanca Station, Salamanca, Spain (2001). *(Source: RTKL)*

The development has a contemporary urban character which is established from the industrial aesthetic of the converted and extended former factory building. The converted factory is a robust simple form, having a masonry base with large, simple, rectangular windows and a top expressed in a lightweight, modular construction of glass and solid panels, with an expressive overhanging roof. The other new buildings continue the robust aesthetic, in simple brick structures adorned with metal canopies and screens. A curved, timber pergola structure partly covers the plaza entrance space.

Mockingbird Station is a suburban example of a mixed-use development providing local community neighbourhood facilities alongside aspirational shops and entertainment facilities. In this example, the station element provides the catalyst for this urban infill development. The retail element is not dependent on the transport to succeed, as is the case with the destination station-type of retail facility. Retail at the neighbourhood station relies on its pull with the local community and surrounding residential population. The station access is an additional benefit and supplements the non-travelling, residential purchasers.

There is a natural synergy between the mixed-use elements of Mockingbird Station, where the project's success relies on the interrelation between the different uses. The sum of the parts is again greater than the total of the individual pieces. With the expansion of the DART network, the project is expected to be a model for other similar station developments.

Salamanca Station, Salamanca, Spain (2001) is another variation of railway station oriented retail facilities. Illustrating the universal potential of this genre, it is found in southern Europe, in the historic city of Salamanca. Here the combined foresight of the Spanish railway company, RENFE, and a private developer, Riofisca, has transformed a basic railway station, with little more than ticketing facilities prior to development, into a community facility and a station building worthy of a major university city. This example combines both destination and neighbourhood station retail facilities, providing for both travelling commuters and non-travelling, local users.

Salamanca Station is located in an urban setting to the east of the historic city centre. The retail development, designed by architects Antonio Fernandez Alba with RTKL, encompasses the main city railway station to provide 11 150 m² (120 000 ft²) of retail and leisure space. The development incorporates a threefold brief: to provide quality railway facilities; new leisure and retail accommodation; and public

Figure 6.38 A two-storey enclosed street leads to the catering, Salamanca Station, Salamanca, Spain. *(Source: RTKL)*

Figure 6.39 Railway related graphics above the shops give an identity to the enclosed space, Salamanca Station, Salamanca, Spain. *(Source: RTKL)*

place making with the incorporation of a new public square. The shopping and leisure facilities are built in a new structure beside and adjoining the railway platforms. The accommodation is arranged in a double height, single-level mall running parallel to the railway tracks. The enclosed interior mall leads from an entranceway at one end, to a food court focus at the other. Anchoring the entrance end is an 1800 m² (19 500 ft²) supermarket. A second entranceway, directly from the main street and taxi area, leads into the middle of the mall via the new entrance piazza.

The shops at Salamanca Station are arranged on each side of the internal street and, (like Manchester Piccadilly) being transport oriented, are smaller than generally found in a traditional mall. The retail mix in Salamanca provides for both travellers and local residents, with the store location determined by the type of shopper it attracts. Retailers targeting train travellers are placed closest to the transit access, while the leisure and local shops are located away from the route to the trains. This arrangement is similar to Manchester Piccadilly Station. Similarly, travellers' ticketing facilities and transport information are strategically positioned directly en route from the entranceway to the train platforms. The restaurants and cafés are arranged at one end of the interior street. Some of the cafés spill out into the mall and the external piazza. The majority of catering units are arranged around a circular court with shared tables and seating. There is

Figure 6.40 The covered entranceway facing onto the street doubles up to provide a civic amenity for the neighbourhood, Salamanca Station, Salamanca, Spain. *(Source: RTKL)*

also internal dining within the larger restaurants. The food court doubles up as a music court for local community events.

Salamanca Station's interior street is robustly finished and flooded with daylight from a combination of shaded, fully glazed, top and clerestory roof lights and large, circular lantern lights arranged in the plaster ceilings. Solid blue blinds with patterned openings suspended beneath the fully glazed areas are features on the ceiling. Polished granite floors and shop divisions are complemented by a palette of lemon-coloured bulkheads, grey canopies and overpanels. Lining the double height walls, above the single-level shop fronts on the platform side of the street, is a series of large, railway related screen prints. These bold graphics are visible from the piazza through the fully glazed entrance screen.

The open piazza space in front of the station is covered by a canopy formed from the extension of the station roof. The covered external space forms a civic entrance to the station and a partially covered local meeting space for the community.

The cantilevered roof canopy is supported on a series of strut columns in the piazza. Part of the roof canopy is open, formed from louvres, and the remainder, over the main entrance, extends the suspended blue feature blinds beneath a solid canopy. A glazed conical tower extends above the canopy to mark the station in the external street. The façades of the building facing on to the external street and piazza are animated by the fully glazed station entrance and the outward facing shop windows of the restaurants and shops. The remainder of the station building is clad in a blond stone which is banded and corresponds with the unifying stone seen throughout the historic centre of the city.

With its canopied entrance piazza, Salamanca Station is a distinctive building representing the glamour of travel and celebrates the sense of arrival. The building is civic, both in its expression of the public transport it fulfils in the city and in the community focus it provides for local residents. The building achieves a balance of retail facilities, providing for city-wide travelling passengers and neighbourhood community needs.

Airport Concourse Retail

Another transport related format which also exploits the large number of passengers using the building, is airport concourse retail. As this mode of travel moves into the 21st century, this shopping format has been simply described as 'shopping malls with runways attached' (Cockram, 2003). Airports are more complex buildings than railway stations and the examination of the retail and the examples described here will reveal that the shops may resemble those of enclosed malls, described earlier on, but are very specific to the airport concourse format.

Since the 1990s, airport buildings have no longer primarily focused on the arrival, departure and transfer of airborne passengers. Airports now depend as much for their revenue from retailers as they do from airline operators. BAA, for example, which operates some of the UK's busiest airports including London's Heathrow, Gatwick and Stansted, and Glasgow, derives more than half its income from the retail operations at these airports (Cockram, 2003).

With the devastating impact of terrorism and its continued threat to aircraft, there has been a momentary dip in air travel. During this unsteady time, airports across the western world have become more reliant on the lucrative revenue from their retail operations. Airport operators are modifying existing airports and planning new ones to incorporate substantial retail facilities, integrally planned with the movement of departing passengers. It is no longer satisfactory or viable simply to fit the retail into where it can go, which commonly has been in under-used parts of the airport concourse. Retail consultants and specialist architects are now involved in the earliest planning stages of new airport facilities. An example of this can be seen in the planning of Heathrow's Terminal 5 – planned for opening in 2008 and designed by architect Richard Rogers Partnership, with Chapman Taylor acting as retail planner.

Incorporating major retail facilities into existing operational airports is complex and requires the skills of programming and construction planning, as well as design. Even with the periodic dips in air travel, the long-term pattern is one of expected growth over the next 20 years. The challenges, therefore, remain the need to build new airports with integral retail facilities and to include new retail accommodation into existing airports as part of their modernisation and expansion plans. An example of meeting this latter challenge can be seen in Heathrow's new international departure lounge at Terminal 3, described later.

With the increased security that airports have adopted since the acts of terrorism of 11 September 2001, the extended check-in procedures require passengers to arrive earlier. Passengers' consequent dwell time in airport lounges has increased accordingly. The average time passengers spend in American airports has been identified as an hour and a half (www.specialityretail.net/issues/October 1999/flying.htm). The increased dwell time by passengers is conveniently located in the passenger lounge or concourse, with the retail facilities, so there is no surprise that this should lead to increased passenger spend.

Airport retail facilities are provided on both the 'landside' and 'airside' of airports. Landside retailing tends to focus on passengers' immediate needs and is secondary to the airside departure retail facilities, which can outwardly resemble a shopping mall. It is the airside departure retail facilities that represent the format of airport concourse retailing reviewed here.

Until relatively recently retail provision at airports was limited and incurred premium prices. Merchandise was restricted to what was available from newsagents – magazines, a few paperbacks and newspapers. Food and beverage choices were also restricted and likely to involve inflated prices. In some airports, local souvenirs might also be available. The first pioneering steps of change were made by the managers of Portland International Airport, Oregon, in 1987 with the introduction of downtown traders into the existing terminal building. Portland established a mix of traders selling local foodstuffs and manufactured products, along with some carefully selected, key national traders (Mander, 1999). The airport's success and its popularity with passengers demonstrated that an alternative revenue

Figure 6.41 Retailing is now integral to the planning of most new airports as illustrated by Richard Rogers proposed design for the concourse of the new Terminal 5, Heathrow, London, UK (planned 2006/2007). *(Source: Richard Rogers Partnership)*

could be obtained, other than from the airline operators. This key point was quickly recognised by other airport operators.

British Airports Authority (BAA), the UK's prime airport operator, was hired in 1992 to run the retail and restaurant operations at Pittsburgh International Airport. BAA introduced some 70 retail operators into the airport, of which 30 were speciality shops, along with an additional 35 catering offers. Pittsburgh established the provision of choice at prices comparable with main street or the mall, in an environment which resembled an upscale shopping centre. Sales at the airport trebled and reinforced the principle of retail operations providing an alternative lucrative source of revenue (Mander, 1999).

Figure 6.43 One of the pioneering examples of high street retailing introduced at Terminal 4, Heathrow, UK (1992). *(Source: BAA)*

Figure 6.42 Pioneering High Street retailing brought to Portland International Airport, Oregon, USA (1987). *(Source: Port of Portland)*

The Portland and Pittsburgh examples may have set the ball rolling but, unusually for once, the mantle was taken up and advanced further in Europe. The development of airport retail is one of the few shopping formats where Europe both kept apace of American trends and also furthered it ahead of the USA. Mark Pullman explained this by the fact that USA consumers already had access to a multitude of good retail facilities and that airport retail was seen as less of an opportunity and was therefore taken up more slowly (Mander, 1999). In Europe, however, where retail facilities generally lagged behind those in the USA, the opportunity was grasped more readily to provide unique and attractive new retail facilities. An example of this readiness is illustrated by the new Terminal 4, Heathrow, London (1992) which incorporated a significant shopping facility – World Class Shopping – as an

integral part of the departure lounge in the planning of the new terminal. Designed by architect Scott Brownrigg, Terminal 4 was one of the first airports with this specifically planned facility.

South Terminal, Gatwick, London (1996) soon followed with the introduction of 6820 m² (73 000 ft²) of shops and catering in a bespoke new departure

Figure 6.44 Departure lounge with ground floor shops and gallery catering, South Terminal, Gatwick, London, UK (1996). *(Source: Chapman Taylor)*

Figure 6.45 Contemporary shops inform the concourse space, Midfield Airport Mall, Detroit Metropolitan Wayne County Airport, USA (2001). *(Source: AP/Wide World Photos)*

lounge arranged on two levels with 35 shop units. Architect Chapman Taylor & Partners designed the new extension to the existing terminal to accommodate 3000 passengers per hour passing through the combined departure lounge and shopping facilities, which incorporated waiting areas and travel information, integrated with the shops and cafés. It is interesting to note that, at the time, the expected passenger dwell time was 50 minutes (Field, 1999).

By the late 1990s airport operators worldwide recognised the lucrative revenue generated by retail

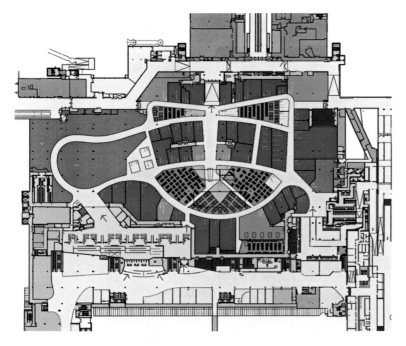

Figure 6.46 Internal plan showing homogeneous arrangement of airport and shopping accommodation, International Departure Lounge, Terminal 3, Heathrow, London, UK (2002). *(Source: CTP)*

operations. All subsequent, new, major airports are now planned to incorporate integral retail facilities into the departure lounges.

A unique quality to note in airport retailing is that once the amount of retail accommodation reaches a certain critical mass, there are diminishing returns from increasing the size further. This is unlike other shopping formats where an increase in size and number of retail offers will automatically attract additional new customers. Airport retailing is a different matter in that their customer base is a captive size, determined by passenger numbers, which are, in turn, related to the flight capacity of the terminal or airport. Once the optimum size is reached, further increases in the number of shops will not increase the number of passengers or retail income.

The key challenge, therefore, with airport retail is for the operator to determine the optimum critical mass of accommodation to suit a particular airport. Observation of certain European and American examples completed to date suggests the optimum figure for a major international airport terminal departure lounge ranges between $6000\,m^2$ ($64\,500\,ft^2$) and $12\,000\,m^2$ ($129\,000\,ft^2$). One of the recently completed larger state-of-the-art retail facilities can be seen at Midfield Airport Mall, Midfield Terminal, Detroit Metropolitan Wayne County Airport (2001) which incorporates $11\,600\,m^2$ ($125\,000\,ft^2$) of retail accommodation for local and national retailers and restaurants (www.specialityretail.net/issues/October99/flying.htm). Another recently completed example is the new International Departure Lounge at Terminal 3, Heathrow which provides $7800\,m^2$ ($84\,000\,ft^2$) of retail accommodation and is described in more detail below.

International Departure Lounge, Terminal 3, Heathrow (2002) is an integral part of BAA's larger plan for the growth and modernisation of London's Heathrow Airport. The project skilfully illustrates the incorporation of contemporary retail facilities into an existing airport building, which remained operational during the works. The design, by architect Chapman Taylor & Partners, maximised expansion at the first floor level by extending the airside face of the building outwards up to the plane stands, and gaining additional space by building across the floor voids. In addition to the extended space, the airport operations were replanned to relocate the security check area, to maximise the space for retail and catering. The new facilities provide $6500\,m^2$ ($70\,000\,ft^2$) of retail accommodation in 50 new units and $1300\,m^2$ ($14\,000\,ft^2$) of catering space in eight new offers. The departure lounge's combined waiting and café seating area provides 1160 lounge seats.

Figure 6.47 Department store-like layout with walkway passing by franchises follow the security control, International Departure Lounge, Terminal 3, Heathrow, London, UK. *(Source: CTP)*

The new airside International Departure Lounge's shopping facilities are formed in a large concourse space situated between the security control and the flight gates leading to the aircraft. The concourse combines shops, cafés, restaurants, bars, travel information, waiting areas and passenger amenities around a giant single-level hall. The character of the hall is comparable to the interior space of a department store, with an open feel and minimal separation between shop displays and circulation routes. Some of the shop displays

Figure 6.48 The catering facilities adjacent to the open seating areas encourage passengers to remain in the shared shopping and waiting space, International Departure Lounge, Terminal 3, Heathrow, London, UK. *(Source: CTP)*

are simply low-level cabinets arranged in the concourse space. Also free-standing and sharing the space, are large areas of lounge seating which are arranged between the retail and catering units. The catering facilities are strategically placed and dispersed among the shops. The integration of the catering with the shops, and the shared use of some of the waiting seating, deliberately encourages passengers to remain in the shopping environment of the lounge, rather than wander off to designated waiting or catering areas before departing for flights. The combination of catering and shops also makes the catering easily accessible and establishes a single synergy between the different activities.

Terminal 3's concourse arranges the pedestrian circulation, from the security zone to the gates, in a circuitous path through the different retail zones, commencing with a path through the open-plan display of low level cabinets in the duty-free area. The journey to the departure gates is predictable and represents a balance between being obvious and encouraging participation in the shopping and catering. The route through the concourse is arranged as a free-flowing, curved racetrack separately finished and identified in natural oak. Perimeter shops define the edges of the outer circuit, with island retail and seating areas encouraging secondary circuits across the concourse space. The island shop units form two separate areas, each with their own catering facilities. The departure gates are centrally located to one side of the concourse. For those passengers of determined persuasion, a more direct path leads from security, across the concourse to the gates. The remaining, less single-minded passengers with dwell time can gently peruse the merchandise or relax in the day-lit seating area in the centre of the space.

A unique characteristic of airport retailing is the captive nature of travelling passengers. With this, airport operators can, to a degree, pre-determine the use of the departure lounge and arrange the layout to encourage customers to spend. The use of passenger profiles also allows tenants to be selected best to match the users of the airport, and for them to plan their merchandising accordingly. At Heathrow's Terminal 3, the tenants have been carefully selected and arranged, with similar tenants grouped together into lifestyle zones. The carefully selected mix of local and international tenants is arranged into four zones: Contemporary; Premium; High Street; and Tourist (see Fig. 6.49). The zones have generally been arranged into the four quadrants of the concourse space.

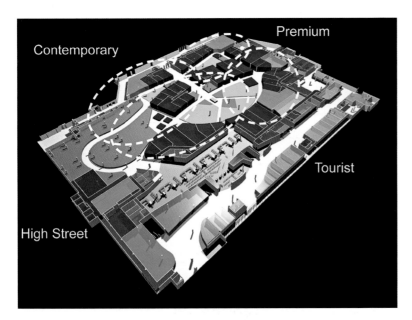

Figure 6.49 Four lifestyle zones order the shopping layout, from bottom left clockwise, high street, contemporary, premium and tourist, International Departure Lounge, Terminal 3, Heathrow, London, UK. *(Source: CTP)*

A further benefit for operators planning airport retailing is the predictable nature of airport customers, allowing the tenant mix and merchandising to be selected to match these needs. For example a proportion of the merchandise at airports, illustrated by

Figure 6.50 The wide open shopfronts encourage entry, International Departure Lounge, Terminal 3, Heathrow, UK. *(Source: Peter Coleman)*

Terminal 3, meets the needs of the following stereotypical passengers:

- tourists buying mementoes of a holiday
- business travellers purchasing a gift for a partner
- guilty parents buying for kids
- impulse purchases of lifestyle products.

Many of the purchases made by these types of passenger will be opportunistic, simply because they are available.

Although airport shopping may outwardly resemble enclosed mall shopping, there are particular qualities of airport shops which differentiate them from their mall or main street cousins. The qualities of airport shops are well illustrated by those in Heathrow Terminal 3. For example, airport shops tend to be smaller than the equivalent mall shop. The shops at Terminal 3 do vary in size, but have a nominal average size of 100 m² (1070 ft²). There are also several shops which are even smaller than this with an average size of 50 m² (540 ft²). The catering units are accommodated in two large restaurants of some 325 m² (3500 ft²), one medium sized operator of 200 m² (2150 ft²), with the remainder of catering offers being housed in average unit sizes of 50 m² (540 ft²). The small size of the shops is determined partly by the premium for space, but also by deliberately keeping the units shallow, to maintain passenger contact and awareness with the concourse and travel information.

Another design quality illustrated by the Terminal 3 shops is the open and readily accessible nature of the shopfronts, which are either completely open to the lounge or have minimal separation from it. This feature is deliberate in order to encourage the passing passenger to browse and wander into the shop. The open frontage allows customers in the shop to remain in contact with the concourse activities. Security is provided by shutters or screens which come down out of trading hours.

A further unique quality of airport shops, illustrated by Terminal 3, is the greater width of the shop fronts. This increased width improves visibility into the shop and allows the passing passenger to see, at a glance, the range of goods on display. The three unique design qualities of airport shops – open frontage, shallow depth and wider frontage – all work together to fulfil the fundamental requirements of airport shopping: free movement, and awareness between the concourse and the shops.

The open quality of airport shops is in many ways similar to the concessions arranged within a department store. This similarity reinforces the earlier comparison between the open nature of the departure lounge of airport concourse retail and the grand open interiors of department stores. The format is a highly successful one, which is demonstrated by the sales per square metre at the new International Departure Lounge, Terminal 3 reaching the highest in the UK, outperforming even Oxford Street (Cockram, 2003).

To maximise the available retail space at airports, the shops rely on minimal storage space. In order to avoid additional individual deliveries and the consequential security issues these incur, central handling of goods deliveries is commonly adopted. This type of central handling from an offsite distribution depot has been adopted at Heathrow Terminal 3's Consolidation Centre. Here, individual tenants make deliveries to the consolidation centre in their own vehicles. The airport operator's agent then delivers from the central depot to each individual shop. The use of a single agent simplifies the security measures and allows deliveries to be efficient. Service lifts from below bring goods up to the departure lounge level. Goods are delivered to the rear of the perimeter shops, which have rear corridors. Deliveries to the island units are serviced from the mall and carefully arranged with the terminal manager.

Airport concourse retailing takes place in an enclosed internal environment which is mechanically vented, heated and chilled. Although the architecture may be relatively simple, airport buildings are inherently complex. This complexity is a direct reflection of the different functions integrated into the building – the operations of the airport, the separate passenger movements for arrivals and departures, and the incorporation of shopping facilities.

Other Emerging Trends

Stores with an Experience

Another separate retail trend is originating from the experiential society, where the change from providing customers with a commodity to an experience

Figure 6.51 The glazed enclosure to the climbing wall is synonymous with the store's image, REI Store, Seattle, USA (1999). *(Source: Mithun)*

Figure 6.52 The climbing pinnacle demonstrates the facility of try before you buy, REI Store, Seattle, USA. *(Source: Mithun)*

Figure 6.53 Elements of the ski lodge (the fireplace) incorporated into the shop interior reflect the aspiration of the leisure shopper, REI Store, Seattle, USA. *(Source: Mithun)*

merchandise acts as a souvenir to commemorate the experience.

Instore Education

Progressing from the recreational experience, retailers in America have also recognised that educational experiences can equally link customers to retailers. For example, in the large DIY store, Home Depot, customers can attend in-store tutorials and demonstrations relating to basic trades and products for sale in the store. This principle of bonding customers to retailers has been developed a stage further in Europe at Amsterdam's Villa Arena in Holland, where, rather than being a mere retailer, the centre provides the facilities for learning skills and product demonstrations. At Villa Arena these facilities are provided in an attractive enclosed public square – De Kunst van het Wonen (The Art of Living) – which is integrally located yet away from the shopping area. The Dutch example illustrates in a different way the principle of 'play before you pay' and the importance of providing enjoyable experiences for customers.

has evolved further into providing a memory or a thought. This can be seen in the American example where customers use the large sportsware stores to learn about the product before purchase and have established the 'play before you pay' principle. In this case, shops provide recreational and enjoyable testing facilities expressed as positive features within the store. An example of this is the flagship REI (Recreational Equipment Incorporated) store, Seattle, where a range of different facilities is incorporated, allowing products to be experienced before purchase. These range from a five-storey glass enclosed rock climbing pinnacle; a mountain bike track; a rain room for testing out waterproof clothing; and a biking trail. At REI the store emphasises the experience as much as the merchandise. Taken to the extreme, some stores are becoming entertainment centres in their own right, where the

Figure 6.54 A monorial above the shops connects the terminals, Detroit Metro Airport, Detroit, Michigan, USA (2001). *(Source: Vito Palmisano)*

References

Beyard, M. (1998). *Developing Urban Entertainment Centres*. Urban Land Institute.

Beyard, M. et al. (2001). *Developing Retail Entertainment Destinations*, 2nd edn. Urban Land Institute.

Boroski, J. and Arrington, G.B. (2002). *Development Case Study* **32** (19), Urban Land Institute.

Cockram, A. (2003). Fly Buy Visits. *Plaza Magazine,* September, p. 26.

Field, M. (1995). Going into a Retail Spin. *The Architects Journal*, **201** (13), 30.

(1999). Flying the Friendly Skies of Airport Retail. *www.specialityretail.net/issues/October 1999/flying.htm*

Mander, E. (1999). New Tactics Help Airport Retail Soar in the United States. *Shopping Centers Today.* January.

PART **3**

The Design Guides

Interior detail of Chapelfield, Norwich, UK (2005). *(Source: Justin Parsons)*

What Makes
a Successful
Shopping Centre

7

Unique Qualities of Shopping Centres

The combination of several characteristics makes shopping centres a unique building type. These include:

- Privately funded buildings with both private and public usage.
- Predominantly commercial use, with some civic functions included in town centre locations. (Principal function to make money for the retailers and owners.)
- Instigated on a speculative basis with the majority of users not known at the outset. (Instigation based on an estimation of retailer and customer demand made by a specialist consultant.)
- The commissioning sponsor is not necessarily the end owner or operator.
- Long gestation and development process.
- Shopping centres are invariably large-scale developments which have a significant and immediate impact upon the local environment and the environment at large.
- The development will benefit the local community's economy and employment opportunities.

Understanding these qualities and their implications will help designers of shopping centres. The private funding means that public spaces are kept to a practical and functional level. The predominantly commercial use means the majority of space is lettable and determined by market and retailer requirements. The speculative nature of the accommodation requires it to be based on derivatives of previous solutions and encourages a formulaic approach. The potential separation of the instigator of the process from the final owner requires the architect to understand the parallel objectives of each of these parties (these objectives are expanded further below). The long gestation and development process also require the architect to have a combination of creative and tenacious skills.

The Different Stakeholders

There are three principal types of stakeholder involved in the formation of a retail development and the needs of all three need to be considered and balanced to achieve a successful shopping centre.

These stakeholders are:

■ developer/owners
■ tenants
■ customers/(custodians).

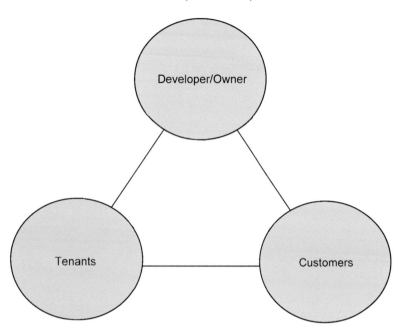

Figure 7.1 The three principal stakeholders. (*Source: BDP*)

Developer/Owners

The instigator of a shopping centre development and the eventual owner of the property can be one and the same or, as frequently occurs, two separate parties. There are several types of client who may instigate the development and commission the architect – a developer, a property company or, sometimes, a funding financial institution. The different types of client organisation are examined in more detail below. Developers are private companies with local knowledge and the skills to seek out an opportunity. Although they are able to instigate projects, they are likely to seek a development partner and a fund (who could be one and the same) to finance the development. Developers are likely to sell the development to a property company or institutional fund who will become the eventual property owner. In this instance, the architect will need to consider the objectives of the two clients.

A property company too could initiate the development and could also remain the eventual owner of the property. Property companies may, being publicly owned listed companies, often be able to finance the development from their own funds. Alternatively, they can seek joint funding of the development (to

avoid tying up large proportions of their capital) and may form a joint venture to retain the property, or sell to a fund on completion.

If the property company funds the development, the architect will have a single client from start to completion. In the case of joint funding, the architect will again need to consider the objectives of both parties.

The third type of instigator of shopping centres are the financial institutions which invest in property as part of their pension investment portfolios. Financial institutions or pension funds, although risk adverse, will, in certain circumstances, instigate shopping centres and frequently remain the owner on completion. In this case, the architect will only have to consider the objectives of a single company. (The different characteristics and priorities of the different types of client are expanded upon later.)

The general objectives of developer/owners, be they developers, property companies or financial institutions are:

■ establishing the overall size and critical mass of the development based on customer and retailer demand within the catchment area
■ obtaining an appropriate planning permission within the policies of use and permitted amount of development
■ minimising risk and financial exposure at each successive stage until the planning permission and key tenants are secured
■ maximising value of the opportunity
■ testing the viability of the development and balancing the development cost with rental return, asset value and profit
■ undertaking land assembly negotiations to define the extent of the site
■ forming a centre which is easy and economical to run and maintain
■ ensuring accessibility by various modes of transport: private cars, buses and other means of public transport
■ forming a unique retail offer and destination of choice, distinct from other nearby retail facilities
■ utilising sustainable materials and energy sources
■ being perceived as a local employer, both training and employing staff from the catchment area.
■ acting as a local contributor by instigating and sponsoring local events and activities
■ to make a profit from the development if it is sold on
■ to achieve a cash income rental return which grows, year on year, as retained asset value.

Tenants

Tenants are the retailers who occupy the shop premises to display and sell goods. The retailers' objective is to attract customers in order to make a profit from selling their wares. The tenants can require a small or medium sized shop selling a single type of product, i.e. fashionware, sportsware, footware, household goods, books or leisure products. (The typical sizes of shops are discussed later.) Some larger tenants will act as anchors to attract customers to visit the centre. The anchor store will be a large variety store or department store selling a wide range of products including fashionware, homeware, electrical products, cosmetics and speciality food stuffs. The majority of tenants occupying the shop accommodation will be part of a national or multinational retail chain. Chain stores will have an objective of expanding to increase sales and will generally have in-house property sections who are familiar with taking on new accommodation. Some individual and local shop operators still exist and are important tenants by providing a unique and distinctive quality to the shopping offer of the centre. It is important that the centre accommodates a wide variety of retailers. The general objectives of the retailer are:

- provision of the appropriate amount of floor space
- provision of floor space that meets the needs of modern retailing, having appropriate column spacing, floor loading and floor to ceiling heights
- having means of easily connecting vertically between the floors if multi-level
- being located in a visible position which is readily accessible, with sufficient pedestrian footfall passing the shop
- being grouped together with other compatible retailers which have a natural synergy with one another
- if a medium space user (MSU), having a strategic location at the end of a run of shops, on a corner, entranceway or change of direction to a public space
- positioning an anchor store strategically at the focus of the shopping centre, visible from key decision points in the centre, having an external presence from the existing town centre and from key points of arrival by car, train or bus
- easily accessible to large amounts of user-friendly car parking
- accommodated in a safe and comfortable shopping environment
- being part of a shopping centre with other leading edge retailers of sufficient critical mass to attract customers from the catchment area

- located in a unique and distinctive shopping centre
- ease of secure goods delivery to the centre
- integral servicing to a designated loading area with a back of house route leading directly to the rear of the shop
- sufficient space and provision for installing own plant with direct routings to the store
- the provision of statutory service and waste connection
- the connection facility to a central security and fire system
- an appropriate and sensible amount of shopfrontage to complete and dress
- sufficient lengths of blank wall space for fitting out with racking and displays.

Customers

Customers are the users of shops and include all social groups and age ranges. Customers are of both genders, although it is widely recognised that women currently visit shopping centres more than men; a fact which is reflected in shops tending to be strongly oriented towards women's fashion. However, this trend is likely to change as more men take more active partner roles and do more shopping for themselves.

Retailers have traditionally tended to focus their products towards distinct age segments, for example young children, teenagers, young professionals, the middle aged and the retired. However, the demographic is shifting towards more people being aged above 45, and more aged over 60 years old. This, combined with people living longer with more active lifestyles, has required a more sophisticated categorising of consumer types to be developed beyond age and income groupings.

According to the Future Foundation (Grosvenor, 2002), a more reliable predictor of behaviour and attitude in social groups is identified through states of life expressed as 'life stages' rather than by age alone. The Future Foundation also points out that lumping together all the over-60s into one bracket is too crude a categorisation and misses the significant spending potential of this affluent growing UK and western age group.

The demographic customer groups identified by the Future Foundation believe that life stage and household circumstances are more accurate predictors of purchasing patterns. The changing 'lifestyles' they have listed are young singles in own homes; older singletons – The Bridget Jones;

more child-free couples; later child birth; kids staying at home longer or returning home; divorce and remarriage. These changing lifestyles reflect that fewer traditional families now make up the customer group and that shopping facilities need to be targeted towards each of these individual groups.

Retailers' product ranges have responded to these specific categories and the more enlightened shopping centres are also beginning to organise similar life stage and lifestyle shops in groups. For example, the New International Departure Lounge, Terminal 3, Heathrow (analysed earlier), has the shops organised into lifestyle zones: contemporary, premium, high street and tourist. The new Bullring in Birmingham (also described earlier), has shops grouped together on a level by level basis into 'high street retailers, young fashion and lifestyle and aspirational' units.

Whatever the lifestyle or the life stage grouping of similar shops, the Future Foundation believes that designers of future shopping centres will need to respond to the more discerning and individualistic customer. It will no longer be sufficient simply to cater for the mass market customer. Future shopping centres will need to group together shops into carefully considered 'lifestyle' groupings, tailored towards specific groups in society. This trend highlights the importance of demographic research into the catchment area, which is discussed later. Customers will vote with their feet and will be attracted to those centres that recognise and cater for their specific, fragmented lifestyle groups.

Customer Influences

The customer's choice and preference as to which shopping centre to use is, of course, influenced by more than just the choice of retail offer provided. Choice and preference of the customer are also influenced by:

- the centre having a sufficient critical mass to provide both a wide range of different retail products and a variety of choice of similar products
- the optimum retail mix should be varied and comprehensive to include lifestyle retailers, a wide choice of comparison retailers and one or more anchor stores
- good quality levels of convenience
- the extent of comfort provided by the interconnecting spaces between the shops
- a sense of safety and security when using all parts of the centre

- the ease of access to the centre by a variety of means of transport: private car, public transport and walking
- the quality and extent of car parking
- the ambience and feel of the centre.

The last quality is particularly important to the more discerning and selective customer, where establishing a distinctive sense of place can leave the customer with a memorable experience of their visit to the centre. The quality of the public facilities – toilets, baby changing, crèche and shop mobility facilities – can also help to make the difference between one centre and another.

Centres that provide a range of different catering facilities encourage customers both to extend their stay while shopping and to visit the centre as part of their leisure time. Additional leisure facilities can also attract customers to visit one centre in preference to another. A natural synergy exists between leisure retailing, catering and leisure uses which can extend the use of the centre into the evenings and encourage day out visits to the centre.

The incorporation of catering and leisure uses and the proximity of cultural facilities found in town centres, allows the customer to visit the centre for one reason and then be able to participate in another activity, either in a planned or an off-chance way. Such a variety of retail, leisure, catering and civic uses allows each visit to the centre to be different and builds in a natural flexibility, allowing the customer choice – a quality which is increasingly appropriate to the discerning and enlightened shopper of today and the future.

Custodians and Social Responsibility

Another external influence on shopping centres, which is part of the public sphere but separate from the customer stakeholder, are the custodians of historical heritage and architectural quality. In Europe these custodial bodies have now been given real teeth and their consultative capacity has significant influence over planning decisions; including how well a development integrates into the surrounding urban environment, the quality of the architecture and public realm and the sensitivity of the development to any retained or nearby historic buildings. The architect, therefore, in addressing the architectural and historical custodians, has a broader responsibility to the public at large.

Government planning policy to encourage greater inclusivity is giving local communities more influence upon shopping centre proposals than they had upon the first generation of development. Modern large-scale shopping centre developments are encouraged to consult with the public and to demonstrate that process has been actively engaged prior to the submission of the planning application. These consultation processes will usually involve a selective representation from all social groups as well as key stakeholder groups from the local community. Participation in these consultation procedures is giving the public an increasing influence upon the form and content of shopping centre proposals. Applicants are encouraged to demonstrate public consultation and its influence upon the scheme as part of the planning application. Demonstrating public participation is influencing the favourable determination of planning decisions and will ensure the ongoing influence of the community upon shopping development.

Above and beyond the influence of the architectural custodians, there is also a growing public awareness which is encouraging development and property companies to adopt socially responsible policies. This intangible public pressure is influencing companies to adopt appropriate sustainable, inclusive and social policies which architects will need to address. For example, the sustainability policy will influence the selection of materials and energy sources; the inclusivity policy will influence provision for the disabled; and the social policy will involve training and employing local staff from the catchment area. Many of these corporate policies are becoming design obligations as a matter of course under the adoption of European legislation.

Interdependence of the Stakeholders

Having examined the issues to be considered with the individual stakeholders, it is important to re-emphasise that the success of a shopping development depends on the requirements of all three stakeholders being equally met and balanced. There are fundamental interrelationships and dependencies between the developer/owner, tenants and customers which necessitate no single stakeholder's requirements being met at the expense of another's.

For example, the developer/owner needs tenants to occupy the accommodation; pay the rental income and service charge in order to cover the

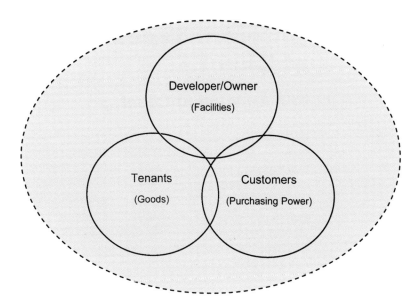

Figure 7.2 The key stakeholders involved in the successful formation and operation of shopping facilities are interdependent upon each other. *(Source: BDP)*

development and running costs; and attract the customers to use the centre and justify the charges to the tenants. The tenants need customers to purchase goods from their stores to operate their business; and the owner to provide an attractive retail mix, and a convenient memorable environment, together with good customer facilities and ease of access to attract customers and encourage their return. The customer benefits from the shopping centre facilities of the owner, and requires the retail goods of the tenant. The interdependence of the stakeholders is shown in Fig. 7.2.

However, if neither the owner/developer nor the tenant has got the retail mix and quality of environment right, the customers can vote with their feet and go elsewhere. Therefore, ultimately, the customer is king and the key stakeholder in helping both to create and judge a successful shopping centre. It is interesting to note that, although the relationship between the developer/owner and tenant is contractual, it is the implicit relationship of these parties with the customer that is the most critical to establish and retain for the long-term success of the centre. Attracting the customer at the outset is only the beginning of this key relationship. Establishing customer loyalty and retaining the attraction requires effective maintenance and a positive approach in an ever-changing and developing market place.

Different Types of Client

The Appointing Client

Although the architect is required to balance the different objectives and requirements of the principal stakeholders outlined above, it is apparent that their needs are interdependent and ultimately lead to the single objective of forming a successful shopping centre. Even with the customer as king and the tenants being vital ingredients, the architect is directly employed and responsible to only one of the stakeholders, the developer/owner who is the instructing client.

The earlier overview of the developer/owner stakeholder identified the different types of client and the possibility of the architect having to work consecutively for two separate parties, and needing to take account of both parties' interests and objectives. The following examines in more detail the interests and skills of the different types of client for whom the architect may find themselves working.

Developers

Developers are usually small to medium sized private companies. They are often locally based with an insight of local knowledge. Their particular skill is in seeking out development opportunities originating from available land and property, and identifying the development potential that may arise from further acquisitions. Developers are likely to manage the development up to the point of selling on the shopping centre to a financial institution or property company, which may be at the opening or earlier. The general objectives, skills and characteristics of developers are:

- to seek out development opportunities
- to make early site acquisitions
- instigating small to large developments
- to maximise value for short-term gain
- persuade and satisfy a fund or property company to invest or purchase the development
- completing a deal with an anchor tenant (thereby securing other tenant interest)
- obtaining planning permission (securing the land value)
- establishing interest in the development from other key retailers

- securing the go-ahead of the development (managing out the risk)
- selling on the development at a key stage, for example:
  - upon identifying the opportunity
  - having obtained planning permission
  - having established a guaranteed price and programme for construction
  - upon completion of construction and opening of the centre
- (if completing construction) securing the letting of all accommodation
- minimising the development cost for maximum value.

Skills and characteristics:

- local knowledge and awareness of opportunities
- likely to be able to devote priority time to initiate and manage the opportunity
- tendency to maximise development opportunity to establish the gross lettable area (GLA) to be developed
- land acquisition and site assembly skills
- able to progress development at minimum internal cost until the opportunity and funding are secured
- ideally suited to small to medium scale development
- may find it difficult to fund the planning and consultation process of large and complex developments
- an opportunistic manager of risk
- may undervalue final quality, maintenance and running costs against other priorities
- unlikely to have in-house skills of research, project management, letting policy, etc.

While the developer's objectives may be to maximise the development value, seek out a purchaser and sell on, the skills are not to be undervalued. A large number of significant major developments have been initiated and led by developers. Their contribution to the development industry is essential and recognised by property companies, financial institutions and funds. Many of the developers' interests and objectives are parallel to those of property companies and financial institutions who joint venture, purchase or fund developers' shopping centres. However, there are subtle differences in the objectives and characteristics of the different types of client. If the developer sells on, the architect will ultimately be responsible to the purchaser and, in these circumstances, it is important for the architect to anticipate the longer term interests of the property company and financial institution, and to recognise where the developer's particular interests may vary or conflict.

To assist with understanding the varying interests of the clients, the different objectives, skills and characteristics of property companies and financial institutions are outlined below.

Property Companies

Property companies are likely to be medium to large sized companies whose overall aim is to improve the value of the property that they own and run. They are often publicly owned, listed companies aiming to increase the share value and dividend payment and are accountable to the shareholders. Property companies can also be privately owned. The property investment portfolio of both types of company is likely to contain other types of commercial property, with a significant proportion invested in retail related property including shopping centres. Some property companies are focused solely on retail property, here referred to as shopping centre property companies. Although focusing their interest on one property area, the objectives of a shopping centre property company are similar to those of a general property company:

- investment in shopping centre property
- development of shopping centres
- being both an owner and manager of shopping centres
- maintaining and improving the asset value of its shopping centres
- establishing successful medium and long-term property interests
- seeking out development opportunities (alone and with developers)
- instigating medium to large-scale developments. Instigating development through a variety of ways including:
  - property acquisition
  - improving the asset value of property
  - limited competitions
  - purchasing development opportunities
  - joint venturing development opportunities
- maximising the development opportunity and value of development (based on research of demand in the catchment area and retailer interest)
- completing a deal with an anchor tenant
- securing commitment from other key tenants
- obtaining interest from other potential tenants
- convincing a fund where joint funding is required

- establishing a fixed cost and a programme for delivery of the development
- trading in poorly performing property to assist the finance of further acquisitions and development
- maintaining ongoing relationships with retailers
- demonstrating socially acceptable policies (employment, sustainability and training).
  Skills and characteristics:
- extensive development skills and knowledge
- support from in-house specialist skills:
  - research
  - letting policy
  - project management
  - asset management
  - public relations
- public perception of the company likely to be important
- ability to convince funds for joint funding
- experience of complex development processes and knowledge of the building type
- recognition of the importance of durability, running costs and maintenance
- managing acquisitions and property sales to finance a rolling programme of acquisitions and development funding
- careful management of risk
- utilisation of research to establish customer demand in the catchment area and retailer demand to define the overall size of the development
- awareness of importance of obtaining the right tenants and retail mix (for asset management)
- understanding of and commitment to planning issues, prepared to undertake public consultation to obtain correct planning permission
- able to sell project management skills to joint venture.
  Additional skills and characteristics of a shopping centre property company:
- highly focused on the qualities of retail design relating to running costs and maintenance
- single focus on shopping centre property and development leads to considerable in-depth knowledge of the building type.

Property companies are diverse and comprehensive companies with a knowledge and interest in all stages of the development and running of shopping centres. They may not be as nimble footed as developers in seeking out development opportunities, but once engaged are thorough and will carefully manage out any risk associated with the development. Property companies' medium and long-term interests in asset management of the shopping centre are likely to ensure that the tenant mix is right and that aspects of running and maintaining the centre are a priority in the design process. Once a property company is committed to a development opportunity, it is likely to see it happen and delivered.

Financial Institutions

Financial institutions invest in property as part of their pension investments. These property investments are part of a diverse portfolio which includes shopping centres and other retail property. By the earnest nature of pension investments, the retail developments undertaken by financial institutions are risk adverse and made with a view to perpetuate success into the long term. The asset income from shopping centre property is a significant part of the investment and safeguarding the asset value and income will be a key objective of these organisations.

Although financial institutions do instigate new development, it is more likely that development will originate as a means of improving or safeguarding the asset value of an existing property by modernisation, extension or even redevelopment. Development may also occur by way of acquisition of a strategic shopping centre with potential, which is then realised by the financial institution.

Objectives:
■ achieving long-term investment value
■ safeguarding the asset value and income from existing property investments
■ instigating development (through selective opportunities), arising from the acquisition of property, and safeguarding the asset value of existing property
■ investment in large, diverse property portfolios with long-term asset interests
■ investment in successful shopping centre developments completed by others
■ to own and manage shopping centres
■ self-finance own development
■ risk aversion and surety of success in development
■ surety of value and cost in construction
■ demonstrate socially acceptable policies.

Skills and characteristics:
■ development based on thorough research of demand in the catchment area and of retailer interest
■ the retail mix and type of tenant will by a high priority to get right from the outset
■ recognition of the importance of durability, running costs and maintenance

■ extensive analysis and research to inform best decision making
■ circumspect and cautious management of risk
■ some additional in-house skills – research, asset management and project management
■ the value of fixed construction cost recognised above lowest price
■ understanding of and commitment to planning issues, prepared to undertake appropriate measures to obtain correct planning permission.

Coexistence and Interdependence

Although developers, property companies and financial institutions represent different generic types of client organisation, they are bound together by the single objective of prospering through shopping centre development. Their specific skills and set up are organised to support the drivers of each organisation. While there is a degree of independence between the organisations, there is also strong interdependence, which is illustrated here.

Property companies and financial institutions welcome the development opportunities introduced to them by developers. Developers, in turn, gain from the introductory fee paid to them for their initiative. Developers require financial institutions to fund the developments which are sold on completion of the shopping centre. Property companies also rely on financial institutions, albeit to a lesser extent, to fund the development either partially or fully. They can also benefit from joint venture and other investment arrangements with the financial institution.

Financial institutions often rely upon developers and property companies to manage the risk in delivering the shopping centre, which they either purchase or invest in respectively. They also benefit from the interest paid when funding developments. Financial institutions can also invest in the property company itself and gain through shareholdings and dividend payments.

With the trend towards fewer but larger town centre shopping centre developments of increasing complexity and risk, more of these projects are undertaken involving joint ventures between property companies, or between a property company and a financial institution. These joint venture arrangements have the advantage of spreading the risk and development opportunity between several parties. The new Bullring, Birmingham is an example of a joint venture between two property companies (Hammerson/Land Securities) and a financial institution (Henderson Global Investors), which was formed at an early stage to undertake the complex redevelopment and extension of the former centre. These agreements are complicated and challenging and require commitment from all involved to resolve an equitable arrangement, in order to balance the different financial interests of the parties.

Financial institutions are unlikely to have the internal resources to seek out, to the same extent, the quick gain opportunities found by developers or, to a lesser degree, property companies. However, the institution will have the availability of funds that developers covet and that property companies call upon. Although financial institutions complete shopping centre development independently in their own right, for them just to develop independently would restrict their development investment potential and would require a significant increase in their own in-house skills. Instead, they add to their own developments by investing, joint venturing or purchasing shopping centres procured by the specialist skills of others. The interdependence of developers, property companies and financial institutions is illustrated in Fig. 7.3.

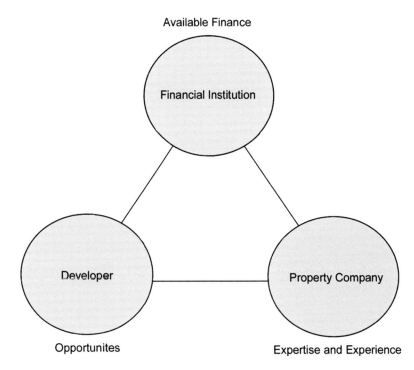

Figure 7.3 The coexistence and complementary skills of the different types of client. *(Source: BDP)*

References

Grosvenor, BSCS (2002). *Shopping Centres Futures*. Future Foundation, p. 9.

The new city library with ground floor shops closes the vista at the end of Hayes Place, St David's Centre, Cardiff, UK (2008). *(Source: Benoy/GMJ)*

Initiating the Project – The Fundamental Issues

8

Starting the Project – The Brief

There are a number of strategic design considerations that designers of shopping centres need to address at the outset of the process. Examined here are some of the key issues that the design team will be involved with at the initiation of the project and at the start of the interactive process of formulating the brief.

There is no standard procedure for initiating a shopping centre and each project is likely to be different. There are, however, some common ways in which projects originate and these are:

- a client owns or acquires an existing shopping centre and intends to improve the asset value by extending it or making improvements
- a development opportunity is identified on an out-of-town, edge-of-town or town centre site and the client initiates a land assembly process
- a local authority seeks a private development partner to develop and regenerate an area of a town centre
- a masterplan has been prepared in which several architects may be invited to complete parts of the shopping centre, or individual buildings which make it up.

Shopping centre brief formulation is an evolving process. It starts with core ideas in the 'primary brief', which covers the issues to allow the planning of the initial layout. As the design progresses the primary brief will gradually expand through each stage of development to include more detailed requirements for areas and elements of the building. Eventually the brief will expand to include the specific requirements of individual tenants, which may involve changes to the shell building.

The Initiating Team

Much of the brief making will be assisted and determined through a process of analysis and the careful interpretation of information provided by specialist consultants who make up the client's team. Design teams for large shopping centre projects can involve a large number of specialist consultants who join the core team to advise the client at different stages of the project. The specialist advisers who commonly advise the client in the formative initiating stage of the project are identified in Table 8.1.

As the project progresses and different skills are required, additional consultants will join the core team and other specialist advisers will contribute to the team at appropriate stages. Traditionally, the coordinating architect will advise the client when it is appropriate for specialist advice to be included. Many clients in the retail industry are, however, sufficiently experienced to take the initiative with many of the specialist advisers involved. A typical list of all the consultants and advisers who may be involved or contribute to the design team during the lengthy process of completing the project is included in Table 8.2.

Table 8.1 The client's initiating team of consultants and specialist advisers

Architect	masterplanning, design and lead consultant
Commercial agent	land and property acquisitions
Commercial agent	retail planning and leasing strategy
Commercial viability adviser	can be commercial agent
Cost planners and surveyors	capital cost estimating
Customer research analyst	demographic analysis
Highway and transport engineers	road access, traffic management, public transport, car parking and service vehicle planning
Legal adviser	land and property assembly, development agreements with joint venture partners
Planning consultant	planning strategy for obtaining planning permission
Planning lawyer	advice on planning law which may affect the planning strategy
Political analyst	advice on national and local political influence
Public relations adviser	managing public consultations
Retail demand analyst	can be commercial agents

Table 8.2 The client's design team of consultants and specialist advisers

Archaeology adviser	
Architect	may be more than one
Acoustic consultant	
Building surveyor	
Catering consultant	
Civil engineer	
Commercial agent	retail planning and leasing strategy leasing may be divided between several agents land and property acquisitions
Commercial viability adviser	
Conservation and historic buildings consultant	
Construction planning adviser	
Cost planners and surveyors	
Customer research analysts	
Environmental impact adviser	
Fabric engineer	external façade design
Fire safety consultant	
Graphic designer	
Health and safety supervisor	
Highway and transport engineers	
Hydraulic engineer	water table, flooding and rivers
Interior designer	
Landscape architect	
Legal adviser	lawyer
Lighting designer	
Planning consultant	strategy
Planning lawyer	can be separate from planning consultant
Political analyst	
Project planners and programmers	
Public art adviser	
Public relations adviser	
Retail demand analyst	can be commercial agent
Services engineers	
Structural engineers	
Tenant shop fitting designer and coordinator	
Topographical surveyors	
Wind tunnel test analysts	

Different groupings from the consultants and specialists will be formed during the process of the project to deal with key issues as they arise; for example viability, planning, retail strategy and lettings, construction and shop fitting through to handing over to the asset management team on completion of the project.

One of the reasons why clients involve and consider a large amount of research and analysis at the formative stage, is that while the planning and building project may take 10 years, the completed projects' retail offer and facilities must be right for the market for the following 10–20 years. With such large sums of money involved in retail development, it is vital that as much anticipation as possible is made of future market and customer requirements.

The Fundamental Issues

This Chapter focuses on the issues that are considered in the formation of the primary brief with the following Chapters examining the detailed issues involved in the different types of accommodation, the public spaces, the elements which make up the public spaces and the back of house (non-public) areas.

The fundamental issues for consideration at the beginning of the project are outlined in Table 8.3.

Table 8.3 Fundamental issues initiating the project

- Establishing the strategic planning constraints
- Understanding the customers in the catchment area
- Analysing the relationship with other developments
- Reviewing the type of shopping format (to match the location)
- Testing the type of location (out-of-town/in-town)
- Checking the retailer demand
- Agreeing the overall size
- Testing the fit with the site
- Preparing a wish list of tenants
- Balancing the mix between unit shops, anchor stores and catering
- Grouping together tenants with a natural synergy
- Providing a range of unit shop sizes which are single and two-level
- Defining the extent of the catchment area
- Establishing the relationship with the different modes of public transport
- Reviewing the requirement for private car access and parking (including existing car parking)
- The inclusion of sustainable alternative modes of transport
- Providing service and fire-fighting vehicle access
- Defining the site boundary
- Assessing the implications of variable site boundaries
- Outlining the strategic objectives for planning the layout
- Examining the factors determining the number of levels and the type of solution
- Establishing the type and nature of shopping environment
- Reviewing the implications of mixed-use development upon shopping facilities

Testing the Location

General Considerations

The location of a proposed shopping centre will have a considerable influence upon the brief for the development. Consideration of location will involve issues within the context of the region and related directly to the site location. A thorough review of the location will help to establish the size of development; first from a strategic aspect as to how much retail growth is permitted and how much demand the catchment will support. Secondly, from a specific and physical aspect, how much can be fitted on to the site and how much will the surrounding infrastructure support. These considerations will influence the type, size and character of the proposed shopping centre.

Strategic Considerations

Generally, government policy in developed countries, in support of environmental policy being less reliant on private car transport, is in favour of town centre development, as opposed to out-of-town retail

development. Regional plans generally identify the strategic policy for retail growth within a region. Growth of retail space is more likely to be encouraged in deprived areas and areas of high unemployment.

A review of a region's strategic planning policy will establish the general policy for either 'growth' or 'consolidation'. This policy is usually based on a demand survey completed periodically by independent consultants. The size of a proposed development should be checked against the regional policy. If the regional strategy is for consolidation, then the size of the proposed development is likely to be carefully reviewed to establish if it is achievable within the limited growth policy. It is worth noting that regional policy can be out of date and may therefore need updating. Policy can be influenced by a further independent demand survey sponsored by the client, and a case prepared by specialist planning consultants. Influencing the alteration of regional strategy will require the support of the local council and can be a lengthy and costly procedure.

It is also important to note that strategic retail demand surveys are academic and, if they support growth, this in itself is not a guarantee that a retail development, sized within the policy, will succeed. The client should complete its own demand survey that relates to both customer demand and retailer requirements at the time of the proposed development. This survey will be more specific to the development and will also relate to the prevailing economic cycle. Such an independent assessment is likely to take account of the demographic information relating to the catchment area (explained below).

Customer Surveys

Demographic surveys, compiled by customer research analysts, are a key part of the background research used by clients and the design team to help establish the brief for a proposed new shopping centre. The survey is based on a statistical analysis of the social character of the resident population within the proposed development's catchment area. The aim of the survey is to try to understand the shopping and leisure requirements of the likely customers. Traditionally, the statistical analysis examined the age and income of the population and interpreted it into a series of categories of potential customers.

The Future Foundation's more recent research for the BCSC has generally established that 'lifestyles' or life stages are a more representative method of categorising the characteristics of the customer group (Grosvenor, 2002).

Figure 8.1 'Premium' shops grouped together to establish a local synergy at the upper level, Bullring, Birmingham, UK (2003). *(Source: Chapman Taylor)*

Figure 8.2 Immediate catchment diagrams from the Almondvale Shopping Centre Extension Report, Livingston, Scotland, UK (planned 2008). *(Source: BDP)*

Customer research analysts will identify the characteristics and categorise the different customers into key groups. For example, of the seven groups identified as likely customers for Bluewater, Greenhithe, Kent, three of the main types were

categorised as follows:

- 'County Classics': a wealthy group, usually married, with wide interests, who are concerned about their appearance, home, family and quality of the purchase.
- 'Club Executives': successful, married, quality conscious, who like to be in control and who are prepared to pay more to save time.
- 'Young Fashionables': image conscious, brand orientated, active, single and likely to be in their early twenties (Lend Lease, 1999).

The demographic survey prepared by specialist consultants interprets the statistics into the qualities and character of the shopping community. A key qualitative aim of the survey is to try to identify the likely shops that will match the catchment population. The identified list of probable shops is then refined into the 'tenant mix', which places shops with similar qualities and a natural synergy into groups. The grouping of shops can be arranged into categories such as 'contemporary', 'premium' and 'high street' retailers as demonstrated at the new Bullring, Birmingham, UK or where each of the three malls of Bluewater, Greenhithe, Kent has been targeted to one of the following tenant markets – 'mass market', 'aspirational' and 'lifestyle'.

Increasingly in mixed-use, town centre development, the survey can also influence the quality and type of other accommodation; for example, the residential, office and civic amenities which might best complement and have the greatest synergy with the retail facilities.

In addition to assisting with defining the qualitative character of the centre, the demographic survey also helps to establish the quantitative size of the development. The size of catchment population is also generally proportional to the size of centre. The size of catchment population will also influence the type of anchor tenant that can be attracted to the centre. For example, a new UK anchor store will require a minimum population of 200 000 residents within a ten minute drive time of the location. The population size will take account of both existing and any planned residential growth for a given area. Areas with planned employment growth, and the consequent likely residential increase, are likely to attract subsequent retail expansion.

Catchment populations can be divided between 'immediate' and 'destination' catchments. Immediate catchment represents customers who are likely to use the centre on a weekly and regular basis and will be defined as customers within a 20 minute car journey. In some cases this is extended to a 30 minute journey. The destination catchment is defined as customers who may use the centre less frequently as a day out destination.

Careful consideration of the demographic survey by the client, commercial agents and architect will help to determine the following qualities of the proposed shopping centre:

- overall size
- type of centre
- nature and character of the centre
- tenant mix.

However, reference to the demographic information is not limited just to the briefing stage of the project. Continual reference should be made to the research to inform subsequent design decisions during design development. For example, the demographic information can be used to inform the design of the overall vision, character of space and the quality of detail.

The essence of the demographic survey is to help the client determine who the customers are and what they want.

The survey will be structured to define:

- the overall size of the current population
- the likely catchment penetration (how far it is likely to extend)
- the types of retailer and other attractions that will appeal to the particular catchment.

The other attractions influenced by the survey, which are included in the brief, can be the extent and type of catering and the size and nature of leisure facilities, where the catchment can extend up to a one or two hour car journey. In making this assessment, the quality of the road network can influence the geographical spread significantly, hence the earlier consideration given to access when reviewing a potential location. Proximity to a good road network will extend the physical catchment and potential resident population. The catchment population identified in the demographic survey will indicate the size of centre that the customer population will be able to support.

It is important to note that in the UK, any retail development greater than $10\,000\,m^2$, $(107\,000\,ft^2)$, requires the local council to consult with central government before any planning permission can be granted.

One of the fundamental requirements of the brief is to determine the type of shopping centre to be provided. The demographic survey will help establish the type and nature of the shopping development. This can be illustrated by the following principles:

- a regional shopping centre – a large retail facility in its base format will suit a densely populated area with little competition

- a regional shopping and leisure centre – will have a wider customer appeal and suit a populated area with competing centres
- a retail entertainment centre will respond well to an immediate resident population with a shortage of leisure and recreational facilities
- a focused retail centre – can suit a specific need or gap in a well populated market.

(The full range of different types of shopping centre has been reviewed in more detail in Part 2 of the book.)

Opinion Based Surveys

In addition to surveys based on statistical analysis, empirical and opinion based surveys can also be helpful in formulating the brief. Opinion based surveys conducted by phone, interviews and workshops, can give an indication of public wishes and preferences. Wishes for particular facilities can influence the type of centre and the inclusion of such facilities. Public preference can also be used to influence the character of a shopping centre. For example, a groundswell of opinion against enclosed shopping centres can influence the provision of a more natural, covered, but still open shopping centre. These opinion based surveys can be compiled by the commercial agents, or customer research analysts.

Relationship with Other Developments

The demographic survey will identify particular characteristics of the customer population. A separate review of existing retail facilities can establish if the characteristic needs of the catchment are being provided for. If it is evident that these needs are not catered for, then the gap can be filled by the new development. For example, in a large affluent residential population, where the fashion retail provision is fragmented and inconveniently arranged, a large new centre solely focused on a collection of fashion retailers would aptly address this need in the form of a 'fashion centre'. Alternatively, in a large, expanding, highly populated area, a 'single focus centre' providing only goods and products for the home, would also appropriately meet a specific demand.

Interpretation of the demographic survey, combined with an assessment of the competing retail facilities, will help the client team identify the unique selling point for each individual shopping centre development.

The success of a shopping centre will depend on it achieving a unique selling point (USP). To help determine the USP for a new development, it is important to review and assess both the competing and complementary developments within the catchment area.

Typical questions to be answered by this type of review are:

■ What is the competition and where is it?
■ What and where is the complementary retailing?
■ What are the strengths and weaknesses of the competition?
■ Are there any gaps in the retail provision?
■ Can a new development compete and win its own loyal customers?

These general criteria apply equally to prospective out-of-town and in-town retail developments. Town centre retail developments, however, also have to work together with existing retailing. In-town developments should therefore take into account the following assessments:

■ Where is the existing prime retail area and how does this relate to the proposed development?
■ Who are the anchor tenants?
■ What is the extent of the current catering provision and how can this be complemented?
■ What is the nature of the leisure offer and can this be extended?
■ What are the principal shopping circulation routes and can these be extended?
■ How well does the existing retail accommodation meet the needs of contemporary retailing trends?
■ How does each of these factors come together to help establish a USP for the new development?

Type of Location

Having examined the big picture issues of strategic, demographic and competitive aspects of the location, it is also necessary to come to an understanding of how the new development will fit into the proposed specific location. This will vary considerably between out-of-town and town centre locations.

Out-of-Town

In out-of-town shopping centre developments it is necessary to consider the qualities of the site and sometimes to consider the merits of alternative sites. The latter is more relevant to countries with an abundance of available land. Whichever is the case, an assessment of the site will need to be completed by reviewing the criteria in Table 8.4.

Table 8.4 Out-of-town criteria

■ How accessible is the site by car, public transport and service vehicles?
■ How close is the site to a primary road network?
■ Is the site prominent and easily seen from the approaching roadways?
■ What is the availability and capacity of mains services to the site?
■ How large is the available site – will it accommodate the proposed development and allow for further growth if required?
■ What is the topography of the site and how developable is the land?
■ How easily can the land be acquired?

A recommendation for a preferred site should be achievable from considering these general criteria.

It is unlikely that a choice of sites will be available in densely populated areas. Available development sites are likely to be located in one of these categories:

■ disused industrial land
■ an enterprise zone
■ a former shopping development
■ occasionally on agricultural land.

Potential out-of-town development sites are likely to require an assessment of the impact of the development on the ecology of the area. Where sustainable environmental planning policies prevail, out-of-town shopping centre development sites are unlikely to be considered.

Town Centre

Shopping centre development in town centre locations is likely to be on brownfield sites which have contained buildings and infrastructure. Town centre

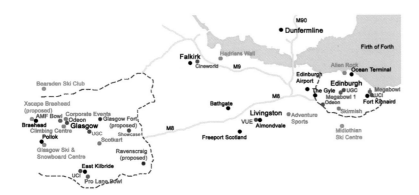

Figure 8.3 Analysis diagram of the competing retail and leisure development adjacent to the Almondvale Centre, Livingston, Scotland, UK. *(Source: BDP)*

sites have additional considerations to understand, such as existing structures, services and the issue of integration within the existing urban fabric.

Much of the site evaluation criteria identified above for out-of-town locations are also relevant to town centre locations. The criteria to consider for a town centre location are listed in Table 8.5.

Table 8.5 Town centre criteria

- How accessible is the site to the primary trunk roads? Customer access to the site by private car and public transport is essential. Service vehicles require access to the shops and fire-fighting and emergency medical vehicles need to be able to access the buildings for public safety
- What is the existing retail provision and how will its proximity influence the new development? It is important to ensure the two complement each other and work together. (The criteria to consider are identified above in Relationship with Other Developments)
- What main services exist and what is their capacity? Any necessary diversions of existing services to clear the site will need to be determined. Service intake positions will need to be established
- Shopping centres consume large amounts of energy and locations for new substations, or retained substations, will need to be planned. Combined heat and power may be appropriate for certain locations and a suitable site location will need to be identified if an alternative electrical source to the national grid is to be used
- An assessment of the surrounding urban structure will be necessary for the development to be integrated into the town centre
- An understanding of the existing shopping pattern and circulation routes will be required for the new centre to successfully extend the shopping circuits
- The new development should also allow for cross routes to surrounding areas to be maintained across the completed development
- Maintaining pedestrian permeability through the town centre is an important consideration
- An assessment of the existing architectural character should be made to establish the key design criteria for the new buildings
- Where historic buildings and conservation areas are involved, the quality and character of retained and adjacent buildings should be understood and carefully integrated within the development
- Where historic buildings are to be demolished, a case will need to be prepared to establish that the existing buildings could not be reused. Specialist historic building consultants can assist in these circumstances
- An assessment should be made of the character of the existing public realm to help determine the requirements for any new public spaces and how these will complement existing spaces
- An assessment of the character and range of uses in the surrounding districts will assist the integration and compatible siting of any new mixed-use elements to be included within the town centre
- Review and establish the location relative to the location of existing public transport and public car parking facilities (see also Accessibility below)

Establishing the Size

The use of demographic research to establish the size of catchment and the direct relationship between catchment size and the size of a potential shopping centre, were referred to above in the review of demographic surveys.

Retailer Demand Surveys

The retailer demand survey is a sort of economic reality test of the statistical analysis. The demand survey is primarily based on retailer research, taken from representative cross sections, using phone and personal interviews to gain responses to set questionnaires. The retailer demand survey is separate from the demographic survey and can be prepared by the commercial agents or specialist retail demand analysts. The development team and commercial agents will determine the optimum size by assessing the information from both the catchment and the demand surveys.

Optimum Size

The optimum size of a shopping centre is established as an amount of retail floor space that can be leased to shop tenants. It is known as the gross leasable area (GLA). The retail brief to the architect is usually expressed as an amount of GLA. It is important, for the purposes of the early site planning exercises, for the architect to convert the GLA into the potential overall gross area. To achieve this conversion simply, an additional area needs to be added to the GLA to allow for service access, means of escape, supporting accommodation, structure and external walls. As a general rule the GLA should represent about 80 per cent of the gross area. It should be noted that the GLA also excludes the public circulation space, service yards and car parking areas which will need to be allowed for. The public circulation space will need to be considered for each project and is influenced by individual site conditions. The inclusion of public circulation space in the gross area will differ between enclosed and open schemes. For example, the public circulation space will be part of the gross building area in an enclosed or covered shopping centre. However, in an open street-based shopping area, the public circulation space will be considered separately, and possibly as an identifiable part of the public realm.

Testing the Site

Having established the retail brief in terms of GLA and converted this to a gross area, the scheme should be tested out on the proposed site with some preliminary sketch options. These early sketch options will establish the land usage and plot density. They will also reveal the number of floor levels likely to be required, as well as any available land for car parking. These early studies should be used to check if the space required in the brief can be arranged on the site in a practical and viable manner.

The optimum size for the proposed shopping centre will need to achieve a balance between these considerations:

- enough critical mass to attract customers
- being achievable within a viable building cost
- generating sufficient rental returns from tenants to achieve a development profit.

The optimum size may need to be reviewed following the early sketch exercises and viability appraisals. Achieving a precise area on a constrained site is not always possible and a compromise on the brief area may need to be made. This can sometimes be advantageous when it comes to letting the centre. For example, a slight under provision in terms of meeting demand will generate leasing competition and assist rental levels. A slight under provision is preferable to over-providing, thus forming a surplus to retailer demand.

Tuning the Tenant Mix

The tenant mix will be influenced by the demographic survey and by the research into the likely demand of potential retailers identified above.

Research Surveys

The research into potential retailers is usually completed by the commercial team and complements the information required to consider the tenant mix. Early research by the commercial agents will establish the expansion requirements of retailers and potential interest in the development. (Retailer research is also reviewed above under Demand Surveys.)

Wish List of Tenants

In the formative stages of a project, it is only the anchor stores and major stores who are likely to show commitment to the project. (Even with these tenants the extent of their commitment may remain, for some time, as only a gentleman's agreement to continue to discuss the progress of the project.) The interest from the remaining shops will, therefore, only be considered as a general indication. The unit shops will probably be unable to commit until an opening date can be guaranteed. The level of interest can only be gauged at this stage and will need to be assessed by the commercial retail team. While the wish list of potential tenants can be prepared, a degree of flexibility with this list will need to be maintained, as a proportion of it will change before completion of the project. Regardless of some inevitable change, a wish list of suitable tenants should be established from the demographic and retailer research. This list will allow various scenarios to be tested out and the character of the shopping centre to emerge.

The tenant mix should be wide-ranging and balanced to attract a wide field of customers. The mix should include a range of retailers to cover comparison fashion, household, leisure, speciality and anchor retailing. From the wish list of tenants, for the purpose of establishing the brief, a broad assessment can be made of the likely spatial, loading, mechanical servicing and delivery requirements of the different tenants.

Balanced Mix

In parallel with the consideration of the optimum overall gross leasable area (GLA), an assessment should be made of the optimum number of shops to be provided. The inclusion of anchor department stores, or an equivalent facility, is necessary in order to attract other tenants to the centre. As an incentive to the department store to come into the scheme, they are offered lower rental arrangements and sometimes financial contributions towards their fit out costs. While the anchors are important, it is also necessary for the centre to have the correct balance of anchors and unit shops, and not to have too large a proportion of anchor units. With the anchor stores paying little rent, it is important that there is sufficient space for the higher rent paying unit shops, in order to make the scheme viable. Experience of successful shopping centres reveals that the proportion of unit shops should be between 55 and 70 per cent of the total GLA for the scheme to be viable.

MINIMUM PROPORTION OF TOTAL
GROSS LETTABLE AREA

IDEAL PROPORTION OF TOTAL
GROSS LETTABLE AREA

Figure 8.4 For large and regional shopping centres to be viable the ideal proportion of unit shops to the total should range between 55 and 70 per cent of the gross lettable area. *(Source: Peter Coleman)*

Figure 8.5 Grouped catering with internal and external seating, The Wintergarden, Bluewater, Greenhithe, Kent, UK (1999). *(Source: Lend Lease)*

Figure 8.6 Cafées, shops, harbour-side buildings and boats form a leisure and entertainment destination at the Victoria and Alfred Waterfront, Cape Town, SA (1996). *(Source: Reid Architecture)*

Catering

While considering the number of shops and optimum area, it is also important to consider the type and extent of catering facilities to be included in the scheme. The catering can range in scale and type from small espresso bars and fast food areas with shared seating, through to large-scale, themed restaurants. An early view should be taken of the range of catering facilities to be provided and this will be influenced by the type and size of the shopping centre being considered. Catering space requirements are reviewed more fully in a following Chapter, but each single unit can vary from 50 m² (500 ft²) to 600 m² (6500 ft²), from a café to a large restaurant. The requirement for a fast food area with shared seating should also be established, along with the number of covers (seats), to be provided.

When considering the catering strategy, a view should be taken as to whether the catering should be grouped together or spread throughout the centre. Catering units tend to pay less rent than shop units, which may influence their location. Catering accommodation also has some requirements that differ from the shops, in that the restaurants and cafés remain open for longer in the evenings. This consideration, together with the opening hours of the centre, may influence the location of the catering. Delivery of food stuffs and removal of wet rubbish should also be considered when positioning catering facilities. The overall brief for these facilities should be considered jointly with the commercial agents.

The tenant mix will need to be carefully considered and monitored throughout the design and development process. It will invariably change from the initial wish list through to the completed project. However, it is important that the intended character and balance of the wish list is maintained, or deliberately varied, during the project.

Tenant Grouping

Although it is possible to achieve a wide mix of tenants without consciously grouping them, their placing should not be left to chance. Centres that have tuned the mix to group together similar tenants and tenants with a natural synergy have a more positive dynamic. Grouping tenants into similar types is more convenient for customers, particularly in the larger centres where this grouping helps to reinforce a local identity and helps with customer orientation. The grouping of tenants can also be extended into the architectural character of the space to reinforce the identity and help customer way-finding around a centre.

The method and categorisation of tenant groupings varies from centre to centre (various approaches are illustrated in the examples in Part 2 and referred to above). Tenant grouping is generally arranged to correspond or reflect a different lifestyle or life stage category. Whatever the approach to the categorisation of the tenant groupings, they tend to be based on the generic types of shops such as:

- youth fashion
- aspirational fashion
- leisurewear and activities
- high street (retailers)
- homeware
- lifestyle
- perishable goods.

Group categories tend to be broad and simplistic to allow for a degree of flexibility on site. In practice, tenant groupings are simplified and tend to be organised into three or four broad types. Generic retailer types are combined together where there is a natural synergy, for example, youth fashion combines with leisurewear, high street combines with perishable foodstuffs.

Tenant groups may be loosely defined at the briefing stage only to be pinned down as leasing agreements are finalised during the later construction stages of the project.

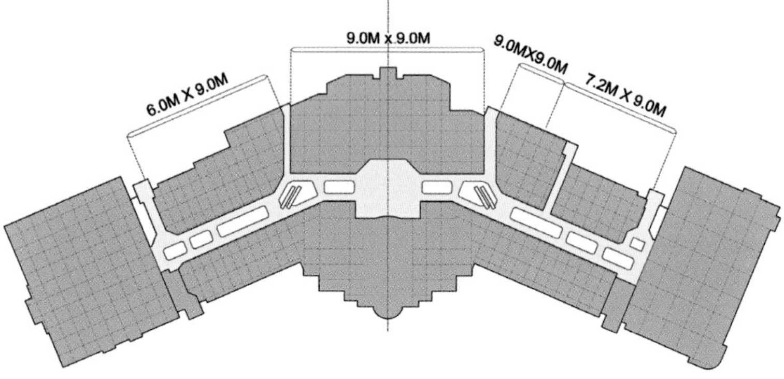

A Range of Shop Unit Sizes

The shop unit accommodation for the tenants should be established at the briefing stage to provide a range of different sized shops. (The range of shop unit sizes are discussed in more detail in Chapter 9.) The standard shop width can vary from one area of the centre to another by moving to a different structural grid. The shop unit principle is based on the adoption of one or two universal shop sizes which are then varied by adjusting the number of multiples of the standard unit. The unit module is usually determined by the structural grid, which can vary from 6.9 m up to 10.8 m. If car parking is located above or below the shops, the module adopted will need to be compatible with a car parking module, to avoid transfer structures.

It is important that the universal unit shop module size adopted is capable of being combined in multiples of the unit and, in the larger format, will still meet the requirements of the retailers. The ability to amalgamate units is fundamental to a successful shopping centre and the ability to provide flexible leasing arrangements. The range of shop sizes should be agreed with the commercial leasing agents.

Two-Level Shops

At the briefing stage a view should be taken on the requirement for some of the units to allow two-level trading accessed from within the shop unit. The provision for this facility meets an increasing demand from retailers. This requirement can be met by allowing for sufficient height within the shop to accommodate a trading mezzanine. This can usually be met within an overall floor-to-floor height of 8–9 m (26–29.25 ft). These double height shop units are best located on an upper floor, to avoid creating too great a difference between the public levels of the centre.

Figure 8.7 Plan layout of the Mall at Cribbs Causeway, Bristol, UK showing variable grids providing different shop unit sizes. *(Source: BDP)*

Figure 8.8 Unit shops increasingly require larger premises and are prepared to trade on two levels with double height shopfronts similar to those at The Bullring, Birmingham, UK (2003). *(Source: Peter Coleman)*

The extent of shop units with the facility for trading mezzanines should be established early on with the client and retail team. In a large scheme it is common for 30 to 50 per cent of the total number of shop units to be provided with this facility. Two-level shops are discussed further in Chapter 9.

Site Accessibility

Site accessibility has been identified as one of the key issues for consideration when assessing the potential location of a shopping centre development. Accessibility directly affects the fundamental workings of a shopping centre. It affects how easily customers can visit and be encouraged to return, how efficiently goods can be delivered to supply the shops and the means of safety and security of the occupants. Understanding how a site location provides for public transport, private cars and service vehicles is essential to establishing the brief for the new facilities in the development. Accessibility includes an understanding of all modes of transport and access to the site which, in

town centre locations, includes pedestrians and cycle-ways.

The brief for the new facilities is likely to include complementing and altering access arrangements and facilities.

Access and Catchment

Access is interrelated with catchment in that it is journey times that establish the catchment population of a shopping centre. For example, the easier the access, the larger, by area, will be the catchment area.

Accessibility will include routes across the greater catchment, as well as the immediate road-ways to the site location. The assessment will review the proximity of motorways, trunk roads and ring roads. The strategic road network will be particularly important when considering access for regional shopping centres.

The size of catchment, which is determined by the road network, will establish the catchment population and the type of customers who will use a centre. The customers will, in turn, influence the nature of the tenants who will occupy the development. Accessibility is therefore a fundamental and interrelated consideration in determining both the size and nature of a shopping centre development. (See also Demographic considerations, reviewed above.)

Specialist Advice

Architects will normally seek specialist advice from highway and transport engineers on accessibility issues to include:
■ determining the size of the catchment area
■ assessment of the greater road network and immediate roadways to handle the traffic generated by the development
■ detailed design of the new road network and junctions
■ alterations to the existing road network and junctions
■ public transport provisions
■ car park capacity, layout design, circulation, access and egress.

Public Transport

Although private cars are traditionally the customer's preferred choice of access, other means of transport must be encouraged and accommodated

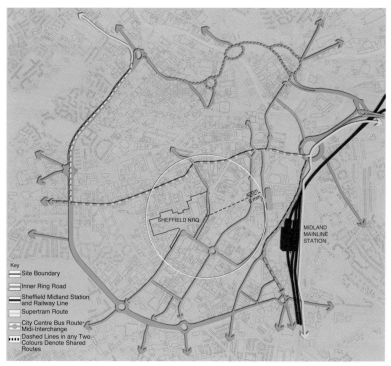

PUBLIC TRANSPORT ACCESS

Figure 8.9 A typical immediate transport and access assessment diagram prepared for the New Retail Quarter, Sheffield, UK (planned 2010). *(Source: BDP)*

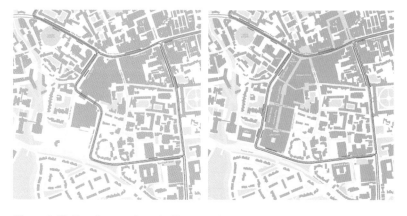

Figure 8.10 Two diagrams from the Westgate Masterplan, Oxford, UK show the difference between the existing and proposed bus routes to enable pedestrianisation of the high street (planned 2010). *(Source: Allies and Morrison/BDP)*

in new shopping centre developments built in a more socially responsible society looking to reduce carbon dioxide emissions. Less dependency on the car is partly met by the trend towards town centre development which is more readily accessible by public transport, pedestrian and cycle-ways.

Public transport includes buses, trams, trains and taxis. When preparing the brief, a review should be completed of each of these facilities, including

any planned changes in the short and long term. A specialist transport consultant will usually assist with this assessment, in particular the capacity of the existing facilities and recommendations for the new proposals. The review will also consider maintaining access to any existing shopping facilities, as well as estimating the requirements for the new development.

Taking account of the inclusion of suitable public transport facilities into a new shopping development is an appropriate and favourable planning consideration in developed countries that are aiming to reduce the dependency on private car usage. Generally, the public are being encouraged to be less car dependent and to make more use of pedestrian access and public transport in urban environments.

New shopping centre development may also have to take into account any local council aspiration for future improvements to public transport, including planned pedestrianisation schemes which may impact on public transport routings. For example, pedestrianisation of a street may involve the re-routing of facilities which will need to be taken into account with the new proposals. Liaison with transport authorities and operating companies will be required where there are any proposals likely to involve the alteration and re-routing of transport facilities.

Buses

Bus facilities range from full bus interchanges, through midi-interchanges, to simple bus stops. Comprehensive interchanges include enclosed waiting areas, passenger facilities, catering amenities, ticketing offices and travel information. Some of these larger interchanges can also include operating staff rest rooms and facilities.

In some towns, new bus facilities show a trend of moving away from large central facilities, which take up large areas of valuable land, towards a series of well distributed midi-interchanges. The midi-interchanges have the benefit of providing a wider distribution of improved facilities to different parts of the town centre. In these cases, bus stations are located at the end of routes and act as terminuses.

Bus facilities represent points of arrival and departure in town centres and shopping centres. Opportunities exist to form appropriate gateways in recognition of this significance. Bus hubs and interchanges can require large amounts of land to accommodate both the passenger facilities and the bus stops and waiting standings. In preparing the brief, it is advisable to establish the requirements from an early stage to allow these facilities to be planned from the outset.

Figure 8.11 New bus facilities, Oldham Bus Station are typical of the extent of contemporary bus facilities incorporated into town centre shopping development, Oldham, Lancashire, UK (2000). *(Source: Austin-Smith Lord)*

Figure 8.12 Inclusive public transport sometimes includes tram facilities needing to be considered and accommodated similar to the Supertram, Sheffield, Yorkshire, UK. *(Source: BDP)*

Bus facilities can be very busy and hazardous, and their location and planning will need careful consideration. Bus facilities located in urban streets can form barriers to pedestrian cross movement and isolate areas beyond the bus facility. Equally buses combined with pedestrianised streets can be hazardous and should be avoided if possible.

Taxis

Taxis provide safe and convenient access to shopping centres from residential districts and nearby transport nodes, such as railway stations. The location and number of existing taxi ranks should be established, together with an assessment of the number of new taxis to be provided for in the new development.

Trams

Some locations have trams in the highways. An assessment of location and existing stops should be undertaken, along with a review to establish if the new development will require any alterations or new facilities to be provided.

Trains

Most town centres have railway stations, but these may be located some distance away from the proposed new shopping centre. The location of the station and its proximity to the proposed development should be noted. The pedestrian route in between should be taken into account and the

need for any improvements considered. Where railway stations are a considerable distance away, facilities for shuttle buses can be considered and appropriately planned into the development.

Typical questions to consider in the access brief:

- What are the existing transport provisions?
- Are there any planned changes in the short and longer terms?
- How do these facilities serve any existing shops?
- What will be required to address the requirements of the proposed new development?
- How will public transport relate to the shopping centre?

Private Cars and Car Parking

Private motor cars are the preferred means of transport for customers visiting a shopping centre. Cars provide a safe, convenient and reliable means of access and, until public transport becomes more economical and convenient, will remain the life blood of shopping centres. No doubt the eventual demise of available petrol and diesel sources will force alternative means to be considered. However, for the foreseeable future the design of shopping centres will need to accommodate the motor car as the means of transporting the majority of customers to the centre.

Accommodating the motor car first requires a suitable road network to distribute the cars to and

Figure 8.13 While private car access remains a shopper's preferred means of transport, shopping facilities will need to provide large user-friendly multi-storey car parks similar to those of The Oracle, Reading, UK (1999–2000). *(Source: Hammerson)*

from the centre, and secondly a means of parking them on arrival.

Car parking to a shopping centre development can be provided in a variety of ways, or in various combinations of:

■ new car parking provided with the shopping centre
■ existing car parking adjacent to the development
■ off-site car parking in a park and ride facility with buses transferring customers from perimeter car parks into the town centre.

In establishing the brief for a new shopping centre, it is important to establish the quality and availability of existing parking, to determine the number of new parking spaces to be provided. In preparing the brief these assessments should be made:

■ Where are the existing car parks?
■ How many spaces do they provide?
■ What is the quality of the existing car parking?
■ How legible is the existing car parking in terms of signposting, accessibility and easiness to understand?
■ Is there a park and ride facility supplementing the town centre parking?

Numerous small car parks can be difficult to understand and direct cars to. It is preferable to have a series of sizeable car parks (larger than 250 spaces) which are strategically located to receive cars arriving from different directions. Automated direction signs, which inform car drivers of where there are available parking spaces are an essential facility in regional and larger centres. Car parks and signage should be coordinated into a coherent system in any one location. If such a system is not available, the development should consider providing for a facility to be installed. Clear signposting and understandable car parking prevent cars needlessly searching and congesting the road network, thereby leaving the network for through traffic.

The amount of new car parking to be provided depends on the size and location of the centre, as well as the proximity of existing parking surrounding the location of the proposed shopping centre. Other factors that will influence the provision of new parking will be:

■ local council planning policy
■ the availability of public transport
■ the integration of the centre with surrounding pedestrian routes leading to other facilities
■ extent of available land
■ the requirements of major anchor tenants
■ the size of the proposed development.

Major anchor tenants will have minimum parking requirements for the number of spaces they wish to be provided on site. This figure can vary, but can be as many as 1000 parking spaces for some major tenants. The British Council of Shopping Centres provides a general rule of two to four spaces per 100 m^2 of new accommodation (British Council of Shopping Centres, 2000). For a typical centre of 50 000 m^2 this could be as many as 1000 to 2000 parking spaces.

Car parking numbers can vary considerably from centre to centre and from out-of-town to town centre locations. The Bluewater shopping centre, Kent, for example has 13 000 new parking spaces; while the development of Southampton city centre has over 6000 parking spaces, including over 4000 new spaces provided within the West Quay shopping centre development. The proposed new retail quarter in Sheffield city centre has a combined total of 4000 car parking spaces, including 2000 from new development.

The quality and quantity of car parking are essential to the success of a shopping centre. Therefore, particular care should be taken in assessing and agreeing the number of parking spaces to be provided for a new shopping development.

The consumer experience of the car park when visiting a shopping centre will frequently be their first and last impression of the centre. The quality of this experience is therefore highly likely to determine if the customer visits a particular centre again. The brief and design for this supporting element of accommodation is vital to the success of the overall development. (See Chapter 10 for the different types of car park facility and detailed design considerations.)

Pedestrian Access

Pedestrian access is particularly relevant to town centre shopping centres and is especially important as an alternative means of access and reducing dependency on private car usage addresses current planning guidance.

The objective for a new town centre shopping development should be for it to be integrated with the surrounding pedestrian routes. To achieve this, an assessment will need to be made of pedestrian circulation and movement in the town centre. Consideration should be given to both where pedestrians are coming from and going to. The places pedestrians are coming from are referred to as 'generators' and include other town centre car parks and transport nodes such as bus interchanges and train stations. Where pedestrians are going to are referred to as 'destinations' and include other shopping centres, major anchor stores, libraries, museums, theatres and concert halls.

The pedestrian routes assessment should also analyse routes leading in from outside the town centre, to include large residential areas, sports arenas and transport nodes. This assessment should look at cross routes through the town centre which will need to be maintained on completion of the development.

Having considered the existing pedestrian routes, it is also necessary to assess the impact the new development will have upon them. To this extent the development will need to take account of its own role as a destination which will require the principal pedestrian routes to be related to and from the development and to entrances. It is important to look at the cross routes through the new development which will need to be maintained to ensure the town centre remains permeable on completion of the new development. It is equally important for the key cross routes to be maintained outside the trading hours of the shopping centre. This will avoid the shopping centre becoming an unusable part of the town

Figure 8.14 Consideration of where pedestrians are coming from and going to is essential to integrating new facilities into town centres. Example diagram of 'generators' and 'destinations' analysis from the New Retail Quarter, Sheffield, UK (planned 2010–2012). *(Source: BDP)*

centre when the shops are closed. Current planning guidelines are encouraging shopping developments to be integrated and vital parts of town centres and not to become large impenetrable blocks during the evening and night-time. Unfortunately, many existing town centre shopping centres have not addressed this issue and form large unusable blocks of town centres from the evening until opening time the next day. New town centre shopping proposals should avoid sterilising large parts of the town centres when the shops close.

When looking at pedestrian access, it is important to consider both the routes of pedestrian access and the interconnecting spaces where routes meet. This is referred to as 'nodal analysis'. Nodal analysis considers the quality, hierarchy and completeness of the pedestrian routes across the town. It is possible to see from the nodal analysis the extent of completeness of the pedestrian routes and then to establish where routes need to be reinforced or completed.

The trend for maintaining pedestrian access, for 18 hours or more, is encouraging shopping centres to be more urban solutions, based on open or covered streets, rather than enclosed shopping

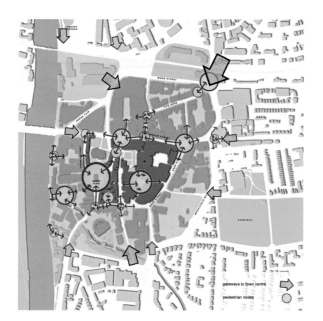

Figure 8.16 Cycle racks, Olivandenhof, Cologne, Germany. *(Source: Peter Coleman)*

Figure 8.15 Assessment of existing pedestrian circulation help with the understanding of local networks. A 'nodal' pedestrian analysis from the Eden Quarter, Kingston, Surrey, UK (planned 2010). *(Source: BDP)*

environments which are closed off outside of trading hours. It is important to realise that pedestrian access is only one of the key ingredients in forming vibrant town centre areas in the evening time; other evening uses must be retained for the town centre to have vitality. These include catering, leisure activities and residential uses (see Mixed uses below for more detail on this).

Cycle-Ways

Cycle-ways and provision for cyclists are other important means of access for town centre shopping centres. Encouraging the use of bicycles provides a further means of alternative access, therefore decreasing the dependence levels on the private car. Town centre shopping development should therefore incorporate cycle-ways and include facilities for cyclists.

An assessment will need to be made of existing cycle routes to take into account:
■ where cyclists are coming from?
■ where cyclists are going?

Consideration will need to be given to the impact the new development will have on these routes, how these routes will be taken into account by the new proposals and how many new cycle parking

facilities will be provided. The design brief will need to take account of new cycle routes and new facilities that will be provided to encourage the use of cycle access to the shopping centre.

In busy pedestrian streets, cycle-ways should be clearly identifiable to avoid hazardous conditions. Separate cycle-ways should be established wherever possible. Where these are not practical in combined pedestrianised streets, cyclists should be required to dismount during shop trading hours.

Cycle facilities can range from the simplest to the more elaborate. Simple cycle facilities will include the minimum of parking racks conveniently distributed around the shopping centre to cater for cyclists' different points of arrival. More elaborate and convenient facilities for cyclists include storage lockers for cycle clothing, changing rooms and shower facilities.

Service Vehicles

Service vehicles include all the various vehicles that service the shops, catering and leisure facilities of the shopping centre. These vehicles represent the functional life blood of a shopping centre and should remain invisible to the customer. They are key to the business of the tenant and to the operation of the landlord/owner's premises.

Along with the assessment of the accessibility of private cars and public transport, an assessment will need to be made of the capacity of the road infrastructure to distribute service vehicles to and from the proposed development. Although service vehicles can share the primary road network to the centre, their points of access should be kept separate from those for private cars and public transport.

Having established the capacity, and any alterations to be made to the access network to accommodate service vehicles, it is then necessary to determine the number of vehicles and a particular method of accommodating them.

The type of service vehicles to be accommodated range from shop delivery vehicles, refuse vehicles and fire-fighting vehicles. As a general guideline, the British Council of Shopping Centres (BCSC) research study 'Service Areas for Shopping Centres' recommends the provision of 5.5– 6.5 vehicle parking bays per 9000 m^2 (100 000 ft^2) of GLA (excluding large department stores) (British Council of Shopping Centres, 1995). Of these service parking spaces, three will be required for articulated vehicles or large rigid trucks. Additionally, large stores and major anchors will require their own dedicated service vehicle parking bays. Parking space will also be required in the unloading yard for refuse compactors and skips which accommodate compacted rubbish, along with parking spaces for the refuse vehicles that remove the skips. For an average sized shopping centre of 45 000 m^2 (500 000 ft^2) the total number of parking spaces can be as many as 30 spaces, plus space for refuse vehicle accommodation. This can require a considerable amount of space and needs careful planning to remain discreet and accessible to all parts of the shopping centre. In some centres it may be necessary to provide several unloading areas to ensure convenience for all the shops. It is also worth bringing in a specialist highways consultant to determine the exact number of service bays to be provided so as to avoid over-sizing the service yard facilities.

It is most likely that for any planned shopping centre, however small, the local highway authority will require integral service vehicle facilities. Early consultation with the highway authority is recommended to establish the requirements for service vehicles and what will be permitted directly off street.

Once the principal requirement for integral vehicle servicing has been established, the method of providing it can be considered. The simplest service yard is one at ground level. This option will suit sites where there is plenty of available land. Town centre sites are likely to need to consider alternative options which leave the ground floor available for shop facilities. Alternative options for service yards are below ground or on the roof. With service vehicles requiring 4.5–5 m clear headroom, this can involve expensive basement construction in order to accommodate a below ground service yard. Rooftop service yards can be unsightly and are unlikely to be suitable in

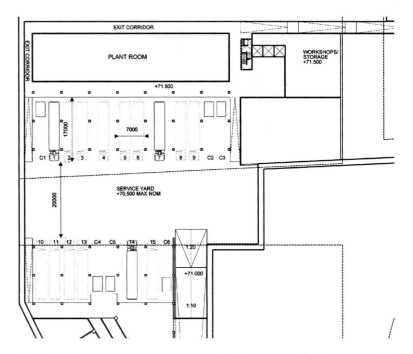

Figure 8.17 An integral basement service yard with square on unloading on two sides, The New Retail Quarter, Sheffield, UK (planned 2010). *(Source: BDP)*

sensitive town centre locations. Where they can be screened from view and are visually acceptable, the construction needs to be able to accommodate the weight of heavy goods vehicles and will need to be suitably waterproofed. Rooftop servicing is also unlikely to be a suitable method in centres addressing the urban agenda of mixed-use town centre development, where the roof of the shops is likely to be used for other accommodation. Both basement and rooftop service yards will require ramps to transfer the vehicles from ground level. These ramps, which should not exceed a gradient of 1 in 10, will take up space which will need to be planned into the centre.

In medium to large sized shopping centres, it is unlikely that the service yard will be able to access all the shops directly from the yard. In these circumstances, a service corridor will be required to lead from the service yard to the rear of the remaining shop units. The service yard will need to be positioned to avoid unnecessarily long delivery distances to the shops. In single-level centres, the maximum distance from the service yard to the furthest shop unit should not exceed 150 m (490 ft). In multi-level arrangements, where goods delivery requires a change of level via a goods lift, then the maximum distance should not exceed 100 m (325 ft). In larger shopping centres more than one service yard may be required to provide convenient access to all the shop units. The service yards should also be arranged to avoid having to handle goods through more than one vertical core to access the shops.

Fire-Fighting Access

The shopping centre will need to be planned to allow for ready access of fire-fighting vehicles to predetermined points around the building or buildings. From these predetermined points of access, hose reels will be required to extend from the fire-fighting vehicles to cover all parts of the shopping centre. Early consultation with the fire service is recommended to establish the permitted maximum lengths of hose reel, in order to determine the degree of access points for the fire-fighting vehicles.

Fire-fighting vehicle access must remain unobstructed and should be of sufficient width to allow for turning if not arranged on a through route. Access routes need to allow for the significant weight of a fire-fighting vehicle.

The other fire-fighting facilities required within the building can also be established from early consultation with the fire service.

Refuse Management and Access

The shops and catering outlets within the shopping centre require the removal of rubbish and waste materials. This is usually provided by the landlord from a central collection point in the service yard.

Waste collection can either be in bins or skips from refuse compactors. Short-term ventilated bin store areas can be provided in more localised areas adjacent to the shops and catering areas for subsequent transfer to the central bin store in the service yard, either by the tenant or centre management.

The trend towards waste recycling has resulted in the segregation of different types of waste into separate paladins or skips and a subsequent increase in the amount of space required for the storage of rubbish. The frequency of refuse collection arranged by the centre management will, however, determine the amount of space that needs to be allowed. Consultation with the property owner or management company will help to establish the intended refuse management and thus the space required.

The service yards need to be planned to allow sufficient separate space for refuse storage and for the vehicles which collect the rubbish. Care should be taken with compactor skip usage to allow the collection vehicle to back up, to align with the skip and ensure there is sufficient headroom above the skip to allow for the lifting action of the collection vehicle.

Defining the Site

Land Assembly

It is a common quality of shopping centre development for the site to be made up from the assembly of several different pieces of land in separate ownerships. The acquisition of the different land ownerships is referred to as the 'land assembly'. The successful assembly of land will determine the extent and boundary of the site. In order to assemble the land for a development, the client will enter into negotiations with the other owners. The ownership of land in a town centre can be more complex than an out-of-town development and is likely to involve several different owners in a complicated process.

During the land assembly process, the site boundary might vary in response to the success or failure of a land negotiation. As a consequence of these negotiations, a unique quality of town centre shopping development arises, which gives the potential for the site boundary to vary during the early design stages. For example, the land assembly negotiation may not reach an amicable agreement and require an alternative alignment to part of a site boundary.

Figure 8.18 Recycling of waste requires separate bins for different materials. Photo of waste storage at the Great Western, Swindon, UK (1999). *(Source: BDP)*

Figure 8.19 Land acquisition diagram for the Fife Road Area, Eden Quarter, Kingston, Surrey, UK. *(Source: Montagu Evans)*

Early in the process of the land assembly it is important to establish ownership of the different land parcels that make up a potential development site. This is usually completed by surveyors and legal advisers within the client's development team. On simple sites, the land ownership diagram can be completed by the architect and the client's legal advisers.

While preparing the design brief, the client should be undertaking negotiations with the different land owners in order to establish the likelihood of assembling the site. The client should regularly update the design team of the progress being made. Assessments should be made with the client of the likely success of assembling all the land to make up a particular site. Alternative scheme options might need to be considered in anticipation of certain land parcels not being obtainable.

Compulsory Purchase

In the larger strategic town centre developments, it is possible for the local council to assist with the acquisition of land. For example, in the UK where development is in line with local planning policy, the local council can instigate a process of compulsory purchase of land that cannot be acquired through the normal negotiation process. The compulsory purchase commences after planning permission has

been granted and is resolved, in a legal process, to establish a fair and appropriate level of compensation to be paid to the former land owner. The compulsory purchase process is a last resort and should be avoided where normal land negotiations are possible.

Some shopping centre developments involve the realignment and building over of public rights of way or highways and require the appropriate agreements to be made with the highway authority. The alteration to highways within a site should also be identified at an early stage and negotiations undertaken with the highway authority to establish the appropriate realignment licence, stopping up order or road closure order.

The final site boundary for the shopping centre development should be agreed with the client and the local council before a planning application is made. Having to alter a site boundary once the planning process has commenced can require the application to be re-submitted, thereby prolonging the process.

The land must be owned by the client before any site work associated with the development can be commenced. The successful completion of the land assembly is also important to release major stage payments from funding institutions, which may be required by the developer or property company.

Layout (Organisational Framework)

Strictly speaking the organisational framework of the layout is more to do with the design of the scheme than the primary brief. The layout is also not necessarily part of the brief given to the architect by the client, but more the architect's own brief and accepted as given by the client. The layout is fundamental to the success of a shopping centre and is therefore considered here as part of the primary brief. The primary brief should start with simple objectives which can evolve as the design progresses. The considerations here have been organised into general objectives for the primary brief. More detailed guidelines for consideration of the organisational framework when designing the layout are examined in the following Chapters.

General Layout Objectives

General objectives relating to the layout to be considered for the primary brief are listed in Table 8.6.

Table 8.6 General layout objectives

- The layout should form a unique and interesting place that is convenient, safe and enjoyable to use
- It should be legible and easy to understand
- The arrangement should establish strong pedestrian flows which will allow customers to pass along all the retail frontages
- Anchor stores should be positioned to generate and reinforce pedestrian flow
- Medium space user stores should also be located to reinforce pedestrian flow
- Other major attractions (leisure facilities and catering areas) can be located to assist pedestrian flow
- Other generators of footfall which include entranceways from car parks, points of access from public transport, vertical circulation points including stairs, escalators and lifts, should be positioned to assist pedestrian flow
- The arrangement of public circulation space should form natural circuits and avoid customers having to retrace steps

Single or Multi-Level

Single or multi-level is the number of publicly accessible circulation levels which should be considered for the shopping centre. This consideration is separate from the number of built levels which might be required to house the retail accommodation.

The publicly accessible levels are those levels on which the customers circulate to access the shops, catering and leisure facilities. The shops and other accommodation may also have several additional levels which are accessible from within the unit. The publicly accessible levels form the armature (organisational framework) which connects together the different elements of the centre and represents the front of house. These levels establish the sense of place and form any lasting memory of the centre's shopping experience.

Key Factors of Influence

Reaching a decision on the number of publicly accessible circulation levels will require the assimilation of a number of individual factors relating to the particular location, the site constraints and the requirements of the brief. The main factors to be considered are discussed below.

Location of the Site

Whether the proposed scheme is an out-of-town centre or town centre location will have considerably different available site areas and constraints. Out-of-town proposals will have relatively less pressure on fitting the required accommodation to the site.

Available Land

In densely populated areas there will be a shortage of available sites to accommodate a large shopping development. Choice will be restricted and may require a multi-level solution to fit the accommodation. Out-of-town locations, and countries with large amounts of available land, will be more readily able to provide large sites which can fit the accommodation on a single level.

The Brief

The brief will determine the amount of accommodation and car parking to be fitted on the site. The brief requirements may necessitate a multi-level solution in order to fit all the accommodation on to the site.

Type of Accommodation

Schemes with requirements for large leisure and catering areas, which may have pressures on available

Figure 8.20 High land values necessitate high density development and generate multi-level retailing, Suria KLCC, Kuala Lumpar, Malaysia (1998). *(Source: Patrick Lim)*

Figure 8.21 Touchwood illustrates a single level scheme with two level shops, Solihull, West Midlands, UK (2001). *(Source: Peter Coleman)*

site area, can utilise the lower value upper levels for this type of accommodation.

Land Value

In the most densely populated countries with high urban land values, adopting multi-level solutions is the only way to fit the accommodation on to the site and achieve sufficient rental returns to make the scheme viable.

Types of Multi-Level Solution

Having examined the individual issues that may influence the adoption of a multi-level scheme, the general types of multi-level scheme, and where they are appropriate, need to be reviewed.

Single Level

These schemes are appropriate on large flat sites which can readily cater for all the accommodation. They are dependent on large amounts of low value land being readily available. Single-level solutions are the simplest, but can result in extreme distances of public circulation space unless circuits are formed.

Two Levels

Two-level solutions are adopted when it is necessary as a means to fit the requirements of the brief on to the available site. These solutions also suit sites where there is a change in ground level of 2.5 m (8 ft) or more across the site. A simple cut and fill solution can be adopted to create two natural ground floor levels. Two-level solutions are commonly adopted and it is reasonably straightforward to achieve equal footfall to both levels. They can be

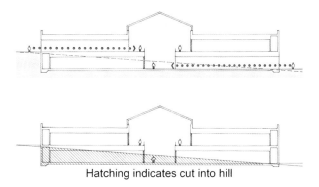

Hatching indicates cut into hill

Figure 8.22 Gently sloping sites can be used to create two equal ground floors at both upper and lower floor levels. *(Source: Peter Coleman)*

more compact than single-level schemes of the same size.

Three or more Levels

These solutions are less common and only considered on sites in high density and high value locations where it is necessary to fit the accommodation. They can more readily be achieved if there is a level change across the site and two ground levels can be accommodated, leaving only one level to be reached solely by vertical circulation. Particular care will need to be given to ensure the third level has sufficient generators and attractions to create pedestrian footfall.

Figure 8.24 A six level vertical mall, Suria KLCC, Kuala Lumpar, Malaysia (1998). *(Source: Patrick Lim)*

Figure 8.23 Three level enclosed centre exploiting level change across the site at The Bullring, Birmingham, UK (2003). *(Source: Peter Coleman)*

Vertical malls in high density urban locations with four to seven or more levels, may have to utilise the more remote levels to accommodate the lower value accommodation, such as catering facilities, leisure accommodation, specialist independent retailers and even access to the department store. Forming strong pedestrian flows in schemes arranged above three

levels is a challenge for multi-level arrangements and will require the most imaginative of solutions.

Multi-Level Schemes

The clear advantage of a multi-level solution is its ability to accommodate more shop unit frontages on a site. The number of levels to be adopted needs to be balanced with the ability to achieve good pedestrian footfall to each level. Rental levels are proportional to footfall, therefore once pedestrian footfall is perceived to reduce, rental levels will be discounted. This is not to say that schemes above three levels should not be considered. It is simply the potential reduced rental levels of such schemes will need to be taken into account in the viability appraisal. Other than in the most dense, high value cities, it is generally unlikely that schemes with more than two or three public levels can be made viable.

The most common solutions likely to be encountered are one and two publicly accessible levels with some three level arrangements. In each case it is vitally important that the different levels have broadly equal amounts of pedestrian footfall if the

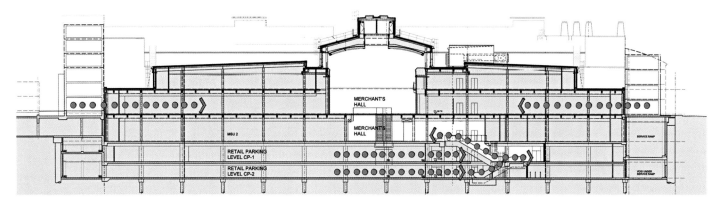

Figure 8.25 Basement car parking can be used to reinforce a lower ground floor as illustrated by the Chapelfield cross section, Norwich, East Anglia, UK (2005). *(Source: BDP)*

rental levels are not to be discounted between the perceived prime and secondary levels. The objective is to try to arrange the anchor elements and generators in such a way as to achieve all publicly accessible levels being ground floors. In reality it is difficult to create more than two equivalent ground floor levels and commonly, where a third level must be adopted, a reduced rental value will need to be used for this floor. This may be a perfectly valid solution, as some tenants and users may well require a lower rental value and such a solution will allow the centre to accommodate a variety of different types of tenant.

Returning to the practicalities of achieving a two-level scheme, ideally it will be preferable to provide a major external entrance to each level. This can more readily be achieved where there is a natural level change across a site and where each level relates to a busy street or footfall generator such as a car park.

If there is still a perceived difference between the levels, other footfall generating elements may need to be positioned at the weaker level to equalise it. Such footfall generators to consider adding are:

- entrances to a major department store
- entranceways from car parks
- food and beverage areas.

Multi-level arrangements are generally more appropriate to larger shopping centres. According to the BCSC, small centres which are less than 20 000 m² (215 000 ft²) GLA are unlikely to be of sufficient size to be viable at more than one level, unless the site location provides strong retail areas at the different levels (British Council of Shopping Centres, 2000).

Open, Covered or Enclosed

Recent Trends in Shopping Environments

Tastes change and recent trends in shopping environments have indeed progressed in such a way as to have moved full circle since the origins of the purpose-built, planned shopping centre 50 years ago. None more so than that of the open or enclosed debate, relating to the nature of public circulation space connecting the different accommodation of shops, cafés, bars and restaurants. The debate and trends for the character of the circulation space continue to evolve, having travelled from open canopied precincts, to enclosed centres with largely solid roofs, to extensively glazed enclosures, to interconnecting armatures creating memorable experiences, to enclosed interior rooms, then hybrids mixing open streets with enclosed interior space and, most recently (addressing the urban agenda), with untempered, open and covered streets.

A Move Away from Enclosed Centres

No doubt the debate on the nature of the public circulation space will continue, with various combinations continuing to evolve into new forms and permutations of public space. The current trend for open

Figure 8.26 An example of open pedestrianised streets fronted by two and three level shops proposed for Broadmead, Bristol, UK (planned 2007–2008). *(Source: Chapman Taylor)*

Figure 8.27 A glazed canopy is proposed to the open William Street, Victoria Square, Belfast, UK (planned 2007). *(Source: BDP)*

streets and untempered covered streets challenges the traditional prime retail precepts of providing climate controlled, enclosed interior space. This trend is borne out by the majority of recently planned new shopping centres in the UK adopting the approach of open and covered streets. These schemes have been encouraged, under planning guidance, in order to be more integrated with the surrounding streets. For this trend to succeed, it will require both customers' and tenants' traditional requirements for prime shopping space to be fundamentally refined and represented in a different package.

Although the recent trends represent a radical departure from the tried and tested, some of the traditional benefits of enclosed shopping centres, such as convenience and safety, can be readily provided in high quality, pedestrianised open streets. Covered streets can also, to a degree, address the requirement for comfort, provided the issue of wind draughts has been adequately designed out at the entrances. For example, a well designed and naturally ventilated covered space will provide protection from the rain and improve upon the ambient external temperatures of both winter and summer. Admittedly it won't provide the same degree of comfort as a fully enclosed, controlled interior space, but there are other advantages to the covered street which need to be balanced against reduced provision of comfort. For example, the shops can be arranged in a natural environment which has greater contact with the external weather, improved integration with the urban context and, consequently, providing the customer with an interesting and memorable experience. A convincing case can be made for the move towards open and covered space, rather than automatically opting for

the blandness of the fully enclosed space, on the basis that it provides a more sophisticated solution and addresses the customer requirement to provide a more individual shopping experience.

When considering alternative options for the public environment in town centre locations, it is important to consider the impact of the shopping centre on its surrounding environment as well as the comparative internal qualities of comfort. The consideration of integration with the surrounding urban environment has introduced a further criterion to be considered in evaluation. When evaluating alternatives, a significant advantage of the open and covered street is its ability to integrate more readily with the surrounding streets of the town centre. By comparison, the enclosed shopping environment can remain detached from the town centre and form a monolithic box. This impenetrable quality is emphasised when the centre closes and becomes an unusable part of the town centre. Open and covered street solutions can more readily remain open and form an integral and usable part of the town centre when the shops close.

When considering public space options the architect may need to broaden the debate and encourage more flexible thinking, away from traditional perspectives. To assist in changing the mindset away from enclosed interiors and prejudices against open streets, examples of some of the more successful open pedestrianised shopping streets are: The Rows, Chester; Gentleman's Walk, Norwich; Buchanan Street, Glasgow; and New Cathedral Street, Manchester. These and other shopping streets are successful open-air shopping environments, because they are carefully considered, quality pedestrianised shopping environments which have used natural materials, integrated street furniture and landscaping to create a public realm to be enjoyed. It is important when considering open street options to demonstrate the need to provide a high quality pedestrianised environment. It should also be noted that enclosed shopping centres were originally formed to provide a convenient and comfortable alternative to the many traffic congested high streets. With new and existing high streets once

Figure 8.28 Marikenstraat, Marienburg, an open two level street integrates with the streets of Nijmegan, The Netherlands (2000). *(Source: Sjaak Henselmans)*

Figure 8.29 Open streets and covered urban spaces integrate with the existing streets, the New Retail Quarter, Sheffield, UK (planned 2010–2012). *(Source: BDP)*

Figure 8.30 A traditional two level street at The Rows, Chester, UK. *(Source: Peter Coleman)*

again returning to focus on the pedestrian, in high quality, public realm environments, the open high street is convincingly able to offer an attractive and more natural alternative to the artificially enclosed shopping interior. At a time of shoppers wanting a more unique and memorable shopping experience, the natural, pedestrianised, open high street, integrated with the civic and cultural qualities of the town centre, is likely to be better equipped to meet this requirement.

The debate between enclosed and open shopping environments will run and run until more of the open street schemes in the pipeline are completed. In the meantime, architects will need to address how to make the urban agenda's requirement for open and covered street-based schemes become a destination of choice and compete against the traditional, enclosed, climate controlled centre.

Return to Mixed Use

Since the first planned town centre retail schemes, there has been a long tradition of incorporating other building uses with shopping facilities. Subsequent to the formative years of shopping centres, a period of largely singular use developments were completed which became isolated areas of town centres when the shops closed. Many recent retail-led regeneration schemes in town centres incorporate a variety of other uses. Retail facilities are being planned combining residential, office and civic facilities to regenerate town centres and achieve vitality throughout the day and evening. When carefully considered and integrated with the shopping centre, other uses can be beneficial to the development.

Earlier Chapters have identified the complementary nature of leisure uses (including cinemas, health clubs and catering) combined with shops in order to achieve a natural synergy between the uses. The benefits of widening the attraction of the centre and increasing the visit time by adding leisure uses have also been previously discussed. The recent urban agenda and return to town centre based schemes requires the incorporation of additional uses to provide city living, working, civic and tourist facilities. When this wider mix of facilities is incorporated, they must be planned in such a way so as not to compromise the shopping centre, and to allow for future flexibility and incremental change.

Some of the key issues to be considered with each of the different uses are now discussed.

Leisure and Catering

Although the cinema, health club, entertainment centre and catering tenants can be treated and organised in the same way as the shop tenants, leisure tenants generally pay considerably less rent than their retail neighbours. Therefore the leisure tenants should be located in the less used parts of the centre. These locations will be the more peripheral parts of the layout and probably the upper levels. Coincidentally, the upper levels are better suited to accommodating the larger space requirements of cinemas and health clubs which can be readily housed there.

Leisure uses tend to continue to operate in to the evening and, with night clubs, extend into the night. These extended hours of use can add life to a centre

Figure 8.31 A proposed two level open street with residential above the shops, New Burgess Street, Sheffield, UK (planned 2010–2012). *(Source: BDP)*

Figure 8.32 Terraced catering area above the shops, WestQuay, Southampton, UK (2000). *(Source: David Barbour/BDP)*

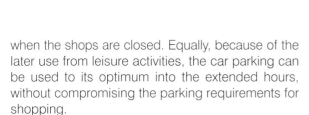

Figure 8.33 Cinemas located above the shops at N1, Islington, London, UK (2002). *(Source: Peter Coleman)*

Figure 8.34 Cafés and bars added at ground floor level animate the riverside walk to the large cinema box, The Oracle, Reading, UK (1999). *(Source: Hammerson)*

centres and clubs also require careful design of the large box enclosures. In some circumstances, the accommodation can be arranged to line the edges of the blank boxes with catering and small shop uses.

when the shops are closed. Equally, because of the later use from leisure activities, the car parking can be used to its optimum into the extended hours, without compromising the parking requirements for shopping.

Leisure activities which extend beyond the shop trading hours also require access to be maintained. The provision of independent access to late night activities can be an advantage. Care needs to be given to the location of some late night uses, when combined with residential uses, to avoid the nuisance of noise.

The means of escape from large leisure uses can be significant and requires careful planning if above the shops. Single zone evacuation policies can avoid doubling up on escape routing, but will need to be negotiated with the fire authority, otherwise separate escape routes will need to be incorporated.

Catering accommodation can be designed with animated and active frontages which positively contribute to the edges of the building. Animating the edges of cinemas is less easy to do without compromising their function. Similarly, entertainment

Residential

City living is once again both desirable and lucrative. Shopping centres in urban locations are likely to need to find ways of accommodating residential uses. The residential accommodation often needs to be both a mixture of private and public in order to be inclusive of all housing needs.

Private apartments and loft style housing are fashionable and in demand. However, while having the potential for an attractive environment, private residential traditionally requires long individual leases which may conflict with the requirement for the flexible resale of a retail property investment asset. To overcome these divergent needs, it is better to plan private residential accommodation with the facility of vertical separation from the main shopping element. The vertical separation will allow the shopping to be independently sold without affecting the residential.

Public housing for students or housing associations can more readily be arranged on short leases and is therefore more flexible. As such, public housing is more suitable to be arranged horizontally above shop facilities. Public housing above shops needs to be carefully designed so as not to detract from the required retail environment. Where housing is arranged above shops, the following issues should be considered and planned into the scheme from an early stage:

■ access to the entrances
■ the inclusion of entranceways while maintaining continuity of shopfronts
■ a separate means of delivery access for large items
■ separate refuse collection
■ car parking if on site or separate
■ isolation of the residential services for maintenance purposes (without needing to disturb shop tenants below the residential, which illustrates the principle of isolating the residential services).

Figure 8.36 The proposed new library above two level ground floor shops, St David's Centre, Cardiff, Wales, UK (planned 2008). *(Source: BDP)*

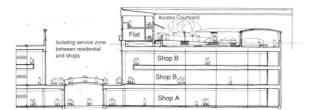

Figure 8.35 An isolating zone for services is recommended between residential and shop uses to avoid any services passing through the shop units, The New Retail Quarter, Sheffield, UK (planned 2010). *(Source: BDP)*

Residential uses above retailing provides activity in the area outside of trading hours and a means of positive security as they overlook the street.

Civic Uses and Libraries

Libraries are another inseparable use from the daily activity of town centres and have been integrally planned with shopping centres since the opening of the first precincts. There was a library in the Precinct in Coventry, one of the first town centre shopping precincts which opened in 1955. Libraries are generally compatible with the institutional requirement for asset flexibility and are usually leased to local councils for them to run. A natural synergy exists between a trip to the library and shopping. Libraries need to be easily accessible and, although the bulk of the accommodation can be above the shops, require a ground floor entrance.

Figure 8.37 A new library is included in the retail led mixed-use development for the Eden Quarter, Kingston, UK (planned 2010). *(Source: BDP)*

Hotels

Hotel accommodation can be leased to a hotel operator on a similar basis to a shop and therefore can coexist above and adjacent to shopping facilities, without compromising the retail property asset. The hotel will, however, require a significant ground floor entrance and a dropping off point. The positioning of the hotel is therefore likely to suit a peripheral location with adjacent road access. If located above the shops, the positioning of vertical service stacks will need to be carefully considered.

Figure 8.38 The Radisson Hotel shares the covered street with the shopping and leisure facilities, The Light, Leeds, UK (2001). (*Source: Peter Coleman*)

Figure 8.39 Underground enclosed shopping at Jubilee Place, Canary Wharf serve the intense office development above, London, UK (2004). (*Source: Peter Coleman*)

Offices

In principle, offices above shops can be developed by the same landlord and arranged with complementary leases. Unfortunately, prime offices principally need to appear as an office building, where the office accommodation and cores are established first and any retail on the ground floor is made to fit around the offices. A shopping centre with offices above tends to give the shop accommodation priority and potentially compromises the office accommodation. In the latter arrangement, the image of the office can be compromised and become secondary to the shopping environment.

While a preference for stand alone offices exists and individual corporate image pervades, offices above shopping centres will tend to be secondary. However, there is a market for this type of office accommodation, for example offices for small tenancies and various types of council accommodation.

Offices above shops require a suitable ground floor entrance and a street address. Consideration will also need to be given to the selection of a structural grid that works with both shops and units and modules of office accommodation.

References

British Council of Shopping Centres (1995). *Service Areas for Shopping Centres*. BCSC.

British Council of Shopping Centres (2000). *A Briefing Guide for Shopping Centre Development*. BCSC. p. 5.

Grosvenor, BCSC (2002). *Shopping Centre Futures*. Future Foundation, p. 13.

Lend Lease (1999). *Vision to Reality*. Lend Lease. p. 60.

Toyo Ito's organically inspired façade to the multi-level store for Tod's, Tokyo, Japan (2004). *(Source: Toyo Ito/Nacasa and Partners Ltd)*

Types of Accommodation

9

The Principal Types of Shop

The shop units form the nucleus of a shopping centre and attract the customers to use the shopping facility. In terms of the function of the building and the rental income, the shop units are the most important accommodation in a shopping centre. The architect does not design the shop unit interior, but instead provides the context and container in shell form for each shop separately and independently to fit out its own interior.

Shop unit accommodation is planned on a speculative basis based on an estimation of retailer demand established by the retail team, who will determine the overall gross leasable area (GLA). Although, at the same time, there may also be a potential wish list of tenants, the planned accommodation is based upon general space requirements prior to any commitment by a tenant to lease specific accommodation. For this reason, the shop accommodation needs to be planned on a generic basis that is sufficiently flexible to house a variety of potential tenants. The shop accommodation also needs to be planned to accommodate the different space requirements of the principal types of shop. There are three principal types of shop:

- unit shops
- medium space users (MSUs)
- anchor stores or department stores.

Each of these three primary types of shop is explained in more detail below.

Unit Shops

Unit shops make up the majority of accommodation in a shopping centre. The unit shop is a standard size which will be readily lettable to a range of potential tenants. A range of different sized unit shops may also be provided to meet more closely the generic space requirements of different retailers. Standard unit shops may also be combined, in part or whole multiples of shop unit, to form large shop units, or combined to become medium space user accommodation. The space requirements for the unit shops can be agreed with the retail team or established from empirical knowledge. Another useful source of information can be found in periodic surveys of tenant requirements which are compiled by the shopping industry.

A survey compiled by the BCSC in 1998 revealed the unit shop requirements shown in Table 9.1.

Table 9.1 Tenant unit shop requirements

- Majority of tenants (63%) seek floor space $95\,m^2$ ($1000\,ft^2$)–$380\,m^2$ ($4000\,ft^2$)
- Strong preference for units in range $190\,m^2$ ($2000\,ft^2$)–$325\,m^2$ ($3500\,ft^2$)
- Small proportion (19%) require units less than $95\,m^2$ ($1000\,ft^2$)
- A proportion (18%) require units larger than $380\,m^2$ ($4000\,ft^2$)

Information for this table taken from Survey of Tenant Requirements, BCSC 1998.

Shop Unit Size

In preparing initial layouts to consider the viability of a shopping centre development, a shop unit module will be established in order to lay out the gross floor area (GLA), having made an allowance for the anchor store requirements. It is important to note here that since the earliest shopping centres of the 1960s, a trend for shops to require increasingly larger premises has emerged through each decade. So consideration of what may now be an appropriate shop unit format will continue to change over time.

However, in taking account of this trend, for initial planning studies, a shop unit module of 7.5 m wide by 30 m deep (24.6 ft × 98.4 ft) providing a nominal area of 225 m² (2420 ft²) GLA is typical current shop requirement. It is likely that more than one shop unit size will be required and that tenant requirements will continue to change. For this reason the design team should, at the project outset, establish with the commercial agents the size and range of sizes for the shop units to be accommodated.

Frontage Module

Another key consideration in shop unit planning will be the dimension of the frontage module. Frontage size has similarly increased with the evolution of shopping centres. The typical shop unit frontage accepted today by tenants is a module between 7.5 and 8 m (24–26.2 ft).

Shop Proportion

Shop unit size is the result of both the frontage width and the depth of a typical rectangular shaped unit. However, the proportion of the shop plan is important to the tenant who requires the interior to appear inviting and not too deep. It is not a simple case of adopting a frontage module and achieving

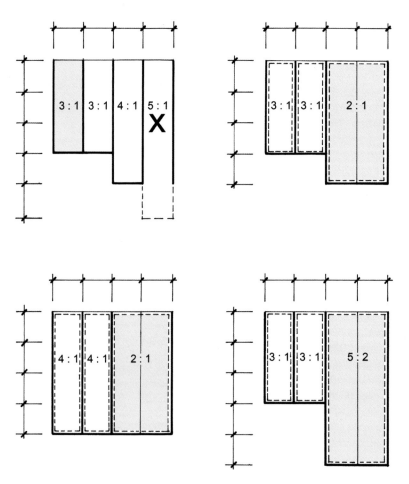

Figure 9.1 Typical shop unit proportions: single shop unit width to depth proportions should not exceed 3:1 or 4:1. Where units are combined to make larger units these proportions still apply. *(Source: Peter Coleman)*

the area by making the unit the required depth regardless of the proportion of the shop. The frontage-to-depth ratio of a typical rectangular shaped shop unit of between 1 to 3 and 1 to 4 will suit most tenants' interior requirements. In some circumstances the frontage-to-depth ratio can be increased up to 1 to 5. This deeper proportion can suit single-level shops with the requirement for on site storage.

Most retailers have traditionally required 25–30 per cent of the GLA for storage. It should, however, be noted that in some shops the requirement for on site storage has been reducing with the use of 'just in time' stock management and the use of computer sales and ordering processes. Storage space can also be provided above or below the shop provided there is a direct vertical stair connection between the two floors. While shop sizes have evolved and increased, the requirement for the correct shop proportion has remained more constant and is likely to remain a universal requirement as shop sizes continue to change in the future.

Shop units can also operate on more than one level and are prepared to trade on two levels or to use the extra level for storage where there is insufficient headroom for a full trading floor. Vertical dimensional requirements are discussed in more detail below. An increasing proportion of shops are prepared to trade on two levels. (The 1998 BCSC Tenant Survey revealed that 50 per cent of tenants were prepared to do so.)

Figure 9.2 Double height shopfronts have a historical precedent, Galeria Vittorio Emmanuelle, Milan, Italy. *(Source: Peter Coleman)*

Multi-Level Shops

It is the tenants with the larger space requirements who are more likely to trade on two levels. It is, therefore, no coincidence that as shop unit size requirements have increased, so has the trend for shops to trade on two levels. Two-level trading shops operate in a variety of different configurations:

- directly repeating the footprint of the shop to trade at another level
- occupying a larger proportion of trading space at the upper level (the additional level of space is likely to be cheaper to rent)
- occupying storage space at another level which is a small proportion of the main floor.

The common occurrence of two-level shops has seen the formation of up and over units where smaller shop units sit beside and beneath the shops with larger space requirements. It has also seen the advent of double height shopfronts and a more dramatic and lively frontage facing on to the high street or shopping mall.

Figure 9.3 Multi-level shops in the high street illustrated by The Gap, Oxford Street, London, UK. *(Source: BDP)*

Figure 9.4 Double height shop and frontage, The Liberty, Romford, UK (2003). *(Source: Peter Coleman)*

The requirement for various vertical combinations of shop unit make it important for the plan layout to remain flexible until the tenants have been finalised and their requirements are known. It is only at the time of the tenants agreeing to lease space that the internal wall and floor opening layout are finalised. Multi-level units require the floors to be designed to be sufficiently flexible to accommodate, at a late stage, the requirements for interconnecting stairs, lifts, escalators and mechanical systems. At the initial stages the design team has to make an informed estimate of the layout for the purposes of viability appraisals, technical feasibility and planning permissions. It is important to understand and accept this, and to have allowed for the fact that changes will take place when the tenants are finalised.

Vertical Dimensions

The shop tenant's principal interest in vertical dimensions is the clear internal height allowed from the finished floor to the underside of the structure. Most tenants require this dimension to be a minimum of 4.0 m (13.1 ft). For the purposes of establishing the floor-to-floor height, an additional allowance for the structure and floor finishes will need to be added to the clear 'floor to underside of ceiling' height. The structural allowance will depend on the structural method and grid dimensions being used, however, for design purposes a floor zone of 750–1000 mm (2.5–3.3 ft) is usually sufficient, establishing a design floor-to-floor height of 4.75–5.0 m (15.6–16.4 ft). Larger structural grids may require the floor-to-floor height to be increased up to 5.5 m (18 ft). The tenant usually completes the screed and floor finish on top of the structural slab and, within the floor zone an allowance of 75 mm (3 inches) is usually made for this. Within the 'clear floor to underside of structure', the tenant usually includes a suspended ceiling and zone for services of 500 mm (20 inches). This allows the tenant a minimum finished 'floor to underside of ceiling' height of 3.5 m (11.5 ft). The typical minimum vertical dimensions are shown in Fig. 9.5.

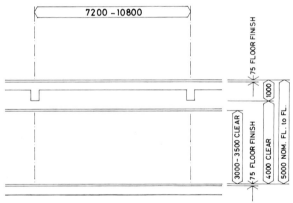

Figure 9.5 Nominal vertical floor-to-floor dimensions for a single level unit shop. *(Source: Peter Coleman)*

Mezzanines and Additional Floors

With tenants' requirements for larger shop units comes a corresponding acceptance of additional storage or trading space to be provided as an additional floor level within the shell unit. Additional storage space can be provided by a mezzanine floor, which typically extends the GLA of the main floor by up to 50 per cent. Additional trading floors can be provided by the provision of an equivalent performing, additional floor level which typically can extend to 80–90 per cent coverage of the main floor GLA. Mezzanine storage floors can be accommodated in an overall floor-to-floor height of no less than 6.5 m (21.3 ft). Additional floors for trading purposes require a larger floor-to-floor height of a minimum of 8.0 m (26.2 ft).

It is important at the briefing stage to establish the extent of additional mezzanine or trading floor cover to be provided within the project, as these areas have to be designed into the scheme and the areas included in the planning application. The vertical dimensions for the inclusion of mezzanine and trading floors within the tenant's shell are shown in Fig. 9.6. It is common for the landlord to build in the extra mezzanine and trading floors, as means of escape needs to be provided from these additional areas.

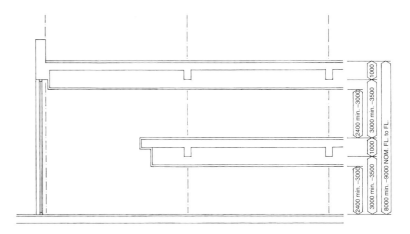

Figure 9.6 Nominal vertical floor-to-floor dimensions for a two level unit shop. *(Source: Peter Coleman)*

Grids

The structural grid for the unit shops usually determines the shop unit width and either directly coincides with it or has an arithmetic relationship with the shop width if different. Shop units can be accommodated within a variety of different structural grids. The grid is usually equal in the northing and easting axes and is set back from the shopfront line. Grid sizes commonly adopted are: 7.5×7.5 m (24.6 ft × 24.6 ft), 7.8×7.8 m (25.6×25.6 ft) and 8×8 m (26.2×26.2 ft). Where car parking is located above or below the shops, there is less flexibility with the grid as it is necessary to consider a grid that is compatible with the parking layout if transfer structures are to be avoided – 8×8 m is an accepted grid which works with both the shop unit module and the layout of the car park. A larger grid of 10.8×10.8 m (35.4×35.4 ft) is used in some instances, which allows the additional flexibility of forming either two or three unit shops per two structural grids. It is important to agree the structural grid with the specialist retail advisers at an early stage of the design.

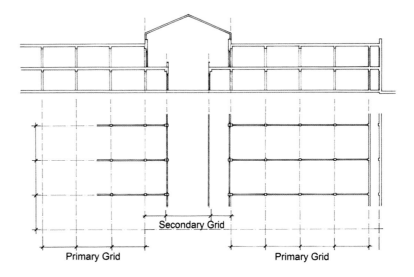

Figure 9.7 Grids are set back from the shopfront. In multi-level schemes the primary grid is usually set out from the upper level, with the lower floor shopfronts set out from a secondary grid. *(Source: Peter Coleman)*

Floor Loading

The floor loading will determine the structural design of the shop floors and can influence the floor-to-floor heights. Acceptable floor loading standards vary. For example:

- British Standard Code of Practice recommends 4 kN m^2 + 1 kN m^2 superimposed and a partition load respectively – a combined loading of 5 kN m^2
- Current common practice frequently works to a combined loading of 7.5 kN m^2

- The BCSC recommend a combined loading of 6–6.5 kN m^2 (BCSC, 2000).

It can be seen from these standards that the combined floor load can vary from 5 to 7.5 kN m^2. In line with more sustainable design practices, it would be sensible not to over-design the structure and to adopt the lower to median universal standard on the general shop floors throughout the centre. Where additional loading is required, this can be added to suit a particular requirement. The only drawbacks of this approach are the need to predetermine where shops with high loadings may be located (e.g. bookshops) and the disruption and delay which may occur from altering the structure on site. The structural loading will need to be agreed with the retail team and structural engineer.

Medium Space User Shops (MSUs)

Many of the principles outlined for unit shops apply to medium space user (MSU) shops. MSU shops are like large shop units which are usually strategically positioned in the layout to act as attractions and to lead the customer from one area to another. A more detailed explanation of the positioning of MSU shops is given in Chapter 10 (see Horizontal circulation and layout).

MSU shops are two or more times larger than unit shops and typically the small to medium MSUs range in size from 460 to 1400 m^2 (5000–15 000 ft^2). Some of the larger MSU shops can extend to 2790 m^2 (30 000 ft^2) and even to 5580 m^2 (60 000 ft^2). Beyond this size they become anchor stores in their own right.

The number and size of MSU shops will vary with each project and will depend upon the size of the project and catchment area. However, as an indication, in a medium sized shopping centre development it would be typical to provide between 6 and 10 small to medium sized MSUs along with 1 or 2 larger size MSUs. The brief for the number and size of MSU shops should be established with the retail team from the outset of the project.

The spatial requirements of the small to medium sized MSU shops can usually be met within the structural loadings, grid and vertical dimensions established for the unit shops. This commonality allows the flexibility of MSU shops being formed by the combination of two or more unit shops. MSU shops commonly occupy more than one level or even multiple levels and are prepared to trade on each

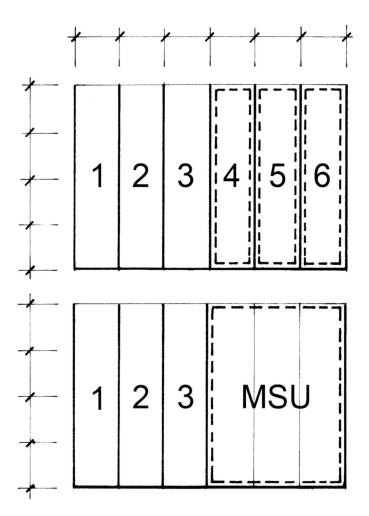

Figure 9.8 Medium space user (MSU) can be formed by the combination of several standard shop units. *(Source: Peter Coleman)*

Figure 9.9 Multiple height shopfront to an MSU at New Cathedral Street, Manchester, UK (2003). *(Source: David Barbour/BDP)*

level. These shops are also prepared to accept a smaller ground floor and utilise a larger amount of space at lower rental levels on an upper level. Two level MSU shops are commonly found with the medium to large MSUs sometimes prepared to trade from three levels. These multiple-level shops can adopt correspondingly high shopfronts and provide the opportunity to form more interesting and animated frontages to the street scene.

The larger MSU shops can occupy deeper floor space than the unit shops provided the proportions of the shop are kept to a similar 1 to 4 or 5 width-to-depth ratio. Within the larger MSU shops, as well as the opportunity of the double height shopfronts, consideration will also need to be given to the overall extent of frontage into which the tenant will be required to fit shop windows, as the shop may not

be prepared to provide and window-dress the whole extent of frontage available. In situations where the tenant is presented with long lengths of shopfront, these can end up being blank and uninteresting and should be avoided where possible.

Anchor Stores

Anchor stores are the third principal type of shop that the shopping centre architect will be required to accommodate within the overall layout. The architect will often then go on to design the shell building. Anchor stores are generally occupied by major retailers who trade in variety goods, fashion and homewares and are sometimes referred to as department stores. Store sizes can vary from

7000 to 23 000 m² (75 000–250 000 ft², a typical anchor store size being 9300–14 000 m² (100 000–150 000 ft²). Developers and owners have traditionally secured a store as a sure way of attracting the other shop tenants into the development. This principle still generally applies, although there are also other large attractions which can generate footfall and reassure other tenants, such as several significant MSUs grouped together or a large leisure facility.

Anchor stores attract customers to visit a centre in their own right and are usually positioned in the layout in order to encourage footfall past the other shop units. These stores are strategically located and are generally one of the key pedestrian circulation drivers. Typical locations for an anchor store would be:

- at the end of a run of shops, thereby drawing customers past the shopfronts
- located at a change of direction in the layout in a way which is clearly visible and draws customers in from both directions
- strategically positioned to form a focus and point of punctuation in a large complex layout.

Anchor stores should be located in positions that are easily understood and achieve good visibility within the internal layout and have an external presence.

Although anchor stores are key to the success of a shopping centre, their size needs to be kept in proportion to the space given to the remaining shop units. This is a viability issue relating to the fact that anchor stores pay less rent per square metre than shop units and the developer/owner needs to earn the lion's share of income from the shop units. Although the proportion of the total GLA occupied by the anchor stores will vary from project to project, a general guide to assist viability will be to keep the proportion given to anchor stores to 30–45 per cent of the total. The size and number of anchor stores to be included in a scheme will be related to the size of project. For example, a scheme will need to be larger than 23 000 m² (250 000 ft²) GLA in order to support a small to medium sized department store and larger than 56 000 m² (600 000 ft²) GLA to support two medium sized or one large sized department store.

Anchor stores will have their own requirements for column spacing, floor-to-floor heights and floor loadings which are generally different from those

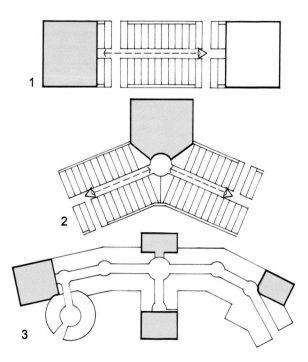

Figure 9.10 The strategic positioning of anchor stores: 1 at the end of a run of shops, drawing customers past the shopfronts; 2 located at a change of direction to draw customers on; 3 strategically positioned forming focus points. *(Source: Peter Coleman)*

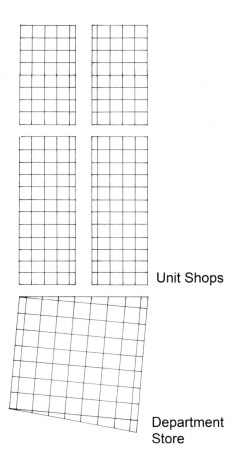

Unit Shops

Department Store

Figure 9.11 Department stores have a separate grid and identifiable footprint from unit shops. *(Source: Peter Coleman)*

provided to the unit and MSU shops. These requirements are discussed in more detail below. It is therefore preferable to give the anchor store its own distinct footprint, which is independent although attached to the remainder of the shopping centre. Department store footprints are usually simple regular shapes with square to rectangular shaped internal trading areas. Rectangular shaped trading areas are acceptable, provided it is a well-proportioned rectangle.

As a consequence of department stores having larger footprints than other stores, they require a larger internal volume of space, which involves a taller floor-to-floor height than the unit shops. Requirements vary but typical floor-to-floor heights that are acceptable to department stores range from 5 to 5.5 m (16.4–18 ft). Where the department store requires the larger floor-to-floor heights of 5.5 m in multi-level shopping centres, this can require a change of floor level in the public spaces to take up the adjustment between the unit shops' and department store floor-to-floor heights. Ramping the public space adjacent to the department store is one way of dealing with this level change. If ramps are not possible, the unit shops can adopt a taller floor-to-floor height to match those of the department store.

The larger floor plate and spaces of the department store are also better suited to a larger structural grid. A larger structural grid will provide the store with a more flexible internal trading arrangement, as well as improving visibility between different sections of the store. Grids that are commonly accepted by department stores range across: 8.4×8.4 m (27.5×27.5 ft), 9.6×9.6 m (31.5×31.5 ft), 9.6 × 10.8 m (31.5×35.4 ft) and 10.8×10.8 m (35.4× 35.4 ft).

Anchor stores generally operate on several floor levels, with a centrally positioned escalator well interconnecting between the floors. The number of floor levels is dependent on the store size and availability of land. Out-of-town and small stores are more likely to require three trading levels, while in-town locations and large stores are more likely to accept four trading levels. Some restricted urban locations with high land values may convince the retailer to accept trading on more than four levels.

The arrangement of the department store's internal departments within the multi-level store will vary depending on the type of store, the number of floor levels, the size of floor plate, whether there is a basement level and which level is perceived as the primary entrance level if the store is entered from

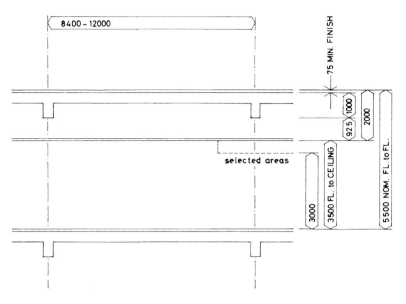

Figure 9.12 Nominal vertical floor-to-floor dimensions for a department store. *(Source: Peter Coleman)*

several different ones. Perfumery and items of personal adornment will usually be arranged on the principal entrance level with the remaining departments arranged to suit the particular store configuration and location. The typical product departments to be arranged within the department store are categorised into general areas such as: perfumery and personal adornment; home and housewares; women's fashionware; men's fashionware; children's clothing; and electrical wares. There may also be a food hall, a café and a restaurant to be accommodated in some department stores. Although the internal arrangement of departments (within the store) will be laid out by the store's in-house design team, it is useful for the shopping centre architect to understand these principles which may require particular requirements of the internal layout to be incorporated into the shell design of the department store.

Within the envelope design of the shell for the department store, the architect will be required to establish the location and design of the entrances. Department stores will usually accept more than one entrance and entrances to be made on several levels. However, because the position and number of entrances will influence the internal store layout, the architect will need to liaise closely with the in-house design team before these can be finalised.

In addition to these considerations, the architect will have to incorporate other general requirements into both the design of the shell for the department store and the general setting of the store. Some of these general requirements are listed in Table 9.2.

Table 9.2 Department store requirements

- Department store buildings usually require their own separate architectural identity, separate from the remainder of the shopping centre
- When viewed from the approaching circulation routes, the main entrances will be required to be clearly visible and free from any obstructions, such as escalators or stairs
- Most stores will require an independent pedestrian entrance which can be reached without having to go through the centre's circulation spaces
- The main entrance will usually be required to be directly located on to the prime circulation space and positioned centrally on to the trading area of the store
- The most influential department stores will require compatible shops to be located adjacent to them in the layout of the shopping centre
- The car parking will be required to be located within close proximity to the store
- Some stores will require direct access from the car parking
- Most stores will have a minimum requirement for the number of car parking spaces to be provided
- Deliveries to, and servicing of, the store will be required from designated loading bays and direct and secure access into the store. The loading bays can be from a shared service yard
- As a convenience to their customers, the larger stores will require a customer collection facility which is usually integral with the store and provides clear and user-friendly means of car access and designated customer parking
- Independent, naturally ventilated space for the store's mechanical services plant, integrally screened within the building envelope, will also be required

Figure 9.13 A specific and individual identity has been given to the Selfridges Store by Future Systems, Birmingham, UK (2003). *(Source: Caroline Field)*

In addition to these general requirements, the developer/owner sometimes provides specific requirements of the store within the building shell to assist the department store's fit out. For example, openings required through the floor slab, tenant's escape stairs and the vertical risers can be included in the shell works once known from the store's layout.

These considerations assume the shopping centre architect will complete the shell building design for the department store. In some schemes, an independent architect may be introduced to design the shell for the department store within an overall masterplan prepared by the shopping centre architect. In these circumstances, the shopping centre architect will be responsible for establishing the overall layout, defining the masterplan requirements, monitoring the compliance of the design with the masterplan and coordinating the detailed design of the department store with the rest of the shopping centre.

Shell Completion to Shops

The developer/owner usually completes the shop units, MSU shops and anchor stores up to the point of a shell standard of finish. The different types of shop tenants then complete their own shop fit out which includes internal finishes, environmental services installations, shop fitting and stocking out with products. The shell finish provided in most formats of shopping centre will include the structure, the weatherproof envelope, floor openings and the supply of capped-off mains and electrical services.

In factory outlet centres, which have shorter-term leases and potentially faster turnover of tenants, the developer/owner (landlord) may also provide an enhanced level of finish which represents a basic finished shop. This basic level of finished shop will include simple floor and wall finishes, primary lighting, power, heating and ventilation to allow the tenant to move in and out quickly with little more to complete than the racking and stock. Factory outlet centre tenants also have the option of supplementing the lighting and finishes to reflect their own brand if required. In factory outlet centres, the additional capital and running costs are reimbursed to the landlord on a pro rata basis per square metre, applied to the rent for the total area let to each tenant.

Generally, in most types of shopping centre development, the shell finish includes terminated mains services connections including water, drainage, electricity and interfaces with the landlord's public address, fire and security systems. It is usually the responsibility of each individual tenant to arrange for their own connection to the telephone network. In some covered and enclosed types of shopping centre, a terminated connection to a sprinkler main will also be included. Shop units that are planned to accommodate catering tenants will also include a terminated gas main connection. The larger shop units, which includes MSU shops and anchor stores, will also include a terminated mains gas supply.

The mains services to each tenancy are separately metered and will require consideration and the provision of space for suitably located and accessible meters for each service to each unit. Meters are usually grouped together by type of mains service and arranged into convenient zones relating to identifiable areas of the centre. (This is discussed in more detail in Back of house areas, further on.)

Shop tenants will complete their own services installations from the point of the capped-off supplies. The heating, cooling and venting to the tenancies is usually provided by an electrically driven, individual heat exchange unit installed at roof level for each shop unit. The individual heat exchange units are connected to the shop units via vertical risers. Space for each tenant's plant will need to be allocated at roof level, which will also include the means of supporting the mechanical kit.

Multi-level shopping centres, with shops arranged above other shops, will need to allow for vertical risers passing from the shop units located at the lower levels, through the upper-level shops in fire resistant enclosures. Riser ducts require the coordination of openings formed in the intervening floor and roof slabs and are usually formed in blockwork masonry. The tenants are usually required to complete the waterproofing around the roof-level opening upon the completion of their installation.

In some shopping centres, either located in particularly sensitive areas or where the roof is required for other areas of accommodation, the roof may not be available for tenants' plant. In these circumstances, the tenants' plant will need to be alternatively accommodated with suitable free air space, or the landlord will have to provide the primary heating, cooling and fresh air supply to each tenancy. If the latter, the tenant will still complete the installation within the shop unit. However, the tenant will reimburse the landlord for the primary environmental supplies by an additional rental contribution based on a pro rata basis per square metre, applied to the amount of floor space occupied. Where the landlord provides capped-off primary heating and cooling supplies to each tenancy, the shopping centre architect will need to plan for suitably located central plant and

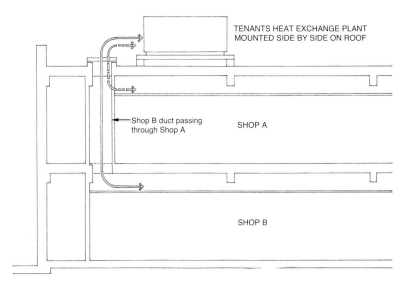

Figure 9.14 In multi-level arrangements vertical risers from ground floor pass through upper shop units to reach plant on the roof. *(Source: Peter Coleman)*

coordinate the primary service routes which lead around the centre to each unit.

Each tenant will be required to complete its shop fitting and installation work in accordance with a shop fitting guide prepared by the landlord's team. The shop fitting proposals of each tenant will also be approved and coordinated by the landlord's team. The shop fitting guide, together with the approval and coordination process, are explained in more detail at the end of this Chapter.

Catering Facilities

Catering areas are other tenant-occupied front of house areas that the architect has to plan within the overall layout and complete to a shell standard of finish. Catering includes the various eating and drinking facilities which are an important attraction for a shopping centre. Catering is an integral part of visiting any shopping and leisure destination and has proven not only to widen the appeal of a particular centre, but also to extend the average stay time and amount of spend per customer per visit.

When considering catering accommodation, the architect will be responding to several social trends – with corresponding lifestyle changes – in order to provide the appropriate range and balance of facilities. Improved general social wealth is allowing more people to eat out which is generating a requirement for more catering facilities and a greater variety of provision. Eating out is no longer reserved for special occasions, but has become a regular leisure pastime. The age range is more diverse and there is a great variety of different lifestyles now eating out, with a need for more socially inclusive catering. Customer expectations have extended beyond the range of catering found in the traditional food court. Today the fast food of the food court is still valid, but needs supplementing by a wider choice of experience and wider range of eating and dining. Food courts are now just a part of a wider catering facility which also includes individual cafés and restaurants which provide medium and long stay dining and a wider selection of food types. Catering also includes individual bars for beverages, which include coffee or soft drinks, as well as licensed premises.

The catering brief for each project will depend on the lifestyle requirements of the catchment population, the location, the size of centre and the availability of existing facilities. The catering facilities make up a proportion of the total accommodation which can range from 2 to 25 per cent of the GLA. Large regional shopping centres which intend to act as day out destinations will provide a full range of catering facilities which may include fast food, medium length of stay value dining, some quality restaurants and individual localised beverage (coffee and juice) bars. These provide a variety of offers which will need to meet the range of aspirations of teenagers, families, the more sophisticated middle-aged and elderly customers. In town centre locations, any existing facilities will need to be taken into account when considering the mix. There is a general trend towards providing more individual cafés and restaurants.

The selection of eating and drinking facilities should ideally be selected and located to correspond with the retail mix, in order to reinforce the synergy between the retail and catering elements. The extent and mix of the catering should be established with the retail team at the briefing stage of the project.

Location Considerations

In addition to locating catering elements in order to establish a natural synergy with the corresponding retail accommodation, there are also some other important general considerations to be taken into account. Catering units are generally prepared to pay less rent than comparable sized shop units. Therefore there will be a loss of premium rent if a catering unit is located among the prime retail units. It is preferable to locate catering facilities nearby or adjacent to the retail units, in a secondary or off-prime pitch location. With some café and restaurants trading out of hours into the evening, these units should have a perimeter location which can

maintain independent access when the shopping centre may be closed. Provided there is sufficient critical mass, a group of catering facilities can become a destination in its own right. However, it makes better economic sense not to locate catering as an isolated dead end, but to position it en route to other facilities in, for example, a leisure facility or external space. Locating catering accommodation on the perimeter of a centre with views over a setting or to an existing local landmark, can be a useful way of reinforcing the identity of a location.

Figure 9.15 Perimeter located catering with external views to The Village, Bluewater, Greenhithe, Kent, UK (1999). *(Source: Peter Coleman)*

External views are also a useful way of providing a break away from the intensity of focused shopping activity. Positioning catering at an upper level can be a useful way of utilising this space and providing additional mass and activity to the building. It is important when catering is located at an upper level that it is clearly visible and physically well-connected to the retail areas and main circulation areas.

Types of Catering Format

The wide range of different types of catering which can be incorporated into shopping developments can be categorised into four basic physical formats for more detailed examination.

1 Food Courts

This format can be summarised as providing fast food, with a limited choice, obtained by self-service and eaten in a communal seating area. In isolation, food courts are outmoded and fall short of meeting the catering requirements of a discerning and mature society, but as part of a more diverse comprehensive catering offer they serve a specific segment of the larger market. Food courts meet the requirement of fast snacks from teenagers and young families, and are only likely to be included as part of a wider catering offer in the largest regional shopping centres and regional shopping and leisure centres.

Food courts are often located as an extension of the shopping centre public circulation space, either in a specially formed focal space or located in a specially formed area adjacent to it. As such, they are an element of the shopping centre accommodation that (provided the architect has interior design and graphic skills) can be fully designed by the architect.

Figure 9.17 Self-service food served from open fronted counters with communal seating, Canal Walk, Century City, Cape Town, SA. *(Source: Peter Coleman)*

Figure 9.16 A foodcourt with a range of fast food in a separately themed area, Canal Walk, Century City, Cape Town, SA (2000). *(Source: Peter Coleman)*

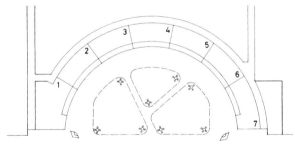

Figure 9.18 A typical food court configuration with the unit counters visible from the entranceway and a larged zoned common seating area. *(Source: Peter Coleman)*

Food courts are based on self-service food served from a range of open-fronted counters which are arranged together. The layout is arranged to present all the counter frontages as a kind of three-dimensional menu for each of the types of food available. Gentle concave curves and horseshoe shaped layouts are commonly adopted. The immediate preparation and serving area behind each counter is relatively small and constrains the choice of food that can be prepared. There will also be additional preparation and storage space arranged out of sight behind the open counter and galley servery. A storage facility will be provided for each unit and will include a preparation workspace with a sink and cupboard space, as well as refrigerated cold storage.

The commonly available catering offers in UK food courts are somewhat formulaic, predictable and tend to be the usual suspects: burgers, pizzas, filled potatoes, Chinese food, fish and chips, rolls and sandwiches, ice creams and juice/beverage bars.

A typical arrangement is likely to include six to eight of these offers where each unit is provided with 40–60 m^2 (430–645 ft^2) of space, serving a communal dining area with tables and chairs for 300–400 people. Seats and tables should generally be robust loose furniture which can allow for easy floor cleaning and maintenance. Some larger food court facilities may be planned to accommodate 600 seats.

Figure 9.19 Large, themed food court, The Orient, The Trafford Centre, Manchester, UK (Chapman Taylor) (1998). *(Source: Chapman Taylor)*

Food courts are arranged with the counters facing the communal seating (see Fig. 9.18). It is also necessary for all the counter frontages to be visible from the approaching point of arrival. A clearly defined pedestrian route is required in front of the counters to provide sufficient queuing and access space. There are usually also defined pedestrian access routes leading through the seating area to allow for easy access and to help form more easily identifiable zones of seating.

The seating area can be at the same level as the counters or slightly terraced down to help form more identifiable seating areas. Any changes of level

Figure 9.20 Two level catering overlooking the water at Ocean Terminal, Leith, Edinburgh, UK (2001). *(Source: Peter Coleman)*

should be clearly defined with balustrading, gentle steps and ramped access.

Food courts are usually run and managed by a single specialist company which arranges and provides supplies to all the individual caterers. Where possible, the final food court layout should be planned together with this specialist management company. Each caterer will have its own cooking and preparation equipment to be accommodated behind the counter.

Food is often served on disposable plates with plastic cutlery which will be centrally collected and disposed of and will require a suitably sized daily collection space located adjacent to the food court. Food can also be served on ceramic plates with metal cutlery which will also be centrally collected and washed, requiring a central washing-up room. The type of cutlery and plates will be determined by the specialist manager of the food court. In planning the food court it is important to establish which of these serving methods will be used, as it will affect the planning and accommodation to be provided. Reusable cutlery, napkins, cups and saucers, condiments, garnishes and milk and sugar are usually made available from island collection stations which are conveniently positioned between the counters and seating areas. Refuse bins are sometimes regularly located around the communal seating allowing customers to dispose of rubbish. This also allows for the central collection of rubbish.

Another communal staff facility to be incorporated behind the servery area is a staff changing and locker room. Communal staff toilet facilities will also need to be planned adjacent to the food court. Having a specialist management company responsible for the running of the food court will greatly assist with the practical management of keeping the communal facilities – the lockers, changing room, toilets, washing up area, rubbish clearance area – neat and tidy. The food court will also require convenient public toilets. Separate toilets will be required, in addition to the main public toilets for the shopping centre, if the latter are not conveniently located.

Food court catering is constantly evolving. Today the food court is no longer the single universal catering facility and is only planned in shopping centres as part of a wider catering offer. Food courts are also particularly associated with significant leisure developments, again as part of a wider catering facility. Food court offers, as outlined above, are restricted and not inclusive of all lifestyle requirements. Further development of food court formats may see the incorporation of more healthy and discerning eating options. Further evolution may see them combine

Figure 9.21 Food being eaten on the premises or sold for use at home, The Wintergarden, KaDeWe Department Store, Berlin, Germany. *(Source: KaDeWe)*

Figure 9.22 A seafood bar for on site eating, KaDeWe, Berlin, Germany. *(Source: KaDeWe)*

quality fresh food, which can either be purchased to take home or consumed on the premises, as already exists in the foodhall of the KaDeWe department store in Berlin.

2 Restaurant Clusters

Restaurants are usually independent catering offers and although they can be individually located, they are usually grouped in a cluster of four to six restaurants to establish a local identity. Restaurants usually occupy a shell space provided by the developer/owner, with the seating integral to the unit. Some of the eating can be arranged externally in a pre-arranged overspill area. The restaurant tenant usually arranges for the completion of the internal fit out in a similar way to those explained above for shop units. However, the shell unit for the restaurant can be more expressive and individual than that required for a standard shop unit.

Figure 9.23 A cluster of restaurants arranged over two levels at the Victoria and Alfred Waterfront, Cape Town, SA (1996). *(Source: Peter Coleman)*

Restaurants provide waitress served food, consumed within the premises from a wide range and variety of choices. In choosing a restaurant the customer has elected for a controlled experience, which can range from a light meal to a full culinary experience. The choice can also be from a wide range of different national cuisines and types of food. Restaurants have the advantage over food courts of being able to provide a greater variety of choice and experience. Restaurants can provide catering that ranges from good value to the exclusive end of prices. Most shopping centre restaurants tend to represent the middle ground, where value and quality will attract more customers than the exotic and exclusive cuisine. Within the range of restaurants selected, there can also be one representing the national fast food chains, thereby allowing the needs of the discerning to be met as equally as those requiring convenience, and for the catering offer to be inclusive of all lifestyles.

The range of restaurants to select from will include the following: American diner, Chinese, fish, French crêperie, Indian, Italian pizzeria or trattoria, Japanese sushi, Mexican, national fast food operators, noodle bars, themed restaurants and traditional English. From this range the retail team will try to select four to six restaurant operations to provide the wide choice which will attract the maximum number of customers within the catchment area of the shopping centre.

The size of accommodation required for a restaurant will vary depending upon the type. For example, a café or small restaurant can be accommodated in a unit of 140 m^2 (1500 ft^2) GLA, while a themed restaurant will require a larger unit – up to 560 m^2 (6000 ft^2) GLA. It is likely that a restaurant cluster will be made up of a range of unit sizes which provides for the smallest to the largest with several medium sized restaurants of 200–400 m^2 (2100–4300 ft^2) GLA. The restaurant sizes should

be agreed with the retail team before space planning. Restaurants ideally prefer all accommodation on one level and at ground level. However, the practicalities of rental levels have required some restaurants to accept accommodation at more than one level or with only a ground floor entrance, with stairs and a lift leading to the majority of the accommodation at another level. Restaurants located at upper levels have the advantage of views and external terraces. Sometimes basement space can be used, provided the space can be serviced and ventilated.

Larger restaurants are prepared to occupy units with more than one level and will even serve

Figure 9.25 A converted boathouse forms a large two level restaurant overlooking the Victoria and Alfred Waterfront, Cape Town, SA (1996). *(Source: Peter Coleman)*

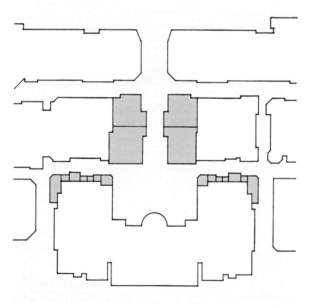

Figure 9.24 A cluster of restaurants face the plaza and street leading to the cinemas, with fast food outlets forming active frontages, The Block at Orange, Orange County, California, USA (1998). *(Source: Peter Coleman)*

Figure 9.26 An individual restaurant at an upper level with seating on the gallery and a separate café on the ground floor overlook an historic part of the city, The Forum, Norwich, UK (2004). *(Source: Peter Coleman)*

food on two levels, provided the second level is visible and easily accessible. In multi-level catering spaces it is important that there is good visual contact between the levels. Floor-to-floor heights between levels can be less than those provided for trading uses in shops and 3–3.5 m (9.8–11.5 ft) will be acceptable. It is preferable for smaller restaurants to be arranged on a single level, although some restaurants may accept storage space and staff facilities on a second level. Individual restaurants will have integral public and staff facilities required for the operation of the restaurant.

The restaurant may need to include within its demised area the following: a reception space, a bar, dining area, kitchen, food preparation and storage space, staff toilet and public toilets. Food deliveries and refuse should ideally be accessed from a separate entrance, which is usually at the rear. Some restaurants can be serviced from a separate off-street entrance. Where rear servicing access is provided from an integral service yard shared with the shops, it is preferable to provide a separate service lift for wet foods and for the removal of restaurant refuse.

Restaurant accommodation is finished to a similar shell standard as unit shops, with each tenant arranging the interior fit out. Restaurants will have the addition of a capped-off gas main included with the other main services. The shop fitting procedure and liaison with the landlord's team is also similar to that for the unit shops.

As well as the advantage of greater variety of choice for the customer, individual restaurants and restaurant clusters generally require less input and involvement from the centre management during their operation. With both commercial and operational advantages, it is not surprising that the popularity of including individual restaurants in shopping developments is growing.

3 Individual Beverage Areas

These catering facilities provide an important additional refreshment of drinks and snacks, which is separate from those provided in food courts or individual restaurants. Beverage areas are a short-stay, less committed refreshment which is self-serviced from a bar or counter. The counter is located within, or to the side of, the public circulation space, allowing the user to retain contact with the shopping activity while taking a fast pick up refreshment, without disturbing the process of shopping.

Figure 9.27 An individual café beverage bar located beneath the knuckle roof, Touchwood, Solihull, UK (2001). *(Source: Peter Coleman)*

Figure 9.28 Spiral Café by Marks Barfield in St Martin's Square, The Bullring, Birmingham, UK (2004). *(Source: Peter Durant/ArcBlue)*

These facilities suit customers who need refreshing but want to get on with their shopping. A specific type of catering is provided at each beverage area. Typical operators will be national coffee or espresso bars, or soft drink or juice bars. Beverages and snacks are ordered at the counter and can be consumed either at the bar or sometimes in adjacent, additional seating at tables which are an identifiable part of the beverage bar. An important requirement of these facilities is for customers using them to be amidst the activity of the street or mall and to overlook their passing fellow shoppers.

The size of space required for beverage bars is very dependent on the amount of seating to be provided. For example, the bar area can be accommodated with 18–20 m² (190–220 ft²). With each seating space requiring 1 m² (10 ft²), the combined bar and seating area for a typical beverage bar with 20–30 seats can be accommodated in 40–50 m² (430–540 ft²).

Beverage bars' proximity and open nature require them to be carefully considered and finished to a high standard. These specialist facilities are often designed by the operator's in-house design team and approved by the landlord's team. The landlord usually identifies a suitable location and provides the available space to include capped-off power, water and drainage supplies to which the tenant connects. In addition to the servery counter, an additional remote wash up and storage area can also be provided for the tenant's use. These remote facilities should be located adjacent to the public circulation space within a reasonable distance of 30–50 m (100–164 ft). The back up space for dishwashing and storage should be a minimum of 15–20 m² (160–215 ft²). Clean crockery and food can be trolleyed to the servery counter.

Beverage bars located within the public circulation space should avoid obscuring views to anchor stores. They can be conveniently located near entranceways to allow an arriving customer to be refreshed and settled after a long journey. Alternatively, they can be positioned midway along the circulation space, thereby allowing customers to be refreshed during their shopping activity.

4 Bar Clusters

This form of catering is focused towards alcoholic beverages and is based on three to four individual bars which are grouped together to establish a local identity. In physical form they are similar to individual restaurants in that they occupy a shell unit provided by the landlord and arrange for their own internal fit out. The focus of customer activity,

however, tends to take place in the evening. Bars and shops are therefore not necessarily compatible when located together. Bars have a great synergy with evening/night-time activities associated with leisure developments. Bar clusters are therefore only likely to be considered in large regional shopping and leisure centres.

Figure 9.29 A cluster of bars aligns the outward facing crescent to The Gateway Theatre of Shopping, Umlanga, SA (2001). *(Source: RTKL)*

The type of tenants who are attracted towards bar clusters in the UK tend to be national wine bars and themed pubs. Both these bar formats have a strong appeal with the youth and young adult age range and their corresponding lifestyles. Most other age and lifestyle groups are not attracted to these establishments. The nature and clientele of these facilities has fuelled a troublesome drink culture associated with bar clusters. The unsociable activities associated with certain bar clusters have only served to reinforce further the incompatibility of these areas with shopping facilities.

Leisure Facilities

General Combinations with Retail Facilities

The earlier Chapters in Part 2 illustrated that there are various ways in which leisure facilities can be combined together with shopping and catering facilities to form very different types of shopping format. The different ways of combining leisure with retail facilities can be summarised into the following formats:

■ Leisure facilities treated as an add-on to a regional shopping centre to form a 'regional shopping and leisure centre'. In this format, the leisure facilities can either have been added to an existing centre or planned in a new centre in a non-integrated way, simply to meet the need of extending the attraction of the centre and to broaden its customer appeal.

■ Leisure facilities integrally planned within a new regional shopping and leisure centre. In this format, the new destination is formed with the leisure elements integrated into the layout of the centre.

■ A leisure focused 'entertainment centre' is a purpose-built leisure development which is formed around a single specialist leisure use and where the retail and catering uses exist principally to support the leisure activity.

■ Leisure planned as an integral part of a 'retail entertainment centre', which is another relatively new format arranged to give equal importance to the three uses of retail, leisure and catering. The aim of retail entertainment centres is to maximise the synergy between these uses. In this format, each tenant in each principal category is carefully selected to ensure their compatibility with the other uses.

It can be seen from the above summary that leisure uses can take several forms and interrelate with shopping and catering in various ways. In its simplest form leisure uses, when treated as add-ons, will extend the attractiveness and widen the appeal

Figure 9.31 Catering in the mall leading to the leisure facilities and stadium, Menlyn Park, South Africa. *(Source: Reid Architecture)*

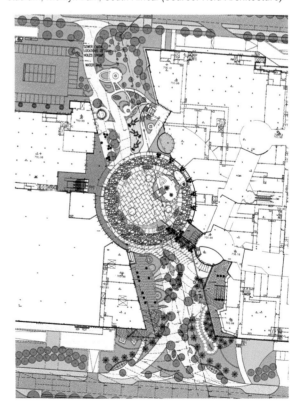

Figure 9.32 The entry plaza between the leisure and retail areas illustrates leisure facilities integrally planned with the regional centre, Tres Aguas, Madrid, Spain (2002). *(Source: BDP)*

Figure 9.30 Stadium leisure facilities added on the roof to the regional centre, Menlyn Park, Johannesburg, SA (2002). *(Source: Peter Coleman)*

Figure 9.33 The stair entrance from the plaza leading to the health club, Tres Aguas, Madrid, Spain. *(Source: BDP/David Barbour)*

Figure 9.34 Leisure as the primary activity at the entertainment centre at Xscape, Milton Keynes, UK (2002). *(Source: Faulkner Brown)*

to more customers in the catchment area. Leisure, when integrally planned within the layout of a centre, can be used as a footfall generator, acting as an attraction to lead customers towards another area. In this way, large leisure elements can sometimes perform a similar role to that of an anchor store. Care should be given when considering this, to ensure that it will generate footfall throughout the day and not just at evening times.

Some leisure uses have a natural synergy with catering and shopping. For example, health and fitness clubs will generate visitors throughout the day and some of these visitors will also actively engage in the shopping centre on some occasions by taking a refreshment or doing some shopping. The same crossover applies between facilities, but to a lesser extent, with multi-screen cinema users.

Where leisure is the primary activity, such as in entertainment centres, the uses tend to be focused towards a specialised single activity – such as real snow skiing, or ice-skating. Sometimes these uses are complemented by the addition of a multi-screen cinema complex. In these leisure focused formats the catering facilities are there to support the leisure activities and any shops will be restricted and specifically related to selling leisure related merchandise.

Retail entertainment centres are newly formed destinations which, in themselves, are aimed at the idea of shopping as a leisure activity. The leisure uses

in this format will be complementary to the catering and retail uses. Compatible leisure uses will tend to be health and fitness clubs and multi-screen cinemas, with the former generating activity and crossover activities and the latter attracting large numbers of

Figure 9.35 Leisure in the trinity of retail, catering and leisure at the retail entertainment centre, The Zone, Rosebank, Johannesburg, SA (2000). *(Source: Peter Coleman)*

Figure 9.36 Leisure in a retail entertainment centre in the downtown Denver Pavilions, Denver, Colorado, USA (1998). *(Source: Entertainment Development Group)*

users who will regularly use the catering facilities, either before or after a viewing. The retailing will be focused towards leisure pastimes (books, music and outdoor activity clothing) and aspirational fashionware, which will both have a synergy with the leisure and catering uses.

One of the significant advantages of leisure activities is that they are performed throughout the day and into the evening. The greater spread of activity can make fuller use of car parking – particularly in the evening, when the car park may not be fully used. Evening leisure uses can also help to support catering facilities – in particular restaurants and cafés and can also encourage the extension of shop trading hours into the early evening. Combining leisure, catering and shopping into town centre developments can be a useful means of generating vitality in a town centre area. Some care will need to be given to the juxtaposition of elements to ensure that they are compatible and there is not a conflicting requirement for the car parking. Multi-screen cinemas' coexistence with shops trading into the early evening can be assisted by the staggering of film start times.

Figure 9.37 Inventive use of the roof top as a drive-in cinema, Menlyn Park, Johannesburg, SA (2002). *(Source: Peter Coleman)*

Leisure facilities often require large amounts of accommodation. This requirement, combine with the fact that leisure tenants pay considerably less rent than retail tenants for comparable floor space, means that leisure facilities, when combined with sizeable amounts of retail space, are invariably planned in the more remote and peripheral locations.

For the same reason, leisure facilities can make use of upper floor levels, provided access to them can be readily achieved. Utilising the potential floor area above the retail can be particularly useful in some urban locations, where additional mass to the building can be required for urban design reasons. Where leisure uses are located above retail, it will be necessary to consider compatible structural grids to avoid complex transfer structures and alternative locations for the retail tenants' plant.

Types of Leisure Facility

Having examined the different combinations that leisure facilities can generally take with shopping centre development, we shall now review some of the specific leisure uses themselves.

Leisure activities associated with shopping developments are commercial leisure activities where the public pay the operator for the use or enjoyment of their facilities. These activities range from the passive to the active, and from the mainstream to the specialist. The different leisure activities are wide-ranging and too extensive to comprehensively review here. (Design guides on most of the leisure uses referred to here can be found in other books.) Instead, some of the characteristics and general considerations associated with the more common leisure activities are examined.

Multi-Screen Cinemas

This cinema format is one of the most common leisure activities combined with shopping development. Multi-screen cinemas have now largely replaced the grand picture palaces and are operated by a fast-changing group of international companies. The multi-screen success is twofold – it gives the visitor a choice of programmes and gives the operator the ability to judge the business potential of each film. This determines which auditorium to show it in to best match public demand. If the film is playing to a half full audience, it can be switched to a smaller auditorium, or vice versa. Blockbuster films can also be shown on more than one screen. The number of screens varies depending on the available catchment, with the smallest viable operations providing a minimum of eight to ten screens and the largest offering up to 20 or more auditoriums. The auditorium sizes will vary to give the operator the necessary flexibility, with the smallest providing a minimum of 100 seats and the largest extending up to 600 seats. In between these benchmark sizes there will also be the requirement for a series of incremental auditorium sizes which may nominally progress as follows – 100, 150, 200, 275, 350, 450

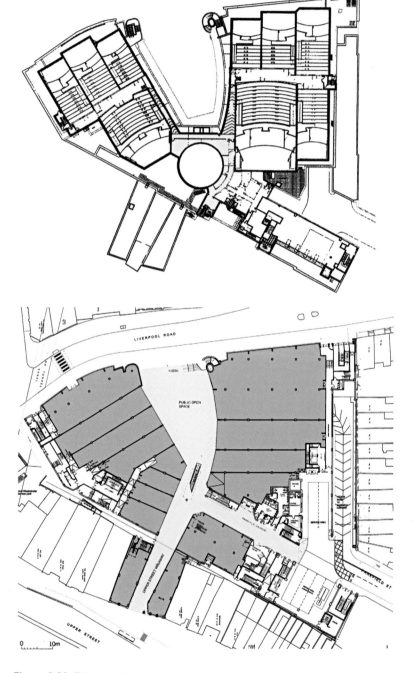

Figure 9.38 The ground and second floor plans of a closely fitted nine screen cinema, arranged above each side of the public square, represents a typical mixed use urban example, Warner Village, N1, Islington, London, UK (2002). *(Source: Chapman Taylor)*

Figure 9.39 A typical multi-screen cinema entrance from the mall of Gateway Theatre of Shopping, Umlanga, SA (2001). *(Source: Peter Coleman)*

and 600 seats. The makeup of sizes will vary with each project. A typical multi-screen cinema may provide two auditoriums at each size of the selected mix.

Cinema operators will have their own specific brief in response to their assessment of the catchment area. Until the cinema tenant is known, the shopping centre architect should work within generic space planning areas. For example, a general area should be allocated with the knowledge that a ten-screen cinema can be accommodated within approximately 4250 m² (45 750 ft²) GLA extending upwards to a 20-screen cinema within approximately 8500 m² (91 5000 ft²) GLA.

It is difficult for the architect to plan space with any certainty until the operator has agreed to lease. Two operators, for example may enter into negotiations to lease the same cinema space, each having different layout requirements. It may be necessary for the architect to work with both operators and test out different options for each before a preferred tenant is selected. It is common for the architect to have to modify the general scheme layout to accommodate the requirements of the cinema operator and for the operator to make some compromises to fit in with the overall scheme and any planning requirements.

Some cinema operators provide a luxury cinema experience for the more discerning customer alongside the standard auditoriums. The more luxurious auditorium will have fixed seats with table space between pairs of seats, and more generous space provided between the rows of seats to allow for waitress service of drinks. The architect should check with the operator if luxury auditoriums are to be provided as these screens will be larger than those required for the same number of tip seats in a stan-

Figure 9.40 Luxurious individual seats, arm-rests and drinks tables provided at the VIP Auditorium, Warner Village, Star City, Birmingham, UK (2000). *(Source: Photogenics)*

dard auditorium. The size of auditorium will therefore depend on the number and type of seat to be used.

Cinemas will have raked floors and the overall height required will be determined by the size of auditorium and the screen format, which in turn will depend on the picture format (e.g. Cinemascope, Cinerama, Todd AO, Circarama, Imax). The distance from the front row seats will be determined by the maximum allowable angle of sight-line to the top of the screen, which should not exceed 35° (Neufert, 1995). An internal clear dimension of 7 m (23 ft) from floor to underside of structure will generally meet the requirement for raked seating in the smaller sized auditoriums, while the larger ones can require a clear dimension of 10 m (32.8 ft), with the heights varying on a pro rata basis for the sizes in between.

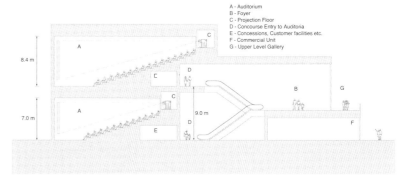

A - Auditorium
B - Foyer
C - Projection Floor
D - Concourse Entry to Auditoria
E - Concessions, Customer facilities etc.
F - Commercial Unit
G - Upper Level Gallery

Figure 9.41 Cross section through a two-level multi-screen cinema showing typical clear vertical dimensions for different size auditoriums. *(Source: BDP)*

The architect will usually work together with the operator's in-house advisers to prepare a layout which coordinates with the building shell and the overall scheme. The layout will need to be efficiently arranged with public circulation space providing access to each auditorium. These are usually arranged on a single level, but in some exceptional urban locations the operators may be convinced to accept two levels of auditoriums to fit the required number on to the site. A general requirement will be to provide ventilation and acoustic separation between each auditorium and between any adjacent alternative uses.

Multi-screen cinemas require an entrance foyer space to accommodate a ticket office, pre-ordered electric tickets, refreshment and confectionery sales, beverage bars and possibly an ice cream bar. A projection room is required at the rear of each cinema and the side-by-side adjacency of some of these projection rooms is sometimes required to allow for the simultaneous projection of selected films. Other additional accommodation to be provided includes public toilets, manager's office, staffroom, store rooms for refreshments and plant rooms. Most multi-screen cinema operators' requirements can be accommodated within a single blank box. This simple form may not be acceptable in urban locations, where it will require the skill of the architect to scale the building by potentially expressing the individual auditoriums and providing some active and animated façades from the entrance and foyer space.

Arthouse Cinemas

These are a scaled down version of multi-screen cinemas and are run by independent operators. They usually provide three to four auditoriums to give the visitor a modest choice of programmes. The general principles of auditorium size and layout that apply to multi-screen cinemas also apply to arthouse cinemas. The independent operator is likely to make these cinemas more individual, which can in turn be expressed in the architecture and interior of the building. The film choice offers an alternative to the mainstream distributors and provides the opportunity to put on film events and festivals, which may celebrate a particular director or allow the continuous showing of several films. The more liberal nature of these cinemas can be expressed in the foyer spaces, which may also include a restaurant and licensed bar.

Figure 9.43 Imax cinemas make object buildings as illustrated by the London Imax Cinema, Waterloo Bridge, London, UK (1999). *(Source: Avery Associates/Richard Holttum)*

Family Entertainment Centres (FECs)

These facilities are modern day amusement arcades which now house a variety of electronic machines, including slot machines, novelty machines, games and simulated rides. The machines can be readily laid out in a large single space, provided there are adequate power supplies. The operator rents the shell space and completes the fitting out and installations. The special requirements vary from operator to operator but can typically require floor space from 930 m² to 3350 m² (10 000 ft²–36 000 ft²). The height required can generally be accommodated within a space similar to that provided for shop units.

Figure 9.42 The entrance foyer to Ster Century Cinemas, Ocean Terminal, Leith, Scotland, UK (2001). *(Source: Peter Coleman)*

Figure 9.44 Simple architecture and applied graphics characterise the Family Entertainment Centre, Tres Aguas, Madrid, Spain (BDP) (2002). *(Source: David Barbour)*

The space can also accommodate columns, provided there are not too many. The proportion of the space should encourage visitors into it, allow most of the machines to be visible and therefore, should not exceed a width to depth ratio of 1:3 if these requirements are to be met.

Bowling Alleys

Facilities for American tenpin bowling are likely to be considered as part of a large leisure destination, either in a regional shopping and leisure centre or a retail entertainment centre. Bowling alleys are operated and fitted out by specialist companies which have specific requirements. These facilities tend to require a large amount of floor space with particular structural requirements. The amount of floor space will be determined by the number of bowling lanes to be accommodated, which can vary from a minimum of eight to upwards of 40 lanes. Each lane has specific dimensional requirements. For general planning purposes, each lane requires an overall clear area of 26.7 m length×1.7 m width (87.5×5.6 ft), which includes the participant area, the bowling lane and space for the pin stacking machinery. The width of the space will be determined by multiples of 1.7 m relating directly to the number of lanes required, plus a minimum allowance of 0.9 m (3 ft) at each end for maintenance. Additional general circulation space will be required to provide access to each bowling lane. The bowling lane area will need to be kept relatively free of structural columns, although lanes can be grouped together with columns located between groups of eight to ten lanes. Bowling alleys suit large span structures, but can sometimes suit large basement areas, provided the structure can be suitably coordinated with the accommodation above. In addition to the playing space, further supporting accommodation will also need to be allowed for which will include ticket office and entrance foyer, shoe distribution room and store, beverage and

Figure 9.45 The large space for bowling alleys can have intermediary columns, illustrated here with four lanes between the structure, Megabowl, Metrocentre, Gateshead, UK (1984–1987). *(Source: Simon Williams)*

licensed bars, restaurant, food and drink stores, public toilets, manager's office, staffroom and plant rooms.

Casinos

Gambling facilities were once only likely to be considered as part of a comprehensive leisure development. Today, with the deregulation of gambling licences, they are becoming increasingly popular and are just as likely to be considered as an individual operation as they are as part of a large leisure destination. Casinos aim to create self-contained internal environments where every facility and convenience is provided to retain the visitor within the controlled and pampered atmosphere. The landlord will provide shell space for the operator to fit out.

The special accommodation will need to allow for a large gaming hall for the various table games and slot machines, which are generally arranged into two areas. The amount of space required will be determined by the number of tables and machines required by the operator. The floor space can range from 2800 m^2 (30 000 ft^2) GLA for a small casino up to 8500 m^2 (91 500 ft^2) GLA for a larger facility. The larger casinos like Montecasino, Fourways, Johannesburg in South Africa, provide 1700 slot machines and 70 card and gambling tables for roulette, poker, blackjack, dice and baccarat (see Figs. 9.46 and 9.47). Good visibility and circulation space are required in the machine and table areas. Additional accommodation will need to

Figure 9.46 An internal environment creates the illusion of a Tuscan Village for shops and gaming rooms 24 hours a day at Montecasino, Fourways, Johannesburg, SA (2001). *(Source: Tsogo Sun Gaming)*

Figure 9.47 Large gaming machine space with a Tuscan theme, Montecasino, Fourways, Johannesburg, SA. *(Source: Tsogo Sun Gaming)*

be allowed to include a variety of restaurants, beverage and licensed bars, public toilets, food and drink storage, management offices, staffrooms and plant space. The large casinos may also include an integral entertainment venue for cabaret and dancing, plus the facility for some specialist shops.

Bingo Halls

The popularity of bingo has allowed bingo halls to survive beyond the occupation of disused cinemas and into successfully occupying purpose-built halls. They tend to be located where there is an adjacent local resident population. Special requirements are dependent on local catchment and determined by a specialist operator. The accommodation is based around the bingo hall, which is a large open space with levelled floor areas for groups of tables and chairs, arranged to focus towards the calling platform. The hall may be a single level or a series of stepped terraces. Additional accommodation to be provided will include a ticket office, entrance foyer, confectionery shops, refreshment facilities, licensed bar, public toilets, management office, stores for drinks and snacks, and plant space. Bingo halls are operated in the afternoon and evenings and can help to bring additional activity to a shopping centre and town centre.

Nightclubs

These tend to be an urban phenomenon which operate, as indicated by the name, from late evening into the early hours of the morning. They need to be easily accessible by a suitable local resident population, but not so close to residential areas as to cause a nuisance. The visitor catchment to night clubs is focused around a youth market and upwards to include thirty-somethings! The spatial requirements vary considerably from operator to operator, with typical nightclubs requiring floor space

Figure 9.48 Night club and casino included in the retail entertainment centre, The Gate, Newcastle, UK (2002). *(Source: Spacedecks)*

from 550 m^2 to 3700 m^2 (6000 ft^2–40 000 ft^2) GLA. Clubs tend to be individually operated with the interior fit outs being designed by specialist designers. These facilities again ideally suit shell space provided by blank boxes, which may have to be scaled and articulated in an urban location. Nightclubs require separate access and servicing to allow for deliveries and refuse collection.

Internally they are arranged to allow for several bar and dance areas, together with casual seating areas, a dining space, kitchen and food preparation area, food and drink stores, public toilets, management office and plant space.

Entertainment Venues

These provide accommodation for audiences to be entertained by live performances. The venue can be an auditorium with a stage or can be arranged for cabaret, with seated dining facing a stage. The latter arrangement is more flexible and more commonly provided. The spatial requirements for entertainment venues vary and are determined by the operator. The typical size of cabaret space may range from accommodating 200–600 diners. The accommodation will be based around the entertainment venue, which will be a large column free space, with good visibility towards the stage. Supporting accommodation will include foyer space with ticket office and cloakroom, bar and drinks store, public toilets, kitchen and food store, manager's office, performers' changing rooms and green room, staffroom and plant rooms. Entertainment venues are accommodated in shell space provided by the landlord and fitted out by the operator. The interior of the venue is sometimes themed, for example at the Barnyard Theatre, Gateway, Umlanga Rocks, South Africa, where the interior is arranged as a farm barn with large wooden tables, timber corrals and straw on the floor (which is replaced daily). Independent access is usually required to allow for flexible opening times together with the provision of servicing access for deliveries and refuse removal.

Health Clubs

These have grown in popularity in conjunction with the general increase in leisure time and greater public awareness of the importance of physical well-being. In response to this popularity, an increasing number of independent health club companies now provide private facilities based on membership subscriptions. (In the UK, for example, these facilities are run by several chains such as Esprit, Fitness First, Holmes Place and Spirit, as well as other independent companies.) Health club facilities are commonly being included in a variety of different shopping centre formats, which range from being part of a comprehensive leisure offer in a regional shopping and leisure centre, part of the 'trinity of synergy' in a

Figure 9.50 Private health clubs provide luxurious public areas illustrated by David Lloyd Leisure, Fulham Broadway, London, UK (2002). *(Source: Platform Group/Carl O'Connell)*

Figure 9.49 Dining and evening entertainment, viewed from the stage, The Barnyard Theatre, Gateway Theatre of Shopping, Umlanga, Durban, SA (2001). *(Source: Catalyst)*

retail entertainment centre, or included as an individual compatible use, alongside shops, in a town centre urban quarter.

The landlord usually provides a suitable shell space for the operators to complete their own interior fit out. The health club should be suitably located to provide convenient visitor access and separate servicing access. It is preferable if the entrance can be positioned so as to be independent of the shopping facilities, to allow for out of trading hours access. The size of shell accommodation depends on the operator, the location and the range of facilities to be provided in the health club. A comprehensive facility can typically require up to 4200 m² (45 200 ft²) or more. Some of the accommodation will require special spatial and structural provision to be made within the shell space, which will need to be considered by the shopping centre architect. Special consideration will need to be given to:

- the provision for the structural loading and space for a small swimming pool which can measure 8.5 × 16.6 m (27.9 × 54.6 ft) or 8.5 × 20 m (27.9 × 65.6 ft) or larger
- a separate hydro pool of 2.4–3 m (7.9–9.8 ft) diameter
- a column free space to accommodate a range of gym equipment to include treadmills, rowing machines, cycles, ski-walkers, weight machines, benches and mat space, where the number of pieces of equipment varying from 24 to 50 or more machines.

Figure 9.52 A column free space accommodating gym equipment in a comfortable environment, David Lloyd Leisure, Fulham Broadway, London, UK. *(Source: Platform Group/Carl O'Connell)*

Other more general accommodation to be included in a health club are entrance foyer and reception desk; male and female changing rooms, with separate access to the swimming pool; public toilets; interview rooms; manager's office; refreshment bar and lounge area; snack and drink store; general aerobic exercise room; other accommodation

Figure 9.51 A column free space accommodates a medium size pool at David Lloyd Leisure, Fulham Broadway, London, UK. *(Source: Platform Group/Carl O'Connell)*

Figure 9.53 Lounge and reception areas in today's health clubs resemble those found in hotels, David Lloyd Leisure, Fulham Broadway, London, UK. *(Source: Platform Group/Carl O'Connel)*

associated with the swimming pool – sauna, steam room, pump and filtration plantroom; general environmental plant space; and interconnecting circulation space between the accommodation.

Rides

These tend to be items of equipment or machine based facilities which are placed into sufficiently sized, covered interior spaces or open-air external spaces. Rides provide general leisure facilities which are focused towards amusing children. The equipment includes roundabouts, ferris wheels, electric carts and scenic railways. Spatial requirements vary depending upon the type and number of rides to be provided. Specific requirements are the provision of adequate power supplies and a suitable surface which is sufficient to bear the load of the equipment. Rides are most likely to be included as a part of a comprehensive leisure attraction and where there is sufficient space. As such, rides are therefore likely to generally be considered for out-of-town regional shopping and leisure centres.

Figure 9.54 A go-cart track and other leisure facilities utilise the roof space at Centro Columbo, Lison, Portugal (1997). *(Source: BDP/Paul Chapman)*

Specialist Leisure Facilities

These facilities group together a range of more specialist leisure pursuits which actively involve the participants and require a change of clothing or the use of specialist equipment. Other common characteristics of specialist leisure facilities are that there is generally a greater risk involved by those participating in them, and that they require specialist instruction and on hand supervision. The specialist skills required to operate these facilities tend to restrict the running of such facilities to a limited number of

Table 9.3 Specialist leisure facility characteristics

- Climbing walls and sculptures provide covered climbing courses for a range of different abilities. Climbing walls take up potentially valuable internal frontage and, consequently, there are fewer suitable opportunities for the formation of this type of facility. Free-standing climbing structures or sculptures can be more readily accommodated within large covered or enclosed public spaces. Free-standing climbing structures can also have purpose-made enclosures built around them, like the REI store in Seattle, for example

- Climbing facilities require changing rooms and supervision which are relatively expensive facilities to provide just for inclusion into the facility. They are, therefore, best suited as part of a large sports shop or as part of another activity-based leisure facility which can help to support the high running costs. For example, the store bears the cost of the climbing sculpture used to help demonstrate the outdoor sports equipment and clothing which it sells. The inclusion of a climbing sculpture has been made possible at the XScape, Milton Keynes entertainment centre as an integral part of the sporting theme associated with the internal ski slope

- Skate board parks tend to be located externally from the shopping facilities and occupy various sculpturally-shaped courses. They can require a sizeable space which will be determined by the location and the operator. However, once in place they require minimal maintenance

- White water rafting courses are external, artificial surfing courses for the initiated. They operate in a similar way to tread mills, except the moving surface is replaced by water which is forced at greater pressure to form sheets of water across a sculptured surface. The water is drained at the rear of the course and then recirculated through the pumping system. Surfers demonstrate their skill by riding across different shaped courses. The water-based activity is animated and provides an interesting spectacle which can form a focal point to be overlooked by several different catering venues. The accommodation requires space for the rides, waiting and instruction space, ticketing, changing rooms and plant space for the pumps. A good example of white water rafting can be found at Gateway Theatre of Shopping, Umlanga Rocks, South Africa

- A four-wheel drive vehicle driving course can be a useful way of utilising unused perimeter strips of land often found on the edges of out-of-town shopping centres. A linear driving course can be incorporated into the external landscaping for use by a specialist operator. This type of facility can usefully be associated together with a specialist vehicle showroom. An example of an adventure driving course can be seen at the Gateway Theatre of Shopping, Umlanga Rocks, South Africa

- Mini go-kart courses can be formed on the large flat roof spaces associated with shopping centres. An example of a roof top go-kart track can be seen at Centro Colombo, Lisbon, Portugal

- Simulated golf driving ranges can be formed with the use of computer software and digital projection screens. These facilities can be accommodated within relatively simple enclosures

Figure 9.55 Climbing wall within the shopping area of Xscape, Milton Keynes, UK (2002). *(Source: Faulkner Brown)*

Figure 9.57 White water surfing at The Gateway Theatre of Shopping, Umlanga, SA (2001). *(Source: Peter Coleman)*

for a standalone entertainment centre, for example real snow ski slopes and ice-rinks which are also discussed separately later. The general characteristics of the different specialist leisure facilities which can be included in certain shopping formats are outlined in Table 9.3.

Leisure for Entertainment Centres

The leisure activities outlined here can either be included as part of a comprehensive leisure destination in a regional shopping and leisure centre, or are sufficiently large attractions to form standalone entertainment centres with their own supporting catering and shopping facilities.

individualistic specialist companies. These facilities are all only likely to be considered as part of a larger comprehensive leisure development which is incorporated into a regional shopping and leisure centre. Some of the larger specialist facilities may also be a sufficiently large attraction to be used as a catalyst

Figure 9.56 Skate Board Park on the roof of Canal Walk, Cape Town, SA (2000). *(Source: Peter Coleman)*

Figure 9.58 The grand space of the indoor ski slope, looking towards the overlooking restaurants, Xanadu, Madrid , Spain (2003). *(Source: Mills Corporation/Parque de Nieve)*

Indoor ski slopes require large amounts of purpose-formed space and plant to create the appropriate environment to support real snow. Indoor ski slopes can extend beyond 200 m (656 ft) in length. As the focus of an entertainment centre, these facilities will have a range of supporting catering facilities, as well as shops related to leisure activity or activity sportswear. There may also be additional leisure facilities which can make use of the space beneath the ski slopes. An example of an entertainment centre based around an indoor ski slope is the XScape, Milton Keynes. An example of a snow ski slope as part of a regional shopping and leisure centre can be seen at Xanadu, Madrid, Spain.

Another leisure activity which requires large specialist facilities and is sufficiently attractive to form an entertainment centre is an ice-skating rink. This facility will require a single span structure across the

Figure 9.60 The first UK ice rink incorporated into a shopping centre, East Kilbride, Glasgow, UK (1989). *(Source: BDP)*

Figure 9.59 Ice rink adjacent to the ground floor shops, The Galleria, Houston, Texas, USA (1970). *(Source: HOK)*

rink, which varies in size from 56 to 60.96 m (184–200 ft) long by 26–30.48 m (85.3–100 ft) wide plus the seating space on either side of the rink. Full sized ice-rinks are most suitably located where there is a requirement from a local ice hockey team who can help to support the use of the facility for training and matches, in addition to the use of the rink for leisure purposes.

Other Leisure Facilities

Covered stadia are another leisure facility which may be located adjacent to a regional shopping and leisure centre or may even be a sufficiently large attraction to be the catalyst around which an entertainment centre may be formed.

These stadia facilities are the type that provide indoor performance venues for a variety of activities, ranging from popular music, sports, circuses, tournaments and other events. These entertainment related venues are likely to seat between 10 000 and 12 000 and can be compatibly located with shopping facilities. With evening performances the stadium can utilise the shopping centre car parking. Conflicts with this requirement for parking can arise when the stadium requires the car parking for weekend afternoon performances and at these times alternative parking will need to be provided. Multi-use stadia are a specialist subject and are not considered in detail here.

Shopping as Leisure

This examines the premise that the pastime of going shopping is in itself a leisure activity. To clarify this generality, 'leisure activity' refers to comparison shopping rather than shopping for practical perishable goods. In addressing the activity of comparison shopping as a leisure activity, consideration needs to be given to the collective experience of using the total shopping facility. The collective shopping experience will involve reviewing every aspect of using the facility from the point of arrival to departure from the customers' perspective and will include:

- the range and quality of the retail offer
- the nature of the public amenities
- the variety and choice of catering
- the provision and compatibility of leisure facilities
- the character of the public spaces, ease of orientation, clarity of circulation and ability to change level
- the amount and quality of car parking, and general level of use
- the ease of access to, and departure from, the car park.

The quality of the public space can be enhanced by allowing other activities to take place and by incorporating qualities which will encourage the visitor to dwell and experience enjoyment of the shopping facilities. The various means of providing for other activities to take place and ways of encouraging visitors to dwell and enjoy the experience are discussed in more detail later on (see Public circulation space – general qualities).

Compatibility with Other Uses

The following examines the general compatibility of leisure uses with shopping and other uses, and reviews some general considerations to take into account when including them. The earlier review of the different types of leisure uses has identified these general placement issues:

- most leisure uses are generally compatible with catering uses
- catering is generally compatible with shopping uses, but some catering may require separate access for out of shopping hours use
- some day and early evening leisure uses are compatible with shopping, although care needs to be taken that sufficient car parking will be provided

- leisure uses taking place in the late evening and beyond, are not compatible with shopping uses
- in mixed-use developments, leisure is generally incompatible with residential uses.

Placement compatibility depends on the actual uses and their specific location, requiring each individual case to be considered in its own right.

Where leisure uses are combined with shopping in mixed-use developments, careful consideration will need to be given to the compatibility of the different uses. Compatibility extends beyond functional uses, to include the compatibility of physical structural requirements when different uses are arranged vertically above each other.

In town centre locations with high land values, leisure uses should be selected which are complementary to the shopping and catering uses, and which can be readily accommodated within the site without resorting to a complex structural solution. Incompatible uses should avoid being located

Figure 9.61 Town centre retail, health club and cinemas, The Light, Leeds, UK (2001). *(Source: Peter Coleman)*

together and leisure uses should be positioned separately from residential when both uses are required by the brief. Leisure uses often require large amounts of floor space and have specific spatial requirements. As such, leisure uses can more readily be accommodated on large out-of-town centre sites. Hence most large regional shopping and leisure centres are located in out-of-town sites. Where leisure uses are integrated into town centre locations, a balance will need to be achieved between the value of the leisure element, the cost of building it and the amount of site it occupies.

The operation issues to be considered in the location of leisure accommodation with shopping, catering and other facilities are listed in Table 9.4.

Certain functional considerations should also be applied to the leisure use before finalising the location of the different uses:

- what are the overall spatial area requirements (GLA)?
- what are the specific volumetric spatial requirements?
- are there any minimum clear span requirements?
- what structural grid requirements are compatible with the internal layout requirements of the leisure uses?
- what are the loading requirements of the leisure uses?
- what are the internal clear floor to ceiling height requirements?

Table 9.4 Leisure accommodation operational considerations

1. What are the operational hours of the different uses?
2. Will there be a requirement for out of hours access to the leisure accommodation?
3. What impact will this have on the other accommodation?
4. Can the extended hours of operation be accommodated within the management regime?
5. Is there a genuine requirement for independent access to the leisure element?
6. Is there a requirement for sound insulation because of the sensitivity of the adjacent use?
7. Will visitors using the leisure facility cause a noise nuisance to the adjacent uses?
8. Will the car parking requirements for the leisure use be complementary or not; and if not, will additional spaces be required?
9. Is there a requirement for separate servicing for deliveries and removal of rubbish?
10. Can good visibility and presence be achieved without compromising prime retail space or retail access?

- are there any special shape requirements for the leisure accommodation (e.g. raked floors)?
- are there any special plant requirements to be accommodated?
- will separate means of escape need to be coordinated through other uses?
- will there be sound insulation requirements between the leisure and other uses?
- will the leisure use require sound insulation from other adjacent uses?
- can separate, easy access be achieved?

Design Guidelines for Tenant Shop Fitting

Tenant's Shop Fitting Guideline

The most important front of house areas are the actual shops themselves, which are the ultimate destination of each customer. While the architect will have considerable influence over the arrangement of the shops, the actual interiors are usually designed by the shop tenant's own in-house design team, who will work within the shell provided by the developer/owner. The different types of shop and their arrangement are described at the beginning of the Chapter. Referred to here are the shop fitting guidelines which are prepared by the developer/owner's architect, within which the shop tenant's team should work. Each scheme will have its own specific tenant's design guideline. Outlined in Table 9.5 is a general indication of the topics to be covered in a typical tenant's shop fitting guide.

Shopfront Guidelines

In addition to the general shop fitting guide, the developer/owner may also prepare a shopfront fitting guide. Shopfront guides are especially relevant in large complex schemes where the quality of the public space will be influenced by the quality of the shopfront. In these instances, the shopfront guideline will indicate a series of approved example types of shopfront which establish a minimum standard rather than a single prescriptive approach. This approach is used to encourage variety and encourage tenants to adopt innovative new formats of shopfront. In shopping centres with open street type public spaces, the shopfronts will form part of

Table 9.5 Contents for a typical tenant's shop fitting guide

The scheme	A general description of the shopping centre, its location, overall layout, quality of public spaces, key tenants, shop unit provision, means of servicing, car parking and the programme for its completion
Landlord's specification	A more detailed description of the landlord's works in the public spaces at the interface with the tenant's area, and general landlord specification of the tenant's area describing the key elements of the building including: The elements of structure and fabric The services installations ■ describes the services provided in the landlord areas, the back of house areas and to the tenancy ■ each service of the tenancy is described including statutory services ■ fire defence strategy, including means of escape, fire suppression, means of access and control, fire-fighting facilities, detection system, smoke venting system
Shell unit specification	A detailed specification to be provided within the tenant's shell describing: The structure and level of finish, floor-to-floor heights, building tolerance Enclosing wall construction and insulation (where relevant) Door construction and ironmongery Enclosing roof construction (where relevant) Shop unit ceiling construction and finish Mall ceiling finish and clearance heights Roof plant area Extent of openings provided in floors and roof Extent of vertical shafts provided (lower floors) Extent of incoming services provided and point of termination for the following:

Statutory services	electrical supply drainage water supply
Landlord supply	fire alarm interfaces security interface public address interface sprinkler supply phone: interface with landlord (individual connection to the phone network is the responsibility of the individual tenant) TV interface (optional)

Diagrams are provided to show points of service entry and points of termination: how foul drainage is capped off

Figure 9.62 A typical simple shop unit shell finish prior to handover to a tenant for fitting out. *(Source: BDP)*

the architecture of the building. Where the shopfront is part of the architecture of the external fabric, it may be more appropriate for the developer/owner to provide the shopfront. Alternatively, in these cases, the shopfront guide will have to be sufficiently prescriptive to comply with the requirements of the external appearance of the building as defined by the planning permission.

Coordinating Site Work

The tenant is expected to complete his proposals and submit them for approval by the developer/owner's team. This process is likely to be interactive

Figure 9.63 The inventive Habitat shopfront at Bluewater, Greenhithe, Kent, UK (1999). *(Source: Lend Lease)*

and will require the involvement of the architect in signing off the tenant's proposals.

With up to, and sometimes over, 100 tenants simultaneously fitting out on site, the developer/owner may often provide a separate coordinating team to assist the tenants. This is particularly appropriate in large multi-level schemes and those involving complex shopfront arrangements.

References

British Council of Shopping Centres (1998). *Survey of Tenant Requirements*. BCSC.

British Council of Shopping Centres (2000). *A Briefing Guide for Shopping Centre Development*. BCSC, p. 5.

Neufert, E. (1995). *Neufert Architects Data*. Blackwell Science, p. 354.

Figure 10.1 The dramatic covered street forms Freemont Street, Las Vegas, USA (1995). *(Source: Buddy Mays/Corbis)*

Front of House Areas – The Public Spaces

10

Public Circulation Space

The Armature (The Organisational Framework)

The Pocket Oxford Dictionary of Current English defines 'armature' as a 'framework for supporting sculpture during construction', which aptly describes the organising role performed by public circulation space in the process of forming a shopping centre. Common to all the different types of shopping centre format (described earlier in Part 2) is the organising role of the accommodation performed by the public circulation space. The organising framework of the public circulation space, and the constituent elements that define it, is arguably the most significant part of a shopping centre designed by the architect. It is also one of the few elements of the building that is designed in full by the architect and not just completed to a shell standard of finish to be completed by another designer, which is the general case with most of the accommodation described in the previous Chapter. The public circulation space is the element that organises and joins together the different parts of a shopping centre. As such the circulation space is partly defined by the different accommodation of shops, anchor stores, catering and leisure facilities. In view of the importance and significance of the role of the public circulation space, the architect will need to demonstrate his greatest skill in addressing this challenging aspect of the building.

The circulation space forms the planning structure and layout and, as such, will determine the building's success. It will establish the circulation of pedestrian footfall and the vertical movement of visitors between the shops, and will determine if visitors can conveniently locate and move between all the different facilities. The organisational framework can adopt a range of different geometric patterns, from a simple linear arrangement to a complex geometry of curves and angles (see Fig. 10.2).

The architect John Jerde is an advocate for complying with the rules of shopping centre design while adopting more complex geometries. Jerde's approach to shopping centre design is based on 'armatures inspired by the patterns established earlier in history' (The Jerde Partnership, 1998). His completed successful shopping centre work demonstrates this, for example Horton Plaza, San Diego, California uses circulation patterns inspired by Italian hill towns (see Figs. 10.3 and 10.4).

In town centre locations, the circulation framework will also establish the degree of integration with the surrounding street pattern. Urban integration is another important consideration when determining the geometry to be adopted.

Another important functional requirement for public circulation spaces is the need for general robustness to handle the large number of daily visitors to a shopping centre. For example, a successful regional shopping centre can have to accommodate more than 100 000 visitors per day in peak times, which equates to the numbers visiting a football stadium or passing through a major railway

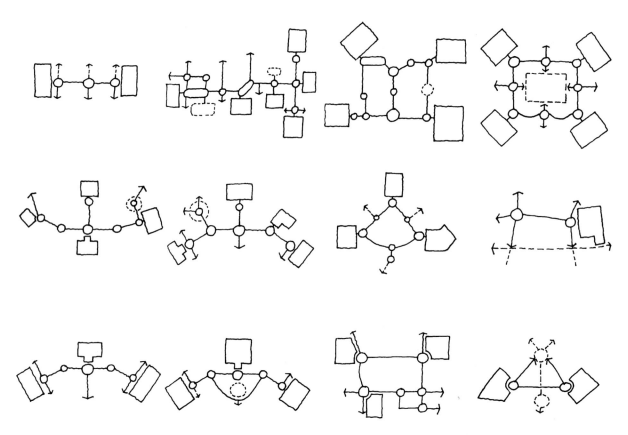

Figure 10.2 The armature of public circulation space establishes the organising geometry of 'linear' and 'circuit' shopping centre layouts. *(Source: Peter Coleman)*

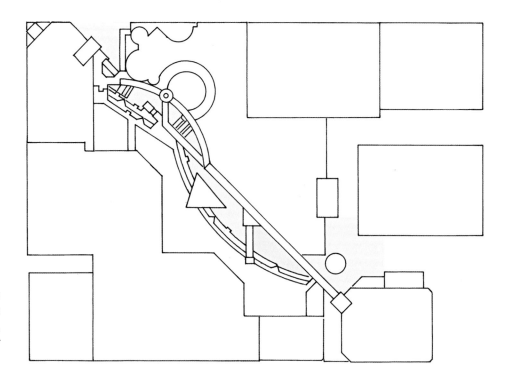

Figure 10.3 Interlocking curves and primary forms are layered into the armature forming the public space through Horton Plaza, San Diego, California, USA (1985). *(Source: Peter Coleman)*

Figure 10.4 The public space of Horton Plaza, San Diego, California, USA. *(Source: Stephen Simpson)*

station on a daily basis. The design of public circulation spaces, therefore, needs to take into account being both sufficiently sized and being durable to accommodate the wear and tear of this large number of daily visitors.

As well as influencing the function of the shopping centre, the circulation space will also establish the character of the centre, thereby having a significant influence over the visitors' qualitative memories of the place. This qualitative aspect is especially important in an age when providing customers with memorable experiences is all important.

Functional and Qualitative Requirements

In considering the organisational framework to be established by the public circulation space the objectives can be separately identified into functional and qualitative requirements. The functional requirements are essential primary planning considerations and the qualitative requirements are recommended (nice to have) secondary planning and more detailed design considerations. The functional and qualitative considerations are summarised in Tables 10.1

Figure 10.5 The durable character of the urban arcade, GUM, Moscow, Russia (original 1893, refurbished 2004). *(Source: Alexei Naroditsky)*

and 10.2. The functional requirements represent the basic and well-established general rules of shopping centre planning. They are essential considerations common to all shopping formats and were referred to earlier Table 10.2 summarises the qualitative considerations which generally give character to a place and help make the facility more memorable and enjoyable. The qualitative requirements tend towards the consideration of the use of the centre from the viewpoint of the customer and are recommended considerations that can make the difference between one centre and another.

Table 10.1 Public circulation space functional requirements: primary planning considerations (essential)

- Establish the organisational framework for all the accommodation
- Form the means of pedestrian access to all the different facilities included in the centre
- Provide an attractive and convenient environment for shopping, catering and leisure activities
- Provide pedestrian access to all facilities which are safe and secure to use
- Form points of pedestrian linkage with the existing streets
- Connect the accommodation with the various means of vehicular access (to include all means of public transport and private cars)
- Strategically arrange the accommodation to ensure footfall passes in front of all the shopfrontes
- Size the circulation space:
  - to accommodate safely and conveniently the volume of visitors in peak periods to allow freedom of movement in all directions
  - to establish also a sense of activity and business in the quieter periods
- Form an organisational arrangement which is easy to understand
- Provide circulation spaces which are well lit by day and night
- Organise the public circulation space into identifiable lengths of shopfront
- Utilise points of punctuation to accommodate changes of direction or to allow different routes to interconnect
- Arrange the circulation space to form natural pedestrian circuits of movement which allow all the frontages to be passed without retracing steps
- Form node spaces (focal spaces/knuckle spaces) at the punctuation points
- Make use of the node spaces to act as points of focus, to lead visitors forward from one place to another
- Strategically locate anchor and MSU stores to lead visitors from one place to another
- Arrange the public circulation space and accommodation to address any level changes which may occur across the site
- In multi-level arrangements:
  - organise the accommodation and vertical circulation to achieve equal footfall to pass all the shops at each level
  - position the different means of vertical circulation to allow convenient access between levels
  - size the space and arrange the accommodation to allow good visibility between the circulation space and shops on a different level
  - position the shops on each side of the space to have good visibility between shopfrontes
  - provide convenient crossing points for access, connecting each side of the gallery opening

Table 10.2 Public circulation space qualitative requirements: secondary planning considerations (recommended)

- Consider giving different areas or individual lengths of circulation space a separate recognisable identity
- Establish a clear hierarchy between the different circulation spaces which correspond to the relative importance of the function of the space
- Provide protection from the weather
- Form a comfortable environment which will be an improvement on the external ambient temperature
- Provide a chilled environment in summer
- Provide a heated environment in winter
- Establish a sense of well-being from a well made and maintained environment
- Provide a positive memorable experience (combining functional and qualitative considerations):
  - general quality and proportion of space
  - form the space to facilitate the occurrence of informal social and civic uses to include:
    - identifiable meeting places
    - space for seating to allow visitors to enjoy the place and watch the activity
    - space for occasional gatherings, events, performances and Christmas displays
    - spontaneous overspill space for tables and chairs to allow street cafés and dining
  - generally encourage the visitor to dwell and experience the place:
    - by inclusion of the above informal spaces
    - provide a quality of detailing, finishes and general workmanship which can withstand scrutiny
    - incorporate aspects of craftsmanship integrated into the finishes (decorative plaques, motifs, decoration)
    - incorporate elements of artwork (stand alone and integrated pieces)
    - provide civic elements (clocks, water sculptures and other features)

All the above facilities, if well considered, will encourage the visitor to engage with the place, enhance their experience and encourage the use of the shopping facility in preference to another

Types of Space

For the purposes of organisation, the different types of public circulation space have been defined by the degree of enclosure provided to the space.

Open Spaces

Open streets and spaces represent the simplest form of public circulation space. These spaces are open ended and predominantly open to the sky, although they can also provide some protection from direct rain by the inclusion of simple canopies. These canopies can either be hung from the surrounding buildings or supported from free-standing structures positioned within the space. These spaces provide little protection from the weather or environmental convenience and comparison shopping activity has to be undertaken in the ambient weather conditions of the season. They suit moderate and temperate climates better than extreme climates where humidity levels, extreme temperatures and high levels of rainfall may make these environments less acceptable or inappropriate.

Figure 10.6 An open street with a glazed canopy supported above the shopfronts, Paradise St, Liverpool, UK (planned 2008). *(Source: BDP)*

Open-air shopping environments traditionally prevail in the high street and are adopted in both simple retail formats (through an economy of means, for example the retail parks and some of the factory outlet centres) and in comparison shopping facilities which consciously form more natural open street environments (lifestyle centres, hybrid centres,

retail entertainment centres and new urban quarters). Examples of each of these different shopping formats are given in Part 2. It should also be noted that the retail park format makes little attempt at providing any definition to the public circulation space.

Open street shopping environments suit some retailers and some of the public who wish to avoid shopping in monolithic, enclosed, shopping mall environments. However, it should also be acknowledged that the majority of multiple shops prefer enclosed or covered shopping environments and most of the public like the convenience of the protected shopping centre. So architects who are proposing open-air shopping environments should be prepared to demonstrate the reasoning for such an approach to the retail team and retailers.

Open street shopping arrangements have the advantage of not requiring any environmental, ventilation or smoke venting installations. However, balancing this omission the space will be defined by buildings which require weatherproof insulated architectural façades and the surface paving will have to be appropriately finished and laid to falls to aid drainage of surface water. All the architectural elements – the balustrades, stairs, lifts, escalators and lighting – will also require upgraded finishes to be suitably robust to resist exposure to the external weather conditions. The external space lighting and illumination of the building façades will also require additional consideration in an open space shopping facility.

Figure 10.7 Natural materials and public art enhance the public realm together with a street café, St Martin's Square, The Bullring, Birmingham, UK (2003). *(Source: Peter Durant/ArcBlue)*

Covered Spaces

This type of space is fully covered over and generally has open ends, with no enclosing doors or mechanical tempering of the internal environment.

Figure 10.8 An open ended covered space between the buildings forms a fine public space, Hays Wharf, London, UK (1988). *(Source: St Martins Property Corporation Ltd)*

Figure 10.9 Steel masts support a stretched Teflon fabric roof to cover the street, Festival Place, Basingstoke, UK (2002). *(Source: PJC)*

Figure 10.10 Simple planar glazed roof with external cable structure, History Museum, Hamburg, Germany. *(Source: Von Gerkan, Marg)*

As a naturally ventilated and unheated space, the environmental conditions are generally a slight enhancement of the ambient summer and winter external air temperature and provide the convenience of protection from the rain and wind. Covered spaces can be formed by covering over existing streets and courtyards, as well as newly formed spaces.

The covering roof can be fully or partly glazed, although each roof covering will have distinctly different spatial qualities. For example, the ambience of a covered external space will be more readily achieved with a fully glazed roof for unobstructed views to the sky above. A solid and partially glazed roof will, on the other hand, achieve the effect of being more of an interior space within a building. Solar gain and glare will need to be carefully considered and appropriate shading and filtering measures incorporated into the roofing solution. A solid and partly glazed roof will achieve sufficient natural daylight and have less solar gain. As well as daylight, the roof covering will also need to allow for natural ventilation. Ventilation can be achieved in a variety of ways. For example, the roof can float like an umbrella above the buildings, with the ventilation occurring between the roof and wall space on either side; the roof can be shaped with a pop-up lantern with ventilation openings on the sides; or the roof can be formed with clear storeys which accommodate ventilation openings. The structure for the roof can be supported directly off the side buildings or from free-standing columns which sit within the space.

Covered spaces tend to be enclosed by buildings with façades formed from external quality materials. The enclosing walls can be part of a single building or made up of several individual buildings. The walls of the buildings will need to be insulated and weatherproofed and can take into account the effective double skin provided by the roof covering.

Figure 10.11 The covered street with external natural materials, The Light, Leeds, UK (2001). *(Source: Peter Coleman)*

The open ends of covered spaces need to be carefully considered to avoid through draughts from the wind causing unacceptable conditions in the space. Desktop and wind tunnel models can be used to determine the wind effect, the extent of opening that can be achieved and to establish if any vertical glazing or other remedial measures will be required. Bearing in mind that a large proportion of shopping is completed during the hours of darkness, the space lighting and illumination of the building façades will also be an important consideration in establishing the character of a covered space shopping facility.

Covered spaces extend the tradition of the nineteenth century arcades and are considered in new projects where there is the requirement for some protection from weather exposure while avoiding becoming a monolithic, enclosed environment. Covered spaces are appropriate for town centre locations where there is a requirement for a new shopping facility to integrate with the existing street pattern.

The shopping environment provided by a covered space will be a compromise between the natural open street, which is exposed to the prevailing weather, and the fully enclosed shopping centre with the convenience of an artificial mall environment. With covered space types of environment offering a degree of customer convenience for comparison shopping, the retail team will be able to attract, at premium rents, most types of shop to take floor space. In view of it not being monolithic and enclosed, the covered space environment may also attract some of the retailers opposed to shopping centre malls.

Enclosed Spaces

Shopping facilities provided within enclosed spaces are similar to covered spaces, with the addition of closure of the ends and enclosing doors. These spaces also have mechanical heating and cooling installations to modify the internal environment and give an interior character. The enclosed space shopping facility provides optimum comfort standards and levels of convenience for the visitor to the centre. However, the internal conditions can also be perceived as both artificial and uniform and not as distinctive and memorable as those formed by both open and covered space centres.

In principle, the roof to enclosed centres is outwardly similar to those described earlier for covered spaces, except this roof is completely weatherproof and sealed to the surrounding buildings. The roofs can be fully or partially glazed and, in some circumstances, can also be solid and fully reliant on artificial lighting with a treated ceiling. Fully and partially glazed roofs will also require supplementary artificial lighting installations and the appropriate consideration of solar gain and glare provision. Ventilation to enclosed spaces is usually by a mechanical installation and integrated into the space. Smoke ventilation can be by natural means, provided sufficient air can be removed and is not disturbed by turbulent air currents caused by surrounding buildings. Automatic opening vents can be readily accommodated within either the glazed or solid elements of the roof. Smoke ventilation often requires mechanical extraction, requiring louvres or screens to conceal the powered extraction motors.

In view of the weather-enclosing nature of the roof and the enclosing ends, the requirement of the side walls is correspondingly reduced and can be contained by wall components with a lower standard of overall performance. The general tendency has traditionally been to finish the side walls with interior quality finishes. The quality of the overall enclosed space has consequently been characterised by having more of an interior nature. There are many existing completed enclosed centres which illustrate this characteristic.

Figure 10.12 An enclosed space with a glazed skylid roof to the upper level of The Bullring, Birmingham, UK (2003). *(Source: Michael Betts/Hammerson)*

Figure 10.13 An enclosed space, with natural materials and a partially glazed clerestory roof, Touchwood, Solihull, UK (2001). *(Source: Peter Coleman)*

Figure 10.14 Mould breaking use of external natural materials to an enclosed space, Touchwood, Solihull, UK. *(Source: Peter Coleman)*

One of the key challenges with enclosed spaces is how to make them more architectural and to break the mould of uniformity which has emerged, where there is little discernible difference between one enclosed shopping centre and another. The fully enclosed nature and uniform character of enclosed shopping centres has given this type of facility the reputation of forming monolithic uniform internal environments. While such an arrangement may be acceptable for out-of-town shopping centres, enclosed facilities are less favourably received for town centres. Enclosed facilities in town centre locations are considered by the planning authority as having less potential for being integrated into the surrounding street pattern and less accessible. Architects presented with delivering an enclosed shopping facility in a town centre in a mature European country with sustainable planning policies, should recognise the challenge that this will present. The process will involve convincing the consultative bodies that an enclosed centre can be integrated and can contribute by making a vital piece of the town centre. In addition to the pressures from the consultative bodies against enclosed shopping facilities, there are additional corporate pressures to reduce energy consumption and emissions, which will cause the further exploration of less energy consuming shopping facilities than those found in typical enclosed shopping centres.

Hybrid Spaces

In today's multifarious world of variety and combinations, different types of shopping environments exist side by side, either arranged independently or consciously planned together in the form of hybrid centres as identified earlier in Chapter 4. The trend for a combination of open and enclosed shopping in hybrid centres offers the best of both worlds. However, if each shopping environment is required to attract similar types of retailer, care needs to be taken to ensure that each environment is perceived in an equal way and is equally utilised by customers to avoid any differential rental levels occurring. For example, the two different environments should each be attractive, even if for different reasons. Open and enclosed environments can be used to complement one another. A successful example which combines both an enclosed and open environment, can be found at the Streets of Southpoint, Durham, North Carolina, USA. Here the individual quality of the external shops is reinterpreted through in to the enclosed internal environment of the mall. The imaginative shop fitting guide allows the individual shops inside to extend their shop fit beyond the normal goalposts and achieve greater vitality and variety. The effect is to achieve the feeling inside of a linear strip mall.

One of the key issues to consider with hybrid arrangements is where customers move from a bright open or covered street into a darker, predominantly artificially lit, enclosed space. In this case, care will need to be given to a gradual move through a transition where contrasting environments can coexist. The immediate transfer between contrasting environments should be avoided where possible.

Different environments can however be used positively to create local identity in larger schemes. The differentiation between shopping environments can be used consciously to provide for the different requirements of retailers. It can also be used deliberately to provide accommodation at different rental levels. If different rental level space is provided, care should be taken to determine the likely amount of space required in order to provide only an appropriate amount.

With the extension and alteration of existing out-of-town enclosed shopping centres, and a general

Figure 10.15 The treatment of the external streets are carried through to influence the enclosed environment at The Streets of Southpoint, Durham, North Carolina, USA (2002). *(Source: RTKL)*

Figure 10.16 The external street proposed for the new urbanised Brent Cross, London, UK (planned 2010–2012). *(Source: BDP)*

move towards urbanising the mall, it is likely that we will see the frequent adoption of open street environments alongside the enclosed mall environment. Hybrid shopping environments are likely to be increasingly appropriate and considered.

Practical and Cost Considerations

It is ironic that architects once had to justify the additional costs associated with the design of a fully enclosed, interior based centre. For example, when compared with the first generation of open-air precincts, additional costs were considered for the enclosing roof, the smoke ventilation and climate control systems, and the interior finishes.

When comparing the cost differences between fully enclosed and open centres, it is not simply a case of today's generation of open centre making a straight omission of the above extras and making a considerable saving on the scheme. For example, in an open street scheme the roof covering would be omitted, but there may also be an add back for the partial roofing over of any covered street or space in the new urban scheme.

The roof spans also tend to be larger in schemes with covered urban spaces, although covered streets will be comparable with the glazed roof area for enclosed mall spaces. The linear length of glazing is, however, likely to be less in the new urban schemes.

Another balancing cost factor to consider with the new open and covered schemes is that, while there would be a saving from the omission of the services installations (for the smoke ventilation and environmental control), the façades of the buildings would need to be of an external wall quality and also likely to be required to provide architectural variety through the provision of individually designed building blocks. So against any saving on installation, there would be an add back for the greater performance and complexity of the external walling.

Similarly, while the interior mall finishes and fittings can be omitted these will be replaced by the inclusion of quality natural materials and street furniture to form the public realm of the streets.

It is also likely that many of the new urban schemes will have two publicly accessible levels. In such schemes there will need to be comparable balustrades and mechanical vertical circulation, so few savings can be made on these elements when compared with those of an enclosed mall.

Finally, it should also be noted that the new urban schemes have more complex plan arrangements

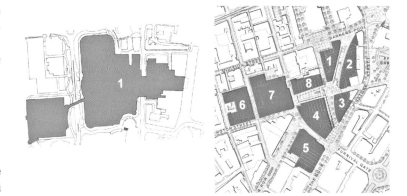

Figure 10.17 Layouts of an enclosed scheme at WestQuay, Southampton and an open street scheme for the New Retail Quarter, Sheffield illustrate the greater length of external wall in 'urban' schemes. *(Source: BDP)*

by being arranged as a series of individual buildings or blocks. The urban arrangements generate greater lengths of external wall and are likely to form more complexity in the roof. Therefore it is likely that many urban proposals will turn out to be more complex than their enclosed cousins. Any savings that may be made are likely to be required to meet the particular requirements of the urban scheme. In conclusion, the construction costs of the urban solution are likely to be similar to their energy consuming forebears. The urban schemes are, however, likely to make considerable running cost savings, without the requirement environmentally to control the public space.

A direct consequence of the greater complexity of the new urban schemes is the likelihood of the viability of these schemes having to work to closer margins. The outcome of having to accommodate closer margins will require these schemes to be larger in order for the developer to make a similar amount of profit. Reflecting this consequence, the generation of open street based urban schemes now in the UK pipeline are considerably larger than the previous generation of town centre based schemes. For example, the average size of the town centre schemes proposed for Sheffield, Cardiff and Liverpool range from 75 000 m² up to 140 000 m² (807 000– 1.5 million ft²), whereas the earlier generation of town centre schemes ranged from 46 000 m² to 75 000 m² (500 000 ft²–807 000 ft²).

Attracting Tenants

Upmarket, fashion based shopping centres have traditionally been enclosed shopping environments. The requirement for enclosure is being challenged under the urban agenda of current planning guidance. Open street and partially covered street based schemes, provided they incorporate levels of convenience, safety and some environmental protection, are forming attractive shopping environments and attracting fashion retailers to commit to them. This move is also being assisted by those fashion retailers, who preferred independence and who traditionally had an aversion to enclosed shopping malls, now being prepared to become involved with an open or covered street based scheme.

The challenge for the new urban schemes is to be able to attract those tenants who have traditionally associated prime retail space with an enclosed shopping environment. In meeting this challenge the new urban schemes will need to achieve a balance between providing a varied retail offer, convenience, safety and an acceptable level of environmental protection.

constraints of the site, and provide a layout (organisational framework) that achieves an individual solution for the project. The layout of the organisational framework and the planning of the horizontal circulation are intrinsically interrelated and influential upon each other.

The general layout objectives were identified in the previous Chapter. The functional and qualitative requirements for public circulation spaces were also examined in the previous section of this Chapter. Here we examine in more detail some of the fundamental rules of retail planning and some of the different types of basic layout, in order to set the groundwork for designers to develop their own solutions.

Layout Guidelines

One of the fundamental ways of establishing strong pedestrian flows is to position carefully the generators of footfall. The stronger retail areas are those perceived as having the most footfall. The generators can be considered as the anchor stores, MSU stores, other major attractions (leisure and catering areas), and the strategic elements relating to access and vertical movement noted above (see Figs. 10.21 and 10.22). The busiest areas naturally occur on the approach to an anchor element and die away beyond the anchor, unless a new attraction, or another anchor, is perceived ahead. Hence, the generators should be consciously positioned to encourage all parts of the centre to be used and

Figure 10.18 Comparison between the convenience of the enclosed shopping environment and the variety offered by a covered open urban environment. The Mall at Cribbs Causeway, Bristol; Martineau Place, Birmingham, UK (1998 and 2001). *(Source: David Barbour/BDP)*

Horizontal Circulation and Layout

The challenge to the designer of each new shopping facility is to establish a unique pattern of geometry to the layout of the horizontal circulation. In order to meet this challenge, the designer will need to understand the rules of retail planning, the requirements of the brief (see Chapter 8) and the

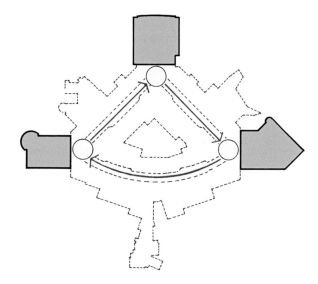

Figure 10.19 The strategic positioning of anchor stores are used to generate footfall around a circuit such as Bluewater, Greenhithe, Kent, UK. *(Source: Peter Coleman)*

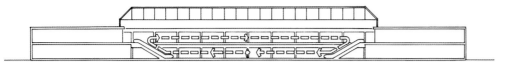

Figure 10.20 Two level dumb-bell arrangements allow circulation past all shopfronts without retracing steps. *(Source: Peter Coleman)*

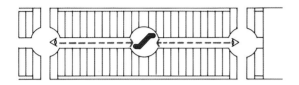

Figure 10.21 Vertical circulation can also be used to draw footfall past unit shops. *(Source: Peter Coleman)*

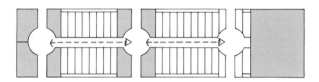

Figure 10.22 The strategic positioning of MSUs can draw footfall past unit shops. *(Source: Peter Coleman)*

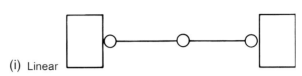

(i) Linear

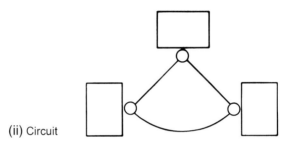

(ii) Circuit

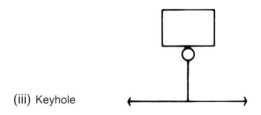

(iii) Keyhole

Figure 10.23 The traditional geometric layouts: i) linear; ii) circuit; iii) keyhole ('in-out' from high street). *(Source: Peter Coleman)*

for the volume of footfall to be evenly distributed past all the shopfronts.

Successful shopping centre layouts are based on the formation of a natural journey, commencing from a point of arrival and leading to a destination. The destination need not be immediately apparent on arrival, but there should be a sufficient attraction, or reason, to lead the customer from one strategic point to another before reaching the destination.

The customer's return journey should equally be considered and should ideally avoid having to retrace exactly the steps of the original journey. In a simple gun-barrel or dumb-bell layout, this can readily be achieved in a two-level arrangement which forms a vertical circuit, the customer arriving on one level and returning on another (see Fig. 10.20). Circuits can also be formed in plan to allow the customer to return to a point of arrival without exactly having to retrace steps. The consideration and formation of vertical or horizontal circuits are fundamental to pedestrian circulation in shopping centres and are considered in more detail below.

Types of Layout

Here we look at some of the principal types of geometric layout that work within the roles of retail planning and also meet the basic functional requirements of the organisational framework.

Linear Arrangements

The simplest organisational layout sets out the circulation space and shopping accommodation in a linear arrangement between two anchor elements. These layouts are referred to as dumb-bell, linear or gun-barrel malls and connect between two points defined by the anchors. This simple arrangement can be varied by one or more points of punctuation formed by node spaces (focal spaces/knuckle spaces). The number of punctuation points along the length of the public circulation space will depend on the amount of accommodation and size of the available site. The node space can be used to introduce an angle into the layout or to accommodate the interconnection of an adjoining circulation route. The node space may also be used to

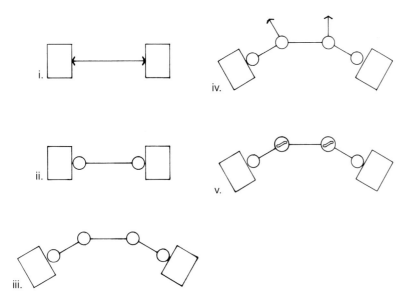

Figure 10.24 Linear arrangements: i) simple dumb-bell between two anchors; ii) dumb-bell with nodes; iii) nodes used to change angle; iv) nodes to receive other routes; v) nodes including vertical circulation. *(Source: Peter Coleman)*

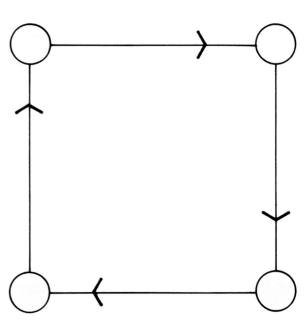

Figure 10.26 A simple 'circuit' layout. *(Source: Peter Coleman)*

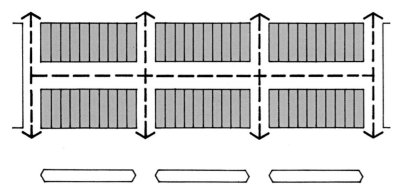

Figure 10.25 Lengths of shopfront form identifiable areas of shops and should be coordinated with maximum fire escape distances. *(Source: Peter Coleman)*

locate elements of vertical circulation. The total length of horizontal circulation space may use node spaces to organise the circulation space into identifiable areas and lengths of shopfront. The optimum length of shopfront varies from project to project, but for the purpose of general guidance 90 m (292 ft), with a tolerance of 10 m (32 ft), can be used. (Fire escape requirements may influence this dimension and should be considered when planning the layout.) (See Fig. 10.25.)

Circuits

The shop units should be laid out in such a way that the public circulation forms a natural flow of pedestrian movement. Circuit patterns of layout

encourage continuous circulation past all the shop frontages and a return back to a point of arrival. The formation of a circuit allows the customer to visit the whole of a shopping centre without having to retrace steps. Circuits can be formed in three dimensions by considering both the vertical and plan arrangement of the layout. Circuits can be singular or multiple by adopting a figure of eight.

Pedestrian flows in circuits are activated by the strategic positioning of an anchor element at the corners to maintain interest. The anchor element should be visible ahead to lead the customer on. Maintaining sight lines and clear visibility from one anchor element to the next are important considerations.

Distances between strategic elements should generally be considered to retain visibility from one point to another. This is not an exact science, but a distance of 90 m with a tolerance of plus-or-minus 10 m is a sensible starting point. The length of linear run can be extended by the careful placement of an anchor element.

In the larger shopping centre arrangements the anchor elements can be considered as points of punctuation to the layout. Pedestrian movement should be encouraged to lead from one point of punctuation to another anchor element in an easy flowing sequence. The positioning of the anchor elements will be more complex in larger arrangements. Care should be given to achieving variety and establishing local orientation.

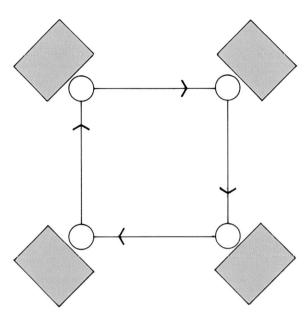

Figure 10.27 Strategic positioning of anchors in a circuit generate footfall. *(Source: Peter Coleman)*

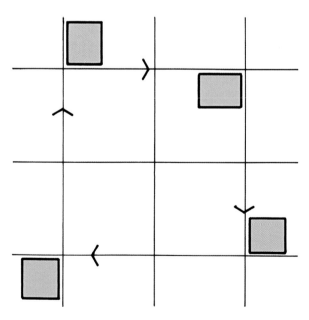

Figure 10.28 Positioning of anchors in a town centre can form 'urban circuits'. *(Source: Peter Coleman)*

Pedestrian circuits can be formed in both out-of-town and town centre shopping layouts. Circuits can sometimes be more easily formed in town centre locations by the integration of the layout within an existing street pattern.

Care needs to be given to these arrangements to avoid repetitive circuits by forming points of orientation and providing areas of different identity.

Node spaces can be introduced to punctuate the total length of circulation space and also provide identifiable areas, in the same manner as identified for linear arrangements above. The formation of natural circuits of pedestrian circulation past all the shops, or in large centres past selected groups of shops, is a fundamental requirement of retail planning. Selected circuits of pedestrian movement should be provided in the layout, regardless of it adopting a physical geometric representation of a circuit.

The generic types of horizontal circulation usually found in town centre locations are discussed below.

Journeys

This horizontal circulation pattern is based on forming a new journey commencing from a recognisable point in the town centre and leading through a newly formed retail area, before leading back to another prime part of the existing town centre. This format of circulation often forms a journey from two separate points in the same high street. Journey circulation patterns usually involve two principal entrances where the route should work equally well when approached from either direction. The circulation route usually leads on to an anchor store destination. There will also be points of interest at each entranceway, along with other retail attractions strategically positioned at intervals to lead the visitor forward and through the facilities. Points of punctuation and node spaces can again be used to organise the journey into recognisable areas of accommodation and to facilitate changes of direction.

Journey organisational arrangements are often U-shaped layouts. Journey layouts, by their directional nature, suit simple, single-level circulation arrangements or multi-level circulation arrangements, where each entrance is related to a different external level. Multi-level arrangements can work particularly well where a central space is used to connect the two principal levels and includes the vertical circulation. Journey types of horizontal circulation can be used in open, covered and enclosed types of space (see Fig. 10.29).

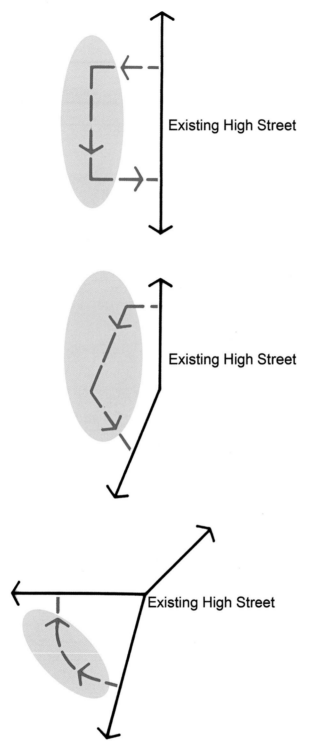

Existing High Street

Existing High Street

Existing High Street

Figure 10.29 A 'journey' can be formed through a new shopping area from an existing high street. *(Source: Peter Coleman)*

Keyholes

This arrangement is based on a single point of entry and return from a high street. The focus of this type of layout is usually one or more large anchor stores located at the end of the circulation route, which attract visitors past all the other frontages on the way to the destination. The single point of entry and return suits a multi-level arrangement of accommodation better, where visitors enter and circulate to the destination on one level and return by another level, thereby avoiding having to retrace steps past the same shops. A means of vertical level change near the entrance will be required, along with the anchor stores having entrances on each circulation level, in order to facilitate entry and return routes being completed at different levels. Keyhole arrangements,

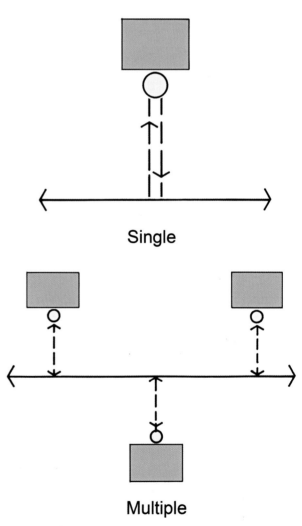

Single

Multiple

Figure 10.30 A single point of entry and return onto a high street can also be used in multiples to form several keyholes. *(Source: Peter Coleman)*

by their nature, are predictable and more successful when arranged on two or more levels. They are also reliant on the quality and drama of the circulation space, along with the quality of the anchor, for their success.

Routes

Like the 'journey' type of layout, these are usually based on arranging the circulation to connect between two existing shopping locations and have entrances to each of these two destinations in the town centre. However, routes differ by being formed between two different parts of the town centre, rather than connecting between two parts of the same high street. Routes also differ by either forming a connection between two existing unconnected destinations or by reinforcing the linkage between two weakly related areas. Routes exploit the potential for a desire line between two destinations and the natural synergy that exists between two areas of vitality in a town centre. The formation of a route can often involve the removal of a previous barrier and improve the integration of facilities across a town centre.

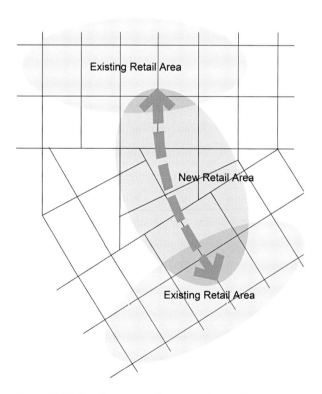

Figure 10.31 Forming a new retail area around a 'route' by connecting two separate retail areas. *(Source: Peter Coleman)*

In a similar way to the journey format, anchor stores can be arranged midway along the route. The inclusion of an anchor is not essential in some smaller schemes, where the strength of pedestrian footfall between two existing destinations is so strong that an anchor is not required. Route layouts of circulation without an anchor are similar to a traditional arcade which also directly connects two busy streets between a city block. It is likely that both anchors and points of punctuation will be required in larger schemes. The length of circulation space can again be organised into recognisable areas by the use of node spaces. Retail attractions can be strategically positioned to lead the visitor from one point to another and generate pedestrian footfall throughout the length of the scheme. The layout and arrangement will again need to be considered so as to work equally well when approached from either direction. In urban based schemes the node spaces will be formed from more urban spaces, such as squares and piazzas.

Routes suit simple single-level and multi-level arrangements of accommodation where each entrance relates to a different principal level. In multi-level arrangements, the use of a central space to connect the two levels can be as effective as in the journey type of layout. Route types of layout improve and facilitate the integration of areas and linkages in existing town centre and urban types of scheme. For example, schemes based on open or covered types of space are better suited to route layouts than enclosed types of space.

Networks

In addressing the urban agenda in town centre locations, the organisational framework for the accommodation and public circulation can be arranged to form a network of circuits and cross routes within the existing street pattern. Network layouts provide an approach for integrating a major shopping facility into a town centre location. In this format, the shopping facility can become an integral part of the town centre and is not just a separate monolithic entity which, when the shops close, becomes an impenetrable area.

The successful integration of a network type of shopping facility requires extensive research and investigation by the developer/owner, the architect and the retail team. For example, it will require:

■ the developer/owner to assemble a sufficiently sized site to accommodate the facilities (a task where the opportunities in major towns and cities are few and far between)

- integration with the existing street pattern will require both an urban and nodal analysis of pedestrian circulation (see Chapter 8) in order to understand the urban form and the pedestrian routes. The pedestrian circulation analysis will need to establish where people are going to and coming from as well as how they go about it
- an analysis of the existing retail facilities will be necessary to understand them sufficiently, so as to enable the new proposals to work together and complement the existing facilities.

With the appropriately sized site and armed with sufficient urban and local research, the opportunity for an integrated shopping facility exists with a network layout. With this type of layout there will be potential for urban integration by:

- continuing or reinstating lost historical routes which pass through the site
- repairing street patterns lost through subsequent urban erosion caused by highways, war damage or previous, insensitive development
- allowing existing routes to cross the site and retain connections both from and to adjacent surrounding neighbourhoods
- forming linkages with means of arrival by public transport and private cars
- integration of the new development with the existing urban street pattern.

Network based layouts can connect to many different parts of the town centre and link together several destinations. As such, they are more complex

arrangements than those for 'journeys' and 'routes'. Shopping facilities arranged as a network that are based on urban design principles require a comprehensive understanding of retail rules, the brief, urban planning and the confidence of knowing where to break the rules in order to achieve a unique and workable solution.

Dimensional Requirements

The dimensional requirements for circulation spaces will vary depending upon a number of different factors:

- the type of shopping centre
- the layout
- proximity of other accommodation
- the number of floor levels
- the volume of pedestrian footfall (peak and quiet times).

Each project will need to be considered on its individual merits and particular circumstances. Considered here, for the purpose of general guidance, are the minimum dimensions for a typical medium sized European regional shopping centre with two public access floors.

Public Circulation Space – Widths

A primary ground floor circulation space should have a minimum clear width of 9 m (29.25 ft). Ideally this dimension should be between 10 m and 12 m (32.5–39 ft). Enclosed ground floor circulation spaces, which are not used for any other purpose or are required to accommodate vertical circulation or other facilities, should not exceed 12 m (39 ft). Open or covered ground floor circulation spaces relating to a town centre location can be more flexible and can respond

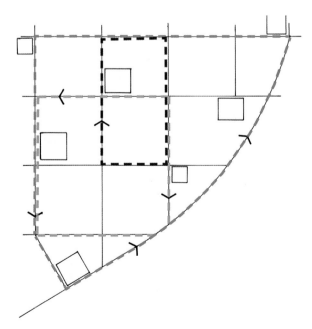

Figure 10.32 A 'network' of urban streets establishes multiple circuits. *(Source: Peter Coleman)*

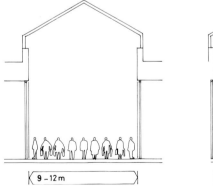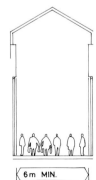

Figure 10.33 Public circulation space dimensions: primary routes 9–12 m; secondary routes 6 m minimum. *(Source: Peter Coleman)*

to the prevailing dimensions of the urban context. Secondary interconnecting routes should not be less than 6 m (19.5 ft) in width. If circulation spaces are used as a means of fire escape, there may also be regulatory minimum dimensions to take into consideration. A hierarchy should be established between primary and secondary routes and the dimensions arranged to correspond with the different requirements.

In multi-level centres where the public circulation space is arranged with upper-level galleries overlooking a ground floor public circulation space below, the primary upper floor gallery circulation space should have a minimum clear width of 4.5 m (14.6 ft). A preferable minimum gallery width is 5 m (16.25 ft) and should be used where space permits.

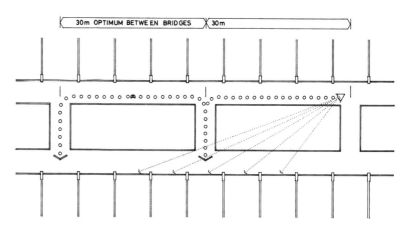

Figure 10.35 The optimum spacing of bridges for convenient crossovers between gallery walkways. *(Source: Peter Coleman)*

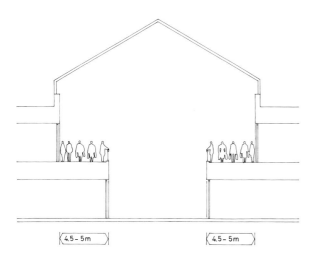

Figure 10.34 Public circulation spaces: minimum gallery widths. *(Source: Peter Coleman)*

Public Circulation Space – Lengths

Ideal lengths of public circulation space have been discussed previously in addressing the requirement to arrange the layout into recognisable areas and to punctuate the circulation space (Types of layout, above).

Bridge Connections

Multi-level arrangements, with upper-level galleries each side of the gallery, will need to be regularly connected to the other side in order to allow customers to cross over conveniently between the shops arranged on each side. These crossing points (bridges) should ideally be positioned at intervals not exceeding 30 m (98 ft).

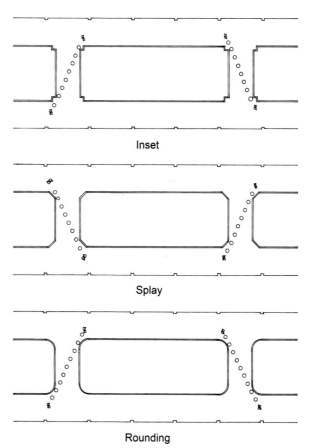

Inset

Splay

Rounding

Figure 10.36 Alternative ways of easing corners to make convenient crossovers between gallery walkways. *(Source: Peter Coleman)*

Visibility between Floors

In multi-level public circulation arrangements, it is important that maximum visibility between the shops on different levels is maintained to encourage visitors to circulate on both levels and establish a combined synergy between the shopping facilities on each level. There are several different factors to take into account when considering the visibility between different floor levels:

■ the vertical dimension between the floors
■ the spatial relationship with the structure
■ the profile of the gallery level edge (bulkhead)
■ the balustrade design.

Each of these influencing factors is considered separately below. The number of floor levels will also obviously influence the visibility between different floors. For the purposes of reviewing each of these factors, visibility is considered here on the basis of an arrangement with two public access levels.

Vertical Dimensions

The floor-to-floor height of the public circulation space is largely determined by the vertical height requirements of the shops accessed from the space.

The vertical dimensions for shops are identified in Chapter 9.

The type and arrangement of accommodation within the shop will significantly influence the vertical dimension between the floor levels of the public space. For example, a typical shop unit with a single level of trading and combined storage can be accommodated within a nominal floor-to-floor height of 4.75–5 m (15.5–16.4 ft). A typical unit shop with single-level trading and storage arranged at a partial upper level, will require a minimum floor-to-floor height of 6.5 m (21.3 ft). Furthermore, a shop with a requirement for trading on two levels within its premises will require a minimum floor-to-floor height of 8 m (26.25 ft). The structure and grid will also determine the vertical dimension. For the purpose of achieving the best visibility between levels, the vertical dimension should be kept to the practicable minimum. It is therefore preferable, wherever possible, to arrange the shops with combined trading and storage in a single level on the lower ground floor and to arrange

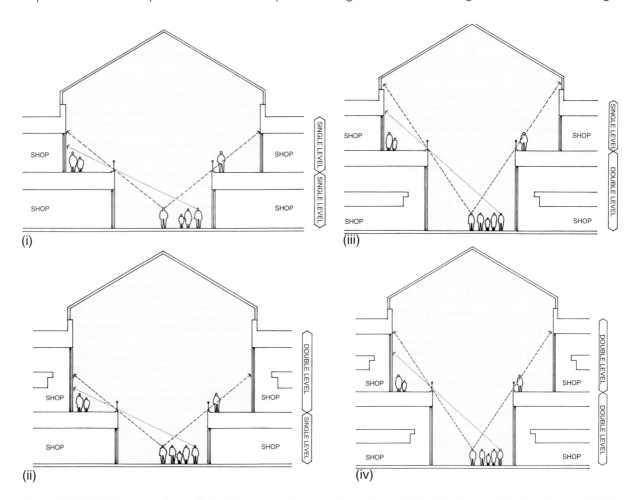

Figure 10.37 Visibility between floors: (i) single level shops at upper and lower floors; (ii) single level shops at the lower floor and double height shops at the upper floor; (iii) double level shops at the lower floor and single level shops at the upper floor; (iv) double level shops at lower and upper floors. *(Source: Peter Coleman)*

the shops with multi-level trading requirements on the upper ground floor. The arrangement and requirement for both single level and two-level shops should be considered with the client and specialist retail consultants at an early stage, as it will fundamentally influence the layout and character of the centre.

Multi-level public circulation spaces with a dimension greater than 5 m (16.4 ft) between the different floor levels can make the levels appear disconnected and detached. In addition, it should be recognised that as the vertical dimension increases the physical connection that can be comfortably achieved by stairs and escalators becomes more challenging and increases the likelihood of the retail facilities becoming more physically remote and it being less convenient to connect between levels.

Particular care should also be given where unit shops are located adjacent to department stores, where each has different vertical dimension requirements. This can result in the floor level of the public circulation space having to take up a vertical level difference between the two elements of accommodation. Small level differences of up to 0.5 m (1.5 ft) can be accommodated by ramping the circulation space over a manageable short length. The level difference can be accommodated by ramping either the upper or lower ground floor of the circulation space.

Spatial Relationship with Structure

This issue concerns the positioning of the supporting structure relative to the public circulation space, where the objective is to maximise visibility to the shopfronts. In single-level access arrangements to the shops, the column position is simply resolved by being positioned just behind the line of the shopfront and setting the grid out from this point on either side. In multi-level shopping spaces, with a gallery level above a lower ground floor and a profiled cross section, it will be necessary to coordinate the position of the structure at both ground and upper floor, and in covered or enclosed spaces, to determine the position of the structure supporting the roof. For example, the projection of the ground floor columns set out just behind the line of the shopfront will result in columns occurring on the upper floor along the gallery edge. Gallery edge columns will restrict both the width of the gallery and the visibility between the different floor levels – in particular where the effect of perspective over the longitudinal views is taken into consideration (see Fig. 10.39). The key decision to resolve in multi-level covered and enclosed spaces is therefore where to position the columns on the upper floor levels and how to support the roof above.

A common solution to achieving good visibility between floor levels is to provide a column free space by setting the column grid out from the upper floor level and to position the columns behind the shopfront line and, where spaces are roofed over, to support the roof structure on the corresponding shopfront line. This clear span approach requires a greater roof structure and involves the lower ground floor columns behind the shopfront being positioned in a different dimension to the normal grid. While a column free space will address the requirement for good visibility, it can also appear to lack scale and feel too open. It is therefore important to address the overall character of the space and achieve a balance with the requirement for visibility. An alternative approach is to consider a more modest roof structure and to minimise obstructions to visibility by adopting an elegant and minimal supporting column structure on line with the upper floor level gallery edge.

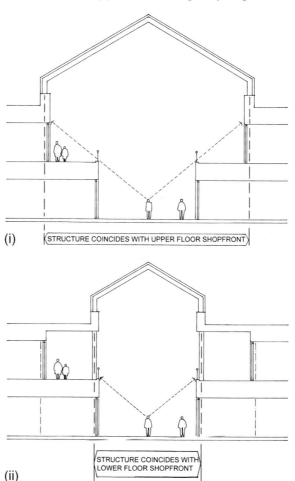

(i)

STRUCTURE COINCIDES WITH UPPER FLOOR SHOPFRONT

(ii)

STRUCTURE COINCIDES WITH LOWER FLOOR SHOPFRONT

Figure 10.38 Spatial relationship and structure: (i) roof structure coinciding with the primary structure where both are set out from the upper floor, with clear visibility to the upper floor; (ii) roof structure coinciding with the gallery edge, set out from lower floor compromises visibility to the upper floor. *(Source: Peter Coleman)*

Figure 10.39 Positioning columns on the gallery edges can obscure the view to the upper level shops, Gateway Theatre of Shopping, Umlanga, SA (2001). *(Source: Peter Coleman)*

Gallery Edge Profiles

Gallery edges apply to arrangements with multi-level access to the shopping facilities. The gallery edge applies to the horizontal edge of the upper floor level. (The gallery floor edge profile is sometimes referred to as a bulkhead.) Traditionally, upper floor galleries have been arranged to maximise lettable floor space and used to accommodate landlord's services, which have resulted in large projecting overhangs and narrow floor openings across the lower ground floor space. In order to maximise the lettable space, traditional upper floor galleries have been arranged to minimise the collective cross-sectional width of the public circulation space. In extreme cases, with galleries forming full canopies, this has resulted in the upper floor shopfront line coinciding with the ground floor shopfront line. These prison-like arrangements have resulted in small openings in the upper floor and poor visibility between the shops on different floor levels. The oppressive nature of overhanging galleries has been emphasised by the additional ceiling hung beneath the floor

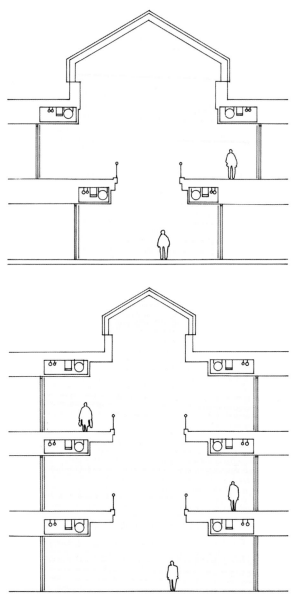

Figure 10.40 Enclosed public spaces provide space for services within bulkheads which in turn influence the gallery edge and spatial quality. *(Source: Peter Coleman)*

containing the public space heating and ventilation services. The resulting combined gallery edge has been profiled and shaped to reduce the apparent size and present an acceptable visual dimension to the floor edge.

The evolution of shopping centres has seen a greater awareness of the importance of the character and quality of the public circulation space, with greater emphasis being placed on visibility over maximising space. However, while full overhanging galleries may be less common, partially projecting gallery floor edges are still used to house landlord services.

In new schemes, the gallery overhang should ideally be kept to a minimum in order to maximise visibility between floor levels. However, in order to ensure the required floor space is achieved, the requirement for visibility will need to be kept in balance with the viability and functional requirements of the scheme. The ideal solution, of having no bulkhead projection at the gallery level above the shops on the lower level, is more readily achieved in the new generation of more urban proposals. For example, naturally ventilated covered spaces (without heating and cooling installations) do not have the same requirement for accommodating services installations and ductwork as a heated and cooled enclosed space. Where bulkheads are required at gallery floor level, the gallery should be profiled to present as thin a visual edge to the floor as possible.

Balustrade Design

Balustrades are an integral part of the gallery floor edge and should be considered together. The balustrade should be as transparent as possible to allow visibility through it. The balustrade supports will need to be designed to comply with the regulatory requirement to withstand the loading from potential crowds.

There are fundamentally two types of balustrade which meet the general requirement for good visibility between the shops on different floor levels – glazed panel and open metal baluster type balustrades. Glazed balustrades are the most transparent but care needs to be given to potential reflections and the need for regular cleaning. It is important to confirm with the client that they are committed to the cleaning regime to ensure glazed balustrades are well maintained. Carefully designed metal balustrades can be effective and require less maintenance than glazed types. However, the cumulative effect of vertical balusters at a maximum spacing of 100 mm (4 inches), when viewed obliquely along the length of the balustrading, can severely restrict visibility between floor levels. Metal balustrading could be considered as less flexible than glazed balustrading and should be considered as part of a total public space solution, which takes into account the combined visibility achieved by the vertical height of the shopfronts at each floor level, the position of the structure and the section profile of the overall space.

Vertical Circulation

Positioning

The successful inclusion of vertical circulation is one of the key enablers to the operation of multi-level shopping layouts and, as such, facilitates shopping development located on high value land. In multi-level schemes, vertical circulation should be considered, equally with horizontal circulation, as the means of structuring the layout and encouraging pedestrians to pass by all the shop units equally. Positioning of vertical circulation has to achieve a balance between facilitating pedestrian footfall and providing a convenient means for visitors to move between different floor levels. Generally, vertical circulation should be organised to allow visitors to pass in front of a recognisable length of shops before changing level and returning past a further length of shopfronts. Equally importantly, the vertical circulation should be positioned so that it is clearly visible and understandable, allowing visitors to stop in a leisurely way having foreseen where to change level. The vertical circulation should also be positioned to encourage visitors to move forward and towards the point of changing level.

Vertical circulation must be conveniently and strategically located. It should be positioned at regular intervals, which generally should not exceed 80–100 m (260–325 ft). The interval positioning of vertical circulation is dimensionally similar to the positioning of punctuation spaces in horizontal circulation. Coincidentally, the vertical circulation can be positioned with the node spaces, provided it is of sufficient size. Alternatively, where the node spaces are kept free, the vertical circulation can be positioned midway between the node spaces in the circulation space. The former arrangement is illustrated by the example of Brent Cross, London (see Fig. 10.42). The latter approach can be seen in the example of Bluewater, Greenhithe, Kent, where the knuckle spaces are kept largely free and the escalators are located in the mall (see Fig. 10.43).

In the formation of multi-level schemes, any existing level changes across the site should be exploited, wherever possible, to feed different floor levels naturally, thereby helping to achieve equal amounts of pedestrian footfall and effectively forming several ground floors (see Fig. 10.44). The objective should be to avoid having to resort solely to using internal level changing devices (stairs, lifts, escalators) in order to form a multi-level scheme. Naturally forming the equivalent of equally served ground floors

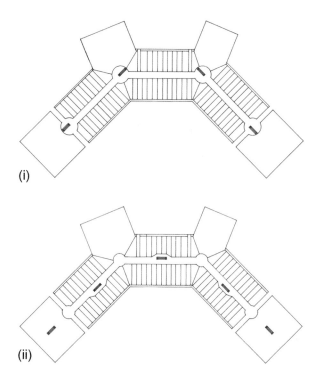

(i)

(ii)

Figure 10.41 Vertical circulation: alternative escalator locations. (i) Escalators located in the node spaces; (ii) escalators located in the malls (can compromise some shops but leave nodes clear). *(Source: Peter Coleman)*

Figure 10.42 Escalators in the node space, Brent Cross, London, UK (1996). *(Source: James Cheung)*

can readily be achieved in two-level schemes. However, the formation of several equally served ground floor levels becomes more challenging above two levels, unless there are considerable level changes across the site. In layouts with more than two levels, the additional floors beyond the

Figure 10.43 Escalators in the Rose Gallery, Bluewater, Greenhithe, Kent, UK (1999). *(Source: James Cheung)*

second level are generally likely to require a major anchor with access from these floor levels to help generate the appropriate levels of footfall. In multi-level schemes, the footfall to a weaker level can also be reinforced by the careful positioning of a secondary anchor; a large catering area, a major leisure facility, the entrance to the car park, or a public transport interchange, which can all assist with generating footfall to the floor.

Figure 10.44 Two natural ground floor levels can be readily formed on a sloping site. *(Source: Peter Coleman)*

The positioning of vertical circulation can influence the footfall dynamics and workings of a centre as much as the plan layout. The objective should be to arrange the layout and utilise the site levels to reduce the need for vertical circulation as much as possible.

General Types of Vertical Circulation

Where vertical circulation is required to provide level changes in the layout, this can be provided by a variety of means. It is usual for a combination of stairs, lifts and escalators to be used to solve the vertical circulation requirements of multi-level shopping facilities. Ramps and sloping the floor are also used readily to accommodate small level changes.

Travelators are used where there is a requirement to transfer vertically large numbers of trolley users; for example, moving visitors from a supermarket or food store to a car park located at a different level. Escalators have become the accepted means of conveniently transferring large numbers of people vertically between levels. Escalators are expensive mechanical installations, however, and need to be carefully considered and sparingly used. Stairs can be a simple and effective means of transferring customers between levels and can readily be inserted as a means of convenient intermediate change of level. Even with stairs and escalators providing convenience and volume of vertical movement respectively, it will also be necessary to include lifts to accommodate the disabled and users with prams and pushchairs. Each of the different means of vertical circulation is examined separately below.

Stairs

Feature stairs within the public circulation space are an appropriate and flexible way of moving visitors vertically between levels and are commonly used and accepted in shopping facilities. Stairs can be located individually or positioned together with escalators in a variety of combinations. For example, stairs can reinforce overall circulation patterns by being located at strategic positions, together with escalators, in node spaces. Alternatively, stairs can be positioned individually midway between the node spaces in the public circulation space or in the node space when the space is kept free of escalators.

Stairs are accommodated into the layout more flexibly than escalators and provide a convenient alternative option for allowing visitors to connect between floors. Escalators are sometimes deliberately kept out of node spaces to allow the space to be enjoyed and used for public seating, and to retain clear views to the adjacent shopfrontages. An elegant feature staircase can more readily be accommodated in a node space while also maintaining the clutter free objective, as illustrated in Bluewater.

Figure 10.46 Feature stair in the knuckle space at the Sun Court, Bluewater, Greenhithe, Kent, UK (1999). *(Source: Lend Lease)*

Figure 10.45 A generously wide mall accommodates a dog-leg feature stair, Metrocentre, Gateshead, UK (1984–1987). *(Source: Simon Williams)*

In the design of the stair, it should be arranged to form convenient lengths of rise between the landings. Because of the large floor-to-floor heights involved in shopping spaces, more than one landing may be required in a single staircase. Where stairs are located in the circulation space, the landing should be arranged to allow sufficient headroom for the public to walk beneath it. The stair should also be designed with a generous width, gentle risers and wide treads to allow comfortable movement. To avoid a feature stair becoming a visual obstruction, careful consideration should be given to the structure, the materials and degree of openness achieved between the treads. Combinations of metal and glass, with natural materials for the tread, are commonly used.

A variety of stair configurations ranging fro straight, dogleg and sweeping flights can be used to suit the individual layout of the centre. Although most feature staircases are free-standing, they can be carefully arranged to run parallel to escalators, as illustrated by the example of WestQuay, Southampton.

Figure 10.48 Staircase running beside the escalators in the main space to WestQuay, Southampton, UK (2000). *(Source: Charlotte Wood)*

Ramps

Independent ramps and sloping the floor of the public space are discreet ways of making up small level differences. Sloping the floor of the space can be used to take up the level difference between:
- existing street level or external level at an entrance-way and an internal floor level
- finished floor levels caused by adjacent shops (beneath the circulation space) with varying floor-to-floor height requirements.

Independent ramps can be used to form a deliberate level change and to help reinforce the separation of circulation space from a seating area. Careful consideration will need to be given to all ramp designs to ensure they comply with the regulatory requirements for accommodating less able persons. Ramp design criteria for general design guidance are included in Table 10.3.

Where the public circulation space is ramped, the shops that are accessed directly from the sloping

Figure 10.47 The feature stair arranged with seating beneath the landing at White Rose, Leeds, UK (1997). *(Source: Roger Ball/Image Photo Ltd)*

Figure 10.49 The sloping mall leading up from the high street, WestQuay, Southampton. *(Source: Joe Low)*

floor will need to be carefully considered. Lengths of sloping floor will require the shop floor levels to step along the length of the ramp, such that the mid-point of each shop unit can be accessed from a nominal level point with the ramp. WestQuay, Southampton is an example where the public circulation space is ramped at 1 in 30 to take up a 3 m level difference from the high street entrance up to the upper ground floor level. (It should be noted that this scheme was completed prior to the new regulatory guidelines.)

While ramping the floors can be a convenient way of accommodating level changes in the floor finish, it should also be recognised that the need to step the shop floor levels along the length of the ramp complicates the method of construction and should only be considered where the added value

Figure 10.50 The double height ramped Wesley Walk, Festival Place, Basingstoke, UK (2002). *(Source: Peter Coleman)*

Table 10.3 General design guidance for ramps

- Sloping surfaces from zero up to a gradient of 1 in 60 are deemed to be a level surface
- Sloping surfaces between gradients of 1 in 60 and 1 in 20 are required to be arranged into lengths of ramp to provide a horizontal landing for each rise up to a maximum rise of 500 mm (1.6 ft)
- Sloping surfaces of 1 in 20 or more should meet the following requirements:
  - where landings are provided they must be a minimum length of 1.5 m (5 ft)
  - handrails must be provided on both sides
  - a 1 in 20 gradient ramp can accommodate a maximum single rise of 500 mm (2.5 ft) in a single length of ramp, extending up to a length of 10 m (32.8 ft) before a landing is required
  - a 1 in 15 gradient ramp can accommodate a maximum single rise of 333 mm (1.1 ft) in a single length of ramp, extending up to a length of 5 m (16.4 ft) before a landing is required
  - a 1 in 12 gradient ramp can accommodate a maximum single rise of 166 mm (6.6 inches) in a single length of ramp, extending up to a length of 2 m (6.6 ft)
  - landings should be level – up to a fall of 1 in 60 with a maximum cross fall of 1 in 40

Source: English Building Regulations 2000: Updated October 2004 Part M Access and Use of Buildings. Further information contained in British Standard 8300: 2001 'Design of Buildings and their Approaches to Meet the Needs of Disabled People – Code of Practice'.

compensates for the additional build cost. Generally, independent ramps and sloping the floor are not practical means to consider when accommodating large level differences, in view of the excessive ramp lengths and added complexity of the construction. An interesting exception to this general guidance is the example of Festival Place, Basingstoke, Hampshire, which has successfully adopted a continuous circuit layout to ramp the lower ground floor up to the upper ground floor without the use of escalators and has effectively formed two ground floor levels (see Fig. 10.50). (This scheme was completed prior to the new regulatory guidelines.)

Escalators

Mechanical moving stairs have been adopted in retail premises for over 100 years, since Bloomingdales installed escalators in its late-nineteenth century New York department store. Since their acceptance in department stores, escalators have come into common use in shopping centres from the period of expansion in 1950s America – with the growth of

the out-of-town regional shopping centre. These early American centres established the escalator as the primary means of transferring large volumes of the shopping public between different shopping levels. Escalators are now accepted and adopted as the primary means of vertical circulation in shopping facilities throughout the world.

Escalators have traditionally been located in the node spaces of the public circulation space. The logic of this arrangement is well established and allows customers to complete the circulation of a run of shops before changing level. It also helps the shopping public to return past another run of shops at a different level, without having to retrace their steps. (The importance of this vertical circuit has also been discussed in Circuits and positioning earlier.)

An alternative to this traditional location is to omit the escalators from the node spaces and to position them within the adjacent department stores. Although the additional footfall passing through the store and clear visibility to the store's frontage can be welcomed by the retailer, it is less flexible and popular with the other shop units, as it requires the department store to remain open at corresponding times to all the remaining retail, catering and leisure accommodation accessible from the circulation space.

Another solution (referred to earlier) is to locate the escalators at the mid-point of the length of public circulation space. Positioning escalators in this way requires careful organisation of the adjacent shops to ensure sufficient circulation space around the escalators and careful positioning and design of the escalators to ensure visibility is maintained to the shops and the continuing sequence of public circulation space.

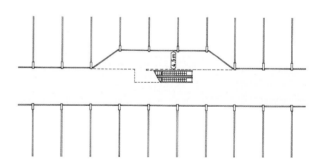

Figure 10.51 Escalators in the mall require the mall to be widened to form sufficient space between the escalators and shopfronts. *(Source: Peter Coleman)*

Escalator Configuration

In addition to the general location of the escalators, the circulation will also be influenced by their configuration. Each shopping centre will require the escalators to be configured to suit the circumstances of the particular layout. Factors that will influence the individual configuration are: the number of floor levels; the position of the escalators in the overall layout; the relationship with other means of vertical circulation; the available space; and the relationship with adjacent accommodation. Some of the most commonly used configurations are outlined here.

Two-Level Configurations

In two-level layouts, the up and down escalators are usually positioned together as a pair. In these arrangements, they require the width for two escalators at each level (two springing points – a point for the up and for the down escalator).

The escalators can be arranged as a parallel pair positioned side by side or separated, where there is a requirement for visibility between them.

The pair of escalators can also be crossed over to allow each level to be circulated to the maximum (Fig. 10.53). This arrangement will require the opening in the upper floor to be extended to the far end of the escalators.

Figure 10.53 A pair of crossed escalators, Great Northern Experience, Manchester, UK (2001). *(Source: Kone)*

Figure 10.52 Escalators in the widened mall space Centre West, East Kilbride, Glasgow, UK (2003). *(Source: Peter Coleman)*

Multiple-Level Configurations

In arrangements where escalators serve more than two levels, consideration will need to be given to the greater complexity of escalators arriving on the middle floor. The middle level, for example, will have to accommodate the springing point of four escalators.

A commonly adopted method is where the escalators are stacked in an arrangement of parallel pairs of escalators superimposed one upon another. This configuration requires the passengers to leave the escalator and consciously return via the floor level before proceeding up or down via the next escalator. As such, the arrangement dissuades continuous vertical movement. This stacked arrangement of parallel pairs of escalators is an efficient use of space. The escalators can be accommodated within an opening that is the width of a single pair of escalators, despite the middle floor/s having to accommodate the springing point of four escalators.

Figure 10.54 A stacked parallel pair of escalators connect the three floor levels at WestQuay, Southampton (2000). *(Source: David Barbour/BDP)*

Figure 10.55 A pair of crossed escalators superimposed one upon another illustrated by the Selfridge's atrium, The Bullring, Birmingham, UK (2003). *(Source: Caroline Field)*

In multi-level arrangements, pairs of escalators can also be crossed over and then another pair of escalators superimposed over the original pair. This configuration forms an interweaved arrangement and is used to provide both a continuous upward moving circulation route and a continuous downward route. The interweaving pattern also allows four escalators to spring from the middle floor within the opening width of a pair of escalators and as such is an efficient use of space. However, it can present a considerable visual obstruction which will need to be taken into account.

A further configuration to consider, which also provides continuous up and down circulation routes, is a double parallel pair. This arrangement has four escalators arriving side by side at the middle floor and therefore requires more space to accommodate it. It does, however, allow greater visibility between the mid-level escalators, which can meet an important requirement for most department stores.

A dramatic escalator arrangement, which can be considered in some multi-level centres, is the formation of a continuous cascade of escalators. In this arrangement there is a continuous flow of circulation in both directions. Cascading escalators, however, tend to compromise the horizontal circulation of the lower and middle level floors by encouraging pedestrian short circuiting all the shopfrontages. Despite

Figure 10.56 A double parallel pair of escalators (split by the lower level) connect between the upper mid and lower levels at The Bullring, Birmingham, UK (2003). *(Source: Peter Coleman)*

the pedestrian footfall shortcoming, a cascade of escalators, arranged in continuous pairs passing continuously from floor to floor, can be efficiently accommodated within an opening width of a single pair of escalators.

The majority of escalator installations are generally straight linear mechanisms which are supported from steel trusses that span between the floor levels. The length of escalator will be determined by the floor-to-floor height and the angle of pitch from the springing point. A further allowance will need to be made to accommodate the driving motor at one end of the escalator. Escalator widths are measured between the treads and between the handrails where the latter is the larger dimension. For the purposes of sizing the escalator, the dimension between the treads is usually adopted. Reference should be made to individual manufacturers' information for specific design details. (The information in Table 10.4 can be used for general design guidance.)

The size and speed of the escalator to be provided will be influenced by the expected volume of customers to be transported. Careful consideration should be given to selecting the escalator speed, as an escalator moving too fast can discourage passengers from using it. The architect should consult with specialist advisers to determine the size of escalator to be provided. Typical escalator tread widths used in regional shopping centres are likely to range from 0.8 to 1.0 m (2.66–3.25 ft) with an overall escalator width ranging from 1.4 to 1.6 m (4.6–5.25 ft) respectively. The visual impact of the escalator should also be considered when determining its width. For example, maintaining visibility to certain key shopfrontages may be an important consideration.

The proximity of other means of vertical circulation, such as an adjacent staircase, may also be a consideration when selecting the width of escalator.

In special circumstances, escalators can be configured in a curved or part-circular arrangement. Curved escalators have been made possibly by the inventiveness of Japanese manufacturers. Although

Figure 10.57 Curved escalators at Nordstrum, San Francisco, USA (1990). *(Source: Peter Coleman)*

curved mechanisms are possible, these escalators are more complicated than straight versions and are made to special order. Consequently, curved escalators are considerably more expensive than standard straight types and should only be considered in special circumstances. The Nordstrum department store in San Francisco installed one of the first curved escalator arrangements in the late 1980s.

Escalator Finishes

The escalator treads are usually finished in a ribbed metal. The balustrades can be glazed or solid metal panels, with a polymer moving handrail. The supporting steel trusses to the moving mechanisms can be clad in a variety of materials including plaster and plasterboard, opaque glass, metal or stone panels. Special escalators can be built which are made to expose the working mechanism and steel truss structure, having glazed sides to make a feature of the installation.

Table 10.4 General design guidance for escalators

- The pitch of the escalator can be up to 35° where the floor-to-floor height is less than 6 m (19.5 ft)
- Where the floor-to-floor height is greater than 6 m, an escalator pitch of 30° is recommended to form a more comfortable arrangement
- Tread widths of escalators vary from a minimum of 0.6 m (2 ft) to a maximum of 1 m (3.25 ft)
- For a passenger to move past a stationary person, an escalator tread width of 1 m will be required

Travelators

Travelators (also referred to as passenger conveyors) are similar to escalators as mechanical means for transporting passengers vertically, except that they have flat floors rather than steps. As a consequence, they are arranged at a shallower pitch and are longer than escalators. As identified earlier, travelators are used where there are large numbers of customers using trolleys to transfer goods to car parking arranged at a different level to the shops. Travelators are commonly provided in shopping facilities that incorporate a large food store or hypermarket.

Travelators are preferably located close to where the trolleys are used to avoid them being wheeled about the rest of the centre. Travelators require longer linear spaces into which to fit the installation and are less flexible to position than escalators. In theory, travelators could be configured in the same variety of ways outlined for escalators. However, taking into account the greater physical requirements to accommodate them, for practical reasons travelators are usually configured in simple parallel pairs, with the up and down routes positioned side by side.

Figure 10.58 A pair of travelators span across the water feature, Blanchards Town, Dublin, Ireland (1996). *(Source: Peter Coleman)*

In multi-level arrangements, travelators can be configured in a stack of parallel pairs superimposed one upon another. This arrangement does not provide continuous up and down routes and requires passengers to return the length of the travelator before being able to join the next flight. In order to provide continuous up and down routes the travelators can be arranged in crossed pairs in the same way as escalators. However, crossed configurations of travelators result in passengers arriving at different ends of the travelator and will also involve some passenger inconvenience by their potentially having to return the length of the travelator in order to reach their destination. Individual manufacturers' details should be consulted for specific design information. For general design guidance the information in Table 10.5 can be used.

Travelators are available in a similar range of tread widths to those available for escalators. The general cladding finishes available are also similar. A noticeable difference to consider, and which influences the visual impact of a travelator, is that the supporting truss is likely to be larger as a consequence of the longer span and greater load. A plastic polymer floor option, as well as a steel ribbed floor, is also available for the conveyor floor of the travelator.

Table 10.5 General design guidance for travelators

- Travelator tread widths are available in sizes which range from 0.6 m (2 ft) to 1.05 m (3.5 ft)
- The angle of gradient is more gradual than escalators and varies depending on the speed of travel of the conveyor
- Any slope (or angle of gradient) from 0 to 8° is permitted with speeds up to 0.9 m (3 ft) per second
- Angles of gradient above 8° up to 12° are required to operate at a maximum speed of 0.75 m (2.5 ft) per second
- Angles of gradients above 12° are not recommended

Lifts

Mechanical passenger lifts or elevators will be required for use by disabled persons and those with prams and pushchairs. The same lifts will also be used for the general convenience of the shopping public. The lifts considered here are those operating between the different floor levels of public circulation space and those areas that extend to the car parking located above or below the shopping facilities. Lifts directly connected to car parking will be a significant generator of footfall and can be strategically located to help balance and distribute pedestrian footfall between different floor levels of a centre. For example, in order to reinforce a particular floor, the car park lifts can be arranged to terminate at a given floor level requiring passengers to circulate the floor before using other means of vertical circulation to move through the facilities. Lifts tend to be the primary means of vertical access from the car park to the shopping facilities, yet are a less prevalent means of vertical circulation in the shopping centre.

Where lifts extend from the shopping areas into the car parking levels, personal security will need to be carefully considered with regard to the positioning and design of the lifts. For example, it should be easy to see into the lift lobbies and hidden corners should be avoided. Visibility can be enhanced by including glazed screens and glazed vision panels in all doors. Good levels of illumination also help to achieve safe and secure lift areas.

Lifts limited to serving the public circulation spaces can either be conventional lifts located to the side of the space, or free-standing feature lifts positioned in the circulation space. Conventional lifts are more practical, accommodate more passengers and can incorporate glazed vision panels to enhance customers' feeling of security. Feature lifts within the circulation space can be extensively glazed but are less practical in that they can accommodate fewer passengers than conventional ones.

Feature lifts need to be carefully positioned to avoid obscuring shopfronts and in view of being smaller and slower to operate, invariably require supplementing with conventional lifts. Feature lifts were traditionally fashionable in the interior focused, enclosed shopping centres of the late twentieth century. More recently, however, the value of feature lifts is increasingly being questioned in favour of more practical lift solutions. Furthermore, with more urban based schemes being considered, feature lifts are likely to be inappropriate.

Figure 10.60 Conventional lifts with glass doors, The Bullring, Birmingham, UK (2003). *(Source: James Cheung)*

Lift motor rooms will be required and will need to be incorporated into the layout. The location and amount of space will depend upon the type of lift installation being used. For example, feature lifts are usually hydraulically driven, where the location of the motor room is more flexible and can be less specifically positioned relative to the lift. Conventional lifts, which are driven by electric motors (with cables and running gear), generally require the motor room to be located directly above the lift. Each lift installation is individually designed and manufacturers should be referred to for each particular case.

Figure 10.59 Square lift in a circular glazed enclosure in the enclosed mall, Smaralind, Reykjavik, Iceland (2001). *(Source: David Barbour/BDP)*

Lifts are usually configured in pairs, to allow the facility to be maintained in the event of a break-down. Lift installations should be designed with the mechanical consultants who will advise on the number and size of lifts required for the project. Their advice will take into account the number of passengers and the appropriate number and size of lifts in order to achieve convenient waiting times.

The finishes inside the lift car will need to be robust and compatible with those used in the public circulation space. Call button markings should be easily understood and coordinated with the signage and way-finding terminology for the shopping centre and, where appropriate, the car parking.

Customer Care Facilities

Customer care facilities, being a facility related to personal hygiene or a personal service, are likely to have a significant influence upon the customers'

memory of a particular centre. In a competitive world and where customers invariably have a choice, the quantity and quality of customer care facilities must not be underestimated. High quality restaurants in major cities have recognised the importance of attention to detail in toilet areas and the effect this has on creating a positive memorable experience. Similar attention to detail in all areas of the shopping experience are required in order to attract, and retain, regular customers to a shopping centre. This attention to detail applies to the consideration of the customer care facilities – the public toilets, baby change, crèche, facilities to assist the mobility impaired visitor and the management facilities with interface with the public.

Public Toilets

The location of public toilets needs to be carefully balanced by being readily accessible, without taking up valuable shopfrontages. Remote cheap space is also inappropriate. Toilets should be conveniently located and can be adjacent to catering

Figure 10.61 Public toilets conveniently located immediately off the public space, The Bullring, Birmingham, UK. *(Source: Amalgam)*

facilities or adjacent to an entranceway. The latter location is convenient for customers arriving or departing.

The number of public toilets should be generous and above the minimum regulation standard. Regulatory standards establish the minimum number of toilets and hand basins to be provided in female toilets and the number of toilets, urinals and hand basins for male toilets. With the majority of shopping being undertaken by women, provision above the minimum standard is particularly relevant to female toilet facilities. Research by the British Council of Shopping Centres has shown that adequate high quality toilets are high on the priority list of shopping centre customers (British Council of Shopping Centres, 2000, p. 29).

Both male and female toilets should include separate cubicles for disabled persons in each of the toilet areas provided. Alternatively, separate disabled toilets can be provided, which have the advantage of allowing a carer of a different sex to assist the disabled person. Baby changing facilities should also be included in both male and female toilet areas. Separate mother and baby rooms can be provided adjacent to the toilets, either as an additional or alternative facility to those included in the main toilets.

A recent trend in providing more easily accessible public toilets has been the adoption of open frontages which lead directly from the public circulation areas. These open entranceways, which are easy to enter, utilise carefully placed privacy screens and wider circulation spaces to avoid the need for traditional separating doors and lobbies.

Toilets are used extensively and should be finished with durable and easily maintained materials. Walls should preferably be finished with easily cleanable surfaces, such as tiling or laminate panels. Walls concealing pipework and other sanitary

Figure 10.63 Contemporary and robust male toilets, The Bullring, Birmingham, UK. *(Source: Amalgam)*

Figure 10.64 Glass shelf wash hand basin, The Bullring, Birmingham, UK. *(Source: Amalgam)*

Figure 10.62 Easy access from the open fronted entrance to the toilets, The Bullring, Birmingham, UK. *(Source: Amalgam)*

plumbing services will require removable access panels for maintenance. Modular panel systems can be used or access panels can be provided in tiled finishes. If modular systems are used, then sanitary ware will need to be planned to suit the modular dimensions. Floors can be finished in a variety of water-resistant finishes, which range from natural stone, ceramic and polymer tiles to *in situ* latex polymer floors. The cubicles can be formed from proprietary systems with formica or similar laminate finishes. The cubicle screens should preferably extend full height from floor to ceiling for privacy and require suitable upstands to allow for floor cleaning.

Multiple wash basins are best set into worktops rather than in free-standing arrangements. Worktops should be robust and of the best affordable quality. Natural stone is the most durable and expensive solution with pre-formed laminate being a more affordable and commonly used worktop solution. Hardwood can also be used with multiple vitreous hand basins, and stainless steel can be used to form a common integrated wash bench where this approach is acceptable.

Along with the worktops and hand basins, the taps should be robust and single mixer taps are preferable. Automatic water sensors can be used to dispense water and save on water consumption. Attention will also need to be given to the soap dispensers, hand dryers and waste bins to provide a neat integrated solution. Soap dispensers, if integrated, should allow for easy replenishment. Plenty of hand dryers should be provided with a combination of hot air and hand towels being the best arrangement. The use of linen or paper towels will need to be determined with the shopping centre management, and if paper towels are adopted, waste storage bins will need to be considered. The hand drying facilities should be placed to avoid obstructing circulation movement. Mirrors above the hand basins are sufficient for grooming in the male toilets, but a separate grooming area and mirror may be considered for the female toilets.

The best designed toilet areas can quickly deteriorate if they are not regularly maintained as intended. It is therefore imperative that all the toilet design proposals and details are understood and the maintenance requirements accepted by the centre management before finalising the details.

Crèches

Providing a crèche facility enables parents with young children to enjoy a period of uninhibited shopping, knowing their children are being entertained in a secure place of care. Providing a crèche is appropriate for larger shopping centres that serve a regional or sub-regional role, in particular those that are located in a catchment area with a young age profile. Crèche facilities are usually operated by independent specialist companies who pay a subsidised rent for the space and charge to look after the children. These companies have to be registered and are subject to compliance with rules enforced by regular inspection.

Figure 10.65 Children's entertainment at a science centre, Canal Walk, Century City, Cape Town, SA (2001). *(Source: Peter Coleman)*

The accommodation for a crèche should be conveniently located in a position which is close to the public circulation space, but which does not occupy prime retail space. Ideally it should be located near an entranceway, which could be en route from a main car park or from a public transport interchange. Positioning in this way will allow parents the convenience of leaving children with the carers on arrival and collecting on departure. Crèche facilities should not be located in the centre of the layout as this would involve parents having to search out the facility and then doubling back to find certain shops.

The ideal size for a crèche, according to the British Council of Shopping Centres (BCSC) is one accommodating up to 40 children. With additional staff facilities, storage and toilets, an area of approximately 175 m^2 (1900 ft^2) is required (British Council of Shopping Centres, 2000, p. 30).

The BCSC Guide also gives the floor space requirements for different ages of children. This information will be useful where the operator has details of the specific age ranges of children likely to be provided for. As an approximate guide for space planning purposes, a figure of 3 m² (32 ft²) per child can be used.

Shopmobility

Shopmobility is a term used for the facilities that assist access to a shopping centre or town centre for the mobility impaired visitor. Shopmobility facilities are commonly provided in new large shopping developments and those in town centre locations often serve the larger community by assisting with access to the remainder of the town centre. These facilities should be located close to a main point of arrival, commonly adjacent to a principal car park. If the shopmobility is serving the remainder of the town centre as well as the new centre, particular attention will need to be given as to how visitors will access both locations. Shopmobility facilities should be located adjacent to the main lifts if the parking is at a different level from the shops or town centre. The facility should also be located so that it is clearly evident on arrival and is directly accessible without having to experience long traffic queues.

Figure 10.66 Shopmobility reception in the entranceway from the car park into the Centre, Touchwood, Solihull, UK (2001). *(Source: Peter Coleman)*

Shopmobility facilities consist of a variety of accommodation to store, maintain and distribute access equipment for the mobility impaired visitor. The accommodation includes a public reception area and staff office for the administration of the facility; a practice space for user familiarisation; a storage area for the equipment; and a maintenance area. The bulk of the accommodation is required for storage of the electrically driven wheelchairs, the charging facilities, ordinary wheelchairs and other general

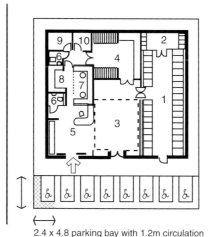

1. Electric Vehicle Room
   Battery powered scooters and
   chairs 1500 x 800 unit size
2. Battery Room
3. Practice Area
4. Folded wheelchairs and workshop
5. Reception
6. Disabled toilet facilities
7. Office
8. Kitchenette
9. Interview Room
10. Storage or services room

2.4 x 4.8 parking bay with 1.2m circulation
to give 3.6 v 6.0m parking bay for disabled person(s)

Figure 10.67 Plan layout showing typical shopmobility facilities – accommodating space to greet visitors, make demonstrations, store the chairs and electric vehicles and room for maintenance. *(Source: BDP)*

walking aids, as well as space for maintenance. The accommodation should be arranged on one level with openings and circulation space sized sufficiently to allow convenient access for these customers. The floor, wall and door finishes up to a height of 900 mm (3 ft) should be sufficiently robust to allow for contact with the various pieces of equipment. It is also beneficial if the shopmobility facility can be planned with easy access to some toilet facilities. If this is not possible, then separate toilet facilities will also be required in this accommodation.

Other Facilities (Centre Management)

Although the management suite's prime purpose is to accommodate the administrative and operational management functions of the shopping centre, it also provides an important interface between the shopping centre and the public by providing customer care and first aid facilities. A part of the management suite is therefore used to provide public facilities for dealing with any problem that the customer may experience. The management suite has to balance the requirements of being publicly accessible, while retaining the operational aspects in a discreet way. It should be inviting to the public, located in a readily accessible location and clearly signposted if not located adjacent to a main public circulation space. The route to the management suite should be appropriately finished and well lit.

Figure 10.68 Management suite waiting area, The Bullring, Birmingham, UK (2003). *(Source: James Cheung)*

providing a separate satellite information kiosk or desk to deal with general queries. Information kiosks provide a personal and more convenient way of informing customers about retailers and events in the centre and can also provide more general information about the local vicinity outside the centre. The information desk can also help to direct customers with more serious problems, or those needing care, to the management suite. Satellite information desks do not altogether replace the customer care role provided by the management suite, but reduce the number of customers needing to find their way to there by dealing with the simple everyday issues.

Information desks should be located centrally in the public circulation space, in positions that are obvious from the entranceways. The desk itself is often manned by more than one person and takes the form of a hotel reception desk with a privacy screen, counter and separate worktop. The information desk can take the form of an island unit or be located to one side of the circulation space.

To accommodate the public interface, the management suite should have a well finished and furnished reception area where people can wait and be dealt with separately. This part of the suite should be separate and independent from the operational and administrative area, although the reception area can be shared. (The operational and administrative areas of the management suite are examined in a subsequent Chapter.)

Some of the larger centres try to avoid the duality of the role performed by the management suite by

Car Parking

Characteristics

Appropriate amounts of good quality car parking are an essential ingredient in forming a successful shopping centre. This is the case, despite the government directing planning policy away from out-of-town shopping to dissuade car usage and encouraging alternative means of access to town centre shopping facilities. A significant proportion of customers will continue to use their cars as the preferred means of access when visiting a shopping centre, be it located in a town centre or elsewhere.

In light of this, the quantity, quality, location and areas used for car parking are important design considerations. Customers will vote with their feet and use an alternative shopping venue if it has better and easier parking facilities. Problems not resolved in the design which result in queuing for a parking space, not being able easily to relocate a car, or long delays when exiting a car park, are all sufficient to deter a customer from re-using a shopping centre and likely to affect its long-term success.

In addition to these examples affecting the success of a centre, the quantity and quality of car parking will also influence the decision of key retailers and anchor stores as to whether to occupy premises in a particular shopping centre. The influence of car parking provision on retailers' decisions, illustrates the direct effect of car parking upon the commercial

Figure 10.69 A satellite information desk located in the mall, Lakeside, Thurrock, Essex, UK (2004). *(Source: Capital Shopping Centres)*

success of the shopping centre. (The importance of anchor stores in the layout of shopping centres has been identified in earlier Chapters.)

Having identified the fundamental importance of car parking to the success of a shopping centre, it is also important to review the different qualities that are inherent to shopping centre car parking and which differentiate this type of car parking from office or industrial car parks.

The car park spaces in shopping centres are frequently used by more than one visitor each day. Each space can be used by as many as five different cars per day. Throughout its daily operation, there will be a flow of incoming and outgoing customers. Shopping centre car park users are also generally less familiar with the car park arrangement. At best, frequent users will use the facility for relatively short stays and may have to use different parts of the car park as spaces cannot be reserved. At worst, visitors will be first time or irregular users of the car park and will be completely unfamiliar with the arrangement and layout.

It is important for designers of car parks to understand these characteristics of a typical shopping centre car park user, in order to understand the requirement for the layout to be simple, comprehensible and to provide good circulation. In addition to these characteristics of the typical user, many users will also be time-pressured families or mothers with young children. This further emphasises the requirement for the parking to be user-friendly and for the pedestrian access to and from the centre to be direct and secure.

The organisation and type of car parking to be adopted will be determined by a variety of factors:

■ the amount of available land in a vicinity
■ the size of site
■ the value of land
■ the type of site and sensitivity of the location.

The different types of car park and where they are most appropriately used are outlined below.

Surface Car Parking

The use of surface car parking immediately adjacent to a shopping centre is the most economical in

Figure 10.70 Semi-mature planting softens and scales large surface car park areas, White Rose, Leeds, UK (1997). *(Source: Roger Ball/Image Photo Ltd)*

construction terms and is well liked by customers. This type of parking will utilise a substantial amount of land and requires a site sufficiently large to allow for it. Where large numbers of cars are accommodated, the effect will be to create a vast sea of cars in front of the centre, which can be unsightly and result in some of the parking being so remote it has unacceptable travel distances to the centre. This arrangement can be suitable in out-of-town locations, where the visual issue can be alleviated by the inclusion of careful landscaping. Surface car parking is unlikely to be appropriate in high value or sensitive town centre locations. In summary, this type of parking can be an economical solution in some locations, but is unlikely to be an appropriate urban solution.

Over the Centre Parking

Over the centre, or rooftop parking, can be effective where land availability is an issue. When restricted to a single level the number of spaces may be restricted once allowance is made for rooftop glazing and tenants' plant. It may be necessary to consider additional decks of parking above the roof or other means of parking to supplement the provision. Access to the rooftop is likely to require long ramps which will require careful location and consideration to avoid the ramp becoming visually obtrusive. Multi-level decks above the shopping centre will impose a discipline over the structural grid to suit the parking module, if transfer structures are to be avoided. Over the centre parking can be acceptable in some town centre locations, but is unlikely to be appropriate in sensitive

Figure 10.71 Roof top car parking arranged around the mall roof light in a robust urban environment, Villa Arena, Amsterdam, The Netherlands (2001). *(Source: Benthem Cornwel)*

locations or locations which are overlooked. Light pollution from car headlights and space lighting will need to be carefully considered in order to avoid environmental problems.

Basement Parking

Below ground level basement car parking is the most expensive and complex parking solution and should only be considered when all other types of solution have been explored and found to be inappropriate. A single parking space in a basement car park can cost three times the price per space of those provided in an above ground, stacked car park. Basement car parking can be an appropriate way of providing parking in a discreet way in sensitive, historic locations or where land values are extremely high and other uses are more viable above ground.

This type of parking will need to be executed to a high standard and will need to incorporate the additional technical requirements of retaining structures and mechanical ventilation in order to encourage customers to use it. Lighting levels will need to be high throughout and good visibility should be achieved across the car park in all directions. As well as the structure being restrained in order to achieve good visibility across the car park, a further discipline will be imposed on the car park structure in order for it to relate to the shop module and structural grid above.

The interrelationship between the structural grid of the car park and the shops above will also impose less flexibility on available choices in both areas and will restrict the available grids for the shops. A grid will need to be chosen which works for the shop units and also relates to a car parking module, in order to avoid the need for a transfer structure between the shop and parking levels.

A structural grid of 7.5 m (24.3 ft) can be used if the corresponding grid in the car park is a clear span arrangement of 15.8–16 m (51.3–52 ft). This arrangement avoids the columns projecting midway into the parking stalls. However, a 7.8 m grid (25.3 ft), or preferably a 7.8 × 9 m (25.3 × 29.25 ft) grid, is a more flexible one to be adopted, as the former will work with the car park layout in both directions where clear spans cannot be achieved. A commonly adopted grid with basement car parking arranged below shop units is 8 × 8 m (26 × 26 ft). These larger grids allow three parking spaces per grid and accommodate a reasonably sized structural column sitting within the parking stalls without unduly obstructing car manoeuvres.

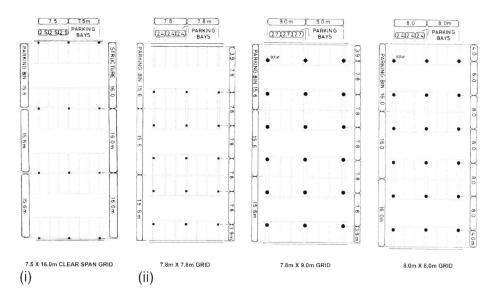

Figure 10.72 Basement parking and structural arrangements: (i) clear span 7.5×16 m grid; (ii) intermediary columns in a variety of grids – 7.8×7.8 m, 7.8×9.0 m, 8.0×8.0 m. *(Source: Peter Coleman)*

Basement car parks should be arranged in simple plan arrangements to assist with the customers' orientation and understanding. Circulation patterns for car movement should be straightforward, with the pedestrian access points leading up to the shopping centre being clearly visible across the car park. The optimum number of basement parking levels is two to three. Additional levels tend not be used and are unpopular with the shopping public. Where basement servicing is used, it is convenient to fit two parking levels within the same height of basement excavation. Careful planning can usually allow the

mechanical ventilation to be achieved from each side of the car park, except for the widest of plan arrangements, thereby avoiding the need for additional floor-to-floor heights to accommodate large ventilation ductwork. Access ramps down to the car park and between levels will need to be planned into the layout. Ramps should be kept within a maximum gradient of 1 in 10.

Decked Parking

Car parking arranged on horizontal decks which are stacked one above another are referred to as multi-storey decked car parks (sometimes called parking garages). Multi-storey decked car parks can be free standing, arranged above the shopping accommodation, or organised in a combination of these two. Multi-storey decked car parks (multi-storey car parks) are commonly found in shopping centre developments and, because of customer familiarity with this format, have become a generally accepted parking format. Multi-storey car parks have several advantages:

- the arrangement makes good use of available land
- in free-standing blocks they do not impose any restrictions on the shopping centre grid
- more of the car parking is made accessible to the shopping centre
- the arrangement can be used to help feed the shopping centre upper ground floor levels and distribute even footfall to an upper level.

Figure 10.73 Simple, well lit and easy to use basement car park beneath the John Lewis store, Kingston, UK. *(Source: Peter Coleman)*

Figure 10.74 An exposed steel frame, car park, Centre West, East Kilbride, Glasgow, UK (2003). (*Source: David Barbour/BDP*)

Figure 10.75 Detail of exposed steel frame and balustrade, Centre West, East Kilbride, Glasgow, UK (2003). (*Source: BDP/David Barbour*)

The maximum number of levels that customers will readily circulate in multi-storey car parks is generally considered to be five to six. While additional levels can be built, these upper levels will remain unused except, perhaps, for the busiest peak periods. The large amount of under-used parking above the sixth level makes building taller arrangements uneconomical. In some sensitive town centre locations it may not be possible even to build a six-level multi-storey car park, as the height may be constrained by the heights of the surrounding buildings.

In town centre locations, multi-storey decked car parks will need to be considered in relation to the scale of their surroundings and designed accordingly. The issue of scaling blank façades, associated with the simple functional expression of car parks, may need to be addressed in urban and sensitive locations. Animating the façades and providing scale to the car park can be achieved by either

Figure 10.76 A well considered urban car park enclosed by metal louvres, Southside, Wandsworth, London, UK (2004). *(Source: Peter Coleman)*

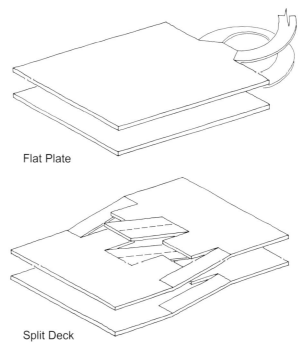

Flat Plate

Split Deck

Figure 10.77 The principle types of decked parking: flat plate and split deck car parks. *(Source: Peter Coleman)*

introducing other uses at the lower levels, such as showrooms or shops, or by lining the entire façade with another building use into a particular street frontage. These other uses can provide accommodation for residential or office space, bringing town centre living and working opportunities respectively.

There are several different formats of multi-storey decked car parks which are outlined below.

Flat Plate Multi-Storey Car Parks

Flat plate multi-storey car parks are formed from a stacked arrangement of two or more parking bins arranged in parallel on a single level. Parking bins are formed by car parking stalls arranged at 90° on either side of the car circulation driveway. Arranging several parking bins together on a single level has the advantage of facilitating good visibility, assisting the shopping centre customer in seeking out an available parking space in unfamiliar surroundings. The stalls and driveway arrangements of the parking bin are discussed in more detail under parking arrangements below. The structural arrangement of the car park across the parking bin can completely

correspond with the parking layout in a clear span, or adopt a separate structural layout which coordinates with the parking.

A separate independent structural arrangement will involve intermediary columns which can be organised in a variety of configurations. In this format the

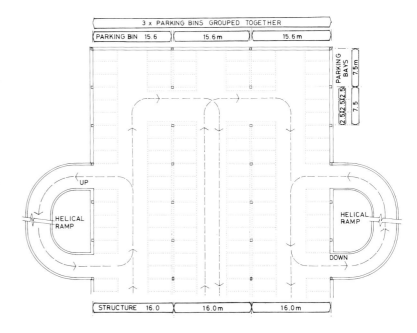

Figure 10.78 Flat plate multi-storey car park with clear span structure (7.5 × 16.0 m grid) with grouped parking bins and separate 'up' and 'down' helical ramps. *(Source: Peter Coleman)*

parking and searching circulation is kept separate from the inter-connecting ramps between each level. The separation of the parking bin from the ramps improves the circulation as well as promoting good visibility. The ramps are usually located outside the parking bin and adopt a helical form at the end of the parking bin, or are arranged parallel to one side of the parking bin.

To assist the circulation flow of flat plate car parks, two separate ramps are usually provided for cars moving upwards in a slow search pattern and for cars moving down in a fast exit pattern. The separate helical ramps are sometimes also referred to as 'D' ramps. An alternative ramp arrangement is to use long straight ramps at the ends or integrally to the car park. However, bearing in mind typical floor-to-floor height of 3 m (9.8 ft), this will require a minimum ramp length of 30 m (98.5 ft) which would only suit a large flat plate car park with three or more parking bins. In the layout of the car park it is important to plan for a clear continuous exit route to allow the car park to clear quickly.

Although helical ramps are usually separated into independent up and down ramps, they can be combined to form a single large drum. Helical ramps can be unsightly and require careful location and treatment of the external form. In some sensitive urban locations, helical ramp forms may be difficult to integrate with their surroundings. The larger form of a combined drum may therefore be unsuitable for some site contexts.

Split Deck Car Parks

Flat plate multi-storey car parks are user-friendly and efficient car park formats, but may prove to be unacceptable in certain sensitive locations. An alternative format of multi-storey car park is a split deck arrangement, which has integral ramps.

This format arranges the next deck of the car park at the half-floor level of the adjacent car deck and utilises integral ramps to connect between the half-floors. The parking bin is used for both general circulation as well as being integral with the vertical movement of the circulating vehicles. This arrangement is efficient in terms of land usage, but the visibility across the car park is constrained by the half-level configuration and is therefore not as user-friendly for the typical, unfamiliar shopping centre car park user. The gradient and length of ramp that can be accommodated along the length of two parking stalls will control the floor-to-floor height which is generally 2.75–3.0 m (9–9.8 ft) maximum. With the

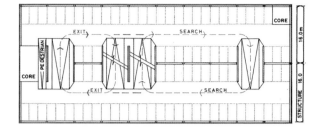

Figure 10.79 Split deck car park: with separate search and fast exit loop ramps. *(Source: Peter Coleman)*

visibility across the car park already constrained by the half-deck configuration, it is preferable to adopt a clear span structure across each parking bin of 15.6–16 m (51.2–52.5 ft) rather than use intermediary columns.

The larger span will invariably require a deeper structure. This factor will need to be balanced with achieving a minimum headroom clearance of 2.1 m (6.9 ft) and with a maximum floor-to-floor height of 3 m (9.8 ft) for the ramps to remain workable. Whichever solution is adopted will involve the end of the ramps extending into the car circulation driveway in order to achieve a suitable gradient.

The ramp configuration and positioning will be critical to the layout of the split deck multi-storey car park format. The ramp will need to be arranged to achieve a balance between providing a search pattern with visibility to the extremes of the car park, and maintaining a fast exit route. It is important that the cars which are exiting have a direct circulation route which does not involve driving the length of the parking bin and that these vehicles have priority over vehicles searching for a space. The priority of the exiting vehicles will help to avoid the car park coming to a standstill. The ramps between each half-level are usually arranged vertically above each other and provide separate ramps for vehicles involved in the upward search, from those involved in the downward exit route.

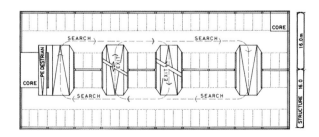

Figure 10.80 Split deck car park: with separate fast exit loop ramps integrated within the overall search pattern. *(Source: Peter Coleman)*

In order to achieve this separation of the ramps it is usual for each intermediary floor in these car parks to have four ramps. The integral ramps involve the loss of parking spaces and require an efficient solution to be adopted in order to maximise the number of parking spaces. The minimum ramp width should not be less than the width of two car spaces, i.e. $2 \times 2.5 \, \text{m}$, which is 5 m overall. This is made up of 3 m for the car and 1 m for kerb and structure each side.

Split deck car parks with the integration of vertical ramps, avoid unsightly external ramps of the flat plate format and are therefore likely to be more acceptable in sensitive urban locations.

Other Arrangements

These alternative car park formats are based on folding plate or continuous ramp forms, where the parking bin is continuously ramped upwards in a dogleg or spiral configuration. In these arrangements the circulation space between the parking stalls is used for circulating, parking manoeuvres, searching, moving up and exiting and has a tendency to become congested with all the various car manoeuvres taking place simultaneously. For example, the two-way driveway between the parking stalls can become blocked by cars waiting or manoeuvring in and out of the stalls. In addition to the congestion that can occur, the parking area is on a continuous slope. Parking on a ramped surface can be problematic with pushchairs, wheelchairs and trolleys, all commonly used by shopping centre customers. Continuous ramp formats of car park are, for reasons of poor circulation, not user-friendly or suited to the unfamiliar customer and are not commonly used or accepted formats for shopping centre car parks.

Having examined the different general formats of car park arrangements for shopping centres the following examines the considerations involved in the design of multi-storey car parks.

Design Considerations

Car Park Capacity

The optimum size for a car park will depend on the location and the capacity of the surrounding road network and its ability to accommodate the number of car spaces being proposed. This calculation is usually assessed with the assistance of a specialist traffic engineer. Entry and exit points should be on to the same roadway to assist the customers' orientation and to allow them to retrace their route of arrival on departure. This may not always be possible and will be dependent on the road capacity as checked by the traffic engineer. It should also be noted that shopping centre car parks will require multiple entrance and exit lanes to each entry and exit. The number of lanes leading to each point will be determined by the method of payment, which is discussed later.

Requirements for accommodating more than 1000 car parking spaces should generally be arranged with more than one entry and exit point on to the road network. (For example, a 4000 space car park would require four separate entrances and exits and should ideally be organised into four identifiable modules of car parking. Alternatively the car parking could be organised into four separate car parks.) Futhermore, these large car parks will require electronic signage and capacity counting to inform the customer of where there are available

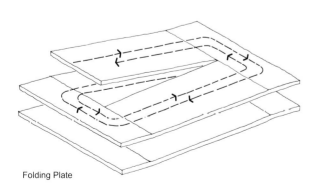

Folding Plate

Figure 10.81 Other types of multi-storey car park – folding plate layout. *(Source: Peter Coleman)*

Figure 10.82 A large car park can be scaled by using the cores, entranceways and ramps as illustrated by the north car park, Brent Cross, London, UK (1996). *(Source: James Cheung)*

spaces. These electronic signage and capacity counting systems are sometimes integrated into larger similar systems for a town centre and are referred to as vehicle management systems (VMS).

Bay Dimensions

Earlier descriptions have identified the general configuration of parking bins as commonly being formed from two rows of parking bays arranged at 90° to a circulation driveway. The dimensions of the parking bays and driveway are examined in more detail here.

The minimum recommended standard for a parking bay or stall in a multi-storey car park is 2.4 m wide by 4.8 m long (7.9 × 15.7 ft) with a two-way circulation space or driveway 6 m (19.7 ft) wide. The combined arrangement of parking bays and driveway produces a parking bin of 15.6 m (51.2 ft) overall width. Ideally, the parking bin should be 16 m (55.5 ft). With European cars generally increasing in size and a growing preference for sports utility vehicles (SUVs), people carriers and four-wheel drive off-road vehicles, larger parking bays of 2.5–2.6 m wide may be more appropriate standards.

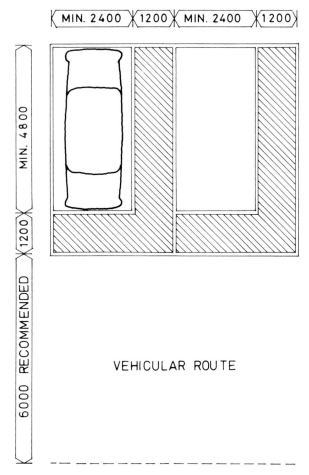

Figure 10.84 Disabled parking bay standards. Hatching shows access zone both between and at the end of designated parking bays. (Dimensions to centre line of road markings.) *(Source: Peter Coleman)*

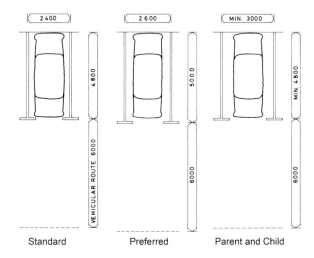

Figure 10.83 Head-on parking bays standards: (i) standard parking bay; (ii) preferred parking bay; (iii) parent and child bay. (Dimensions to centre line of road markings.) *(Source: Peter Coleman)*

Disabled parking bays are required to be wider to accommodate wheelchair users and a minimum width of 3.5 m (11.5 ft) is recommended. In the UK, a minimum number of disabled parking spaces is required which represents 4 per cent of the total number of parking spaces plus an additional four spaces.

A similar ratio of 4 per cent of the total number of parking spaces is also recommended for larger sized parking bays for parent-and-child spaces. These spaces should be 3–3.5 m (9.8–11.5 ft) wide.

For early space planning purposes an allowance for 8 per cent of the total number of parking spaces should be used for disabled and parent-and-child spaces. The requirement for a proportion of parking bays to be larger than the minimum recommended standard will reduce the net total of spaces. The disabled and parent-and-child spaces should be located close to the pedestrian access points of the shopping facilities.

Ramps

These are the means by which the cars transfer from one level of a multi-storey car park to another. The type of ramp is dependent on the format of the car park and was generally identified above. For an efficient and user-friendly car park, the ramps should be separate from the parking bays and separate ramps should be provided for the search and exit routes, which correspond to the upward and downward circulating cars respectively. Flat plate car parks have separate helical shaped D ramps and, sometimes, separate spiral shaped exit ramps. Split deck car parks have integral straight ramps between the half-levels. Straight ramps are sometimes used in flat plate car parks where the dimensions are large enough. Straight ramps should be 3.6 m (11.8 ft) wide between structure with a clear road width between kerbs of 3.0 m (9.8 ft). Spiral ramps should have a preferred minimum radius to the outside of the road of 12 m (39.33 ft) with an additional allowance for kerbs. Ramp lengths will depend on floor-to-floor height, but should not exceed a gradient of 1 in 10.

Designers in the UK should refer to the design guidance in the publication 'Design Recommendations for Multi-Storey and Underground Car Parks' (The Institution of Structural Engineers, 2002).

Pedestrian Circulation

These routes lead from the parking bays to the cores or entranceways into the shopping centre. The public circulation should be simply laid out and easy for customers to understand. The route should be clearly identified by separate coloured or treated surfaces from those used on the vehicle driveways. In split-level car parks, separate pedestrian ramps should lead to the core areas (where the lifts do not provide direct access to each half-level).

Figure 10.85 A clearly identified pedestrian route helps to provide a user-friendly car park. *(Source: David Barbour)*

Vertical Circulation

Multi-storey car parks require well finished lifts and stairs to connect the different levels of the car park directly to the shopping centre, or to street level where the car parks are separate buildings. The vertical circulation areas or cores should be easily seen from within the car park and visible from outside when located on the façade of the building. Visibility into the core area discourages unsocial behaviour and enhances customer security. Glazed screens should be considered between the parking area and the public lobby of the core. When considering glazed screens, care will need to be taken to achieve the appropriate levels of fire compartmentation and to provide safe escape routes.

Figure 10.86 Glazed entranceways from the car park encourage surveillance, Centre West, East Kilbride, Scotland, UK (2003). *(Source: David Barbour)*

Considerable care and attention to detail should be given to these areas as they represent important points of arrival to the primary destination. They are often the first and last impression of a shopping centre and should be finished and lit to a standard comparable to the main shopping centre's pedestrian circulation spaces. These entrance cores act as gateways to the shopping facilities and town centres and should be designed to reflect the significance of this role. The entrance cores to the car parks should re-establish some of the traditional excitement of transport termini and express the importance of this preferred mode of transport.

Lighting

Because of their size, multi-storey car parks will need to be lit artificially. This should balance the requirements of providing a safe and secure internal environment and avoiding the generation of external light pollution. The British Council of Shopping Centres (BCSC, 2000) recommends a minimum level of illumination of 150–200 lux which is distributed evenly across the car park avoiding any dark spots. This level of illumination is a minimum standard and should be exceeded wherever possible. The guide also recommends that the lighting levels be increased to the pedestrian circulation routes, inside the stair and lift cores and at the entranceways into the shopping centre. Care should be taken with the selection and location of light fittings to ensure good distribution of light and to prevent glare. The soffits of the car park decks can be painted to improve their appearance and increase the light reflection of the interior.

Signage

The signage referred to here concerns pedestrian way-finding which is required to work in the two directions of arriving and departing by car. It must clearly guide the customer from the car parking to the destination of the shopping centre, and back again. The most effective symbols to be used in way-finding signage are primary elements which include words, numerals, letters and colours. Symbols are sometimes also used in signage to add personality to the place, but can be misinterpreted and should be used carefully. Location and legibility of the signage are other important considerations and they need to be both strategically and locally positioned.

The extent of information to be conveyed in the signage depends upon the size and complexity of the car park arrangement. For example, in large complex arrangements which involve several car parks, the signage may have to identify information such as:

- the area of the shopping centre   West Street
- the car park identification   Car Park A
- the car park level   Level 1
- the zone of the car park   Yellow zone.

Figure 10.87 Separate layers of graphic information help to identify car park areas. *(Source: David Barbour)*

The other aspect of signage is vehicular signage, which needs to be communicated to the driver when arriving and departing in the car. This signage needs to be considered off site with the highway network, within the local road network, as well as within the car park itself. Off site signage will need to be coordinated and approved by the local council and highway authority. In large shopping centres and town centres with several car parks, vehicle management systems (VMS), which include vehicle counting systems, are used to direct cars to where there are available spaces and to signal where car parks are full.

Directional signage will also be required within the car park to communicate the layout and circulation pattern of the car park. The internal vehicular signage will involve a mixture of signs and road markings. Careful consideration will be required with the placement and type of sign to ensure both searching and departing vehicles are informed. The colour and markings of the signage need to be considered together with the levels of illumination and the surface treatment of the sign locations.

Payment Systems

In the design and layout of the car park, the designer will need to consider the method of payment to be adopted and to take account of the different implications of each system. Only out-of-town shopping centres are likely not to involve a payment system for car parking. Here, free parking is used to maximise the convenience and attractiveness of the centre. Elsewhere, payment systems will involve allowing sufficient space for the payment machines, space for customers to queue and pay, and pedestrian movement to and from the payment areas. The payment system can also influence the number of vehicle lanes required at the entrance and exit and therefore should be established as early on as possible in the planning process. The implications of the different payment systems are noted in Table 10.6.

Barrier Capacity

The assessment of the barrier capacity at the entrance and exit is assisted in a shopping centre car park as peak usage times are spread more throughout the day than those of an office car park. Shopping centre peak times are mid-morning and in the period close to closing time. This means that shopping centre car parks are not required to empty completely over a short period of time.

For the purpose of calculating the required entry and exit capacity, the BCSC identifies that it is reasonable to work on the basis of accommodating 60 per

Figure 10.88 Pay-on-foot pay machine conveniently located in an entranceway. *(Source: David Barbour)*

cent of the total parking provision over the space of one hour (British Council of Shopping Centres, 2000, p. 36).

It should be noted that these figures are given for general guidance and a specialist traffic engineer will work with the architect to determine the number of entry and exit lanes required.

Based on the vehicle movements per barrier per hour identified, a pay-on-foot payment system will generally require less exit barriers than a pay-on-exit arrangement to clear a similar sized car park. For this reason pay-on-foot payment systems are more commonly accepted and operated in car parks to large shopping facilities.

Management

To overcome the public's natural reluctance to use multi-storey car parks, consideration should be given to ways of reducing the opportunity for car theft

Table 10.6 Car park payment systems

Pay and Display
This system is simple to install and does not require any barriers at the exit and entry points. Payment is made on arrival but requires a decision to be made at the outset regarding the length of stay for each visit. The system inhibits shopping activity and also requires policing and the imposition of penalties. Both of these qualities are somewhat counter-productive when the objective is to encourage customers to extend their stay and enhance their enjoyment. Pay and display systems tend to suit simple surface car park arrangements, in particular those run by local authorities. The location of the machines, the display of tariffs and pedestrian access need to be considered in the layout where this system is to be used.

Pay-on-Exit
This payment system requires ticket collection on entry and payment facilities at the exit barriers. Payment at the exit barrier can be by machine with a change-giving facility or by a manned kiosk, both of which can cause congestion and delay on leaving the car park. Congestion is a particular problem with this system at peak times. Pay-on-exit systems suit small car parks where each barrier can handle 180–200 vehicles per hour.

Pay-on-Foot
This system separates the process of payment from the barriers. The entry barriers involve the collection of a ticket and the exit barrier has a reading facility which verifies that payment has been made. The payment machines are separately located, either in the lobby of the car park which leads to the shopping centre or in the shopping centre itself. Payment is made at the machine on the return journey to the car from the shopping centre. This method allows customers the freedom to determine the length of stay and payment is made by the hour. The payment machines accept cash or credit payment and have change-giving facilities. The isolation of the payment activity allows the barriers to be swift at both entry and exit points. A single barrier can accommodate 300–330 vehicle movements per hour. This system requires that all return routes from the shopping area to the car park have conveniently located payment machines to allow payment to be made, which validates the ticket and allows the exit barrier to open. Despite the relative simplicity of this system, provision will need to be made for a separate lay-by at the exit with a payment machine or call point for customers unfamiliar with the system or for those who have forgotten to validate their ticket.

and encouraging personal security. Mention has been made earlier with regard to the inclusion of passive design measures (for example, simple layout, good visibility, careful selection of the structural grid to avoid too many large columns, high levels of illumination and the avoidance of hidden corners). Consideration is given here to the importance of active management systems such as closed-circuit television (CCTV) and patrols. CCTV coverage of the car park and lobby areas is both a deterrent and a reassuring component when the cameras are readily visible and acknowledged as being connected back to a permanently manned security office. Personal security can also be reinforced by the centre arranging for the car park to be regularly patrolled by management or specially hired security staff. Further active measures in the form of help call-points with intercoms linked to the management office and the provision of an escort-to-car service will also help to reassure customers.

A good design guide for different types of car park, which identifies the issues to be considered in the design of car parks, can be found in the 'Park Mark Safer Parking' Guidelines prepared by the Association of Chief Police Officers (ACPO, 2004).

References

Association of Chief Police Officers (ACPO) (2004). *Safer Parking Scheme Assessment Guidelines 'Park Mark Safer Parking'*. British Parking Association (BPA).

British Council of Shopping Centres (2000). *A Briefing Guide for Shopping Centre Development*. BCSC.

The Institution of Structural Engineers (2002). *Design Recommendations for Multi-Storey and Underground Car Parks*. ISE.

The Jerde Partnership (1998). *Visceral Reality*. L'Arca Edizioni, p. 9.

Figure 10.89 View looking towards the north western façade showing the main entrance and the semi-transparent screen enclosing the 600 space car park. Paradise Street Car Park, Liverpool, UK (2006). *(Source: Wilkinson Eyre Architects/James Brittain)*

ETFE covered street to new extension, Almondvale, Livingston, Scotland, UK (2008). *(Source: BDP/Miller Hare)*

11

The Elements and Features of Public Spaces

Roofs

The roof is one of the most important architectural elements that determines the very nature and character of the public space. The nature of the roof (in fact its very existence) and its influence upon the fundamental type of space were referred to earlier under 'Types of space'. Here we consider the influence of the roof upon the character of covered and enclosed spaces. In view of the increasing number of open street schemes and the requirement for protection from the rain, partial roof coverings are also examined. Before examining the different types of roof, the primary performance requirements for roofs are:

- protection from the wind and rain
- defining the space
- providing high levels of natural daylight
- controlling the amount of direct sunlight
- protecting from solar gain
- providing a reflective surface for illumination
- incorporating a means of ventilation
- where necessary, facilitating smoke ventilation.

Types of Roof

Partially Covered Spaces

This type of roof attempts to provide some weather protection and convenience from direct exposure to rain in open street based schemes. Partially covered

Figure 11.1 A steel cantilevered glazed canopy provides a degree of protection in the two level open street to upper and lower ground levels, The Beursplein, Rotterdam, The Netherlands (1996). *(Source: Peter Coleman)*

spaces include canopies which provide limited rain protection and little screening of the wind. Canopies can be supported directly from adjacent buildings or from free-standing structures in the space. Canopies can be solid, or fully glazed with transparent or opaque glass.

The following types of roof apply to covered and enclosed spaces.

Fully Glazed Roofs

These roof types are used to achieve the effect of retaining a natural sky above the space. This effect is equally appropriate for urban based covered streets and for the more traditional, enclosed shopping spaces. Glazed roofs are suitable for spaces with heating and cooling and for untreated environments. These roofs can be configured to allow natural

Figure 11.2 A glazed vaulted roof with secondary perforated metal coffers forms integrated solar shading, The Bentall Centre, Kingston, Surrey, UK (1992). *(Source: Andy Borzyskowski/BDP)*

Figure 11.3 A fully glazed roof with perforated metal shading encloses the shopping centre, The Mall, Cribbs Causeway, Bristol, UK (1998). *(Source: Charlotte Wood)*

ventilation by a variety of integral opening lights or louvres, open ends and openings elsewhere in the building. This type of roof requires an exposed structure (see Types of roof structure below).

Fully glazed roofs need to address the issue of solar gain, which is discussed separately below (see shading devices). The inherent nature of the transparent roof facilitates plenty of natural daylight during the daytime, but requires consideration to be given to the black hole effect of plain glazing and to illuminating space effectively at night-time. Glass is a hard reflective acoustic surface and will also require the consideration of the sound absorbing qualities of the other materials in the space to avoid the 'swimming pool' acoustic effect. To avoid condensation, single skin glazing will need to be carefully considered in heated and natural spaces. Open-ended, covered, glazed spaces will require wind modelling studies to check for the occurrence of uncomfortable draughts in the space and to establish the need for vertical glazing at the entrances.

Partially Glazed and Solid Roofs

A solid roof with 20 to 30 per cent of the roof area glazed will provide sufficiently high levels of natural daylight to the space, while also providing a surface for night-time illumination. Partially glazed roofs have traditionally suited enclosed spaces and schemes that are intended to have an interior character.

However, before deciding on the appropriate type of roof, it should also be borne in mind that partially glazed roofs have historically been successfully used in open-ended arcades and market buildings both of which have more natural urban qualities. There are several advantages of using this type of roof. For example, partially glazed roofs

Figure 11.4 The partially glazed and solid 'handkerchief' form to the roof above the Guild Hall, Bluewater, Greenhithe, Kent, UK (1999). *(Source: Lend Lease)*

Figure 11.5 Bands of glazing in the solid roof over the central space allow controlled natural daylight, WestQuay, Southampton, UK (2000). *(Source: Charlotte Wood)*

reduce solar gain and, if appropriately ventilated, the requirement for space cooling; so space cooling and heating are required only in the extremes of temperatures. The amount of natural daylight can also be varied to differentiate between spaces and to emphasise a greater significance, for example, recognising a punctuating node space by increasing the proportion of glazing.

Ventilation of the space can be included by the incorporation of opening lights in the glazing or openings elsewhere in the building. Where the solid parts of the roof can be lined, the roof structure can be concealed if required. Partially glazed and solid roofs are particularly appropriate where the primary structure is exposed and the secondary structure is concealed.

Solid Roofs and Glazed Clerestories

Spaces with this type of roof tend to have the character of an interior type of space and, as such, this roof type suits enclosed shopping spaces. The environmental benefits identified above for partially glazed roofs are further reinforced with solid and glazed clerestory roofs. There will, for example, be minimal solar gain and condensation to deal with, and acoustic insulation can be incorporated into the lining of the solid roof. The solid roof can also be used to assist with the indirect, reflective illumination of the space. Furthermore, the roof can be fully insulated to minimise the requirement for space cooling and heating to only the extremes of weather temperatures.

Figure 11.6 Clerestory glazing in the Poplar Arcade, Touchwood, Solihull, UK (2001). *(Source: Peter Coleman)*

Figure 11.7 Varying clerestory glazing from a monopitched roof, Flat Iron Crossing, Broomfield, Colorado, USA (2000). *(Source: Callison/Chris Eden)*

Ventilation and smoke ventilation can be readily incorporated by the inclusion of louvres in the vertical clerestory. The louvres will need to be glazed to retain natural daylighting and electronically operated to facilitate both natural and smoke ventilation. Additional powered smoke ventilation openings may also need to be incorporated. A drawback of this type of roof is its greater reliance on artificial lighting. The nature of the roof lining is also less readily disposed to exposing the roof structure, although the primary structure can be more easily exposed if required.

Types of Roof Structure

The roof structure can be exposed and expressed as an integral part of the design of the space, or remain hidden and concealed behind a secondary lining. Exposed roof structures can be internal or external to

Figure 11.8 An external steel structure has been adopted for the 'skylid' glazed roof, The Bullring, Birmingham, UK (2003). *(Source: Michael Betts/Hammerson)*

the space. An interesting example of an exposed external roof structure is the 'skylid' glazed roof to the new Bullring, Birmingham. This roof has a structure-free interior, with the glazing extending between the internal façades, formed by structural glazing supported directly from the primary external steel trusses.

Fully glazed roofs or other roofs where the structure is exposed, require all aspects of the structure to be considered, including any secondary structural

Figure 11.9 Laminated timber structure supporting the glazed roof, Castlemall, Norwich, Norfolk, UK (1993). *(Source: Peter Coleman)*

Figure 11.10 Timber struts support a timber lined roof, Chequers, Maidstone, Kent, UK (1997). (*Source: Andy Borzyskowski/BDP*)

Roof Glazing Materials

Laminated glass should be used for all glazing that is located above a public space. Double and single glazing can be used depending on the type of space. For example, enclosed spaces with tempered environments are more likely to suit double glazing, while covered spaces with open ends will be more suited to single glazing. However, regardless of this generalisation, each case will have to be assessed on its own merits and designed to comply with the appropriate regulations in place at the time.

An interesting lightweight alternative to a traditional glass roof, which retains transparency to the sky, is an inflated polymer roof (technically referred to as an ETFE roof). This polymer roof consists of a

Figure 11.11 ETFE inflated roof over the concourse, Piccadilly Station, Manchester, UK (2002). (*Source: Peter Coleman*)

Figure 11.12 ETFE inflated roof with variable shading treatment following the roof geometry, Villa Arena, Amsterdam, The Netherlands (2001). (*Source: Benthem Cronwel*)

elements. In fully glazed roofs, it is especially important that the glazing structure and primary structure are coordinated. There can be advantages with the integration of these two elements when the glazing and roof structure are coordinated by a single specialist sub-contractor. The careful integration and minimalist solution of the Bullring's skylid roof is an example of a single company being responsible for the roof structure and glazing over the public spaces. Primary structures can be made of either steel or timber, the selection being determined by the required aesthetic for the space.

In addition to the structure supporting the enclosing skin and any internal linings above the public spaces, the following will also need to be accommodated:

- space lighting
- event lighting gantries
- any heating and cooling installations
- fixings for decorations and banners
- access for cleaning
- access for roof maintenance and replacement of light fittings.

double skin construction which is constantly inflated to form a convex cushion panel supported between a metal structure. The polymer skin can incorporate reflective layers to improve the thermal and reflective internal qualities of the roof. Care will need to be taken when integrating the air supply hose which feeds each inflated panel. Opening lights and louvres can be included in specific customised glazed panels within the overall structure.

Shading Devices

The simplest shading can be achieved by integrating reflective filters and insulating film into the laminated make up of the glass. Some of these reflective filters colour the glass and can detract from the inherent natural transparency of the glass. Particular care will therefore need to be taken in selecting the laminate make up, to ensure the intended effect of the glass is maintained. Glass can also incorporate a seraphic film in its manufacture, which can be plain in varying degrees of opacity, or incorporate decorative motifs – to help reduce solar gain and improve the internal reflective quality for night-time illumination.

However, it may not always be possible to achieve acceptable internal conditions by the use of integral laminating films. In these circumstances it may be necessary to provide additional shading by the application of external or internal screening. External shading is more effective as it prevents heat from reaching the space. External louvres can be an effective means of preventing solar gain, but will complicate the external cleaning of the glass. Internal shading can also reduce solar gain (if not preventing direct heat gain) and can be provided by blinds, louvres and perforated metal panels. Blinds need to be automated to allow for the ongoing intermittent benefit of natural daylight. Automated blinds can become problematic and should be very carefully specified. Fixed internal louvres are effective, but can be inflexible when required to respond to differing daylighting conditions.

Figure 11.13 Seraphic shading treatment to the glazed roof, Centre West, East Kilbride, Scotland, UK (2003). *(Source: David Barbour/BDP)*

Figure 11.14 External fabric blinds shade the glass roof lights from the direct Iberian sun, La Vaguada, Madrid, Spain (1983). *(Source: Peter Coleman)*

The application of perforated metal panels to a proportion of the glazed area can effectively reduce solar glare, while still retaining filtered and direct natural daylight. Perforated metal panels also provide a surface for night-time reflective illumination and help to avoid the black effect (at night-time) of large areas of glazing. Perforated metal panel shading devices are illustrated by the examples at The Mall at Cribbs Causeway, Bristol and at the Bentall Centre, Kingston.

Roof Linings

Partially glazed and solid roofs can be lined on the inside with a variety of decorative and insulated materials such as:

- plasterboard and plaster
- pre-formed glass reinforced gypsum plaster (GRG)
- acoustic insulation panels
- plain and perforated metal panels
- treated timber panels
- treated strips of timber.

While individual aspects of the roof are referred to above, it is important to consider each individual roof design as a total solution. Roofs require an integrated solution which meets the performance criteria and solves the issues of structure, glazing, shading, ventilation, illumination, installation, lining and maintenance.

Figure 11.15 Perforated metal coffers partially shade the glazed roof, The Bentall Centre, Kingston, London, UK (1992). *(Source: Andy Borzyskowski/BDP)*

Figure 11.16 Various types of solid roof linings: (i) plasterboard and plaster; (ii) glass reinforced gypsum; (iii) acoustic insulation panel; (iv) perforated metal panel; (v) treated timber panels; (vi) treated strips of timber. *(Source: BDP)*

Floors

The floor finish of the public space is another significant element that influences the visitor's perception of the overall quality of the shopping centre. Some would even argue that more attention is given by visitors to the floor finish (which can be overlooked) than the roof. The large number of visitors and the need for longevity of the floor finish require it to be hard wearing and robust. Floor finishes in shopping centres are generally not expected to require replacement within a normal refurbishment programme (approx 10–20 years). This requires the floor finish to be carefully considered.

The selection of floor finish will be influenced by the type of space, the extent of enclosure and the intended character of the space. Character can be selected from a variety of key qualities ranging from urban-sophisticated to organic-informal. The character of the floor finish (and space) may also be selected to reflect a type of retailer grouped together

Figure 11.18 Patterned terrazzo floor in the enclosed mall of Vasco da Gama, Lisbon, Portugal (1999). *(Source: Peter Coleman)*

Figure 11.17 Concentric ring pattern in brickwork, Kalvertoren, Amsterdam, The Netherlands (1997). *(Source: Peter Coleman)*

Figure 11.19 Patterned natural stone floor to the open street, The Beursplein, Rotterdam, The Netherlands (1996). *(Source: AM Developments)*

Figure 11.20 Limestone with inset granite forming the floor to the enclosed Thames Walk, Bluewater, Kent, UK (1999). *(Source: Lend Lease)*

in the space. The retailers themselves address either a customer life stage, or lifestyle, which have been referred to in earlier Chapters (see Chapters 5 and 8).

The floor finish required for an urban, open type of space will be very different from that required for an enclosed interior. The requirements for a covered space, without environmental treatment, will be somewhere in between these extremes and is likely to be influenced by the character of the adjacent architecture of the space.

In addition to the character and aesthetic requirements of the floor finish, these general performance issues should also be taken into account:

- robustness and durability
- safety and degree of slipperiness
- easy to clean
- readily repairable
- ability to make services available
- incorporation of thermal movement joints
- inclusion of structural joints.

Figure 11.21 Natural stone floor to the covered street, Hays Wharf, Bermondsey, London, UK (1988). *(Source: St Martins Property Corporation Ltd)*

Figure 11.22 High quality public realm in natural stone, Exchange Square, Manchester, UK (1999). *(Source: David Barbour/BDP)*

Figure 11.23 Brick paving to the lower level and natural stone used on the gallery, Marienburg, Nijmegen, The Netherlands (2000). *(Source: Sjaak Henselmans)*

Types of Floor Finish

Alongside the general evolution of different types of shopping centre there has been a corresponding growth in the different types of floor finish being used. The materials used for the public space floor finish in traditional shopping centres were stone, marble, *in situ* terrazzo, terrazzo tiles and ceramic tiles. All these floor finishes are still suitable for enclosed spaces, along with the selective use, in limited areas, of natural timber and carpet. In addressing the move towards open urban streets and covered streets, appropriate floor finishes have broadened to include natural stone slabs and paviours, concrete slabs and blocks, as well as brick paving. Particular care needs to be taken where public spaces transfer from the open air to a covered or an enclosed space and the conditions affecting the floor finishes may change from wet to dry. Carefully sized transition zones with suitably sized and detailed floor mats should be considered.

Figure 11.24 Continuity of stone floor finish and pattern moving from outside to inside, The Streets of Southpoint, Durham, North Carolina, USA (2002). *(Source: RTKL)*

Practical Considerations

In a traditional enclosed space, an allowance of 75 mm (3 inches) on top of the structural slab for the screed and floor finish is generally suitable. The allowance for the screed and floor finish is likely to need to be increased in more urban schemes, in order to accommodate the additional thickness of natural external materials. A further allowance may be necessary to facilitate the floor being laid to falls to allow for the drainage of surface water.

Floor finishes in open street spaces may have to incorporate statutory services and services for the shops. Consideration should be given to allowing for regular maintenance of these services. This can be provided by access manholes with the finishes recessed into the cover. Alternatively, it may also be worth considering an accessible coordinated service trench, with regular manholes, to help avoid continual disruptive maintenance damaging expensive natural floor finishes.

Figure 11.25 Uncoordinated manhole in The Blue Carpet pavers, city centre, Newcastle upon Tyne, UK (2002). *(Source: Thomas Heatherwick Studio)*

Balustrades and Handrails

Balustrades

Balustrades define the edge of upper level spaces in public spaces with more than one accessible level. Balustrades are applied where one public level overlooks another – for example gallery edges of upper floor levels, bridges which cross the space and staircases which connect between different floors. As such, they form a significant architectural element in multi-level public spaces.

Figure 11.26 Balustrades have a significant influence upon the character of multi-level spaces, GUM Arcade, Moscow (2004). *(Source: Alexei Naroditsky)*

At a practical level, gallery spaces are considered as places of public assembly which require the balustrade to be designed to withstand the applied load from a gathered crowd. Under the UK Building Regulations, a balustrade is required to withstand a load of 3 kN per linear metre applied at the level of the handrail. Such a practical consideration requires a balustrade to incorporate into its design suitable, regularly spaced uprights securely fixed to the gallery edge. (Staircases in the UK have a reduced loading requirement of 0.75 kN per linear metre.)

The importance of balustrades allowing good visibility between different floor levels has been identified earlier (see Chapter 10, Visibility between

floors). The requirement for a high degree of transparency between floors rules out solid or opaque panel balustrades and narrows the choice to a glazed or metal railing type of balustrade, combined with an appropriate handrail. The requirement for metal balustrades to be arranged vertically at not more than 100 mm (4 inches) apart, means that glass balustrading generally achieves better visibility than compliant metal types. Glass balustrades can be cantilevered upwards from a suitable continuous floor edge fixing provided heat soaked, toughened glass is used and the appropriate crowd loading is achieved (Figs. 11.28 and 11.29). If a glass balustrade is supported on all edges, then laminated glass can be used.

The balustrade design should avoid any opportunity for climbing up. For this reason, horizontal bars and stretched cables should be avoided in balustrades for public buildings.

Figure 11.27 Metal balustrade with vertical divisons in the Rose Gallery, Bluewater, Greenhithe, Kent, UK (1999). *(Source: Lend Lease)*

Figure 11.28 Glass balustrade with supporting balusters, The Mall at Cribbs Causeway, Bristol, UK (1998). *(Source: BDP/David Barbour)*

Figure 11.29 Balustrade detail, The Mall at Cribbs Causeway, Bristol, UK. *(Source: David Barbour)*

Handrails

Handrails should be sized to be a suitable scale in relation to the space. The handrail should run continuously along the top of the balustrade and be shaped and sized to be comfortable to grasp. The handrail must be smooth and free from any sharp projections which can arise from changes of direction and where staircases or bridges join the gallery. Particular care should be given to where gallery balustrades are stopped to allow for the landing of an escalator. The handrail material should be robust to resist heavy usage and suitable for the type of environment in which it will be used. Naturally finished metal, plated

Figure 11.30 Balustrade and escalator handrail junctions need to be carefully layered, GUM, Moscow, Russia (2004). *(Source: Alexei Naroditsky)*

Figure 11.31 Layered balustrade detail, Villa Arena, Amsterdam, The Netherlands (2001). *(Source: Benthem Cronwel)*

Table 11.1 Different types of handrail

Painted steel	This is the most economical handrail solution. However, it is prone to wear and will need regular re coating. Re-coating and repairs can be readily made *in situ*
Powder coated steel	This finish is more resilient than painted steel, but is suspect in areas of heavy wear. It is less convenient to repair and maintain and has to be removed for factory re-finishing
Natural metals	Stainless steel, polished brass and bronze are expensive, but durable choices which can be used in external and internal environments. These materials require regular wiping to remain at their best
Finished metals	Chrome plated metal and polished brass are durable and long lasting. The finish is best suited to covered or enclosed spaces. These finishes require regular wiping to maintain the desired polished finish
Natural hardwoods	These natural materials are visually warmer and more tactile. Oak, cherry, ash and beech are commonly used. They are best suited to covered or enclosed spaces, although teak can be used externally. Natural timber can be susceptible to vandalism. However, this can generally be kept to an acceptable level when used in locations which are well used and overlooked

Figure 11.32 A 1.5m raised balustrade with a separate lowered handrail to the high gallery of Peter Jones, Chelsea, London, UK (2003). *(Source: BDP)*

metal, powder coated and painted metal, along with natural hardwood, handrails can all be used. However, each type of handrail has particular considerations and these are outlined in Table 11.1.

When selecting handrail materials that are required to extend between different environmental conditions, care will need to be taken that a uniform choice of material will be appropriate for the conditions in each environment.

Practical Considerations

In the detailed design of the balustrade, the base detail with the floor must be formed to ensure that no gap exists, in order to prevent small items falling through onto the public below. The upstand detail must also prevent any water from cleaning solutions running down the bulkhead and shopfront below.

Balustrades are required to be a minimum of 1.1 (44 inches) high and, in circumstances with high

galleries, the balustrade height must be increased to 1.5m (5ft), with a separate handrail being provided at 1.1m height.

Walls, Pilasters and Bulkheads

Walls, pilasters and bulkheads form the remaining internal elements of the public spaces in traditional enclosed shopping centres. In enclosed spaces the majority of the wall frontage will be made up of the tenants' shopfronts. The tenants are usually encouraged (within shop fitting guidelines) to animate their frontage with imaginative shopfronts. The collective effect formed from groups of shopfronts will establish the retail statement for the space. There are, however, some remaining surfaces which form the visual framework for the shops and which have an influence on the quality of the

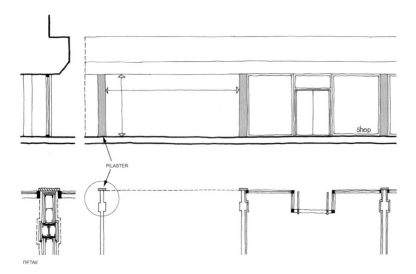

Figure 11.33 Elevation and plan show tenant's shopfront defined by vertical pilasters and a horizontal bulkhead (the landlord's 'goal post'). *(Source: BDP/Sean Dooley)*

public space. These elements are completed by the developer and take the form of minor walls, the pilasters between the shops and bulkheads, which are each examined here.

Walls

Once all the shopfronts have been installed, there will inevitably be some left over wall space which, even though kept to a minimum, will need to be appropriately finished. Some of these wall surfaces can be utilised to provide space for cash machines, information screens and telephones. The remaining walls will need to be carefully finished in a suitably robust material. Walls in contact with the public can be lined with natural stone, ceramic tiles, composite panelling, fairface brickwork or painted plasterwork. High-level walls can be more simply finished with painted plasterwork, acoustic panels and composite panels.

Pilasters

These elements form the dividing wall between each shopfront and form the framework for the shops. They also establish the rhythm for the shops. The BCSC has identified some useful design guidelines which ensure good visibility between shopfronts (British Council of Shopping Centres, 200, p. 20). These guidelines are summarised in Table 11.2.

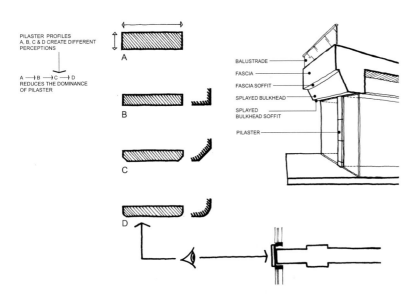

Figure 11.34 Sketch shows the principal of a pilaster division between individual shopfronts and different pilaster profiles to ease visibility to the shop frontage. *(Source: BDP/Sean Dooley)*

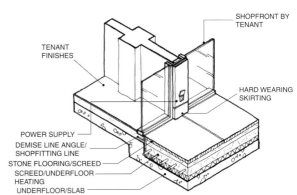

Figure 11.35 Sketch of a typical pilaster base and the interface with the mall floor. *(Source: BDP/Sean Dooley)*

Figure 11.36 Double height pilaster framework with stone bases, The Bullring, Birmingham, UK (shopfronts screened) (2003). *(Source: BDP)*

The pilaster guidelines and recommendations are readily achievable in an enclosed space with an interior character. However, they are less practical in open or covered street types of spaces where the dividing walls between the shops will be part of the external

Table 11.2 Pilaster design guidelines

- Pilasters should not project more than 250 mm (10 inches) in front of the shop
- The pilaster width should not be wider than 300 mm (1 ft)
- The pilaster should not be too decorative or assertive in order to allow the shop display to dominate
- The pilaster base could be made of the same material as the floor finish
- The pilaster should be made of a robust material up to a minimum height of 1.5–2.0 m (5–6.6 ft)
- The pilaster should be easily removable to allow any damaged part to be repaired or replaced
- Suitable materials for pilasters are natural stone, cast terrazzo, metal and timber

building fabric and, as a result, more substantial. In these more urban types of space, the external walling will invariably meet the requirement for robustness.

Bulkheads

These elements form the vertical face and return to the ceiling of gallery and roof edges in enclosed spaces. Bulkheads have traditionally been used to house the landlord's services in the public space. In enclosed spaces with heating and cooling installations the spaces behind the bulkhead are likely to continue to be used in this way. Care should be taken to avoid the front face of the bulkhead profile from becoming too deep. This will ensure the gallery edges remain thin and elegant. Bulkheads have also traditionally been profiled to assist the visibility between shopfronts on one level and another. Bulkhead profiles can be kept elegant by stepping back or curving the profile between the floor edge and ceiling. Careful attention to this detail will help to minimise the visual impact of gallery floors and maintain an elegant interior space.

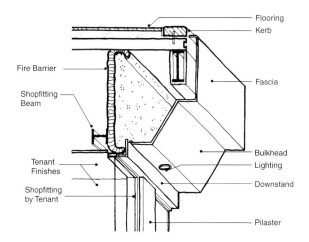

Figure 11.37 Sketch section illustrating a typical gallery edge bulkhead above a lower ground floor shop, providing space for landlord's services and lighting. *(Source: BDP/Sean Dooley)*

Traditional bulkheads concealing services can be finished in painted plasterboard or preformed glass reinforced gypsum (GRG). The bulkheads should incorporate regular integral access panels for easy maintenance of the services.

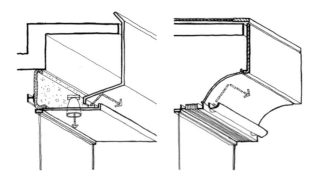

Figure 11.38 Typical alternative bulkhead profiles showing the principles of reducing the mass of the floor edge while accommodating landlord's space for lighting and ventilation. *(Source: BDP/Sean Dooley)*

Figure 11.39 The floor bulkhead between levels is split and recessed to maintain an elegant floor edge, Villa Arena, Amsterdam, The Netherlands (2001). *(Source: Benthem Cronwel)*

In contemporary urban shopping spaces formed in partially covered or covered spaces (without heating or cooling installations), bulkheads can be avoided and edge profiles kept very simple. There is a trend away from projecting gallery edges as spaces become single level access spaces or, at most, two-level schemes. In these cases, the upper floor edge is kept almost flush with the lower-level

shopfronts – in a keyhole cross section profile. These simple, profiled, two-level spaces are more urban in character and maximise the visibility between the different levels.

Features

Purpose-designed features in the form of sculpture, clocks, water features and other artworks can add civic interest to the public spaces and help to establish a unique sense of place. Well-considered features establish an individual character and assist in making a visit to a shopping centre a memorable experience. Incorporating the provision of a memorable experience has previously been identified as one of the key challenges for designers of shopping centres. It is important that any features are carefully considered and researched and that they have a relevance to the location. Features that fail to form an association and have no relevance to the particular shopping centre are prone to become patronising gestures. Most features will involve the architect working together with artists and craftsmen or specialist companies. The architect will usually be required to help prepare the brief, identify the location, coordinate the feature into the building and liaise between the artist/specialist and the building contractor.

Also included here are other items which are not essential to the working of the shopping centre, but contribute to the quality of the public spaces. For example, seating which provides a useful purpose and planting which complements the spaces.

Water Features

These features are diverse in type and can be a delightful and refreshing addition to the public spaces. It is important to recognise that water features involve several technical and operational issues which will need to be considered and resolved. Some of the technical issues to be solved include water supply, pumping and filtration plant, waterproofing, drainage, public health and public safety. In view of these practical considerations grand scale and large expanse water features are likely to be more problematic and, therefore, inappropriate. However, carefully considered, suitably sized water features, which utilise computer-controlled software for effect and variety, can achieve a worthwhile civic quality in both internal and external locations.

An excellent external example of a water feature incorporated into an open shopping street can be found in the Beursplein, Rotterdam (see Chapter 5). This playful water feature is integrated beneath the stone paving of the urban street and remains invisible when the feature is not operating. Apart from some small openings in the stone, the paving remains flush with its surroundings and pedestrians simply walk over it when it is switched off. This water feature is computer-controlled to propel single jets of water upwards, through small openings in a precise projectile which falls into a correspondingly small opening in the paving. As water projects out from apparently random openings and disappears into the paving it appears animated and engages all ages.

Figure 11.41 The light wall in the colonnade to the car park, The Precinct, Coventry, UK (2002). *(Source: TUI Interactive)*

Figure 11.40 Children enjoy the water feature in the stone paving to the Peace Gardens, Sheffield, Yorkshire, UK (1998). *(Source: Sheffield City Council)*

Sculpture

The different types of sculpture feature are equally diverse and can take the form of figurative pieces or more abstract representations incorporated into the fabric of the building. In either form it is important that the sculpture relates to the location and the shopping centre. The background and history of the location should be carefully researched to help prepare a suitable brief for an artist or craftsman. The relevance of the sculpture to a particular location may be derived by a variety of means, including local history, famous persons, inventions, manufacturing or a characteristic associated with the area.

Sculpture integrated into the building can be incorporated into any of the elements, such as glazing, brickwork, pre-cast panels, flooring, or balustrading. The architect will need to liaise between the artist

Figure 11.42 Detail of the light wall in the colonnade to the car park, The Precinct, Coventry, UK (2002). *(Source: TUI Interactive)*

Figure 11.43 Martin Donlin's enamelled glass artworks animate the river frontage, The Oracle, Reading, UK (1999). *(Source: Martin Donlin/Hammerson)*

and contractor to help coordinate the work and assist with its integration.

Clocks and Instruments

Clocks have traditionally been used to create a focus to a civic space, as well as providing a useful purpose. Clocks can fulfil a similar role within the public spaces of a shopping centre. The focus

Figure 11.44 24 hour calendar clock in the Guild-Hall, Bluewater, Greenhithe, Kent, UK (1999). *(Source: Lend Lease)*

Figure 11.45 Solar clock in the Sun Court, Bluewater, Greenhithe, Kent, UK. *(Source: Lend Lease)*

of the clock forms a local identity and areas adjacent to clocks become useful meeting points. Clocks can be formed to include a regular event which can become an attraction to visitors. Clock features cover instruments measuring other than time including aspects of astrology, international time zones and the seasons.

Seating

The provision of seating should be considered as a basic customer facility and included in the public space. It provides an opportunity for visitors to relax and encourages more prolonged visits. An important consideration with the layout of seating is that it should not encourage down-and-outs. The BCSC recommends seating should be arranged facing outwards rather than inwards facing each other, so as to discourage close interaction. BCSC also suggests that seating should be laid out to discourage interaction between more than four to six people and that convex curves of seating are preferable to concave arrangements (British Council of Shopping Centres, 2000, p. 25).

Seating layouts should be prepared together with the client, making sure that the management issues of the proposal are understood. The seating layout should be positioned so as not to conflict with pedestrian movement between the shops and routes to node spaces. The type of seating will be determined by the type of space in which it will be located. For example covered but open spaces will require more robust seating than enclosed spaces where domestic type sofas can be used. Seating in open spaces will need to be hard-wearing and durable.

Figure 11.46 Formal bench seating, Tres Aguas, Madrid, Spain. *(Source: David Barbour/BDP)*

Figure 11.47 Informal seating, The Bullring, Birmingham, UK (2003). *(Source: Caroline Field)*

Planting

The inclusion of soft landscaping provides a complementary and softer element against the architecture of the buildings or interior spaces. Planting introduces a natural element into the public space. The psychological benefit to the visitor of adding a natural element to an otherwise commercially driven environment should not be underestimated. The types of planting will be determined by the types of space, which are individually considered below.

In open street settings, planting can be considered together with the public realm. Planting can be selected to suit the urban quality of the streetscape and the architecture of the buildings. In tree selection and placement care should be taken not to obscure the visibility to the shopfronts and anchor stores.

In covered spaces, more careful consideration will need to be given to the suitability of the trees and planting to the environmental conditions. For example,

although the environment will be marginally better than the external summer and winter temperatures, the lighting levels may need to be checked for particular species and additional artificial lighting provided as necessary.

Figure 11.49 Planting in an open-air covered space, ABC, Beirut, Lebanon (2003). *(Source: Raf Makda/BDP)*

Enclosed spaces require the greatest consideration with regard to whether the interior conditions provide suitable lighting for the proposed planting. Additional artificial lighting may be need to be

Figure 11.48 Soft landscaping planted flush with the surface treatment complements the street and architecture, Above Bar, Southampton, UK (2000). *(Source: David Barbour)*

Figure 11.50 Trees planted flush with the terrazzo floor, White Rose, Leeds, Yorkshire, UK (1997). *(Source: BDP)*

added to supplement the natural daylight. This is particularly likely in spaces with partially glazed roofs and those with solid roofs and glazed clerestories. In view of the overriding requirement for visibility, trees are less likely to be appropriate in an enclosed space, in particular multi-level spaces requiring visibility between levels.

Where trees are planted, these should be flush with the floor finish to avoid obstructing pedestrian movement or reducing the effective width of the space. Flush planting requires a tree pit and sufficient space beneath the tree and requires careful consideration where it is not located at ground level. For example, where the public space is located above other accommodation, the tree pits will have an impact on the accommodation beneath the space. For general guidance, tree pits usually project downwards some 2 m (6.6 ft). Planting trees in large pots or containers above the finish level can overcome the adverse effect on accommodation

Figure 11.51 Imported mature trees in pots in the enclosed space, The Mall, Cribbs Causeway, Bristol, UK (1998). *(Source: Roger Ball/Image Photo Ltd)*

beneath the tree. However, with this solution care will need to be taken to consider the visual effect and impact on the spatial dimensions. At least with trees in large pots there is the flexibility of being able to reposition or remove the trees if necessary.

Whichever type of space, consideration will need to be given to ensure that regular watering and maintenance can be completed. Furthermore, the introduction of access for the bringing in of seasonal planting may also need to be considered. Routine watering can be facilitated by automatic water systems, provided these are integrated into the building. Maintenance and seasonal planting are normally undertaken by specialists who will require ready access to the planters and tree pits. Additional water supplies and wash down drainage should be included if natural planting is to be included in the space.

Lighting

Lighting is a key design element in determining the character of the public space. Public space lighting is made up of a combination of both natural daylight and artificial lighting. The amount of natural daylight is determined by the nature of the space and the type of roof, both of which have been reviewed earlier. The artificial lighting is usually of a supplementary nature during the daytime and gradually takes over for the hours of darkness.

Lighting is fundamental to the public space of a shopping centre. This fundamental relationship is reflected in the key evolutionary stages of shopping centre development. For example, the evolutionary stages identified earlier can be characterised as:

Stage 1 commencing with the early shopfront dominated subdued spaces

Stage 2 developing into the dramatic, fully glazed, interior spaces

Stage 3 evolving into the partially glazed, more modest and practical interior spaces (rooms)

Stage 4 the urban stage of open streets and glazed covered spaces maximising natural daylight.

Whether the public space is enclosed, covered or open, the fundamental requirement for the quality of lighting will be to achieve an inviting, interesting and safe environment both during the day and evening.

The energy used by lighting makes up a significant proportion of a shopping centre's energy load. For example, 50 per cent of the electrical energy used in a shopping centre is in lighting systems and 67 per cent of that lighting is consumed in the public spaces (British Council of Shopping Centres, 2000). With 25 per cent of the electrical energy typically being used to light artificially the public spaces, lighting design must be carefully considered, particularly when addressing sustainability and improving the energy efficiency of a shopping centre.

With the variability of natural daylight and the majority of shopping occurring during the hours of darkness, the natural lighting will have to be

Figure 11.52 The transition of lighting an enclosed space – from natural lighting, combined daylight and artificial lighting through to artificial lighting at night-time, Bentall Centre, Kingston, Surrey, UK (1992). *(Source: Peter Durant/ArcBlue)*

supplemented by artificial lighting (even in spaces designed to make the maximum use of natural day-light). Artificial lighting is therefore particularly important in shopping centres. This is illustrated in the northern hemisphere where the period of peak shopping takes place in the winter, which coincides with the shortest days and extended evening trading. In these locations, the greatest need occurs when natural daylight is least effective and operation is dependent upon artificial lighting. Recognising that shopping activity takes place daily, throughout the year, it can be demonstrated that shopping spaces rely equally on a combination of natural and artificial lighting and that both are of equal importance and should be considered together in the design of public spaces. Consideration of the combined lighting effect is fundamental to both the character and commercial success of the shopping centre.

Natural daylighting and artificial lighting are usually designed with the assistance of a specialist lighting consultant. In considering the lighting design, the architect will need to balance a series of issues. The main issues are outlined below.

In the process of achieving a balanced natural and artificial lighting installation, it will be necessary to consider the effect of the combined lighting under different and changing external conditions. A combination of three-dimensional scaled models and computer modelling can be used to explore the lighting effect during different seasons and at different times of day.

In addition to considering the lighting under different static conditions, the response of the artificial lighting to changing external conditions will also need to be taken into account. Solar cells and an energy management system, for example, can be used to control and subdue artificial lighting when there is sufficient natural daylight. This helps avoid circumstances where the artificial lighting is on full in bright daylight. Equally the switch-over process which occurs during dusk when natural light gives way to artificial lighting will also need to be considered and controlled. For example, during twilight there should be a gradual change-over rather than a sudden switchover from daylight to artificial lighting. The change-over can be controlled by the building management system to allow the artificial lighting gradually to increase in response to the declining daylight. This arrangement requires the selection of dimmable luminaires (discussed further on) and separately switched circuits.

The design of the artificial lighting will need to achieve a balance between the general lighting and feature lighting (the types of lighting are expanded below). The combined installation will need to be achieved with an economy of means. The selection and positioning of luminaires should take account of availability and the requirement for regular replacement. In addition to the space lighting, the external lighting of the building façades may also be an important part of the lighting installation. The external façade lighting is likely to be a particularly important consideration in urban schemes with open streets and covered spaces.

Figure 11.53 External lighting to the entrance façade provides night-time animation, The Mailbox, Birmingham, UK (2000). *(Source: Birmingham Picture Library)*

The vogue for lighting installations designed around the dominance of the shopfront display are consigned to history and memory. Public spaces have become increasingly interesting in their own right, corresponding with grander shopfronts achieved through a combination of increased vertical size, greater visibility into the shop and more imaginative window displays.

Artificial lighting installations are made up from a combination of three principal types of lighting:

■ background and general lighting
■ feature lighting
■ effect lighting.

Each of these different types of lighting should be arranged on separately controllable circuits to allow for flexibility and events.

Background and General Lighting

This part of the installation provides the functional lighting to the public space, is usually arranged with controlling sensors and utilises luminaires which

Table 11.3 Types of luminaire

Background lighting	
Tungsten GLS lamps	ordinary domestic type lightbulbs generally not permitted under the Building Regulations
Fluorescent lamps	available in a wide choice of formats and power
	can be dimmed
	flexible format
	suitable for direct and indirect lighting
	excellent colour rendition and efficiency
	linear types suit indirect lighting
	popular choice for background lighting
	very long life
High pressure mercury lamps	can give a bluish white rendition
	wide power range available
	require time to warm up
	reasonable colour rendition and efficiency
	favoured in car parks
High pressure sodium discharge lamps	efficient lamp life
	wide power range available
	require careful selection to obtain good colour rendition
	when combined with daylight and can be slightly yellow
	require time to warm up not dimmable
	utility character – suits warehouses
Metal halide	high power range available
	efficient to use and good life expectancy
	good colour rendition
	(can also be feature lighting in low wattage version)
Feature lighting	
Tungsten halogen	wide power range
	require regular replacement
	not efficient if used extensively
	excellent colour rendition
	dimmable
	can only make up 5% of lighting load
	produces focused beam and sparkle
Low voltage diochroic	wide choice of available formats
	suitable for highlighting features
	excellent colour rendition
Fibre optics	(not the primary source which is remote: usually metal halide or tungsten halogen)
	single source used to illuminate multiple fittings
	useful where light fittings need to be in inaccessible locations
	discreet
	useful where lots of points of light required for effect
	can be used to introduce colour
	low efficiency (approx 20% of lamp output at fitting)

are dimmable (see below for types of luminaire). Background lighting is usually responsive to external daylight conditions and arranged gradually to go up and down.

Feature Lighting

This is used to highlight specific areas and features. Brighter areas may be used to identify entrances, node spaces and connecting public circulation spaces. Features to be highlighted can be natural landscaping, feature staircases, works of art, insets in the flooring, entranceways and architectural features. Feature lighting is used to create variety and contrast to the general lighting. Feature lighting may be switched off in bright daylight conditions. Sometimes feature lighting is arranged on gantries and treated like theatre stage lighting. This can be particularly effective for lighting events held in the larger public spaces.

Effect Lighting

The third part of the installation is an optional decorative element which is used to add character and identity to specific places. Effect lighting is used to create drama. Effect lighting can be used to add colour to selective architectural elements, such as a floor edge, a wall surface or an entranceway. It is generally used to identify selective areas to emphasise a local identity or particular use, for example, to identify and differentiate a catering area or leisure use.

Types of Luminaire

Artificial lighting is a specialised and technical subject which is continually progressing and evolving. In the design of a shopping centre the architect is likely to work with a specialist lighting consultant who will assist with technical matters. To assist this collaborative process, the general types of luminaire and the characteristics of each type are outlined in Table 11.3.

References

British Council of Shopping Centres (2000). *A Briefing Guide to Shopping Centre Development*. BCSC.

Security is a key consideration in the operation of contemporary shopping centres, involving accommodating multiple monitors, as part of the management facilities. *(Source: Getty Images)*

Back of House Areas and Installations

12

Characteristics and Types of Area

The back of house areas of shopping centres have a tendency to be a hidden world which is generally not accessible to the general public, but is integral to the operation and safety of the building. In a large shopping centre these areas will be used by several thousand shop staff, along with the management, maintenance, cleaning and security staff who assist with the operation of the centre. There will also be external users who will have access to some of the back of house areas, such as delivery vehicle drivers, refuse collectors, utility service suppliers, maintenance contractors and shop fitters. These facilities are separate from the front of house areas, so the visiting public are only likely to encounter them in the event of an emergency and, for this reason, they tend to be basic and unfinished.

Although the back of house areas tend to be secondary or service spaces to the principal accommodation, they are fundamental to the functioning and operation of the building and must be properly considered and planned. These areas represent the life blood of supplies for the delivery of goods and simultaneously provide the means of removing waste and surplus goods from the centre. They are also the primary source of services to the public spaces. Many of the corridors provide means of escape to ensure the public get safely away from the building in an emergency. In addition to the horizontal corridors are the vertical routes, lifts, stairs and risers which interconnect between the different levels to form a coordinated network for delivery, building services and escape. The back of house areas also include the plant rooms and plant space and the points of connection to the highway network.

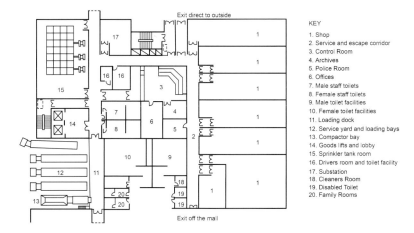

Figure 12.1 Plan identifying the various back of house areas to be accommodated in a typical large or regional shopping centre. *(Source: BDP/Sean Dooley)*

The different back of house areas and the interconnections between them are arranged into four principal categories shown in Table 12.1 and are each examined separately.

Table 12.1 The different back of house areas

Management facilities
- Management suites (administrative offices)
- Control rooms
- Staff rooms
- Maintenance facilities

Access and deliveries
- Service yards
- Service corridors (deliveries)
- Service lifts
- Interconnecting stairs

Plant and installations
- Service corridors (services distribution)
- Riser ducts
- Landlord's plant rooms
- Tenants' plant space and provisions

Fire safety
- Means of escape
  - service corridors
  - escape corridors
  - escape stairs
- Smoke control
- Fire prevention (sprinklers)
- Fire-fighting facilities

Management Facilities

Activities and Responsibilities

The management facilities need to accommodate a multitude of different activities. These can broadly be divided into activities relating to the public and operational activities involved with the day-to-day running of a complex building. Public facilities were examined in a previous chapter. Examined here are the different facilities required for the running of the centre.

The management suite will need to provide the centre management staff with all the necessary accommodation and facilities to allow them to run and manage the centre, which generally includes the public spaces/malls; customer facilities; the structure and fabric of the buildings; the environmental, safety and security installations; the entrances, service yard and deliveries; and the operation of the car parks.

The specific management responsibilities include:
- the security, safety and well-being of the public
- monitoring the safety and security systems and coordinating the response to the emergency services

- cleaning of the public and landlord areas
- managing the delivery of goods to the centre
- managing the removal of waste from the centre
- liaison with customers, visitors and tenants
- the operation and maintenance of the building fabric and installations
- liaison with maintenance contractors, suppliers and utility services
- managing the services and charges to the tenants
- communicating with the tenants and immediate community.

Management Accommodation

Location

The management suite does not have to be prominently located in the public space. The centre management can achieve an effective presence in the public space through the regular attendance of its staff and through the existence of an information desk. However, the management suite does need to be publicly accessible to enable customers and visitors to locate it once given directions.

Size

The size of any management facility is related to the size and complexity of the retail facilities.

Figure 12.2 Comfortable and welcoming management suite reception area, The Bullring, Birmingham, UK (2003). *(Source: James Cheung)*

BCSC advises that a small open centre up to 15 000 m² (161 400 ft²) is likely to require only a small office and some storage space for maintenance equipment, whereas a larger covered shopping centre will require a management suite and other supporting accommodation. For example, a typical management suite will occupy an area of 200–250 m² (2150–2700 ft²) (British Council of Shopping Centres, 2000).

Typical Facilities

The typical facilities to be included within a management suite are listed in Table 12.2. Control rooms within the management suite will control and monitor all the environmental, safety and security installations of the building. As such, the control room will be the nerve centre for the total building. The equipment and facilities within the control room are becoming increasingly sophisticated and extensive with banks of monitors and control consoles requiring several staff to manage them. The management

staff are required to work for long hours and it is important that their working environment is properly considered and allocated sufficient space. The control room should allow staff to operate the nerve centre of the building in an efficient and comfortable environment – similar to commercial offices.

(The various installations controlled from the control room are listed in Table 12.2 and outlined in more detail later under Plant and Installation Space: Control Rooms.)

In addition to the accommodation included within the management suite, there will be a requirement for other remote supporting accommodation to assist with the day-to-day operation and maintenance of the centre. This additional storage and workshop space can be located elsewhere in the centre and is identified in Table 12.3. While most of the additional accommodation does not have a specific location requirement, the cleaners' rooms and stores for cleaning equipment and machines should be located conveniently close to the public spaces. The rest of the accommodation can be

---

Table 12.2 Typical management suite facilities

- Reception area and desk for greeting retailers and contractors (space and facility shared with public facility)
- Office administration space to include:
  - general office space
  - conference rooms for meetings (meetings held with retailers to resolve issues, contractors for maintenance, staff induction and external communications)
  - centre manager's office
- Small kitchen facility
- Staff toilets
- First aid and medical room
- Control room, accommodating:
  - environmental and security controls
  - public address system for voice messages
  - address system for broadcast of music
  - building management system – controlling heating, cooling, ventilation and lighting
  - fire safety system – monitors and controls for detection, alarms, sprinklers and ventilation
  - security controls – screen monitors from CCTV surveillance network (likely to be a large number of screens each with a multi-screen facility)
  - controls are usually arranged with a consul and chairs
  - some control rooms include a pedestrian counting system
  - centres operating a 'shop-alert' system to assist combating crime will have a facility to notify tenants
  - centres with turnover rental arrangements will have additional digital lines connected to the tenancies to transfer cash turnover information to centre management
- Staff room
  - with lockers, toilets, showers and changing facilities
- Secure room
  - for financial information and records

Table 12.3 Other management accommodation

- General store for Christmas decorations, display screens, safety barriers, emergency signs
- Store for hazardous materials
- Store for bulky items: ladders, scaffold towers, gantries and maintenance equipment – scissor platforms and floor cleaning machines
- Workshop for minor repairs which facilitate the continual safe operation of the centre
- A satellite control/security room to oversee the service yard operation
- Cleaners' rooms with sink, toilets, lockers, equipment and materials storage
- Store for the public space cleaning machines with battery charging and washdown facilities

located adjacent to the service yard or elsewhere provided there is a reasonable means of access. If the storage is remotely located from the public spaces access will entail the need for sufficient manoeuvring space around corridors, doors wide enough and the potential use of service lifts.

Access and Deliveries

Importance of Deliveries

Shopping centres contain a multitude of businesses which are represented by different individual shops. Access and deliveries are the means of supplying goods to allow these retail businesses to operate. Access and deliveries usually stem from the service yard, leading, via a network of corridors,

Figure 12.3 Typical service yard illustrating unloading bays to a raised dock and designated doorways with separate areas for recycled materials and delivery trolleys. *(Source: David Barbour)*

to the rear of each shop unit. If the life blood of a shopping centre is fed from the service yard, then the delivery corridors (service corridors) are the arteries leading to the shops.

Service Yards

The significance of service yards to the operation, their alternative locations, and their positioning and sizing have been identified previously (Chapter 8, Site accessibility: service vehicles). Examined here are the activities and interrelationships involved, to assist with the more detailed design and layout of the service yard.

The service yard is the shopping centre's means of connection to the highway and transport network which, in turn, connects with the distribution warehouses and manufacturers that supply the retail industry (Fig. 12.3). The service yard also has to be the means of removing waste and refuse from the shopping centre. Delivery and refuse vehicle areas therefore need to be clearly delineated and arranged into separate areas. In addition to delivery and refuse vehicles, the yard will also need to accommodate vehicles for shop fitters and maintenance contractors, and the vans used by the statutory authorities and services suppliers. Service yards can be a hive of activity where all and sundry goes on. It is important that the centre layout discourages the public from having access to them. To this end, it is recommended that service vehicle and car park vehicle access is kept separate wherever possible. Where separate points of access to the highway are not possible and where a shared access road cannot be avoided, access to the car park should not be from any part of the service yard. In this case, access to the car park should be reached before the service yard entrance.

Positioning

Chapter 8 identified that service yards should be positioned within 150 m or 100 m of the furthest shops for single or multi-level shopping arrangements respectively. Additional service yards will need to be provided if these distances are significantly exceeded. The service yard should be positioned so as to provide safe and secure unloading and delivery of goods to the rear of each shop. Another important consideration in positioning the service yard, which can affect the layout of the centre, is to ensure that deliveries can be made to the rear of each shop without having to cross any of the public circulation spaces. Additional service yards may have to be provided if the shops on each side of the public space cannot be separately accessed. It is generally unacceptable to deliver goods across or via the public circulation spaces, except in the case of delivering to small island units or kiosks.

Types of Yard

Service yards are usually arranged in combined areas, large enough for several vehicles, where these can enter and exit from the same point of access. In these layouts, the loading bays are usually organised to allow the vehicles to back up perpendicularly to a loading dock – also referred to as head-on parking. Sufficient space will be required for manoeuvring and for the parked vehicle. Service yards can be arranged with head-on unloading bays on a single side, or in a double-sided layout, depending on the shop layout, the number of service yards and the amount of available space. An alternative to large

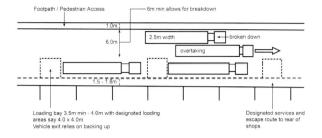

Figure 12.5 A linear 'side-on' unloading arrangement where unloading is lowered from the vehicle directly on to the road. (NB less efficient unloading than with a dock.) *(Source: BDP)*

service yards with perpendicular, head-on unloading bays are more linear arrangements, regularly arranged along the length of a one-way service road. In these arrangements, the parking bays form lay-bys which are parallel to the road and the vehicles back into the bay. The roadway is arranged with sufficient space to allow for other vehicles to pass when a vehicle is unloading. Having unloaded, the vehicles move out in a forward direction and continue along the service road to the point of exit. This arrangement can be made to work with separate or combined points of entry and exit to the highway network. On restricted sites requiring two-way entry and exit roads or ramps, traffic lights can be used to control vehicular flow.

In addition to the parking bays, it will also be important to allow for sufficient manoeuvring and turning space to enable the vehicles to gain access, park up and leave in an unhindered manner, while other vehicles are parked. It will be important to consider the structural requirements and positioning of columns when assessing vehicular movements in covered or basement service yards. Articulated vehicles require parking bays which are 15–16.5 m (49.2–54.1 ft) long by 3–5 m (9.8–16.4 ft) wide, depending on the manoeuvring space in front of

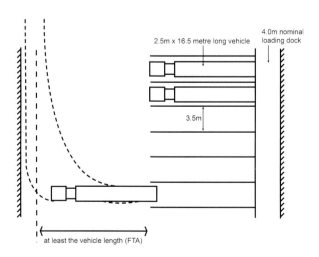

Figure 12.4 A single-sided unloading yard with 'reverse-in' parking bays. *(Source: BDP)*

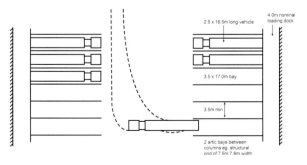

Figure 12.6 A typical double-sided unloading yard with 'reverse-in' parking bays to unloading docks on each side. *(Source: BDP)*

the parking bay. The wider parking bay requires less forward manoeuvring space in front of the parked vehicle which will vary from 12.4 to 17.4 m (40.7–57 ft). As well as providing space for the largest articulated vehicles, some of the bays will be required for smaller vans and maintenance vehicles. In the design of the service yard, consideration should be given to the trend for vehicles to become both longer and taller.

Refuse Space

Chapter 8 identified the requirement for refuse vehicles and compactors. Sufficient space must also be provided for the storage of refuse prior to collection. The amount of storage space will be determined by the frequency and method of refuse collection, which should be agreed with the owner and refuse collector early on in the design process. Space should be provided in the service yard for general bins and cardboard compactors. Wet and dry rubbish

Figure 12.8 Typical recycled refuse storage with separate bins for individual materials. (*Source: David Barbour*)

should be separately stored, especially where there are sizeable catering facilities. Space should also be considered for recycling identifiable materials such as cardboard, glass, metals and plastics, and this should be separate from other waste material. Localised refuse storage space can sometimes be provided close to the rear of the shops for periodic transfer, by the centre management, to the service yard. Localised refuse stores should be agreed with the owner beforehand.

Unloading Docks

Generally, delivery vehicles unload from the back of the vehicle, directly on to a raised unloading dock which is 1–1.1 m (3.3–3.6 ft) above the road surface of the yard. The unloading dock needs to be sufficiently wide to allow unloading to take place and facilitate trolleys to pass by from another unloading vehicle – 3 m (9.8 ft) is recommended as the minimum width for an unloading dock. With most delivery

Figure 12.7 A cardboard compactor located in the service yard. (*Source: David Barbour*)

Figure 12.9 A raised loading dock with an access ladder. (*Source: David Barbour*)

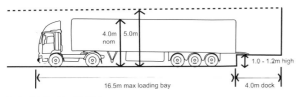

Typical Articulated Vehicle

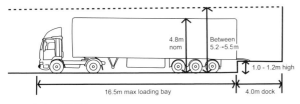

Tall Articulated Vehicle

Figure 12.10 Sections showing plan and vertical dimensions for typical and tall articulated vehicles. *(Source: BDP)*

Figure 12.11 Designated unloading docks to a department store with shuttered openings which correspond with the rear of the vehicle. *(Source: David Barbour)*

vehicles having levelling platforms, not all service yards are provided with a raised unloading dock. Some unloading areas are arranged flush with the surface of the yard, which can simplify its construction. In these arrangements, caged and trolleyed goods cannot be wheeled directly out from the back of the vehicle and have to be lowered from the vehicle onto the ground. Flat unloading areas restrict the unloading to the maximum amount that can be stacked onto the vehicle's levelling platforms and tend to be less efficient than raised dock arrangements. The reduced efficiency of the unloading may be especially critical in a town centre location, where the faster turn around of vehicles may assist with the optimum use of the yard and thereby allow a smaller yard to be provided.

Security

Security is an important issue in the delivery and unloading of shop goods. Unloaded goods are usually transferred by shop staff from the service yard to the shop unit. In view of the fact that the majority of shop units will unload in an undesignated part of the service yard, the unloading is restricted by the amount that can be securely handled and immediately taken to the store. The remaining goods will be kept securely in the vehicle until they can be safely transferred to the shop unit. The department stores and larger stores will have designated unloading bays with direct access into the back of the store premises, providing secure unloading.

Some stores will require shuttered openings at the rear of the store, which correspond with the openings in the rear of the delivery vehicle, to facilitate

Figure 12.12 Dock leveller making up the difference between the truck and store to allow trolleyed deliveries direct into the department store. *(Source: James Cheung)*

rapid secure unloading (see Fig. 12.11). In these circumstances, a raised unloading dock will not be required, but the store's finished floor level will be raised above the service yard by a similar amount, in order to allow caged goods and trolleys to be wheeled directly from the vehicle into the unloading and storage area of the store. These direct and designated unloading arrangements are secured by a hood which fits over the roof of the vehicle and the building door openings, corresponding with the opening on the back of the vehicle. Some stores' delivery vehicles are arranged with two levels of goods. Once the first level is unloaded, the upper level is mechanically lowered down and then unloaded. These taller articulated vehicles are refilled with empty cages, level by level in reverse, before returning to the distribution depot.

The unloading dock or area should connect directly to the rear of the immediate shop units and, in larger centres, to a network of secure delivery corridors (service corridors), which lead to the rear of the other shops. In multi-level shopping centres or where the service yard is at a different level to the shops, goods lifts are used to transfer the goods to the appropriate level.

Service corridors and lifts are discussed separately below.

Management

Service yards should be controlled by the shopping centre management to help ensure that the spaces are used efficiently. It is common practice for busier service yards to require delivery vehicles to phone in advance of their arrival to check the availability of parking spaces. Entry into the service yard is sometimes controlled by an intercom system positioned at the entrance to the service yard or access road. Closed-circuit television (CCTV) is also used to monitor vehicular movement approaching, leaving and using the yard.

Service yards are dangerous places and rely largely upon the quality of the individual driver to maintain safety and operation levels. Traffic management and signage will assist with operation of the yard. For example, different service yards should have an understandable identity and individual parking bays should be clearly numbered and marked to assist centre management to direct vehicles to the correct bays.

With the aid of modern technology, service yards can be managed from remote control rooms in the management suite. Some of the larger shopping centres may require a separate control office located within the service yard to help manage the vehicles

in the yard. Some service yards provide the delivery drivers with toilet and washing facilities, which are directly accessible from the yard.

Lighting

Enclosed service yards require artificial lighting and ventilation for their operation. Care will need to be taken to ensure any installations do not obstruct the clear headroom requirement of larger vehicles. Open-air and roof-level service yards will require artificial lighting for occasional night-time deliveries. Any lighting of open service yards should be used carefully to avoid light pollution in sensitive town centre locations.

Finishes

Service yards are simply and robustly finished. The road surface of the yard must be sufficiently hard wearing to resist the forces from the turning action of 38–40 tonne vehicles. The structure and building fabric of the service yard should be robust, with corners and exposed edges protected with kerbs and barriers against vehicle impact. Any walls or doors likely to come into contact with trolleys should also have rub rails and protective plates. The edges ofraised loading docks should have a continuous rub rail.

Delivery Corridors (Service Corridors)

The delivery corridors (service corridors) also double up as the means of distributing statutory and other supply services to the shops. As the means of providing for both the delivery of goods and the power, communications, security and safety installations, the analogy of service corridors being the arteries bringing life blood to the shops, is further reinforced. Furthermore, service corridors in many instances also act as the means of escape in the event of a fire, both from the rear of the shops and from the public circulation spaces. These corridors are sometimes also referred to as 'service and escape corridors', but for the purposes of this book are referred to as 'service corridors'. (The other functions of service corridors for the distribution of services and as a means of escape are discussed separately further on.)

Service corridors should be arranged to lead directly from the service yard to the rear of each shop unit and provide an integral, secure delivery arrangement. If the service yard is at a different level to the shops, service lifts and access stairs will connect vertically between the various levels. Retailers prefer goods to be handled vertically in a lift only once before delivery to the shop. The service yards and service corridors should be designed and laid out to meet this preference.

In view of the service corridor's combined use as a means of escape, its width is primarily determined by the requirement for fire safety (see below). Service corridors must not be used for storage purposes and must generally be kept free of any obstructions. A notional zone is, however, permitted to the side of the corridor to allow goods in transit to stand while being delivered into the shop. This goods in transit zone is 0.5 m (1.6 ft) wide, providing the minimum escape distance is maintained. Corridors which serve as a delivery route should be sufficiently wide to allow for trolleys to pass in opposite directions – 1800–2000 mm (6–6.3 ft) minimum clear width for example. Corridor clear dimensions should take into account the requirement for rub rails. Walls should ideally be free of any projections (such as columns) and be flush.

Service corridors are used by centre management and shop staff and, with the exception of emergency escape, are not accessed by the public. Service corridors are also used for the removal of rubbish and the return of empty trolleys to the service yard. These spaces are basically finished with fairface or painted blockwork walls, unfinished, exposed structure ceilings and screed floors which are either sealed or sometimes finished with a polymer or with vinyl tiles. Walls should be protected with rub rails and all doors fitted with crash plates. Any projecting corners should be fitted with corner guards. Service corridors used for the return of wet rubbish from catering areas should have the walls and floors sealed for reasons of hygiene and ease of maintenance.

Service Lifts

Where shops are located at a different level to the service yard, service lifts are installed to transfer goods vertically to the level of the appropriate service corridor. It is usual to provide more than one lift to ensure deliveries can be maintained in the event of a breakdown. Goods lifts should be suitably sized and robustly finished to handle the type of goods likely to be transported in them. In a medium sized shopping centre, for example, it would be common to provide two goods lifts, each with a bearing capacity of 2 tonnes (approx 2 tons), in each service yard with a requirement for vertical

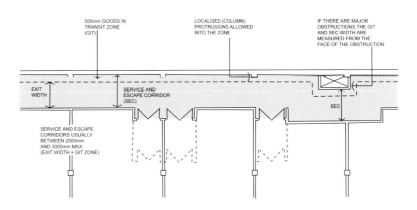

Figure 12.13 Typical delivery corridor (service corridor) layout showing access arrangements to the rear of shop units. *(Source: BDP/Sean Dooley)*

transfer. The architect would usually consult with a mechanical engineer to determine the number and size of service lifts to be required for the project. Where a large catering area is included at a different level from the service yard, it is good practice to provide a separate wet lift for the exclusive use of the catering area.

Interconnecting Stairs

Where shops are located at a different level to the service yard and in multi-level shopping centres, it is necessary to provide staircases which connect between the different levels. Some of these interconnecting stairs are likely to double up as means of escape stairs and will need to be sized and designed to comply with the regulatory requirements. Where tenants' plant is located at roof level, the interconnecting stairs will also need to provide access from the shop level up to the roof level. Escape stairs can be arranged in 'scissor' configurations to maximise the escape potential for each stair. Interconnecting stairs are often grouped with service risers and service lifts to form vertical cores.

Plant and Installation Space

Service Distribution (Corridors and Risers)

Earlier reference has been made to the service corridors' function as the primary means of distributing services horizontally around the centre to each of the shop units. Pipes, cable trays' conduits and trunking services run at high level in the service corridor and must be arranged so that each service is easily accessible. For example, if services are stacked at different levels there must be access from the side.

Figure 12.14 Electrical cable trays and water distribution pipes at high level in a service corridor. *(Source: James Cheung)*

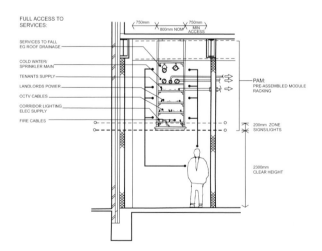

Figure 12.15 Typical cross section through a delivery corridor (service corridor) showing high level accessible service trays. *(Source: BDP/Sean Dooley)*

Figure 12.16 Incoming meters for tenancies with gas supplies. *(Source: David Barbour)*

Figure 12.17 Electrical transformer used to supply power to a department store. *(Source: David Barbour)*

Service corridors act as the horizontal supply route to the tenants' shops for a variety of services, which include statutory services (water, electricity and gas), landlord services (sprinklers, smoke alarms, security installations) and landlord provisions (telecommunications). Landlord provision includes cable trays for the tenants to use, but it is the responsibility of the tenant to arrange for the installation of telephone and cable connections. Where appropriate, the service corridors are also used to run the landlord's services from the plant rooms to the malls and public spaces. The landlord's services include heated and chilled air ducts, smoke ventilation ducts, power, lighting, smoke detection, surveillance and public address systems. Corridors combining the full range of both landlord and tenant services require careful coordination.

Vertical risers or ducts are used to route services between different levels of service corridor. The vertical risers considered here are those completed by the landlord to supply the shop shells and service the landlord's areas. (Vertical risers within the shop units are completed by the tenant and considered separately.)

The landlord's vertical risers should be separately organised from those distributing services to tenants' shop units. Gas services should be separated from any electrical services. The landlord's vertical risers should be arranged to allow access to each service, with access doors and panels included for maintenance. Where the vertical risers pass through compartments, the riser will need to be constructed of fire resistant materials. Vertical risers are usually grouped together and located conveniently beside the service corridor. Sometimes vertical risers are grouped with the interconnecting stairs to form consolidated vertical cores.

Vertical risers located beside the service corridors and stairs tend to be positioned at the rear of the shops. While these locations are convenient for the tenants' supplies, they can be remote from the public spaces. Vertical risers with services supplying public spaces are sometimes more conveniently located closer to the public spaces than to the rear of the shops. Finding an acceptable location which is closer to the public spaces without compromising the shop footprints or losing high value space will need to be carefully considered.

When positioning vertical risers, consideration should be given to where and what type of plant room the services are coming from. For example, vertical risers for statutory and supply services leading to tenanted shop units will tend to connect to intake and meter rooms. On the other hand, vertical risers for landlord services to public spaces and tenanted shops tend to lead back and connect to the various plant and management control rooms, as well as meter rooms.

Landlord's Plant Rooms

The plant rooms considered here are the landlord's plant rooms and the landlord's obligations to provide for tenants' plant. (Tenant's plant is separate, usually located at roof level and is considered later.)

Plant rooms for shopping centres come in all shapes and sizes and are located in various parts of the building. The type and number of plant rooms depend on the nature and size of the shopping centre. For example, an open street based scheme without heating and cooling will have simpler installations and less plant than a comparable sized enclosed type of centre. The plant rooms mentioned here will not apply to all types of shopping centre and are listed for the purpose of identifying the range of potential facilities that may be encountered. The ones listed here are, however, likely to apply to a large, enclosed, regional shopping centre. The different plant rooms considered here are:

- statutory service connections
- water storage
- storm water holding
- emergency generators
- lift motor rooms
- space heating and cooling
- air handling (ventilation)
- smoke ventilation
- combined heat and power
- working space.

Statutory Service Connections

These are sometimes also referred to as the public utility supply services and include water, gas and electricity. For each service they require the facility for making the intake connection, subdividing the service between the various tenant and landlord areas, and individually metering the consumption of each supply. Provision will need to be made for intake rooms for each service, with sufficient adjacent space for individual meter reading. Digital reading meters take up less space than mechanical meters and can be housed in cupboards or rooms beside the service corridors. Meters need to be located so that they can be reasonably accessible from the service yard where the suppliers' vehicles will be parked.

Incoming electricity suppliers often require a transformer before the separation into metered supplies. Transformers should be positioned to be accessible, preferably ventilated naturally and located in such a way that the equipment can be replaced when necessary. Electricity supplies are usually separated into high and low voltage supplies, with individual switch rooms required for each. High voltage electricity supplies are required for large mechanical installations such as lifts, escalators, fans and heat exchange units. The landlord will require both levels of supply and the shop units are usually provided with a low voltage supply. Large anchor stores are sometimes provided with their own high voltage supply requiring a transformer to convert the supply for low voltage services (see Fig. 12.17).

Water Storage

Space will need to be allocated for water storage tanks to supply water to the landlord's installations, which include public and staff toilets, washrooms, cleaners' cupboards and wash down facilities in the service yard and car parks. Where sprinkler installations are required, space will also need to be considered for sprinkler tank water storage. Sprinkler tanks are substantial in size and weight and their placement requires careful consideration. Further space will also need to be provided for water pumps and, because of the public safety aspect, stand-by pumps and power generation will also need to be considered.

Storm Water Holding Tanks

Some water authorities will not permit large volumes of surface water to discharge directly into the sewer system. In view of the large site areas covered by shopping developments, they will require the provision of a holding tank which will gradually release the drained surface water into the sewer network. The stored surface water (sometimes referred to as grey water) can be put to good use for flushing WCs and for vehicle wash downs. Storm water holding tanks can sometimes be located beneath the ground floor slab or in other voids that are not suitable for occupation.

Emergency Generators

Fire safety installations and escape routes must be maintained in the event of a power failure. Space for emergency generators and fuel storage must be provided to maintain power supplies to the mechanical smoke ventilation, emergency lighting and sprinkler installations (mentioned previously). These generators are usually powered by diesel driven motors which are often located on the roof of the building for easy ventilation. They need to be located conveniently enough to allow for regular maintenance and eventual replacement.

Figure 12.18 Motor driven emergency generators and fuel storage. *(Source: David Barbour)*

Figure 12.19 Stand-by batteries for power generation in an emergency. *(Source: David Barbour)*

Lift Motor Rooms

Lifts are operated by either electric motor driven cables or electric pumped hydraulic rams. Motorised cable driven lifts traditionally require plant rooms positioned directly above the lift shaft. In some instances, particularly within shop tenancies, a new prefabricated type of cable driven lift with the motors arranged on the side of the lift, omits the plant requirement above the shaft, but requires careful sizing of the shaft itself.

Hydraulic lifts (which generally have less capacity) are more flexible with regard to the positioning of the motor plant and do not require the plant to be directly over the lift. These lifts require the facility for the hydraulic extending ram to be accommodated beneath the lift and plant space for the motor to be reasonably close to the installation.

Space Heating and Cooling

In enclosed centres, the landlord usually heats and cools the public spaces in order to provide a comfortable environment for the visiting public. The landlord also tempers the environment in the service corridors, public toilets, crèche, management suite and other inhabited management facilities. Traditionally, shopping centre installations have used boilers for primary heating and water-cooled evaporative cooling towers for air-conditioning. Air handling units were used to transfer the primary source to air which was blown by fans to the treated space. Water-based cooling towers have become unpopular cooling sources (because of the associated Legionnaires' disease) and most new installations are now using air-cooled chillers for cooling the air. A convenient energy-saving variant on the air-cooled chiller is an air-cooled heat pump, which can provide both cooling and heating from a single piece of equipment. In view of a shopping centre's primary requirement being the need to cool the space, it has become commonly accepted to use air-cooled heat pumps to provide both cooling and heating sources and thus avoid the need for boilers.

In enclosed centres with the requirement to heat and cool the public spaces, provision will need to be made to accommodate air-cooled heat pumps which come in prefabricated, packaged units. Where the air-cooled heat pumps do not include air handling plant, additional space will need to be allocated for this plant. The air handling units transfer the primary source to the air, which is then blown by fans into ducts which lead to the tempered space.

Ideally, air-cooled heat pumps and air handling units should be located near the space that is being treated to reduce the size of the ductwork, and as close together as possible to reduce the length of the primary heating and chilling pipework. Air handling units need to be located with access to fresh air and the facility to extract air to the outside. Locating air handling units close to the outside of the building will reduce the need for large supply and extract ductwork. Air handling units can be in plant space located on the roof or beside external walls, behind louvred screens. Air supplies must be fresh and this can be more readily achieved in an elevated location.

The location and placement of air cooled heat pumps and air handling plant must allow for both maintenance access and the eventual replacement of plant. With air-cooled heat pumps being used as the primary means of space heating, it is sometimes more practical to service the more remote areas of the building by using small individual boilers for space heating and instantaneous water heaters for hand washing facilities.

Figure 12.20 Packaged air cooled heat pumps for space heating and cooling of the public spaces, Bluewater, Greenhithe, Kent, UK (1999). *(Source: James Cheung)*

Ventilation Plant

Air handling plant may also be required to ventilate spaces that are not heated or chilled, for example, below ground car parking will require mechanical ventilation. The motorised fans to ventilate below ground car parks can be arranged horizontally or vertically, provided suitable access can be achieved for maintenance and replacement. A common arrangement in below ground parking is to locate the fans at both the supply and extraction ends of the ductwork, to draw air into and across the space before mechanically extracting it. General ventilation fans (provided they have sufficient capacity) can also be doubled up and used at a greater speed for smoke ventilation. For example, fans operating at six air changes per hour for venting the car park can act at ten air changes per hour for smoke extraction. The size of fan used for ventilation of a below ground car park can be 6–9 m (20–30 ft) long and they can be grouped together in a bank, thus the space required to house them will be considerable.

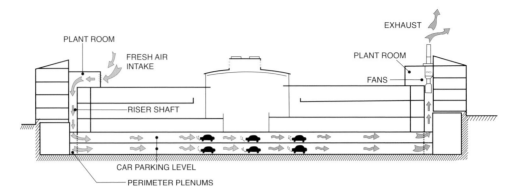

Figure 12.21 Cross section through a basement car park ventilated by pulling air across the space from fans on one side, Chapelfield, Norwich, UK (2005). *(Source: BDP/Sean Dooley)*

Smoke Ventilation

Enclosed and covered public spaces will need to be provided with smoke ventilation. If smoke ventilation cannot be achieved by natural means, a mechanical system will need to be installed and plant space allocated to house the extraction fans. The most efficient arrangement is to connect the extraction fans directly to the space and to discharge at roof level, thereby keeping the ductwork to a minimum. This type of arrangement requires sufficient adjacent space to be available at roof level. Alternatively, large ducts connected to remote fans will need to be accommodated. The ductwork in this case will be large and the routing will require careful consideration.

Combined Heat and Power

With increasing social and corporate pressure for the use of more sustainably sourced energy, combined heat and power (CHP) plant will become more commonly used. As an alternative electricity source

Figure 12.22 Roof mounted smoke extraction fans for the public spaces, WestQuay, Southampton, UK (2000). *(Source: David Barbour)*

to the national grid, CHP is especially relevant in mixed-use development where there is a potential demand for residential property to utilise the surplus heat from the generation of electricity. With an increasing number of mixed-use schemes combining retail and residential uses in the pipeline, CHP is likely to be used increasingly in the future. Where CHP is a possibility, space for plant will need to be considered and planned into the layout from the outset.

Working Space

An important consideration with all plant is to allow sufficient working space for maintenance, repairs, access and eventual replacement. The provision of working space is as important as the actual space for the plant itself.

Provision for Tenants' Plant

The fact that tenants complete their own plant and service installations has been referred to earlier (see Unit shops). Although the landlord does not complete the tenants' plant installation, provision will have to be made in the building and sufficient space allowed to enable the tenant to do so. Each tenancy will have a riser duct with a temporary hood fitted across the opening at roof level, along with an adjacent rooftop area allocated for the tenant's plant. The tenants' roof top plant usually consists of a packaged air-cooled heat pump which, like the landlord's plant adopted for its convenience, is commonly used to space heat and cool each shop unit on an individual basis. The roof plant usually supplies fan coil units located in the ceiling of the shop. With shopping centres commonly containing 50 to 80 tenants or more, this can give rise to a considerable amount of

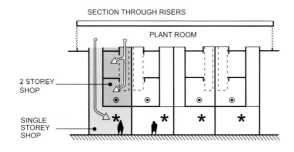

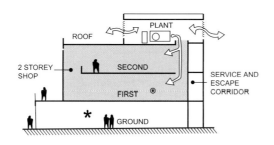

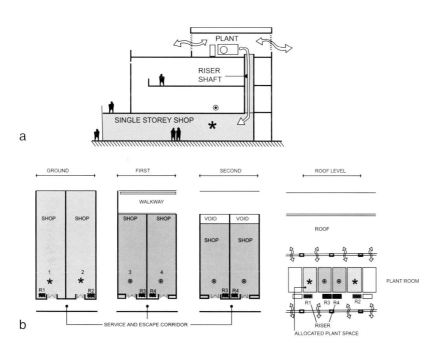

Figure 12.23 (a) Cross sections and (b) plan diagram of multi-level shopping arrangements, with separate shops stacked upon another requiring vertical access to roof located plant. *(Source: BDP/Sean Dooley)*

plant space to be accommodated on the roof. The architect, together with the services engineer, will therefore need to plan the service routing from the shop unit, up to the roof and then to the tenant's plant area. The tenant will be required to complete the installation and waterproofing around the riser opening (see Figs. 12.23 and 12.24).

With the tenants' plant sitting on the roof the landlord will need to make provision to protect the roof's waterproofing, still allowing the tenant to fix the plant, and to allow for the continual maintenance of the roof. There are several commonly used ways of meeting these conflicting requirements. The first approach requires the landlord to provide stub

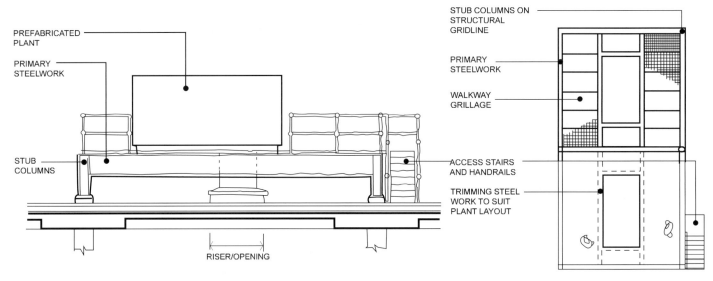

i) STEEL FRAMEWORK ONTO STUB COLUMNS

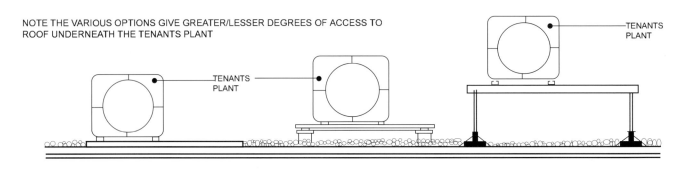

ii) DIRECTLY ONTO PAVING SLABS

iii) PROPRIETARY BEARERS AND FRAMEWORK SUPPORTED ON CONCRETE PADS

iv) PROPRIETARY PADS AND SUPPORTING FRAMEWORK ONTO INSULATION SLABS

Figure 12.24 Supporting tenants roof top plant: (i) steel framework onto stub columns; (ii) directly onto paving slabs; (iii) proprietary bearers and framework supported on concrete upstands; (iv) proprietary pads and supporting framework onto insulation slabs (upside down roof). *(Source: BDP/Sean Dooley)*

Figure 12.25 Tenants' packaged heat exchange units resting on paving slabs, WestQuay, Southampton, UK (2000). *(Source: David Barbour)*

columns and a raised steel platform onto which the tenant fixes the plant installation. A second option is to have raised plinths which the tenant frames across the plant. A third option is to provide a paved area for the tenant to fix plant to. The final option involves the tenant providing a raised platform on to which the plant is fixed (see Fig. 12.24).

All these approaches avoid plant being fixed directly to the roof and retains the integrity of the roof's waterproofing. The architect will also need to plan a suitably finished access route which leads from the access stair to each plant area at roof level. Roof top plant is usually screened by vertical louvres. It is becoming increasingly common in town centre schemes, in sensitive locations and where other

Environmental Issues

With changing regulations, more stringent standards for energy consumption and requirements for more sustainable design, large shopping environments of the future will need to incorporate a wide range of sustainable and low-energy features to meet these new targets.

The environmental issues considered here focus on sustainable energy and reducing energy usage, rather than those relating to visual impact.

The requirement to reduce the generation of carbon dioxide and other emissions associated with certain manufacturing processes and the production and consumption of energy have become widely accepted as part of the effort to minimise the effects of global warming.

Environmentally damaging emissions are primarily caused by the by-products of producing electricity from carbon based fuels such as coal and gas, the exhaust fumes of vehicles and chemicals used in manufacturing processes. Reducing the energy consumption at each stage of a shopping centre's life cycle – during building construction, while the centre is in operation and its dependence on vehicular access – will all fundamentally reduce the level of emissions. Some of the ways in which emissions generated by the formation and running of a shopping centre can be reduced are discussed briefly here, but this is a specialist topic and subject to continual change, so specialist advice should be sought.

Figure 12.26 Tenants' plant screened by louvred roof in the foreground with unscreened plant beyond, New Catherdral Street, Manchester, UK (2003). *(Source: Peter Coleman)*

uses overlook, to enclose fully both landlord's and tenants' plant space with louvred enclosures. It is no longer acceptable in urban locations to let the services 'hang out' (see Fig. 12.26).

Control Rooms

The control room is an integral part of the landlord's plant and functions as the nerve centre of the building. All the landlord's different plant installations controlling the environment, safety and security of the centre, will be wired back to the building management and control systems located in the control room. Control rooms should be centrally positioned wherever possible, to minimise the wiring installations.

The control room will have the monitoring and control facilities for the space heating and cooling; daylight and artificial lighting; fire and smoke detection; sprinklers; natural and artificial ventilation; and security and public address system.

Typical Energy Use

Shopping centres are invariably large scale developments with significant energy demands and their consequent implications for the environment. In the early design stages, consideration should be given to ways of reducing energy consumption both from the formation and operation of the building. The different ways in which energy is directly used in a typical shopping centre are:

- during the construction and formation of the building
- from the various manufacturing processes associated with the materials and installations to form the building
- the energy consumed from heating, cooling, venting and lighting the building in operation – in both the public and tenanted areas
- the energy consumed by the consumers and employees

- the energy used in delivering goods by the vehicles accessing the building.

Design decisions that have the effect of reducing the emissions caused by any of these factors will have both local and global benefits. Careful planning and design should try to minimise to a benign level the effect from energy emissions.

Primary Energy Source

The prime energy source of a shopping centre is generally electricity, with some gas usage. Electricity is used to drive the heating, cooling, venting, lighting, lifts, escalators, mechanical installations, security and information systems. The most convenient way of sourcing electricity is to connect up to the national grid which is run by a network of power stations. Power stations are driven by fuels from a variety of sources, but with a high dependence on carbon based fuels. However, some alternative and renewable sources are starting to be used. Furthermore electricity from the national grid is an inefficient source of supply. More efficient supplies such as combined heat and power (CHP) should be considered at an early stage.

Location

Government planning policy in favour of town centre development has been adopted in most European countries. This is in recognition of the need to reduce travel distances and vehicle dependency by customers and shop staff.

Material Selection

Materials and components which perform equally and which can be locally or regionally sourced should be chosen in preference to items from overseas.

Other environmental considerations (apart from those associated with energy usage) are the general impact and effect on the environment of the manufacture and processing of materials. Materials should preferably be selected from renewable sources rather than artificial materials which involve chemical processes with harmful emissions. Particular care should be taken to understand the manufacturing processes involved with materials in order to avoid the selection of materials that involve wasteful energy processes.

Consideration of its reusability may also be influential in the selection of a material. Natural materials,

for example, are more likely to be reuseable for an alternative use at the end of a building's lifetime.

Evaluating the full environmental consequences of obtaining, processing, delivering and reusing a particular material, will add to the performance criteria when evaluating the merits of alternative materials.

Component Design

In the design of component assemblies made up from different materials, consideration should also be given to the potential recycling and use of the component or its constituent materials. For example, consideration should be given to the ease of removal and disassembly, as well as the general potential to allow for ease of future use.

Avoiding Waste

Avoiding waste involves efficient design both to fulfil the functions of the building and to avoid wastefulness on site. In the design process, materials should be used effectively and not over-designed. A balance will need to be achieved between the visual and the performance requirements of the component.

Operational Efficiency

Shopping centres consume large amounts of energy in operating the building. Energy is primarily consumed in heating, cooling, venting and lighting the accommodation, together with running the mechanical installations which assist vertical movement and the security and information systems that are necessary. The design of the building, together with its systems and controls, will influence the energy consumed by the front of house, back of house and, to a lesser extent the tenanted areas. It has previously been identified that the tenant designs and fits out the shop units (within the shell provided by the landlord). In this regard, the architect has a limited influence over the fabric and power source to the tenanted areas.

In preparation of the brief, the architect and design team should consider ways of reducing the energy consumed in the operation of the building. Ways of reducing the energy load can be identified as:

- use of a more efficient prime energy source
- the extent to which heat is lost and gained (transferred) through the building fabric

- the efficiency of the plant systems and controls tempering the environment of the building
- mitigating the effect of heat gained through the operation of the building, for example from the lighting installations and occupants
- setting sensible internal comfort standards for both the tempering and lighting of the internal environment.

Alternative Energy Sourcing

Although the heating and cooling of the landlord and anchor tenant areas may use alternative energy sources such as gas and CHP as the primary source to temper the environment, it is important to convince the landlord to supply the tenants with an alternative primary electricity source. A fundamental consideration at the outset of the project is the use of an on site CHP installation as a means of providing electricity in a more efficient way. Electricity that is sourced from renewable sources such as wind and hydraulic power, is less polluting than electricity from traditional fossil fuel driven power stations and should also be investigated if a CHP source is inappropriate.

Heat Transfer

Reducing the heat transfer through the building fabric will help to optimise the energy required to heat and cool the internal environment of the building. The insulation quality of the roof, floor, walls and windows will influence heat transfer and should have high insulation characteristics. National building regulation standards should be considered as only a minimum benchmark and higher standards should be used. In shopping centres, the requirement for cooling is often more relevant than the need for heating. Although the cooling requirement is largely driven from the internal lighting installations and occupants, it is important to minimise external heat gain through the building fabric.

Efficient Systems and Controls

As well as efficient energy sources, it is important to select efficient boiler heaters and space heating systems to reduce the energy used to run the installations. The control system should allow the system to respond to changing external environmental conditions and internal occupancy levels. These controls range from simple timing programmes, thermostatic temperature controls, daylight sensors – modulating shading devices and internal artificial lighting, through to rain and wind sensors which optimise ventilation openings.

Mitigating Heat Build Up

One of the most effective means of reducing the energy load in an enclosed shopping centre is the careful adoption of a combination of passive and active measures to reduce heat build up. The objective behind reducing heat build up is to mitigate the requirement for cooling and air-conditioning.

One of the largest energy requirements in a shopping centre is generated by the display and space lighting. Consequently, one of the most significant ways of reducing running costs and energy consumption is the use of low energy lighting.

Further information and advice on energy efficient lighting for retail accommodation can be found in Josephine Prior's book 'Sustainable Retail Premises, an Environmental Guide to Design, Refurbishment and Management of Retail Premises' (1999).

Sensible Comfort Standards

Guidance on the acceptable internal temperatures to be provided in enclosed shopping environments can be found in Energy Efficiency Best Practice, GIR 31 'Avoiding or Minimising the Use of Air-conditioning' (DETR, 1995).

The Future

There is both increasing social awareness and a corresponding corporate pressure for shopping centre owners to demonstrate energy reducing policies and to create sustainable buildings. From 2006, European legislation will require public buildings to display openly their energy usage, in a similar way to the labels on electrical appliances.

Fire Safety

Regulations

Shopping centres are fundamentally large complex buildings occupied by considerable numbers of the general public and shop staff. These buildings must be planned to be safe and, in the event of an emergency or fire, allow for fast and safe evacuation from the building by all its occupants. In the design of the practical issues, fire safety is one of the most important and complex considerations. Fire safety requirements will be more onerous for enclosed and covered shopping centres than for open street based schemes. There are many regulations and guidance documents which vary from country to country. In the UK the two most significant documents are the Building Regulations and the code of practice BS 5588 – Fire Precautions in the Design, Construction and Use of Buildings: Part 10 – Code of Practice for Enclosed Shopping Centres. These regulations and guidelines are regulated by local authority building control who are responsible for the enforcement of the legislation with the fire service acting as a consultant to the local authority. The fire officer (of the Fire Service) has a pivotal role in the interpretation of the code of practice as the guide to developing a fire safety strategy for the building.

The fire safety strategy and design will have to be agreed and approved by the local building control and usually involves a process of negotiation, which is continuous throughout the development of the design. The architect will need to comply with the regulations and satisfy the fire service, which will involve a common interpretation and understanding being reached between both parties. In view of the building complexity and the extent of legislation, specialist fire consultants often join the design team to advise on the interpretation of regulations, to develop the fire safety strategy and negotiate with the local authority. In the design process, early and regular discussions are recommended with the controlling authority in order to formulate the fire safety strategy. Invariably the final strategy will involve a combination of application of the regulations, the adoption of a sensible interpretation of the codes and a degree of negotiation.

The process of interpretation and negotiation in reaching a fire safety strategy will be determined by a combination of the following factors:
- means of escape
- control of smoke
- prevention of fire spread
- access for fire-fighting facilities
- management systems and procedures.
  Each of these factors is examined further below.
  It is also worth noting that in large centres the fire safety strategies are usually based on some commonly agreed fundamental principles which are:
- the building will be subdivided into several zones for the purpose of establishing escaping populations and smoke extraction zones

- for the purpose of assessing means of escape and smoke ventilation, a fire will occur in one zone at a time
- evacuation of the building will be phased and organised one zone at a time. (Phased evacuation prevents the instantaneous evacuation of the whole centre.)

These common principles significantly help with the sizing of the means of escape, as the population is divided into manageable zones.

Means of Escape

The routes of escape to places of safety outside the building include purpose-made escape routes, the service corridors, interconnecting stairs and the public circulation spaces themselves.

The provision of the means of escape is determined by several key factors:
- the number of people escaping – the population
- the distance of travel to a place of safety
- the time taken to evacuate the building.

These factors can be applied to determine the escape requirements for a particular zone of the building. The code of practice BS 5588 Part 10 (the Code) allows the mall exit widths to be calculated from either the population in the mall or from the population in the shop units, whichever is the greater. The occupancy factor for the malls is set out in the Code (square metres/per person) which defines the occupancy rates for the shops. In some circumstances, where the tenant is known at the design stage, it may be beneficial to negotiate a lower occupancy rate which is specific to the shop. However, at the design stage it is wise to adopt the standard Code occupancy rate, as this will build in future flexibility to allow different types of shop to occupy the unit, should tenants change in the future.

The time taken to evacuate a zone of its population will significantly influence the width of the means of escape routes. Traditionally 2.5 minutes has been the required evacuation time, which has resulted in large escape corridors of 5 m wide and scissor stair arrangements to transfer the population vertically. More recently, specialist fire consultants have presented a reasoned case for the use of 5 minute evacuation periods, which the fire service has accepted in negotiation, and correspondingly the size of the corridors and stairs have been reduced.

The maximum travel distance from a mall to an escape exit is 45 m (146 ft) (assuming there is an alternative exit in the other direction). This establishes that escape routes must not be positioned more than 90 m apart along the length of the circulation space.

While the unit shops use the communal escape routes and stairs to the outside of the building, the large MSUs and department stores must provide integral escape stairs and routes (see opposite). In these stores the escape stairs and corridors must be self-contained and capable of handling the population of the store. In determining the population of these stores, the standard occupancy rate may be too dense for the actual store and it could be worth negotiating with the fire service. The fire safety specialists may prepare a case based on evidence from other stores to help negotiate a reduced occupancy rate and thereby help to achieve realistic escape provisions.

All the unit shops, MSUs and department stores will be required to obtain their own individual approval from building control for the means of escape from the shop unit. Although shopping centre architects are not generally required to design the escape routes within the stores, they must be able to understand these requirements to make provision for the stores to be able to do so in a practical manner.

Control of Smoke

It is well recorded that inhalation of smoke and hot gases are the primary causes of death in a fire. The building must therefore be designed to provide safe and smoke free escape routes. Designing the building to control smoke is especially critical where the public spaces will be used as a means of escape. In these cases, the interior space will have to be designed to control and channel away the smoke from the clear escape zone and to release it to the open air. An important aspect of controlling smoke in public spaces will be the formation of a 3.5 m (11.7 ft) high clear zone for the public to escape through. The clear zone is achieved by the formation of sufficient space above the public space to hold the smoke before it is extracted to the open air. This holding space is referred to as a 'smoke reservoir'. Public spaces are usually given volume as part of the design, which can be put to a very practical use by providing sufficient space for the smoke reservoir (see Fig. 12.29).

In shopping centres, the most likely source of a fire is from within the shops. For the purpose of smoke control and extraction, the building will generally be designed to deal with the fire load from a single fire occurring in any one of the shop units. The control of the smoke, the smoke reservoir and extraction is designed to accommodate a standard fire load of 5 megawatts.

It is important to note that the large MSU and department stores are generally required to deal

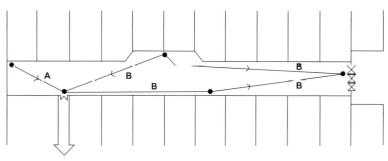

A - 18 metres in 1 direction

B - 45 metres in 2 directions

Figure 12.27 Maximum escape distances in a public space/mall. *(Source: BDP/Sean Dooley)*

with smoke extraction independently and extract their smoke directly through ducts which lead to the outside air.

There are two general strategies that can be used for the removal of smoke from the building (see Fig. 12.31). The first has been alluded to above, whereby the smoke from the source in the shop is allowed to discharge into the public space from which it is then controlled and extracted. This is a commonly adopted practice, where the discharged smoke in the mall is controlled from spreading by the use of screens that are either fixed or drop down automatically when activated by smoke detectors. The screens channel the smoke, limit cold air dilution and ensure the smoke plume has sufficient heat and buoyancy to move out beyond the shop, rise up into the smoke reservoir and then to be extracted into the open air by natural or mechanical

Figure 12.28 A smoke control glazed downstand used to control the smoke towards the extraction fans. *(Source: Richard Allen)*

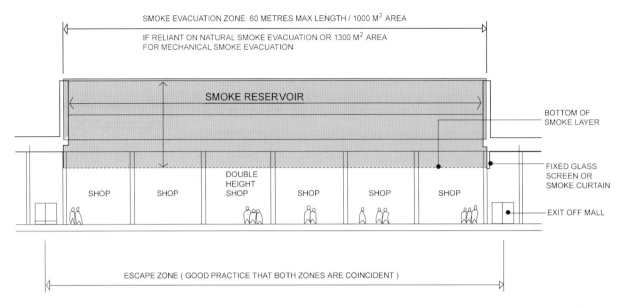

SMOKE EVACUATION ZONE: 60 METRES MAX LENGTH / 1000 M² AREA

IF RELIANT ON NATURAL SMOKE EVACUATION OR 1300 M² AREA
FOR MECHANICAL SMOKE EVACUATION

SMOKE RESERVOIR

BOTTOM OF
SMOKE LAYER

FIXED GLASS
SCREEN OR
SMOKE CURTAIN

SHOP   SHOP   DOUBLE
HEIGHT
SHOP   SHOP   SHOP   SHOP

EXIT OFF MALL

ESCAPE ZONE (GOOD PRACTICE THAT BOTH ZONES ARE COINCIDENT)

Figure 12.29 Longitudinal section illustrates the principle of a smoke reservoir above the shops. *(Source: BDP/Sean Dooley)*

Figure 12.30 A light, elegant glass smoke screen defining the smoke reservoir into a controllable area, WestQuay, Southampton, UK (2000). *(Source: David Barbour)*

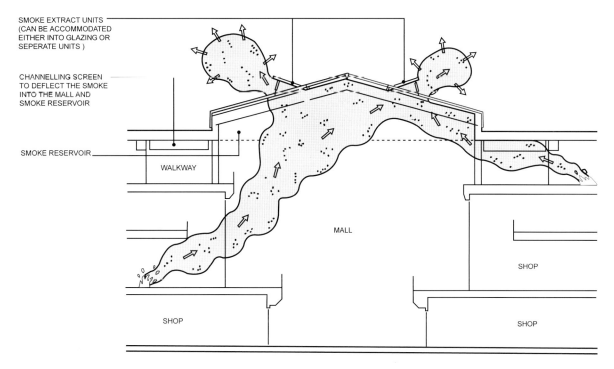

SMOKE EXTRACT UNITS
(CAN BE ACCOMMODATED
EITHER INTO GLAZING OR
SEPERATE UNITS)

CHANNELLING SCREEN
TO DEFLECT THE SMOKE
INTO THE MALL AND
SMOKE RESERVOIR

SMOKE RESERVOIR

WALKWAY

MALL

SHOP

SHOP

SHOP

NATURAL VENTILATION / MECHANICAL VENTILATION
BULKHEADS/CEILINGS GREATER THAN 1500MM - CHANNELLING SCREENS REQUIRED TO STOP
a   SMOKE RACING ALONG THE UNDERSIDE OF CEILING

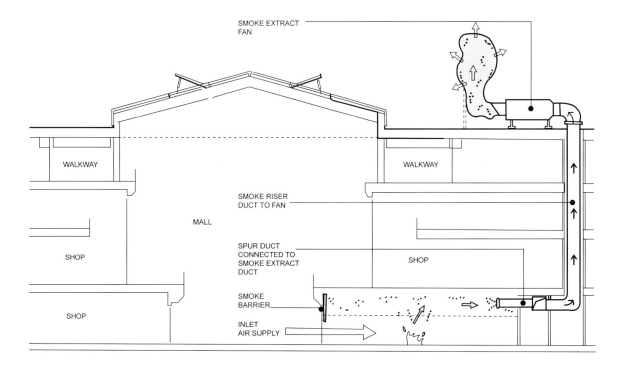

SMOKE EXTRACT
FAN

WALKWAY

WALKWAY

MALL

SMOKE RISER
DUCT TO FAN

SHOP

SPUR DUCT
CONNECTED TO
SMOKE EXTRACT
DUCT

SHOP

SMOKE
BARRIER

SHOP

INLET
AIR SUPPLY

MECHANICAL VENTILATION

b

Figure 12.31 Alternative ways for venting smoke from a fire in a shop: (a) through the front of the shop and out via the public space; (b) through the shop unit and taken out via ducts at the rear. *(Source: BDP/Sean Dooley)*

ventilation. Generally, the smoke's natural buoyancy will readily discharge it beyond a projecting bulkhead up to 1.5 m (5 ft) long. Where the overhang in front of the shop is greater than 1.5 m additional screens will be required to channel the smoke outwards and up into the public space.

In the control of smoke in the public space, the roof area will need to be subdivided by vertical screens or smoke curtains to form smoke reservoirs which are no more than 60 m (180 ft) long. The smoke reservoirs are controlled in size in order to retain the clear zone beneath the smoke layer. The public space may be formed into a series of smoke reservoirs, where each one is treated as an individual smoke control zone. Ideally, the zone for smoke control should coincide with the zone established for the means of escape (see Fig. 12.29). Given that the maximum distance between escapes is 90 m, some balancing and compromise is likely to be needed in the public space design. The mismatch of dimensions can, however, readily be designed out by the use of screens or smoke curtains to achieve a coordinated design.

Having formed the smoke reservoir, the smoke has to be extracted through the roof. The rate of extraction will be determined by the volume of smoke, the height to the point of extraction and the minimum height of the smoke layer required to maintain the clear zone. In view of this calculation being influenced by the height and volume of the space, it is beneficial for the roof space to be significantly higher than the occupied space.

Natural smoke venting of the space can be used provided sufficient openings can be made in the roof space and where the external air flows around the roof are not influenced by surrounding buildings. It is common for the smoke to be mechanically extracted in the more complex schemes and in those located in town centre locations with surrounding tall buildings.

The alternative smoke control strategy is generally to leave the public space free of any discharging smoke and to extract the smoke mechanically from the shop unit via ductwork, to discharge at roof level (see Fig. 12.31b). Even with the use of common vertical smoke extraction ducts (reducing the number of large ducts passing upwards through the building), this approach is a more complex arrangement. Common riser ducts, for example, require fire proofing and dampers to prevent the spread of fire between units. In addition, a fire resistant downstand (of approximately 1 m deep) is required at the front of each shop to prevent smoke escaping into the public space and allow the upper

part of each shop to become the smoke reservoir. While this approach imposes restrictions on the tenant's ceiling and shopfront design, it limits the extent of damage caused elsewhere in the centre and can reduce the possibility of panic among the escaping population.

When considering the virtues of these two approaches to the control of smoke, the use of the mall to extract the smoke is generally understood and accepted to work well in spaces with up to two publicly accessed shopping levels. However, in view of smoke plumes cooling and losing buoyancy as they progress vertically, the mall extraction approach has limitations. Larger and more complex spaces with more than two levels are likely to require the lower levels to have the smoke extracted without discharging into the mall and the hybrid solution may be considered. WestQuay, Southampton, which has a four-level space, adopts a hybrid solution, with the lower ground floor extracting smoke through the shops, while the upper floors operate on the principle of discharging smoke into the public space. An extensive glazed screen spanning 50 m, subdivides the roof void into two separate smoke reservoirs (see Fig. 12.30). Although the discharge of smoke into the mall can generally be expected to work in schemes with up to two levels, with the trend for shops having mezzanine trading floors and shops becoming taller, the buoyancy of the smoke in some two-level schemes will need to be carefully examined.

Whichever method of smoke control and extraction is adopted, provision will need to be made for replacement air to balance the removed smoke. The replacement air can usually be achieved by the inclusion of automatic entrance doors and opening windows in entrance screens.

Although the smoke control strategy can be tested through desk top analysis, it is common practice for large enclosed or covered schemes to have the smoke control strategy verified by way of a laboratory wind tunnel test undertaken on a scaled model. These model wind tests are especially useful to verify if a natural smoke venting solution will work in a town centre location.

Prevention of Fire Spread

Public spaces and malls are generally constructed from non-combustible materials and, unless used for trading, are considered by the fire service as a low risk. (The implication of retail activity in the mall is discussed further on.) The principal area to prevent

Figure 12.32 Sprinkler distribution main adjacent to main tanks serving a typical shopping centre. *(Source: David Barbour)*

Figure 12.33 Water storage tanks for sprinkler supplies. *(Source: David Barbour)*

the spread of fire is, therefore, from shop to shop. The construction of the shop shell must be of fire-resistant material which must extend to include sealing between walls and floors and all openings where connections pass between compartments. Fire dampers must be included in any ductwork that connects shop units.

Generally, the fronts of shops are separated by public spaces which are sufficiently wide for there not to be a risk of fire jumping between shops. In narrow public spaces with fully glazed shop windows facing each other, it may be necessary to install fire shutters or drenchers to prevent fire spreading from one shop to another across the space. (The risk of fire spread from one unit to another will be determined by the size of shop unit.) Extinguishing by water can be an effective means of controlling the spread of fire and can be achieved in a variety of ways. Small fires can be dealt with by hand-held extinguishers and the use of hose reels. In covered and enclosed shopping centres, sprinkler systems are likely to provide the primary means of fire control.

Sprinkler systems within shop units are usually installed by the tenant by connecting up to a sprinkler main provided by the landlord. To achieve sufficient water pressure it is common practice for the landlord to provide sprinkler storage tanks and a pumped sprinkler supply. Stand-by pumps and stand-by power generation will also need to be installed if the sprinkler supply is to be pumped. Large stores may also require their own sprinkler tank.

Sprinkler protection of the public spaces in covered shopping centres will generally not be required if the space is only used as a circulation space. Where the public space is to be used for any retailing activity, sprinkler protection will be required. It is essential to establish with the client and retail advisers if any retail use is intended for the public space in both the immediate and longer terms. A dilemma can arise post-completion when subsequent asset management teams wish to add kiosks to an unsprinklered space in order to provide additional revenue.

Access for Fire-Fighting Facilities

The need to provide road access and space for fire-fighting vehicles has previously been identified (Initiating the project – site accessibility).

Access routes for fire-fighting vehicles must be provided to predetermined points agreed by the fire

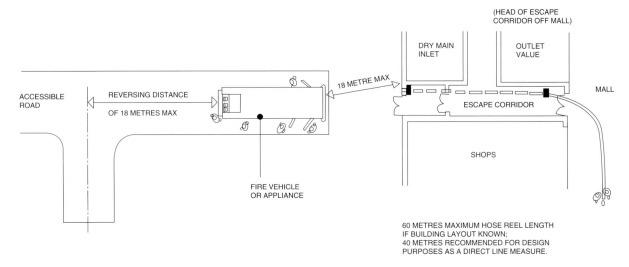

Figure 12.34 Fire-fighting vehicles should be able to gain access to within 18 m of the building, with sufficient points of access to allow 60 m hose lengths to cover all parts of the building. *(Source: BDP)*

service. The access layout must ensure that all parts of the building or buildings can be covered by the fire-fighting vehicles or provide easy access to stair cores within the building. Access routes must be kept free of any obstructions at all times. The location and number of points of access will be determined by the size of centre and the length of hose reels (60 m maximum) used on the appliances.

Fire-fighting vehicles are heavy and large and must be given sufficient manoeuvring space for the largest vehicles to get within 18 m of the building.

As well as making provision for access by fire-fighting vehicles, other fire-fighting facilities may be required in the building for use by the fire service. These facilities can include dry risers, hose reels, hydrants and fire-fighting lifts. These will need to be easily accessible and conveniently located near the vehicular access points to assist the fire service to fight a fire.

The fire service is likely to require automatic fire indicator panels at the agreed fire call points and often also repeater panels at entranceways. All the alarm and detection systems from the individual tenants and from the landlord's areas will be integrated and connected back to the monitoring systems in the management control room. The alarm and detection systems will need to be agreed with the fire service, as well as the procedure for how the management staff will work together with the fire service in the event of a fire.

Early consultation with the building control and fire service is recommended to agree the vehicular access and fire-fighting strategies.

Management Systems and Procedures

In preparing the fire safety strategy, the fire consultant will also consider the benefit of having management staff to hand in the event of a fire. For example, the fire service has the opportunity to influence the management procedures in the event of a fire. The procedural activities which the fire service may wish to influence are:

■ immediate checking if the alarm is for a real fire and rectifying the system if it is a false alarm
■ utilising the public address system to advise the public to evacuate the building (rather than the use of a general alarm)
■ providing management staff to prevent further public access to the building or the zone where the fire has been identified
■ providing management staff to help guide the public to the escape routes.

Although none of these measures directly influences the design of the building, they are responsive human measures which assist public safety and may be taken into account in considering the overall fire safety strategy.

References

British Council of Shopping Centres (2000). *A Briefing Guide for Shopping Centre Development.* BCSC, p. 31.

DETR (1995). *Energy Efficiency Best Practice, GIR31, Avoiding or Minimising the Use of Air Conditioning.* DETR.

Prior, J. (1999). *Sustainable Retail Premises, An Environmental Guide to Design, Refurbishment and Management of Retail Premises.* BRE Publications, pp 13-16.

The fully let mixture of shops and cafés facing onto the open entrance space, Chapelfield, Norwich, UK (2005). *(Source: BDP/David Balbour)*

Economic and Commercial Considerations

13

Overall Objectives

The developer's and investor's objective will be to produce a shopping development that is both profitable on completion and successful in operation. It should be noted that the developer's interest will be focused towards making a short-term development profit and the investor more focused towards achieving a successful, long-term investment. While these roles are often combined, there will inevitably be some divergence of interest between the developer and investor. (The different interests and characteristics of the types of client were examined in more detail in Chapter 7.)

The common commercial considerations examined here are considered under the following topics:

- finding the opportunity
- assessing if a project will be successful
- managing the process and risk.
- making a profit.
- other considerations and drivers.

Finding the Opportunity

Opportunities generally arise through three different routes: local authority/public sector promoted opportunities (generally in some form of competition); redevelopment or extension of an existing shopping centre; or by an entrepreneur recognising the potential of a site and promoting it for development.

Of these three possibilities the first is by far the most common. Not only is it most likely that the opportunity is recognised by the local authority in its own town or city but it also has, via its planning and compulsory purchase powers, the ability to reduce key uncertainties that inhibit or delay development.

However, with the first generation of UK shopping centres now over 40 years old (and many no longer truly fit for purpose), there is a growing likelihood that existing centres will be redeveloped or significantly extended – the best recent example of this trend being The Bullring in Birmingham.

Figure 13.1 36 years after the opening of one of the first enclosed shopping centres in the UK, the joint venture company, The Birmingham Alliance (two development companies and an institution, see Chapter 5), commenced the demolition in order to redevelop The Bullring with a 110000 m², £500 million, town centre development. Illustrated here at its opening launch in 2003, The Bullring, Birmingham, UK. *(Source: Ravi Deepres)*

Examples of entrepreneurs finding and promoting sites are less common currently than was the case in the past. Several of the larger out-of-town shopping centres or mega-malls were the brainchild of individual entrepreneurs – the MetroCentre (Sir John Hall), Meadowhall (Eddie Healey) and Trafford (John Whittaker) being eminent examples. However, with the planning policy of successive governments favouring in-town retail development over out-of-town, the scope for individual entrepreneurs has diminished, although not entirely disappeared. There are still opportunities (in town or out) that are recognised by the property industry but not actively promoted by local authorities. The Oracle, Reading (see Chapter 5) is an example of a scheme that was promoted by the developer (Hammerson) and, although it enjoyed support from the council, it was a privately promoted scheme.

Once a suitable opportunity has been recognised, by whichever route, it is almost inevitable that the support or cooperation of the local authority will be required since the land is unlikely to be in single ownership and therefore compulsory purchase powers are likely to be required.

Assessing if a Project will be Successful

The challenge for developers and investors is in finding development sites in suitable locations which can also be purchased for a reasonable price. Few development opportunities arise from a single land purchase. Invariably development sites are assembled from several acquisitions where the developer's skill will be to assess the likelihood of assembling the remainder of the site while securing the major opportunity.

Opportunities arise where customer demand is not being met. This assessment can be made from researching the catchment population to establish the consumer demand and surveying the existing retail facilities. The combination of demographic research and understanding of existing retail facilities can help to determine what opportunities exist to provide new and additional facilities in order to meet the aspirations of the catchment. (Demographic surveys and assessments of existing retailing are examined in Chapter 8.)

Surveys establish, *inter alia*, available spend and existing rental levels. From this information a developer will be able to determine the prospects for future rental growth. The best opportunities occur where there is a strong level of projected growth.

Having identified the development and market opportunity, it will also be necessary to assess the likely success of the development and refine the type of retail to be provided. Much of this assessment will be established from more detailed research of the catchment population and market potential.

Understanding the number and nature of the customers in the catchment will be assisted by demographic profiling prepared by specialist analysts (see Chapter 8). This information will help to establish the type of shops that are required and likely to succeed.

The retail agents will also advise on the level of demand for space from retailers, which will be an important determinant of the total amount and type of space that is supportable.

Managing the Process and Risk

A key factor in determining the success of the development (and the level of profit it is likely to make) is the mitigation and management of risk. Development risk can occur in a variety of areas. The principal issues are planning, site assembly, efficient design, delivery time, completion dates, funding and leasing (or letting risk) and these are overlaid with the time the project will take to complete. These issues and their interrelationship are considered below.

Planning

The primary consideration will be to establish the likelihood of achieving planning permission for the proposed development. This will be influenced by the fit with both strategic planning guidance for additional retail growth and the sensitivity of the particular site.

Strategic planning guidance considerations:
- the location of the site
  - with current guidance favouring in-town development
- the size of development
  - is the size of development supported by the strategic growth for the region and particular area?
- will the size of development be referred to the strategic planning body (even where the growth is supported)?
- is the development considered strategic and likely to involve consultation with the custodians of the built environment (e.g. Commission for Architecture and the Built Environment (CABE))?
- is the development in an historic town and likely to involve historic building and conservation consultees (e.g. English Heritage (EH))?

Consultation with each of the above strategic bodies will add a level of complexity to the application.

In addition to the strategic planning issues, the local context and site sensitivity will need to be assessed.

- It will be necessary to assess the local sensitivity and the likely consultations that will be necessary
- Can local hearts and minds be won over?

Planning risk can be reduced by careful consideration of the issues and by establishing a strategy to address each issue at the earliest stage.

Working closely with the local planning authority throughout will also help achieve planning permission. Large-scale development can be assisted by the planning authority working with the developer to prepare a development framework or masterplan, which can be adopted as long-term planning guidance for the development and the surrounding context.

Such an approach is time consuming and requires a commitment from the developer, but may be the surest route to success.

Applications for large developments are encouraged to engage in local consultation and demonstrate local influence. An auditable consultation process is likely to assist a successful application.

Site Assembly

Assembling town centre development sites can take some time to complete. Much of the site can often be secured through negotiation. However, it is highly likely on larger projects that the site can only be completed through a compulsory purchase order (CPO). Where a CPO is required, this can only proceed once planning permission has been gained and, by its nature, with the assistance of the local authority or Regional Development Agency. Large developments can take several years to secure planning permission with the site assembly only finalised following a set period after the planning permission. The developer will often, therefore, have to manage the development risk some way into the project. In the development timescale, this can be more than halfway through the overall process. More importantly, the developer can be working and expending costs for a considerable time.

Land acquisitions are sensitive and developers will usually seek to pay current market values as opposed to completed development values. Developers therefore often aim to secure or obtain options on as much of the site as possible prior to planning permission being granted. For developers, exclusive options on sites are attractive arrangements, whereby site purchase is only completed once the developer is sure the development will proceed. Option arrangements on land allow developers to minimise upfront financial outlay and help

to reduce interest payments during the period before which returns can be expected.

Efficient Design

Improving the net to gross areas of a scheme can significantly increase the viability of the project. Efficient design is achieved by keeping the dimensions of public spaces to the minimum required for them to operate safely as intended. Design expenditure should be planned to achieve maximum effect and add value to the project. For example, materials and details should be influenced by their location – 'front of house' areas being more elaborate than the 'back of house' areas. Failure to recognise these design drivers as part of managing the process can result in frustrating and lengthy value engineering, at a later stage, in order to make the scheme viable.

Delivery Time

Large-scale development can take an average of 10 years to complete. Since any financial outlay by the developer will affect the profitability of the project and will attract interest on the money expended, the developer will be keen to limit expenditure until there is certainty that the project will proceed.

The periods of high expenditure should also be kept as short as possible to reduce the interest payments on land/property exchanges and capital expenditure. For example, land exchange deals should be managed to be as late as possible in the process and construction periods should be as short as practically possible.

Once land deals are completed and construction is underway, the overall aim will be to ensure that returns and income can be achieved as quickly as possible.

Given that shopping centres are usually required to meet the prime annual trading periods, construction programming is usually sequenced working backwards from a completion date which allows the tenants to open in time to benefit from Christmas trading, which commences in October. Construction programmes, funding agreements, development agreements and property exchanges are arranged, and sometimes delayed, to meet the specific Christmas trading period. In some instances where the Christmas period cannot be achieved, completion dates are sequenced to coincide with the Easter trading period.

Completion Dates

Finalising the completion date is critical to the funding becoming unconditional, and allows the tenant leasing negotiations to be completed. Meeting the completion date will be critical (to both the developer and funding partner) as it will confirm the timing of the return on the investment and any agreement is also likely to incur penalties if the date is not met.

Commitment to the start of the building contract is a key milestone in a shopping development. Commitment to the building contract is perhaps more significant in large retail developments than on other projects, in that it is tied in with other legal arrangements including:

- the shop unit leasing agreements with tenants
- the property and land exchanges
- the development agreement with the local authority
- the completion of the funding agreement where the developer hands over the ownership to the fund on completion.

The timing of the signing of the contract will often involve the legal team in a period of frantic activity in order to have the other legal agreements in place, ready to sign simultaneously. Once these commitments are made there is no going back and significant risk is then passed to the contractor to deliver the building on time and within budget. Because of the critical nature of the building contract commencement, all parties wish to ensure that all aspects are safely secured.

Funding

Financing the project is critical to retail development. The arranging and releasing of funds will be a key driver of the process and progress of the project. Funding will be critical to enable the project to enter subsequent stages. While some developers finance a project from their own resources or by bank borrowing, the majority of large retail developments are also funded by at least a partial equity investment by one or more institutional investors, such as insurance companies or pension funds. Funding from a financial institution is usually delivered in stages, once major milestones have been reached. The funding will not normally become unconditional until the developer has secured completion of the site assembly, the signing of the building contract, finalisation of key lettings and the legal agreements for the development. At this stage the fund will allow the developer to draw down the money to acquire the site and, thereafter, draw down in stages the money required to pay the building contractor, the professional fees and other costs.

Funding is interlinked with the key drivers of retail development:

- land assembly
- the development agreement
- leasing
- building construction.

The interrelationships are examined separately below.

External financing from a funding partner for the project only usually becomes available once certain conditions have been achieved. These can include:

- obtaining planning permission
- establishing the principles for the heads of terms agreement with the anchor tenant or even a binding but conditional agreement for lease in place
- agreeing the principles of the heads of terms agreement with the development partner and/or local authority
- a proportion of other tenants showing a commitment to the development (see below for when tenants can formally commit to the project)
- a costed scheme
- a realistic and achievable opening date
- site assembly or agreed options on land/property to allow full acquisition to be completed at short notice.

External funding will be secured from an institution or fund through a funding agreement. Developers usually arrange for the funding to coincide with the point when major expenditure is required. This usually occurs at a simultaneous point, for example when the construction contract is signed and contracts to acquire the site are exchanged.

It is common for developers to self-fund the scheme up to the 'tipping point' of major expenditure. This point (as explained above) coincides with most of the development risks being managed out or largely achieved. On large-scale developments some developers may seek a joint venture partner to share the risk up to the funding agreement. Such a joint venture may be with another developer or an investing institution. It can take several years to reach the milestone of securing the funding agreement. The lengthy and unsure process emphasises the need for the developer to minimise costs up until this moment. Developers will usually reimburse architects costs up to this point. It is important for the architect to understand the pressures on the developer and to expect only a reasonable proportion of the fee until this critical milestone has been reached.

Anglican Cathedral   Paradise Street   Police HQ   Line of Old Dock   Albert Dock   The River Mersey   Law Courts   Site 14 - Shops

Line of original   Site 13C - 2 Levels Retail   Site 13D - Underground Carpark / Service infrastructure   Site 15 - Debenhams   Site 13A - Retail / Cinemas
'Pool' of Liverpool

Figure 13.2 Construction of the 140 000 m² Paradise Street development involves multiple site activities, with the simultaneous construction of several individual buildings and the surrounding infrastructure commonly generating a monthly construction expenditure of more than £10 million. Paradise Street Development Area, Liverpool, UK (planned 2008). *(Source: BDP)*

Leasing

Mention has been made above of the interrelated nature of the key drivers of retail development. Leasing is a key driver and both the developer and funding partner will have an interest in securing a level of commitment from retailers before proceeding with a project. Funding agreements usually require, for example, a proportion of the tenant leasing to be committed prior to release of funding. For a developer to attract interest in a scheme from a financial institution requires commitment from at least the anchor tenants. Final stage funding will ideally involve an indication of commitment to the development from a good proportion of the retailers. Most unit shop retail tenants will not be able to agree formally to take space in a development until the opening date can be fixed and many shop unit tenants are unable to commit to leasing a shop two or three years in advance. Most tenant agreements can therefore only be signed once the building contract is in place and the construction is in progress. Undertaking the building contract and funding therefore have to be arranged on the basis of tenants giving an indication of interest. Binding but conditional agreements for lease with the anchor tenants and potentially heads of terms agreements with other retailers can, however, usually be agreed on the basis of a target completion date.

Making a Profit

Development Appraisals

The key aim of the developer will be to maximise profit upon completion of the shopping centre.

Development profit can be simply expressed as how much money will be made on the sale of the development having met all the costs, including land, the building construction, interest payments on the finance and payment of the professional consultants' fees. The assessment of the viability of a project is referred to as a development appraisal (Figs. 13.3 and 13.4).

Put simply

Development Profit = Development Value less Development Cost

Figure 13.3 Development appraisals

The development appraisal can be structured and reviewed to analyse a range of outputs, e.g. on residual site value and development profit.

A key measure used by developers is development yield (Fig. 13.5).

Terminology

The important elements for consideration in an appraisal are described below.

Development (or Capital) Value

This is the value of the development when completed (often assessed one year after practical completion, by which time retentions under the building contract have been released, rent free periods to tenants expired and the centre should be fully let and income-producing). The value is calculated by estimating the rents that will be achieved and the return that an investor would require (e.g. 5.75%). By dividing the rental value (ERV) by the investment yield required,

Figure 13.4 Development yield.

one arrives at a gross value from which purchasers' costs need to be deducted to arrive at a net value.

Interest

Whether schemes are funded by a financial institution, a bank, a combination of both or (less commonly) by the developer from his own resources, interest needs to be calculated from when expenditure is incurred to the point when the development is assumed to be completed. To estimate this in advance, and to monitor expenditure during the development period, the developer will construct a cashflow financial model drawing upon a construction cost cash flow prepared by the quantity surveyor. An estimate of when other expenditure will be incurred will then be prepared. This will allow the developer to assess accurately the cost of borrowing the money as well as monitoring the outlay against budget.

Tenant Incentives

Since the developer has assumed in the estimate of development (or capital) value that the centre will be fully income-producing, any rent-free periods or capital incentives paid to retailers to take space within the scheme will need to be included in the estimate of development cost. Since the shop units are provided as a bare shell, it is common practice for retailers (in particular the anchor tenants) to ask for a rent-free period and/or a capital contribution to assist with the cost of fitting out their unit.

Development Profit

As set out above this is a product of deducting all of the development costs (usually referred to as total development cost (or TDC)) from the capital value. While the cash value of the profit is of interest, most developers will be more interested in considering the profit as a percentage of their financial outlay to allow them to assess whether they are being adequately rewarded for the risks they are taking. In our example, the profit of £34.6m represents an 18 per cent profit on cost (i.e. 34/188×100) and this would be within the range

Floor Areas/ Components	GIA ft²	Av Rate Rent/ ft²	ERV	Investment Yield	Gross Capital Value	Purchaser's Costs	Net Capital Value
						5.7625%	
Extension							
Dept. Store	150,000	£8.00	£1,200,000				
MSUs	120,000	£25.00	£3,000,000				
Retail Units	250,000	£37.44	£9,360,000				
Sub Total	520,000		£13,560,000	5.75%	£235,826,087		£222,977,000
Development Value					£235,826,087		£222,977,000
Land Assembly							
Acquisition of Car Park Site					£9,500,000		
Rehousing of ambulance station					3,850,000		
Allowance for buying out existing tenants				say	2,700,000		
Cost of freehold					13,500,000		
Purchasers costs on all above at 5.7525%					1,702,819		
					£31,252,819		
Predevelopment Costs							
Demolitions + site clearance					£5,200,000		
Diversion of existing services					900,000		
Surveys				say	75,000		
Planning				say	100,000		
Section 106				say	1,500,000		
Research/ Promotion				say	50,000		
					£7,825,000		
Construction							
Dept Store					£12,000,000		
Retail - new construction					30,600,000		
MSU - new construction					14,200,000		
Mall - new construction					7,250,000		
Other Indicative Allowances					£20,000,000		
					£84,050,000		
Contingency @		5.0%			4,202,500		
					£4,202,500		
Consultants Fees							
Professional Fees		15.5%			£13,679,138		
Letting Costs							
Letting Fees		15.0%			£2,034,000		
Legal Fees		3.0%			406,800		
Tenants incentives including rent free					22,040,000		
Marketing				say	500,000		
					£24,980,800		
Project Contingency		5.0%			£6,736,872		
Net Development Costs					£172,727,128		
Interest on expenditure per cash flow		6.5%			£15,655,016		
GROSS DEVELOPMENT COSTS							£188,382,144
Development Profit (Cash)					£34,594,856		
Development Profit (%)					18.36%		
Return on Cost (Development Yield)					7.20%		

Programme

Start land purchase	June 2006
Start on Site	December 2007
Practical Completion	December 2009
Valuation PC + i	December 2010

Notes and Assumptions
Costs provided by QS on 22 October 2004 - Current Day
ERVs based on Clark Kent Plans 100-102 Rev 1- Current Day
assume 18 month incentives for unit shops on new proposal

Figure 13.5 Example development appraisal.

(say 15–20 percent) that most developers would consider acceptable.

Development Yield (Return on Cost)

This is an alternative indicator of whether the developer is being adequately rewarded for the risks undertaken. It is calculated by dividing the rents receivable by the total development cost. This allows the developer (and any funding partner) to calculate the return they receive on the capital they have invested. In our example, the total expenditure incurred is £188m and the income receivable is £13.56m per annum, thus a return on cost of just over 7 per cent is achieved on the money invested.

In more recent years, many developers and funders have used an additional method of assessing the viability of projects utilising the internal rate of return (IRR). This allows a more readily measurable comparison between the true return over time of investing in developing a shopping centre against available alternative investments, such as equities. It is a method of assessing the value today, of making a series of payments and receiving a series of income payments over fixed periods of time, and is closely linked to the concept of net present value.

Net Present Value

This is the value that can be calculated today of the property (or site) taking into account future expenditure and anticipated income, over a fixed period, allowing the investor to achieve a desired level of return.

Rental Returns

These are a key measure and are the product of lettable floor space against the rental levels anticipated.

The Bottom Line Influence

It can be seen from the commercial considerations outlined above that the building cost is likely to be capped by a variety of commercial factors. For example, the building cost can be influenced by:
- the level of development profit expected by the developer
- the development yield (expected by the developer and investor)
- the rental levels and amount of lettable floor space.
  As a simple generalisation, the more profitable and successful a development appears at the viability appraisal stage, the greater amount there will

be to expend on the building.

Retail buildings are significantly influenced by the commercial drivers and the inevitable bottom line.

Architects are more likely to influence the level of building quality by understanding the commercial factors and working together with the retail team to bring added value to the development.

Other Considerations and Drivers

Size of Development

Developers and investors will be looking for opportunities to provide a dominant retail offer in the catchment area. In this case size matters and being able to provide the customer with a wide range of offers is important. Becoming or establishing the dominant offer in the catchment is a key development objective.

Economic Cycles

With the average retail development taking up to 10 years to complete from inception, it is difficult to plan for the development completion to meet an upswing in the economy. Retail development, however, usually extends across normal economic cycles and projects are usually completed when there is reasonable consumer demand. Developers do need to research the likelihood of major recessions, as a sudden downturn in the market can affect demand and rental levels. As a general rule, it is prudent to plan to under-supply and for demand to exceed shop space availability. With under-supply, there is greater prospect of maintaining rental expectations.

Development Agreement

Town centre development agreements normally involve the freehold being held by the local authority with a long lease granted to the developer. Development agreements are entered into between developers and local authorities to include the following principles:
- conditionality
- freehold transfer to the authority
- arrangements for long leasehold to the developer – annual ground rental levels and future income share

- site assembly provisions including CPO
- construction and design obligations
- completion dates
- future management provision.

Funding Agreements

These agreements are entered into between developers and a funding partner and establish the following principles.

- the conditions for staged payments
  - i pre-planning application
  - ii post-planning permission up to construction
  - iii construction through to project completion.

  The conditions that commonly apply to these stages are:
- institutions release initial funding on achievement of planning permission provided the following conditions are met:
  - a heads of terms agreement is reached with an anchor store
  - a proportion of retailers have committed to the development
  - a programme for completion of the project exists
  - a cost plan has been agreed for the development
  - the development agreement is unconditional
- funding for the construction stage can include the following conditions:
  - vacant possession of the site
  - committed programme and completion date
  - a fixed construction price
  - unconditional development agreement
  - all planning conditions are met
  - anchor stores have been let
  - a proportion of retailers have committed to signing leases in the scheme.

Proposed entrance and naturally ventilated arcade, Westgate, Oxford, UK (2010). *(Source: BDP)*

14

Future Places for Shopping

Continual Evolution

Although long-term predictions are invariably uncertain, an undoubted reality of the future of shopping facilities will be their continual evolution in response to ongoing social and economic development. Future leading edge shopping will involve the evolution and emergence of new shopping formats, as yet unknown. While the future state-of-the-art shopping facilities are likely to be unrecognisable from what is known today, many of the formats identified here will be relevant in the future. Other certainties are the requirement for existing shopping centres to be upgraded and extended and for shopping facilities to remain integral to the heart of urban centres. A consistent challenge to the designers of future shopping facilities will also be to make going out to shop a more enjoyable experience.

So can we begin to address how future shopping facilities might develop? It may be both rash and inappropriate to try to make precise predictions. It is probably wiser and more realistic to look at current trends and examine where these issues might lead. The evolving trends are examined under the following three broad categories of driver:

- environmental
- market
- customer.

Environmental Drivers

Planning

While planning policy remains to be led by sustainable issues, such as discouraging use of the private car, shopping facilities will follow these patterns:

- a focus towards town centre development
- greater integration with the urban fabric
- more open and covered street public spaces

- fewer enclosed interior environments
- layouts being urban design led
- an emphasis towards variety and design quality.

Although open street urban design-led shopping is currently *de rigueur*, over time and the establishment of these developments, there is likely to be a gradual return and acceptance of more plural shopping environments and the advent of a selective number of well-considered, enclosed or covered shopping facilities. These future enclosed environments will have to be well integrated with their urban context and better designed than their predecessors. The mixture of both enclosed and open shopping environments will go some way towards meeting the customer's increasing wish for comfort and convenience.

Town centre retail development has a regenerative quality and is also likely to include other elements in a mixed-use development, incorporating urban living, leisure facilities, employment and civic uses.

Environmental Awareness

The future is likely to see increasing corporate and social pressure for shopping facilities to be more sustainable. This will require buildings to be designed that consume less energy and potentially use more efficient energy sources. New legislation will require energy labelling of public buildings which will reinforce corporate pressure to achieve energy efficiency. In addition to the pressure on corporate landlords, their tenants will also seek greater operational efficiency to reduce service charges and running costs.

Shopping facilities are encouraged to be accessible to different modes of transport, which will especially involve the incorporation of public transport facilities. Public transport nodes will themselves be opportunities for retail development.

Market Drivers

Maturity of the Market

As opportunities are completed the market matures and competition increases. Furthermore, there will be fewer large new opportunities resulting in a move towards making better use, and expansion, of existing shopping facilities.

Intensification

Retail development adjacent to or nearby to existing shopping facilities will drive older facilities to catch up with the competition. Mature markets will require better use and intensification of both existing town centre and out-of-town shopping facilities. Refurbishment, extension and redevelopment of existing facilities will therefore be common in the future.

Research Analysis

Increasing knowledge and understanding of the market go hand in hand in mature developed countries. With fewer opportunities, development will be more reliant on the findings of research analysis to confirm demand and assess what the customers want. Research analysis will be increasingly used to enable the retail offer to be targeted toward a particular catchment area's needs. Tenants will continue to be more readily selected in response to catchment research.

In the organisation and layout of shops, tenants with a natural synergy will be grouped together. These groupings will be used to form local identity to areas within larger developments and to form individual specialised centres. Tenant groupings will be arranged both to reflect customer aspirations in the retail offer and to influence the character of the shopping environment.

Comprehensive Development

Shopping developments have, over time, increased in size. This trend is likely to continue in order for the more complex town centre schemes to be viable and to provide an attractive wide-ranging retail offer. Regional centres will continue to include selective leisure facilities to increase their appeal beyond the local catchment.

Comprehensive town centre developments are likely to be more complex and will involve great commitment and organisational skills from the developer's team. Only the larger development companies will have the development and project management skills that are necessary to complete large comprehensive developments. There are, therefore, likely to be fewer single development companies able to undertake comprehensive developments and more joint ventures formed to share the risk.

Specialised Development

While general shopping developments increase in size, some of the new formats, which have evolved from targeting specific and selective customer requirements, are adopting small to mid-size development. Research of the market to provide for selective needs will allow specialised developments to succeed on a smaller scale. For example, developments will be biased towards leisure retailing

Figure 14.1 Retail entertainment centres' – The Zone, Rosebank, Johannesburg, SA (2000) is an example of the type of carefully targeted, new, urban shopping format which will respond to the future environment, market and customer drivers. (*Source: Peter Coleman*)

(incorporating a synergistic trinity of retail, catering and leisure facilities) and form 'retail entertainment centres' geared towards highly populated areas.

As the economies of industrialised countries move more towards service industries, another selective new format (aimed at the professional middle class) that is likely to occur more commonly are 'lifestyle centres'. These facilities cherry-pick aspirational retailers and caterers to form highly convenient, main street, open-air environments which are targeted to reflect the aspirational lifestyles of a particular customer.

Middle-of-the-road generalised shopping facilities will not, in themselves, be sufficient to attract enough customers to allow regional centres to survive. Large regional centres will be made up of some middle-of-the-road, mainstream shopping combined with identifiable areas of targeted aspirational retailers and caterers to broaden their attractiveness to a wider portion of the catchment market.

Regional Control

Operational property companies are attracted towards achieving a greater share of regional turnover. In mature markets this can be a way of their being able to manage an increase in turnover. Consequently, it is more likely, in future, that we will see more single companies taking control of major portions of town centre retailing in partnership with local authorities. An alternative, which gives the same result, is for an operating company to own both the town centre and the out-of-town competing centres, in order to manage and control a catchment's turnover.

Bigger Shops

Unit shops for multinational retailers are becoming bigger to allow tenants to provide a full product range and to benefit from the operational efficiencies of scale. The accommodation of these larger shops is leading towards centres becoming larger, yet providing a similar wide variety of offers. (Centres are reluctant to provide fewer offers in order to accommodate these larger shops within the same area, recognising the overall retail offer and attractiveness will be reduced.) Designers will therefore need to find ways of accommodating larger shops both in plan and by the use of multi-level shops.

Customer Drivers

Experiential

In the previous half-century, the act of shopping has evolved from a basic activity of purchasing products, through giving service, to providing an experience and stimulating a memorable thought. Today's shops and public spaces need to be more than safe and convenient places to shop. Shopping environments should establish a sense of place and create a local identity. Achieving a unique sense of place that is inclusive to a wide range of the public and does not alienate, will remain a key challenge to shopping centre designers.

Informative

As the activity within shops becomes more informative, it is likely that the experience of using the public space that connects the shops will need to take account of this. How the public spaces may respond is examined further below.

With increasing competition from alternative shopping sources the process of going shopping

Figure 14.2 Customers will become increasingly more discerning, expecting to be informed and stimulated in the process of purchasing as demonstrated by Nike Town, Oxford Circus, London, UK (1999). *(Source: Adrian Wilson)*

has become more than 'feeling' and 'collecting' the merchandise. Increasingly, shops use the display of full product ranges to create drama and inform the customer. The development of the setting and display of merchandise is likely to continue and become increasingly important and sophisticated. The development of shop interiors resembling showrooms, museums and galleries is likely to continue and grow. The trend for some retailers to educate and inform the customer, seen in the elaborate displays of Nike Town stores or the incorporation of presentation spaces such as the Apple Store, Regent Street, London, will spread to other retailers.

Being able to try out the product before purchase is another benefit of visiting a shop over the Internet. These facilities are available in many stores already, like the Apple Store, London, and the elaborate climbing facilities and outdoor leisurewear weather testing areas of the REI Store, Seattle. These try out facilities and others like them will be increasingly common in stores of the future.

The experiential and informative nature of shops is likely to have an influence on the public spaces leading to them. This influence may encourage the incorporation of more civic and cultural information relating to the history of the place. Alternatively, the interconnecting spaces may generally increase in quality and sophistication and remain neutral, allowing the shops to set the character.

User-Friendly and Convenient

The requirement for shopping facilities to be convenient and enjoyable to use will become increasingly important in a pressurised society, where available time is scarce and shopping is increasingly available through other means (other centres, supermarkets, Internet and mail order). Future shopping formats will need to provide wide-ranging, conveniently arranged and carefully selected retail offers, in a comfortable and secure environment. Going to the shops will need to provide a clear advantage of choice, convenience, contentment, value and experience over the alternative formats, if it is to avoid falling into decline.

Convenience and ease of use will need to apply from the point of arrival through to departure. The experience will include the type and organisation of the shops, ease of movement, the quality of the amenities and the means of finding a particular product. Providing 'choice' and 'variety of experience' will become increasingly important criteria in a discerning and individualistic society.

Going Forward

In this brief examination of the evolution of places for shopping, we have seen shops gradually develop from secondary spaces shared within other buildings, such as those in the medieval market and town halls, to become splendid individual buildings with their own identity in the Middle Eastern Bazaars. This was followed by the European arcades of the late eighteenth and nineteenth centuries.

The twentieth century established the contemporary purpose-planned shopping facility, with the suburban malls of America and the precincts repairing the war damaged cities of Europe. More recently, new generations of specifically targeted retail formats have emerged from the universal regional suburban and town centre malls. They range from retail entertainment centres and lifestyle centres to (single product) focused retail centres and transport oriented retail. Traditional town centre malls are re-inventing themselves as mixed-use urban quarters integrated with the surrounding streets. Edge of town malls are being urbanised to provide a hybrid of main street and enclosed interior environments with the best of both worlds.

Assuming that the current pattern of change and evolution continues, the future will see ever more sophisticated new formats emerge and existing formats re-invent themselves as exciting new types. With the continual emergence of new types and with shopping development being integral to the formation of town centres, the future represents an exciting and inventive time for those involved in the design and formation of shopping environments.

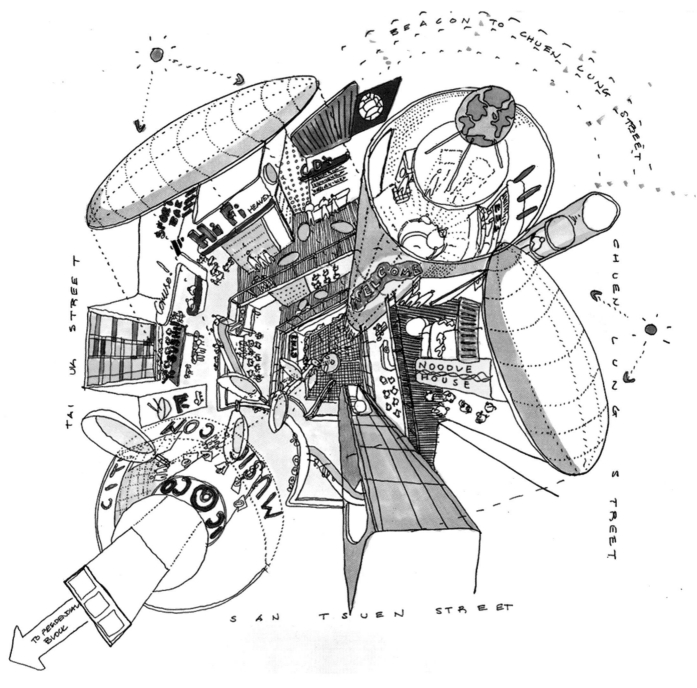

Figure 14.3 The conceptual proposal for Chuen Lung Street, Hong Kong illustrates the opportunity for a selective, few, enclosed shopping environments, which will maintain the difference between competing Internet shopping and that of a comfortable and enjoyable environment. *(Source: Stephen Anderson/BDP)*

Index

(Figures and Tables are in *italic*)